LP-Gas Code Handbook

NINTH EDITION

Edited by

Theodore C. Lemoff, P.E.
Principal Gases Engineer, NFPA

With the complete text of the 2011 edition of NFPA® 58, *Liquefied Petroleum Gas Code*

National Fire Protection Association®
Quincy, Massachusetts

Product Manager: Michael S. Barresi, Jr.
Developmental Editor: Irene Herlihy
Production Editor: Khela Thorne
Permissions Editor: Josiane Domenici
Copy Editor: Kathleen Allain

Composition: Modern Graphics, Inc.
Art Coordinator: Cheryl Langway
Cover Design: Lana Kurtz Design
Manufacturing Manager: Ellen Glisker
Printer: Courier/Westford

Notice Concerning Code Interpretations: This ninth edition of the *LP-Gas Code Handbook* is based on the 2011 edition of NFPA 58. All NFPA codes, standards, recommended practices, and guides ("NFPA Documents") are developed in accordance with the published procedures of the NFPA by technical committees comprised of volunteers drawn from a broad array of relevant interests. The handbook contains the complete text of NFPA 58 and any applicable Formal Interpretations issued by the NFPA. This NFPA Document is accompanied by explanatory commentary and other supplementary materials.

The commentary and supplementary materials in this handbook are not a part of the NFPA Document and do not constitute Formal Interpretations of the NFPA (which can be obtained only through requests processed by the responsible technical committees in accordance with the published procedures of the NFPA). The commentary and supplementary materials, therefore, solely reflect the personal opinions of the editor or other contributors and do not necessarily represent the official position of the NFPA or its technical committees.

The following are registered trademarks of the National Fire Protection Association:
National Fire Protection Association®
NFPA®
Building Construction and Safety Code® and NFPA 5000®
Life Safety Code® and 101®
National Electrical Code®, NEC®, and NFPA 70®

NFPA No.: 58HB11
ISBN (book): 978-0-877659-099
ISBN (electronic product): 978-0-877659-105
Library of Congress Card Control No.: 2010929123

Printed in the United States of America

11   12   13   14   15   5   4   3   2   1

Contents

iv   Contents

Preface

The ninth edition of the *LP-Gas Code Handbook* continues the tradition begun by Wilbur L. Walls, editor of the first edition in 1986. The handbook provides commentary that brings the legalistic language of the code to life. The code must be written using a technically clear, usable, and enforceable style. It cannot include the guidance and explanations that the Technical Committee on Liquefied Petroleum Gases would like to include.

The purpose of this handbook is to assist you, the enforcer or user of NFPA 58, *Liquefied Petroleum Gas Code.* The commentary and supplements provide guidance, recommendations, and common practices for the use of LP-Gas as a fuel.

The 2011 edition of the code contains several important changes, including the following:

1. New requirements for installation and ongoing inspection of cathodic protection of underground propane storage containers
2. New requirement for the location of storage containers used for emergency generators, which are common at many cell phone tower locations
3. Deletion of the requirement for pressure relief valve "stacks"
4. Deletion of the requirements for operation of small LP-Gas pipeline vapor systems with 10 to 99 users (such as might be located at a mobile home park)

An NFPA code handbook is never complete. In order to stay current, it must change as technology and code requirements change. Users will find that problems they encounter may not be addressed fully in the handbook commentary, tables, illustrations, or photographs, or that the commentary appears incomplete when applied to real problems. Therefore, the editor invites suggestions, examples, new illustrations, and photographs from all readers for use in the next edition.

History of NFPA 58

NFPA standards concerned with gases date from 1900, only four years after the establishment of NFPA itself. The first standards were concerned with acetylene, which was actually used in those days as a household cooking, lighting, and heating fuel, and with manufactured, or "city," gas derived from coal and oil.

The NFPA Technical Committee on Gases developed the early standards. By 1924, the use of liquefied petroleum gas (LP-Gas), primarily as a cooking and heating fuel in rural areas, had become common, and the need for a national fire safety standard was recognized. The LP-Gas for these systems was stored in compressed gas cylinders. Because of their cylindrical shape, the LP-Gas they contained was widely referred to simply as "bottled gas," an identification rather lacking in specificity (acetylene was also a "bottled gas") but one still used today.

In 1927, the Committee on Gases secured NFPA approval of the first NFPA standard on LP-Gas, a four-page document with a title — *Regulations for the Installation and Operation of Compressed Gas Systems Other than Acetylene for Lighting and Heating* — that comprised a fair proportion of the text of the standard itself. The standard covered only systems in which

EXHIBIT P.1 Early Magazine Advertisements for Acetylene Lighting and Cooking.

the LP-Gas was stored in cylinders fabricated to regulations of the U.S. Interstate Commerce Commission (ICC), today known as the U.S. Department of Transportation (DOT).

In those days, NFPA published its standards only in the Proceedings of the Annual Meeting at which the standards were adopted. To make them more available to users, the National Board of Fire Underwriters (NBFU), now known as the American Insurance Association, obtained NFPA permission to publish many of them in pamphlet form. These were identified as standards of the NBFU "as recommended by the NFPA." In those days, NFPA did not identify many of its standards by number. However, the NBFU did, and the standard was thus designated NBFU 52. Amended editions of the standard were adopted in 1928, 1933, and 1937.

Because the LP-Gas "bottles" had to be refilled (in those days, only at a plant built for that purpose), which required the use of a much larger container for plant storage, new specifications had to be developed. In addition, major consumers found a container larger than an ICC cylinder to be advantageous. These larger containers required different design and siting criteria.

In 1931, NFPA tentatively adopted *Regulations for the Design, Installation and Construction of Containers and Pertinent Equipment for the Storage and Handling of Liquefied Petroleum Gases*, which was officially adopted at the next NFPA meeting in 1932. This standard covered the larger containers, which are the ASME containers of today. Also published by the NBFU, under the designation NBFU 58, this standard had 14 pages, 10 more than NBFU 52.

At the 1931 Annual Meeting, committee chairman Harry E. Newell of the NBFU noted in his report that the proposed standard had been prepared by a joint subcommittee of the Committee on Gases and the Committee on Flammable Liquids. He attributed this to the fact that "it was difficult to decide whether liquefied petroleum gases were flammable liquids or gases." Even today, confusion exists on this score. Some municipal ordinances, undoubtedly of considerable vintage, equate them, and many communities have failed to adopt LP-Gas regulations under the erroneous impression that their flammable liquid regulations apply to LP-Gas.

For many years, the Committee on Gases was composed of 11 to 20 members. In 1932, there were 15 members, representing the Associated Factory Mutual Fire Insurance Companies, American Gas Association, Board of Fire Underwriters of Allegheny County, Western Factory Insurance Association, Conference of Special Risk Underwriters, Manufacturing Chemists Association, Boston Board of Fire Underwriters, International Acetylene Association, Underwriters Laboratories Inc., Compressed Gas Manufacturers Association, American Petroleum Institute, Railway Fire Protection Association, and the U.S. National Bureau of Standards, as well as the NBFU. With 6 of the 15 members, including the chairman, representing the insurance industry, the standard could be presumed to be rather conservative and thus lacked the balance of interests that is required under today's NFPA procedures.

The extreme versatility of "gas in a bottle" soon led to more and more complex uses, and the Committee on Gases was hard-pressed to keep up. Amended editions of the 1931 standard were adopted in 1934, 1937, 1938, and 1939.

In 1935, a standard on LP-Gas cargo vehicles, whose use had become widespread in the early 1930s, was adopted and published by NBFU as NBFU 59. In 1937, a standard was adopted to regulate the use of LP-Gas as a fuel to power vehicles, a practice that had become prevalent by the mid-1930s. In 1938, however, this became a part of the ASME Code container standard (NBFU 58).

By now, it was apparent that the various standards contained considerable duplicate material and could be combined into a single standard. This was done in 1940. The resulting 47-page standard (in the NBFU 58 pamphlet version) combined the 1937 edition of NBFU 52 and the 1939 editions of NBFU 58 and 59. This single standard also replaced the *Liquefied Petroleum Gas Code*, which was adopted in 1937 in response to a request by regulatory and insurance interests to provide container siting and basic fabrication criteria that were not as detailed as those found in the existing standards. This code ultimately proved inadequate from the industry's point of view, and it was withdrawn when the combined standard was introduced. The 1943 edition of the standard was the first edition to be designated NFPA 58. The first pamphlet edition of NFPA 58 was published in 1950.

The dates of each edition of NFPA 58 are given in the "Origin and Development" section of each edition. To date, there have been 31 editions since the 1940 edition, an average of about one every two years. From 1950 to 1961, in fact, a new edition was adopted each year. This is a very high rate, and it placed an impossible burden upon its usefulness as a public safety regulatory instrument. Since 1961, new editions have been adopted about every three years, except for the 2008 edition, which took four years due to controversy, which resulted in a last-minute deletion of proposed coverage of cabinet heaters.

The Committee on Gases itself developed NFPA 58 until 1956. By that time, the number and variety of NFPA standards covering various gases had grown so large that the size of the committee was becoming difficult to manage. The solution was to establish a number of smaller committees, known as sectional committees, composed of experts on the different gas applications. The developmental and interpretative responsibilities for NFPA 58 were thus assigned to the Sectional Committee on Liquefied Petroleum Gases. However, the sectional committee could only recommend amendments, Formal Interpretations, or Tentative Interim Amendments (TIAs) for adoption by the Committee on Gases.

Because the sectional committee lacked authority, its membership essentially duplicated that of the Committee on Gases, and the purpose of the sectional committee was defeated. It was also becoming evident that the Committee on Gases seldom overturned a sectional committee recommendation.

In 1966, the sectional committees — there were four at the time — were organized into three full-fledged technical committees, and the Committee on Gases ceased to exist. NFPA 58 thus became the complete responsibility of the Technical Committee on Liquefied Petroleum Gas.

From 1940 to 1969, NFPA 58 consisted of a chapter entitled Basic Rules, followed by a number of chapters entitled Divisions and by appendixes. The Introduction and Basic Rules included all material common to all applications, such as scope statements, retroactivity, definitions, odorization, approval requirements, container fabrication, siting, design criteria for piping, valves, hoses and fittings, filling levels, and ignition source controls. The eight divisions amplified and sometimes modified the basic provisions for specific applications, some on the basis of kinds of containers and others on the basis of the environment in which the system was used.

As a new application was developed, it was essentially treated as a package and added as a new division, which was easier to do and allowed for the timely inclusion in the standard of new applications. The problem with this approach was that similar hazards were being treated differently, and the basic rules were becoming less and less basic.

In the late 1960s, the Technology and Standards Committee of the National Propane Gas Association (NPGA) undertook the development of a format that would provide consistency in hazard evaluation, would reduce the extent to which particular interests would have to study the entire standard, and would make the format more like that used in other NFPA standards.

In the current format, Chapters 1 through 4 include only material truly relevant to all applications.

Chapters 5 and 6 address the fundamental breakdown of interest that experience has shown exists between manufacturers of equipment and those who assemble this equipment into systems and actually install them. Fire experience clearly reveals that incidents are nearly always due to failure to comply with one or more provisions and that many of these failures are the result of confusion between manufacturers and installers as to who should do what. To help reduce this confusion, Chapter 5 is aimed at the equipment manufacturer and Chapter 6 at the installer.

The same experience has also shown that the great majority of nonappliance-related accidents occur when LP-Gas liquid is being transferred from one container to another. An essential aspect of such operations is the presence and performance of a person or persons conducting the transfer operation: An accident generally involves human behavior, as well as equipment. Chapter 7 addresses LP-Gas liquid transfer.

Chapter 8, Storage of Cylinders Awaiting Use, Resale, or Exchange, and Chapter 9, Vehicular Transportation of LP-Gas, retain the old format of Divisions V and III.

Chapter 10 was essentially new in the 1972 edition. Earlier editions had not considered the role of the structural behavior of a room or building in an explosion.

Chapter 11 was created in the 1992 edition by relocating the coverage of engine fuel systems from Chapter 6 to this chapter.

Drawn largely from NFPA 59 and NFPA 59A, Chapter 12 was added in the 1989 edition to provide requirements for the new coverage of refrigerated storage containers.

Coverage of marine shipping and receiving was relocated from Chapter 4 to create Chapter 13 in the 1992 edition.

Chapter 14, Operations and Maintenance, was added in the 2001 edition. It contains only operations and maintenance requirements that were new in the 2001 edition. In the current edition, a new section was added, Small LP-Gas Systems, covering vapor systems of 10 to 99 users connected to a common supply system. These requirements essentially duplicate requirements in U. S. Federal Law applicable to these pipeline systems. The intent is to make them more easily available to operators of these relatively small systems, which may be located in mobile home parks, campgrounds, and housing developments.

Chapter 15 was added in the 1998 edition. It consists of tables used to size propane vapor piping. The tables were extracted from NFPA 54, *National Fuel Gas Code*. The chapter was added because some pipe sizing in buildings is now included in the scope of NFPA 58, because it was deleted from NFPA 54 in the 1996 edition.

While the 1972 edition went a long way toward bringing the format of NFPA 58 into line with other NFPA standards, it still did not properly segregate mandatory and nonmandatory provisions, and it used a different paragraph numbering system. These differences were corrected in the 1983 edition.

Experience with the format of the 1972 edition and with subsequent editions indicates that it has led to improved comprehension and application. However, it is more difficult to review existing provisions to see if a new application is in fact already covered than it is to start from scratch. Furthermore, there is always pressure to include all provisions applicable to a new and "hot" application in one place. This temptation must be resisted lest the standard evolve into the conflicting and cumbersome document it once was.

The administration of the committees responsible for NFPA 58 has been remarkably stable over its history. Harry E. Newell of the NBFU was chairman from 1932 until 1956, when he retired from NBFU. As an indication of the respect the committee and NFPA had for him, the position of honorary chairman was created for him, the only time this position has existed. He served in this capacity until 1958.

Newell's dedication was even more remarkable in that he also performed the chores of committee secretary, albeit anonymously. It wasn't until 1954 that NFPA was able to assign a staff member, Clark F. Jones, as committee secretary. Jones served in this post until his untimely death in 1962. Wilbur L. Walls succeeded him in September 1962. Walls was the committee secretary until his retirement from NFPA in 1984. From May 1985 through October 2010, when he retired from NFPA, Theodore C. Lemoff served as the NFPA staff secretary. In Nov 2010, Denise M. Beach became the staff secretary.

Franklin R. Fetherston succeeded Newell as chairman of the Committee on Gases in 1956. Initially representing the Liquefied Petroleum Gas Association (now the National Propane Gas Association), he later represented the Compressed Gas Association until he retired in 1966. During Fetherston's tenure, the Sectional Committee on Liquefied Petroleum Gases was chaired by Harold L. DeCamp of the Fire Insurance Rating Organization of New Jersey from 1956 to 1964, and by Myron Snell of the Hartford Accident and Indemnity Company from 1964 to 1966.

Hugh V. Keepers of the Fire Prevention and Engineering Bureau of Texas became the first chairman of the current committee in 1966 and served for 10 years until his retirement. He was followed by Connor Adams of the City of Miami, who served as chair from 1975 to 1996. The immediate past chairman, E. E. (Al) Linder, a safety consultant and former propane company employee, took over the reins in 1996 and served through the 2004 edition. He was replaced by Frank Mortimer of Federated Mutual Insurance Company.

Acknowledgments

A book that compiles the history, intent, and application of an NFPA standard, as the *LP-Gas Code Handbook* does, is the work of many contributors, many of whom are members of the Technical Committee on Liquefied Petroleum Gases, and all of whom work with LP-Gas daily. The foundation for this sixth edition was laid by the three authors who contributed to the first edition in 1986: Wilbur L. Walls, who represented, at the time, the expertise of NFPA on flammable gases; Walter H. Johnson, who possessed a broad knowledge of the LP-Gas industry from the industry association viewpoint; and H. Emerson Thomas, who offered his perspective as one of the founders of the propane industry in the United States.

The preparation of this ninth edition was enhanced by the contributions of Richard Fredenburg, LP-Gas Engineer, North Carolina Department of Agriculture and Consumer Services, as the contributing editor, provided draft commentary on the entire code and made many important contributions, which are appreciated by the Editor. In addition, I wish to thank the many contributors of new artwork that makes this handbook more useful. These contributors include the following companies and individuals: Al-Gas SDI; Anderson Greenwood; Amano Pioneer Eclipse Corporation; AmeriGas; ASCE; Blackmer, a Dover Company; Brian Clayton; Cavagna North America, Inc.; CENEX, a brand name of CHS Inc.; ChefMaster, a division of Mr. Bar-B-Q, Inc.; CleanFuel USA; Corken, Inc., a member of Liquid Controls Group; Dead River Company; Eastern Propane Corp; Elster Gas North

America; Ely Energy; Emerson Process Management Regulator Technologies, Inc.; Engineered Controls International, Inc.; Ferrellgas; Flame Engineering; Richard Fredenburg, North Carolina Dept. of Agriculture and Consumer Services; Full Circle; Gas Equipment Co., Inc. and Rochester Gauges, Inc.; Gastite Division, Titeflex Corporation; Heath Consultants Incorporated; H&H Gas; Illinois Propane Gas Association; Richard A. Hoffmann, P.E., Hoffmann & Feige; IMPCO Technologies, Inc.; Independent Propane Co.; LabelMaster®; LEHR; Lin's Propane Trucks; Liquid Controls, Inc.; Manchester Tank; Mississippi Tank Co.; National Board of Boiler and Pressure Vessel Inspectors; National Propane Gas Association; the Propane Education and Research Council (PERC); Propane Technical Services; Quality Gas Service; Ransome Manufacturing; Revere Gas & Appliance; R.W. Lyall & Company, Inc.; Screen Graphics of Florida; SEA-3 Inc.; Sensidyne; Sensit Technologies; Sherwood Valve, LLC, a Division of TWI; Smith Precision Products Co., Inc.; Superior Energy Systems; Texas Trailer Corp.; Trinity Containers, LLC; U.S. DOT; Wilbur Walls; Worthington Cylinder Corp.

I especially thank Emerson Process Management Regulator Technologies, Inc., and Engineered Controls International, Inc., for their assistance in adapting their original artwork for this handbook.

This handbook is built on the foundation laid by the Technical Committee on Liquefied Petroleum Gases, which writes NFPA 58. I appreciate the work the committee members do in carefully considering each proposal and comment and the discussions on other topics, which are the basis of the book.

I would also like to again thank Wilbur Walls, NFPA gases engineer emeritus, who, though retired, volunteered his time and energy to assist me when I took over the staff role for the NFPA gases project. Bill continues to be a valuable resource for the historical questions that arise.

I also appreciate the efforts of the NFPA staff who made this book possible. Particular thanks go to Josiane Domenici, permissions editor, Kathleen Allain, copy editor, Irene Herlihy, developmental editor, Khela Thorne, production editor, and Mike Barresi, product manager.

Finally, I offer my best wishes to the new staff secretary, Denise Beach, as she becomes the bearer of the flame.

Theodore C. Lemoff, P.E
Editor

About the Contributor

Richard Fredenburg

Richard Fredenburg has been with the North Carolina Department of Agriculture and Consumer Services since 1994 as the LP-Gas Engineer. He supervises eight field inspectors who inspect bulk plants, dispensing sites, delivery trucks, and consumer sites for compliance with state law and the *LP-Gas Code*. Calls from consumers, industrial customers, propane dealers, and government officials at all levels come in for Richard to handle. He serves on the National Fire Protection Association Technical Committees for LP-Gas and for LP-Gases at Utility Gas Plants, the UL Standards Technical Panels for valves and safety relief valves, and the National Propane Gas Association Technology, Standards, and Safety Committee.

Mr. Fredenburg has a bachelor of science degree in nuclear engineering from the University of Virginia and a master of science degree in engineering administration from the University of Tennessee. He worked at the Tennessee Valley Authority in their nuclear power program for 15 years.

About the Editor

Theodore C. Lemoff, P.E.

After graduating from the City College of New York with a Bachelor of Engineering (Chemical) degree, Theodore C. Lemoff was employed in the chemical and petrochemical industry by Proctor and Gamble Company, Sun Chemical Corporation, and Badger Engineers, Inc., in various engineering positions. He joined NFPA in 1985 and served as NFPA's principal gases engineer until his retirement from NFPA in November 2010. He also served as the NFPA staff liaison to the National Fuel Gas Code Committee, and he was also responsible for other NFPA standards on flammable gases.

In addition to being the editor of the *LP-Gas Code Handbook*, Lemoff is the editor of the *National Fuel Gas Code Handbook* and co-author of the *NFPA Pocket Guide to Fuel Gas Storage and Use*.

Mr. Lemoff represented NFPA on the ASME Code for Pressure Piping Committee (National Interest Review Group) (B31), the pipeline safety advisory committee of the U.S. Department of Transportation, and the IAPMO Mechanical and Plumbing Code Committees.

Mr. Lemoff is a registered professional engineer in the Commonwealth of Massachusetts and is a member of the American Institute of Chemical Engineers and Society of Fire Protection Engineers, the American Society of Plumbing Engineers, and the International Association of Plumbing and Mechanical Officials. In 2010, Mr. Lemoff received the Howard Card Safety Award from the New Jersey Propane Gas Association.

In Memoriam

This handbook is dedicated to the memory of Carlos de León of Mexico City, Mexico. Carlos was a member of the NFPA Technical Committee on Liquefied Petroleum Gases from 1993 until 2007. He represented the Mexican Association of Gas Distributors and was responsible for several revisions to the code that recognized safe practices that have been in use in Mexico. Carlos introduced NFPA to propane distributors and government officials in his country, and his personal initiatives led to the greater use of NFPA 58 in Mexico. His down-to-earth approach to all aspects of committee work will be missed by all those who worked with him.

Este manual lo dedicamos a la memoria de Carlos de León de ciudad de México, México. Carlos fue miembro del Comité Técnico de la NFPA de Gases Licuados de Petróleo de 1993 al 2007. Representaba a la Asociación Mexicana de Distribuidores de Gas y fue responsable de varias revisiones al código, las cuales reconocieron prácticas seguras que ya estaban en uso en México. Carlos presentó a la NFPA a distribuidores de propano y oficiales gubernamentales en su país. Sus iniciativas personales resultaron en un mayor uso del NFPA 58 en México. Cabe mencionar, su actitud práctica hacia todos los aspectos del trabajo del Comité serán extrañados por todos aquellos que trabajaron con él.

PART ONE

NFPA® 58,
Liquefied Petroleum Gas Code,
with Commentary

Part One of this handbook includes the complete text of the 2011 edition of NFPA 58, *Liquefied Petroleum Gas Code,* which is made up of 15 mandatory chapters and 12 nonmandatory annexes. Working within the framework of NFPA's consensus codes- and standards-making process, the Technical Committee on Liquefied Petroleum Gases prepared the mandatory provisions found in Chapters 1 through 15.

The Technical Committee on Liquefied Petroleum Gases also developed the material found in the annexes of the code. The annex material is designed to assist users in interpreting the mandatory code provisions. It is not considered part of the requirements of the code; it is advisory or informational in nature. An asterisk (*) following a code paragraph number indicates that advisory annex material pertaining to that paragraph appears in Annex A. For the reader's convenience, in this handbook Annex A material has been repositioned to appear immediately following its base paragraph in the body of the code text.

The explanatory commentary in this handbook was prepared by the handbook editor, with the assistance of those persons mentioned in the acknowledgments, and is intended to provide the reader with an understanding of the provisions of the code and to serve as a resource and reference for implementing the provisions of or enforcing the code. It is not a substitute for the actual wording of the code or the text of the many codes and standards that are incorporated by reference. The commentary immediately follows the code text it discusses and is set in blue type for easy identification.

This edition of the handbook includes a frequently asked questions feature. The marginal FAQs are based on the questions most commonly asked of the NFPA 58 staff. The handbook also features a tool designed to help users easily identify important new or revised elements in the code from the previous edition. Changes other than editorial are indicated by a vertical rule beside the paragraph, table, or figure in which the change occurred. Where one or more complete paragraphs have been deleted, the deletion is indicated by a bullet (•) between the paragraphs that remain.

Administration

Chapter 1 provides the requirements for administering the provisions of NFPA 58, *Liquefied Petroleum Gas Code*, hereinafter referred to as the code. The requirements in Chapter 1 are essential for establishing a framework for enforcing the code, which the authority having jurisdiction needs in order to avoid conflicts and overlaps with other codes or standards that may have been adopted.

Chapter 1 includes the following administrative topics:

- Scope (See Section 1.1.)
- Purpose, which is reserved for future use (See Section 1.2.)
- Application, including non-application (See Section 1.3.)
- Retroactivity (See Section 1.4.)
- Equivalency (See Section 1.5.)
- Units and Formulas, which is reserved for future use (See Section 1.6.)
- Enforcement (See Section 1.7.)

These sections are important because they lay the ground rules by which the code is enforced. These rules are necessary in order to achieve uniformity in enforcement between jurisdictions, which assists the users of the code in complying with its provisions.

1.1* Scope

This code applies to the storage, handling, transportation, and use of LP-Gas.

A.1.1 *General Properties of LP-Gas.* Liquefied petroleum gases (LP-Gases), as defined in this code *(see 3.3.34)*, are gases at normal room temperature and atmospheric pressure. They liquefy under moderate pressure and readily vaporize upon release of the pressure. It is this property that allows the transportation and storage of LP-Gases in concentrated liquid form, although they normally are used in vapor form.

For additional information on other properties of LP-Gases, see Annex B.

NFPA 58 addresses virtually every aspect of LP-Gas distribution and use, but it does not cover the production of the gas itself. However, the actual scope of application, including exclusions, is delineated more precisely by the lists in 1.3.1 and 1.3.2. LP-Gas storage, handling, and transportation are described in the following commentary.

STORAGE

One way to categorize the different types of storage locations is to use the three types of propane storage facilities: primary, secondary, and tertiary.

Primary Storage. Primary storage involves large storage facilities [hundreds of thousands or millions of gallons (liters)], including underground salt caverns, refrigerated storage containers, and large tank farms. Primary storage also includes storage that is associated either with the production of LP-Gas or with marine or pipeline transportation, before the product is transferred to the retail market.

Secondary Storage. Secondary storage usually refers to bulk and industrial plants, in which the LP-Gas is typically stored in pressure vessels with water capacities usually ranging between 10,000 gal (38 m³) and 90,000 gal (340 m³). The product in secondary storage facilities is held until it can be used or delivered to the end user's facility, where it is typically used as a fuel.

Tertiary Storage. Tertiary storage refers to the storage located at the end user's facility. In residential installations, containers may range in size from as small as a 100 lb (45 kg) propane capacity cylinder to a 4000 gal (15.1 m³) ASME tank. Commercial, industrial, and agricultural users typically have storage capacity of 18,000 gal to 30,000 gal (68 m³ to 114 m³), and some have multiple 30,000 gal tanks. There are some larger installations with single or multiple 60,000 gal and 90,000 gal tanks.

HANDLING

The term *handling* of LP-Gas applies to operations associated with the transfer of liquid LP-Gas from one container to another. Because LP-Gas is a flammable material, the code requires all persons performing transfer operations to be trained to do so.

TRANSPORTATION

FAQ ▶
How do NFPA 58 requirements correlate with the hazardous materials transportation regulations contained in Title 49 of the Code of Federal Regulations?

Although NFPA 58 contains provisions for transporting LP-Gas, it must be recognized that in the United States, the U.S. Department of Transportation (DOT) is the primary authority for regulation of transporting hazardous materials in commerce. The term *in commerce* generally applies to the transportation of all hazardous materials by companies in the hazardous materials business. It also applies to vehicles that transport LP-Gas as a "material of trade," such as by a roofing company that uses LP-Gas as a fuel during the normal conduct of its business. Title 49 of the Code of Federal Regulations, "Transportation" [1], contains the provisions enforced by DOT for transporting LP-Gas. Therefore, any transportation of LP-Gas by any method in commerce in the United States must be in compliance with Title 49 (many other countries have similar requirements). However, additional requirements that are contained in NFPA 58 and that do not conflict with Title 49 must be complied with as well. In addition, NFPA 58 establishes the requirements for the private transportation of LP-Gas, which is not governed by Title 49; for example, a customer transporting a gas grill cylinder for refilling or exchange. See also the commentary following 1.3.1(2).

Federal Regulations. Regulations of the U.S. Department of Transportation (DOT) are referenced throughout this code. Prior to April 1, 1967, these regulations were promulgated by the Interstate Commerce Commission (ICC). The Federal Hazardous Substances Act (15 U.S.C. 1261) requires cautionary labeling of refillable cylinders of liquefied petroleum gases distributed for consumer use. They are typically 40 lb (13 kg) and less and are used with outdoor cooking appliances, portable lamps, camp stoves, and heaters. The Federal Hazardous Substances Act is administered by the U.S. Consumer Product Safety Commission under regulations codified at 16 CFR 1500, Commercial Practices, Chapter 11, "Consumer Product Safety Commission."

1.2 Purpose. (Reserved)

The NFPA *Manual of Style for NFPA Technical Committee Documents* [2] requires that all NFPA codes and standards use Section 1.2 for a statement of the purpose of the code or standard. Not all NFPA technical committees for codes and standards, including the committee responsible for NFPA 58 (Technical Committee on Liquefied Petroleum Gases), have elected to include a statement of purpose. Therefore, Section 1.2 is reserved for future use.

1.3 Application

The Technical Committee on Liquefied Petroleum Gases recognizes that it is not feasible to apply NFPA 58 to all LP-Gases and their uses, for a number of reasons. First, because of the great versatility of LP-Gases, the number and variety of their applications are large and have steadily increased since their original commercial use as a residential fuel. This increase is especially true in industry, where LP-Gases have a great variety of uses, such as fuel, refriger-ant, solvent, or chemical feedstock. Second, the committee's expertise has always been con-centrated on the distribution and use of propane as a fuel.

The applications not covered by NFPA 58 often are addressed by other NFPA technical committees, by standards-making bodies, or by technically qualified groups. Where the tech-nical committee responsible for NFPA 58 considers those other standards adequate, it has been the practice to reference those standards in NFPA 58. In instances where the standards are written in a mandatory format that can be adopted as law, the referenced standards are located in the code (Chapters 1 through 15). Where standards are referenced, and NFPA 58 is adopted as a law, the referenced document has equal status (unless the adopting agency states otherwise). In cases where the standard is not written in mandatory form (usually a recom-mended practice or guide), it is referenced in Annex A to advise the user of its availability. Although recommended practices and guides are valuable, they cannot be referenced in NFPA 58 because doing so would mandate items that were not intended to be mandatory.

When other standards or documents cover an LP-Gas application, it is important that the scope be carefully correlated with that of NFPA 58 to avoid conflicts. This task is not always easy because of the large number of standards-making bodies, but the effort has been rather successful because the spirit of cooperation among these bodies has always been high.

1.3.1 Application of the Code.

This code shall apply to the operation of all LP-Gas systems, including the following:

(1) Containers, piping, and associated equipment, when delivering LP-Gas to a building for use as a fuel gas.
(2) Highway transportation of LP-Gas.

Until the mid-1990s, NFPA 58 was a primary document for addressing the transportation of LP-Gas, particularly intrastate transportation. The jurisdiction of DOT extended only to the interstate commercial transportation of LP-Gas. In the mid-1990s, Congress extended the jurisdiction of DOT to cover intrastate as well as interstate transportation. As a result, if there are any conflicts between the requirements of NFPA 58 and DOT in Title 49 of the Code of Federal Regulations with respect to the transportation of LP-Gas in commerce, the provisions of DOT must take precedence. The transportation of LP-Gas in a private vehicle is not regu-lated by DOT and therefore falls under the scope of NFPA 58.

(3) The design, construction, installation, and operation of marine terminals whose primary purpose is the receipt of LP-Gas for delivery to transporters, distributors, or users, except for marine terminals associated with refineries, petrochemicals, gas plants, and marine terminals whose purpose is the delivery of LP-Gas to marine vessels.

Marine and pipeline terminals, such as the one shown in Exhibit 1.1, are included in the scope of NFPA 58 because these facilities are storage and transfer facilities similar to those covered elsewhere in the code. Prior to the 1989 edition, when marine and pipeline coverage was added to the code, owners, operators, and authorities having jurisdiction were applying NFPA 58 and NFPA 59, *Utility LP-Gas Plant Code* [3], even though coverage of marine and pipeline terminals was specifically excluded. Previous editions of NFPA 58 contained no specific re-quirements and simply referred the reader to the American Petroleum Institute's API 2510, *Design and Construction of LPG Installations* [4].

The exception of marine terminals supplying refineries, petrochemical plants, and gas plants recognizes that these facilities are frequently designed and integrally associated with the refinery, petrochemical plant, or gas plant. If a refinery, petrochemical plant, or gas plant has the capability of supplying LP-Gas to other uses by truck- or rail-loading facilities, those loading facilities come under NFPA 58 if they are separate.

The exception of marine terminals that load ships recognizes that safety standards for marine terminals in the United States are written by DOT and are enforced in the United States by the U.S. Coast Guard. If a terminal is used for truck or rail loading incidental to its main use, NFPA 58 applies to those truck- or rail-loading facilities.

(4)* The design, construction, installation, and operation of pipeline terminals that receive LP-Gas from pipelines under the jurisdiction of the U.S. Department of Transportation (DOT) whose primary purpose is the receipt of LP-Gas for delivery to transporters, distributors, or users. Coverage shall begin downstream of the last pipeline valve or tank manifold inlet.

A.1.3.1(4) For further information on the storage and handling of LP-Gas at natural gas processing plants, refineries, and petrochemical plants, see API 2510, *Design and Construction of LP-Gas Installations.*

Pipelines in the United States are constructed in accordance with Part 192 of Title 49, "Transportation," of the U.S. Code of Federal Regulations [5]. Propane vapor piping distribution systems may also be subject to Part 192 if they serve more than nine customers, or if any portion of the piping system is located in a "public place," which would include streets. Pipeline terminals associated with refineries, petrochemical plants, and gas plants have pipelines built to conform with other standards, usually ASME B31.8, *Gas Transmission and Distribution Piping Systems* [6].

1.3.2 Nonapplication of Code.

This code shall not apply to the following:

(1) Frozen ground containers and underground storage in caverns, including associated piping and appurtenances used for the storage of LP-Gas

Frozen ground containers, as referenced in 1.3.2(1), are a type of refrigerated LP-Gas container made by excavating an open pit, lining the pit with a nonpermeable barrier (such as a plastic sheet), covering it with a gastight cap, and freezing the ground to provide containment. The Technical Committee on Liquefied Petroleum Gases does not prohibit or discourage the use of such containers. However, if these containers are used, other standards must be used for their construction and maintenance.

(2) Natural gas processing plants, refineries, and petrochemical plants

Refineries, petrochemical operations, and gas plants are excluded from the scope of NFPA 58 for a number of reasons, including the following:

1. The storage and processing equipment is usually integrated, and it is difficult for enforcement officials to determine which vessels, equipment, and piping come under NFPA 58.
2. Safety is frequently achieved in these complex facilities by a combination of design and operational features that, by their nature, would be unnecessarily restrictive for most facilities covered by NFPA 58.
3. No incidents have occurred at these facilities that have warranted additional coverage by NFPA codes.

Information on these facilities can be found in API 2510. API also publishes API 2510A, *Fire Protection Considerations for the Design and Operation of Liquefied Petroleum Gas (LPG) Storage Facilities* [7], which supplements API 2510.

(3) LP-Gas (including refrigerated storage) at utility gas plants *(see* NFPA 59, *Utility LP-Gas Plant Code)*

The exclusion of nonrefrigerated and refrigerated storage, vaporization, and mixing of LP-Gas with air at utility gas plants recognizes that NFPA 59 is written for these facilities, which mix LP-Gas and air for use to supplement natural gas supplies in pipeline transportation systems.

LP-Gas storage at utility gas plants is covered by NFPA 59, which is adopted by reference in NFPA 58. There is extensive overlap of membership of the Technical Committee on Liquefied Petroleum Gases, responsible for NFPA 58, and the Technical Committee on LP-Gas at Utility Gas Plants, responsible for NFPA 59. From 1966 to 1993, the Technical Committee on Liquefied Petroleum Gases wrote both NFPA 58 and NFPA 59. Following their separation in 1993, the two committees have met jointly. As a result, both documents are continuously monitored to maintain consistent provisions. This process is expected to continue.

The need for NFPA 58 and NFPA 59 as separate documents has been considered and rejected several times in the past, most recently during the development of the 2001 editions. NFPA 59 has changed its revision cycle to be one year following NFPA 58's revision cycle. This allows the NFPA 59 committee to review the published changes in NFPA 58 to determine which are applicable to NFPA 59.

(4)* Chemical plants where specific approval of construction and installation plans, based on substantially similar requirements, is obtained from the authority having jurisdiction

A.1.3.2(4) The exclusion of the use of LP-Gas as a chemical reactant (feedstock) or in processes recognizes the unique and complex fire hazard problems that often exist in a chemical plant. The term *chemical plant* includes all facilities owned by chemical companies where LP-Gas is used primarily as a chemical reactant, process solvent gas, or solvent. However, there is no standard definition of a chemical plant, and facilities in which few or no chemical reactions are carried out may be called chemical plants.

This new annex text formerly appeared as handbook commentary. It was relocated to Annex A to provide this relevant explanation of the reason for the exclusion to readers of the code, rather than only the handbook readers.

(5)*LP-Gas used with oxygen

A.1.3.2(5) For information on the use of LP-Gas with oxygen, see NFPA 51, *Standard for the Design and Installation of Oxygen–Fuel Gas Systems for Welding, Cutting, and Allied Processes*, and AWS Z49.1, *Safety in Welding, Cutting and Allied Processes*.

The burning of LP-Gas with oxygen rather than air is most commonly associated with the flame cutting of metal in industry and construction. These operations are widespread, and the two standards referenced in A.1.3.2(5) cover them. Both NFPA 51, *Standard for the Design and Installation of Oxygen–Fuel Gas Systems for Welding, Cutting, and Allied Processes* [8], and AWS Z49.1, *Safety in Welding, Cutting and Allied Processes* [9] are consensus standards. Therefore, these documents can be used, although their use is not mandated because the subject is outside the scope of NFPA 58.

Unfortunately, NFPA 58's exclusion of LP-Gas used with oxygen and the specific scopes of NFPA 51 and AWS Z49.1 technically have left some areas of fire safety uncovered. These areas include small jewelry and glass-forming operations (often in shopping malls having considerable public exposure) and the use of oxy-propane torches by plumbers and do-it-yourselfers. Manufacturers of oxy-propane torches customarily obtain product listings. To date, their use has not been a significant problem. However, regulatory authorities have had difficulty with small mercantile operations, such as those using propane cylinders in shopping malls where the use is not easily observed. Used with judgment, many of the provisions in NFPA 51, NFPA 58, and AWS Z49.1 are appropriate, especially those concerned with LP-Gas and oxygen storage.

(6)*The portions of LP-Gas systems covered by NFPA 54 (ANSI Z223.1), *National Fuel Gas Code*, where NFPA 54 (ANSI Z223.1) is adopted, used, or enforced

A.1.3.2(6) Several types of LP-Gas systems are not covered by NFPA 54, *National Fuel Gas Code*, as noted. These include, but are not restricted to, most portable applications; many farm installations; vaporization, mixing, and gas manufacturing; temporary systems, for example, in construction; and systems on vehicles.

NFPA 54, *National Fuel Gas Code* [10], traces its beginnings to early in the 20th century, when it covered the installation of fuel gas piping and appliances in buildings. In the early days, the fuel gas was manufactured gas used for cooking and lighting, and the buildings were residential and commercial in character. At that time, manufactured gas, which was available in cities, was more expensive than other heating fuels such as coal and oil. Some natural gas was used, but usually only in locations relatively close to the gas wells. After World War II, natural gas replaced most manufactured gas in the United States, and by the early 1960s, industrial gas systems were added to NFPA 54.

In the 1950s, NFPA 52, *Liquefied Petroleum Gas Piping and Appliance Installations in Buildings* [11], was developed to provide similar coverage for undiluted LP-Gas piping and appliances in residential and commercial buildings. It was soon recognized, however, that, with the exception of the piping materials and testing of piping for leaks, NFPA 52 and NFPA 54 were similar. Differences were resolved in the 1959 edition of NFPA 54, when its scope was expanded to include LP-Gas systems in buildings, and NFPA 52 was withdrawn.

Still, with very few minor exceptions, NFPA 54 is restricted by its scope to the installation of fixed-in-place appliances and other gas-consuming equipment connected to a building's gas piping system. Furthermore, many specialized types of farm equipment, such as incubators, are not covered even though they are fixed in place in a building and connected to a piping system in that building. These systems are customarily LP-Gas systems rather than natural gas systems. Although the great majority of LP-Gas piping and appliance installations in completed buildings require the application of NFPA 54 to part of the system, it is necessary to refer to paragraph 1.1.1 in NFPA 54 to make this determination. In this respect, A.1.3.2(6) of NFPA 58 should be considered as only a rough guide.

Today, NFPA 58 covers the installation of propane containers and the first- and second-stage pressure regulators. NFPA 54 covers the piping from the outlet of the final stage pressure regulator (usually the second-stage regulator) and all piping and appliances downstream of that point. Prior to the 1996 edition of NFPA 54, the split was the discharge of the first-stage pressure regulator. This change was made following the revision in the 1995 edition of NFPA 58 to require two-stage pressure regulation for building piping systems. It means that, in most cases, all piping and equipment outside a building falls under NFPA 58, and piping and equipment inside a building falls under NFPA 54. This separation is consistent with code enforcement practice since NFPA 58 is usually enforced by fire officials or a state propane agency and NFPA 54 is usually enforced by building officials.

In recent years, the use of "2 psi regulator systems" has become more common. These systems incorporate a first-stage regulator, a 2 psi regulator, and one or more line pressure regulators that reduce the 2 psi pressure to appliance pressure. In these systems, the scope of NFPA 54 begins at the outlet of the 2 psi regulator and includes the line pressure regulators.

Exhibit 1.2, parts (a) and (b), illustrate the division of scope between NFPA 54 and NFPA 58.

◄ **FAQ**
How can one determine where the scope of NFPA 58 ends and the scope of NFPA 54 begins?

(7) Transportation by air (including use in hot air balloons), rail, or water under the jurisdiction of the DOT

DOT has the primary jurisdiction in the United States for the transportation of LP-Gas where DOT's jurisdiction is valid. (See Chapter 9, Vehicular Transportation of LP-Gas, for more information.)

Hot air ballooning is a popular sport that uses propane to heat the air in the balloon. In the United States, the Federal Aviation Administration, a part of DOT, regulates the use of propane cylinders used in balloons in flight or in flight preparation. The storage of propane cylinders used in hot air balloons (when not in flight or in preparation thereof) falls under NFPA 58. The same rules apply to the storage of cylinders used for hot air ballooning (when they are not in the balloon basket) as to any other propane cylinder.

(8)*Marine fire protection

A.1.3.2(8) For information on the use of LP-Gas in vessels, see NFPA 302, *Fire Protection Standard for Pleasure and Commercial Motor Craft*.

LP-Gas is a popular fuel for galley stoves, cabin heaters, and other appliances on motor vessels that fall within the scope of NFPA 302, *Fire Protection Standard for Pleasure and Commercial Motor Craft* [12]. NFPA 302 applies to motor vessels of less than 300 gross tons (849 m³) that are used for pleasure and commercial purposes. LP-Gas use on such vessels is extensive enough to represent substantial public safety exposure. As the subject is outside the scope of NFPA 58, NFPA 302 is not a referenced standard, but it can be used.

(9) Refrigeration cycle equipment and LP-Gas used as a refrigerant in a closed cycle

The expertise of the NFPA 58 committee is in the storage and handling of LP-Gases and not in their use in closed process systems. Propane, butane, and other flammable liquefied gases have physical properties that may make them advantageous as refrigerants. The exclusion stated in 1.3.2(9) applies to the refrigeration equipment in which LP-Gas is being used. It does not include the storage of refrigerant LP-Gas, which is still within the scope of NFPA 58.

(10) The manufacturing requirements for recreational vehicle LP-Gas systems that are addressed by NFPA 1192, *Standard on Recreational Vehicles*

All aspects of recreational vehicles (RVs), including propane systems, are covered in NFPA 1192, *Standard on Recreational Vehicles* [13]. Propane is a preferred fuel for RV appliances, such as furnaces, stoves, and refrigerators, because it is widely available. Some RVs, because

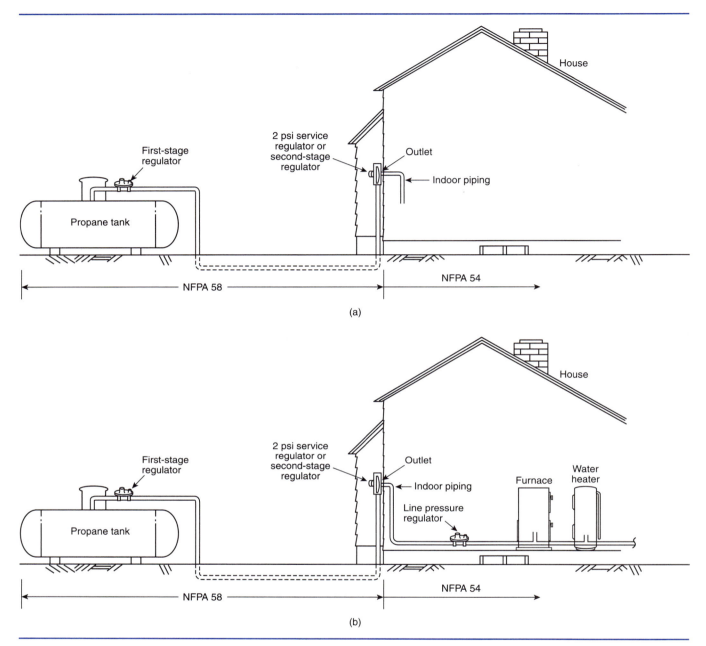

EXHIBIT 1.2 *Split of Scope Between NFPA 54 and NFPA 58 Showing a 2 psi House Piping System.*

of their compact size, have difficulty complying with the spacing requirements of NFPA 58. Some of these spacing requirements may be different in NFPA 1192.

(11) Propane vehicle fuel dispensers located at multiple fuel refueling stations shall comply with NFPA 30A, *Code for Motor Fuel Dispensing Facilities and Repair Garages*

This exclusion refers the user to NFPA 30A, *Code for Motor Fuel Dispensing Facilities and Repair Garages* [14], which addresses the use of LP-Gas as a motor fuel in locations that are open to the public and dispense other fuels such as gasoline, diesel fuel, compressed natural gas, and hydrogen. The text of 1.3.2(11) was revised in the 2011 edition to clarify that the exclusion applies only to propane vehicle fuel dispensers, and not to dispensers filling only portable cylinders at service stations.

This exclusion recognizes that two NFPA codes cannot cover the same installations. In previous editions, NFPA 58 had established spacing at vehicle refueling stations between propane dispensers and liquid fuel dispensers. NFPA 30A had different requirements for that spacing. It was determined that with increased dispensing of compressed natural gas (CNG) and the possible expansion of hydrogen as a vehicle fuel, it made more sense to have one code cover the subject. Note that if propane is the only vehicle fuel dispensed, NFPA 58 is the applicable document. Dispensers for propane are common at many propane bulk plants and dispensing stations.

Most of the information on the installation and placement of LP-Gas dispensing equipment is found in Chapter 12 of NFPA 30A. NFPA 30A excludes propane dispensing located at least 50 ft (15 m) from any other aboveground motor fuel storage or dispensing equipment and refers back to NFPA 58 for such applications. This referral back to NFPA 58 recognizes that where sufficient separation exists, propane dispensing equipment should come under NFPA 58 and not NFPA 30A.

1.4 Retroactivity

The provisions of this code reflect a consensus of what is necessary to provide an acceptable degree of protection from the hazards addressed in this code at the time it was issued.

Retroactivity is an important provision because NFPA 58 is so widely adopted by public safety regulatory agencies and is frequently cited in litigation. Over the more than 70 years of the code's existence, the technical committees responsible for NFPA 58 have consistently taken the approach that when an amendment should be applied retroactively, the amendment will so state. Typically, the applicability of retroactive requirements has taken the form of stipulating a certain date by which something must be accomplished. The date is retained in subsequent editions of the code for many years.

1.4.1 Unless otherwise specified, the provisions of this code shall not apply to facilities, equipment, appliances, structures, or installations that existed or were approved for construction or installation prior to the effective date of the code. Equipment and appliances include stocks in manufacturers' storage, distribution warehouses, and dealers' storage and showrooms in compliance with the provisions of this code in effect at the time of manufacture. Where specified, the provisions of this code shall be retroactive.

An example of a requirement for retrofitting equipment, as referenced in 1.4.1, is Table 5.7.4.2. The table contains a retroactive requirement that existing container installations exceeding 4000 gal (15.1 m^3) in water capacity must have installed on the liquid outlet connection by July 1, 2011, either an internal valve or one of the alternatives as described in Table 5.7.4.2. The retroactive requirement will result in all large LP-Gas containers having the capability to remotely close liquid withdrawal openings by July 2011. The committee believes that this requirement will greatly reduce the amount of liquid released in the event of piping system failure, thereby minimizing the severity of accidents.

◄ **FAQ**
What is an example of a retroactive requirement?

1.4.2 In those cases where the authority having jurisdiction determines that the existing situation presents a distinct hazard to life and property, the authority having jurisdiction shall be permitted to apply retroactively any portions of this code that are deemed appropriate.

The phrase "distinct hazard to life and property" is very subjective and difficult to quantify. It is uncommon for authorities having jurisdiction to impose retroactive provisions where none are required in NFPA 58. Although some code provisions may provide an additional degree of safety over what is currently being used, the functional and economic burdens of retrofitting equipment usually make such retrofits impractical when weighed against the safety that would be realized. It is not the intent of this provision to enable an authority having jurisdiction to apply portions of the code retroactively to installations that complied with the edition in effect when the installation was built. In cases where that may have been necessary, the code was usually revised to make the specific requirement retroactive.

1.4.3 Where the application of the retroactivity requirements of this code are determined to be impractical in the judgment of the authority having jurisdiction, alternate requirements that provide a reasonable degree of safety shall be provided by the authority having jurisdiction.

Similar to 1.4.2, paragraph 1.4.3 requires the parties involved to make a judgment as to what the term *impractical* means. As a rule of thumb, if a particular requirement that is required to be applied retroactively is difficult to comply with and the result would have minimal positive effect on the safety of an installation, the authority having jurisdiction may waive the requirement.

The requirement of 1.4.3 was revised in the 2011 edition to clarify the intent. The current text more clearly states that the authority having jurisdiction is the only entity that can allow alternate provisions.

1.5 Equivalency

Nothing in this code is intended to prevent the use of systems, methods, or devices of equivalent or superior quality, strength, fire resistance, effectiveness, durability, and safety over those prescribed by this code.

1.5.1 Technical documentation shall be submitted to the authority having jurisdiction to demonstrate equivalency.

Technology is continually changing, and code writing often lags behind development. NFPA 58 recognizes this fact and permits the approval of alternative materials and systems that provide the minimum required performance characteristics as specified in Section 1.5, even though that material, product, or system may not be specifically required or even addressed by the code.

1.5.2 The system, method, or device shall be approved for the intended purpose by the authority having jurisdiction.

FAQ ▶
What technical documentation can support the use of an alternative material, product, or system?

Technical documentation may take one or more of the following forms:

1. Engineering calculations
2. Company research or evaluation report
3. Performance evaluation or research report written by a qualified, independent third-party testing or engineering agency and describing testing or modeling performed to demonstrate the performance characteristics of the material, product, or system

The approval of an equivalent product or system is always the prerogative of the authority having jurisdiction. The authority having jurisdiction also determines what evidence or documentation is acceptable to justify the alternative system.

If the documentation required in 1.5.1 is submitted to the authority having jurisdiction, then the alternative product or system can be approved. Eventually, the technology may make its way into the code, and the technical committee encourages all who are involved with such situations to advise the committee of alternatives by the use of a public proposal for the next edition of NFPA 58. Proposal forms are included in the code and their use is encouraged. Proposal forms are also available on the NFPA web page, http://www.nfpa.org/assets/files/PDF/CodesStandards/NFPAProposalForm.doc, and proposals can be submitted on-line by going to the following link: http://submissions.nfpa.org/onlinesub/onsubmain.php.

The special software required to submit proposals on-line is available from the site at no cost.

1.6 Units and Formulas. (Reserved)

1.7 Enforcement

This code shall be administered and enforced by the authority having jurisdiction designated by the governing authority. *(See Annex J for sample wording for enabling legislation.)*

In order for NFPA 58 to be enforceable, it must be adopted and enforced by a governmental jurisdiction, such as a state, city, or county. The sample wording for enabling legislation in Annex J, referenced in Section 1.7, is intended to assist jurisdictions in this process. The administration and enforcement of the provisions of the code are left with that authority, which must make decisions on how to interpret the document as well. The handbook is intended to assist users of the code in making those important decisions by attempting to provide some historical background to the actual code provisions.

REFERENCES CITED IN COMMENTARY

1. Title 49, Code of Federal Regulations, "Transportation," U.S. Government Printing Office, Washington, DC.
2. NFPA *Manual of Style for NFPA Technical Committee Documents,* 2003 edition, National Fire Protection Association, Quincy, MA.
3. NFPA 59, *Utility LP-Gas Plant Code,* 2008 edition, National Fire Protection Association, Quincy, MA.
4. API 2510, *Design and Construction of LP-Gas Installations,* 2001 edition, American Petroleum Institute, Washington, DC.
5. Title 49, Code of Federal Regulations, Part 192, U.S. Government Printing Office, Washington, DC.
6. ASME B31.8, *Gas Transmission and Distribution Piping Systems,* 2007 edition, American Society of Mechanical Engineers, New York, NY.
7. API 2510A, *Fire Protection Considerations for the Design and Operation of Liquefied Petroleum Gas (LPG) Storage Facilities,* 1996 edition, American Petroleum Institute, Washington, DC.
8. NFPA 51, *Standard for the Design and Installation of Oxygen–Fuel Gas Systems for Welding,* Cutting, and Allied Processes, 2007 edition, National Fire Protection Association, Quincy, MA.
9. AWS Z49.1, *Safety in Welding, Cutting and Allied Processes,* 2005 edition, American Welding Society, Miami, FL.
10. NFPA 54, *National Fuel Gas Code,* 2009 edition, National Fire Protection Association, Quincy, MA.
11. NFPA 52, *Liquefied Petroleum Gas Piping and Appliance Installations in Buildings,* 1956 edition, National Fire Protection Association, Boston, MA (withdrawn).
12. NFPA 302, *Fire Protection Standard for Pleasure and Commercial Motor Craft,* 2010 edition, National Fire Protection Association, Quincy, MA.

13. NFPA 1192, *Standard on Recreational Vehicles,* 2008 edition, National Fire Protection Association, Quincy, MA.

14. NFPA 30A, *Code for Motor Fuel Dispensing Facilities and Repair Garages,* 2008 edition, National Fire Protection Association, Quincy, MA.

Referenced Publications

Chapter 2 provides a list of the publications that are referenced in the mandatory part of NFPA 58. Virtually all of these publications are codes, standards, or federal regulations.

The sections in Chapter 2 include the following documents that are referenced elsewhere in NFPA 58:

- Codes and standards referenced in NFPA 58 that are published by NFPA (See Section 2.2.)
- Codes and standards referenced in NFPA 58 that are published by other organizations (See Section 2.3.)
- Regulations published by the U.S. federal government and found in the Code of Federal Regulations (See Subsection 2.3.12.)
- References for extracted code in mandatory sections (See Section 2.4.)

2.1 General

The documents or portions thereof listed in this chapter are referenced within this standard and shall be considered part of the requirements of this document.

The documents that are included in this chapter are mandatory references — that is, to the extent that a reference to a code, standard, or regulation is made in this code, the provisions of that code, standard, or regulation are to be treated as requirements that must be complied with.

The term *code* is defined in NFPA 58 as:

> **3.2.3* Code.** A standard that is an extensive compilation of provisions covering broad subject matter or that is suitable for adoption into law independently of other codes and standards.

In order to be "suitable for adoption into law," the code, and its referenced codes and standards, must be written in a mandatory form with clear and unambiguous language. The Technical Committee on Liquefied Petroleum Gases reviews referenced codes and standards to ensure that they, like NFPA 58, are written in mandatory format. At one time it was common for codes and standards to mix mandatory requirements with recommendations, which are unenforceable. If the technical committee wishes to reference a document not written in mandatory form it can do so, but must place the reference in one of the annexes, not in a numbered chapter of the code.

Note that the scope of the mandatory requirement of the referenced standard is limited to the original scope of reference from NFPA 58. For example, 6.23.8 requires that a fire extinguisher installed in a mobile cooking unit be rated not less than 10-B:C in accordance with the requirements of NFPA 10, *Standard for Portable Fire Extinguishers* [1]. The "mandatory requirement" in this case is to use a fire extinguisher that has the required rating according to NFPA 10. No other requirements in NFPA 10 are mandatory for users of NFPA 58.

2.2 NFPA Publications

National Fire Protection Association, 1 Batterymarch Park, Quincy, MA 02169-7471.

NFPA 10, *Standard for Portable Fire Extinguishers,* 2010 edition.

NFPA 13, *Standard for the Installation of Sprinkler Systems,* 2010 edition.

NFPA 15, *Standard for Water Spray Fixed Systems for Fire Protection,* 2007 edition.

NFPA 25, *Standard for the Inspection, Testing, and Maintenance of Water-Based Fire Protection Systems,* 2011 edition.

NFPA 30, *Flammable and Combustible Liquids Code,* 2008 edition.

NFPA 30A, *Code for Motor Fuel Dispensing Facilities and Repair Garages,* 2008 edition.

NFPA 51B, *Standard for Fire Prevention During Welding, Cutting, and Other Hot Work,* 2009 edition.

NFPA 54, *National Fuel Gas Code,* 2009 edition.

NFPA 55, *Compressed Gases and Cryogenic Fluids Code,* 2010 edition.

NFPA 59, *Utility LP-Gas Plant Code,* 2008 edition.

NFPA 70®, National Electrical Code®, 2011 edition.

NFPA 99, *Standard for Health Care Facilities,* 2005 edition.

NFPA *101®, Life Safety Code®,* 2009 edition.

NFPA 160, *Standard for the Use of Flame Effects Before an Audience,* 2011 edition.

NFPA 220, *Standard on Types of Building Construction,* 2009 edition.

NFPA 251, *Standard Methods of Tests of Fire Resistance of Building Construction and Materials,* 2006 edition.

NFPA 1192, *Standard on Recreational Vehicles,* 2008 edition.

2.3 Other Publications

2.3.1 ANSI Publications.

American National Standards Institute, Inc., 25 West 43rd Street, 4th Floor, New York, NY 10036.

ANSI Z-21.80, *Standard for Line Pressure Regulators*, 2005.

2.3.2 API Publications.

American Petroleum Institute, 1220 L Street, N.W., Washington, DC 20005-4070.

API-ASME *Code for Unfired Pressure Vessels for Petroleum Liquids and Gases*, Pre-July 1, 1961.

API 607, *Fire Test for Soft-Seated Quarter Turn Ball Valves*, 2008.

API Standard 620, *Design and Construction of Large, Welded, Low-Pressure Storage Tanks*, 2008.

API Publication 1632, *Cathodic Protection of Underground Petroleum Storage Tanks and Piping Systems*, 2002.

2.3.3 ASCE Publications.

American Society of Civil Engineers, 1801 Alexander Bell Drive, Reston, VA 20191–4400.

ASCE 7, *Minimum Design Loads for Buildings and Other Structures*, 2005.

2.3.4 ASME Publications.

American Society of Mechanical Engineers, Three Park Avenue, New York, NY 10016-5990.

"Rules for the Construction of Unfired Pressure Vessels," Section VIII, *ASME Boiler and Pressure Vessel Code*, 2007.

ASME B31.3, *Process Piping*, 2008.
ASME B36.10M, *Welded and Seamless Wrought Steel Pipe*, 2004.

2.3.5 ASTM Publications.

ASTM International, 100 Barr Harbor Drive, P.O. Box C700, West Conshohocken, PA 19428-2959.

ASTM A 47, *Standard Specification for Ferritic Malleable Iron Castings*, 2009.
ASTM A 48, *Standard Specification for Gray Iron Castings*, 2008.
ASTM A 53, *Standard Specification for Pipe, Steel, Black and Hot-Dipped, Zinc-Coated Welded and Seamless*, 2007.
ASTM A 106, *Standard Specification for Seamless Carbon Steel Pipe for High-Temperature Service*, 2008.
ASTM A 395, *Standard Specification for Ferritic Ductile Iron Pressure-Retaining Castings for Use at Elevated Temperatures*, 2009.
ASTM A 513, *Standard Specification for Electric-Resistance-Welded Carbon and Alloy Steel Mechanical Tubing*, 2008.
ASTM A 536, *Standard Specification for Ductile Iron Castings*, 2009.
ASTM B 42, *Standard Specification for Seamless Copper Pipe, Standard Sizes*, 2002.
ASTM B 43, *Standard Specification for Seamless Red Brass Pipe, Standard Sizes*, 2004.
ASTM B 86, *Standard Specification for Zinc-Alloy Die Casting*, 2009.
ASTM B 88, *Standard Specification for Seamless Copper Water Tube*, 2003.
ASTM B 135, *Standard Specification for Seamless Brass Tube*, 2008.
ASTM B 280, *Standard Specification for Seamless Copper Tube for Air Conditioning and Refrigeration Field Service*, 2008.
ASTM D 2513, *Standard Specification for Thermoplastic Gas Pressure Pipe, Tubing and Fittings*, 2009.
ASTM D 2683, *Standard Specification for Socket-Type Polyethylene (PE) Fittings for Outside Diameter Controlled Polyethylene Pipe*, 2004.
ASTM D 3261, *Standard Specification for Butt Heat Fusion Polyethylene (PE) Plastic Fittings for Polyethylene (PE) Plastic Pipe and Tubing*, 2003.
ASTM F 1055, *Standard Specification for Electrofusion Type Polyethylene Fittings for Outside Diameter Controlled Polyethylene Pipe and Tubing*, 2006.
ASTM F 1733, *Standard Specification for Butt Heat Fusion Polyamide (PA) Plastic Fitting for Polyamide (PA) Plastic Pipe and Tubing*, 2007.

2.3.6 CGA Publications.

Compressed Gas Association, 4221 Walney Road, 5th floor, Chantilly, VA 20151-2923.

CGA C-3, *Guidelines for Visual Inspection and Requalification of Low Pressure Aluminum Compressed Gas Cylinders*, 2005.
CGA C-6, *Standard for Visual Inspection of Steel Compressed Gas Cylinders*, 2007.
ANSI/CGA C-7, *Guide to the Preparation of Precautionary Labeling and Marking of Compressed Gas Containers*, 2004.
CGA S-1.3, *Pressure Relief Device Standards, Part 3 — Stationary Storage Containers for Compressed Gases,* 2008.
CGA V-1, *Standard Compressed Gas Cylinder Valve Outlet and Inlet Connections*, 2008.

2.3.7 CSA America Publications.

CSA America, Inc., 8501 East Pleasant Valley Road, Cleveland, OH 44131-5575.

ANSI/CSA 6.26 (LC 1), *Interior Fuel Gas Piping Systems Using Corrugated Stainless Steel Tubing*, 2005.

ANSI Z21.18/CSA 6.3, *Gas Appliance Regulators*, 2007.

ANSI Z-21.80/CSA 6.22, *Standard for Line Pressure Regulators*, 2003.

2.3.8 NACE Publications.

NACE International, 1440 South Creek Drive, Houston, TX 77084-4906.

RP-01-69, *Standard Recommended Practice, Control of External Corrosion of Underground or Submerged Metallic Piping Systems*, 2007.

RP-02-85, *Standard Recommended Practice, Corrosion Control of Underground Storage Tank Systems by Cathodic Protection*, 2002.

2.3.9 NBBPVI Publications.

National Board of Boiler and Pressure Vessel Inspectors, 1055 Crupper Avenue, Columbus, OH 43229.

ANSI/NB23, *National Board Inspection Code*, 2007.

2.3.10 UL Publications.

Underwriters Laboratories Inc., 333 Pfingsten Road, Northbrook, IL 60062-2096.

ANSI/UL 21, *Standard for LP-Gas Hose,* 2007.

ANSI/UL 125, *Standard for Valves for Anhydrous Ammonia and LP-Gas (Other than Safety Relief)*, 2009.

ANSI/UL 132, *Standard for Safety Relief Valves for Anhydrous Ammonia and LP-Gas*, 2007.

ANSI/UL 144, *Standard for LP-Gas Regulators*, 1999, revised 2002.

ANSI/UL 147A, *Standard for Nonrefillable (Disposable) Type Fuel Gas Cylinder Assemblies*, 2005, revised 2006.

ANSI/UL 147B, *Standard for Nonrefillable (Disposable) Type Metal Container Assemblies for Butane*, 2005, revised 2006.

UL 514B, *Conduit, Tubing, and Cable Fittings*, 2004.

ANSI/UL 567, *Standard for Pipe Connectors for Flammable and Combustible Liquids and LP-Gas*, 2003, revised 2004.

ANSI/UL 569, *Standard for Pigtails and Flexible Hose Connections for LP-Gas*, 1995, revised 2001.

ANSI/UL 651, *Schedule 40 or 80 Rigid PVC Conduit and Fittings*, 2005, revised 2008.

ANSI/UL 1660, *Liquid-Tight Flexible Nonmetallic Conduit*, 2004.

ANSI/UL 1746, *External Corrosion Protection Systems for Steel Underground Storage Tanks.*

ANSI/UL 1769, *Cylinder Valves*, 2006.

ANSI/UL 2227, *Standard for Overfilling Prevention Devices*, 2007, revised 2008.

2.3.11 ULC Publications.

Underwriters' Laboratories of Canada, 7 Underwriters Road, Toronto, ON, Canada M1R 3A9

ULC S603.1-M, *Standard for Galvanic Corrosion Protection Systems for Steel Underground Tanks for Flammable and Combustible Liquids*, 2000.

2.3.12 U.S. Government Publications.

U.S. Government Printing Office, Washington, DC 20402.

Title 49, Code of Federal Regulations, "Transportation." (Also available from the Association of American Railroads, American Railroads Bldg., 1920 L Street, N.W., Washington, DC 20036 and American Trucking Assns., Inc., 2201 Mill Road, Alexandria, VA 22314.)

Federal Motor Carrier Safety Regulations.

Interstate Commerce Commission (ICC) *Rules for Construction of Unfired Pressure Vessels,* U.S. Department of Transportation, Washington, DC.

2.3.13 Other Publications.

Merriam-Webster's Collegiate Dictionary, 11th edition, Merriam-Webster, Inc., Springfield, MA, 2003.

2.4 References for Extracts in Mandatory Sections

NFPA 1901, *Standard for Automotive Fire Apparatus,* 2009 edition.

REFERENCE CITED IN COMMENTARY

1. NFPA 10, *Standard for Portable Fire Extinguishers,* 2010 edition, National Fire Protection Association, Quincy, MA.

Definitions

Since the 2004 edition, all definitions that apply to subjects covered throughout the code have been located in Chapter 3.

The sections in Chapter 3 are outlined as follows:

- General (See Section 3.1.)
- NFPA Official Definitions, which apply to all NFPA codes and standards (See Section 3.2.)
- General Definitions, which apply to NFPA 58 only (See Section 3.3.)

3.1 General

The definitions contained in this chapter shall apply to the terms used in this standard. Where terms are not defined in this chapter or within another chapter, they shall be defined using their ordinarily accepted meanings within the context in which they are used. *Merriam-Webster's Collegiate Dictionary*, 11th edition, shall be the source for the ordinarily accepted meaning.

Generally, if terms used in the code are not defined in Chapter 3, then *Merriam-Webster's Collegiate Dictionary* [1] is the source for common usage.

3.2 NFPA Official Definitions

Section 3.2 contains definitions that are used in other NFPA documents and are not specifically related to the propane industry. NFPA attempts to make all of its documents consistent with respect to terms used to describe the enforcement authority and approval process.

3.2.1* Approved. Acceptable to the authority having jurisdiction.

A.3.2.1 Approved. The National Fire Protection Association does not approve, inspect, or certify any installations, procedures, equipment, or materials; nor does it approve or evaluate testing laboratories. In determining the acceptability of installations, procedures, equipment, or materials, the authority having jurisdiction may base acceptance on compliance with NFPA or other appropriate standards. In the absence of such standards, said authority may require evidence of proper installation, procedure, or use. The authority having jurisdiction may also refer to the listings or labeling practices of an organization that is concerned with product evaluations and is thus in a position to determine compliance with appropriate standards for the current production of listed items.

Equipment, materials, or services can be listed, approved, or both. *Listed,* defined in 3.2.5, means that the item has been reviewed by an independent testing organization that evaluates products and continues to evaluate their production. Listed products are included in "lists" maintained by the testing agency. *Approved*, as defined in 3.2.1, means that the equipment, material, or services have been accepted by the authority having jurisdiction. Listed products

◄ **FAQ**
What is the difference between the terms *listed* and *approved*?

must comply with standards, while approved products may or may not comply with standards.

3.2.2* Authority Having Jurisdiction (AHJ). An organization, office, or individual responsible for enforcing the requirements of a code or standard, or for approving equipment, materials, an installation, or a procedure.

A.3.2.2 Authority Having Jurisdiction (AHJ). The phrase "authority having jurisdiction," or its acronym AHJ, is used in NFPA documents in a broad manner, since jurisdictions and approval agencies vary, as do their responsibilities. Where public safety is primary, the authority having jurisdiction may be a federal, state, local, or other regional department or individual such as a fire chief; fire marshal; chief of a fire prevention bureau, labor department, or health department; building official; electrical inspector; or others having statutory authority. For insurance purposes, an insurance inspection department, rating bureau, or other insurance company representative may be the authority having jurisdiction. In many circumstances, the property owner or his or her designated agent assumes the role of the authority having jurisdiction; at government installations, the commanding officer or departmental official may be the authority having jurisdiction.

FAQ ▶
What is the meaning of "authority having jurisdiction" as used in NFPA 58?

An authority having jurisdiction is a governmental agency responsible for protecting the public welfare through its activities to enforce the codes and standards that have been enacted into law. The propane industry can be regulated through a number of governmental agencies, including the state or local fire marshal's office, the state or local building department, or the federal or state department of transportation. Notably, many enforcement agencies, including the U.S. Occupational Safety and Health Administration, promulgate rules that reference earlier editions of NFPA 58 than the 2011 edition. As noted in A.3.2.2, nongovernmental bodies can be the authority having jurisdiction by virtue of the conditions of a private contract (e.g., an insurance policy).

Each propane retail marketing business should become familiar with which authorities have jurisdiction over each operation of its business. The following are examples of authorities having jurisdiction for different parts of a propane business:

- Bulk plant — Fire marshal or fire chief
- Vehicles — State vehicle bureau or state police
- Residential installations — Building or gas official

3.2.3* Code. A standard that is an extensive compilation of provisions covering broad subject matter or that is suitable for adoption into law independently of other codes and standards.

A.3.2.3 Code. The decision to designate a standard as a "code" is based on such factors as the size and scope of the document, its intended use and form of adoption, and whether it contains substantial enforcement and administrative provisions.

3.2.4 Labeled. Equipment or materials to which has been attached a label, symbol, or other identifying mark of an organization that is acceptable to the authority having jurisdiction and concerned with product evaluation, that maintains periodic inspection of production of labeled equipment or materials, and by whose labeling the manufacturer indicates compliance with appropriate standards or performance in a specified manner.

FAQ ▶
What information should be on a label?

A product is labeled to indicate that a third-party, independent agency has either conducted testing or otherwise evaluated the performance or the design of a product or system. The label indicates the name of the evaluating organization (such as Underwriters Laboratories Inc. or CSA-America) as well as the manufacturer's name or trademark and the model number and/or serial number and should list the applicable standard under which the product or equipment was evaluated or tested.

3.2.5* Listed. Equipment, materials, or services included in a list published by an organization that is acceptable to the authority having jurisdiction and concerned with evaluation of products or services, that maintains periodic inspection of production of listed equipment or materials or periodic evaluation of services, and whose listing states that either the equipment, material, or service meets appropriate designated standards or has been tested and found suitable for a specified purpose.

A.3.2.5 Listed. The means for identifying listed equipment may vary for each organization concerned with product evaluation; some organizations do not recognize equipment as listed unless it is also labeled. The authority having jurisdiction should utilize the system employed by the listing organization to identify a listed product.

The AHJs customarily accept or even require (depending on whether or not NFPA 58 requires) the use of listed equipment whenever it is available. In the United States and Canada, the major LP-Gas equipment listing agencies customarily recognized as such by the authorities having jurisdiction are Underwriters Laboratories Inc., Underwriters' Laboratories of Canada, FM Global, CSA-International, and others. Many other organizations perform such services, however, and equipment listed by them is acceptable provided that the organization is acceptable to the authority having jurisdiction.

A point of some confusion is that not all the above organizations use the term *listed*. For example, CSA-America uses the term *certified* and FM Global uses the term *approved*. The terms *certified* and *approved* are synonymous with the term *listed* in this definition.

3.2.6 Shall. Indicates a mandatory requirement.

3.2.7 Should. Indicates a recommendation or that which is advised but not required.

3.3 General Definitions

3.3.1 Actuated Liquid Withdrawal Excess-Flow Valve. A container valve that is opened and closed by an adapter, incorporates an internal excess flow valve, and is used to withdraw liquid from the container.

The definition of *actuated liquid withdrawal excess-flow valve* was added in the 1995 edition. These valves are required in ASME containers of 125 gal to 2000 gal (0.5 m³ to 7.6 m³) water capacity manufactured after July 1, 1961. The valve is designed to eliminate the need to roll a container on its side to remove liquid from it. Since the early 1960s, at least three manufacturers have made valves that accomplish the requirements related to this definition under names such as Check-Lok® and Check-Mate®. Prior to the 1995 edition, this specific function valve had no name or definition. The term *actuated* is used to indicate that the valve remains closed until the insertion of the mating connection opens it.

3.3.2 Anodeless Riser. A transition assembly used between underground polyethylene or polyamide pipe and aboveground metal piping or equipment, and terminating aboveground outside of a building.

An anodeless riser is a piping component that connects to polyethylene (or polyamide) pipe under ground and terminates in a metal threaded connection above ground (see Exhibit 3.1). It is anodeless because it provides no metallic surface that contacts the soil, thereby protecting the riser against corrosion. Typically, anodeless risers are manufactured of steel-encased polyethylene liners. The steel is coated with an epoxy covering that protects the inner components. (See 6.9.4.3.)

3.3.3 ANSI. American National Standards Institute.

EXHIBIT 3.1 *Cutaway View of Riser Assembly. (Courtesy of R.W. Lyall & Company, Inc.)*

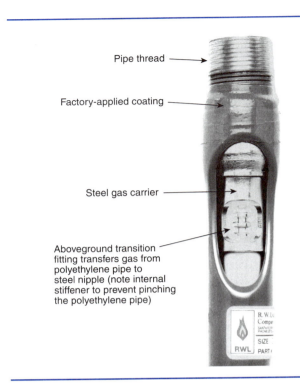

Pipe thread

Factory-applied coating

Steel gas carrier

Aboveground transition fitting transfers gas from polyethylene pipe to steel nipple (note internal stiffener to prevent pinching the polyethylene pipe)

The American National Standards Institute (ANSI) is a private, nonprofit organization that administers and coordinates the U.S. voluntary standardization and conformity assessment system. ANSI does not develop its own standards but sanctions those prepared by committees and organizations that are ANSI members and that use procedures approved by ANSI.

NFPA is recognized as a standards-developing organization under ANSI and issues codes and standards with the ANSI designation because its regulations are accepted by ANSI.

3.3.4 API. American Petroleum Institute.

The American Petroleum Institute (API) is a trade association composed largely of U.S. oil companies. Many oil companies produce and distribute LP-Gas because it is a byproduct of the refining of crude oil as well as the processing of natural gas. API also develops standards that can be useful for those involved in the LP-Gas industry.

3.3.5 API-ASME Container (or Tank). A container constructed in accordance with the pressure vessel code jointly developed by the American Petroleum Institute and the American Society of Mechanical Engineers.

Until 1961, a joint API-ASME code was used for designing propane tanks. A small number of these vessels are still in service, and they remain acceptable for service. After the joint code was discontinued, API addressed the refining industry's need for large storage vessels, while ASME addressed pressure vessels for all applications.

3.3.6 ASME. American Society of Mechanical Engineers.

The American Society of Mechanical Engineers (ASME) is a membership organization of mechanical engineers.

3.3.7 ASME Code. The American Society of Mechanical Engineers *Boiler and Pressure Vessel Code*.

3.3.8 ASME Container. A container constructed in accordance with the ASME Code.

3.3.9 ASTM. American Society for Testing and Materials.

The American Society for Testing and Materials (ASTM) promulgates the largest body of private-sector standards in the United States. As is evident in 2.3.5, many ASTM standards that address piping and castings are adopted by mandatory reference in NFPA 58.

3.3.10* Bulk Plant. A facility where the primary function is to store LP-Gas prior to further distribution. LP-Gas is received by cargo tank vehicle, railroad tank car, or pipeline, and then distributed by portable container (package) delivery, by cargo tank vehicle, or through gas piping.

A.3.3.10 Bulk Plant. Bulk plants receive gas through a variety of methods, such as railroad tank car, transport, cargo tank vehicle, gas piping, or watercraft. These plants are generally utilized for domestic, commercial, agricultural, institutional, and industrial applications or for the storage of product awaiting delivery to the end user. A facility that transfers LP-Gas from railroad tank cars from a private track directly into cargo tank vehicles is also considered a bulk plant. Such plants could have container-filling and truck loading/unloading facilities on the premises. Normally, no persons other than the plant management or plant employees have access to these facilities.

As defined in 3.3.10, bulk plants are facilities where LP-Gas is stored before it is delivered to the end-use customer. Frequent liquid transfer operations take place at bulk plants. These include cylinder filling, transport truck unloading, rail tank car unloading, and bobtail (retail bulk delivery truck) filling. See Exhibit 3.2 for an example of a typical bulk plant. Exhibit 3.3 shows a larger bulk plant with the capability to unload LP-Gas from rail cars. See also F.I. 58-04-3.

◀ **FAQ**
What is meant by the term *bulk plant*?

3.3.11 Cargo Tank. A container that is used to transport LP-Gas as liquid cargo that either is mounted on a conventional truck chassis or is an integral part of a cargo transporting vehicle.

Cargo tanks are typically installed on truck chassis (cargo tank motor vehicles), which are built to comply with DOT requirements (MC-330 and MC-331 specifications) [2,3]. Cargo

EXHIBIT 3.2 *Aerial View of a Bulk Plant. (Courtesy of Revere Gas and Appliance)*

EXHIBIT 3.3 *Large Bulk Plant. (Courtesy of Eastern Propane Corp.)*

Formal Interpretation
NFPA 58
Liquefied Petroleum Gas Code
2011 Edition

Reference: 3.3.10

F.I. No.: 58-04-3

Question: Is it the intent of the Committee, based on the definition provided in 3.3.10 of NFPA 58, that a building, at a bulk plant, containing cylinders for distribution or buildings at bulk plants where LP-Gas cylinders are filled, is part of the bulk plant?

Answer: Yes

Issue Edition: 2004

Reference: 3.3.10

Issue Date: November 30, 2005

Effective Date: December 19, 2005

tank vehicles include bobtails (see Exhibit 3.4) and transports (see Exhibit 3.5). Cargo tanks differ from DOT containers, which are "portable" and are transported on trucks.

3.3.12 CGA. The Compressed Gas Association.

In 1913, a nonprofit service organization was incorporated in New York as the Compressed Gas Manufacturers' Association to promote, develop, represent, and coordinate technical and standardization activities in the compressed gas industries in the interest of safety and effi-

EXHIBIT 3.4 Bobtail. (Courtesy of CENEX, a brand name of CHS Inc.)

EXHIBIT 3.5 Transport Vehicle. (Courtesy of Mississippi Tank Co.)

ciency. Today, among the Compressed Gas Association's (CGA's) members are companies and individuals producing compressed, liquefied, and cryogenic gases and their containers (including cargo containers), container appurtenances, and other system components.

From its inception, a major activity of CGA has been the development of standards through the efforts of more than 40 technical committees. The 1932 edition of what is now NFPA 58 was based on a draft prepared by CGA's Test and Specification Committee in 1930 and 1931. (See "History of NFPA 58" in the Preface.) Much of this work has now passed on to the National Propane Gas Association (NPGA). CGA continues to provide valuable technical assistance to the NFPA Technical Committee on Liquefied Petroleum Gases.

3.3.13 Container. Any vessel, including cylinders, tanks, portable tanks, and cargo tanks, used for the transporting or storing of LP-Gases.

As noted in the definition of *container,* there are several different pressure containers used to store and transport LP-Gas, and each must comply with specific fabrication requirements. The word *container* is a generic description in NFPA 58 for pressure vessels that store LP-Gases and is used by itself in the code whenever it is not necessary to cite a specific type. A container may be either a DOT cylinder or an ASME tank.

3.3.14 Container Appurtenances. Devices installed in container openings for safety, control, or operating purposes.

3.3.15 Container Assembly. An assembly consisting of the container and fittings for all container openings such as shutoff valves, excess-flow valves, liquid level gauging devices, pressure relief devices, and protective housings.

3.3.16 Cylinder. A container designed, constructed, tested, and marked in accordance with U.S. Department of Transportation specifications, Title 49, *Code of Federal Regulations*, or in accordance with a valid DOT special permit.

The definition of *cylinder* was revised in the 2011 edition to recognize that DOT allows cylinders to be manufactured to its requirements in the Code of Federal Regulations, or by special permits, formerly called exemptions. Nonmetallic composite cylinders are being manufactured to U.S. DOT special permits.

> **3.3.16.1 Universal Cylinder.** A cylinder that can be connected for service in either the vertical or the horizontal position, so that the fixed maximum liquid level gauge, pressure relief device, and withdrawal appurtenances function properly in either position.

A universal cylinder is shown in Exhibit 3.6.

3.3.17 Design Certification. The process by which a product is evaluated and tested by an independent laboratory to affirm that the product design complies with specific requirements.

Design certification and listing or approval go hand in hand. See 3.2.1 and 3.2.5 for more information.

3.3.18 Direct Gas-Fired Tank Heater. A gas-fired device that applies hot gas from the heater combustion chamber directly to a portion of the container surface in contact with LP-Gas liquid.

3.3.19 Dispensing Station. Fixed equipment in which LP-Gas is stored and dispensed into portable containers.

The fundamental feature differentiating vehicle fuel dispensers and dispensing stations from bulk plants or industrial plants is that persons other than management or employees have access to the dispensing facility. The distinct provisions for dispensing fuel into portable containers are included in Section 6.24.

Dispensing stations include cylinder refilling facilities, which are open to the public; cylinder refueling facilities at recreational vehicle parks; facilities at hardware, equipment rental, and sporting goods stores for filling gas grill cylinders; and facilities at marinas. Refueling of industrial truck cylinders could be at a bulk plant where exchange cylinders are refilled or at an industrial plant where either exchange cylinders or containers mounted on the industrial truck are refilled.

Another dispensing facility just coming into use provides motor fuel for the public. With the push for alternative fuels, some vehicles are being produced or modified to run on propane. While these dispensers are accessible to the public, their use by those not trained to fill containers is restricted by NFPA 58.

3.3.20 DOT. U.S. Department of Transportation.

3.3.21 Filling.

All LP-Gas containers have a maximum permitted filling limit to prevent the container from becoming "liquid full" if the temperature of the gas rises. If a container becomes "liquid full,"

EXHIBIT 3.6 *Universal Cylinder. (Courtesy of Worthington Cylinder Corp.)*

gas can be released into the atmosphere, possibly resulting in a fire or explosion if a source of ignition is present. If liquid LP-Gas is released through a pressure relief valve, it will expand to 270 times its liquid volume. Two fundamental methods are allowed for filling LP-Gas containers — *volumetric* and *weight.*

> **3.3.21.1 Volumetric Method Filling.** Filling a container to not more than the maximum permitted liquid volume.

Volumetric method filling limits the volume of liquid LP-Gas to 80 percent for cylinders and smaller ASME containers, or to a level determined by the density and temperature of the liquid LP-Gas for ASME containers over 1200 gal (4.5 m³) (see 7.4.3). Volumetric filling is typically performed using a fixed maximum liquid level gauge, which comprises a dip tube protruding into the container and a knurled nut or slotted screw that opens the dip tube to the atmosphere. When the liquid LP-Gas level contacts the bottom of the dip tube, liquid is transported out of the cylinder and vaporizes outside the cylinder at the lower pressure of the atmosphere. The act of vaporization causes moisture in the surrounding air to condense and appear as a white fog. The appearance of this fog indicates that the container has been filled to its maximum limit.

> **3.3.21.2 Weight Method Filling.** Filling containers to not more than the maximum permitted filling limit by weighing the LP-Gas in the container.

The weight method for filling cylinders is used for smaller size cylinders and limits the amount of liquid propane gas to 42 percent of the water capacity (in pounds) marked on the cylinder. Using the weight filling method for cylinders requires the use of a scale to measure the weight of the gas in the container.

In either filling method, stopping the filling process when the container is at the full level is important to safety. Dispenser operators have at times tilted cylinders in an attempt to get more fuel into cylinders equipped with overfilling prevention devices (OPDs). Some, but not all, OPDs can be partially defeated by tilting the cylinder, resulting in cylinders that can be dangerously overfilled if the temperature increases. Refer to 3.3.45 for the definition of *overfilling prevention device* and to 7.4.4, where it is clearly stated that the OPD cannot be used to determine when a cylinder is full.

3.3.22* Fire Protection. Includes fire prevention, fire detection, and fire suppression.

A.3.3.22 Fire Protection. The term *fire prevention* covers measures directed at avoiding the inception of fire or the escalation of an incident following the accidental or inadvertent release of LP-Gas. Such measures could include product control equipment and the insulation, mounding, or burial of containers.

The term *fire detection* covers equipment that detects the presence of fire or heat either to initiate automated operation of the product control or other process equipment or to initiate local or remote alarms.

The term *fire suppression* covers means of supplying water or other agents providing for fire control, exposure protection, or fire extinguishment.

The definition of *fire protection* was added to the code in 2004 to clarify the intent of the term as it relates to the provisions contained in Section 6.25, Fire Protection. It was revised in the 2011 edition to be more specific. Fire protection systems include methods for fire prevention, fire detection, or fire suppression. Methods of fire prevention include requirements that are specified in the code, such as restricting the separation distance between propane containers and combustible materials or tanks containing flammable liquids. Fire detection methods may be traditional systems, such as smoke or heat detectors, but they may also be systems specifically required by the code, such as thermal activation links for internal valves and emergency shutoff valves. Fire suppression systems are traditionally recognized as being active systems, such as water spray or deluge systems. However, "passive" systems, such as insulating, burying, or mounding containers, also fall into this category.

•

3.3.23 Flexible Connector. A short [not exceeding 60 in. (1.52 m) overall length] piping system component that is fabricated from a flexible material and equipped with connections at both ends.

The definition of *flexible connector* recognizes an increase in the permitted length up to 60 in. (1.52 m) because flexible connectors are necessarily longer than 36 in. (0.9 m) in order to achieve the necessary separation between the containers and the appliances they connect to. Previously, the 36 in. maximum was insufficient to maintain the 36 in. separation required by the code. Flexible connectors in permanent installations are restricted to flexible metallic connectors for durability.

> *3.3.23.1 Flexible Hose Connector.* A component fabricated from LP-Gas hose that is made from a material that is compatible with LP-gas.

The definition of *flexible hose connector* was simplified in the 2011 edition. References to standards to which connectors are constructed, which are found in 5.9.6, were removed.

> *3.3.23.2 Flexible Metallic Connector.* A component fabricated from metallic material that provides liquid and vapor LP-Gas confinement and is provided with connections on both ends.

> *3.3.23.3 Metallic-Protected Flexible Hose Connector.* A flexible hose connector that is provided with a metallic material over wrap that provides mechanical protection of the inner hose but does not provide fluid confinement.

In the 2011 edition, the definition of *flexible metallic connector* was revised to add more description and a new definition of *metallic-protected flexible hose connector* was added to clearly show that metallic-protected hoses are not flexible metallic connectors.

Flexible hose connectors or flexible metallic connectors are allowed for portable and exchange cylinder connections to building piping systems. This construction is successfully used in many applications, including recreational vehicles. Flexible hose connectors up to 60 in. (1.52 m) in length would only be used for portable exchange cylinders. Flexible hose connectors and flexible metallic connectors longer than 36 in. (1 m) are successfully being used in areas subject to seismic forces for piping system flexibility. The additional length avoids overstressing the connector in order to maintain required separation distances between the appliance and the container. Metallic-protected flexible hose connectors are new to the code and are allowed for compressors in 6.17.3.2.

3.3.24 Gallon, U.S. Standard. 1 U.S. gal = 0.833 Imperial gal = 231 in.^{3} = 3.785 L.

3.3.25* Gas (for the purposes of this code). Liquefied petroleum gas in either the liquid or vapor state.

A.3.3.25 Gas (for the purposes of this code). The more specific terms *liquid LP-Gas* or *vapor LP-Gas* are used for clarity.

3.3.26* Gas–Air Mixer. A device or a system of piping and controls that mixes LP-Gas vapor with air to produce a mixed gas of a lower heating value than the LP-Gas.

A.3.3.26 Gas–Air Mixer. A gas–air mixture normally is used in industrial or commercial facilities as a substitute for another fuel gas.

Gas–air mixers are used to provide substitute fuel gas in natural gas systems. They are commonly referred to as "peak shaving" installations where the economics of the system make the temporary or permanent use of diluted LP-Gas more economically attractive than using natural gas.

3.3.27 Gauge.

> **3.3.27.1 *Fixed Liquid Level Gauge.*** A liquid level indicator that uses a positive shutoff vent valve to indicate that the liquid level in a container being filled has reached the point at which the indicator communicates with the liquid level in the container.
>
> **3.3.27.2 *Fixed Maximum Liquid Level Gauge.*** A fixed liquid level gauge that indicates the liquid level at which the container is filled to its maximum permitted filling limit.

An *outage gauge* is a common term for a fixed maximum liquid level gauge. A *10 percent gauge* is a common term for a fixed maximum liquid level gauge located at the 90 percent fill level of a container (leaving 10 percent empty space). A *20 percent gauge* is a common term for a fixed maximum liquid level gauge located at the 80 percent fill level of a container (leaving 20 percent empty space). Exhibit 3.7 shows the components of a fixed maximum liquid level gauge.

> **3.3.27.3 *Float Gauge.*** A gauge constructed with an element installed inside the container that floats on the liquid surface and transmits its position to a device outside the container to indicate the liquid level.
>
> **3.3.27.4 *Magnetic Gauge.*** See 3.3.27.3, Float Gauge.

A *magnetic gauge* is a type of float gauge that relies on a magnetized coupling to display the liquid level in the container. With a magnetic gauge, there is no possible leakage of LP-Gas through a seal since there is no penetration of the container wall.

> **3.3.27.5 *Rotary Gauge.*** A type of variable liquid level gauge that indicates the liquid level on a dial gauge installed on an ASME container by manually rotating an open ended tube inside the container, which is connected to a positive shutoff vent valve.

The definition of *rotary gauge* was revised in the 2011 edition to provide a better description of the gauge. A rotary gauge is a manually operated gauge that is used in both stationary and mobile storage containers. It consists of a vent to the atmosphere (a small tube with a valve) that is normally closed and a tube within the container that is manually rotated from outside. The gauge is operated by locating the tube in its uppermost position and opening the valve. A small stream of LP-Gas vapor is released, which is not visible. The tube is rotated until the stream turns white, indicating that liquid is being released, and the position of the gauge is read from the scale. For a more accurate reading, the tube rotation is continued, and the point at which the stream turns clear again is noted. Or, the tube rotation is reversed until the stream again turns white and the position is noted. (This method releases less liquid product.) The two measurements are averaged, compensating for any bending of the tube in the container.

> **3.3.27.6* *Slip Tube Gauge.*** A variable liquid level gauge in which a small positive shutoff valve is located at the outside end of a straight tube that is installed vertically within a container.
>
> **A.3.3.27.6 *Slip Tube Gauge.*** The installation fitting for the tube is designed so that the tube can be slipped in and out of the container and so that the liquid level at the inner end of the tube can be determined by observing when the shutoff valve vents liquid.
>
> **3.3.27.7 *Variable Liquid Level Gauge.*** A device that indicates the liquid level in a container throughout a range of levels.

3.3.28 GPA. Gas Processors Association.

3.3.29 ICC. U.S. Interstate Commerce Commission.

3.3.30 Ignition Source. See 3.3.64, Sources of Ignition.

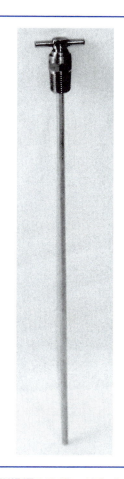

EXHIBIT 3.7 *Fixed Maximum Liquid Level Gauge.*

3.3.31 Industrial Occupancy. Includes factories that manufacture products of all kinds and properties devoted to operations such as processing, assembling, mixing, packaging, finishing or decorating, and repairing.

Industrial occupancies may sometimes have large LP-Gas storage on hand. In that respect, an industrial occupancy may be similar to a retail bulk plant. The primary difference between the two is that a retail bulk plant typically has many more liquid transfer operations.

The LP-Gas storage at an industrial plant may be the primary source of fuel for space heating, process heating, or part of the process (if a blowing agent), or the storage may be a standby or backup source if the plant's natural gas supply is restricted.

This definition is taken from *NFPA 5000®, Building Construction and Safety Code®* [4], and is also used in NFPA *101®, Life Safety Code®* [5].

3.3.32 kPa. Absolute pressure in kilo-Pascals.

3.3.33 kPag. Gauge pressure in kilo-Pascals.

3.3.34 Liquefied Petroleum Gas (LP-Gas). Any material having a vapor pressure not exceeding that allowed for commercial propane that is composed predominantly of the following hydrocarbons, either by themselves or as mixtures: propane, propylene, butane (normal butane or isobutane), and butylenes.

FAQ ▶
Is propane the same as LP-Gas?

LP-Gas can comprise any of a number of different hydrocarbons, but within the scope of NFPA 58, it is limited to a material with a vapor pressure for commercial propane. ASTM D 1835, *Standard Specification for Liquefied Petroleum Gases* [6], defines the vapor pressure for commercial propane to be 208 psig at 100°F (1.43 MPag at 38°C). By the same standard, commercial propane must be "predominantly propane," while HD-5 propane grade must be at least 90 percent propane.

3.3.35* Low Emission Transfer. Establishes a maximum fugitive emissions standard for certain product transfer operations. Low emission transfer specifications might be employed to comply with environmental regulations or to determine certain minimum distance requirements.

A.3.3.35 Low Emission Transfer. Specifications for low emission transfer might be employed to comply with environmental regulations or to determine certain minimum distance requirements.

Low emission transfer is a method of transferring LP-Gas into containers with significantly reduced emission of hydrocarbon vapors. It is accomplished with specialized dispensing nozzles and corresponding transfer fittings that limit the amount of vapor released to the atmosphere to 0.24 in.^{3} (4 cc) of product (liquid equivalent).

3.3.36 LP-Gas System. An assembly consisting of one or more containers with a means for conveying LP-Gas from a container to dispensing or consuming devices that incorporates components that control the quantity, flow, pressure, and physical state (liquid or vapor) of the LP-Gas.

LP-Gas systems include LP-Gas transfer facilities such as bulk plants. An LP-Gas system also includes every installation of a tank and piping to serve an appliance or appliances at a business, residence, church, club house, or other consumer site.

3.3.37 Maximum Allowable Working Pressure (MAWP). The maximum pressure at which a pressure vessel is to operate as described by the ASME *Boiler and Pressure Vessel Code*.

3.3.38 Mobile Container. A container that is permanently mounted on a vehicle and connected for uses other than supplying engine fuel.

The term *mobile container* defines permanently mounted, non-engine fuel containers on vehicles, such as recreational and catering vehicles. Exhibit 3.8 shows a mobile container designed for use in recreational vehicles. The definition does not include cargo tank motor vehicles.

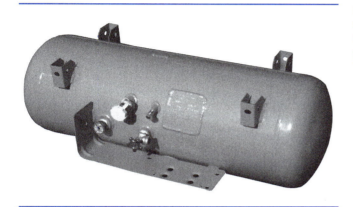

EXHIBIT 3.8 *Mobile Container Used on Recreational Vehicles. (Courtesy of Manchester Tank)*

3.3.39 Mounded Container. An ASME container designed for underground service installed above the minimum depth required for underground service and covered with earth, sand, or other material, or an ASME container designed for aboveground service installed above grade and covered with earth, sand, or other material.

Mounded containers are aboveground or partially aboveground containers covered with earth, sand, or other material so that the container itself is not visible. Mounding provides protection from exterior flame impingement.

3.3.40* Movable Fuel Storage Tender. A container equipped with wheels (including a farm cart) not in excess of 1200 gal (4.5 m³) water capacity that is moved from one location to another.

A farm cart is shown in Exhibit 9.12. Its use on public roads when it is a "non-specification container," an ASME tank, is permitted under a special permit issued by DOT that is explained in the commentary following 9.3.4.

Some farm carts are used to transport anhydrous ammonia. In the past, these carts were sometimes used interchangeably with anhydrous ammonia and propane. A tentative interim amendment (TIA) prohibiting conversion was issued in 2008.

A.3.3.40 Movable Fuel Storage Tender. Movable fuel storage tenders or farm carts are basically non-highway vehicles but can occasionally be moved over public roads or highways for short distances to supply fuel for farm tractors, construction machinery, and similar equipment.

3.3.41 MPa. Absolute pressure in mega-Pascals.

3.3.42 MPag. Gauge pressure in mega-Pascals.

3.3.43 NFPA. National Fire Protection Association.

3.3.44 NPGA. National Propane Gas Association.

The National Propane Gas Association (NPGA), originally the National Bottled Gas Association and later the National LP-Gas Association, is the national association for the liquefied petroleum gas industry. NPGA members include producers of LP-Gas, wholesale and retail marketers, gas appliance and equipment manufacturers and distributors, tank and cylinder fabricators, transport firms, and others. NPGA has 3500 members throughout the United States and 228 other countries.

One of the primary reasons for the association's establishment in 1931 was to afford all interested segments of the industry full opportunity to aid in making the rules that safeguard it. The NPGA was first affiliated with the Compressed Gas Manufacturers' Association (now the Compressed Gas Association), the only technical association in existence that could manage the problems involving gases in cylinders, the primary method of handling LP-Gases at that time.

Today, the NPGA is a separate and distinct organization that carries on its own technical activities through its technical committees. One of these committees, the Technology, Standards, and Safety Committee, has engineering and technical representation from all segments of the industry. (The name of the committee was changed from Technology and Standards Committee in June 2007 with the closing of the Education, Safety, and Training Committee. It was important to the members of the association that the word "safety" appear in the name of a standing committee.) In addition, there are advisory members representing other related industry associations, testing laboratories, regulatory officials, insurance organizations, and others that greatly assist the technical committee in its standards development work. The technical committee initiates many recommendations for new provisions and amendments of existing provisions in NFPA 58 as industry-sponsored recommendations. The NFPA Technical Committee on Liquefied Petroleum Gases, which reflects a broader interest, in turn considers these recommendations. Because the NPGA Technology, Standards, and Safety Committee has at its disposal a large amount of technical talent, the NFPA Technical Committee on Liquefied Petroleum Gases has at times referred matters to this group for initial study and recommendations.

3.3.45 Overfilling Prevention Device (OPD). A safety device that is designed to provide an automatic means to prevent the filling of a container in excess of the maximum permitted filling limit.

The definition of *overfilling prevention device (OPD)* was added in the 1998 edition to describe a device that is required in cylinders with a propane capacity of 4 lb (2 kg) through 40 lb (18 kg) and in engine fuel containers fabricated after January 1, 1984. There are different designs in use, but all of them shut off flow into the container when the liquid within reaches a specific level. (See 5.7.3, 11.4.1.15, and 11.4.1.16 for requirements for overfilling prevention devices.) Exhibit 3.9 shows an OPD.

3.3.46 Overpressure Shutoff Device. A device that shuts off the flow of LP-Gas vapor when the outlet pressure of the regulator reaches a predetermined maximum allowable pressure.

NFPA 58 requires protection against excessive vapor pressure in propane piping systems in buildings. This protection is in the form of an overpressure shutoff device, which is usually incorporated into pressure regulators used in vapor distribution systems. The outlet pressure of a first-stage pressure regulator is 10.0 psig (69 kPag), and a second-stage pressure is 11 in. water column (2.7 kPag). Regulators require a feature (which can be an overpressure shutoff device) to prevent the pressure at the discharge of the second-stage regulator from exceeding 2.0 psig (14 kPag). [See 5.8.1.2(2) and its related commentary.]

3.3.47 Permanent Installation. See 3.3.67, Stationary Installation.

3.3.48 Permitted. Allowed or acceptable, and not requiring a permit (a document granting permission) to be secured.

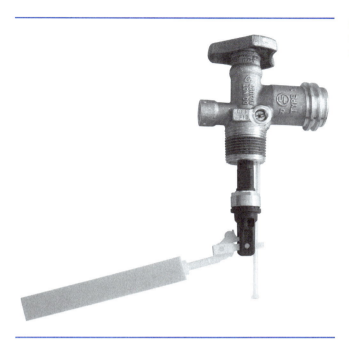

EXHIBIT 3.9 *Overfilling Prevention Device. (Courtesy of Cavagna North America, Inc.)*

The definition of *permitted* is intended to clarify a misconception regarding the issuance of formal permits. The term, as used in NFPA 58, does not require or imply a need for a permit from a local or state official. It means that something is permissible according to NFPA 58.

3.3.49 Piping Systems. Pipe, tubing, hose, and flexible rubber or metallic hose connectors with valves and fittings made into complete systems for conveying LP-Gas from one point to another in either the liquid or the vapor state at various pressures.

3.3.50 Point of Transfer. The location where connections and disconnections are made or where LP-Gas is vented to the atmosphere in the course of transfer operations.

Point of transfer is a term used to identify the location of the temporary connection between a liquid transfer supply tank, such as a bobtail or a dispenser tank, and the storage container that is being filled. (See Exhibit 3.10.) This connection establishes the point from which clearance must be maintained to sources of ignition and other equipment. It was introduced in the 1972 edition of NFPA 58.

3.3.51* Portable Container. A container designed to be moved readily, as opposed to a container designed for stationary installations.

A.3.3.51 Portable Container. Portable containers, designed for transportation, include cylinders, cargo tanks, and portable tanks, which are defined separately in this code. Containers that are designed to be readily moved from one location of use to another but that are substantially empty of product are portable storage containers and are also defined separately in this code.

3.3.52* Portable Storage Container. A container that is designed and constructed to be moved over a highway from one usage location to another.

A.3.3.52 Portable Storage Container. Portable storage containers have legs or other supports attached or are mounted on running gear (such as trailer or semitrailer chassis), with suitable supports that can be of the fold-down type. Such supports allow the containers to be placed on a reasonably firm and level surface. For large-volume, limited-duration product

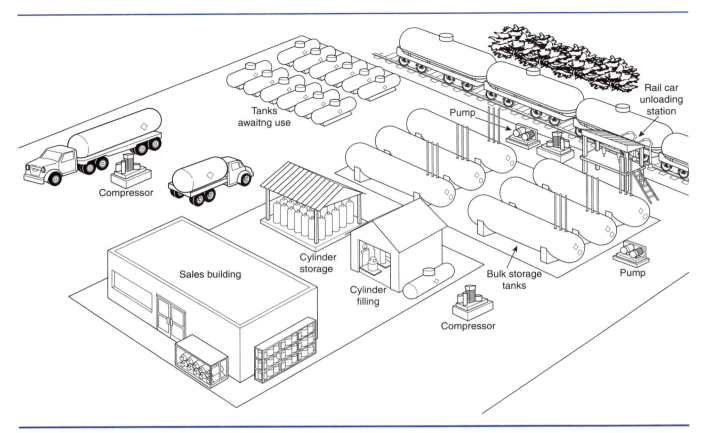

EXHIBIT 3.10 *Points of Transfer at a Propane Bulk Plant. (Redrawn courtesy of Blackmer, a Dover Company)*

usage (such as at construction sites normally used for 12 months or less), portable storage containers serve as permanently installed stationary containers.

3.3.53 Portable Tank (or Skid Tank). A container of more than 1000 lb (454 kg) water capacity that is equipped with protected container appurtenances, is used to transport LP-Gas, and is designed and fabricated with permanently mounted skids or runners or is fabricated and installed within a full framework.

FAQ ▶
What is the difference between a portable storage container and a portable tank?

The definition of *portable tank* is consistent with the terminology used by DOT in Title 49 of the Code of Federal Regulations. A portable tank differs from a portable storage container in that the portable tank complies with DOT requirements and can be shipped entirely filled with LP-Gas. However, a portable storage container is an ASME container but not an approved DOT shipping container and therefore must be transported with no more than 5 percent liquid within it.

3.3.54 Pressure Relief Device. A device designed to open to prevent a rise of internal pressure in excess of a specified value.

FAQ ▶
When is a pressure relief device likely to activate?

All cylinders and ASME containers used for LP-Gas are equipped with pressure relief devices. These are designed to prevent failure of the container due to overpressurization. Overpressurization may occur when the container becomes "liquid full," due to the heating of the container by a fire or, in some cases, if the container has been overfilled. Once a container becomes "liquid full," the pressure rises incredibly fast with a small increase in temperature — faster than a human can respond. The only method to prevent failure of the container is for the relief valve to release product. Although opening of the pressure relief device will prevent the container from failure due to overpressure, the released flammable LP-Gas may also present a hazard.

In addition to containers, pressure relief devices are used in segments of hose or piping where liquid can be trapped between shutoff valves.

3.3.55 psi. Pounds per square inch.

3.3.56 psia. Pounds per square inch, absolute.

3.3.57 psig. Pounds per square inch gauge.

Units of pressure measurement used in the code are pounds per square inch (psi) and Pascals (Pa). When metric units of measurement were added to the code in the 1980s, pressure measurements were converted into Pascals (and kilo-pascals and mega-pascals because the Pascal is a small unit). Pressure measurements are usually given in one of two forms, either gauge or absolute. *Absolute pressure* is the pressure of the gas in the container plus the atmospheric pressure. *Gauge pressure* is the absolute pressure of a gas minus the local atmospheric pressure, or the pressure one would read on an accurate gauge connected to a tank. A pressure gauge at sea level will read 0, even though a pressure of 14.7 psi is present. Traditionally, pressure in tanks and piping systems is expressed in gauge pressure.

◀ **FAQ**
What is the difference between absolute pressure and gauge pressure?

3.3.58 Quick Connectors. Fittings used to connect hose assemblies to piping and valves without the use of tools.

Quick connectors are used to connect transfer hose to piping and valves for loading and unloading cargo tank vehicles or railroad tank cars. They can also be used as connectors on swivel-type transfer piping. Quick connectors are also used in other LP-Gas systems, such as those used for engine fuel refueling and cylinder filling, connecting cylinders to gas-fired barbecue grills, and connecting gas systems between two sections of mobile homes.

3.3.59* Refrigerated LP-Gas. LP-Gas that is cooled to temperatures below ambient to maintain the product as a liquid with a vapor pressure of 15 psig or less.

A.3.3.59 Refrigerated LP-Gas. LP-Gas can be refrigerated to reduce its vapor pressure to near atmospheric up to 15 psig. Refrigerated LP-Gas containers are typically constructed to API 620 and are maintained at less than $^1/_2$ psig and use a container fabricated of significantly thinner steel than a pressure vessel. Refrigerated LP-Gas can also be stored in ASME containers above 15 psig, and this is called semi-refrigerated LP-Gas.

Refrigerated LP-Gas is just what the term implies — LP-Gas that has been refrigerated or cooled. When the gas is propane, the liquid is typically at a temperature of about –40°F (–40°C). At that temperature, propane is a liquid that exerts no pressure on its container (except for static head pressure), thus providing a way to store propane in a nonpressurized (and usually insulated) container, which is less expensive than a pressure vessel. The economics are such that refrigerated storage is normally used for very large containers [1,000,000 gal (3785 m^3) is not unusual], and refrigerated LP-Gas storage is normally found at pipeline and marine terminals and occasionally at larger storage facilities.

The definition of *refrigerated LP-Gas* was revised in the 2011 edition to remove a requirement, because requirements are not allowed in definitions in accordance with the NFPA *Manual of Style for NFPA Technical Committee Documents* [7]. Previously, the definition required that the pressure not exceed 15 psig (103 kPag). It was revised by relocating the part of the definition that was additional information to the new Annex A paragraph. This pressure criterion is coordinated with the ASME *Boiler and Pressure Vessel Code* [8], Section VIII, which is not applicable to pressures below 15 psig. The pressure of refrigerated propane in storage is a function of the liquid temperature, and if it exceeds 15 psig, ASME containers must be used.

Cylinder 2

Cylinder 1

EXHIBIT 3.11 *Automatic Changeover Regulator. (Courtesy of Cavagna North America, Inc.)*

EXHIBIT 3.12 *Cutaway of First-Stage Regulator. (Courtesy of Engineered Controls International, Inc.)*

3.3.60 Regulator.

The various types of regulators defined in NFPA 58 are shown in Exhibits 3.11 to 3.14 and listed in Commentary Table 3.1.

3.3.60.1* Automatic Changeover Regulator. An integral two-stage regulator that combines two high-pressure regulators and a second-stage regulator into a single unit designed for use with multiple cylinder installations.

A.3.3.60.1 Automatic Changeover Regulator. An automatic changeover regulator incorporates two inlet connections and a service-reserve indicator. The system automatically changes the LP-Gas vapor withdrawal from the designated service cylinder(s) when depleted to the designated reserve cylinder(s) without interruption of service. The service reserve indicator gives a visual indication of the cylinder(s) that is supplying the system.

3.3.60.2 First-Stage Regulator. A pressure regulator for LP-Gas vapor service designed to reduce pressure from a container to 10.0 psig (69 kPag) or less.

3.3.60.3 High-Pressure Regulator. A pressure regulator for LP-Gas liquid or vapor service designed to reduce pressure from the container to a lower pressure in excess of 1.0 psig (6.9 kPag).

3.3.60.4 Integral 2 psi Service Regulator. A pressure regulator for LP-Gas vapor service that combines a high-pressure regulator and a 2 psi service regulator into a single unit.

3.3.60.5 Integral Two-Stage Regulator. A pressure regulator for LP-Gas vapor service that combines a high-pressure regulator and a second-stage regulator into a single unit.

3.3.60.6 Line Pressure Regulator. A pressure regulator in accordance with the *Standard for Line Pressure Regulators*, ANSI Z-21.80/CSA 6.22, with no integral overpressure protection device for LP-Gas vapor service designed for installation inside a building to reduce a nominal 2 psi inlet pressure to 14 in. w.c. (4.0 kPa) or less.

3.3.60.7 Second-Stage Regulator. A pressure regulator for LP-Gas vapor service designed to reduce first-stage regulator outlet pressure to 14 in. w.c. (4.0 kPag) or less.

3.3.60.8 Single-Stage Regulator. A pressure regulator for LP-Gas vapor service designed to reduce pressure from the container to 1.0 psig (6.9 kPag) or less.

EXHIBIT 3.13 *Integral Two-Stage Regulator. (Courtesy of Engineered Controls International, Inc.)*

COMMENTARY TABLE 3.1 *Regulators*

Type	Location	Description or Use
Automatic changeover (Exhibit 3.11)	Outdoor	Changes service cylinder to reserve cylinder automatically
First stage (Exhibit 3.12)	Outdoor	Reduces tank pressure to 10 psig (69 kPag) or less
High pressure	Outdoor	Reduces tank pressure to lower pressure above 1 psig (7 kPag)
Integral 2 psi service	Outdoor	Reduces tank pressure in two stages to 2 psig (14 kPag)
Integral two-stage (Exhibit 3.13)	Outdoor	Reduces tank pressure in two stages to 11 in. w.c. (2.7 kPag)
Line pressure Second-stage (Exhibit 3.14)	Outdoor/indoor*	Reduces first-stage pressure to 11 in. w.c. (2.7 kPag)
Single-stage	Outdoor	Reduces tank pressure to 11 in. w.c. (2.7 kPag)
2 psi service	Outdoor	Reduces first-stage pressure to 2 psig (4 kPag)
2 psi system	Outdoor/indoor**	Reduces first-stage pressure to 2 psig (4 kPag)

*Regulator vent is piped to outdoors.
**Only the line pressure regulator is installed indoors.

EXHIBIT 3.14 *Second-Stage Regulator. (Courtesy of Engineered Controls International, Inc.)*

3.3.60.9 2 psi Regulator System. An LP-Gas vapor delivery system that combines a first-stage regulator, a 2 psi (14 kPag) service regulator, and a line pressure regulator(s).

3.3.60.10 2 psi Service Regulator. A pressure regulator for LP-Gas vapor service designed to reduce first-stage regulator outlet pressure to a nominal 2 psig (14 kPag).

3.3.60.11 Two-Stage Regulator System. An LP-Gas vapor delivery system that combines a first-stage regulator and a second-stage regulator(s), or utilizes a separate integral two-stage regulator.

3.3.61 SCFM. Standard cubic feet per minute.

3.3.62 Service Head Adapter. A transition fitting for use with polyethylene or polyamide pipe or tubing that is recommended by the manufacturer for field assembly and installation at the aboveground termination end of an anodeless riser.

A service head adapter is a fitting that connects plastic pipe or tubing inserted inside a non-pressure-containing steel jacket to steel piping.

3.3.63 Skid Tank. See 3.3.53, Portable Tank.

3.3.64 Sources of Ignition. Devices or equipment that, because of their modes of use or operation, are capable of providing sufficient thermal energy to ignite flammable LP-Gas vapor–air mixtures when introduced into such a mixture or when such a mixture comes into contact with them, and that will permit propagation of flame away from them.

Although the code has addressed the control of ignition sources since its inception, this definition for *sources of ignition* was added in the 1979 edition. The definition became necessary because of the existence of electrical devices and equipment that could ignite a flammable LP-Gas–air mixture under certain conditions. In addition, the definition clarifies that other devices might produce ignition but would not permit a flame to propagate away from them, in which case they are not a hazard. Examples of such devices include certain Class I,

Division 1, Group D electrical equipment in which devices are installed in enclosures using gap flame-quenching principles and devices or enclosures equipped with flame arresters.

Some sources of ignition are as follows:

- Devices or equipment — such as gas- or oil-burning appliances, torches, matches, and lighters — producing, or capable of producing, flame
- Devices or equipment — such as motors, generators, switches, lights, and wiring and welding machines — producing, or capable of producing, electrical arcs or sparks of sufficient energy (Devices or equipment listed for Class I, Group D locations are not sources of ignition when properly used and maintained in the classified areas prescribed in this code.)
- Devices or equipment having, or capable of having, surfaces at temperatures exceeding 700°F (371°C)
- Devices or equipment — such as grinders, metal saws, chipping hammers, and flint lighters — producing, or capable of producing, mechanical (struck) sparks of sufficient energy (Unpowered hand tools used only by one individual at a time and for their intended purposes are not considered sources of ignition.)
- Cigarettes and other smoking materials
- Gravity or mechanical air intakes and exhaust terminals of ventilation systems for structures housing the ignition sources described, because they constitute a readily communicating pathway (These include air intakes and exhaust terminals for gas- or oil-burning appliances such as those for direct-vent appliances, and air intakes and exhaust terminals for air conditioners.)

Operating spark-ignition internal combustion engines do not appear, based on experience, to be an ignition source. However, they have been an ignition source during the act of being started and their exhaust systems can easily exceed 700°F. Operating diesel engines have been identified as the ignition source in fire reports, usually as the result of burning carbon being blown out of their exhausts. Such engines tend to speed up when LP-Gas is drawn into their intake manifolds.

3.3.65* Special Protection. A means of limiting the temperature of an LP-Gas container for purposes of minimizing the possibility of failure of the container as the result of fire exposure.

A.3.3.65 Special Protection. Where required in this code, special protection consists of one of the following:

(1) Applied insulating coating
(2) Mounding
(3) Burial
(4) Water spray fixed systems
(5) Fixed monitor nozzles that meet the criteria specified in this code
(6) Any means listed for this purpose

See Section 6.25 for more information on fire protection and special protection.

In the late 1960s and early 1970s, the propane industry in the United States experienced a number of BLEVEs (Boiling Liquid Expanding Vapor Explosions) of LP-Gas railroad tank cars (some following derailments). Most of these incidents were caused by container failure from overheating of the container metal (steel) through contact with flames from flammable or combustible materials released from other cars. These incidents were accompanied by fire fighter fatalities.

Although this hazard was beyond the scope of NFPA 58, these accidents resulted in widespread fear of all large LP-Gas containers among the fire service and the public. Notable in this respect was an increasing reluctance by fire fighters to approach an LP-Gas container exposed to fire in order to limit the container temperature by the application of water from hose streams. Because this procedure was, and is, a fundamental and universal BLEVE prevention tactic, the NFPA Technical Committee on Liquefied Petroleum Gases and the industry were concerned that a reduction in its use would increase the frequency and severity of BLEVEs.

A joint task force of the NFPA technical committee and the NPGA's Technology and Standards Committee (augmented by representatives of railroad and DOT groups studying the tank car problem) concluded that additional provisions were needed to reduce the chances for BLEVEs caused by fire exposure. As a result, the following two provisions were first included in the 1976 edition of NFPA 58.

1. The first provision was for the installation and use of emergency shutoff valves as described in Section 6.10. These valves were considered important enough to require retroactive installation in all of the larger facilities as prescribed in Section 6.10.
2. The second provision was for special protection as stipulated in 6.25.5. It is noted, however, that the need for this protection is predicated on the results of a required fire safety analysis.

The six modes of special protection cited in A.3.3.65 represent those currently recognized and for which standards exist. However, the definition is broad enough to recognize other means, provided those means are listed for the purpose.

3.3.66 Standard Cubic Foot (SCF). The volume of gas in cubic feet at the standard atmospheric conditions at 60°F (15.6°C) and 14.7 psia (101 kPa).

3.3.67 Stationary Installation (Permanent Installation). An installation of LP-Gas containers, piping, and equipment for indefinite use at a particular location; an installation not normally expected to change in status, condition, or location.

3.3.68 UL. Underwriters Laboratories Inc.

Founded in 1894, Underwriters Laboratories Inc. (UL) was chartered as a not-for-profit, independent organization performing testing for public safety. The organization maintains laboratories for the examination and testing of devices, systems, and materials to determine their relation to life, fire, casualty hazards, and crime prevention.

UL-listed materials within the scope of NFPA 58 are included in the following UL Product Directories: *Hazardous Location Equipment* [9]; *Marine Products* [10]; *Automotive, Burglary Protection, and Mechanical Equipment* [11]; and *Flammable and Combustible Liquids & Gases Equipment* [12].

Where NFPA 58 requires listing of a product, any listing agency acceptable to the authority having jurisdiction can be used.

◄ **FAQ**
Is UL the only agency that can test and list products, devices, and systems for use within the scope of NFPA 58?

•

3.3.69 Valve.

3.3.69.1 Emergency Shutoff Valve. A shutoff valve incorporating thermal and manual means of closing that also provides for remote means of closing.

3.3.69.2 Excess-Flow Valve (or Excess-Flow Check Valve). A valve designed to close when the liquid or vapor passing through it exceeds a prescribed flow rate.

3.3.69.3 Filler Valve. A valve that is designed to allow liquid flow into a container.

3.3.69.4 Internal Excess-Flow Valve. An excess-flow valve constructed and installed so that damage to valve parts exterior to the container does not prevent closing of the valve.

3.3.69.5* Internal Valve. A container primary shutoff valve that can be closed remotely, which incorporates an internal excess flow valve with the seat and seat disc

EXHIBIT 3.15 *Internal Valve. (Courtesy of Cavagna North America, Inc.)*

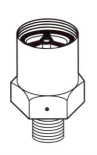

FIGURE A.3.3.69.6.1
External Pressure Relief Valve.

FIGURE A.3.3.69.6.2
Flush-Type Full Internal Pressure Relief Valve.

located within the container so that they remain in place should external damage occur to the valve.

A.3.3.69.5 Internal Valve. An internal valve has provision for the addition of a means of remote closure. An internal valve closes when flow through the valve exceeds its rated excess-flow capacity or when the pump actuation differential pressure drops to a predetermined point.

An internal valve is a valve that is installed in ASME container openings. It is typically installed in the liquid inlet/outlet of propane containers of 4000 gal (15.1 m³) and larger, but can also be used to protect openings used for vapor inlet and outlet. An internal valve allows flow to be stopped remotely in the event of failure in the piping system. Remote operation can be by a mechanical, pneumatic, or electrical means. Internal valves are required in all new installations of containers larger than 4000 gal (15.1 m³) and must be installed on all existing containers larger than 4000 gal (15.1 m³) by July 1, 2011 (see 5.7.4.2).

By halting the flow of gas, a fire or the potential fuel for a fire is eliminated. In addition, internal valves can be operated at their installed locations, and they have an excess flow valve incorporated into them to stop the flow should it exceed the rating of the valve. Exhibit 3.15 shows an internal valve.

3.3.69.6 Pressure Relief Valve. A type of pressure relief device designed to both open and close to maintain internal fluid pressure.

3.3.69.6.1* External Pressure Relief Valve. A pressure relief valve where all the working parts are located entirely outside the container or piping.

A.3.3.69.6.1 External Pressure Relief Valve. See Figure A.3.3.69.6.1.

3.3.69.6.2* Flush-Type Full Internal Pressure Relief Valve. An internal pressure relief valve in which the wrenching section is also within the container connection, not including a small portion due to pipe thread tolerances on makeup.

A.3.3.69.6.2 Flush-Type Full Internal Pressure Relief Valve. See Figure A.3.3.69.6.2.

3.3.69.6.3* Full Internal Pressure Relief Valve. A pressure relief valve in which all working parts are recessed within a threaded connection of the valve, and the spring and guiding mechanism are not exposed to the atmosphere.

A.3.3.69.6.3 Full Internal Pressure Relief Valve. See Figure A.3.3.69.6.3.

3.3.69.6.4* Internal Spring-Type Pressure Relief Valve. A pressure relief valve that is similar to a full internal relief valve except the wrenching pads and seating section are above the container connection in which the adjusting spring and the stem are below the seat and are not exposed to the atmosphere.

A.3.3.69.6.4 Internal Spring-Type Pressure Relief Valve. See Figure A.3.3.69.6.4.

3.3.70 Vaporizer. A device, other than a container, that receives LP-Gas in liquid form and adds sufficient heat to convert the liquid to a gaseous state.

Vaporizers are heat exchangers that transfer heat to convert LP-Gas liquid to vapor, just as boilers convert water into steam. The heat provided to a vaporizer converts the liquid to a gaseous state in pipes, coils, or chambers within the vaporizer. There are several styles of listed vaporizers that perform this function. Section 5.21 provides detailed requirements for different vaporizer styles.

Exhibit 3.16 shows principal features and operating characteristics of a typical vaporizer installation. Liquid flows from the bottom of the tank into the direct-fired vaporizer (shown on the left). A float controls the liquid level in the vaporizer. Flames provide heat to the liquid through the shell. Vapor travels from the upper part of the vaporizer to a tee where it goes to the equipment. Excess pressure is returned to the tank through the optional vapor line. If the tank pressure is high enough, it will supply the load, and the vaporizer will no longer be required to operate.

> ***3.3.70.1 Direct-Fired Vaporizer.*** A vaporizer in which heat furnished by a flame is directly applied to a heat exchange surface in contact with the liquid LP-Gas to be vaporized.

Direct-fired vaporizers convert liquid propane into propane vapor, just as boilers convert water into steam. In a direct-fired vaporizer the flame is directed on piping or a vessel containing liquid propane. This differs from an indirect vaporizer where the liquid propane is vaporized in a coil immersed in a heated fluid (see 3.3.70.3).

Submerged combustion vaporizers are vaporizers in which a flame is directed into a nonflammable fluid, usually water, which surrounds pipe coils containing liquid propane. This type of vaporizer is usually used for very large vaporizing loads. Although they do not meet the definition of direct-fired vaporizers in 3.3.70.1, for purposes of this code, submerged combustion vaporizers may be treated as direct-fired.

> ***3.3.70.2 Electric Vaporizer.*** A vaporizer that uses electricity as a source of heat.

Because electric vaporizers can be designed so that they are not a source of ignition (unlike a vaporizer using fuel-fired burners), they can be installed differently and thus need to be defined separately. Electric vaporizers are separated into two types — direct immersion, described in 3.3.70.2.1, and indirect, described in 3.3.70.2.2.

> ***3.3.70.2.1 Direct Immersion Electric Vaporizer.*** A vaporizer wherein an electric element is immersed directly in the LP-Gas liquid and vapor.

> ***3.3.70.2.2 Indirect Electric Vaporizer.*** An immersion-type vaporizer wherein the electric element heats an interface solution in which the LP-Gas heat exchanger is immersed or heats an intermediate heat sink.

> ***3.3.70.3 Indirect (or Indirect-Fired) Vaporizer.*** A vaporizer in which heat furnished by steam, hot water, the ground, surrounding air, or other heating medium is applied to a vaporizing chamber or to tubing, pipe coils, or other heat exchange surface containing the liquid LP-Gas to be vaporized; the heating of the medium used is at a point remote from the vaporizer.

> ***3.3.70.4 Waterbath (or Immersion-Type) Vaporizer.*** A vaporizer in which a vaporizing chamber, tubing, pipe coils, or other heat exchange surface containing liquid LP-Gas to be vaporized is immersed in a temperature-controlled bath of water, water-glycol combination, or other noncombustible heat transfer medium that is heated by an immersion heater not in contact with the LP-Gas heat exchange surface.

A waterbath vaporizer is shown in Exhibit 3.17.

3.3.71 Vaporizing Burner (Self-Vaporizing Liquid Burner). A burner that also vaporizes liquid LP-Gas prior to burning it.

3.3.72 Vehicle Fuel Dispenser. A device or system designed to transfer and measure LP-Gas into engine fuel and mobile containers on vehicles.

3.3.73 Volumetric Loading. See 3.3.21.1, Volumetric Method Filling.

3.3.74 Water Capacity. The amount of water at 60°F (16°C) required to fill a container.

The water capacity of a container is the maximum amount of water the container can hold at 60°F (16°C). The water capacity (full of water) is expressed in pounds (kilograms) for cylinders and gallons (cubic meters) for ASME containers.

FIGURE A.3.3.69.6.3 *Full Internal Pressure Relief Valve.*

FIGURE A.3.3.69.6.4 *Internal Spring-Type Pressure Relief Valve.*

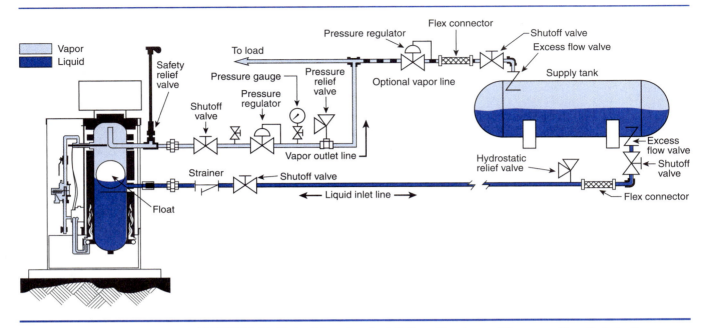

EXHIBIT 3.16 *Typical Vaporizer Installation. (Courtesy of Ransome Manufacturing)*

EXHIBIT 3.17 *Waterbath Vaporizer. (Courtesy of Ransome Manufacturing)*

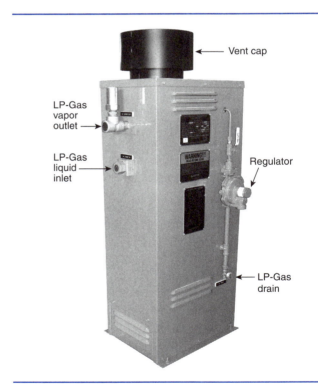

The water capacity is different from the propane capacity of a container. Water capacity is measured with the container 100 percent full, whereas the maximum permitted filling limit allowed for propane is typically set at 80 percent of the water capacity, although there are exceptions to this practice as described in Chapter 7. For example, the typical 1000 gal

(3.8 m³) water capacity ASME container is allowed to hold about 800 gal (3.0 m³) of propane (80 percent). However, a 30,000 gal (114 m³) container can be filled to 25,800 gal (98 m³) (86 percent at 40°F) of propane because its large size minimizes extreme swings in the temperature of the product (and therefore expansion and contraction are minimized) due to daytime solar heating and night cooling.

The maximum propane capacity of a cylinder is also based on its water capacity, but since the water capacity is given in pounds (kilograms), the multiplying factor for propane is 42 percent because propane is about half the density of water. If the water capacity of a cylinder is marked as being 48 lb (36 kg), the propane capacity is 42 percent of 48 lb (36 kg), or about 20 lb (9 kg).

REFERENCES CITED IN COMMENTARY

1. *Merriam-Webster's Collegiate Dictionary,* 11th edition, Merriam-Webster, Inc., Springfield, MA, 2003.
2. Title 49, Code of Federal Regulations, Part 178, U.S. Government Printing Office, Washington, DC.
3. Title 49, Code of Federal Regulations, Part 178.337, U.S. Government Printing Office, Washington, DC.
4. *NFPA 5000®, Building Construction and Safety Code®,* 2009 edition, National Fire Protection Association, Quincy, MA.
5. NFPA *101®, Life Safety Code®,* 2009 edition, National Fire Protection Association, Quincy, MA.
6. ASTM D 1835, *Standard Specification for Liquefied Petroleum Gases,* 2005 edition, American Society for Testing and Materials, West Conshohocken, PA.
7. NFPA *Manual of Style for NFPA Technical Committee Documents,* 2003 edition, National Fire Protection Association, Quincy, MA.
8. ASME *Boiler and Pressure Vessel Code,* 2007 edition, American Society of Mechanical Engineers, New York, NY.
9. UL Product Directory, *Hazardous Location Equipment,* 2007 edition, Underwriters Laboratories Inc., Northbrook, IL.
10. UL Product Directory, *Marine Products,* 2006 edition, Underwriters Laboratories Inc., Northbrook, IL.
11. UL Product Directory, *Automotive, Burglary Protection, and Mechanical Equipment,* 2007 edition, Underwriters Laboratories Inc., Northbrook, IL.
12. UL Product Directory, *Flammable and Combustible Liquids & Gases Equipment,* 2006 edition, Underwriters Laboratories Inc., Northbrook, IL.

General Requirements

Chapter 4 covers general requirements that apply to the entire code. In the 2001 and previous editions of the code, these requirements were included in Chapter 1. The sections in Chapter 4 cover the following:

- Acceptance of Equipment and Systems (See Section 4.1.)
- LP-Gas Odorization (See Section 4.2.)
- Notification of Installations (See Section 4.3.)
- Qualification of Personnel (See Section 4.4.)
- Ammonia Contamination (See Section 4.5.)
- Minimum Requirements (See Section 4.6.)

4.1 Acceptance of Equipment and Systems

4.1.1 Systems or components assembled to make up systems shall be approved as specified in Table 4.1.1. Where necessary to alter or repair such systems or assemblies in the field, approved components shall be used.

Approval of systems using cylinders applies to the following:

- The cylinder itself, which must meet DOT specifications and have the dates of manufacture and retest (if done) stamped in the collar, as shown in Exhibit 5.13 (See Annex C for information on requalification of cylinders.)

TABLE 4.1.1 Containers

Containers Used	Water Capacity		Approval Applies to . . .
	gal	m³	
Cylinders	<120	<0.445	Container valves and connectors
			Manifold valve assemblies
			Regulators and pressure relief devices
ASME containers	≤2000	≤7.6	Container system,* including regulator, or container assembly* and regulator separately
ASME containers	>2000	>7.6	Container valves
			Container excess-flow valves, backflow check valves, or alternate means of providing this protection, such as remotely controlled internal valves
			Container gauging devices
			Regulators and container pressure relief devices

*Where necessary to alter or repair such systems or assemblies in the field in order to provide for different operating pressures, change from vapor to liquid withdrawal, or the like. Such changes are permitted to be made by the use of approved components.

- Cylinder valves, which must comply with DOT regulations, which reference CGA V-1, *Standard Compressed Gas Cylinder Valve Outlet and Inlet Connections* [1]
- Cylinder connectors, manifold valve assemblies, regulators, and pressure relief devices, which must be approved
- The approval of systems using ASME containers of 2000 gal (7.6 m^3) or less includes one of the following:
- The container, which must be designed, fabricated, and marked in accordance with the ASME *Boiler and Pressure Vessel Code* [2], and its appurtenances, which may be approved as a unit
- The container, which may be approved separately, in which case the container appurtenances and pressure regulator must also be approved separately

The approval of systems using ASME containers of more than 2000 gal (7.6 m^3) includes the following:

- Container valves
- All other container appurtenances, as listed in Table 4.1.1, and the pressure regulator(s)

Larger systems using ASME containers with capacities greater than 2000 gal (7.6 m^3) capacity are not approved as a system. Instead, the individual parts are approved. The reason is that there are many variations on how a container may be used, and approval of the entire unit as a system would be very difficult, possibly requiring many different approvals to cover all possible applications.

4.1.2 Where it is necessary to alter or repair such systems or assemblies, approved components shall be used.

4.1.3 Acceptance applies to the complete system or to the individual components of which it is comprised as specified in Table 4.1.1.

4.2 LP-Gas Odorization

4.2.1* All LP-Gases shall be odorized prior to delivery to a bulk plant by the addition of a warning agent of such character that the gases are detectable, by a distinct odor, to a concentration in air of not over one-fifth the lower limit of flammability.

A.4.2.1 It is recognized that no odorant will be completely effective as a warning agent in every circumstance.

   It is recommended that odorants be qualified as to compliance with 4.2.1 by tests or experience. Where qualifying is by tests, such tests should be certified by an approved laboratory not associated with the odorant manufacturer. Experience has shown that ethyl mercaptan in the ratio of 1.0 lb (0.45 kg) per 10,000 gal (37.9 m^3) of liquid LP-Gas has been recognized as an effective odorant. Other odorants and quantities meeting the provisions of 4.2.1 can be used. Research on odorants has shown that thiophane (tetrahydrothiophene) in a ratio of at least 6.4 lb (2.9 kg) per 10,000 gal (37.9 m^3) of liquid LP-Gas might satisfy the requirements of 4.2.1.

FAQ ►
Why is ethyl mercaptan a good choice for an odorant in propane?

The note to A.4.2.1 provides additional information on the important subject of odorization. It must be remembered that the code requires the gas to have an odor that serves as a "distinctive" warning agent, but it does not specify the type of odorant or the quantity of odorant. While specific recommendations for odorization levels are made in A.4.2.1, LP-Gas is required to be odorized prior to delivery to a bulk plant or other bulk storage where a bulk plant is bypassed in the chain of distribution. There are several odorants that have been tested through many research projects, but ethyl mercaptan remains as the odorant of choice for its distinctive smell and its chemical and physical properties, which match up well with those of propane. (See the commentary following A.4.2.3.)

NOTE: Odorant research includes *A New Look at Odorization Levels for Propane Gas*, BERC/RI-77/1, United States Energy Research and Development Administration, Technical Information Center, September 1977.

4.2.2 Odorization shall not be required if it is harmful in the use or further processing of the LP-Gas or if such odorization will serve no useful purpose as a warning agent in such further use or processing.

LP-Gas used as a feedstock in the manufacture of petrochemicals, as an aerosol propellant, and as a blowing agent in the manufacture of plastic foam products are three examples of situations in which the gas is not required to be odorized. Another potentially large application of propane in the future may be the fuel cell. Fuel cells convert hydrocarbon fuels to electricity through a chemical process. LP-Gas is being considered as a potential fuel for this application, but the sulfur added in the form of odorant to the gas and other impurities may present a problem for the internal fuel cell parts and can possibly damage the fuel cell. Therefore, it may be necessary to strip the odorant and sulfur from LP-Gas prior to introducing it to the fuel cell. This procedure, however, would most likely have to be done on site and as part of the fuel conversion process to remain in compliance with the code requirement for odorant to serve as a warning agent.

4.2.3* If odorization is required, the presence of the odorant shall be determined by sniff-testing or other means, and the results shall be documented as follows:

(1) When LP-Gas is delivered to a bulk plant
(2) When shipments of LP-Gas bypass the bulk plant

A.4.2.3 Another method of determining the presence of odorant is the stain tube test. This method involves using a small hand-held pump to draw a sample across a filled glass tube and reading the length of color change. For additional information, see GPA Standard 2188, *Tentative Method for the Determination of Ethyl Mercaptan in LP-Gas Using Length of Stain Tubes,* and CAN/CGSB-3.0 No. 18.5, *Test for Ethyl Mercaptan Odorant in Propane, Field Method*. At the time of the preparation of this code, additional analytical methods were under development.

LP-Gas is stored in pressure vessels, or containers, that contain both liquid LP-Gas and vapor. The pressure in the container depends on the temperature of the LP-Gas in the container, with higher pressure at higher temperature. (See Annex B for pressure–temperature charts.) When this pressure is reduced (e.g., by vapor being drawn out of the container to supply an appliance), the liquid in the container begins to boil, producing additional vapor to raise the pressure back to equilibrium. In the process of this boiling, the temperature of the liquid is reduced as it vaporizes, which in turn reduces the equilibrium vapor pressure. This temperature reduction is sometimes seen as ice forming on the outside of a container on a humid day.

The odorant used with propane is ethyl mercaptan, which is a liquefied flammable gas that is mixed with the liquid propane and which, in turn, boils with the propane. The boiling point of ethyl mercaptan is higher than that of propane [95°F (35°C) for ethyl mercaptan versus –44°F (–42°C) for propane], which means that as propane is first withdrawn from a full cylinder with ethyl mercaptan more propane will boil than ethyl mercaptan. The result is that 15 to 25 percent of the amount of ethyl mercaptan in the liquid (depending on the temperature of the propane) is found in the vapor. More ethyl mercaptan than propane is left in the container, and the concentration of ethyl mercaptan in the vapor increases as more propane is vaporized and will exceed the concentration added to the liquid near the end of vapor withdrawal. The amount of ethyl mercaptan added to the propane takes this fact into account.

◀ **FAQ**
How does the odorant in LP-Gas get into the vapor?

A sufficient amount of odorant is in the gas phase, throughout the entire useful temperature range to meet code requirements.

Determining the presence of an odorant in LP-Gas is important and is required by the code to be done on each shipment to a bulk plant. Shipments that bypass a bulk plant and are delivered directly to the end user must also be tested. Sniff testing, in which a human with a normal sense of smell verifies the odor, is common practice. In some cases, however, an evaluation method with a quantifiable result may be desired.

The odorization of gas started as early as 1880 in Europe, where it was used to prevent injuries or fatalities resulting from escaping gas. The first reported odorant used was ethyl mercaptan, a prevalent compound still used to odorize LP-Gas. Ethyl mercaptan has a characteristic smell that has been described as garlic or rotten eggs. Regardless of dosage levels, it is impossible to warn 100 percent of the population of gas leaks by the use of odorant systems. Some individuals may simply not be able to discern the odor. Others may have their sense of smell temporarily impaired due to a cold, sickness, or other condition. Odorization is a valuable practice, because it does serve as a useful warning in the vast majority of cases. In a study conducted by inserting a "scratch and sniff" card in its magazine, National Geographic reported that the fuel gas odor was one of the most recognized odors [3].

Odorization for bottled propane and LP-Gases began in the late 1920s and early 1930s in the United States. Around this same time, the companies that sold LP-Gases into home-use markets began using odorants. The work of the Bureau of Mines [4], which was funded by the American Gas Association, and research conducted by those companies developing this new market showed that ethyl mercaptan was the best odorant for propane because of its volatility, odor properties, and chemical properties. The concentration of ethyl mercaptan required was also determined by research and calculation during this same period.

Ethyl mercaptan and later thiophane (tetrahydrothiophene or THT) were used at a rate of at least 1.0 lb per 10,000 gal (0.45 kg per 37.9 m³) until the late 1970s, when an industry group funded a study at the Bartlesville Energy Research Center [5]. The main action resulting from this study was an increase in the amount of THT from 1.0 lb per 10,000 gal (0.45 kg per 37.9 m³) to 6.4 lb per 10,000 gal (2.9 kg per 37.9 m³) of propane (0.012 kg/m³ to 7.7 kg/m³). This study measured values for the distribution coefficients of ethyl mercaptan and THT from propane at a variety of temperatures. Because THT has a much higher boiling point than ethyl mercaptan, its odor is not as striking as that of ethyl mercaptan. For this reason and because of its cost, THT is not used in the U.S. propane market.

Further research funded by companies that were part of the propane industry — the Gas Processors Association (GPA), the Canadian Propane Gas Association (CPGA), and the National Propane Gas Association (NPGA) — and by the Consumer Product Safety Commission (CPSC) indicated that there was a potential problem with "odor fade" in the use of ethyl mercaptan in propane. The GPA, CPGA, and the NPGA funded another series of tests, which evaluated alternative odorants for use in propane. This study and the results of the summation of industry research were synthesized into a document issued by the Joint Industry Task Force on Propane Odorization [6]. This group verified that ethyl mercaptan was the best choice for propane odorization.

A result of an engineering study funded by the CPSC was the incorporation of 4.2.3 into NFPA 58 [7]. This requirement stipulates that the presence of odorant in LP-Gas should be determined and also documented. Although the code requires only that the presence of odorant be verified, there are laboratory methods and field test methods that may be used to determine the amount of odorant present in the gas. The note to A.4.2.3 contains information regarding "length-of-stain" tube tests, which were developed by the GPA and by the CPGA, as part of the activity of the Joint Industry Task Force on Propane Odorization. In the stain tube test, a sample of the propane is drawn through a glass tube (see Exhibit 4.1), which changes color in the presence of ethyl mercaptan or other mercaptan. The length of the changed color indicates the concentration of the odorant.

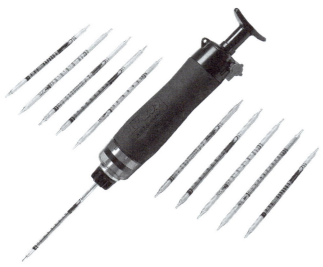

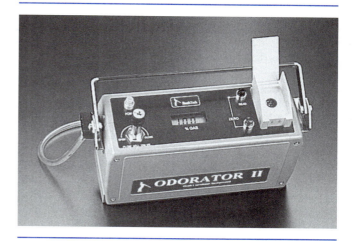

EXHIBIT 4.2 *Odorator®. (Courtesy of Heath Consultants Incorporated)*

EXHIBIT 4.1 *Stain Tubes and Pump. (Courtesy of Sensidyne, LP, www.Sensidyne.com)*

The odorant level can also be determined through the use of an instrument called an Odorator®, which is shown in Exhibit 4.2. The Odorator mixes odorized gas with air in varying amounts, as the operator sniffs the gas. When the odor is detected, the operator presses a button and reads the concentration of the odorant.

Another method used to verify the odorant concentration is by the gas chromatographic analysis of a liquid propane sample. This laboratory method takes more time and is complicated by sampling and shipping issues. A knowledgeable chemist, familiar with the properties of propane and odorants, should be consulted before taking samples of propane for gas chromatographic analysis.

Those interested in odorization are encouraged to review the latest available work in the field. The *National Fuel Gas Code Handbook* [8] includes a supplement, "Fuel Gas Odorization," which covers the odorization of both natural gas and LP-Gas. Also, "Additional Readings on Odorization," a list of published papers and magazine articles on the subject, is included at the end of this chapter.

The odorants utilized for odorizing natural gas or propane can be deodorized in a number of ways. Odors can be in the form of vapors from odorant-containing equipment, residual odorant in old drums, residual odorant in old equipment, or odorant on tools, rags, or clothing.

Large quantities of odorant should not be reacted with oxidants or oxidizing agents, as there is a very large heat of reaction. This heat of reaction will substantially increase the temperature of the mixture and can put a large amount of odorant into the vapor phase. This will have significantly undesirable results. If one has large quantities of odorants, or large vessels that have contained odorants, strong consideration should be given to hiring a company with experience in this type of disposal.

Tools, equipment, rags, empty drums, containers, and clothing can be deodorized with oxidizing agents, such as bleach, hydrogen peroxide, calcium hypochlorite (HTH), or other oxidizer. These should all be diluted to 3 percent or less in order to minimize any heat of reaction. Calcium hypochlorite should not be used without dissolving it in water to a concentration of around 3 percent. Failure to do so will generate a significant amount of heat, potentially enough to cause a fire.

◄ **FAQ**
What can a gas company do to remove odorant that may have spilled, or that may be present in used propane containers?

Several different bacterial solutions also exist that can perform the deodorization of odorant-contaminated equipment or drums. The bacterial solutions tend to be slower than the chemical methods, but if time is not an object, they will oxidize the odorant materials. Many of these bacterial products will incorporate an odor-masking agent.

Charcoal canisters or drums are available that can be used to control the vapor leaving a vessel that contains these odorants. Many odorization stations are in small buildings that can be ventilated through charcoal. The spent charcoal will need to be disposed of in an environmentally responsible fashion.

Masking agents are also sold, which may give some immediate relief to an odor problem. This should not be considered to be a solution, as it is just a stop-gap measure. Treatment of the odorant to render it non-odorous is the only permanent solution.

Anyone handling odorants in bulk quantities should heed manufacturers' suggestions regarding leaks and spill control. Having the materials available to deal with a leak or a spill will save a significant amount of worry [9].

4.3 Notification of Installations

4.3.1 Stationary Installations.

Plans for stationary installations utilizing storage containers of over 2000 gal (7.6 m³) individual water capacity, or with aggregate water capacity exceeding 4000 gal (15.1 m³), and all rooftop installations of ASME containers shall be submitted to the authority having jurisdiction by the person or company that either installs or contracts to have the containers installed, before the installation is started. *[See also 6.19.11.1(F).]*

Plans should be submitted to the authority having jurisdiction (AHJ), which is usually a fire department or state fire marshal. In the absence of specific requirements from the AHJ, plans should include a site plan showing key distances and references to the code, along with information regarding key equipment (i.e., container specifications, investigation of reused equipment, etc.). Subsection 6.25.3 also requires a written fire safety analysis to be submitted for installations that have an aggregate water capacity of more than 4000 gal (15.1 m³) subject to exposure from a single fire in heavily populated or congested areas. (See Supplement 1, "Guidelines for Fire Safety Analysis," and the *Fire Safety Analysis Manual for LP-Gas Storage Facilities* [10] for more information.)

The technical committee has discussed the wording of 4.3.1 during the past few cycles. Some members have expressed the opinion that the AHJ should be required to approve these sites before installation begins. However, because of differences in how the AHJ's office is organized in each state or locality, and because of the difficulty some propane companies have experienced in receiving an acknowledgment from the AHJ that the plans were even received, it was decided that approval from the AHJ would not be a code requirement. It is left for each state or locality to determine how to implement the requirements of this subsection.

FAQ ▶
Why are plans only required to be submitted for installations of containers of over 2000 gal (7.6 m³) individual water capacity or 4000 gal (15.1 m³) aggregate water capacity?

Installations smaller than 2000 gal individual/4000 gal aggregate do not require plans to be submitted because they are relatively simple and standard installation procedures are used. Smaller installations include most one- and two-family homes and typical smaller commercial services that use DOT cylinders and/or ASME 500 gal or 1000 gal (3.8 m³) capacity containers. Some authorities, however, do require approval of these small installations in heavily populated or congested areas. In such instances, the authorities will either amend 4.3.1 or adopt specific wording in the document that requires approval.

Some local authorities need to know of small tank installations for specific reasons. One reason that some localities require permits or notification of these small tanks is to verify that tanks installed in flood-prone areas are properly anchored to prevent flotation. (See 6.6.1.6 for the requirements regarding preventing flotation of underground and mounded containers.)

Some coastal communities inspect tanks for nothing other than proper anchoring in areas they consider to be flood prone.

4.3.2 Temporary Installations.

4.3.2.1 The authority having jurisdiction shall be notified of temporary installations of the container sizes covered in 4.3.1 before the installation is started.

4.3.2.2 Where temporary installations exceed 12 months, approval shall be obtained.

Subsection 4.3.2 was revised in the 2011 edition by separating the requirement into the two current subparagraphs and by adding a specific requirement for approval when temporary installations exceed 12 months.

Subsection 4.3.2 recognizes that some installations are of a temporary nature. These temporary installations of the sizes covered in 4.3.1 must be brought to the attention of the AHJ both (1) prior to installation, so that the fire service can be made aware of them, and (2) if the installation exceeds 12 months and is no longer temporary. When this happens, the AHJ should consider all factors, including public safety, the probable life of the facility, and the need for the installation in determining if the installation must meet all code requirements. Such notice is especially important for emergency response planning. Temporary installations are found at construction sites if temporary heating is needed. They are also found at fairs, where they are used for heating tents and cooking, and at other similar locations.

Twelve months became the maximum period for temporary installations in the 2008 edition, to resolve a conflict that existed in the 2004 edition, where temporary installations were defined as 6 months in one section and 12 months in another. Twelve months was chosen because many construction projects use propane for heating during the construction phase, which often takes longer than 6 months to complete. However, it is not unusual for a new permit application to be submitted after the 12-month period has expired, due to the fact that the job may be ongoing. Under such circumstances, the authority would conduct a review of the submittal as if it were a new temporary installation.

Specific requirements for containers in all temporary services are found in 5.2.7.2 and 6.6.5.

Installations that are removed and then reinstalled in the same specific location might not be considered temporary. For example, a 5-month installation at a cabin used only in the winter might not be considered temporary beyond the first year if the installation is removed after the heating season. However, many summertime fairs require propane for cooking, and these installations are made and removed after a few days in the same location year after year. These are temporary installations and must be approved by the AHJ every year. The AHJ is responsible for determining the nature of all such installations.

◄ FAQ
What happens after the 12-month period for a temporary installation has passed?

4.3.3 Notification of intent for transfer of LP-Gas directly from railcar to cargo tank shall be submitted to the authority having jurisdiction before the first transfer. The authority having jurisdiction shall have the authority to require inspection of the site or equipment for such transfer prior to the initial transfer.

Subsection 4.3.3 was added to the 2008 edition, the same edition where the requirements of 7.2.3.9 were added. Subsection 4.3.3 requires anyone planning to transfer LP-Gas directly from a railcar to a cargo tank to notify the AHJ of the installation. Paragraph 7.2.3.9 requires that anyone wishing to transfer between cargo vehicles must provide certain safeguards during the transfer process, including notifying the AHJ of this temporary operation. These two requirements addressing similar processes came from two different sources, one an AHJ who was concerned about large and frequent transfers occurring in a small town from railcars to cargo tank vehicles, and the other an industry group responding to the effects of an incident where damage and injury occurred because the safeguards specified in the new paragraph were not provided.

The AHJ can require that the system be inspected before the first transfer. This requirement applies to both transfers from a railcar to a cargo tank vehicle at rail sidings and to such transfers at a bulk plant. The intent of this requirement is not to discourage such transfers, as long as all the required safety equipment is in place, but to ensure that the AHJs are aware of them.

While not specifically stated in the code, in an emergency situation where the transfer must be done promptly, such as a derailment, notification should be as soon as practical following the incident, which may be the following day or the following business day.

4.4* Qualification of Personnel

Persons who transfer liquid LP-Gas, who are employed to transport LP-Gas, or whose primary duties fall within the scope of this code shall be trained in proper handling procedures. Refresher training shall be provided at least every 3 years. The training shall be documented.

A requirement for training in proper handling and operation procedures has been included in NFPA 58 since the first edition in 1932. This requirement has been revised over the last decade, as shown in Commentary Table 4.1.

COMMENTARY TABLE 4.1 Changes in Qualification of Personnel Requirement

Edition Year	Nature of Change
1992	Each employee required to carry written certification of his or her job qualifications issued by the training agent or to carry a written document issued by the authority having jurisdiction identifying the functions each employee is authorized to perform
1995	Training required to be documented, but employee no longer required to carry proof of training
1998	Required training limited to those — Who transfer liquid LP-Gas — Who are employed to transport LP-Gas — Whose primary duties fall within the scope of NFPA 58
2001	Refresher training required every three years added

The evolution of the requirements of Section 4.4 shows how difficult it can be to convey the intent of any technical committee. The change in 1992 that required documentation of training was well received by all parties as a way to verify that training was being conducted. The requirement to carry proof of training, however, was not well received, except in areas that had state licensing requirements in place. Because it merely duplicated employee and company records, the requirement was removed in 1995.

FAQ ▶
Are all employees of a propane company required to be trained to handle LP-Gas?

Questions regarding who should be trained led to the 1998 revision, which excluded those who handle cylinders as an incidental part of their jobs from being trained in the hazards of LP-Gas. For example, drivers of propane-powered industrial trucks who exchange fuel cylinders and clerks at retail stores who exchange empty propane cylinders for full ones are exempt from the training requirements. By the same token, office workers in a propane plant are not required to be trained to fill cylinders if that operation is not associated with their job.

Some companies and states prohibit new employees from operating on their own until the required training is complete and documented. Until then, they must operate in a training mode under the observation of a person whose training is complete and documented.

An incident in Ghent, West Virginia, in January 2007 that led to the complete destruction of a store and to multiple deaths was partially attributed to an employee whose training was not complete. The incident was investigated by the U.S. Chemical Safety Board, and a video on the incident is available at: www.csb.gov/videoroom/detail.aspx?vid=15&F=0&CID=1&pg=1&

The requirement for refresher training every three years recognizes that ongoing reinforcement of training is needed, especially for tasks that are not normally part of the job function, but that the employee may be called on to do. For example, a bobtail driver may occasionally be called on to fill cylinders at a dispensing station at the propane company's plant. The driver clearly must have been trained on filling stationary tanks, but must also be trained to fill cylinders.

Complete retraining of all employees on a three-year cycle is not required. Refresher training should cover the normal job functions the employee is expected to perform, any new equipment and procedures introduced since the last training, any code changes that affect the employees' duties, and the operating procedures established by the company. Note that Chapter 14, Operations and Maintenance, requires each LP-Gas bulk plant and industrial plant to have an operating plan and a maintenance plan. Training should follow the procedures in these plans.

A.4.4 Examples of training programs are as follows:

(1) Certified Employee Training Program available from the Propane Education and Research Council (PERC), www.propanecouncil.org
(2) Programs developed by propane companies
(3) Programs developed by government entities

The term *refresher* indicates that the periodic training could be less intensive than the original training, since the primary purpose of periodic training is to reinforce initial training rather than repeat it.

Note that recommendations on training programs were added to A.4.4 in the 2011 edition as a direct result of the 2007 incident described in the commentary on Section 4.4. The Certified Employee Training Program, developed by the Propane Education and Research Council, is the most widely used training for propane employees in the United States. It is important that all employees who transfer liquid LP-Gas, transport LP-Gas, or whose primary duties fall within the scope of NFPA 58 be trained, and the training be validated in some manner, before they work independently.

4.5* Ammonia Contamination

A.4.5 To test for the presence of ammonia, allow a moderate vapor stream of the product to be tested to escape from the container. A rotary, slip tube, or fixed level gauge is a convenient vapor source. Wet a piece of red litmus paper by pouring distilled water over it while holding it with clean tweezers. Hold the wet litmus paper in the vapor stream from the container for 30 seconds. The appearance of any blue color on the litmus paper indicates that ammonia is present in the product.

NOTE: Because red litmus paper will turn blue when exposed to any basic (alkaline) solution, care is required in performing the test and interpreting the results. Contact with tap water, saliva, perspiration, or hands that have been in contact with water having a pH greater than 7, or with any alkaline solution, will produce erroneous results.

Because anhydrous ammonia and LP-Gas are liquefied gases that have about the same vapor pressure characteristics at the same temperature, the same transportation and storage equipment can be used for either ammonia or LP-Gas. In warmer months, when the demand for

LP-Gas for heating falls, LP-Gas tanks are commonly used for ammonia in agricultural areas where ammonia is used as a fertilizer. When switching from ammonia back to LP-Gas service, the tank must be cleaned properly. If not cleaned properly, serious consequences can result.

Specifically, brass fittings are commonly used on tanks in LP-Gas service, particularly on consumers' and dealers' containers. Ammonia can cause these brass fittings to fail while in service through a process known as stress corrosion cracking. If ammonia gets into an LP-Gas distribution system, the ammonia will spread through the system and may damage any brass fittings it contacts.

The maximum concentrations of ammonia that can be tolerated in LP-Gas have been determined through a research project, "A Study of Cleaning Methods for LP-Gas Transports," conducted by Battelle Memorial Institute of Columbus, Ohio [11]. This research indicates that the red litmus paper test for ammonia in LP-Gas, if performed properly, is a much better indicator than simply trying to detect the absence of ammonia odor, and it will ensure that tolerable limits are not exceeded. Litmus paper will detect ammonia to a concentration of 1 to 2 parts per million. This procedure is referenced only in A.4.5 because the test is not mandated for ammonia but rather is informative material for the user. Other test methods can be used, and it is the responsibility of the user to verify that any alternative method will be equally effective in identifying ammonia concentrations that will cause corrosion.

4.5.1 LP-Gas stored or used in systems within the scope of this code shall contain less ammonia than the quantity required to turn the color of red litmus paper to blue.

4.5.2 The initial fill of LP-Gas in a transportation or storage system that has been converted from ammonia to LP-Gas service shall be tested for ammonia contamination prior to being used or transferred from that system.

Testing for ammonia is not required to be performed prior to or after every transfer of LP-Gas from one container to another. Subsection 4.5.2 does require, however, that a test be performed on the LP-Gas transferred into a container that has just undergone a change in service from ammonia to LP-Gas.

4.6* Minimum Requirements

For any purpose or application addressed within the scope of this code, where the minimum requirements of the code are met, additional features or components of equipment not prohibited by the code shall be permitted to be used.

A.4.6 The installation of safety-enhancing equipment that is not otherwise required by the code is permitted by the code. This includes any device that performs a safety-related function even though the device is designed or named to perform a required function. For example, an emergency shutoff valve (ESV) is installed in a location where it is not required to provide all the safety functions of an ESV. Even though the installer uses it to provide a specific feature that can be common to all ESVs, the code would still not require compliance with all of the ESV provisions — for example, the closing requirements described in 5.12.4.

Section 4.6 was added to the 2004 edition. It is intended to permit the installation and use of equipment that is not specifically required by the code, even if that particular piece of equipment, which may be commonly used within a specific system, is not installed with the other components of that system. For example, if an installation were made using an emergency shutoff valve where the code did not necessarily require one to be installed, the installation could be made without requiring a thermal element to be installed to operate the valve in the event of a fire.

REFERENCES CITED IN COMMENTARY

1. CGA V-1, *Standard Compressed Gas Cylinder Valve Outlet and Inlet Connections,* 2005 edition, Compressed Gas Association, Chantilly, VA.
2. ASME *Boiler and Pressure Vessel Code,* 2007 edition, American Society of Mechanical Engineers, New York, NY.
3. Gilbert, A. N., and C. J. Wysocki. "The Smell Survey Results." *National Geographic* 172, 4 (1987) 514–526.
4. Fieldner, A. C., et al. "Warning Agents for Fuel Gases." U.S. Bureau of Mines, Monograph 4 (1931).
5. Whisman, M. L., J. W. Goetzinger, et al. "A New Look at Odorization Levels for Propane Gas," BERC/RI-77/1 (September 1977), Bartlesville, OK.
6. *Proceedings of the Symposium on LP-Gas Odorization Technology,* Gas Processors Association, National Propane Gas Association, Propane Gas Association of Canada, April 18–19, 1989 and October 10–11, 1990.
7. "Status Report on LP-Gas Residential Heating Equipment" (1986), U.S. Consumer Product Safety Commission.
8. *National Fuel Gas Code Handbook,* 2009 edition, National Fire Protection Association, Quincy, MA.
9. Guidance on dealing with excess odorant provided by Dr. John Roberts, personal communication.
10. Raj, P. K., and T. C. Lemoff. *Fire Safety Analysis Manual for LP-Gas Storage Facilities* (2004). Available from www.nfpa.org.
11. "A Study of Cleaning Methods for LP-Gas Transports" (1969), Battelle Memorial Institute, Columbus, OH.

Additional Readings on Odorization

Andreen, B. H., and R. L. Kroencke. "Stability of Mercaptans Under Gas Distribution System Conditions." *Proceedings of the American Gas Association* 136 (1964). Covers oxidation, odor fade, natural gas, odorant, alkyl mercaptans, t-butyl mercaptan, ethyl mercaptan.

Andreen, B. H., and R. L. Kroencke. "Stability of Mercaptans Under Gas Distribution System Conditions." *American Gas J* 48 (May 1965). Covers natural gas, odorant, mercaptan, oxidation, iron oxide, odor fade.

Arthur D. Little, Inc. "Development of New Gas Odorants." *Arthur D. Little Report to Gas Research Institute,* GRI Contract No. 5010-352-0047. Covers oxidation, odor fade, natural gas, mercaptans, iron oxides, amyl mercaptans, adsorption.

ASTM D 5305-92, *Standard Test for Determination of Ethyl Mercaptan in LP-Gas Vapor* (January 1992), American Society for Testing and Materials, West Conshohocken, PA. Covers stain tube, LP-Gas, propane, ethyl mercaptan, odorant, and analysis.

Bacha, John D. "Chevron/Gulf Studies Regarding LPG Odorants." *Proceedings of the Symposium on LP-Gas Odorization* 43 (1989). Covers ethyl mercaptan, alternate, TBM, t-butyl mercaptan, odor fade, IGT, odorants, oxidation.

Barclay, A. T., et al. "Rail Car Field Test Evaluating Ethyl Mercaptan Odorant in Propane." *Institute of Gas Technology Odorization Symposium* (1990). Covers LP-Gas, oxidation, odor fade, treatment, tank, propane, ethyl mercaptan, odorant.

Beltis, Kevin J., and Daniel J. Ehntholt. "Characterization of LP-Gas Odorant Fade." *Proceedings of the Symposium on LP-Gas Odorization* 43 (1989). Covers odor fade, ethyl mercaptan, oxidation, adsorption, surfaces, concrete, propane, LP-Gas.

Bergqvist, L. "LPG Odorization in Europe: No Apparent Cause for Concern." *Proceedings of the Symposium on LP-Gas Odorization* 88 (1989). Covers propane, odorant, ethyl mercaptan, odor fade, oxidation.

Bullerdiek, W. Alan. "LP-Gas Detection: Odorization and Electronic Methods." *Proceedings of the Symposium on LP-Gas Odorization* 94 (1990). Covers gas detectors, alarms, propane, LP-Gas, odorant, ethyl mercaptan, warnings.

Cain, William S., and Amos Turk. "Smell of Danger: An Analysis of LP-Gas Odorization." *American Industrial Hygiene Association* 46 (3), 115 (1985). Covers ethyl mercaptan, LP-Gas, propane, odorant, oxidation, odor intensity, odor fade.

Campbell, Ian D. "Factors Affecting Odorant Depletion in LPG." *Proceedings of the Symposium on LP-Gas Odorization* 28 (1989). Covers oxidation, barbeque cylinders, 5-gallon cylinders, 20-pound cylinders, ethyl mercaptan, odor fade, propane.

Campbell, Ian D. "Research Proposal: LPG Odorant Fade in Consumer Tanks." *Proposal of the Petroleum Gas Association of Canada.* Covers odor fade, ethyl mercaptan, oxidation, tanks, barbeque cylinder, 20-pound cylinders, 5-gallon cylinder.

Campbell, Ian D., et al. "The Chemical Oxidation of Ethyl Mercaptan in Steel Vessels." *Institute of Gas Technology Odorization Symposium* (1994). Covers odor fade, diethyl disulfide, DEDS, barbeque cylinders, 5-gallon cylinders, 20-pound cylinders.

Chowdiah, Prasan, and Amir Attari. "Stability of Gas Phase Odorant Compounds." *Proceedings of the Institute of Gas Technology Odorization Symposium* (1992). Covers adsorption, oxidation, aluminum, carbon steel, stainless steel, and odor fade.

Cooper, L. S., et al. "Some Aspects of the Reception and Transmission of North Sea Gas." 34th Autumn Meeting, Institution of Gas Engineers. Covers wet gas, natural gas, high BTU, odor fade hydrates, absorption, liquids.

Elf, Atochem. "Odor Fade." *Skunk Tips,* 1.2. Covers odorants, odor fade, oxidation, adsorption, absorption.

Gavrilov, L. E. "American Studies of the Stability of Odorants Added to Natural Gas." *Gazovoe Delo* 12, no. 20 (1971). Covers odorant, stability, oxidation, ethyl mercaptan, natural gas.

Goetzinger, J. W., and D. L. Ripley. "Effect of Ammonia on LP-Gas Odorant." *GPA Technical Publication TP-20* (May 1996). Covers ammonia, ethyl mercaptan, odorant, LP-Gas, propane.

Goetzinger, J. W., and D. L. Ripley. "A Study of Passivation Agents for Odorized Propane Containers." *GPA Research Report RR-143* (March 1994). Covers propane, LP-Gas, odorants, ethyl mercaptan, tanks, passivation, treatments, corrosion inhibitors.

Goetzinger, John W., et al. "Vapor-Liquid Equilibrium Data of Ethanethiol and Tetrahydrothiophene in Propane." *Chemical Engineering Data* 22, no. 396 (1977). Covers LP-Gas, propane, THT, thiophane, vapor liquid equilibrium, ethyl mercaptan, vaporization.

Henderson, E. L. "Odorization of Gas." *Operating Section Meeting, American Gas Association* (1952). Covers literature references, soil adsorption, natural gas, odorants, practices, odor fade, testing, leak complaints, equipment, new odorant research.

Hines, William J., and Carl G. Hefley. "Field Test Program of Measuring Odorant in Continuous Use Tank LP-Gas Tanks." *Proceedings of the Symposium on LP-Gas Odorization* 32 (1990). Covers analysis, length-of-stain tubes, propane, LP-Gas, odorant, ethyl mercaptan, continuous use, level, concentration.

Holmes, S. A., et al. "Laboratory and Field Experience with Ethyl Mercaptan Odorant in Propane." *Proceedings of the Symposium on LP-Gas Odorization* (1990). Covers propane, LP-Gas, odorizing, odorization, odorant, ethyl mercaptan, odor fade, oxidation, railroad cars.

Jacobus, O. John, and David Swienton. "Odorant Vapor–Liquid Equilibria: A Generalized Treatment." *Proceedings of the Symposium on LP-Gas Odorization* 79 (1990). Covers vapor–liquid equilibrium K-factor, propane, LP-Gas, ethyl mercaptan, THT, DMS, blends, alternates, thiophane, dimethyl sulfide, concentration.

Jacobus, O. John, and John Roberts. "What Constitutes Adequate Odorization of Fuel Gases?" *Institute of Gas Technology Odorization Symposium,* Chicago, IL (August 1995). Covers mostly natural gas, but discusses odor intensity and concentration issues.

Jacobus, O. John, and John Roberts. "Relationship Between Gas Composition and Odor Intensity." *Institute of Gas Technology Odorization Symposium,* Chicago, IL (July 1996). Covers mostly natural gas, but discusses odor intensity and concentration issues.

Jentoft, R. E., and S. A. Olund. "Solubilities of Odorants in Liquid Petroleum Gas." *Proceedings of the American Chemical Society Chicago Meeting,* Chicago, IL (August 30, 1964). Covers odorants, solubility, solubilities, LP-Gas, propane, butane, ethyl mercaptan, isopropyl, thiophane.

Johnson, James L. "1965 Report on Project PB-48, Stability of Odorant Compounds." *Proceedings of the American Gas Association Conference* (1966). Covers oxidation, kinetics, rust, hydrated, Fe_2O_3, ferric oxide, natural gas, mercaptan, disulfide, odor fade, ethyl, methyl, isopropyl, t-butyl, TBM, IPM.

Johnson, S. J. "Ethyl Mercaptan Odorant Stability in Stored Liquid Propane." *Proceedings of the Symposium on LP-Gas Odorization* (1989). Covers oxidation, new tank, steel, carbon, ethyl mercaptan, disulfide, diethyl, purge, purging, analysis, odor fade.

Kemp, Daniel W. "An Overview of Odorization Technology." *Proceedings of the Symposium on LP-Gas Odorization* 1 (1989). Covers odor fade, ethyl mercaptan, oxidation, alternates, blends, adsorption.

Kniebes, Duane V., and Robert C. Stubbs. "Odorant Concentration in Partially Full LPG Tanks." *Proceedings of the Symposium on LP-Gas Odorization* 54 (1989). Covers LP-Gas, propane, tanks, K-factor, Kd's, ethyl mercaptan, odorants, concentration, vapor–liquid equilibria.

Kuhlman, Michael R. "LP-Gas Odorant Stability Under Simulated Residential Conditions." *Proceedings of the Symposium on LP-Gas Odorization* (1990). Covers odorant, odor fade, ethyl mercaptan, LP-Gas, propane, adsorption.

Maddox, R. N. "Odorization of Hydrocarbon Fuel Gases." *Proceedings of the LP-Gas Odorization Symposium.* Covers LP-Gas, propane, odorization, ethyl mercaptan, alternate blends, odorants.

Marshall, M. D., and C. A. Palladino. "Analysis of Long Term Degradation of LP-Gas Odorants." *Proceedings of the Symposium on LP-Gas Odorization* 69 (1989). Covers propane, LP-Gas, ethyl mercaptan, vapor, used, new, tanks, sampling, sample, analysis, odor fade, oxidation, adsorption.

Marshall, M. D., and C. A. Palladino. "Field Testing for Ethyl Mercaptan in LP-Gas Storage Tanks in Four Marketing Areas." *Proceedings of the Symposium on LP-Gas Odorization* 22 (1990). Covers odor fade, testing, LP-Gas, propane, ethyl mercaptan, odorant level.

Marshall, M. D., and C. A. Palladino. "Ethyl Mercaptan Stability After Refill of New and Air-Exposed Used LP-Gas Service." *Proceedings of the Symposium on LP-Gas Odorization* 54 (1990). Covers oxidation, odor fade, ethyl mercaptan, tanks, new, used.

Matson, A. F., and R. E. DuFour. "Persistency of Odor of Accidentally Released Pyrofax LPG." *Underwriters Laboratories Inc., Research Bulletin* 37 (1946). Covers LP-Gas, propane, odorant, ethyl mercaptan, stratification.

McCullough, J. P., et al. "Ethanethiol: Thermodynamic Properties in the Solid, Liquid and Vapor States." *American Chemical Society* 74 (1952):2801–2804. Covers ethanethiol properties, thermodynamic, physical, ethyl mercaptan.

McHenry, William B., and H. M. Faulconer. "Summary Report on Odorant Investigations." *Proceedings of the Symposium on LP-Gas Odorization* 1 (1990). Covers joint task force report, odorant, odorizing, propane, LP-Gas, ethyl mercaptan, alternates.

Moshfeghian, Mahmood, et al. "Prediction of Odorant Distribution in LP-Gas Tanks." *Proceedings of the Symposium on LP-Gas Odorization* 87 (1990). Covers vapor–liquid equilibrium, equilibria, propane, LP-Gas, ethyl mercaptan, alternates, t-butyl, tertiary, THT, tetrahydrothiophene, thiophane.

MSA Research Corporation. "Test Ethyl Mercaptan Concentration." *Final Report to National Propane Gas Association.* Covers propane, ethyl mercaptan, odorant, odor fade, continuous service, out-of-service, LP-Gas, stain tube.

Nevers, Ashley D., and W. H. Oister. "Problems in the Critical Comparison of Odor Intensities." *Operating Section Proceedings of the American Gas Association* 65-P-126 (1965). Covers natural gas, odorants, thresholds, levels, intensity, concentration, olfactometer, ethyl mercaptan.

Osborn, Ann G., and Donald R. Douslin, Jr. "Vapor Pressure Relations of 36 Sulfur Compounds Present in Petroleum." *Chemical Engineering Data* 11, no. 502 (1966). Covers vapor pressure, measurement, mercaptans, ethyl mercaptan, isopropyl, t-Butyl, sec-butyl, sulfides, disulfides, thiophane.

Pickard, Andrew J. "Test Methods for Ethyl Mercaptan Odorant In Propane." *Proceedings of the Symposium on LP-Gas Odorization* (1989). Covers ethyl mercaptan, propane, LP-Gas, analysis, length of stain, stain tube.

Present, Paula A. "Consumer Survey of Households with Gas Appliances." *CPSC Report* (June 1986). Covers CPSC, odorant, lighting, out of gas, pilot lights, odor fade, LP-Gas, propane.

Ripley, D. L., et al. "Untrained Panel Determinations of Odorant Warning Levels." *Proceedings of the Symposium on LP-Gas Odorization* 12 (1990). Covers warning level, odorant, LP-Gas, propane, ethyl mercaptan, THT, thiophane, t-butyl, tertiary, isopropyl.

Ripley, Dennis L., and John W. Goetzinger. "LP-Gas Odorants." *Proceedings of the Institute of Gas Technology Odorization Symposium* (August 1992). Covers LP-Gas, propane, odorants, ethyl mercaptan, alternate.

Roberts, John S. "Propane Odorant Blends: Panacea or Mythology." Institute of Gas Technology First Annual Conference and Exhibition on Natural Gas Technologies (September 30–October 2, 2002).

Roberts, John S. "Thiols." In *Kirk-Othmer Encyclopedia of Chemical Technology,* 4th ed., 24, 19. New York: John Wiley and Sons, Inc. (1997). Covers mercaptan properties and chemistry (very general).

Roberts, John S. "Thiols." In *Kirk-Othmer The Concise Encyclopedia of Chemical Technology,* New York: John Wiley and Sons, Inc. (1998). Covers mercaptan properties and chemistry (very general).

Roberts, John S., and Daniel W. Kelly. "Selection and Handling of Natural Gas Odorants." *Odorization III, Proceedings of the Institute of Gas Technology* 29, Chicago, IL (1993). Covers toxicity of odorants, ethyl mercaptan included.

Roberts, John, and John Jacobus. "Case Study: The Effect of Propane Tanks on Odorants." *Institute of Gas Technology Odorization Symposium,* Chicago, IL (July 1997). Covers oxidation of propane odorants in new tanks.

Schumacher, John L., and John M. Freeman. "Confirmation of Odor Fade of Ethyl Mercaptan in New and Used LP Tanks." *Natural Gas & LP Odorization Case Study and Best Practices Workshop* (July 21–22, 2003).

Stubbs, Robert C. "Pitfalls in Odorization." *Odorization III,* ed. Wilson & Attari, *Proceedings of the Institute of Gas Technology* 7 (1993). Covers propane, LP-Gas, ethyl mercaptan, blends, alternates, oxidation, adsorption, absorption, soil, odor intensity, thiophane, t-butyl.

Suchomel, Frank H. "Odor Fading and Supplemental Odorization." *Proceedings of the Institute of Gas Technology Symposium on Odorization* (July 12, 1976). Covers odor fade, natural gas, supplemental odorization, methods, oxidation, adsorption, absorption, iron oxides.

Sullivan, Frederick. "Development of New Gas Odorants." *Arthur D. Little Report to GRI,* GRI Contract No. 5010-352-0047. Covers natural gas odorants, alternates, oxidation, odor fade, ferric oxide, ferrous oxide, Fe_2O_3, hydrated, $FeO(OH)$, t-Amyl mercaptan.

Sullivan, Frederick. "New Gas Odorants." *Odorization II,* ed. Wilson & Attari, *Proceedings of the Institute of Gas Technology* 209 (1987). Covers amyl mercaptans, t-butyl, soil penetrability, adsorption, oxidation, odor fade.

Switzer, Donald W. "Engineering Hazard Analysis of Residential LP-Gas Use." *CPSC Report on Contract CPSC-C-85-1131,* Bullerdiek. Covers CPSC, odorant, LP-Gas, propane, odor fade, ethyl mercaptan, out of gas, relight, gas detector.

Switzer, Donald W. "CPSC Fuel Gas Study." *Proceedings of the Symposium on LP-Gas Odorization* (1989). Covers CPSC, propane, LP-Gas, odorants, ethyl mercaptan, odor fade.

"Tentative Method for the Determination of Ethyl Mercaptan in LP-Gas" (January 1988). *GPA 2188-88.* Covers analysis, LP-Gas, propane, odorant, stain tube, length of stain, ethyl mercaptan.

Thomas, E. R., et al. "VLE Data and Correlations for Odorants in Propane." *Proceedings of the Symposium on LP-Gas Odorization* 25 (1989). Covers propane, LP-Gas, odorants, vapor–liquid equilibrium, K-factors, Kd's, TBM, MES, IPM, ethyl mercaptan, t-butyl, methyl ethyl sulfide, isopropyl, blends, dimethyl sulfide.

Thompson, C. J. "A New Look at Odorization — Revisited." *Proceedings of the Symposium on LP-Gas Odorization* 4 (1989). Covers BERC, 1977 Bartlesville, OK, study on ethyl mercaptan, thiophane, warning level, detection, directed, misdirected, threshold.

Whisman, M. L., et al. "A New Look at Odorization Levels for Propane Gas." *USERDA Document,* BERC/R1-77/1 (1977). Covers ethyl mercaptan, THT, thiophane, LP-Gas, propane, odorant level, detection, threshold, warning, odor fade, oxidation, absorption, adsorption.

LP-Gas Equipment and Appliances

Chapter 5 provides the information necessary for the design, manufacture, marking, and performance requirements for individual LP-Gas components or complete systems, with the exception of cargo tank vehicles, which are covered in Chapter 9, and engine fuel systems, which are covered in Chapter 11.

The chapter is organized by numbering many of the sections to align with the sections in Chapter 6, Installation of LP-Gas Systems. This organization makes it easy to go from product to installation requirements, because they will carry similar numbering. For example, Section 5.9, Piping (Including Hose), Fittings, and Valves, contains the requirements for all piping materials, and Section 6.9, Piping Systems, contains requirements for the installation of piping systems. Because of the alignment of subject matter, a number of sections in Chapter 5 are reserved (not used).

Chapter 5 includes detailed information and requirements for the following topics:

- Containers — cylinders and ASME containers (See Section 5.2.)
- Container appurtenances, such as pressure relief devices, regulators, pressure regulators, overfilling prevention devices, container connections, and various gauges (See Section 5.7.)
- Pressure regulators and regulator vents (See Section 5.8.)
- Piping (including hose), fittings, and valves (See Section 5.9.)
- Valves other than container valves (See Section 5.12.)
- Hydrostatic relief valves (See Section 5.13.)
- Equipment, such as pumps, compressors, meters, engines, and sight flow indicators (See Section 5.17.)
- Appliances (See Section 5.20.)
- Vaporizers, tank heaters, vaporizing burners, and gas–air mixers (See Section 5.21.)

5.1* Scope

This chapter applies to individual components and components shop-fabricated into subassemblies, container assemblies, and complete container systems.

A.5.1 The field assembly of components, subassemblies, container assemblies, or complete container systems into complete LP-Gas systems is addressed in Chapter 6. *(See 3.3.36, LP-Gas System.)*

Note that for most propane installations, both Chapters 5 and 6 must be used because both contain relevant requirements. The chapters are organized to enable the user to find the requirements easily. The sections in Chapters 5 and 6 have coordinated numbers; for example, the requirements for propane storage containers are located in Section 5.2, and the container installation requirements are located in Section 6.2. Note that when there are no equipment requirements in Chapter 5 for some of the installation subjects covered in Chapter 6, the equivalent section in Chapter 5 is reserved. For example, Section 6.3 covers container separation distances, but because there are no material requirements for separation distances, Section 5.3 is reserved.

5.2 Containers

5.2.1 General.

5.2.1.1* Containers shall be designed, fabricated, tested, and marked (or stamped) in accordance with the regulations of the U.S. Department of Transportation (DOT); the ASME *Boiler and Pressure Vessel Code*, Section VIII, "Rules for the Construction of Unfired Pressure Vessels"; or the API-ASME *Code for Unfired Pressure Vessels for Petroleum Liquids and Gases*, except for UG-125 through UG-136.

DOT has approved a new type of cylinder for use in the United States — a composite cylinder fabricated from reinforced fiberglass. Only composite cylinders fabricated under a DOT special permit can be used. They have a 15-year service life and must be requalified every 5 years (DOT may review the service life and requalification interval at some time in the future). These cylinders can be used for all applications not prohibited by NFPA 58, such as outdoor gas grills, industrial trucks, and other applications not located in buildings.

(A) Used containers constructed to specifications of the Association of American Railroads shall not be installed

This prohibition was added to the code in the 2011 edition in response to questions on the safety of using propane tanks taken from tank cars as stationary storage containers. Tank car tanks are not constructed to the ASME *Boiler and Pressure Vessel Code* [1], rather, they are constructed to a code of the Association of American Railroads (AAR) [2]. The AAR code is concerned with the forces that a tank car will experience over its life. Tank cars can be used for 40 years and then must be removed from service.

(B) Adherence to applicable ASME Code case interpretations and addenda that have been adopted and published by ASME 180 calendar days prior to the effective date of this code shall be considered as compliant with the ASME Code.

The text of 5.2.1.1(B) ensures that the NFPA Technical Committee on Liquefied Petroleum Gases had an opportunity to review any "code case" amendments to the ASME *Boiler and Pressure Vessel Code* [1] before being accepted in NFPA 58. According to ASME procedures, a code case (similar to NFPA's Tentative Interim Amendment) is effective when issued by the ASME committee.

(C) Where containers fabricated to earlier editions of regulations, rules, or codes listed in 5.2.1.1, and of the Interstate Commerce Commission (ICC) *Rules for Construction of Unfired Pressure Vessels*, prior to April 1, 1967, are used, the requirements of Section 1.4 shall apply.

The intent and application of 5.2.1.1 (C) are often misinterpreted with regard to containers that were built to the API-ASME Code (specifications U-200 and U-201) and pre-1949 editions of the ASME Code (specifications U-68 and U-69). Because these ASME containers have a very long service life when properly maintained, many remain in use and are sometimes relocated and reinstalled. However, not all containers built to these older editions of the ASME Code can be continued in use and reinstalled, regardless of their condition. Before it is filled, a container must be found suitable for continued use, as required in 7.2.2, which states:

7.2.2 Filling and Evacuating of Containers.

7.2.2.1 Transfer of LP-Gas to and from a container shall be accomplished only by qualified individuals trained in proper handling and operating procedures meeting the requirements of Section 4.4 and in emergency response procedures.

7.2.2.2 When noncompliance with Section 5.2 and Section 5.7 is found, the container owner and user shall be notified in writing.

7.2.2.3 Injection of compressed air, oxygen, or any oxidizing gas into containers to transfer LP-Gas liquid shall be prohibited.

7.2.2.4 When evacuating a container owned by others, the qualified person(s) performing the transfer shall not inject any material other than LP-Gas into the container.

7.2.2.5* Valve outlets on refillable cylinders of 108 lb (49 kg) water capacity [nominal 45 lb (20 kg) propane capacity] or less shall be equipped with a redundant pressure-tight seal or one of the following listed connections: CGA 790, CGA 791, or CGA 810, as described in CGA V-1, *Standard Compressed Gas Cylinder Valve Outlet and Inlet Connections.*

7.2.2.6 Where redundant pressure seals are used, they shall be in place whenever the cylinder is not connected for use.

7.2.2.7 Nonrefillable (disposable) and new unused cylinders shall not be required to be equipped with valve outlet seals.

7.2.2.8 Containers shall be filled only after determination that they comply with the design, fabrication, inspection, marking, and requalification provisions of this code.

7.2.2.9 Prior to refilling a cylinder that has a cylinder sleeve, the cylinder sleeve shall be removed to facilitate the visual inspection of the cylinder.

7.2.2.10 "Single trip," "nonrefillable," or "disposable" cylinders shall not be refilled with LP-Gas.

7.2.2.11 Containers shall comply with the following with regard to service or design pressure requirements:

(1) The service pressure marked on the cylinder shall be not less than 80 percent of the vapor pressure of the LP-Gas for which the cylinder is designed at 130°F (54.4°C).
(2) The maximum allowable working pressure (MAWP) for ASME containers shall be in accordance with Table 5.2.4.2.

7.2.2.12 Transfer of refrigerated product shall be made only into systems that are designed to accept refrigerated product.

7.2.2.13 A container shall not be filled if the container assembly does not meet the requirements for continued service.

7.2.2.14 Transfer hoses larger than ½ in. (12 mm) internal diameter shall not be used for making connections to individual cylinders being filled indoors.

A.5.2.1.1 Prior to April 1, 1967, regulations of the U.S. Department of Transportation were promulgated by the Interstate Commerce Commission. In Canada, the regulations of the Canadian Transport Commission apply and are available from the Canadian Transport Commission, Union Station, Ottawa, Canada.

Construction of containers to the API-ASME *Code for Unfired Pressure Vessels for Petroleum Liquids and Gases* has not been authorized after July 1, 1961.

The requirements for the construction of pressure vessels used to store LP-Gases are referenced in 5.2.1.1. (Requirements for nonpressurized refrigerated containers are located in Chapter 12, Refrigerated Containers.) The referenced codes provide a level of safety such that the NFPA Technical Committee on Liquefied Petroleum Gases has not needed to develop its own requirements for pressure vessels for LP-Gas. In referencing the ASME *Boiler and Pressure Vessel Code* [1], the committee has made an exception to sections UG-125 through UG-136, which cover pressure relief devices. The requirements for pressure relief devices in the ASME *Boiler and Pressure Vessel Code* are more conservative than those in ANSI/UL 132, *Standard for Safety Relief Valves for Anhydrous Ammonia and LP-Gas* [3], which requires larger pressure relief valves.

Pressurized LP-Gas containers in the United States, Canada, and other countries served by marketers based in the United States and Canada comply with 5.2.1.1. Many other countries that use NFPA 58 have their own container requirements. In the event that a container constructed to a different standard, such as one used in a foreign country, is to be filled in a jurisdiction that enforces NFPA 58, approval to fill that container must be obtained from the authority having jurisdiction. For cylinders, the authority having jurisdiction is the U.S. Department of Transportation (DOT), and approval to fill is not likely to be given. Given the relatively low cost of cylinders, it is easier to purchase a new cylinder than to petition DOT for a variance. Small foreign vessels and campers that travel internationally provide a source of cylinders built to specifications of other countries. Cylinders manufactured to other than DOT specifications can be used in the United States but cannot be refilled.

An example of a difference in cylinder requirements in other countries has become apparent since the requirement for the overfilling prevention device (OPD) in NFPA 58 following the mandatory retrofit date of April 1, 2001. U.S. cylinders are required to meet DOT cylinder construction testing requirements and any additional requirements imposed by NFPA 58. Canadian cylinders are required to meet Transport Canada (TC) requirements and any additional requirements imposed by CSA B149.2, *Propane Storage and Handling Code* [4]. The respective federal standards are very similar, and it is understood that they are essentially the same. For decades these cylinders have been transported across the long land border between the United States and Canada by campers and others, and filled in either country with no significant problems. With the introduction of the OPD in the United States and its characteristic triangular shaped valve handwheel, it became easy to differentiate Canadian cylinders, especially with the prohibition of filling non-OPD cylinders in the United States after April 1, 2001. Campers and others using Canadian cylinders could no longer have their cylinders refilled in the United States. This forced many Canadians to purchase a second cylinder, built to DOT specifications with an OPD, in order to obtain propane in the United States. The Canadian standard has since been revised to require OPDs, so the problem has been resolved.

FAQ ▶
Is it permissible to use containers that have been fabricated and marked in accordance with regulations in foreign countries?

If the container is a pressure vessel, the authority having jurisdiction is the state in which the container is installed. Because most states adopt and enforce the ASME *Boiler and Pressure Vessel Code* [1], the state boiler agency must be contacted. For example, when packaged propane equipment is imported with propane tanks, the authority having jurisdiction should be contacted to determine how to proceed. The following paragraphs provide more detailed information on the specific types of containers used in the LP-Gas industry.

U.S. Department of Transportation (DOT) Cylinders. DOT cylinders first used for LP-Gas were built to specifications of the Interstate Commerce Commission (ICC). DOT restricts cylinders to 1000 lb (454 kg) water capacity or less. Prior to 1967, ICC specifications were used, but they have not been used for many years. The current basic cylinders for reusable service are DOT 4BA-240 (steel construction) and DOT 4E (aluminum construction) cylinders, specifications for which are found in 49 CFR 178.50 [5] and 49 CFR 178.68 [6], respectively. Disposable cylinders, such as hand torch cylinders, have different DOT specifications.

The regulations for DOT cylinders [and similar cylinders built to Transport Canada (TC) specifications] are concerned with transportation, whereas much of NFPA 58 is concerned with container usage and storage. Several DOT/TC cylinders are shown in Exhibits 5.1 and 5.2. Nevertheless, there are compelling reasons why NFPA 58 must recognize these cylinders as storage containers. Because DOT specifications are developed for transportation applications only, the NFPA technical committee continuously monitors DOT and TC standards to ensure that the standards are adequate for the applications covered by NFPA 58. For example, the committee did not permit the use of 4E (aluminum) cylinder for several years, until the cylinder's use and storage safety were demonstrated by tests and experience.

All DOT/TC cylinders are portable and designed to be transported when filled with product. Cylinders hold from 1 lb to 420 lb (0.5 kg to 191 kg) of propane. (See Exhibit 5.3.)

EXHIBIT 5.1 *DOT/TC Cylinders. Top: Typical Industrial Truck Motor (Engines) Fuel Cylinders; Bottom: Typical Stationary and Portable Cylinders for Residential and Commercial Uses. (Courtesy of Manchester Tank)*

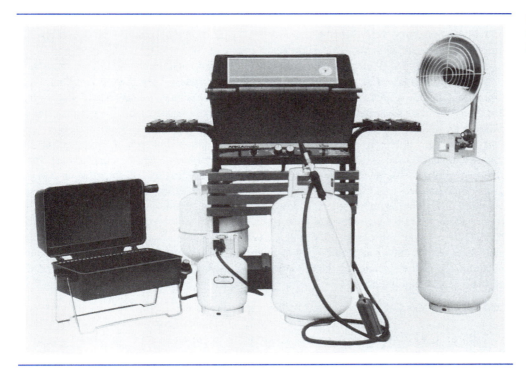

EXHIBIT 5.2 *DOT/TC Cylinders. (Courtesy of Manchester Tank)*

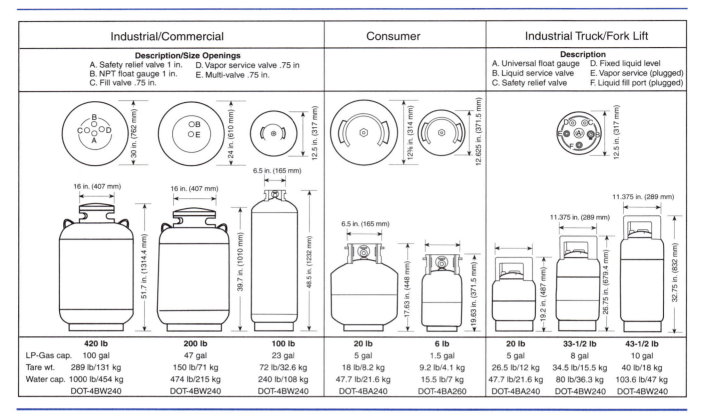

EXHIBIT 5.3 *Dimensions and Capacities of Typical DOT Cylinders. (Courtesy of Worthington Cylinder Corp.)*

Cylinders can be moved with reasonable ease by an individual or by vehicles that are equipped with lifting devices that can transport the larger portable cylinders.

Cylinders are also filled at the location where they are installed or used. It is common to see 100 lb (45 kg) and 420 lb (191 kg) cylinders "permanently" installed at residential and commercial locations being filled there. When the cylinder is permanently installed, the standard cylinder valve is normally replaced with a multipurpose valve so that the cylinder can be refilled without disconnecting the piping.

Commentary Table 5.1 lists types of popular cylinders, their applications, water and propane capacities, and specification numbers. The information listed in Commentary Table 5.1 is especially useful because the capacity of cylinders is rated by weight, in pounds (kilograms), and their spacing is determined by the volumetric capacity, in gallons (cubic meters), by Table 6.3.1. Commentary Table 5.1 allows conversions from pounds to gallons so that the proper spacing distances can be easily determined.

A DOT cylinder must be marked with certain information, usually on the cylinder itself or on its collar, as shown in Exhibit 5.4. This information is especially vital in determining the suitability of the cylinder for continued service, as indicated by the date of manufacture and the requalification date.

ASME Containers. ASME containers, often referred to as bulk containers, are unfired pressure vessels built to the ASME Code, Section VIII, Division 1 or 2. Division 1 is a "prescriptive" approach to container design that lays out the requirements in "cookbook" fashion. Division 2 is a "performance" approach that allows the designer more latitude in the choice of materials, but requires a more extensive analysis to demonstrate compliance. ASME Code

COMMENTARY TABLE 5.1 DOT/TC Cylinder Applications

Type of Service	Typical Use	Propane Capacity			Water Capacity			Common DOT Mfg. Code
		Pounds	Kilograms	Gallons	Pounds	Kilograms	Gallons	
Stationary	Homes, business	420	191	99	1000	454	119	4B, 4BA, 4BW
Stationary	Homes, business	300	136	71	715	324	86	4B, 4BA, 4BW
Stationary	Homes, business	200	91	47	477	216	57	4B, 4BA, 4BW
Stationary	Homes, business	150	68	35	357	162	43	4B
Exchange	Homes, business	100	45	24	239	108	29	4B, 4BA, 4BW
Exchange	Homes, business	60	27	14	144	65	17	4B, 4BA, 4BW
Engine fuel	Forklift	43.5	19.7	10	104	47	12	4B, 4BA, 4BW, 4E
Engine fuel	Forklift	33.5	15.2	8	80	36	9.6	4B, 4BA, 4BW, 4E
Engine fuel	Forklift	20	9	4.7	48	22	5.7	4B, 4BA, 4BW, 4E
Engine fuel	Forklift	14	6.4	3.3	34	15.4	4.1	4B, 4BA, 4BW, 4E
Portable	Rec. vehicles	40	18	9.5	95	43	11	4B, 4BA, 4BW, 4E
Portable	Rec. vehicles	30	13.6	7.1	72	32.7	8.6	4B, 4BA, 4BW, 4E
Portable	Rec. vehicles	25	11.3	5.9	59.5	27	7.1	4B, 4BA, 4BW
Portable	Rec. vehicles, grills	20	9	4.7	48	22	5.7	4B, 4BA, 4BW, 4E
Portable	Rec. vehicles, and small appliances	10	4.5	2.4	23.8	10.8	2.8	4B, 4BA, 4BW, 4E
Portable	Indoors, trailers	5	2.3	1.2	12	5.4	1.4	4B, 4BA, 4BW, 4E
Portable	Torches, RV	0.93	0.42	0.2	2.2	1	0.3	39 (disposable), 4B240 (refillable)

containers are usually found in stationary installations but can also be mounted on trucks for use as a cargo tank motor vehicle. (See Exhibit 5.5.)

Prior to World War I, the first LP-Gas bulk containers in use were riveted, but keeping these containers leak-free around the rivets and the seams was difficult. Forge-welded containers came into use after World War I as the technology became available in the United States. In the 1930s, the current-style fusion-welded pressure vessels were used. At that time, the ASME Code specifications were U-68 and U-69. These specifications had a design margin (safety factor) of 5 to 1 — the ratio of the theoretical burst pressure to the design operating pressure. The normal working pressure of U-68 and U-69 containers was 200 psig (1.4 MPag). At that time, NFPA 58 allowed the pressure relief valve setting to be 125 percent of the working pressure, or 250 psig (1.7 MPag). Pressure relief valves prevent the excessive buildup of pressure in the containers in case of overfilling, or excessive heating of the propane due to fire impingement on the container.

ASME specifications U-200 and U-201, which were developed in conjunction with the American Petroleum Institute (API), were also applied prior to 1949. ASME specifications U-200 and U-201 were known as the API-ASME Code. These API-ASME Code specifications applied to containers that were restricted in use to installations such as refineries, gas processing plants, and tank farms.

In 1949, ASME adopted a design margin (safety factor) of 4 to 1. At that time, the requirement for the pressure relief valve setting was changed to the working pressure of a container, 250 psig minimum (1.7 MPag minimum) for propane. In effect, the 4 to 1 safety factor and the previous 5 to 1 safety factor are comparable, with the same ultimate burst pressure, as 250 × 4 and 200 × 5 both equal 1000. Many pre-1949, 200 psig (1.4 MPag) ASME tanks are still in service.

In the mid-1990s, the ASME Code design margin (formerly called safety factor) was further reduced from 4 to 1 to 3.5 to 1. The ASME Boiler and Pressure Vessel Code Committee took this action because of the improvement in both material quality control and welding technology since the 1950s. The design margin in pressure vessel design anticipates minor

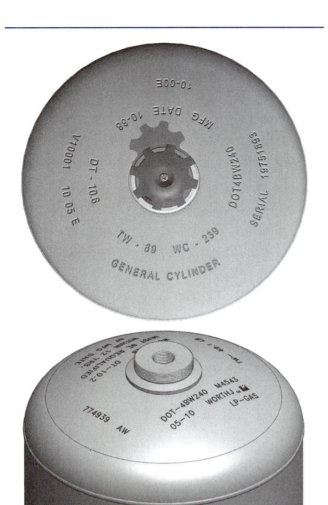

EXHIBIT 5.5 *Small ASME Container Commonly Used in Residential and Commercial Applications. (Courtesy of Trinity Containers)*

EXHIBIT 5.4 *Typical DOT Cylinder Marking. (Courtesy of Worthington Cylinder Corp.)*

defects in materials (thickness variation, imperfections, and inclusions in the metal) as well as less than perfect welding. Because both materials and welding have improved since the 1950s, it was determined that the design margin was excessive and was reduced. This reduction does not decrease safety in pressure vessels designed to the ASME Code. [See Annexes C and D for further descriptions of DOT (ICC) and ASME containers.]

The decrease in the design margin and improvements in steel production have resulted in thinner container walls. If the container is damaged by gouging or corrosion, the wall thickness is further decreased. At some point, the wall can become too thin to reliably contain the pressure of the liquefied gas inside, especially if the container is exposed to fire. Fire has the double impact on the container of raising the pressure inside and of weakening the metal. (See also the commentary following 5.2.1.4.) Because of this concern, sometimes inspectors will condemn a tank because of severe pitting or damage from impact. The owner may have the option to perform a minimum wall thickness calculation to determine whether, in fact, the wall thickness has been decreased to the point of being unsafe. Typically, these calculations would be submitted to the authority having jurisdiction as justification for continuing the container in service. Some states may require certification of these calculations by a registered professional engineer or ASME-certified technician.

Commentary Table 5.2 shows popular ASME container sizes, their applications, and their water and propane capacities. The table also lists the capacities, in pounds, of smaller size containers for easy comparison to cylinder capacities. It is important to note that the ranges given for LP-Gas capacity in the table are not all at the same reference temperature. For example, the LP-Gas capacity for a bulk plant tank of 12,000 gal (45.4 m³) is shown to be 10,800 gal (41 m³), which is 90 percent of the container water capacity. However, 7.4.3.2(B), and referenced Table 7.4.2.3(b), only permit volumetric filling to 90 percent when the propane is at a temperature of 70°F (21°C). Therefore, it is important to realize that the capacities shown in Commentary Table 5.2 are those at assumed propane temperatures.

Intermodal Containers. Intermodal containers, as shown in Exhibit 5.6, are shipping containers larger than cylinders that are mounted within a frame for shipment on railcars, trucks, and ships. The containers are similar to dry shipping containers. The United Nations accepts intermodal containers for international shipping. These containers must meet DOT specifications and ASME Code requirements. LP-Gas is shipped via intermodal containers to islands and inland areas that are accessible only by rivers or other bodies of water.

Container Ownership. Usually, the LP-Gas marketer leases residential and commercial LP-Gas containers to the customer. However, neither NFPA 58 nor other laws prevent consumers from purchasing their own containers. Industrial and other large users are more likely to own their containers. When residential consumers and industrial LP-Gas users own their containers, they are responsible for complying with the code requirements concerning container maintenance. The propane supplier is responsible for taking reasonable steps to verify that a container is fit for service before filling it and should not fill a container that is unfit for service. This applies equally to a 20 lb (9.1 kg) gas grill cylinder, a 500 gal (1.9 m³) ASME container at a residence, and a 30,000 gal (14 m³) ASME container at an industrial facility.

With the new requirement for the installation and periodic testing of cathodic protection systems on underground containers in the 2011 edition, ownership of underground containers may blur the implementation of the new inspection requirements. It is understood that many underground containers installed at homes are sold to the homeowner (for commercial rea-

COMMENTARY TABLE 5.2 *Typical Stationary ASME Container Applications*

Service	Water Capacity Gallons	Water Capacity Liters or Cubic Meters	LP-Gas Capacity Gallons*	LP-Gas Capacity Liters or Cubic Meters	Pounds
Domestic	100	379 L	80	301 L	338
Domestic	125	473 L	100	379 L	423
Domestic	150	568 L	120	454 L	508
Domestic	250	946 L	200	757 L	848
Domestic	325	1230 L	260	984 L	
Domestic	500	1893 L	400	1514 L	
Domestic	1,000	3.8 m³	800	3 m³	
Industrial/agricultural/commercial	1,000–5,000	3.8–19 m³	800–4,500	3–17 m³	
Service stations	1,000–6,500	3.8–24.6 m³	800–5,850	3–22 m³	
Bulk plant or standby storage	12,000–18,000	45.4–68 m³	10,800–16,200	41–61 m³	
Bulk plant or standby storage	20,000–30,000	76–114 m³	18,000–27,000	45.4–102 m³	
Bulk plant or standby storage	30,000–60,000	114–227 m³	27,000–54,000	102–204 m³	
Bulk plant or standby storage	60,000–120,000	227–454 m³	48,000–96,000	182–364 m³	

*Based on propane specific gravity of 0.508 at 70°F (21°C). Actual filling level depends on the specific gravity and temperature of the propane.

EXHIBIT 5.6 *Intermodal Container. (Courtesy of Permagas)*

sons). While NFPA 58 requires periodic inspection, it does not specify who should do (or pay for) the inspection. This is consistent with the philosophy of NFPA 58 to provide necessary safety requirements, but not to specify who is responsible to meet the requirements. A tank filler is prohibited from filling a container that is not suitable for continued service by 7.2.2.13, which states:

> **7.2.2.13** A container shall not be filled if the container assembly does not meet the requirements for continued service.

Clearly, the vast majority of homeowners are not capable of testing a cathodic protection system. While employees of propane marketers can easily be trained to do the inspection, they may charge for the service. Further, it is not clear how the required record keeping will be done. Record keeping may be especially important if the homeowner who owns the underground container changes propane suppliers.

5.2.1.2 Containers that have been involved in a fire and show no distortion shall be requalified for continued service before being used or reinstalled.

(A) Cylinders shall be requalified by a manufacturer of that type of cylinder or by a repair facility approved by DOT.

(B) ASME or API-ASME containers shall be retested using the hydrostatic test procedure applicable at the time of the original fabrication.

Older containers can continue to be used when evidence of design or construction flaws, or dents, pits, and corrosion, is not evident. When these containers were built, they incorporated the latest technology in design, metallurgy, and fabrication methods. Although technology has improved significantly over the years, there is no evidence that older containers are less safe now than when they were built, as long as they have been properly maintained.

Other nondestructive test methods may be considered as alternatives to the hydrostatic test required in 5.2.1.2(B). The following methods are listed in the ASME *Boiler and Pressure Vessel Code* [1] and may be useful for finding flaws in the container that would prevent it from being placed back into service after a fire:

- Radiography
- Ultrasonics
- Magnetic particle

- Liquid penetrants
- Visual inspection
- Leak testing
- Electromagnetic testing
- Acoustic emission

It is important to remember that the ASME Code is a construction code, and not a maintenance or an inspection code, and other codes (e.g., DOT, National Board Inspection Code, NFPA 58) may allow or require hydrostatic pressure testing as a nondestructive test when needed. While a hydrostatic pressure test is considered nondestructive, it can result in damage to the pressure vessel if a significant flaw is detected. The person performing such tests must be familiar both with the code requirements used to construct the container and with the test methods used to test the container.

(C) All container appurtenances shall be replaced.

(D) DOT 4E specification (aluminum) cylinders and composite cylinders involved in a fire shall be permanently removed from service.

If a cylinder has been subjected to fire, the shell, which is usually steel, aluminum, or fiberglass, can be weakened, and the cylinder must be requalified by a properly qualified repair facility authorized by DOT (in the United States) or TC (in Canada). When an ASME container has been subjected to fire, it must be retested using the hydrostatic test procedure applicable at the time the container was originally made. The testing is required because the fire heat can alter the properties of the steel, reducing its ability to contain pressure. Container appurtenances must also be replaced after a container has been exposed to fire.

DOT 4E aluminum cylinders may not be returned to service after a fire because exposure to even moderately high temperatures can affect the structural properties of aluminum and severely decrease its tensile strength. Composite cylinders exposed to fire can also be weakened, and the manufacturer should be consulted for guidance.

Exhibit 5.7 shows a container that has been exposed to fire.

EXHIBIT 5.7 *ASME Container Damaged by Fire. (Courtesy of Independent Propane Co., Pine, CO)*

5.2.1.3 ASME paragraph U-68 or U-69 containers shall be permitted to be continued in use, installed, reinstalled, or placed back into service. Installation of containers shall be in accordance with all provisions listed in this code. *(See Section 5.2, Table 5.2.4.2 and Table 5.7.2.5(A), and Annex D.)*

FAQ ▶
Can ASME containers con-
structed to U-68 and U-69 requirements be installed into a
new service?

The requirement in 5.2.1.3 clearly and specifically states ASME paragraph U-68 or U-69 containers may be continued in service and reinstalled. This addition to the 1995 edition of NFPA 58 was intended to clarify the NFPA technical committee's opposition to one state's interpretation of the code that would not permit ASME containers built under ASME U-68 and U-69 to be reinstalled. [See the commentary following 5.2.1.1(C) for more information on ASME U-68 and U-69.]

5.2.1.4 Containers that show excessive denting, bulging, gouging, or corrosion shall be removed from service.

All containers that show excessive dents, bulges, gouges, or corrosion must be removed from service because these defects can reduce the pressure capability of the container. Once removed from service, the container should be scrapped, or repaired using methods that are in accordance with the code of manufacture.

5.2.1.5 Except for containers used in cargo tank vehicle service, ASME containers of 3000 gal (11.4 m^3) water capacity or less used to store anhydrous ammonia shall not be converted to LP-Gas fuel service.

This new requirement first appeared as a Tentative Interim Amendment (TIA) to the 2008 edition of NFPA 58. It addresses problems that have occurred with portable pressure vessels, of 3000 gal (11.4 m^3) or less, mounted on wheels used at farms for both propane and ammonia at different times. These containers are sometimes called "nurse tanks." The committee was made aware that three fatal accidents occurred when propane tanks that had formerly been in ammonia service failed. Larger containers are also used for both ammonia and propane, but because there have been no incidents reported with larger containers, the restriction applies only to containers of 3000 gal (11.4 m^3) or less.
The following are safety hazards associated with converting tanks:

1. Potential overfilling of the container due to inappropriate dip tube length
2. Container failure from stress caused by corrosion cracking due to prior ammonia service
3. Improper sizing or material of relief valves (propane containers can use steel or brass valves, while ammonia tanks can only use steel valves because ammonia corrodes brass)
4. Accumulation of rust, which can form if the container is left open during a changeover and can lead to odor fade

5.2.1.6 Repairs or alteration of a container shall comply with the regulations, rules, or code under which the container was fabricated. Repairs or alteration to ASME containers shall be in accordance with the *National Board Inspection Code*.

5.2.1.7 Field welding shall be permitted only on saddle plates, lugs, pads, or brackets that are attached to the container by the container manufacturer.

The heat of welding directly to the container can affect the strength of the material and change its characteristics so that it may no longer meet the requirements of the ASME *Boiler and Pressure Vessel Code* [1]. Such heating can set up localized stresses that can reduce the material's strength. Repairs to pressure vessels must meet the requirements of the *National Board Inspection Code* (NBIC) [7], and must be performed by a repair organization accredited by the National Board and authorized to utilize the "R" code symbol stamp. Following a repair and final inspection by a National Board Commissioned Inspector, the repair organization will affix to the pressure vessel a "Repair" that is similar to the ASME nameplate. (The ASME nameplate is not removed or altered.) The requirements in the NBIC were developed to maintain the integrity of the pressure vessel after it has been placed in service. (See Exhibit 5.8.)

5.2.1.8 Containers for general use shall not have individual water capacities greater than 120,000 gal (454 m^3).

REPAIRED BY

CERTIFICATE HOLDER

NATIONAL BOARD R
CERTIFICATE NUMBER

DATE REPAIRED

EXHIBIT 5.8 *National Board "R" Stamp. (Reprinted with permission of the National Board of Boiler and Pressure Vessel Inspectors)*

Containers installed for general use and in dispensing stations are limited in size per 5.2.1.8. However, the number of containers in general use is not limited. The term *general use*, which is not defined in the code, refers to installations where LP-Gas is being stored for an end use application, such as for use as a fuel. Thus an LP-Gas bulk plant, where most employees can be expected to be aware of the proper procedures for handling LP-Gas, is not general use, whereas a container used as an alternate fuel supply at a manufacturing plant, whose product is not related to LP-Gas, would be considered to be general use.

5.2.1.9 Containers in dispensing stations not located in LP-Gas bulk plants, industrial plants, or industrial applications shall have an aggregate water capacity not greater than 30,000 gal (114 m³).

The 30,000 gal (114 m³) water capacity limit on total storage in dispensing stations provides a limit on storage capacity at locations where only cylinders are filled or LP-Gas is dispensed.

5.2.1.10 Heating or cooling coils shall not be installed inside storage containers.

Internal container components, such as heating and cooling coils, can be inspected only when the container is emptied, purged, and declared safe for entry. It is possible that a container's components may not be inspected during the container's normal life of service. If not inspected, corrosion or other container component failure will not be observed. If heating or cooling coils installed inside the storage container leak, the gas could enter the piping of the heating or cooling system, because the LP-Gas pressure is normally higher than the pressure in the internal coil. Leakage into the system could result in a pressure that could rupture or create leaks in the heating or cooling system. Even if a break does not occur, a flammable product will be present in the heating or cooling system that could escape near an ignition source.

5.2.1.11 ASME containers installed underground, partially underground, or as mounded installations shall incorporate provisions for cathodic protection and shall be coated with a material recommended for the service that is applied in accordance with the coating manufacturer's instructions.

This new requirement for underground containers recognizes a long-standing practice to provide corrosion protection — in addition to paint. The method used is called *cathodic protection*, and utilizes a metal that is more electrochemically reactive than steel so that it "sacrificially corrodes" instead of the steel tank. Such systems are used on metal ships, which rely on blocks of zinc bolted to the hull. The zinc corrodes, but the metal hull does not.

Typically, magnesium is used with underground containers of all types. For more information on cathodic protection, see Supplement 5, Cathodic Protection.

> Subsection 5.2.1.11 was revised by a tentative interim amendment (TIA).

5.2.2 Cylinders.

5.2.2.1* Cylinders shall be continued in service and transported in accordance with DOT regulations.

A.5.2.2.1 See CGA C-6, *Standard for Visual Inspection of Steel Compressed Gas Cylinders*, or CGA C-6.3, *Guidelines for Visual Inspection and Requalification of Low Pressure Aluminum Compressed Gas Cylinders*, for further information regarding cylinder inspection.

5.2.2.2 A cylinder with an expired requalification date shall not be refilled until it is requalified by the methods prescribed in DOT regulations.

An important safety provision of NFPA 58 is that all LP-Gas containers be safe before they are filled. Cylinders that are built to DOT requirements can be filled for 12 years from the date of manufacture and subsequently must be recertified periodically. Until the 2004 edition, the question of recertification of cylinders that were used outside of the scope of DOT (not in transportation) was not completely clear. This issue has been resolved by 5.2.2.2 and 5.2.3, which address cylinders that are filled on site and not subject to DOT regulation.

There are three different methods by which to requalify a cylinder:

Requalification Method	Time Before Next Recertification
Water-jacket hydrostatic test method	12 years
Modified hydrostatic	7 years
Visual	5 years

Refer to Annex C for a detailed description of these methods.

Requalification of cylinders under DOT regulations using the visual method could have been done by anyone up until August 8, 2002, when DOT issued Final Rule HM-220D, which requires registration of requalifiers using the visual method. The rule requires facilities or individuals that requalify cylinders to register with DOT in order to obtain a requalification identification number (RIN) Registration of a business facility covers individual employees at the facility. The following also applies to cylinder requalification using the visual method:

- Beginning May 31, 2004, only facilities that held a RIN, issued by the U.S. Department of Transportation, were permitted to requalify cylinders by external visual inspection.
- Inspections must have been be performed in accordance with CGA C-6, *Standard for Visual Inspection of Steel Compressed Gas Cylinders* [8], and/or C-6.3, *Guidelines for Visual Inspection and Requalification of Low Pressure Aluminum Compressed Gas Cylinders* [9].
- Cylinders passing requalification by external visual inspection must be marked as described below.
- Cylinder markings must be made by stamping, engraving, scribing, or any other method that produces a legible, durable mark. Interpretations obtained from DOT allow the mark to be on a "durable pressure adhesive label."
- Each facility that requalifies cylinders must maintain records at the facility where the requalification is performed.

The requirement for a RIN applies only to those who requalify cylinders for use "in transportation" and does not apply to those who visually inspect stationary cylinders per the procedures in 5.2.3.

The following is reprinted from 49 CFR Part 180.213 [10]:

49 CFR Part 180 — CONTINUING QUALIFICATION AND MAINTENANCE OF PACKAGINGS

Subpart C — Qualification, Maintenance and Use of Cylinders

180.213 Requalification markings.

(a) *General*. Each cylinder or UN pressure receptacle requalified in accordance with this subpart with acceptable results must be marked as specified in this section. Required specification markings may not be altered or removed.

(b) *Placement of markings*. Each cylinder must be plainly and permanently marked on the metal of the cylinder as permitted by the applicable specification. Unless authorized by the cylinder specification, marking on the cylinder sidewall is prohibited.

(1) Requalification and required specification markings must be legible so as to be readily visible at all times. Illegible specification markings may be remarked on the cylinder as provided by the original specification. Requalification markings may be placed on any portion of the upper end of the cylinder excluding the sidewall, as provided in this section. Requalification and required specification markings that are illegible may be reproduced on a metal plate and attached as provided by the original specification.

(2) Previous requalification markings may not be obliterated, except that, when the space originally provided for requalification dates becomes filled, additional dates may be added as follows:

(i) All preceding requalification dates may be removed by peening provided that —

(A) Permission is obtained from the cylinder owner;

(B) The minimum wall thickness is maintained in accordance with manufacturing specifications for the cylinder; and

(C) The original manufacturing test date is not removed.

(ii) When the cylinder is fitted with a footring, additional dates may be marked on the external surface of the footring.

(c) *Requalification marking method*. The depth of requalification markings may not be greater than specified in the applicable specification. The markings must be made by stamping, engraving, scribing or other method that produces a legible, durable mark.

> [NOTE: Although DOT has not published a rulemaking to this effect, it has stated in letters to the propane industry that a "durable pressure adhesive label is acceptable" to be used to mark the cylinder]

(1) and (2) [not applicable to propane cylinders]

(3) For a composite cylinder, the requalification markings must be applied on a pressure sensitive label, securely affixed in a manner prescribed by the cylinder manufacturer, near the original manufacturer's label. Stamping of the composite surface is not authorized.

(d) *Requalification markings*. Each cylinder successfully passing requalification must be marked with the RIN set in a square pattern, between the month and year of the requalification date. The first character of the RIN must appear in the upper left corner of the square pattern; the second in the upper right; the third in the lower right, and the fourth in the lower left.

Example: A cylinder requalified in September 2006, and approved by a person who has been issued RIN "A123", would be marked plainly and permanently into the metal of the cylinder in accordance with location requirements of the cylinder specification or on a metal plate permanently secured to the cylinder in accordance with paragraph (b) of this section. An example of the markings prescribed in this paragraph (d) is as follows:

A1
9   06 X
32

◄ **FAQ**
How must the requalification identification number (RIN) be applied to a cylinder?

Where:

"9" is the month of requalification,

"A123" is the RIN,

"06" is the year of requalification, and

"X" represents the symbols described in paragraphs (f)(2) through (f)(9) of this section.

(1) Upon a written request, variation from the marking requirement may be approved by the Associate Administrator.

(2) *Exception.* A cylinder subject to the requirements of §173.301(l) of this subchapter may not be marked with a RIN.

(e) *Size of markings.* The size of the markings must be at least 6.35 mm (¼ in.) high, except RIN characters must be at least 3.18 mm (⅛ in.) high.

(f) Marking illustrations. Examples of required requalification markings for DOT specification and special permit cylinders are illustrated as follows:

(1) For designation of the 5-year volumetric expansion test, 10-year volumetric expansion test for UN cylinders and cylinders conforming to §180.209(f) and (h), or 12-year volumetric expansion test for fire extinguishers conforming to §173.309(b) of this subchapter and cylinders conforming to §180.209(e) and 180.209(g), the marking is as illustrated in paragraph (d) of this section.

(2) and (3) [not applicable to propane cylinders]

(4) For designation of the proof pressure test, the marking is as illustrated in paragraph (d) of this section, except that the "X" is replaced with the letter "S".

(5) For designation of the 5-year external visual inspection for cylinders conforming to Sec. 180.209(g), the marking is as illustrated in paragraph (d) of this section, except that the "X" is replaced with the letter "E".

(5) through (9) [not applicable to visual requalification of propane cylinders]

DOT initially underestimated the number of companies that would be registering as cylinder requalifiers and ran out of four-digit numbers to assign. A seven-digit numbering system was started. Facilities using the seven-digit number must display it, along with the date of inspection, using one of the following formats:

V100001	0907	V100001 0907
0907	V100001	

5.2.3 Cylinders Filled on Site at the Point of Use.

FAQ ▶
Are all cylinders, whether or not they are under DOT jurisdiction, required to be requalified in accordance with DOT procedures?

Subsection 5.2.3 addresses the need to inspect stationary cylinders and provides a method to recertify cylinders filled where they are used. Cylinders not "in transportation" are not subject to DOT regulations for recertification; however, they are required to be recertified by NFPA 58. Cylinders "in transportation" include cylinders transported by common carriers (trucking companies); by someone in the LP-Gas business; or by those who use them as a material of trade, such as a caterer or a roofer using propane fuel.

The subsection was further revised in the 2011 edition by changing the title from "Cylinders Filled on Site" to "Cylinders Filled on Site at the Point of Use." This change was also made throughout the code in response to some misinterpretation of the meaning of "on site." The term originated in the propane industry, where "on site" meant a site other than the filling site. The intent has always been to indicate the point where the cylinder was used, and not central filling locations, but some users did not understand the distinction. The revision makes it clear that this subsection does not apply to dispensing stations and central filling locations. The need for this requirement, which differs from DOT regulations, stems from the difficulty involved in recertifying cylinders filled on site without disconnecting piping, emptying the cylinder, and inspecting and weighing the cylinder, as required by DOT regulations. Weighing is deleted here, because the committee was advised that CGA C-6, *Standard for Visual Inspection of Steel Compressed Gas Cylinders* [8] (which is referenced by DOT), was being revised to drop the re-weighing requirement, and the committee saw potential safety disadvantages to the additional gas transfers that emptying the cylinder would require.

5.2.3.1 DOT cylinders in stationary service that are filled on site at the point of use and, therefore, are not under the jurisdiction of DOT shall comply with one of the following criteria:

(1) They shall be requalified in accordance with DOT requirements.
(2) They shall be visually inspected within 12 years of the date of manufacture and within every 5 years thereafter, in accordance with 5.2.3.2 through 5.2.3.4.

5.2.3.2 Any cylinder that fails one or more of the criteria in 5.2.3.4 shall not be refilled or continued in service until the condition is corrected.

5.2.3.3 Personnel shall be trained and qualified to perform inspections. Training shall be documented in accordance with Section 4.4.

Per 5.2.3.3, training received by persons visually inspecting stationary cylinders filled on site must be documented. As with any documentation required by the code, training documentation should be placed in the employee's file so that it can be located if needed. Copies of documentation can also be kept by employees.

5.2.3.4 Visual inspection shall be performed in accordance with the following:

(1) The cylinder is checked for exposure to fire, dents, cuts, digs, gouges, and corrosion according to CGA C-6, *Standard for Visual Inspection of Steel Compressed Gas Cylinders*, except that 4.2.1.1(1) of that standard (which requires tare weight verification) shall not be part of the required inspection criteria.
(2) The cylinder protective collar (where utilized) and the foot ring are intact and are firmly attached.
(3) The cylinder is painted or coated to minimize corrosion.
(4) The cylinder pressure relief valve indicates no visible damage, corrosion of operating components, or obstructions.
(5) There is no leakage from the cylinder or its appurtenances that is detectable without the use of instruments.
(6) The cylinder is installed on a firm foundation and is not in contact with the soil.
(7) A cylinder that passes the visual examination is marked with the month and year of the examination followed by the letter E (e.g., "10-01E", indicating requalification in October 2001 by the external inspection method).
(8) The results of the visual inspection are documented, and a record of the inspection is retained for a 5-year period.

The procedures for visual inspection listed in 5.2.3.4 are simple and will identify cylinder defects and conditions that require correction. Several are taken from CGA C-6 [8], the standard for visually inspecting steel cylinders.

Note the phrase "minimize corrosion" in 5.2.3.4(3). The technical committee intends that the painting or coating prevent excessive corrosion from occurring.

The intent of 5.2.3.4(5) is that instruments are not required to be used to determine if the cylinder is leaking. Leak detection can be done by using the sound or smell of a leak detected by a person's senses. Use of liquid leak detection instruments is allowed. More sensitive instruments can lead to a false positive if used immediately after the cylinder is filled or is attached to the piping.

Paragraph 5.2.3.4(6) addresses an important installation requirement, namely, that the cylinder be installed on a firm foundation, not in contact with the soil. "Firm" is not defined but in the context of the usage, it is intended to require the foundation to remain substantially intact and level while it supports the cylinder. One state (North Carolina) defines "firm" to mean that the foundation material has a level top surface; rests on solid ground; and is constructed of a masonry material or wood treated to prevent decay by moisture rot and will not settle, careen, or deteriorate. Another state (Maine) allows only masonry foundations for cylinders. Other states may have different interpretations.

The marking requirements of 5.2.3.4(7) are similar to those used for cylinders that are requalified. An important difference is that a requalification identification number (RIN) is not an appropriate marking to apply, because the inspection is different from that performed for requalification of the cylinder. In fact, if the cylinder is inspected using the method outlined in this section, then it does not meet the DOT requirements and the RIN should not be applied. It is also important to note that the person who performs this inspection is not required to have a RIN. Applying the RIN would imply that the cylinder had received a requalification according to the requirements outlined in 5.2.2.2.

Paragraph 5.2.3.4(8) provides a definite 5-year term for retaining the records of all inspected cylinders.

5.2.4 Container Service Pressure.

5.2.4.1 The service pressure of cylinders shall be in accordance with the appropriate regulations published under 49 CFR, "Transportation."

See Annex C, Design, Construction, and Requalification of DOT (ICC) Cylinders, for information on the DOT requirements for cylinder design and fabrication.

5.2.4.2 The maximum allowable working pressure (MAWP) for ASME containers shall be in accordance with Table 5.2.4.2.

FAQ ▶
Can a container having a maximum allowable working pressure of 200 psig (1.4 MPag) be used in propane service?

Table 5.2.4.2 provides minimum MAWP for ASME containers in LP-Gas service. Most containers require a MAWP of 250 psig (1.7 MPag). The higher pressure of 312 psig (2.2 MPag) [125 percent of 250 psig (1.7 MPag)] is now required for all engine fuel container installations, including automobiles, industrial trucks, buses, recreational vehicles, school buses, and multipurpose passenger vehicles.

TABLE 5.2.4.2 *Maximum Vapor Pressure and Maximum Allowable Working Pressure (MAWP)*

Maximum Vapor Pressure		MAWP					
		Current ASME Code[a]		Earlier Codes			
				API-ASME		ASME[b]	
At 100°F (psig)	At 37.8°C (MPag)	psig	MPag	psig	MPag	psig	MPag
80	0.6	100	0.7	100	0.7	80	0.6
100	0.7	125	0.9	125	0.9	100	0.7
125	0.9	156	1.1	156	1.1	125	0.9
150	1.0	187	1.3	187	1.3	150	1.0
175	1.2	219	1.5	219	1.5	175	1.2
215	1.5	250	1.7[c]	250	1.7[c]	200	1.4
215	1.5	312	2.2[c]	312	2.2[c]	—	—

Note: See Annex D for information on earlier ASME or API-ASME codes.

[a]ASME Code, 1949 edition, paragraphs U-200 and U-201, and all later editions. *(See D.2.1.5.)*

[b]All ASME codes up to the 1946 edition and paragraphs U-68 and U-69 of the 1949 edition. *(See D.2.1.5.)*

[c]See 6.23.3.1(A), 6.23.3.1(C), and 6.23.3.1(D) for required MAWP for ASME engine fuel and mobile containers.

Note that containers constructed to the ASME *Boiler and Pressure Vessel Code* [1] up to the 1946 edition, and paragraphs U-68 and U-69 in the 1949 edition, are permitted to be used even though the MAWP is 200 psi. The reason for this allowance is due to the design margin (safety factor) of 5 that was used to design those containers. The recognized benefits of modern technologies and material science have resulted in a reduced design margin for the current ASME *Boiler and Pressure Vessel Code.*

5.2.4.3 In addition to the applicable provisions for horizontal ASME containers, vertical ASME containers over 125 gal (0.5 m³) water capacity shall comply with 5.2.4.3(A) through 5.2.4.3(E).

(A) Containers shall be designed to be self-supporting without the use of guy wires and shall be designed to withstand the wind, seismic (earthquake) forces, and hydrostatic test loads anticipated at the site.

(B) The MAWP *(see Table 5.2.4.2)* shall be the pressure at the top head, with allowance made for increased pressure on lower shell sections and bottom head due to the static pressure of the product.

(C) Wind loading on containers shall be based on wind pressures on the projected area at various height zones above ground in accordance with ASCE 7, *Minimum Design Loads for Buildings and Other Structures.* Wind speeds shall be based on a mean occurrence interval of 100 years.

(D) Seismic loading on containers shall be in accordance with ASCE 7, *Minimum Design Loads for Buildings and Other Structures.* A seismic analysis of the proposed installation shall be made that meets the approval of the authority having jurisdiction.

(E) Shop-fabricated containers shall be fabricated with lifting lugs or other means to lift the container.

Where a container is installed in a vertical rather than a horizontal position, the loading dynamics of the container differ. The methods of support for the vertical container must be designed to account for the increased possibility of toppling the taller container in high wind and seismic conditions. These methods of support are addressed further in 5.2.7.1.

The intent of 5.2.4.3(B) is to require that a container be designed with a maximum allowable working pressure sufficient to encompass all of the pressures present at the bottom of the container.

Paragraph 5.2.4.3(E) requires lifting lugs, but does not require the lugs to carry a specific weight. It should be assumed that the lifting lugs are not adequate to carry the entire weight of the container when filled with LP-Gas or water, so additional support, such as a strapping system, must be used to lift ASME tanks that contain product.

5.2.4.4* ASME engine fuel and mobile containers shall have a MAWP of 312 psig (2.2 MPag) or higher.

A.5.2.4.4 ASME mobile fuel containers constructed prior to April 1, 2001, were required to have a maximum allowable working pressure (MAWP) of 250 psig (1.7 MPag).

The higher pressure of 312 psig (2.2 MPag) is consistent with NFPA 1192, *Standard on Recreational Vehicles* [11]. The following two safety benefits result from the higher design pressure:

1. The higher design pressure provides a stronger container, which could be important in a vehicle accident.
2. The higher design pressure reduces the remote possibility of the pressure relief valve opening in the event of high internal vehicle temperature.

5.2.4.5 Cylinders shall be designed and constructed for at least a 240 psig (1.6 MPag) service pressure.

5.2.5 ASME Container Openings.

5.2.5.1 ASME containers shall be equipped with openings for the service for which the container is to be used.

NFPA 58 does not limit the number of container openings because a properly installed plug, cap, or blind flange will provide an effective seal to maintain the integrity of the container.

5.2.5.2 The openings required by 5.2.5.1 shall be located either in the shell, in the heads, or in a manhole cover.

5.2.5.3* ASME containers of more than 30 gal through 2000 gal (0.1 m^3 through 7.6 m^3) water capacity that are designed to be filled volumetrically shall be equipped for filling into the vapor space.

A.5.2.5.3 Prior to December 1, 1963, ASME containers of greater than 30 gal (0.1 m^3) water capacity, up to and including 2000 gal (7.6 m^3) water capacity, were not required to be equipped for filling into the vapor space of the container.

FAQ ▶
Why is it desirable to fill into the vapor space of the container rather than the liquid space?

Filling only into the vapor space, but not into the liquid space, more rapidly achieves equilibrium between the vapor and the liquid in the container. Lower container pressure results when filling into the vapor space, compared to filling into the liquid space. Filling only into the vapor space allows containers to be filled more rapidly, because the pump does not have to overcome a greater pressure in the container.

5.2.5.4* ASME containers of 125 gal through 2000 gal (0.5 m^3 through 7.6 m^3) water capacity shall be provided with an opening for an actuated liquid withdrawal excess-flow valve with a connection not smaller than ¾ in. (19 mm) national pipe thread (NPT).

A.5.2.5.4 Containers fabricated on or before July 1, 1961, are exempt from this requirement.

An actuated liquid withdrawal excess-flow valve is defined in Chapter 3 as follows:

> **3.3.1 Actuated Liquid Withdrawal Excess-Flow Valve.** A container valve that is opened and closed by an adapter, incorporates an internal excess flow valve, and is used to withdraw liquid from the container.

This valve (see Exhibit 5.9), which is required by 5.2.5.4, is needed to remove liquid from ASME containers before they are transported to another location. The DOT regulations require that such tanks only be transported when the liquid volume is 5 percent or less of the water capacity of the tank. However, Special Permit No. 13341 was issued by DOT in 2006 that allows the transportation of ASME containers with more than 5 percent liquid volume in the container, subject to several limitations. The special permit may be obtained at the following website: http://hazmat.dot.gov/sp_app/special_permits/spec_perm_index.htm

The actuated liquid withdrawal excess-flow valve is more commonly known by the trade names Chek-Lok®, Checkmate®, and SafEvac®, as well as by "liquid withdrawal valve with excess flow." An actuated liquid withdrawal valve is operated by removing the valve cap and threading a pipe nipple or adapter, available from the manufacturer, with a manual valve attached to the liquid withdrawal valve. As the nipple or adapter turns, the valve opens, and liquid flows through the liquid withdrawal valve until the the just-attached adapter and valve are filled. The manual valve on the adapter is then opened to verify that the excess flow feature works. When flow exceeds the excess flow rating, the excess-flow valve closes. The manual valve is then closed. A small flow through a bypass allows a small amount of product to bypass the excess-flow valve, and pressure increases on the outlet side of the adapter. When pressure on both sides of the excess flow disc is about equal, the excess-flow valve opens with

EXHIBIT 5.9 Actuated Liquid Withdrawal Excess-Flow Valve; Old Style (Left) and Current Style (Center and Right). (Courtesy of Engineered Controls International, Inc.)

an audible click. The hose to the container to be filled is attached and the manual valve is opened to remove the liquid.

Section A of Exhibit 5.10 shows an excess-flow valve in the open position, with a manually operated shutoff valve connected also in the open position. The flow through the excess-flow valve is less than the rate that will close the valve. Section B shows an excess-flow valve in the closed position, because the flow has exceeded the rate that will close the excess-flow valve. Note that a small amount of propane, shown as a blue line, continues to flow through the closed excess-flow valve through a designed bypass, such as a small hole drilled in the valve. The manually operated valve remains in the open position. Section C shows the shutoff valve closed, which has allowed the bypass flow to begin to pressurize the space between the shutoff valve and the excess-flow valve. The spring tension retains the excess-flow valve in the closed position. Section D shows the shutoff valve closed, which has allowed the bypass flow to fully pressurize the space between the shutoff valve and the excess-flow valve. With equal pressure (force) on both sides of the excess-flow valve, the spring tension opens the excess-flow valve. The shutoff valve can now be opened (slowly) to restart the flow.

In 5.7.4.1(B) and 5.7.4.1(D), the code recognizes that the valves are usually intended for only occasional use and that the valve manufacturer may or may not recommend them for continuous use.

◀ FAQ
Can an actuated liquid withdrawal excess-flow valve be used on a permanent basis to convert a container to liquid withdrawal service?

5.7.4.1(B) Containers of 125 gal through 4000 gal (0.5 m³ through 15.2 m³) water capacity shall be provided with an actuated liquid withdrawal excess-flow valve with a connection not smaller than ¾-in. NPT (19 mm)

5.7.4.1(D) The actuated liquid withdrawal excess-flow valve shall not be connected for continuous use unless the valve is recommended by the manufacturer for such service.

To the editor's knowledge, the major valve manufacturers recommend that the old-style actuated liquid withdrawal excess-flow valves shown in Exhibit 5.9 (left) should not be used for continuous liquid withdrawal operations. The new-style valves, shown in Exhibit 5.9 (center and right), are more robust, and according to the editor's information, the manufacturers do recommend these new, listed valves for continuous service. To be sure, check with the valve manufacturer.

There is a difference between 5.2.5.4 and 5.7.4.1(B). The latter paragraph recognizes that residential customers' tanks sometimes exceed 2000 gal (7.6 m³), and therefore the assumed upper limit for vapor service residential customers was increased to 4000 gal (15 m³). Tanks larger than 4000 gal (15 m³) were treated as a bulk plant or dispenser tank, for the purposes of establishing the requirements for appurtenances in 5.7.4.1. This difference is minor, as there are relatively few containers in the size range greater than 2000 gal (7.6 m³) up to 4000 gal (15 m³).

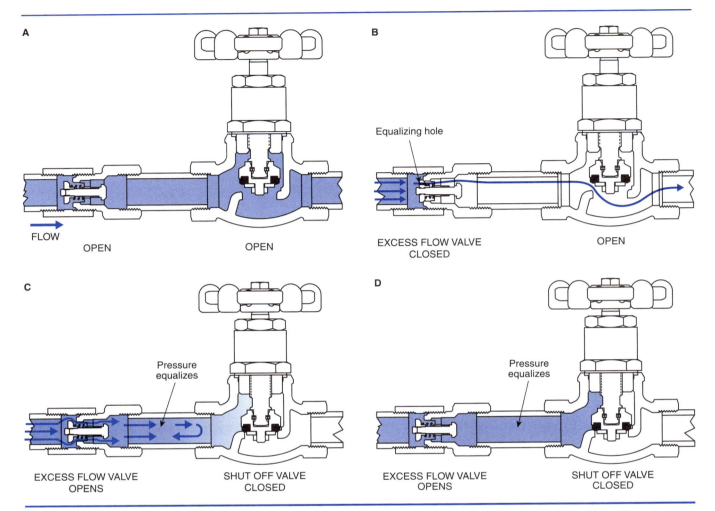

A

FLOW
OPEN   OPEN

B

Equalizing hole

EXCESS FLOW VALVE
CLOSED   OPEN

C

Pressure
equalizes

EXCESS FLOW VALVE
OPENS   SHUT OFF VALVE
CLOSED

D

Pressure
equalizes

EXCESS FLOW VALVE
OPENS   SHUT OFF VALVE
CLOSED

EXHIBIT 5.10 *Operation of an Actuated Liquid Withdrawal Excess-Flow Valve. (Courtesy of Emerson Process Management Regulator Technologies, Inc.)*

5.2.5.5* ASME containers of more than 2000 gal (7.6 m³) water capacity shall have an opening for a pressure gauge.

A.5.2.5.5 See 5.7.8.7 for the pressure gauge requirement.

Knowledge of the pressure in larger containers is useful, especially during liquid transfer operations. When installing a pressure gauge, reference should be made to 5.7.6.2, which reminds the user of an important safety feature requiring either a maximum opening of a No. 54 drill size between the container and the pressure gauge or installation of an excess-flow check valve. This safety feature prevents discharge of significant amounts of LP-Gas in case the pressure gauge is broken off.

5.2.5.6 ASME containers in storage or use shall have pressure relief valve connections that have direct communication with the vapor space of the container.

(A) If the pressure relief valve is located in a well inside the ASME container with piping to the vapor space, the design of the well and piping shall have a flow capacity equal to or greater than that of the pressure relief valve.

(B) An enclosure that protects a pressure relief valve shall be painted, coated, or made from corrosion-resistant materials.

(C) The design of an enclosure that protects a pressure relief valve shall permit inspection of the pressure relief valve.

(D) If the pressure relief valve is located in any position other than the uppermost point of the ASME container, the connection shall be internally piped to the uppermost point practical in the vapor space of the container.

By discharging vapor through the relief valve, the total quantity of LP-Gas escaping to the atmosphere is reduced, compared to discharging liquid, and the pressure within the container is reduced more quickly. Because of the high liquid-to-vapor expansion ratio of LP-Gas (270 to 1 for propane), a liquid discharge through the relief valve represents a much greater quantity of gas discharging into the atmosphere. If vapor is discharged, the pressure is reduced inside the container and the remaining liquid boils, cooling the liquid and thus reducing the pressure in the container. If liquid is discharged, the following results:

◀ **FAQ**
Why is it important that the relief valve be in communication with the vapor space of a container?

- Vaporization occurs outside the container.
- There is no cooling effect from vaporization inside the container.
- Container pressure is higher.

These factors are significant if the valve is discharging as a result of fire exposure.

The relief valve must either be located at the uppermost point of the container or be internally piped to the uppermost point practical in the vapor space of the container. This provision recognizes that some containers used for engine fuel and recreational vehicle applications have been manufactured with the relief valve located just above the 80 percent liquid level. The provision that the relief valve be piped to the uppermost point practical in the container recognizes that, in some containers — for example, portable lift truck cylinders that are stored vertically and used horizontally — the relief valve inlet cannot be located at the uppermost point for use in both positions.

Note that the text of 5.2.5.6 was revised in the 2011 edition to clarify that where pressure relief valves are installed in an enclosure, the enclosure must be protected from corrosion.

5.2.5.7* ASME containers to be filled on a volumetric basis shall be fabricated so that they can be equipped with a fixed maximum liquid level gauge(s) that is capable of indicating the maximum permitted filling level(s) in accordance with 7.4.2.3.

A.5.2.5.7 Containers fabricated on or before December 31, 1965, are exempt from this requirement.

Variable liquid level gauges indicate liquid level over most of the container's capacity range but are not completely reliable. The float may develop a leak, the float arm may sag over time, the mechanism may bind, the magnetic coupling between the float mechanism and the indicator may not work, or the gauge may otherwise indicate an inaccurate reading. Therefore, a fixed maximum liquid level gauge is required by 5.2.5.7 to allow the variable liquid level gauge to be calibrated and to prevent overfilling of the container.

5.2.6 Portable Container Appurtenance Physical Damage Protection.

5.2.6.1 Cylinders of 1000 lb (454 kg) water capacity [nominal 420 lb (191 kg) propane capacity] or less shall incorporate protection against physical damage to cylinder appurtenances and immediate connections to such appurtenances when not in use by either of the following means:

(1) A ventilated cap
(2) A ventilated collar

The cap or collar described in 5.2.6.1 and shown in Exhibit 5.11 is required to provide physical protection for the valves and any other appurtenances connected to the cylinder.

EXHIBIT 5.11 Cylinder Collars. (Courtesy of Manchester Tank)

Collar

Cylinders are portable and normally are transported from their normal use point to a filling point; there are inevitable occurrences where the cylinder is involved in a transportation incident, falls over, or is dropped. If a removable cap is used, it must be in place prior to moving the cylinder. The cap also provides a lifting point for the cylinder. The valve must never be used for lifting a cylinder. Ventilation openings are required to permit discharge from the pressure relief valve to dissipate.

5.2.6.2 Protection of appurtenances of portable containers, skid tanks, and tanks for use as cargo tanks of more than 1000 lb (454 kg) water capacity [nominal 420 lb (191 kg) propane capacity] shall comply with 5.2.6.2(A) through 5.2.6.2(C).

(A) Appurtenance protection from physical damage shall be provided by recessing, by protective housings, or by location on the vehicle.

(B) Appurtenance protection shall comply with the provisions under which the containers are fabricated.

(C) Appurtenance protection shall be secured to the container in accordance with the ASME code under which the container was designed and built.

Paragraph 5.2.6.2(C) refers to the code under which the container was built, instead of specifying the safety factors to be used. As the appurtenance protection is usually installed by the container manufacturer or assembler of a portable tank unit, it is reasonable to assume that the fabricator has access to the container construction code. Also, this provision allows protection built to older editions of the construction code to continue in service.

5.2.7 Containers with Attached Supports.

5.2.7.1 Vertical ASME containers of over 125 gal (0.5 m³) water capacity for use in permanent installations in stationary service shall be designed with steel supports that allow the container to be mounted on and fastened to concrete foundations or supports.

(A) Steel supports shall be designed to make the container self-supporting without guy wires and to withstand the wind and seismic (earthquake) forces anticipated at the site.

(B) Steel supports shall be protected against fire exposure with a material having a fire resistance rating of at least 2 hours.

(C) Continuous steel skirts having only one opening of 18 in. (460 mm) or less in diameter shall have 2-hour fire protection applied to the outside of the skirt.

Vertical containers, as shown in Exhibit 5.12, are used where space is not available for horizontal containers. Because the failure of a vertical tank's structural supports can result in severe damage to the container when it falls, there are special fire protection requirements for the supports. The two-hour fire resistance rating is obtained by using a protective material that has been tested to the requirements of ASTM E-119, *Standard Test Methods for Fire Tests of Building Construction and Materials* [12], a standard used to determine the fire resistance rating of structural elements. Vertical tanks are most often located at propane vehicle refueling stations where space is usually at a premium. Larger vertical tanks have also been installed where land cost is very high, such as near New York City.

EXHIBIT 5.12 *Vertical Container.*

Paragraph 5.2.7.1(C) addresses vertical tanks equipped with continuous steel skirts, which are not normally found at propane dispensing locations, but are more common in refineries. Their use is permitted where the skirt is protected with fire resistance–rated insulation on its exterior.

5.2.7.2 ASME containers to be used as portable storage containers, including movable fuel storage tenders and farm carts for temporary stationary service (normally not more than 12 months duration at any location), shall comply with 5.2.7.2(A) through 5.2.7.2(D).

Notification of temporary installations is required by 4.3.2, and notification is required for all installations of 12 months or less. (See the commentary following 4.3.2 for additional information.)

(A) The legs or supports, or the lugs for the attachment of legs or supports, shall be secured to the container in accordance with the ASME code under which the container was designed and built.

(B) The attachment of a container to either a trailer or semitrailer running gear, or the attachments to the container to make it a vehicle, so that the unit can be moved by a conventional over-the-road tractor, shall comply with the DOT requirements for cargo tank service.

(C) The unit specified in 5.2.7.2(B) shall be approved for stationary use.

(D) Movable fuel storage tenders, including farm carts, shall be secured to the trailer support structure for the service involved.

Paragraph 5.2.7.2 references the edition of the ASME *Boiler and Pressure Vessel Code* [1] to which a portable storage container was built. Note that these containers are subject to the time limitations of temporary service. As they are portable, they can be moved easily.
   See Exhibit 9.12 in Chapter 9 for a photo of a farm cart.

5.2.7.3 Portable tank design and construction of a full framework, skids, or lugs for the attachment of skids, and protection of fittings shall be in accordance with DOT portable tank specifications. The bottom of the skids shall be not less than 2 in. (50 mm) or more than 12 in. (300 mm) below the outside bottom of the tank shell.

Paragraph 5.2.7.3 uses the words "full framework" to make the requirement consistent with Title 49 of the Code of Federal Regulations.

5.2.8 Container Marking.

5.2.8.1 Cylinders shall be marked as provided in the regulations, rules, or code under which they are fabricated.

(A) Where LP-Gas and one or more other compressed gases are to be stored or used in the same area, the cylinders shall be marked "Flammable" and either "LP-Gas," "Propane," or "Butane," or shall be marked in accordance with the requirements of 49 CFR, "Transportation."

(B) When being transported, cylinders shall be marked and labeled in accordance with 49 CFR, "Transportation."

By referencing the code of fabrication for marking requirements, NFPA 58 defers to the requirements of other codes. ASME containers require a nameplate with all required markings, while DOT cylinders require stamping in the head and other markings.
   The requirements of DOT regulations can be difficult to understand. Markings and labeling of cylinders have specific meanings within the context of the DOT, as the following two paragraphs explain.

Labels. Hazardous materials labels are normally printed on or affixed to cylinders containing hazardous materials. They are color- and symbol-coded to afford easy and immediate recognition of the existing hazards. Cylinders containing propane require the label to appear as a diamond with a red background and to be at least 3.9 in.^{2} (2516 mm^2), unless the neck ring listed in CGA-Pamphlet 7 shown in Exhibit 5.13 is used. The "2" represents the hazard class, which is "compressed gas." Sometimes the number "2.1" will appear instead of "2." The "2.1" represents the hazard class division and denotes "flammable gas."

EXHIBIT 5.13 Neck Ring and DOT Flammable Gas Label (Red). (Courtesy of LabelMaster)

Markings. Markings are printed on or affixed to packages of hazardous materials such as propane cylinders to convey additional information about the hazardous material being transported. Cylinders that contain hazardous materials must be marked with the proper name of the material (either "Liquefied Petroleum Gas" or "Propane" and the shipping identification number, usually "1075" but may also be "1978").

5.2.8.2* Cylinders shall be marked with the following information:

(1) Water capacity of the cylinder in pounds
(2) Tare weight of the cylinder in pounds, fitted for service

A.5.2.8.2 The tare weight is the cylinder weight plus the weight of all permanently attached valves and other fittings but does not include the weight of protecting devices that are removed in order to load the cylinder.

Exhibit 5.14 illustrates a typical DOT cylinder marking. Note that the cylinder manufacturer's name, serial number, DT specification number, tare weight, and water capacity are shown. The date of manufacture and the retest date are of special importance. NFPA 58 prohibits the refilling of a cylinder if the requalification or inspection date of the cylinder has passed, but does not prohibit the use of cylinders that were filled prior to the requalification date.

EXHIBIT 5.14 DOT Cylinder Marking. (Tank courtesy of Worthington Cylinder Corp.)

5.2.8.3* The markings specified for ASME containers shall be on a stainless steel metal nameplate attached to the container, located to remain visible after the container is installed.

(A) The nameplate shall be attached in such a way as to minimize corrosion of the nameplate or its fastening means and not contribute to corrosion of the container.

(B) Where the container is buried, mounded, insulated, or otherwise covered so the nameplate is obscured, the information contained on the nameplate shall be duplicated and installed on adjacent piping or on a structure in a clearly visible location.

(C) Stationary ASME containers shall be marked with the following information:

(1) Service for which the container is designed (e.g., underground, aboveground, or both)
(2) Name and address of container supplier or trade name of container
(3) Water capacity of container in pounds or U.S. gallons
(4) MAWP in pounds per square inch
(5) Wording that reads "This container shall not contain a product that has a vapor pressure in excess of ___ psig at 100°F" *(see Table 5.2.4.2)*
(6) Outside surface area in square feet
(7) Year of manufacture
(8) Shell thickness and head thickness
(9) OL (overall length), OD (outside diameter), and HD (head design)
(10) Manufacturer's serial number
(11) ASME Code symbol
(12) Minimum design metal temperature ___°F at MAWP ___ psi
(13) Type of construction "W"
(14) Degree of radiography "RT-___"

(D) In addition to the markings required by this code, nameplates on cargo tanks shall include the markings required by the ASME *Boiler and Pressure Vessel Code* and the DOT.

This new requirement was added to make users aware that the U.S. Department of Transportation has marking requirements in the Code of Federal Regulations, Title 49, Part 178.133-17, for cargo tank motor vehicles that transport propane. In addition to the ASME nameplate provided with the tank, a specification plate must be permanently attached to the cargo tank by brazing or welding on the left side near the front, so that it is accessible for inspection. The specification plate must have the following information stamped, embossed, or otherwise marked into the metal of the plate, in characters at least $\frac{3}{16}$ in. (188 mm) high:

1. Cargo tank motor vehicle manufacturer (CTMV mfr.)
2. Cargo tank motor vehicle certification date (CTMV cert. date)
3. Cargo tank manufacturer (CT mfr.)
4. Cargo tank date of manufacture (CT date of mfr.), month and year
5. Maximum weight of lading (Max. Payload), in pounds
6. Lining materials (Lining), if applicable
7. Heating system design pressure (Heating sys. press.), in psig, if applicable
8. Heating system design temperature (Heating sys. temp.), in degrees Fahrenheit, if applicable
9. Cargo tank serial number (CT serial), assigned by cargo tank manufacturer, if applicable

All plates must be maintained in a legible condition.

A.5.2.8.3 Head design refers to the shape of the head. Shapes include hemispherical, semi-ellipsoidal, and others. *(Refer to the API-ASME Code for Unfired Pressure Vessels for Petroleum Liquids and Gases for more information.)*

The container nameplate, as shown in Exhibit 5.15, must be stainless steel and must be attached to the container in order to eliminate the possibility of corrosion to the nameplate, fasteners, or the container. Container corrosion can occur if water is trapped between the nameplate and the container. The nameplate is usually attached to the container using a continuous stainless steel weld around the nameplate to comply with the requirement in 5.2.8.3(A) that the attachment not contribute to corrosion of the container. Because the ASME Code requires the nameplate to be attached to a container, the need for this provision

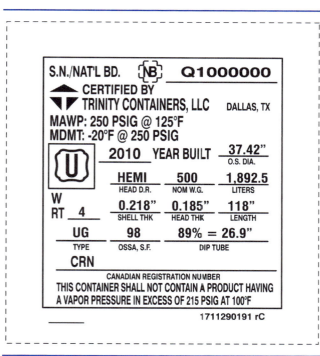

EXHIBIT 5.15 *Optional Container Listing on Container Nameplate. (Courtesy of Trinity Containers, LLC)*

is consistent with the long service life of propane containers. This requirement exceeds the ASME Code requirements, which do not specify how the nameplate is attached. This provision is not in conflict with the ASME Code, but it is important to be aware of the provision if ordering a propane container from a fabricator that does not normally fabricate propane containers.

This requirement was added to NFPA 58 in the 1989 edition. Tanks built under previous editions of the code typically had painted steel nameplates that were attached to the container by tack welds at the corners of the nameplate. Corrosion led to nameplates falling off the container and often being lost. As the ASME Code requires an original nameplate, such containers could no longer be used as propane tanks.

Nameplates provide the operating parameters used in the design of the container and information on the materials used. If the nameplate is missing, the container cannot be used as a pressure vessel. If the manufacturer is still in business, and records of the container construction are available, it is relatively easy to obtain a replacement nameplate. If the manufacturer is no longer in business, it is more difficult or may even be impossible to obtain a replacement nameplate.

Some states also have their own rules for attaching a replacement nameplate. These nameplates might not be recognized outside of the state that did the replacement.

The rules of the National Board of Boiler Inspectors restrict who may attach a replacement nameplate. The AHJ must be involved and approve and, possibly, witness the attachment.

The requirement for a nameplate in the ASME Code is of great importance, and removal of a nameplate for any reason is not permitted. When repainting ASME containers, the nameplate should be taped over to prevent obscuring the markings on the nameplate. If it is intended to remove a nameplate temporarily for container painting, contact the National Board of Boiler and Pressure Vessel Inspectors to determine whether and how it can be done.

The provisions for buried or mounded tanks in 5.2.8.3(B) require that duplicate nameplate information be provided in a visible location if the original nameplate is obscured. This additional marking permits verification of the container nameplate information without

◄ **FAQ**
Can a container without a nameplate be used in LP-Gas service?

digging up an underground container, which could damage the container; the protective coating; or a cathodic protection system, if one is used.

The information required by 5.2.8.3(C)(12) through 5.2.8.3(C)(14) was revised in the 2004 edition and was inserted to make the requirements of NFPA 58 consistent with the manufacturers' requirements in the ASME *Boiler and Pressure Vessel Code* [1]. Containers manufactured prior to this edition of NFPA 58 are not required to display this new information on the nameplate.

5.2.8.4 Warning labels shall meet the following requirements:

(1) Warning labels shall be applied to all cylinders of 100 lb (45.4 kg) propane capacity or less that are not filled on-site.
(2) Warning labels shall include information on the potential hazards of LP-Gas.

The requirements in 5.2.8.4 recognize the need to provide warning to users who are not familiar with the properties and potential hazards of propane. A variety of labels address various container sizes and uses. Exhibits 5.16 and 5.17 show examples of different types of warning labels. This requirement was clarified in the 2008 edition by deleting "LP-Gas capacity" and substituting "propane capacity" as propane and butane, which are both LP-Gases, have different densities and therefore different weights for a full cylinder of the same volume. The term *filled on site* means filled at the usage site and typically applies to cylinders permanently installed at buildings that are filled by a propane delivery truck (bobtail). Cylinders that are filled on site do not require a warning label because the consumer does not handle or install the cylinder.

FAQ ►
What kind of warning label is
needed on a propane tank?

Warning labels are required only on portable cylinders of 100 lb propane capacity (45.4 kg water capacity) or less, because these are the containers that are most likely to be used by consumers of gas who may not be familiar with the hazards associated with LP-Gas. Larger cylinders are assumed to be handled only by propane companies, although this may not be the case universally.

The code does not specify the text of a label. The label must include information on the potential hazards of LP-Gas as well as other information. Many labels include a warning that the cylinder must not be brought into buildings. This is true for most cylinders, but not all. In

EXHIBIT 5.16 *Sample Warning Label Intended for Gas Grill Cylinders. (Courtesy of Screen Graphics of Florida)*

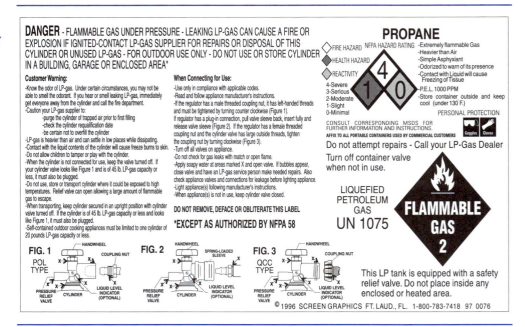

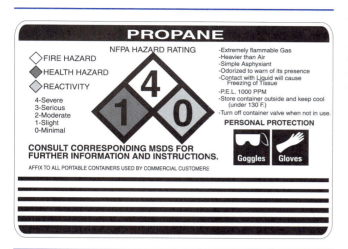

EXHIBIT 5.17 Sample Warning Label Intended for Use on Cylinders in Commercial or Industrial Service. (Courtesy of Screen Graphics of Florida)

accordance with Section 6.19 certain cylinders may be brought into buildings. A warning stating that the cylinder may not be brought into buildings should not be placed on such cylinders. Although this may seem obvious, problems have arisen when inspectors have found cylinders that are permitted by Section 6.19 to be used in buildings that have labels stating that they must not be used in buildings. This situation occurs because the most common size of propane cylinders is 20 lb (9.1 kg) and their most common use is with gas grills. Cylinder manufacturers usually provide a warning label that anticipates use of the cylinder with gas grills, unless otherwise specified.

The code does not specify the form of the label, only that it be applied to the cylinder. Applied means "to put on." Therefore, the label can be glued to the container or be attached by a mechanical means such as a plastic strip. If the label is not on the cylinder, but on an enclosure holding the cylinder, or on a cylinder cover or other container, it has not been applied to the cylinder and does not meet the requirement of 5.2.8.4. Therefore, if a decorative cover or plastic sleeve is used to cover a cylinder, the required label must be on the decorative cover, in addition to the label on the cylinder, as the warning must be visible to anyone using the cylinder.

◄ **FAQ**
Can the warning label required for cylinders of 100 lb (45 kg) or less be applied on an enclosure holding the cylinder or on another cylinder cover?

5.2.8.5 All containers that contain unodorized LP-Gas products shall be marked NOT ODORIZED. The marking shall have a contrasting background surrounded by a rectangular border in red letters and red border in the sizes shown in Table 5.2.8.5. The markings shall be on both ends or on both sides of a container or on both sides and the rear of cargo tanks.

TABLE 5.2.8.5 *NOT ODORIZED Label Size*

Water Capacity		Letter Height		Border Width	
gal	*L*	*in.*	*cm*	*in.*	*cm*
≥499	≥1881	4	10.0	½	1.3
49–498	184–1880	1½	3.7	⁵/₁₆	0.8
2.6–48	10–183	¾	1.8	¼	0.6
1–2.5	4–9	³/₈	1.0	¹/₁₆	0.2

Are any special precautions needed when storing LP-Gas that has not been odorized?
◄ **FAQ**

The marking NOT ODORIZED on ASME containers of unodorized propane provides important information to emergency responders. (See Exhibit 5.18.) The lack of odorant in a storage container adds to the potential hazard that both users and emergency responders face. By

EXHIBIT 5.18 *ASME Containers Marked NOT ODORIZED.*

providing a visible marking, everyone working around stationary containers holding unodorized LP-Gas is made aware of the absence of odorant. If leakage is suspected, alternate sensing devices can be used to locate the leak.

Note that the paragraph applies to both ASME containers and cylinders. Table 5.2.8.5 recognizes that 2 in. (51 mm) letters would not fit on smaller containers.

Unodorized propane is also likely to be found at refineries, import terminals, pipeline terminals, and other similar locations. Odorant is normally added to bulk shipments of propane leaving these facilities.

Odorized LP-Gas cannot be used in a few applications; for example, where propane is used as a chemical feedstock and the odorant could poison a catalyst; where butane is used as a foaming gas in the manufacture of styrene trays used to package meats for retail display or for making plastic foam products, such as kneeling pads and flotation devices for swimming; and where butane or propane is used as a propellant in filling aerosol cans.

5.3 Reserved

5.4 Reserved

5.5 Reserved

5.6 Reserved

5.7 Container Appurtenances and Regulators

The distribution of propane began with most of the gas being distributed to consumers — residential, commercial, and industrial — in cylinders. As the use of propane increased prior to World War II, cylinders continued to be the most common means of distribution to residential and commercial users; however, industrial users began a transition to bulk delivery for their larger use. After World War II, the use of propane expanded, and many residential and commercial users changed to bulk delivery. Originally, each container assembly of 1200 gal (4.5 m³) [and subsequently 2000 gal (7.6 m³)] water capacity or less had to be tested and listed, or inspected and approved. Each appurtenance and regulator on larger containers also had to be listed. Many LP-Gas distributing companies and container fabricators had their own systems listed by Underwriters Laboratories Inc. (UL). Today, the individual appurtenances are tested and listed and either shop-installed by container fabricators or field-installed. Section 5.7 addresses criteria for such appurtenances, which are used as a basis for testing laboratories, manufacturers, and installers.

5.7.1 Materials.

5.7.1.1 Container appurtenances and regulators shall be fabricated of materials that are compatible with LP-Gas and shall be resistant to the action of LP-Gas under service conditions. The following materials shall not be used:

(1) Gray cast iron
(2) Nonmetallic materials, for bonnets or bodies of valves or regulators

Gray cast iron is prohibited because cast iron can be subject to cracking and failing from mechanical shock and from severe thermal shock under fire conditions. The requirement for using metallic materials for the bodies of valves and regulators ensures that exposure of the device to the elements, a fire, or mechanical abuse will result in a reasonable expectation that the device will continue to function without creating a safety hazard. Although there have been considerable improvements in the temperature and pressure capabilities of plastic materials, these materials still do not approach the melting or softening point of metals.

◄ **FAQ**
Can cast iron be used as a material to construct an appurtenance for an ASME container?

5.7.1.2* Pressure-containing metal parts of appurtenances shall have a minimum melting point of 1500°F (816°C), except for the following:

(1) Fusible elements
(2) Approved or listed variable liquid level gauges used in containers of 3500 gal (13.2 m³) water capacity or less

A.5.7.1.2 Materials with melting points exceeding 1500°F (816°C) include steel, ductile (nodular) iron, malleable iron, or brass, as follows:

(1) Ductile iron should meet the requirements of ASTM A 395, *Standard Specification for Ferritic Ductile Iron Pressure-Retaining Castings for Use at Elevated Temperatures,* or equivalent and malleable iron should meet the requirements of ASTM A 47, *Standard Specification for Ferritic Malleable Iron Castings,* or equivalent.
(2) Approved or listed variable liquid level gauges used in containers of 3500 gal (13.2 m³) water capacity or less are exempt from the minimum melting point requirement.
(3) Cast iron should not be used.
(4) Nonmetallic materials should not be used for bonnets or bodies of valves or regulators.

The melting-point criteria for metal parts of appurtenances in 5.7.1.2 are intended to provide a degree of structural integrity in the event of exposure to fire and the application of water for fire control. However, appurtenance configuration, mass, and location on the container affect the degree of hazard to the appurtenance. Paragraph 5.7.1.2(2) for liquid level gauges on smaller containers reflects this consideration.

Note that metal used for pressure-containing parts is required to have a melting point of at least 1500°F (816°C). Most metals and alloys become structurally unusable at temperatures approaching one-third to one-half their Fahrenheit melting points, making materials with melting points below 1500°F (816°C) a potential safety concern should the appurtenance be exposed to fire.

5.7.1.3 Container appurtenances shall have a service pressure of at least 250 psig (1.7 MPag).

5.7.1.4 Gaskets used to retain LP-Gas in containers shall be resistant to the action of LP-Gas.

(A) Gaskets shall be made of metal or other material confined in metal having a melting point over 1500°F (816°C) or shall be protected against fire exposure.

(B) When a flange is opened, the gasket shall be replaced.

(C) Aluminum O-rings and spiral-wound metal gaskets shall be permitted.

(D) Gaskets for use with approved or listed liquid level gauges for installation on a container of 3500 gal (13.2 m³) water capacity or less shall be exempt from the minimum melting point requirement.

LP-Gas systems must be able to maintain their integrity when subjected to fire. Therefore, the requirement in 5.7.1.4 that gaskets maintain their integrity when subjected to a temperature of 1500°F (816°C) limits their use to those materials that have the best chance of maintaining their integrity in a fire. Other gasket materials, such as Teflon® and rubber, are permitted only when the flange containing the gasket is protected against fire exposure. This protection, although not specified, must safeguard the gasket from temperatures that would degrade it in a reasonably expected fire condition. A thermal insulating material that would not be degraded in a fire situation can be used.

When a flange is opened, the gasket can be damaged, and the damage may not be visible to the person opening the flange. Therefore, gasket replacement is required.

Aluminum O-rings and spiral-wound metal gaskets are permitted because of long and successful experience with this equipment, which has been listed for many years. The manufacturer's instructions concerning reuse of these gaskets should be followed. Because these types of gaskets are designed to be deformed when tightened to seal, it is good practice to replace them when a flange is opened, as the gasket manufacturer may recommend.

5.7.2 Pressure Relief Devices.

See Section 5.13 for hydrostatic relief valves.

Subsection 5.7.2 applies to pressure relief devices that relieve vapor only. Hydrostatic relief valves, which release liquid, are not addressed here, but are addressed in Section 5.13.

5.7.2.1 ASME containers shall be equipped with one or more pressure relief valves that are designed to relieve vapor.

The requirement in 5.7.2.1 restates a key safety requirement, namely, that one or more pressure relief valves are required on all ASME containers. The number of valves is not important, as long as adequate relief capacity (flow) is provided. Pressure relief valves open when the pressure in the container reaches the rated pressure of the relief valve. The valves are required to be in communication with the vapor space of the container so that they release vapor, not liquid LP-Gas.

5.7.2.2 Cylinders shall be equipped with pressure relief valves as required by DOT regulations.

In the 2004 edition of the code, a requirement that appeared in previous editions stating that the start-to-discharge pressure for spring-loaded pressure relief valves used to protect cylinders must be between 75 percent and 100 percent of the minimum required test pressure for the cylinder was deleted. Although no longer included in the code, this provision is still a requirement because the DOT regulations specify the relief valve setting through a reference to CGA S-1.1 *Pressure Relief Device Standards, Part I — Cylinders for Compressed Gases* [13]. The NFPA Technical Committee on Liquefied Petroleum Gases simply felt that it was inappropriate to re-state this requirement. Because cylinder pressure relief valves are provided with cylinders, the requirement is for the cylinder manufacturer, rather than the propane user, and is not needed in NFPA 58.

Most propane cylinders have a service pressure of 240 psig (1.6 MPag). Therefore, DOT requires the test pressure for these cylinders to be at least 480 psig (3.3 MPag). Based on the requirement in CGA S-1.1, the start-to-discharge setting for pressure relief valves in these cylinders would be between 360 psig (2.5 MPag) and 480 psig (3.3 MPag). In actual practice, many of these relief valves are set at 375 psig (2.6 MPag).

5.7.2.3 Composite cylinders shall not be equipped with fusible plugs.

This new requirement prohibits the use of fusible plugs in composite cylinders. Composite cylinders made of nonmetallic materials (other than cylinder valves) have been approved for use in the United States and are currently available in 10, 20, and 33 lb (2, 9, and 15 kg) sizes for portable applications, gas grills, and propane forklift trucks, respectively. They are also available in other countries; in the Scandinavian countries, they have been used for over 10 years. Fusible plugs are not needed in this type of composite cylinder, as fire testing has demonstrated that in a fire the cylinders fail so that the propane contained is released over a 10- to 15-minute period as the resin separates from the fibers. A fusible plug, if opererated by heat, would allow the propane to be released quickly and could accelerate a building fire.

5.7.2.4 DOT nonrefillable metal containers shall be equipped with a pressure relief device(s) or system(s) that prevents propulsion of the container when the container is exposed to fire.

DOT regulations in 49 CFR 173.301(f) require that cylinders in butane and propane service be equipped with one or more pressure relief devices selected and tested in accordance with CGA S-1.1, *Pressure Relief Device Standards* [13]. A pressure relief valve (see Exhibit 5.19) is always required, and a fusible plug can be installed in addition to the pressure relief valve. The pressure relief device system must be capable of preventing rupture of the normally charged cylinder when the cylinder is subjected to a bonfire fire test conducted in accordance with CGA C-14, *Methods for Hydrostatic Testing of Compressed Gas Cylinders* [14].

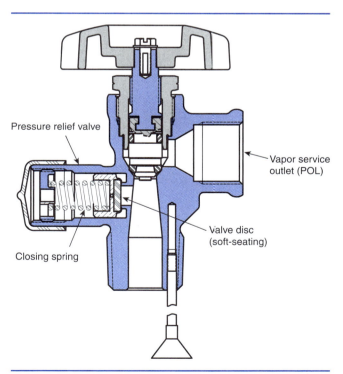

Pressure relief valve

Closing spring

Vapor service outlet (POL)

Valve disc (soft-seating)

EXHIBIT 5.19 *Pressure Relief Valve on DOT/TC Cylinder. On these cylinders, the relief valve is part of a fitting that includes the manual shutoff valve. (Courtesy of Engineered Controls International, Inc.)*

DOT-specification 2P and 2Q nonrefillable metal containers are used primarily for aerosol products. The 2P and 2Q containers have also been used with LP-Gas, specifically butane, for portable butane-fired appliances and for refilling butane cigarette lighters.

In 5.7.2.2, all cylinders are required to have relief devices. In accordance with 49 CFR 173.304(d)(3)(ii) [15], DOT 2P and 2Q nonrefillable metal containers are authorized for LP-Gas. However, depending on the pressure and the quantity of gas, cylinders may not be required to be equipped with a relief device. The LP-Gas committee believes, however, that any container for LP-Gas must contain a relief device or system to help prevent failure or propulsion of the container. Small LP-Gas cylinders can be very dangerous in warehouse fires because they have been known to "rocket" and spread the fire laterally. Sprinkler systems are not always able to contain warehouse fires that involve aerosol containers, resulting in the loss of the structure. Requiring cylinders to have relief devices prevents such incidents involving butane containers. There are at least two ways to prevent "rocketing" of cylinders exposed to fire, as follows:

- A designed point of weakness in the cylinder that forces the failure mode by overpressure and causes the partial separation of the bottom or top of the cylinder (This method results in the gas being released quickly over a large area with little propelling force. Some butane 2P and 2Q containers being sold for use with portable cooking stoves contain a weakness point at one seam that provides pressure relief without rocketing. See Exhibit 5.20, in which small dents at the top seam of a butane cylinder can be seen. These weakness points provide the pressure relief.
- An inert, porous fill in the cylinder that slows the release of gas in the event of cylinder failure

EXHIBIT 5.20 *Indentations on the Upper Rim Seal of a Listed Butane Cylinder.*

5.7.2.5 ASME containers for LP-Gas shall be equipped with direct spring-loaded pressure relief valves conforming with the applicable requirements of ANSI/UL 132, *Standard for*

Safety Relief Valves for Anhydrous Ammonia and LP-Gas, or other equivalent pressure relief valve standards.

(A) The start-to-leak setting of the pressure relief valves specified in 5.7.2.5, in relation to the pressure rating of the container, shall be in accordance with Table 5.7.2.5(A).

TABLE 5.7.2.5(A) *Start-to-Leak Pressure Settings of Pressure Relief Valves in Relation to Container Pressure Rating*

Containers	Minimum (%)	Maximum (%)
All ASME codes prior to the 1949 edition, and the 1949 edition, paragraphs U-68 and U-69	110	125*
ASME Code, 1949 edition, paragraphs U-200 and U-201, and all ASME codes later than 1949	100	100*

*Manufacturers of pressure relief valves are allowed a plus tolerance not exceeding 10 percent of the set pressure marked on the valve.

The provision in 5.7.2.5 specifically states that spring-loaded pressure relief valves must comply with ANSI/UL 132, *Standard on Safety Relief Valves for Anhydrous Ammonia and LP-Gas* [3], or its equivalent. This requirement was revised in the 2011 edition to properly recognize that the UL standard referenced is an ANSI standard. ANSI/UL 132 is essentially an exception to the mandatory reference to the ASME Code in 5.2.1.1, which states in part:

> Containers shall be designed, fabricated, tested, and marked (or stamped) in accordance with the regulations of the . . . ASME *Boiler and Pressure Vessel Code*, Section VIII, "Rules for the Construction of Unfired Pressure Vessels"; . . . except for UG-125 through UG-136.

This exception recognizes differences between the ASME Code and ANSI/UL 132. The difference between the pressure relief valve requirement of the ASME *Boiler and Pressure Vessel Code* [1] and ANSI/UL 132 is that ASME requires a larger pressure relief valve because of its more conservative testing method, which requires larger pressure relief valves than those required by ANSI/UL 132.

Exhibit 5.21 shows a pressure relief valve that is used with a relief valve manifold for a large ASME container and Exhibit 5.22 shows an external pressure relief valve for an older, small ASME container. The manifold allows the pressure relief valves to be removed individually for testing or replacement without emptying the container of propane.

A difference still exists between the ASME Code and other standards: the official capacity of the valves. The ASME Code requires 10 percent derating of the average test capacities of three samples to determine the official capacity of the valve. NFPA 58 and ANSI/UL 132 do not require such derating.

Reference is made to "direct spring-loaded pressure relief valves" to describe accurately the type of relief valve desired on ASME containers used in installations covered by NFPA 58. Various types of direct spring-loaded pressure relief valves exist, such as flush-type internal pressure relief valves used on cargo containers and full internal-type pressure relief valves for engine fuel containers. (See Exhibit 5.23 and 11.4.1.7.) More complex types, such as pilot-operated pressure relief valves, are not needed, are unlikely to receive adequate maintenance, and could result in undesirable frequent premature operation in facilities covered by NFPA 58. Pilot-operated pressure relief valves can be used only on containers larger than 40,000 gal (151 m³) because of their excellent history of use on these larger containers. Simpler devices also exist; for example, burst discs that fail catastrophically at the relief set pressure and cannot reclose. Burst discs are not permitted because the entire contents of the container would be released if the disc opens.

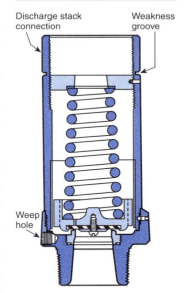

EXHIBIT 5.21 *External-Type Pressure Relief Valve for Large Stationary ASME Container for Use with a Relief Valve Manifold. (Courtesy of Engineered Controls International, Inc.)*

EXHIBIT 5.22 *External-Type Pressure Relief Valve for Older, Small ASME Container. (Courtesy of Engineered Controls International, Inc.)*

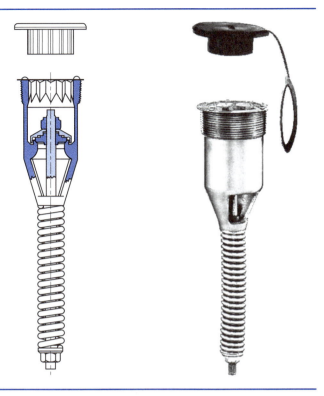

EXHIBIT 5.23 *Flush-Type Internal Pressure Relief Valve Used on Cargo Containers. All working parts are within the container or below the container shell. Stacks are not used. (Courtesy of Emerson Process Management Regulator Technologies Inc.)*

(B) Containers of 40,000 gal (151 m³) or more water capacity shall be equipped with either a spring-loaded pressure relief valve or a pilot-operated pressure relief valve, as follows:

(1) The pilot-operated relief valve shall be combined with, and controlled by, a self-actuated, direct, spring-loaded pilot valve that complies with Table 5.7.2.5(A).

(2) The use of a pilot-operated pressure relief valve shall be approved.

(3) Pilot-operated pressure relief valves shall be inspected and maintained by persons with training and experience and shall be tested for operation at intervals not exceeding 5 years.

The requirement in 5.7.2.4(B) recognizes that direct spring-loaded pressure relief valves may not be available in the larger sizes required by larger containers. Large installations that use 40,000 gal (151 m³) storage containers are more likely to comply with the testing and training conditions specified in 5.7.2.4(B)(3).

FAQ ▶
What is a "pilot-operated" pressure relief valve?

Exhibit 5.24 shows a pilot-operated relief valve typically used on very large containers. Exhibits 5.25 and 5.26 show a pilot-operated relief valve in the closed and open (relieving) position, respectively. In the closed position, pressure from the pressure relief valve inlet at the bottom of the valve is transmitted through the tube to the pilot at the right. The pressure is below the set pressure and is transmitted to the top of the pressure relief valve piston. Because the area of the piston at the top is larger than the area of the piston at the bottom, the force is down, holding the valve closed.

In Exhibit 5.26, the pressure has exceeded the set pressure, and the pilot piston moves up, releasing the pressure through the pilot discharge (shown at the left of the pilot). This reduces the pressure to the top of the piston, and it moves up very quickly.

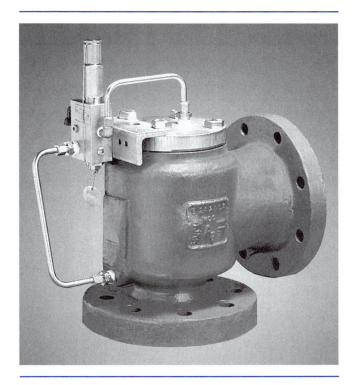

EXHIBIT 5.24 *Pilot-Operated Relief Valve. (Courtesy of Anderson Greenwood)*

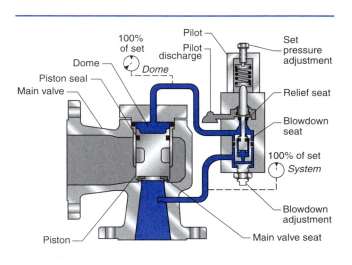

EXHIBIT 5.25 *Pilot-Operated Relief Valve in the Closed Position. (Courtesy of Anderson Greenwood)*

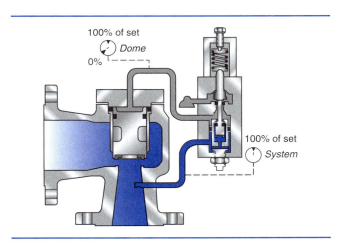

EXHIBIT 5.26 *Pilot-Operated Relief Valve in the Open Position. (Courtesy of Anderson Greenwood)*

5.7.2.6 The minimum rate of discharge of pressure relief valves installed in ASME containers shall be in accordance with Table 5.7.2.6 or shall be calculated using the following formula:

$$F = 53.632 \times A^{0.82}$$

where:

F = flow rate (SCFM air)

A = total outside surface area of container (ft^2)

TABLE 5.7.2.6 *Pressure Relief Valve Flow Capacity as a Function of Container Surface Area*

Surface Area (ft²)	Flow Rate (SCFM)	Surface Area (ft²)	Flow Rate (SCFM)	Surface Area (ft²)	Flow Rate (SCFM)
≤20	≤626	170	3620	600	10,170
25	751	175	3700	650	10,860
30	872	180	3790	700	11,550
35	990	185	3880	750	12,220
40	1100	190	3960	800	12,880
45	1220	195	4050	850	13,540
50	1330	200	4130	900	14,190
55	1430	210	4300	950	14,830
60	1540	220	4470	1000	15,470
65	1640	230	4630	1050	16,100
70	1750	240	4800	1100	16,720
75	1850	250	4960	1150	17,350
80	1950	260	5130	1200	17,960
85	2050	270	5290	1250	18,570
90	2150	280	5450	1300	19,180
95	2240	290	5610	1350	19,780
100	2340	300	5760	1400	20,380
105	2440	310	5920	1450	20,980
110	2530	320	6080	1500	21,570
115	2630	330	6230	1550	22,160
120	2720	340	6390	1600	22,740
125	2810	350	6540	1650	23,320
130	2900	360	6690	1700	23,900
135	2990	370	6840	1750	24,470
140	3080	380	7000	1800	25,050
145	3170	390	7150	1850	25,620
150	3260	400	7300	1900	26,180
155	3350	450	8040	1950	26,750
160	3440	500	8760	2000	27,310
165	3530	550	9470	—	—

For SI units, 1 SCFM = 0.0283 m³/min.
Note: Flow rate in SCFM air.

Although a pressure relief valve can function for other reasons (hydrostatic pressure buildup due to overfilling, for example), the minimum relieving capacity required is based on fire exposure. In the fire exposure scenario, the calculation of relief valve capacity assumes that the container is exposed to fire on the entire surface area and the vaporization rate is calculated from the heat transfer from the fire into the container over the entire surface area of the container. CGA publications describe the factors involved.

The equation in 5.7.2.6 is used to calculate the required relief valve rating based on the flow of air through the relief valve. The flow of air is used rather than the flow of propane for two reasons. First, it is simpler, safer, and less expensive for valve manufacturers to test their products using air rather than propane. Using air eliminates the need to introduce a flammable gas into manufacturing facilities that otherwise do not need propane as a test gas, and helps keep the cost of producing valves down. Furthermore, using air prevents propane release into the atmosphere. Second, the valves can be used for other services such as ammonia and other gases. Conversions are available for the flow of air to the flow of propane, ammonia, and other gases. Table 5.7.2.5 provides the minimum airflow rate required for pressure relief valves based on the surface area of ASME containers. Although there is no advantage to testing relief valves with propane, testing with propane is not prohibited.

Exhibit 5.27 shows ASME container relief valve manifolds. The container shown requires three relief valves. The manifold contains four. By operating the handwheel or lever, an internal valve is rotated to isolate any one zof the four relief valves so that it can be removed for testing, maintenance, or replacement, while having the required three valves connected to the container and available, should they be needed.

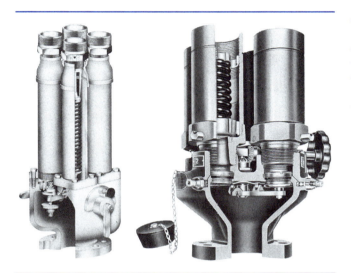

EXHIBIT 5.27 *ASME Container Relief Valve Manifolds. [Courtesy of Emerson Process Management Regulator Technologies Inc. (left) and Engineered Controls International, Inc. (right)]*

5.7.2.7 Relief valves for aboveground ASME containers shall relieve at not less than the flow rate specified in 5.7.2.6 before the pressure exceeds 120 percent of the minimum permitted start-to-leak pressure setting of the device, excluding the 10 percent tolerance in Table 5.7.2.5(A).

Pressure relief valves for ASME containers that are fabricated to current codes must begin to open at no less than 100 percent of the container design pressure, which is usually 250 psig (1.7 MPag). A tolerance of 10 percent is allowed per Table 5.7.2.5(A); therefore, the valve can begin to open between 250 psig and 275 psig (1.7 MPag and 1.9 MPag). Making pressure relief valves that begin to open at exactly 250 psig (1.7 MPag) would be very expensive, even if it could be done in mass production. The tolerance is allowed to exceed the design pressure of the ASME container to prevent unneeded release of propane into the atmosphere. Allowing the ASME container to reach a pressure of 10 percent above its design pressure is recognized by the ASME *Boiler and Pressure Vessel Code*, and is not a threat to safety. Remember that the ASME containers are now built with a design margin (formerly called safety factor) of 3.5 to 1, so the container should maintain its integrity to a pressure of 875 psig (6.0 MPag), assuming no excessive corrosion, dents, pits, or other imperfections are present.

◀ **FAQ**
Why does Table 5.7.2.5(A) permit a tolerance on the pressure settings of relief valves?

5.7.2.8 The flow capacity of pressure relief valves installed on underground or mounded containers shall be a minimum of 30 percent of the flow specified in Table 5.7.2.6.

This requirement was revised in the 2011 edition to more clearly state that the sizing of pressure relief valves on underground containers can be reduced to flow as little as 30 percent of the amount of air flowed by a pressure relief valve on an aboveground container.

Pressure relief valves are sized to allow sufficient gas flow to prevent overpressure under all operating conditions. These conditions include the following:

- Overfilling, followed by heating the liquid in the tank. When this occurs, the liquid level can rise to the top of the tank, and further heating will cause a significant pressure rise and opening of the pressure relief valve.
- Fire impinging over the entire container surface, where overheating quickly leads to rapid pressure rise.
- Out-of-specification propane, with a higher content of hydrocarbons that boil at lower temperatures.

Of these conditions, fire impingement over the entire surface results in the largest flow and is the design basis used for sizing pressure relief valves. Because underground containers cannot be exposed to fire in the same manner as an aboveground container, their required pressure relief valve capacities are 30 percent of those specified in Table 5.7.2.6.

If a container designed for underground installation with a reduced-capacity pressure relief valve is installed aboveground, the relief valve must be replaced with one properly sized for aboveground service. The editor is aware of a case in which local laws were revised to relocate all underground fuel tanks (including propane) above ground, based on concerns about potential gasoline and other liquid fuel contamination of groundwater. This law resulted in the relocation of propane containers above ground. (Note that propane is exempt from the EPA requirements for leaking underground storage tanks because it is not a toxic substance and does not contaminate groundwater.) Propane containers for underground service are usually painted or coated in black or dark color as part of their protective coating. Since dark colors are highly absorptive of heat when exposed to sunlight or another radiative source, installing these tanks above ground may result in occasional relief valve operation. Therefore, if an underground propane container is relocated above ground, the pressure relief valve must be resized in accordance with the requirements for aboveground containers.

5.7.2.9 Each pressure relief valve shall be plainly and permanently marked with the following:

(1) Pressure in psig at which the valve is set to start-to-leak
(2) Rated relieving capacity in SCFM air
(3) Manufacturer's name and catalog number

5.7.2.10 Shutoff valves shall not be installed between pressure relief devices and the container unless a listed pressure relief valve manifold meeting the requirements of 6.7.2.9 is used.

5.7.2.11 Pressure relief valves shall be designed to minimize the possibility of tampering.

Most pressure relief valves used on propane containers have nonadjustable internal springs that prevent tampering. Some older containers may have pressure relief valves that do not have tamper-proof adjustable springs. If the pressure setting on these valves is in doubt, the valves should be tested or replaced.

5.7.2.12 Externally set or adjusted valves shall be provided with an approved means of sealing the adjustment.

5.7.2.13 Where used on aboveground ASME containers of 1200 gal (4.5 m^3) or less water capacity in addition to spring-loaded pressure relief valves, fusible plugs shall meet the following criteria:

(1) They shall have a yield point between 208°F and 220°F (98°C and 104°C).
(2) They shall have a total discharge area not exceeding 0.25 in.^{2} (1.6 cm^2).
(3) They shall communicate directly with the vapor space of the container.

Note that fusible plugs are allowed to be used in some applications for additional pressure relief capacity for smaller tanks, but they cannot replace spring-loaded pressure relief valves. (Note that 5.7.2.3 prohibits the use of fusible plugs in composite cylinders; also see the commentary following 5.7.2.4.)

5.7.2.14 All cylinders used in industrial truck service (including forklift truck cylinders) shall have the cylinder's pressure relief valve replaced by a new or unused valve within 12 years of the date of manufacture of the cylinder and every 10 years thereafter.

Pressure relief valves on cylinders used in industrial truck service are exposed to the truck's operating environment in industrial facilities where foreign material may enter the relief valve. This condition could prevent normal operation of the pressure relief valve. Industrial truck maintenance procedures should include a periodic visual inspection so that any accumulated foreign material can be removed, and to ensure that a relief valve protective cover has been installed over the relief valve outlet.

◄ FAQ
Why are relief valves on cylinders used in industrial truck service required to be changed periodically, although other relief valves are not?

Paragraph 5.7.2.14 requires that the pressure relief valve be replaced within 12 years of the date of manufacture of the cylinder and every 10 years thereafter. The first replacement coincides with the first required requalification of the cylinder, which is also 12 years after the date of manufacture. Thereafter, the containers are normally recertified by a visual inspection every 5 years, and the relief valve is replaced on each second requalification. This replacement should be marked on the cylinder. Markings are not permitted on the body of the cylinder, but can be made on the cylinder's collar, which is not a pressure-containing part.

5.7.3 Overfilling Prevention Devices.

Overfilling of cylinders can result in the release of liquid propane through the relief valve. An overfilled propane cylinder that is heated can lead to expansion of the liquid propane in the cylinder. If the liquid expands to the point where it fills the cylinder, the pressure is relieved through the cylinder's pressure relief valve, a very dangerous situation under a number of typical use and transportation conditions.

The vast majority of propane cylinders in use today are small cylinders in the range of 4 lb through 40 lb (1.8 kg through 18 kg) propane capacity. These cylinders are used with propane barbecue grills (i.e., gas grills) and other outdoor appliances (e.g., camping equipment, patio heaters, and mosquito traps) and for providing energy for space heating, water heating, and cooking in recreational vehicles.

In response to the problem of overfilled cylinders, the 1998 edition of NFPA 58 first required new small portable cylinders to be equipped with an OPD (see Exhibit 3.8). There are some exceptions to this requirement that are detailed in 5.7.3.5. In addition to new cylinders, all existing cylinders were required to be retrofitted in accordance with 5.7.3.2 by April 1, 2001. It is important to note that the OPD is not the primary means by which the proper cylinder fill level is to be determined. The OPD is intended to serve as a secondary safety measure to the primary means of filling a cylinder by weight or by volume, as described in Chapter 7.

At the time of publication of this edition of the handbook, OPDs have been required for 11 years for new cylinders and 8 years for all cylinders. A number of cylinders without OPDs remain in use, but their numbers are decreasing each year as they are being replaced. Data are available on fires caused by gas grills of all types, including propane. Rather than provide numbers and an analysis here, a new supplement has been added to the 2011 edition of the handbook to provide an overview of the subject. Refer to Supplement 6, Home Fires Involving Grills, for more information on the subject.

While the improvement in safety that occurred with the introduction of the OPD is recognized and appreciated, it should be noted that the introduction of the OPD was mandated as a hardware fix to a problem resulting from both mechanical failures and inadequate training. Some dispenser operators were intentionally overfilling a cylinder to "give the customer a special deal" or "to help a friend." Many were not aware that they could have been the direct cause of a possible propane release and possible fire on the way home if the cylinder warmed in the car. The OPD solved that problem for the most part, but it is a mechanical device that can fail. Cylinders with OPDs can be overfilled if the mechanism fails, if the dispenser operator takes certain steps to defeat the OPD, or, on some older OPD models, if the filling continues for a while after the OPD activates. While data on OPD failures are not available, they do not appear to be occurring in significant numbers at this time, Recognizing that OPDs are not perfect, NFPA 58 requires that OPDs not be the primary method of determining when a cylinder is filled. See 7.4.4.1 for the requirement to fill according to other accepted means.

5.7.3.1 Cylinders with 4 lb through 40 lb (1.8 kg through 18 kg) propane capacity for vapor service shall be equipped or fitted with a listed overfilling prevention device that complies with ANSI/UL 2227, *Standard for Overfilling Prevention Devices*, and a fixed maximum liquid level gauge. These devices shall be either separate components or combined in the container valve assembly.

Portable cylinders in the 4 lb to 40 lb (1.8 kg to 18 kg) propane capacity range are those that are most likely to be overfilled. The fixed maximum liquid level gauge has been used for many years to determine that the cylinder is properly filled by the volumetric method. In Exhibit 5.28, note the plastic dip tube to the right of the lower part of the valve. When the screw seen on the valve body is turned, it opens a pathway from the bottom of the dip tube through the valve body to the atmosphere. The OPD, which is the lower part of the valve assembly, is a secondary safety device that prevents overfilling. Note that the OPD is required only for cylinders used in vapor service, not those used in liquid service.

EXHIBIT 5.28 Cylinder Valve with Overfilling Prevention Device. Note the triangle-shaped handwheel, which identifies the OPD valve. In addition to the unique handwheel, the valve is also stamped "OPD." (Courtesy of Sherwood Valve LLC, Division of TWI)

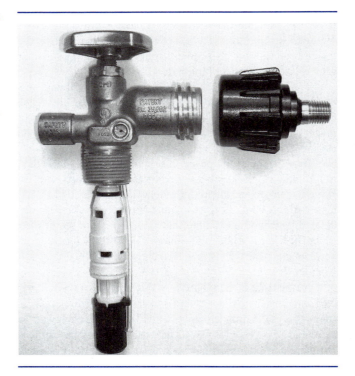

All OPD valves are required to be listed to ANSI/UL 2227, *Overfilling Prevention Devices* [16]. Prior to the 2008 edition, OPD valves were still required to be listed, but there was no reference to a standard.

5.7.3.2* Cylinders requalified after September 30, 1998, shall be equipped with a listed overfilling prevention device and a fixed maximum liquid level gauge, sized in accordance with 7.4.3.2(A) or Table 5.7.3.2, prior to being filled.

Paragraph 5.7.3.2 is one of the few retrofit provisions that are contained in NFPA 58. The matter of requiring overfilling protection on cylinders is so significant that the industry de-

TABLE 5.7.3.2 *Recommended Dip Tube Lengths for Various Cylinders*

Propane Cylinder Size (lb)	Material	Cylinder I.D. (in.)	Cylinder Water Capacity (lb)	Dip Tube Lengths for Various Cylinders (in.)
4.25	Steel	8.9	10.2	2.2
5	Steel	7.8	11.9	3.0
6	Steel	7.5	15.5	3.2
10	Steel	8.9	26.1	3.6
11	Steel	8.9	26.2	3.6
11	Steel	12.0	26.2	3.0
11.5	Steel	12.0	27.3	3.2
20	Steel	12.0	47.6	4.0
25	Steel	12.0	59.7	4.8
30	Steel	12.0	71.5	4.8
40	Steel	12.0	95.3	6.5
6	Aluminum	6.0	15.0	4.8
10	Aluminum	10.0	23.6	4.0
20	Aluminum	12.0	47.6	4.8
30	Aluminum	12.0	71.5	6.0
40	Aluminum	12.0	95.2	7.0

For SI units, 1 lb = 0.454 kg; 1 in. = 25 mm.

Note: This table indicates the approximate fixed maximum liquid level gauge dip tube lengths to be used for retrofitting cylinders with valves incorporating an overfilling prevention device. This table does not cover every cylinder design or configuration. If the dip tube length that is marked on the cylinder does not appear in Table 5.7.3.2, use the next longer dip tube shown in the table.

cided to require even existing cylinders to be retrofitted with OPD valves when they were due for requalification. Refer to the commentary on 5.7.3 for information on the reduction in home fires since the introduction of OPDs.

A.5.7.3.2 Example: When the dip tube length marked on the cylinder is 3.8 in. (97 mm), use a 4.0 in.(102 mm) dip tube for the retrofit.

If the dip tube length is not marked on the cylinder, contact the manufacturer for the recommended dip tube length.

5.7.3.3 No cylinder shall be filled unless it is equipped with an overfilling prevention device and a fixed maximum liquid level gauge. The length of the fixed maximum liquid level gauge dip tube shall be in accordance with 7.4.3.2(A) or Table 5.7.3.2.

5.7.3.4 Cylinders required to have an overfilling prevention device installed shall be equipped with either a CGA connection number 791 or a CGA connection number 810 as described in CGA V-1, *Standard Compressed Gas Cylinder Valve Outlet and Inlet Connections*.

Paragraph 5.7.3.4 restricts the type of cylinder valve that can be used with an overfilling prevention device, which has a unique connection thread or quick coupler, specified by CGA V-1, *Standard Compressed Gas Cylinder Valve Outlet and Inlet Connections* [17]. The CGA designation numbers refer to two specific connection designs, both of which were developed for use with outdoor cooking gas appliances such as grills [see Exhibit 5.28, which shows a CGA 791 connection (Type I) with matching nut]. The performance requirements for each

◄ **FAQ**
Why can only certain types of cylinder connections be used with cylinders having OPD valves?

CGA designation require the cylinder connection device to provide three important safety attributes:

1. A "positive seal," which will not permit gas to flow from the cylinder to the appliance unless the connection is properly made
2. An excess flow feature, which will stop the flow of gas should a hose separation occur downstream of the cylinder connection
3. A thermal link that will shut off gas flow from the cylinder if the temperature of the link reaches 300°F–400°F (150C°–205°C), which would occur if there was a fire in close proximity to the connection

5.7.3.5 The following types of cylinders shall be exempt from the requirements of 5.7.3.1 through 5.7.3.4 for installing a listed overfilling prevention device:

(1) Cylinders used in industrial truck service and cylinders identified and used for industrial welding and cutting gases

FAQ ▶
Are cylinders used for floor buffer machines required to be fitted with an OPD before they are filled?

Industrial truck cylinders used in liquid service are exempt from the OPD requirement per 5.7.3.5(1), and now so are industrial truck cylinders in vapor service. It is important to note that cylinders used in engine fuel service on vehicles, including floor buffer machines, are also exempt from the OPD requirements, per 5.7.4.1(E). This exception to the OPD requirement for cylinders used in industrial truck service and industrial welding and cutting recognizes the different characteristics of these cylinders, which have a higher level of quality control during the filling process and are therefore not subject to the same threats of overfilling that has occurred in grill cylinders.

- Cylinders used in industrial truck service are universal cylinders that can be filled or used in either the horizontal or the vertical position. They are exempt from the OPD requirements because an OPD is not available for universal cylinders [see 5.7.4.1(E)].
- Cylinders used with floor maintenance machines are usually equipped for vapor withdrawal and are exempt from the OPD requirement because of the higher flow required, which cannot be met with some OPD valves.
- Cylinders used in industrial welding and cutting gas service are exempt from the OPD requirement due to the higher gas flow required in cutting and welding, which cannot be met with some OPD valves.

(2) Cylinders manufactured prior to October 1, 1998, and designed for use in the horizontal position and where an overfilling prevention device is not available

Horizontal cylinders manufactured prior to October 1, 1998, are exempt from the OPD requirement because the connections for these cylinders are located on the head, which is on the side when the cylinder is in use. Horizontal cylinders manufactured after October 1, 1998, incorporated an OPD valve. The design of an OPD for a horizontal cylinder is different and more complicated than an OPD for a vertical cylinder, because each horizontal cylinder requires an opening in the head to accommodate the OPD. It would be prohibitively costly to empty, purge, and weld a new connection to a horizontal cylinder manufactured before the OPD was required. In addition, several styles of horizontal cylinders are no longer made, and replacement cylinders may not fit in the compartments of boats, recreational vehicles, and trailers that accommodate them. Because fewer horizontal cylinders are made, they are more expensive than gas grill cylinders — as much as 10 times more in some cases. This combination of hardships created by the unavailability of replacement cylinders in usable sizes, the high cost of such cylinders, and the relatively small number of horizontal cylinders in use led to their exemption from the OPD requirement.

5.7.3.6 Exempted horizontal cylinders shall be marked with a label to indicate that they are not equipped with an overfilling prevention device.

Note that horizontal cylinders not equipped with an OPD are required be marked so that the filler is aware that the cylinder is not equipped with an OPD and that extra care must be taken not to overfill the cylinder. The code does not state who is responsible for adding the label to cylinders not equipped with an OPD. Anyone — the cylinder owner, the filler, or any other party — can add this label, after determining that an OPD is not required for the cylinder (see 5.7.3.5).

5.7.4 Container Valves and Other Appurtenances.

5.7.4.1 Containers of 2000 gal (7.6 m³) water capacity or less shall be fitted with valves and other appurtenances in accordance with Table 5.7.4.1. Shutoff, filler, check, and excess-flow valves shall comply with ANSI/UL 125, *Standard for Valves for Anhydrous Ammonia and LP-Gas (Other than Safety Relief)*, except that shutoff valves used on DOT cylinders shall comply with ANSI/UL 1769, *Cylinder Valves*. Containers of 2001 gal through 4000 gal (7.6 m³ through 15.1 m³) water capacity in bulk plant and industrial plant service shall be fitted with valves and other appurtenances in accordance with Table 5.7.4.2. Containers of 2001 gal through 4000 gal (7.6 m³ through 15.1 m³) water capacity in other than bulk plant and industrial plant service shall be in accordance with Table 5.7.4.1.

Paragraph 5.7.4.1 is based on distinctions between the size of containers and the type of service for which they are used. The committee assumed that containers 2000 gal (7.6 m³) and under are not used in bulk plant operations. In addition, a distinction is made in 5.7.4.2 between containers 4000 gal (15.2 m³) or less used in bulk plant service and those that are not. This distinction is due to the fact that bulk plant equipment is subject to many more liquid transfer operations than a typical residential or commercial customer facility. For that reason, the product control and appurtenance requirements in Table 5.7.4.2 (covering containers installed in bulk plants and industrial plants) are more rigorous than those appearing in Table 5.7.4.1. Industrial plants have historically been grouped with bulk plants, and Table 5.7.4.2 continues that tradition because the quantities of LP-Gas stored are similar.

Table 5.7.4.1 was completely revised in the 2008 edition to provide performance requirements only and not to attempt to cover all possible combinations, which makes it easier to use. The table has columns for cylinders, 2 lb through 240 lb (14 kPag to 1.6 MPag), ASME containers through 4000 gal (15.1 m³), and engine fuel/mobile containers, compared to six types of containers previously. It also has nine appurtenances (rows), compared to fourteen previously.

(A) ASME containers having a propane capacity not greater than 100 gal (0.45 m³) shall be permitted to have an external pressure relief valve. The relief valve shall be permitted to be part of a multiple-function valve. Underground containers and containers originally equipped with an external pressure relief valve shall be permitted to have an external relief valve.

This requirement was revised in the 2011 edition to allow external pressure relief valves to be used on ASME containers of 100 gal (0.45 m³), which was previously prohibited. The committee recognized that ASME containers 100 gal or smaller are portable containers with a protective dome or collar, similar in use to cylinders. As cylinders normally have external pressure relief valves, there is no safety difference between cylinders and these smaller ASME containers. This change does not affect the differences in the pressure relief setting of these pressure relief valves, with cylinders at 375 psig (2.6 MPag) (per DOT requirements) and this type of ASME container at 250 psig (1.7 MPag). Underground containers have used external pressure relief valves, because the valve is in the container dome, which is below ground level and is therefore protected from being broken by vehicle impact.

(B) Containers of 125 gal through 4000 gal (0.5 m³ through 15.2 m³) water capacity shall be provided with an actuated liquid withdrawal excess-flow valve with a connection not smaller than ¾ in. NPT (19 mm).

TABLE 5.7.4.1 *Container Connection and Appurtenance Requirements for Containers Used in Other Than Bulk Plants and Industrial Plants*

Part	Appurtenance	1 *Cylinders 2 lb Through 420 lb Propane Capacity*	2 *Stationary ASME Containers ≤ 4000 gal Water Capacity[a]*	3 *DOT and ASME Engine Fuel and Mobile Containers*
A	Vapor shutoff valve[b]	R (CGA 555 outlet prohibited)	R	R with internal excess-flow valve
B	Liquid shutoff valve[b]	R with CGA 555 outlet and internal excess flow shutoff	R with internal excess flow shutoff	R with internal excess-flow valve
D	Pressure relief valve	R *(See 5.7.2.2.)*	R[c] *[See 5.7.4.1(A).]*	R full internal or flush-type full internal pressure relief valve *[See 5.7.4.1(J) for DOT cylinders used on industrial trucks.]*
E	Fixed maximum liquid level gauge	R (filled by volume) R (filled by weight, ≤ 40 lb and > 100 lb) *[See 5.7.4.1(H).]*	R	R
F	Overfilling prevention device	R (4 lb through 40 lb) *(See 5.7.3.)*	NR	R (ASME only) *[See 5.7.4.1(E).]*
G	Actuated liquid withdrawal excess-flow valve	NR	R (≥ 125 gal) *[See 5.7.4.1(B) through 5.7.4.1(D).]*	NR
H	Float gauge	NR	R (> 124 gal only)	NR
I	Filler valve *[See 5.7.4.1(F).]*	R (for ≥ 100 lb cylinders that are filled on site at the point of use)	R	R (for ASME containers only)

For SI units, 1 lb = 0.454 kg; 1 gal = 0.0045 m³.

R: Required. NR: Not required.

[a]All ASME container capacities are water capacity.

[b]Where installed.

[c]Aboveground ASME containers, internal spring-type pressure relief valves only.

(C) An actuated liquid withdrawal excess-flow valve shall not be required on container connections equipped for liquid withdrawal with a positive shutoff valve that is located as close to the container as practical in combination with an excess-flow valve installed in the container connection.

A positive shutoff valve and an excess-flow valve in the container provide the same function as an actuated liquid withdrawal excess-flow valve. The term *positive shutoff valve* means a valve where the operation of the handle, wheel, or lever directly opens or closes the flow path.

(D) The actuated liquid withdrawal excess-flow valve shall not be connected for continuous use unless the valve is recommended by the manufacturer for such service.

Refer to the commentary following 5.2.5.4 for information on continuous service of actuated liquid withdrawal excess-flow valves.

(E) An overfilling prevention device shall not be required for engine fuel cylinders used on industrial (and forklift) trucks powered by LP-Gas or for engine fuel cylinders used on vehicles (including floor maintenance machines) having LP-Gas–powered engines mounted on them.

Refer to the commentary following 5.7.3.5(1) for an explanation of why overfilling prevention devices are not required for these vehicle applications.

(F) A filler valve shall incorporate one of the following:

(1) Double backflow check valves of the spring-loaded type
(2) Manual shutoff valve with an internal backflow check valve of the spring-loaded type
(3) Combination single backflow check valve of the spring-loaded type and an overfilling prevention device designed for containers

Subparagraph 5.7.4.1(F) is new in the 2011 edition. It complements the new definition of *filler valve* in 3.3.69.3 and provides the requirements for these devices. A filler valve is allowed to have different attributes as described in the new subparagraph because all of those described have been used to safely transfer LP-Gas into containers. A positive shutoff valve provides the same level of safety as a backpressure valve, and an OPD device can be tested to ensure that it serves as a backpressure valve.

(G) Manual shutoff valves in vapor service shall be equipped with one of the following:

(1) Orifice between the container contents and the shutoff valve outlet, not exceeding $\frac{5}{16}$ in.(8 mm) in diameter, and an approved regulator directly attached, or attached with a flexible connector, to the manual shutoff valve outlet
(2) Excess-flow valve

The wording of 5.7.4.1(G) was revised in the 2011 edition to more clearly state the option of an orifice or an excess-flow valve. This paragraph serves as an alternative to the requirement for an excess-flow valve because it provides a "passive" restriction to the flow of gas should the line become severed downstream of the regulator, due to the restrictive orifice and pressure regulator.

◄ **FAQ**
Why is an excess-flow valve not required when a regulator with ⁵⁄₁₆ in. (8 mm) flow orifice is connected to a container?

(H) Overfilling prevention devices shall be required on cylinders having 4 lb through 40 lb (1.8 kg through 18 kg) propane capacity for vapor service. *(See 5.7.3.)*

See the commentary following 5.7.3 for an explanation of why overfilling prevention devices are only required on cylinders in the 4 lb to 40 lb (1.8–18 kg) range.

(I) Cylinders greater than 40 lb through 100 lb (18 kg through 45 kg) propane capacity filled by volume shall have a fixed maximum liquid level gauge.

Note that only cylinders with capacities greater than 100 lb (45 kg) that are filled by volume are required to have a fixed maximum liquid level gauge. This is because it is common practice of many companies where cylinders are exchanged, to fill all cylinders by the weight method, making the fixed maximum liquid level gauge unneeded. The requirement also recognizes that in the fuel gas distribution business, it is common to fill cylinders with capacities of greater than 40 lb through 100 lb (18 through 45 kg) by volume, especially at sites where the cylinder remains at the point of use.

(J) Pressure relief valves installed in multiple function valves in single opening cylinders used in industrial truck service shall have the springs and guiding mechanism on the container pressure side of the seats, such that the springs and guiding mechanism shall not be exposed to the atmosphere. Such multiple function valves shall meet the following requirements:

(1) In accordance with 5.7.2.13, the pressure relief valve shall either be replaced with a multiple function valve that incorporates the pressure relief valve described in 5.7.4.1(J) or it shall have the means to be replaced without removing the multiple function valve body from the cylinder.
(2) The multiple function valve shall incorporate an internal excess flow valve for the liquid or vapor withdrawal service valve outlet.
(3) The multiple function valve shall incorporate a weak section on the service valve outlet connection to mitigate product loss.
(4) The internal excess flow valve incorporated into a multiple function valve shall not restrict the flow to the pressure relief valve.
(5) Multiple function valves shall be listed.

This new requirement provides an alternative to the requirement for internal pressure relief valves in Table 5.7.4.1, Row D, Column 3. It was introduced to allow all composite cylinders to be used in engine fuel applications, such as industrial trucks. Metal industrial truck cylinders have multiple openings and can accommodate internal pressure relief valves. There are currently two types of nonmetallic composite cylinders, one of which (two piece) can be provided with multiple openings for appurtenances, while the other (one piece) can have only one opening. Because the cylinder collar provides protection to external valves if the cylinder is dropped, double protection from breaking is not needed for the pressure relief valve, just as it is not needed for the cylinder valve. Note that where the pressure relief valve is incorporated into a multiple function valve, the pressure relief valve must be replaceable without replacing the multiple valve assembly. In industrial truck service, pressure relief valves must be replaced after 12 years from the date of manufacture and every 5 years thereafter in accordance with 5.7.2.14.

5.7.4.2 ASME containers over 4000 gal (15.2 m³) water capacity shall be equipped in accordance with 5.7.4.2(A) through 5.7.4.2(G) and Table 5.7.4.2.

FAQ ▶
Are there any differences between the requirements in 5.7.4.2 and those in Table 5.7.4.2?

The provisions in 5.7.4.2(A) through (G) are identical to the requirements shown in Table 5.7.4.2. The technical committee duplicated this information in the table because many users find it an easier format to understand. Note that the requirements in 5.7.4.2(H) and (I) are not applicable to the smaller containers covered in Table 5.7.4.1.

Paragraph 5.7.4.2 is intended to address containers used in bulk plant and industrial installations. It recognizes that the internal valve incorporates all of the safety features that are available, including providing protection for the container opening in the event the valve is sheared off; thermal protection that would automatically close the valve if it is subjected to fire; and excess-flow protection and remote shutoff capability. However, the code also recognizes that many existing installations provide similar protection and, therefore, does permit certain alternatives to be used instead of an internal valve. Those alternatives are described in 5.7.4.2(A) through (I).

Internal valves can be operated in various ways. See Exhibits 5.29, 5.30, 5.31, and 5.32 for examples of the different types of internal valves.

(A) Vapor withdrawal openings shall be equipped with either of the following:

(1) A positive shutoff valve located as close to the container as practical in combination with an excess-flow valve installed in the container
(2) An internal valve

The requirements for container appurtenance protection reflect the hazard presented by failure downstream of the connection. Vapor withdrawal lines carry much less propane than

TABLE 5.7.4.2 *Connection and Appurtenance Requirements for New and Existing Container Installations in Bulk Plants and Industrial Plants*

Service	2001 gal through 4000 gal W.C.* (7.6 m³ through 15.1 m³)	Greater Than 4000 gal W.C.* (>15.1 m³)	Requirements for Containers of Greater Than 4000 gal W.C. (>15.1 m³) With and Without Internal Valves†	
			Without Existing Internal Valves (by 7/1/11)	*With Existing Internal Valves*
Vapor inlet	Option A or Option B or Option C	Option A or Option B or Option C	See Note	See Note
Vapor outlet	Option B or Option C	Option B or Option C	See Note	See Note
Liquid inlet	Option A or Option B or Option C	Option D or Option E	Option D or Option E or Option F or Option G	RT
Liquid outlet	Option B or Option C	Option E	Option E or Option H	RT

Option A: Positive shutoff valve installed as close as practical to a backflow check valve installed in the container.

Option B: Positive shutoff valve installed as close as practical to an excess-flow valve installed in the container and sized in accordance with 5.7.8.1(E).

Option C: Internal valve installed in the container or an excess-flow valve in accordance with 5.7.4.2(I).

Option D: Positive shutoff valve installed as close as practical to a backflow check valve designed for the intended application and installed in the container.

Option E: Internal valve installed in the container equipped for remote closure and automatic shutoff using thermal (fire) activation within 5 ft (1.5 m) of valve or an excess-flow valve in accordance with 5.7.4.2(I).

Option F: Emergency shutoff valve equipped for remote closure and automatic shutoff using thermal (fire) activation installed in the line upstream as close as practical to an existing positive shutoff valve/excess-flow valve combination.

Option G: Backflow check valve designed for the intended application and installed in the line upstream as close as practical to the existing positive shutoff valve/excess-flow valve combination.

Option H: Emergency shutoff valve equipped for remote closure and automatic shutoff using thermal (fire) activation, installed in the line downstream as close as practical to an existing positive shutoff valve/excess-flow valve combination.

RT: Equipping an existing internal valve for remote closure and automatic shutoff using thermal (fire) actuation within 5 ft (1.5 m) of the internal valve.

Note: Vapor connections on containers installed prior to the effective date of the 2001 edition of NFPA 58 are not required to be modified.

*Applicable to installations constructed on or after the effective date of this code.

†Applicable to installations constructed prior to the effective date of this code.

liquid withdrawal lines of the same size. Internal valves are not required but are allowed. An excess-flow valve will close in the event the piping system is compromised and the flow exceeds the design flow of the excess-flow valve. It is important to remember that excess-flow valves cannot provide complete safety, as the flow from a container is a function of the pressure in the container, which is temperature dependent. On colder days, container pressure may not be sufficient to develop a flow that will close the excess-flow valve. Excess-flow valves may also not close if the pipe area is reduced by breakage that restricts flow.

(B) Liquid withdrawal openings in new installations shall be equipped with an internal valve that is fitted for remote closure and automatic shutoff using thermal (fire) actuation where the thermal element is located within 5 ft (1.5 m) of the internal valve.

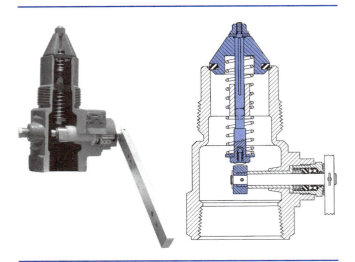

EXHIBIT 5.29 *Lever-Operated Internal Valve for Threaded Installation. (Courtesy of Engineered Controls International, Inc.)*

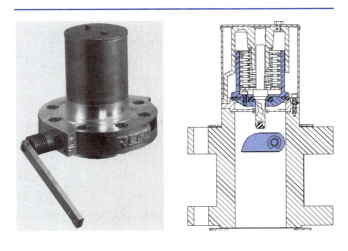

EXHIBIT 5.30 *Lever-Operated Internal Valve for Flanged Installation. (Courtesy of Engineered Controls International, Inc.)*

EXHIBIT 5.31 *Pneumatically Operated Internal Valve. (Courtesy of Engineered Controls International, Inc.)*

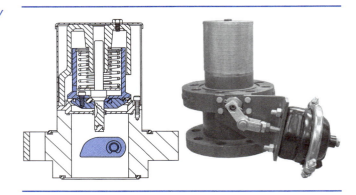

Liquid withdrawal lines present a greater potential hazard than vapor withdrawal lines, and the requirement for the container appurtenance is more stringent. An internal valve is required.

(C) Liquid withdrawal openings in existing installations where the container is equipped with an internal valve that is not fitted for remote closure and automatic shutoff using thermal (fire) actuation shall be equipped for remote and thermal closure by July 1, 2003.

Although the July 1, 2003, date has passed, it is kept in the code to provide guidance to jurisdictions that may not yet have adopted the 2004 edition. This date is also prior to the retrofit date that appears in 5.7.4.2(D) because of the relative ease by which compliance with this paragraph can be achieved. Since the internal valve is already present in the tank, only the remote closure and thermal activation features need be installed.

(D) Liquid withdrawal openings in existing installations shall be equipped with either of the following by July 1, 2011:

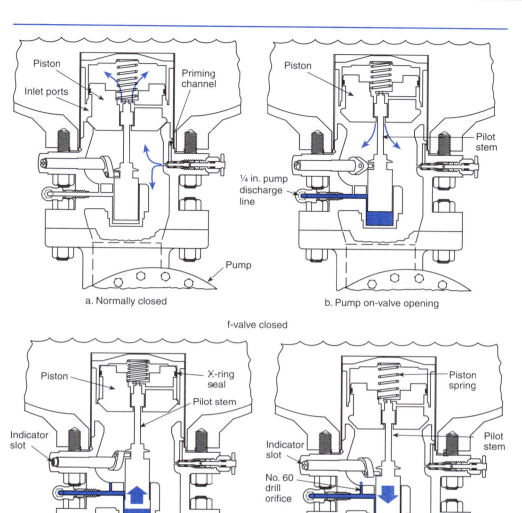

(1) An internal valve that is fitted for remote closure and automatic shutoff using thermal (fire) actuation where the thermal element is located within 5 ft (1.5 m) of the internal valve

(2) An emergency shutoff valve that is installed in the line downstream as close as practical to a positive shutoff valve in combination with an excess-flow valve installed in the container

A substantial amount of time for compliance is given for this retrofit provision for existing installations. To add an internal valve, the container must be emptied of all product to remove the existing valve from the container. Seals and gaskets may be made of materials having low melting points that could potentially be affected when exposed to heat. The maximum 5 ft (1.5 m) distance for the location of the thermal element is intended to keep the activation element close to the valve itself, to avoid heat affecting the ability of the valve to retain product while in the "open" position.

(E) Vapor inlet openings shall be equipped with either of the following:

(1) A positive shutoff valve that is located as close to the container as practical in combination with either a backflow check valve or an excess-flow valve installed in the container
(2) An internal valve

The container appurtenance requirement for vapor withdrawal openings is the same as vapor inlet openings, because the potential consequences are the same.

(F) Liquid inlet openings in new installations shall be equipped with either of the following:

(1) An internal valve that is fitted for remote closure and automatic shutoff using thermal (fire) actuation where the thermal element is located within 5 ft (1.5 m) of the internal valve
(2) A positive shutoff valve that is located as close to the container as practical in combination with a backflow check valve that is designed for the intended application and is installed in the container

The container appurtenance requirements for liquid inlet openings in new installations allow either an internal valve or a positive shutoff valve and a check valve in the container. A check valve will allow flow only in one direction and will allow propane to enter the container, but not to leave. Check valves are not perfect, but experience with them has been better than with excess-flow valves, as their operation will occur over a much wider flow range than that of an excess-flow valve. Note that 6.12.9 requires that check valves used as container appurtenances be checked for proper operation annually.

See 5.7.4.2(H) for requirements effective in 2011 for container appurtenances for all containers.

(G) Liquid inlet openings in existing installations where the container is equipped with an internal valve that is not fitted for remote closure and automatic shutoff using thermal (fire) actuation shall be equipped for remote and thermal closure by July 1, 2003.

Internal valves are required by NFPA 58 to provide a higher level of safety than provided by excess-flow valves, but they do so only when someone is present to operate the internal valve. The remote operating point must be installed properly. Installation distances are provided in 6.11.4. The requirement for installation by July 1, 2003, was added in the 2001 edition to require that remote operating stations be installed for all internal valves.

(H) Liquid inlet openings in existing installations shall be equipped with any of the following by July 1, 2011:

(1) An internal valve that is fitted for remote closure and automatic shutoff using thermal (fire) actuation where the thermal element is located within 5 ft (1.5 m) of the internal valve
(2) An emergency shutoff valve that is installed in the line upstream as close as practical to a positive shutoff valve in combination with an excess-flow valve installed in the container
(3) A positive shutoff valve that is located as close to the container as practical in combination with a backflow check valve that is designed for the intended application and is installed in the container
(4) A backflow check valve that is designed for the intended application and is installed in the line upstream as close as practical to a positive shutoff valve in combination with an excess-flow valve installed in the container

Note that these requirements are retroactive to all existing containers on July 1, 2011. This date was selected when the requirement was added in the 2001 edition to allow a 10-year period to modify all existing containers.

The options for liquid inlet openings are as follows:

- An internal valve
- An internal check valve with a positive shutoff valve
- An internal check valve with a positive shutoff valve and an external excess-flow valve
- An internal excess-flow valve with a positive shutoff valve and an external check valve.

These requirements are similar to those for liquid withdrawal openings, with the addition of another option, a check valve. Check valves can be used only on inlet openings because they will not allow liquid both into and out of a container.

(I) Container openings that are not compatible with internal valves shall be permitted to utilize both an excess-flow valve installed in the container and a valve complying with API 607, *Fire Test for Soft-Seated Quarter Turn Ball Valves*, with the following features:

(1) The valve shall be activated either hydraulically or pneumatically and shall fail in the closed position.
(2) The valve shall be equipped for remote closure and thermal actuation with a thermal element located within 5 ft (1.5 m) of the valve.

This provision recognizes that threaded internal valves are available in sizes up to 3 in. (75 mm) and flanged internal valves are available in sizes up to 4 in. (100 mm) Larger size container openings are found typically in containers used in high-volume commercial or industrial installations and propane terminals. The option of an internal excess-flow valve with an external valve meeting API 607, *Fire Test for Soft-Seated Quarter Turn Ball Valves* [18], provides a similar level of safety for these larger container openings. See Exhibit 5.33 for an API 607 valve.

EXHIBIT 5.33 *Tank Valve Complying with API 607. (Courtesy of Superior Energy Systems)*

5.7.4.3 Appurtenances used on inlet and outlet connections of containers larger than 2000 gal through 4000 gal (7.6 m^3 through 15.1 m^3) water capacity shall be in accordance with Table 5.7.4.1. Appurtenance requirements for inlet and outlet connections of containers in bulk plant and industrial plant service shall be in accordance with Table 5.7.4.2.

Containers falling within the size range of greater than 2000 gal through 4000 gal water capacity are required to comply with either Table 5.7.4.1 or Table 5.7.4.2, depending on how

Why are containers between 2000 gal and 4000 gal water capacity required to comply with different provisions, depending on whether they are used in residential/commercial service or bulk plant/industrial service?

◄ **FAQ**

they are being used. Because of more frequent liquid transfers to and from containers in bulk plant service, these containers must comply with Table 5.7.4.2 for the installation of internal valves or specified alternatives, rather than the less stringent requirements in Table 5.7.4.1.

5.7.4.4 ASME containers over 4000 gal (15.1 m³) water capacity shall also be equipped with the following appurtenances:

(1) An internal spring-type, flush-type full internal pressure relief valve, or external pressure relief valve *(see Annex E)*
(2) A fixed maximum liquid level gauge
(3) A float gauge, rotary gauge, slip tube gauge, or a combination of these gauges
(4) A pressure gauge
(5) A temperature gauge

Since containers used in bulk plant and industrial service are not within the scope of Table 5.7.4.1, the requirements listed in 5.7.4.4 specify the types of appurtenances that must be installed on containers greater than 4000 gal water capacity.

FAQ ▶
Does NFPA 58 require a broken or unreadable pressure or temperature gauge to be replaced?

Although not explicitly required by 5.7.4.4, each of the listed appurtenances must function properly in order to comply with the code (i.e., merely being present is not enough).

5.7.4.5 The appurtenances specified in Table 5.7.4.1 and 5.7.4.3 shall comply with the following:

(1) Manual shutoff valves shall be designed to provide positive closure under service conditions.

The term *positive closure* means the valve should be leak-free across its seat, throughout its entire working pressure range.

(2) Excess-flow check valves shall be designed to close automatically at the rated flows of vapor or liquid specified by the manufacturer.
(3) Excess-flow valves shall be designed with a bypass that shall not exceed a No. 60 drill size opening to allow equalization of pressure.
(4) Excess-flow valves of less than ½ in. NPT (13 mm) shall have a bypass that limits propane vapor flow to 10 scf/hr at 100 psig (690 kPag).

An excess-flow check valve remains in the open position until the flow of liquid or vapor passing through the valve exceeds its designed closing flow rate. The small bypass is a hole or "nick" in the valve seat disc that allows a very small amount of LP-Gas to "leak." This feature is not required for all excess-flow valves, but is required for excess-flow valves in LP-Gas service. This leak is the means by which the valve is reopened, because excess-flow valves do not have a manual means of opening (no valve handle). To reopen a closed excess-flow valve, a valve downstream of the excess-flow valve is closed, and the leakage accumulates between the excess-flow valve and the closed manual valve, increasing the pressure downstream of the excess-flow valve. When the pressure on the downstream side is about equal to the pressure on the upstream side, the valve is no longer held closed and opens with an audible "click." (See Exhibits 5.34, 5.35, and 5.36.)

Some other characteristics that apply to all excess-flow valves include the following:

• Excess-flow valves are designed to close automatically at the rated flow of vapor or liquid specified by the manufacturer. If there is only a partially broken hose or piping system and it does not allow the specified rated flow for closure, the excess-flow valve will not close.
• If the temperature of the liquid is extremely low, there may not be enough pressure in the container to reach the required differential pressure to close the valve even if there is complete breakage of the hose or piping system.

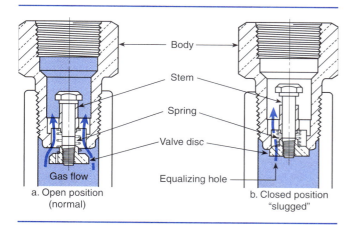

Body
Stem
Spring
Valve disc
Gas flow
Equalizing hole
a. Open position (normal)
b. Closed position "slugged"

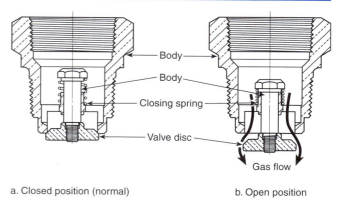

Body
Body
Closing spring
Valve disc
Gas flow
a. Closed position (normal)
b. Open position

EXHIBIT 5.34 *Operation of Excess-Flow Check Valve. After the spring-loaded excess-flow valve nas closed due to excessive flow above the manufacturer's flow rating, the closing of the downstream valve will allow pressure on both sides of the excess-flow check mechanism to equalize through the equalizing hole and the spring loading will cause the excess-flow check to reopen. (Courtesy of Emerson Process Management Regulator Technologies Inc.)*

EXHIBIT 5.35 *Operation of Backflow Check Valve. (Courtesy of Emerson Process Management Regulator Technologies Inc.)*

(5) Backflow check valves shall be of the spring-loaded or weight-loaded type with in-line or swing operation and shall close when the flow is either stopped or reversed.

(6) Internal valves *(see 3.3.69.5, Internal Valve)*, either manually or remotely operated and designed to remain closed except during operating periods, shall be considered positive shutoff valves.

The code specifically states that an internal valve is considered to be a "positive shutoff valve." When it is closed, no flow is passing through the valve. If an internal valve is left open and no flow occurs, it is not a positive shutoff valve, and the installation of another valve may be needed.

Installers should be aware that an internal valve does not necessarily provide positive shutoff in both flow directions. Consider an internal valve installed in the liquid outlet of a container. When closed, the internal valve will not allow flow out of the container but can allow flow into the container where more than one container is connected to a common manifold, especially in a container that has been taken out of service and depressurized. In such installations, a gate or globe valve should be installed with the internal valve.

5.7.5 Liquid Level Gauging Devices.

5.7.5.1 Liquid level gauging devices shall be installed on all containers filled by volume.

5.7.5.2 The gauging devices shall be either fixed maximum liquid level gauges or variable gauges of the slip tube, rotary, or float type (or combinations of such gauges).

5.7.5.3* Every container designed to be filled on a volumetric basis shall be equipped with a fixed maximum liquid level gauge(s) to indicate the maximum filling level(s) for the service(s) in which the container is to be filled or used. *(See 7.4.3.3.)*

A.5.7.5.3 Containers fabricated on or before December 1, 1965, were exempt from this requirement.

EXHIBIT 5.36 *Various Excess-Flow Check Valves. (Courtesy of Emerson Process Management Regulator Technologies Inc.*

5.7.5.4 ASME containers shall have permanently attached to the container adjacent to the fixed maximum liquid level gauge, or on the container nameplate, markings showing the percentage of capacity that is indicated by that gauge.

5.7.5.5 Cylinders shall have the letters DT stamped on them followed by the vertical distance (to the nearest tenth of an inch), measured from the top of the boss or coupling into which the gauge, or the cylinder valve of which it is a part, is installed to the end of the dip tube.

5.7.5.6 Cylinders equipped with a fixed maximum liquid level gauge where the dip tube is not welded to the inside of the cylinder shall be permanently marked adjacent to the gauge.

(A) Cylinders designed to be filled in one position shall be marked as follows:

(1) The marking shall be the letters DT followed by the dip tube length to the nearest tenth of an inch.
(2) The dip tube length shall be measured from the top center of the cylinder boss or coupling where the gauge is installed to the maximum permitted filling level.

(B) Universal-type cylinders, where the dip tube is not welded to the inside of the cylinder and that are permitted to be filled in either the vertical or horizontal position, shall be marked as follows:

(1) Vertical filling: With the letters VDT followed by the vertical distance (to the nearest tenth of an inch), measured from the top center of the coupling where the gauge is installed to the maximum permitted filling level
(2) Horizontal filling: With the letters HDT followed by the vertical distance (to the nearest tenth of an inch), measured from the centerline of the coupling opening into which the gauge is installed located at the maximum filling level in the horizontal position, to the inside top of the cylinder

Universal cylinders are commonly used in recreational vehicle applications and also in fork-lift truck applications because they allow filling to take place while the cylinder is still in its installed position. When filled in the horizontal position, a universal cylinder must be oriented correctly around its circumference in order to properly fill the cylinder. The proper orientation is usually indicated by a pin in the mounting fixture that fits into an opening in the cylinder collar.

5.7.5.7 Cargo tanks and ASME containers utilizing multiple fixed liquid level gauges shall have the loading percentage (to the nearest ²/₁₀ percent) stamped adjacent to each gauge.

Liquid level gauges are needed on all containers that are filled volumetrically to enable proper filling. The two types of liquid level gauges are the following:

- Fixed, which measure only one level in the container
- Variable, which measure and indicate all liquid levels in the container

Two types of variable gauges commonly used in LP-Gas service are the rotary type and the float type, as shown in Exhibits 5.37 and 5.38. Because variable gauges can be inaccurate, it is necessary to have a fixed maximum liquid level gauge installed in all containers for calibration purposes. The fixed maximum liquid level gauge is used to determine maximum filling levels if the variable gauge is inoperative and to calibrate the variable gauges to prevent inadvertent overfilling.

Fixed maximum liquid level gauges incorporate dip tubes at the 80 percent liquid level of the container. Exhibit 5.39 shows a schematic drawing and a photograph of a fixed maximum liquid level gauge. The marking on the disk in the photograph reads, "STOP FILLING WHEN LIQUID APPEARS." Exhibit 5.40 shows a multiple function container valve assembly that incorporates a fixed maximum liquid level gauge. The dip tube is connected to a valve that allows a small amount of vapor or liquid to be discharged to the atmosphere when

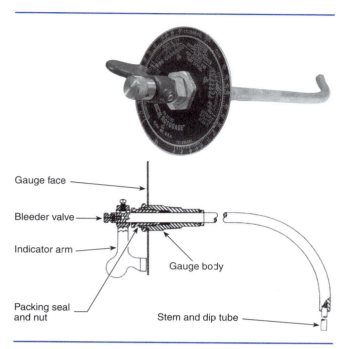

EXHIBIT 5.37 *Rotary Type of Variable Liquid Level Gauge. (Courtesy of Engineered Controls International, Inc.)*

Gauge face

Bleeder valve

Indicator arm

Gauge body

Packing seal and nut

Stem and dip tube

opened. The gauge discharge is invisible if vapor is emitted, but a white fog of condensed water vapor is created in the air by the refrigeration effect caused by the vaporizing liquid when it is discharged into the atmosphere.

The location of fixed maximum liquid level gauges in different containers is shown in Exhibit 5.41. Paragraphs 5.7.5.4 through 5.7.5.7 provide marking requirements for containers equipped with fixed maximum liquid level gauges to readily indicate the length of the dip tube or the percentage fill indicated by the fixed level gauge.

5.7.5.8 Variable liquid level gauges shall comply with the following:

(1) Variable liquid level gauges installed on containers over 1200 gal (4.5 m^3) water capacity shall be marked with the maximum liquid level, in inches, metric units, or percent of capacity of the container on which they are to be installed.

(2) If temperature correction markings are provided on variable liquid level gauges on containers greater than 1200 gal (4.5 m^3) that will be used for volumetric filling as allowed by 7.4.3.2(A), 7.4.3.2(B), and 7.4.3.3, the markings shall indicate the maximum liquid level at liquid temperatures in accordance with Tables 7.4.3.3(b) or 7.4.3.3(c). Temperature markings shall be from 20°F to 115°F (−6.7°C to 46°C), with increments not to exceed 20 F° (11.1°C) for propane, for 50/50 butane-propane mixtures, and for butane.

(3) Dials of magnetic float gauges or rotary gauges shall indicate whether they are for cylindrical or spherical ASME containers and whether they are for aboveground or underground service.

(4) The dials of gauges for use only on aboveground containers of over 1200 gal (4.5 m^3) water capacity shall be so marked.

In the 2011 edition, subparagraphs (1) and (2) were revised and former subparagraph (3) was deleted. These changes make the requirement consistent with the requirements in Chapter 7

EXHIBIT 5.38 *Float Type of Variable Liquid Level Gauge (Top) and Dial Faces (Bottom). (Courtesy of Gas Equipment Co., Inc. and Rochester Gauges, Inc.)*

EXHIBIT 5.39 *Fixed Maximum Liquid Level Gauge. [Courtesy of Emerson Process Management Regulator Technologies Inc. (left) and Engineered Controls International, Inc. (right)]*

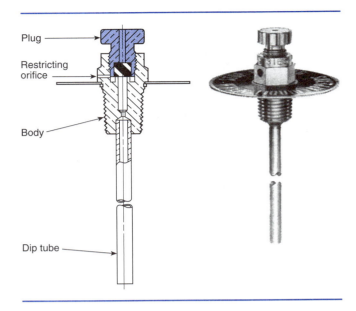

EXHIBIT 5.40 *Multiple Valve for 100 lb to 200 lb (45 kg to 91 kg) Cylinder with Fixed Maximum Liquid Level Gauge (Dip Tube) and Separate Inlet and Outlet Connections. (Courtesy of Sherwood Valve LLC, Division of TWI)*

for filling of containers. Paragraph 7.4.3.2(C) requires that containers of 1200 gal (4.54 m³) or less be filled using a fixed maximum liquid level gauge and allows larger containers to be filled using a variable liquid level gauge. The former subparagraph (3) has been incorporated into new subparagraph (1).

Variable liquid level gauges are normally found on larger containers with capacities over 2000 gal (7.6 m³) (see Exhibit 5.42), and must be marked so that they can be easily read. Markings are required for propane, butane, and 50 percent propane/50 percent butane mix, as these are commonly used. The gauge scale must also provide for the variation in density from

EXHIBIT 5.41 *Locations of Fixed Liquid Level Gauges. (Courtesy of Mississippi Tank Company)*

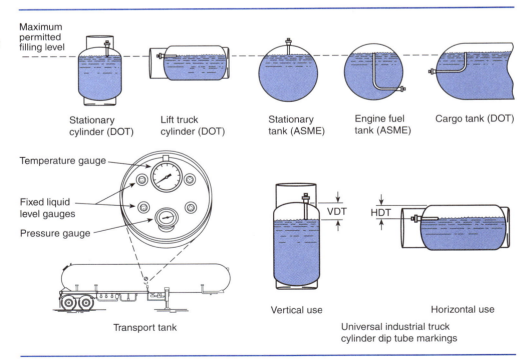

EXHIBIT 5.42 *Variable Liquid Level Gauge. (Courtesy of Eastern Propane Corp.)*

20°F to 130°F (–7°C to 54°C), in increments no larger than 20°F (11°C) so that the container can be properly filled at any temperature within this range. Because the shape of the container (cylindrical or spherical) affects the gauge reading, the type of container for which the gauge is calibrated must be indicated.

5.7.5.9 Variable liquid level gauges shall comply with the provisions of 7.4.3.2(B) if they are used for filling containers.

5.7.5.10 Gauging devices requiring bleeding of product to the atmosphere, such as fixed liquid level, rotary tube, and slip tube gauges, shall be designed so that the bleed valve maximum opening to the atmosphere is not larger than a No. 54 drill size.

A No. 54 drill size has a diameter of 0.055 in. (1.4 mm). It is a very small opening that allows sufficient flow of liquid through to see the fog caused by the liquid boiling to vapor and cooling the air to form minute ice particles, even in low humidity. The amount of propane that is released will not allow a significant amount of flammable propane–air mixture to be formed and is not a fire hazard. The amount is not believed to cause negative environmental consequences; however, the use of these gauging devices should be minimized, as even small releases of propane can add up.

5.7.6 Pressure Gauges.

5.7.6.1 Pressure gauges shall be attached directly to the container opening or to a valve or fitting that is directly attached to the container opening.

5.7.6.2 If the cross-sectional area of the opening into the container described in 5.7.6.1 is greater than that of a No. 54 drill size, an excess-flow check valve shall be provided for the container connection.

Pressure gauges are connected to container openings, and because they extend outward, they can be broken off easily. Pressure gauges must be protected to minimize leakage in the event of accidental breakage. If a break should occur, the leakage is minimized by restricting the opening to the size of a No. 54 drill (see the commentary following 5.7.5.10) or by installing an excess-flow valve, which will close automatically if excessive flow passes through it.

5.7.7 Other Container Connections.

5.7.7.1 Other container openings shall be equipped with any of the following:

(1) Positive shutoff valve in combination with either an excess-flow check valve or a back-flow check valve
(2) Internal valve
(3) Backflow check valve
(4) Actuated liquid withdrawal excess-flow valve, normally closed and plugged, with provision to allow for external actuation
(5) Plug, blind flange, or plugged companion flange

5.7.7.2 Any of the valves listed in 5.7.7.1(1), (2), or (3) that are not connected for service shall be plugged or capped.

5.7.8 Container Appurtenance Installation.

5.7.8.1 All container openings except those used for pressure relief devices, liquid level gauging devices, pressure gauges, double-check filler valves, combination backflow check and excess-flow vapor return valves, actuated liquid withdrawal excess-flow valves, and plugged openings shall be equipped with internal valves or with positive shutoff valves and either excess-flow or backflow check valves.

(A) Valves in ASME containers, where excess-flow or backflow check valves are installed between the LP-Gas in the container and the shutoff valves, shall be installed either inside the container or at a point immediately outside where the line enters or leaves the container.

An excess-flow valve is used where flow is in either direction through a given connection. A backflow check valve can be used where flow is intended only into a container and where outflow must be prevented. It is preferable (and required in most cases) to have an excess-flow valve or backflow check valve installed inside the container so that if the piping outside of the container breaks, the safety device will not be adversely affected.

(B) If excess-flow and backflow check valves are installed outside the container, installation shall be made so that any strain beyond the excess-flow or backflow check valves will not cause breakage between the container and the valve.

(C) All connections that are listed in the ASME Manufacturers' Data Report for the container shall be considered part of the container.

(D) If an excess-flow valve is required for cylinders other than for mobile or engine fuel service, it shall be permitted to be located at the outlet of the cylinder shutoff valve.

FAQ ▶
Why are excess-flow valves installed in cylinders used in mobile and engine fuel service not permitted to be installed at the outlet of the cylinder shutoff valve?

Cylinders in mobile and engine fuel service are more prone to damage, by the very nature of the service they are in. To reduce the possibility of an excess-flow valve being sheared or otherwise disabled on these cylinders, the code requires them to be installed within the container or immediately outside the container in accordance with 5.7.8.1(A) and (B).

(E) Shutoff valves shall be located as close to the container as practical.

(F) Shutoff valves shall be readily accessible for operation and maintenance under normal and emergency conditions.

FAQ ▶
Can a lock be placed on the dome of a container to keep people from interfering with the shutoff valve or to prevent unauthorized filling of the container?

Subparagraph 5.7.8.1(F) makes it clear that the dome on a container must not be locked closed and therefore made inaccessible. Access for operation and maintenance under normal and emergency conditions must be provided. Some propane companies lock the dome closed to prevent tampering and unauthorized filling. Also, in places of high public usage (such as a highway rest area), some officials provide a fence with a locked gate to prevent unauthorized operation of the container service valve. (Closing the valve could affect operation of building heating or water heating systems.) Neither of these practices is permitted by NFPA 58. However, where officials agree that a hazard exists if access is allowed, preventing access may be permitted if fully coordinated with emergency responders and if approval is obtained from the authority having jurisdiction.

(G) Shutoff valves either shall be located in a readily accessible position less than 6 ft (1.8 m) above ground level; shall have extension handles, stairs, ladders, or platforms for access; or shall be equipped for remote operation.

(H) The connection or line that leads to or from any individual opening shall have a flow capacity greater than the rated flow of the excess-flow valve protecting the opening.

An excess-flow valve will shut off the flow of product only if the flow rate is in excess of the valve's flow rating. The sizing of excess-flow valves is critical to their performance. The valves must be sized above the normal design flow rating of the system, but also below the maximum flow capacity of the piping system. The flow of gas in a system can exceed the normal flow, especially during startup when there is no pressure in the system. This condition can cause the excess-flow valve to close when container valves are opened. One solution to this problem is to specify an excess-flow valve with a higher flow rating, but the flow selected must never exceed the maximum design flow capacity of the system. Finding an excess-flow valve with a higher capacity and lower than the maximum system capacity can be difficult, because excess-flow valves are only available with a limited number of flow ratings. The best solution to the problem may be to partially open the valve to avoid pressure spikes until the system reaches operating pressure.

Excess-flow valves are especially effective to control product after hose or piping systems have totally separated. If a partial break in a line occurs that will not allow a flow up to the rated capacity, the excess-flow valve will not close. Many designers and operators believe that an excess-flow valve provides 100 percent protection in case of a pipe break, but this is true only if the break will permit enough flow to operate the excess-flow valve. Because container pressure is a function of temperature, pressure in and flow from a container will be lower at lower temperatures. For this reason, it is well known that excess-flow valves cannot provide 100 percent assurance of stopping product flow. This problem became evident after an incident involving the unintended release of liquid during unloading of a transport truck. Other means of stopping flow in the event of this unintended discharge are now required by DOT for cargo tank vehicles, and by NFPA 58 (internal valves) for larger container installations. Bobtails must have a remote means of closure of the container liquid withdrawal valve within 20 seconds of unintended release of the liquid. This closure is most commonly accomplished with the use of a radio remote shutoff button carried by the operator. Transports require a "passive" shutdown device, which is one that operates without human intervention. Additional information on this subject can be obtained from DOT.

It is also important to size the piping downstream of the excess-flow valve so that it does not restrict the flow of product and thereby prevent the excess-flow valve from closing. If the pipe size is reduced in a branch pipe, the excess-flow valve in the main line will probably not close if the branch pipe is broken, because the flow will probably be less than the closing flow of the excess-flow valve in the main line. Branch lines that are reduced in size from the main line must be equipped with a separate excess-flow valve that is sized for the smaller flows in the branch line.

5.7.8.2 Valves, regulators, gauges, and other container appurtenances shall be protected against physical damage.

Paragraph 5.7.8.2 does not intend that appurtenances must be provided with covers or other protection for all installations. The requirement is intended to apply to those installations where extraordinary circumstances may present the threat of physical damage to appurtenances. For example, an installation where material handling is routinely performed above or immediately adjacent to the container may present the need for additional protection.

5.7.8.3 Valves and other appurtenances that are part of the assembly of portable multicylinder systems shall be arranged so that replacement of cylinders can be made without shutting off the flow of gas in the system.

Paragraph 5.7.8.3 recognizes that where practical, locating the components in a system so that the system need not be shut off to replace cylinders will avoid the necessity of performing a leak check as required by NFPA 54, *National Fuel Gas Code* [19], after an interruption of service has occurred.

5.7.8.4 Connections to ASME containers installed underground shall be located within a substantial dome, housing, or manhole and shall have a cover.

(A) Underground containers shall be installed so that all connections for hose and any opening through which there can be a flow from pressure relief devices or pressure regulator vents are located above the normal maximum water table.

(B) Such manholes or housings shall be ventilated.

(C) The area of ventilation openings shall equal or exceed the combined discharge areas of the pressure relief devices and other vent lines that discharge into the manhole or housing.

The housing around appurtenances on underground containers is subject to the accumulation of water and debris. Provisions must be in place to permit the proper operation of safety systems for the installation.

5.7.8.5 Container inlet and outlet connections on ASME containers of more than 2000 gal (7.6 m^3) water capacity shall be labeled either on the container service valve or on the container to designate whether they communicate with the vapor or liquid space.

This paragraph was reorganized in the 2011 edition, but the intent is unchanged. The container connections not required to be labeled were relocated to a new 5.7.8.6. Note that Exhibit 5.43 shows a typical method of identifying liquid and vapor lines at a bulk plant. Not only is the piping system identified by a label, but the liquid and vapor pipes are color-coded as well. The requirements of 5.7.8.5 can help avoid an incident due to the misidentification of a pipe or valve.

EXHIBIT 5.43 *ASME Container with Labeled and Color-Coded Connections. (Courtesy of Richard Fredenburg, North Carolina Department of Agriculture and Consumer Services)*

5.7.8.6 Connections for pressure relief devices, liquid level gauging devices, and pressure gauges shall not be required to be labeled.

5.7.8.7 Every ASME storage container of more than 2000 gal (7.6 m³) water capacity shall be provided with a pressure gauge.

5.7.9* Container Refurbishment.

To prevent the intrusion of foreign matter and physical damage during the container refurbishment process, either of the following shall be required:

(1) The container appurtenances shall be removed and the container openings shall be protected

(2) The container appurtenances shall be protected.

A.5.7.9 Container refurbishment includes activities such as sand blasting and spray painting.

5.8 Regulators and Regulator Vents

5.8.1 Regulators.

An LP-Gas pressure regulator, commonly referred to simply as a regulator, is designed to control propane vapor pressure. Propane appliances in buildings typically operate at 11 in. w.c. (2.7 kPa) (about ½ psi), so the vapor pressure of the propane in the container must be reduced to a much lower pressure for the appliance to operate safely. Regulators also incorporate devices designed to prevent excessive pressure from reaching appliances installed in buildings. Regulators are the key to the safe use of propane in buildings. Exhibit 3.11 shows a first-stage regulator for vapor service. Exhibit 3.13 shows a second-stage regulator. Although these regulators look very similar, they operate at different pressures. Exhibits 5.44 and 5.45 illustrate how regulators work. The regulator also incorporates a pressure relief function, which is illustrated in Exhibit 5.45.

Since the 1995 edition, two-stage pressure regulation systems have been required for most fixed propane installations in buildings. The regulators used in two-stage regulator systems are designed to reduce propane container pressure to an intermediate pressure of 10 psig (69 kPag), and then further reduce pressure to 11 in. w.c. (2.7 kPag). This is accomplished with the use of two separate regulators (first- and second-stage), or with one single unit, an integral two-stage regulator.

See Exhibit 5.46, where the second stage is the large regulator and the first stage is bolted on at the right. The second-stage bonnet with the vent pointing to the left can be seen above the two pressure taps, which are used for reading first-stage and second-stage regulator outlet pressures. The first-stage regulator is at the threaded inlet with the vent pointing down.

5.8.1.1 Pressure regulators with a maximum rated capacity of 500,000 Btu/hr (147 kW/hr), except for line pressure and appliance regulators, shall comply with ANSI/UL 144, *Standard for LP-Gas Regulators*. Line pressure regulators shall comply with ANSI Z21.80/CSA 6.22, *Standard for Line Pressure Regulators*. Appliance pressure regulators shall comply with ANSI Z21.18/CSA 6.3, *Gas Appliance Regulators*.

This new paragraph in the 2011 edition recognizes ANSI/UL 144, *Standard for LP-Gas Regulators* [20], as the standard for LP-Gas pressure regulators. Now regulators either listed to ANSI/UL 144 or determined to comply with ANSI/UL 144 can be used. Formerly, specific requirements in ANSI/UL 144 were cited, and the authority having jurisdiction would have had to review test reports to determine whether compliance with the cited sections of ANSI/UL 144 was achieved.

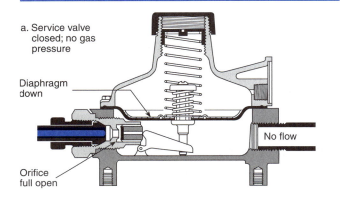

a. Service valve closed; no gas pressure

Diaphragm down

Orifice full open

No flow

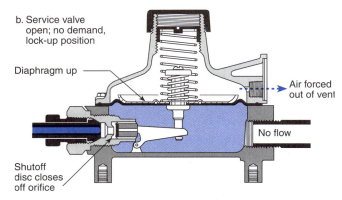

b. Service valve open; no demand, lock-up position

Diaphragm up

Air forced out of vent

No flow

Shutoff disc closes off orifice

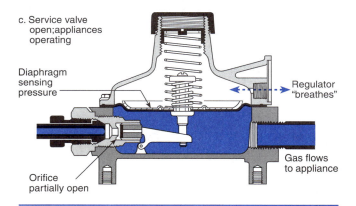

c. Service valve open; appliances operating

Diaphragm sensing pressure

Regulator "breathes"

Orifice partially open

Gas flows to appliance

EXHIBIT 5.44 *Regulator Operation. (Courtesy of National Propane Gas Association)*

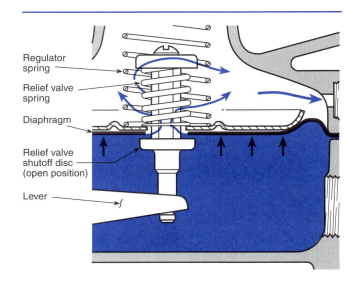

Regulator spring

Relief valve spring

Diaphragm

Relief valve shutoff disc (open position)

Lever

EXHIBIT 5.45 *Operation of Regulator Relief Valve. (Courtesy of National Propane Gas Association)*

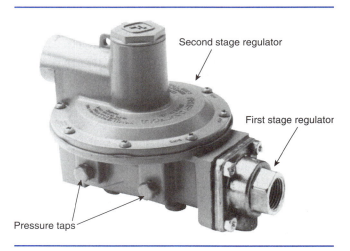

Second stage regulator

First stage regulator

Pressure taps

EXHIBIT 5.46 *Integral Two-Stage Regulator. (Courtesy of Emerson Process Management Regulator Technologies Inc.)*

5.8.1.2 Single-stage regulators shall have a maximum outlet pressure setting of 1.0 psig (7 kPag) and shall be equipped with one of the following (*see 6.8.1.5 for required protection from the elements*):

(1) Integral pressure relief valve on the outlet pressure side having a start-to-discharge pressure setting within the limits specified in ANSI/UL 144, *Standard for LP-Gas Regulators*

(2) Integral overpressure shutoff device that shuts off the flow of LP-Gas vapor when the outlet pressure of the regulator reaches the overpressure limits specified in ANSI/UL 144,

Standard for LP-Gas Regulators, and does not open to allow flow of gas until it has been manually reset

Single-stage regulators are permitted in limited applications. (See 6.8.1.9 for applications in which single-stage regulation is permitted.) The design requirements required by 5.8.1.2(2) are intended for the regulator manufacturer and not for the user.

5.8.1.3 Second-stage regulators and integral two-stage regulators shall have a maximum outlet pressure setting of 16 in. w.c. (4.0 kPag) and shall be equipped with one of the following *(see 6.8.1.5 for required protection from the elements)*:

Integral two-stage regulators, as shown in Exhibit 3.12 — sometimes called "piggyback" regulators — consist of first-stage and second-stage regulators in the same body. They are sold and installed as one unit. To determine outlet pressure of the first-stage regulator portion, a plugged opening with a restrictive orifice for a pressure gauge or a permanently installed pressure-indicating device is included with the integral two-stage regulator.

(1) An integral pressure relief valve on the outlet pressure side having a start-to-discharge pressure setting within the limits specified in ANSI/UL 144, *Standard for LP-Gas Regulators*, that limits the outlet pressure of the second-stage regulator to 2.0 psig (14 kPag) or less when the regulator seat disc is removed and the inlet pressure to the regulator is 15.0 psig (103.5 kPag), as specified in ANSI/UL 144

(2) An integral overpressure shutoff device that shuts off the flow of LP-Gas vapor when the outlet pressure of the regulator reaches the overpressure limits specified in ANSI/UL 144, *Standard for LP-Gas Regulators*, and does not open to allow flow of gas until it has been manually reset

The requirements in 5.8.1.2(1),5.8.1.2(2),5.8.1.3(1), and 5.8.1.3(2) are intended to prevent overpressure in building piping systems. Overpressure can force flames to protrude beyond an appliance and ignite nearby combustibles or otherwise give unsafe, inefficient combustion performance. Prevention of overpressure in the system begins by mandating two-stage regulation in most applications in buildings and by mandating the first-stage outlet pressure to be set at 10 psig (15 kPag) or less. Second-stage regulators must be designed to limit pressure in the building piping to 2 psig. This is accomplished by making the second-stage regulator relief capacity large enough to prevent pressure from exceeding 2 psig in the event of failure to control the flow of gas. The 2 psig limit is also in ANSI/UL 144 [20], for second-stage pressure regulators. The seat is the resilient sealing component in the regulator. This 2 psig overpressure criterion was chosen because it should not cause appliance controls to fail. Appliance control standards require that they not leak when exposed to 2 psig.

Overpressure in piping systems can result from the failure of a regulator component or, in some cases, from blockage of the regulator vent in the regulator housing. Components that can fail include all the components of the regulator: seats, diaphragms, linkages, and other mechanical elements. Although a failure of one of these components may occur, it is not likely to happen. Insect nests built in the screen or opening, or freezing water may cause blockage of a regulator vent. Outdoor installation of regulators must comply with 6.8.1.5, which states in part that they be "designed, installed, or protected so their operation will not be affected by the elements." Regulators constructed and tested in accordance with ANSI/UL 144 have a test for vent blockage caused by freezing rain and require a vent screen to prevent insect blockage to protect the regulators. Unusual weather conditions can cause ice buildup of such thickness that it is beyond the testing mandated by ANSI/UL 144. For example, one highly unusual storm in Cape May, New Jersey, in March 1984, reportedly resulted in ice thickness of about one inch.

The maximum discharge pressure from a second-stage regulator is limited to a 14 in. (4.0 kPag) water column. To the editor's knowledge, no regulators are available in the United States with an integral overpressure shutoff device for use in LP-Gas systems. The drawback of overpressure shutoff devices, in addition to their higher manufacturing cost, is that once the gas flow is shut off, it must be manually reset. The system thus experiences an "interruption of service," which then requires a leak check to be performed (per NFPA 54). Currently, all regulators use an integral full-capacity relief valve that prevents the outlet pressure from exceeding 2 psig (3 kPag), even with total regulator seat failure.

5.8.1.4 Second-stage regulators with a rated capacity of more than 500,000 Btu/hr (147 kW/hr) shall either comply with ANSI/UL 144, *Standard for LP-Gas Regulators*, with respect to an integral pressure relief device or an overpressure shutoff device, or shall have a separate overpressure protection device complying with 5.9.2 of NFPA 54, *National Fuel Gas Code* (ANSI Z223.1). The overpressure protection devices shall limit the outlet pressure of the regulator to 2.0 psig (14 kPag) or less when the regulator seat disc is removed and the inlet pressure to the regulator is 15.0 psig (103.5 kPag).

Regulators with capacities over 500,000 Btu/hr (147 kW/hr) are exempt from the required integral overpressure protection provisions because, with an engineered system, one can use a special separate overprotection device that is addressed in NFPA 54. Information on sizing independent pressure relief valves can be found in the article "Sizing of Independent Pressure Regulators for Large Propane Systems," located at www.nfpa.org/58HB. Paragraphs 5.9.2 through 5.9.8 of NFPA 54, *National Fuel Gas Code*, state the following:

5.9.2 Devices.

5.9.2.1 Pressure relieving or pressure limiting devices shall be one of the following:

(1) Spring-loaded relief device
(2) Pilot-loaded back pressure regulator used as a relief valve designed so that failure of the pilot system or external control piping will cause the regulator relief valve to open
(3) A monitoring regulator installed in series with the service or line pressure regulator
(4) A series regulator installed upstream from the service or line regulator and set to continuously limit the pressure on the inlet of the service or line regulator to the maximum working pressure of the downstream piping system
(5) An automatic shutoff device installed in series with the service or line pressure regulator and set to shut off when the pressure on the downstream piping system reaches the maximum working pressure or some other predetermined pressure less than the maximum working pressure This device shall be designed so that it will remain closed until manually reset.
(6) A liquid seal relief device that can be set to open accurately and consistently at the desired pressure

5.9.2.2 The devices in 5.9.2.1 shall be installed either as an integral part of the service or line pressure regulator or as separate units. Where separate pressure relieving or pressure limiting devices are installed, they shall comply with 5.9.3 through 5.9.8.

5.9.3 Construction and Installation. All pressure relieving or pressure limiting devices shall meet the following requirements:

(1) Be constructed of materials so that the operation of the device is not impaired by corrosion of external parts by the atmosphere or of internal parts by the gas.
(2) Be designed and installed so they can be operated to determine whether the valve is free. The devices shall also be designed and installed so they can be tested to determine the pressure at which they operate and be examined for leakage when in the closed position.

5.9.4 External Control Piping. External control piping shall be protected from falling objects, excavations, or other causes of damage and shall be designed and installed so that damage to any control piping shall not render both the regulator and the overpressure protective device inoperative.

5.9.5 Setting. Each pressure limiting or pressure relieving device shall be set so that the pressure shall not exceed a safe level beyond the maximum allowable working pressure for the piping and appliances connected.

5.9.6 Unauthorized Operation. Precautions shall be taken to prevent unauthorized operation of any shutoff valve that makes a pressure relieving valve or pressure limiting device inoperative. The following are acceptable methods for complying with this provision:

(1) Lock the valve in the open position. Instruct authorized personnel in the importance of leaving the shutoff valve open and of being present while the shutoff valve is closed so that it can be locked in the open position before leaving the premises.

(2) Install duplicate relief valves, each having adequate capacity to protect the system, and arrange the isolating valves or three-way valve so that only one safety device can be rendered inoperative at a time.

5.9.7 Vents.

5.9.7.1 The discharge stacks, vents, or outlet parts of all pressure relieving and pressure limiting devices shall be located so that gas is safely discharged to the outdoors. Discharge stacks or vents shall be designed to prevent the entry of water, insects, or other foreign material that could cause blockage.

5.9.7.2 The discharge stack or vent line shall be at least the same size as the outlet of the pressure relieving device.

5.9.8 Size of Fittings, Pipe, and Openings. The fittings, pipe, and openings located between the system to be protected and the pressure relieving device shall be sized to prevent hammering of the valve and to prevent impairment of relief capacity. [**NFPA 54,** 2009]

5.8.1.5 Integral two-stage regulators shall be provided with a means to determine the outlet pressure of the high-pressure regulator portion of the integral two-stage regulator.

5.8.1.6 Automatic changeover regulators shall be exempt from the requirement in 5.8.1.5.

5.8.1.7 Integral two-stage regulators shall not incorporate an integral pressure relief valve in the high-pressure regulator portion of the unit.

5.8.1.8 First-stage regulators shall incorporate an integral pressure relief valve having a start-to-discharge setting within the limits specified in ANSI/UL 144, *Standard for LP-Gas Regulators*.

5.8.1.9 High-pressure regulators with a rated capacity of more than 500,000 Btu/hr (147 kW/hr) where permitted to be used in two-stage systems shall incorporate an integral pressure relief valve or shall have a separate relief valve.

Regulators larger than 500,000 Btu/hr (147 kW/hr) can have a separate pressure relief valve or a separate overpressure shutoff device. Information on sizing independent pressure relief valves can be found in the article "Sizing of Independent Pressure Regulators for Large Propane Systems," located at www.nfpa.org/58HB.

5.8.1.10 First-stage regulators shall have an outlet pressure setting up to 10.0 psig (69 kPag) in accordance with ANSI/UL 144, *Standard for LP-Gas Regulators*.

5.8.1.11 First-stage regulators with a rated capacity of more than 500,000 Btu/hr (147 kW/hr) shall be permitted to have a separate pressure relief valve.

5.8.1.12 Regulators shall be designed to drain condensate from the regulator spring case when the vent is directed vertically down.

5.8.1.13 Two-psig service regulators and integral 2-psi regulators shall have a maximum outlet pressure setting of 2.5 psi (17 kPag) and shall be equipped with one of the following:

(1) An integral pressure relief valve on the outlet pressure side having a start-to-discharge pressure setting within the limits specified in ANSI/UL 144, *Standard for LP-Gas Regulators*. This relief device shall limit the outlet pressure of the 2 psig service regulator to 5.0 psig when the seat disc is removed and the inlet pressure of the regulator is 15.0 psig (103.5 kPag) as specified in ANSI/UL 144.

(2) An integral overpressure shutoff device that shuts off the flow of LP-Gas vapor when the outlet pressure of the regulator reaches the overpressure limits specified in ANSI/UL 144. Such a device shall not open to permit the flow of LP-Gas vapor until it has been manually reset.

The requirement in 5.8.1.13 preserves the overpressure protection limits to interior piping and appliances that have already been established in the code where 2 psi (14 kPa) systems are used. These 2 psi systems have the advantage over 11 in. w. c. systems in larger piping systems because smaller piping can be used. This difference can result in lower material costs. In addition, corrugated stainless steel tubing commonly is used with 2 psi systems. This material is not rigid, so it offers the advantages of design flexibility, fewer fittings and joints, and a substantial decrease in installation time.

This paragraph was revised in the 2011 edition to include integral 2 psi regulators, as the requirements for 2 psi service regulators are equally applicable.

The 2 psi systems are three-stage regulator systems comprised of a 10 psi (69 kPa) regulator at the container, a 2 psi regulator at the outside of the building, and a line pressure regulator located in the building and near the appliance. NFPA 58 covers the first- and second-stage regulators. NFPA 54, *National Fuel Gas Code* [19], covers the line pressure regulator.

5.8.2 Pressure Regulators. (Reserved)

5.8.3* Pipe for Regulator Venting.

A.5.8.3 Listed rigid PVC electrical conduit in accordance with ANSI/UL 651, *Schedule 40 or 80 Rigid PVC Conduit*, has been designed, manufactured, and tested for use in a wide variety of operating conditions, including low temperatures and exposure to sunlight and outdoor weather. ANSI/UL 651 conduit is widely available and can be purchased in hardware and electrical supply stores, where it is usually sold as electrical conduit.

5.8.3.1 Pipe or tubing used to vent regulators shall be one of the following:

(1) Metal pipe and tubing in accordance with 5.9.3
(2) PVC conduit meeting the requirements of ANSI/UL 651, *Schedule 40 or 80 Rigid PVC Conduit and Fittings*

FAQ ▶
Can plastic pipe or tubing be used to vent regulators? If so, what type of plastic pipe or tubing is permitted?

Permitting the use of PVC in the requirements for regulator venting was added in the 2001 edition to provide an alternative to the pressure piping materials listed in the code for regulator relief valve vent piping. It is noted that PVC complying with ANSI/UL 651, *Schedule 40 and 80 Rigid PVC Conduit* [21], is tested and listed for outdoor use. The PVC electrical conduit is also ultraviolet-resistant and does not crack at subzero temperatures. These properties provide advantages over steel pipe, which will probably corrode over time if installed outdoors.

Note that in the 2011 edition a new subparagraph (3) allows flexible conduit meeting the requirements of UL 1660, *Liquid-Tight Flexible Nonmetallic Conduit* [22], with fittings meeting the requirements of UL 514B, *Conduit, Tubing, and Cable Fittings* [23]. Note that listing is not required. These products were intended for electrical applications, but are usable as nonpressurized vent piping material for regulator vents. In many installations, flexible conduit is much easier to install when obstructions are present. Testing of flexible conduit under UL 1660 is similar to the testing of rigid conduit under UL 651. Normally such conduit will have the mark of the testing agency and the code to which it is listed printed on the conduit.

(3) Flexible conduit meeting the requirements of UL 1660, *Liquid-Tight Flexible Nonmetallic Conduit,* with nonmetallic fittings meeting the requirements of UL 514B, *Conduit, Tubing, and Cable Fittings*

5.8.3.2 Other PVC piping materials and polyethylene and polyamide pipe and tubing shall not be permitted to be used to vent regulators.

5.9 Piping (Including Hose), Fittings, and Valves

The term *piping*, as used in NFPA 58, includes pipe, tubing, hose, and fittings used in the piping system. Minimum requirements for this equipment are given in Section 5.9 for use by manufacturers in producing piping system components. Guidelines, both for testing laboratories to list equipment for possible acceptance by authorities having jurisdiction and for users to select proper materials when making a piping installation, are also included. The requirements for valves used in a piping system are located in Section 5.12.

5.9.1 General.

5.9.1.1 Material specifications for pipe, tubing, pipe and tubing fittings, valves (including hydrostatic relief valves), hose, hose connections, and flexible connectors shall be in accordance with Section 5.9.

5.9.1.2 Piping, pipe and tubing fittings, and valves used to supply utilization equipment within the scope of NFPA 54, *National Fuel Gas Code*, shall comply with that code.

Most LP-Gas building piping systems downstream of the second-stage regulator are subject to the provisions of NFPA 54. Therefore, reference should be made to NFPA 54 to determine whether the particular installation (primarily a permanent building piping system) is subject to that code. However, some jurisdictions have other requirements for determining the point of delivery and for compliance for gas piping in buildings. The installer must determine what code applies to the piping for the installation.

Where an LP-Gas system serves a building, piping between the container and the second-stage regulator is within the scope of NFPA 58, and piping downstream of the second-stage regulator is within the scope of NFPA 54. However, LP-Gas piping in buildings for agricultural applications — for example, brooders, dehydrators, dryers, and irrigation equipment — falls under NFPA 58 even when those buildings are served by fixed piping because NFPA 54 excludes piping serving farm equipment. [See 1.1.1.2(2) in NFPA 54.] Coverage by NFPA 58 is necessary because natural gas mains rarely serve farms, and NFPA 54 has specifically excluded farm equipment. Other piping systems beyond the second-stage regulator in applications not usually served by natural gas mains are covered under NFPA 58. These systems include piping systems serving railroad switch heaters and heaters that keep microwave antennae free of ice.

5.9.1.3 Pipe and tubing shall comply with one of the following requirements:

(1) Pipe and tubing shall comply with 5.9.3.
(2) Pipe and tubing shall be recommended for that service by the manufacturer and shall be approved.

5.9.1.4 Piping that can contain liquid LP-Gas and that can be isolated by valving and that requires hydrostatic relief valves, as specified under Section 6.13, shall have an operating pressure of 350 psig (2.4 MPag) or a pressure that is equivalent to the maximum discharge pressure of any pump or other source feeding the fixed piping system if it is greater than 350 psig (2.4 MPag).

Liquid piping that can be isolated by valves can experience high pressures if the liquid is heated. Although Section 6.13 requires a hydrostatic pressure relief valve to prevent pipe failure, a higher pipe design pressure of 350 psig (2.4 MPag) is specified. There is no potential threat to the integrity of a piping system designed to 350 psig (2.4 MPag) with a pressure relief valve setting up to 400 psig (2.8 MPag).

5.9.2 Reserved.

5.9.3 Pipe and Tubing.

5.9.3.1 Pipe shall be wrought iron or steel (black or galvanized), brass, copper, polyamide, or polyethylene and shall comply with the following:

(1) Wrought iron: ASME B36.10M, *Welded and Seamless Wrought Steel Pipe*
(2) Steel pipe: ASTM A 53, *Standard Specification for Pipe, Steel, Black and Hot-Dipped, Zinc-Coated Welded and Seamless*
(3) Steel pipe: ASTM A 106, *Standard Specification for Seamless Carbon Steel Pipe for High-Temperature Service*
(4) Brass pipe: ASTM B 43, *Standard Specification for Seamless Red Brass Pipe, Standard Sizes*
(5) Copper pipe: ASTM B 42, *Standard Specification for Seamless Copper Pipe, Standard Sizes*
(6) Polyamide and polyethylene pipe: ASTM D 2513, *Standard Specification for Thermoplastic Gas Pressure Pipe, Tubing and Fittings*, and shall be recommended by the manufacturer for use with LP-Gas

5.9.3.2 Tubing shall be steel, stainless steel, brass, copper, polyamide, or polyethylene *(see 6.9.4)* and shall comply with the following:

(1) Brass tubing: ASTM B 135, *Standard Specification for Seamless Brass Tube*
(2) Copper tubing:
    (a) Type K or L: ASTM B 88, *Standard Specification for Seamless Copper Water Tube*
    (b) ASTM B 280, *Standard Specification for Seamless Copper Tube for Air Conditioning and Refrigeration Field Service*
(3) Polyamide and polyethylene tubing: ASTM D 2513, *Standard Specification for Thermoplastic Gas Pressure Pipe, Tubing and Fittings*, and shall be recommended by the manufacturer for use with LP-Gas
(4) Corrugated stainless steel tubing: ANSI/CSA 6.26 (LC1), *Interior Fuel Gas Piping Systems Using Corrugated Stainless Steel Tubing*

Provisions for plastic pipe and tubing were first incorporated in the 1979 edition of the code. Pipe and tubing were limited to polyethylene (PE) meeting certain ASTM standards and recommended for propane service by the manufacturer. Since the 2004 edition, the code now permits the use of polyamide (PA, or nylon) pipe and tubing as well. The technical committee reviewed data on the performance of PA with respect to temperature and pressure ratings and resistance to LP-Gas, and determined that PA is suitable to be used for LP-Gas applications. In practice, it is not anticipated that PA tubing will be widely used, because it is more costly than PE. PA does have the advantage of being able to operate at higher pressure than PE and may find some application in higher pressure systems, where higher pressure can be used.

5.9.4 Fittings for Metallic Pipe and Tubing.

Fittings shall be steel, brass, copper, malleable iron, or ductile (nodular) iron.

Subsection 5.9.4 provides the material requirements for pipe and tubing fittings. The pressure limitations for piping materials were reorganized into table format in the 2001 edition, mak-

TABLE 5.9.4.1 *Service Pressure Rating of Pipe, Tubing Fittings, and Valves*

Service	Minimum Pressure
Higher than container pressure	350 psig (2.4 MPag) or the MAWP, whichever is higher, or 400 psig (2.8 MPag) WOG rating
LP-Gas liquid or vapor at operating pressure over 125 psig (0.9 MPag) and at or below container pressure	250 psig (1.7 MPag)
LP-Gas vapor at operating pressure of 125 psig (0.9 MPag) or less	125 psig (0.9 MPag)

ing the requirements easier to locate (see Table 5.9.4.1). No changes were made to the requirements themselves.

5.9.4.1 Pipe fittings shall have a minimum pressure rating as specified in Table 5.9.4.1 and shall comply with the following:

(1) Cast-iron pipe fittings shall not be used.
(2) Brazing filler material shall have a melting point that exceeds 1000°F (538°C).

Brazing is an acceptable method of joining fittings to pipe and, more commonly, to tubing when the filler alloy has a melting point in excess of 1000°F (538°C). Nearly all brazes meet this requirement, because a braze is defined as a metal alloy with a melting point above 850°F (454°C). Any filler metal with a lower melting point is defined as solder. The lower melting point prohibits soldering as a method of joining LP-Gas fittings to pipe and tubing. The 1000°F (538°C) minimum temperature is intended to ensure the integrity of a gas piping system when exposed to fire.

Although brazing alloys are not specified in this code, NFPA 54 states that brazing alloys must not contain more than 0.05 percent phosphorus because this can lead to a deterioration of the joint. The editor is advised that all brazing materials available at the time of publication meet this phosphorus level requirement.

5.9.4.2 Metal tube fittings shall have a minimum pressure rating as specified in Table 5.9.4.1.

Paragraph 5.9.4.2 is silent on the fabrication and use of flared fittings. Flared fittings are fabricated when installed in the field and do not require approval.

5.9.5* Fittings for Polyethylene and Polyamide Pipe and Tubing.

Joints in polyamide and polyethylene pipe and polyethylene tubing shall be made by heat fusion, by compression-type mechanical fittings, or by factory-assembled transition fittings.

(A) Polyethylene pipe shall not be joined by a threaded or miter joint.

(B) Polyamide and polyethylene fusion fittings shall be recommended by the manufacturer for use with LP-Gas and shall conform to one of the following:

(1) ASTM D 2683, *Standard Specification for Socket-Type Polyethylene (PE) Fittings for Outside Diameter Controlled Polyethylene Pipe*
(2) ASTM D 3261, *Standard Specification for Butt Heat Fusion Polyethylene (PE) Plastic Fittings for Polyethylene (PE) Plastic Pipe and Tubing*
(3) ASTM F 1055, *Standard Specification for Electrofusion Type Polyethylene Fittings for Outside Diameter Controlled Polyethylene Pipe and Tubing*
(4) ASTM F 1733, *Standard Specification for Butt Heat Fusion Polyamide (PA) Plastic Fitting for Polyamide (PA) Plastic Pipe and Tubing*

(C) Installation instructions specific to the type and grade of polyethylene being joined shall be provided with heat fusion fittings.

(D)* Mechanical fittings shall comply with Category 1 of ASTM D 2513, *Standard Specification for Thermoplastic Gas Pressure Pipe, Tubing and Fittings,* and the following:

(1) Mechanical joints shall be tested and recommended by the manufacturer for use with polyethylene pipe and tubing.

An example of a mechanical fitting is shown in Exhibit 5.47.

EXHIBIT 5.47 *Mechanical Fitting for PE Tubing. (Courtesy of Elster Gas North America)*

(2) Compression-type mechanical fittings shall include a rigid internal tubular stiffener, other than a split tubular stiffener, to support the pipe.
(3) Gasket material in the fitting shall be resistant to the action of LP-Gas and shall be compatible with the polyamide or polyethylene pipe material.

Prior to the 1992 edition of NFPA 58, the use of PE and PA piping in LP-Gas service was not allowed except by approval from the authority having jurisdiction. The use of PE piping was restricted because compression-type mechanical fittings were prohibited until the publication of the 1992 edition of NFPA 58. Thus, there was no way to transition from PE pipe to steel pipe and be in compliance with NFPA 58, because transition fittings were considered to be compression-type fittings. Since 1992, with the allowed use of compression-type mechanical fittings, the underground use of PE tubing in LP-Gas piping systems has grown at a very rapid rate. In the 2004 edition, the use of PA in addition to PE pipe and tubing was added, but widespread use of PA is not anticipated due to its higher cost.

The use of compression-type mechanical fittings provides a more practical joining method for propane system installers, because only a few inexpensive special tools are required and training and certification of the installers are easily accomplished. Compression-type mechanical fittings must comply with Category 1 of ASTM D 2513 [24], be tested and recommended for use with LP-Gas by the fitting manufacturer, and be installed in accordance with the fitting manufacturer's instructions. All installers must be trained appropriately, and the training must be documented. These qualifications are consistent with Section 4.4, Qualification of Personnel. (See Formal Interpretation 92-1.)

**Formal Interpretation
NFPA 58
Liquefied Petroleum Gas Code
2011 Edition**

Reference: 5.9.5

FI 92-1

Question: Was it the intention of the Technical Committee on Liquefied Petroleum Gases, when they adopted 5.8.5 in the 1992 edition of NFPA 58, to restrict the choice of any, or all, of the materials that might be utilized in the several components that comprise the total assembly of mechanical joints to those specifically "listed" or mentioned in the ASTM Standard D2513-90.

Answer: No.

It was not the intent of the committee in 5.8.5 to specify materials of construction. Materials of construction of mechanical fittings are covered in 5.8.4 where it was the committee's intent to limit fittings to be constructed of materials listed in ASTM D2513, except for gasket materials, which are covered in 5.8.5.

In 1-2.4, Alternate Materials and Provisions, the committee provides a method of use of alternate materials when supported by sufficient evidence acceptable to the authority having jurisdiction.

Issue Edition: 1992

Reference: 2-4.4(c)(2)

Issue Date: January 15, 1993

Effective Date: February 3, 1993

(E) Anodeless risers shall comply with the following:

(1) The metal-gas carrying portion of the anodeless riser after the transition shall have a wall thickness equal to Schedule 40 pipe.
(2) Factory-assembled anodeless risers shall be recommended for LP-Gas use and shall be leak tested by the manufacturer in accordance with written procedures.
(3) Field-assembled anodeless risers with service head adapters shall be equipped with moisture seals and shall be recommended for LP-Gas use by the manufacturer and shall be design certified to meet the requirements of Category 1 of ASTM D 2513, *Standard Specification for Thermoplastic Gas Pressure Pipe, Tubing and Fittings*; U.S. Department of Transportation, 49 CFR 192.281(e), "Transportation"; and 6.9.4.3 and 6.9.4.4.
(4) The manufacturer shall provide the user qualified installation instructions as prescribed by U.S. Department of Transportation, 49 CFR 192.283(b).

This provision allows the use of assembled anodeless risers, which are piping system components used to transition between underground PE and PA piping systems and aboveground metallic piping systems. Risers have been in use in the natural gas service for many years.

The term *anodeless*, used in conjunction with riser, indicates that the riser is designed to retard corrosion without the use of a sacrificial anode. Sacrificial anodes are used with

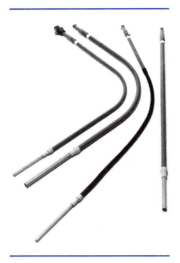

EXHIBIT 5.48 *Factory-Assembled Risers. (Courtesy of R. W. Lyall & Company, Inc.)*

underground propane containers. Risers are protected from corroding by a factory-applied, epoxy-based painted coating.

The two types of risers permitted are described as follows:

- A factory-assembled riser that requires only connection to the PE or PA pipe or tubing under ground and to metallic piping above ground. (See Exhibit 5.48.)
- A field-assembled riser with a flexible metallic or metallic casing incorporating the transition from the PE or PA pipe or tubing to the metal piping above ground. This transition is to be made in the field. The riser consists of a transition fitting (see Exhibit 5.48) and a prefabricated, pre-bent steel riser casing or a flexible metal riser casing. The PE or PA pipe or tubing is inserted up through the casing until it exits the upper end. The transition fitting is installed on the top of the casing, completing the connection from belowground PE or PA to aboveground steel pipe. The transition fitting must be located above ground to minimize corrosion to the steel pipe threads. A metallic or flexible metallic casing protects the PE pipe or tubing, and a moisture seal is installed at the lower end of the casing to prevent water from entering the riser. This type riser is an exception to the rule that PE or PA be used only below ground, but safety is not compromised because the PE or PA is encased with flexible metal or steel pipe and thus protected from mechanical and environmental damage.

A.5.9.5 Persons joining polyethelene pipe should be trained under the applicable joining procedure established by the manufacturer, including the following:

(1) Appropriate training in the use of joining procedures
(2) Making a specimen joint from pipe sections joined according to the procedures
(3) Visually examining these joints during and after assembly

A.5.9.5(D) 49 CFR 192.281(e) states the following:
Mechanical joints — Each compression-type mechanical joint on plastic pipe must comply with the following:

(1) The gasket material in the coupling must be compatible with the plastic.
(2) A rigid internal tubing stiffener, other than a split tubular stiffener, must be used in conjunction with the coupling.

49 CFR 192.283(b) states the following:

Mechanical joints — Before any written procedure established under 192.273(b) is used for plastic making mechanical plastic pipe joints that are designed to withstand tensile forces, the procedure must be qualified by subjecting five specimen joints made according to the procedure to the following tensile test:

(1) Use an apparatus for the test as specified in ASTM D 638, *Standard Test Method for Tensile Properties of Plastics* (except for conditioning).
(2) The specimen must be of such length that the distance between the grips of the apparatus and the end of the stiffener does not affect the joint strength.
(3) The speed of testing is 5.0 mm (0.2 in.) per minute, plus or minus 25 percent.

PE joints in PE and PA pipe and tubing can be made by heat fusion and by compression-type mechanical fittings meeting ASTM D 2513, *Standard Specification for Thermoplastic Gas Pressure Pipe, Tubing, and Fittings* [24]. Factory-assembled transition fittings may also be used. The use of PE pipe and tubing is limited to vapor (no liquid) and must not exceed 30 psig (208 kPag). The system can only be installed outside and under ground.

Fusion joints are made by inserting the ends of either PE or PA tubing sections into a fitting, and then heating the fitting using a special electrically heated tool or by butting the tubing ends in a heating tool and forcing the hot ends together. These methods are used widely for PE tubing in natural gas service, where the vast majority of this piping material is used.

An installer using this equipment must be trained, certified, and experienced in its use in order to make leak-free joints.

Fittings that do not require special heating tools include the following:

- Fittings made of nonmetallic thermoplastic materials, other than PE, that comply with ASTM D 2513 [24] for selection of materials
- PE or PA compression-type mechanical fittings to join PE piping materials
- Risers that provide the transition from PE or PA pipe under ground to metallic pipe above ground [See 5.9.5(E) for information on risers.]

(4) Pipe specimens less than 102 mm (4 in.) in diameter are qualified if the pipe yields to an elongation less than 25 percent or failure initiates outside the joint area.

(5) Pipe specimens 102 mm (4 in.) and larger in diameter shall be pulled until the pipe is subjected to a tensile stress equal to or greater than the maximum thermal stress that would be produced by a temperature change of 55°C (100°F) or until the pipe is pulled from the fitting. If the pipe pulls from the fitting, the lowest value of the five test results or the manufacturer's rating, whichever is lower, must be used in the design calculations for stress.

(6) Each specimen that fails at the grips must be retested using new pipe.

(7) Results obtained pertain only to the outside diameter and material of the pipe tested, except where testing of a heavier wall pipe is used to qualify pipe of the same material but with a lesser wall thickness.

5.9.6 Hose, Quick Connectors, Hose Connections, and Flexible Connectors.

5.9.6.1 Hose, hose connections, and flexible connectors *(see 3.3.23, Flexible Connector)* shall be fabricated of materials that are resistant to the action of LP-Gas both as liquid and vapor.

The requirement in 5.9.6.1 recognizes that the hose used to transfer propane to and from containers and propane trucks includes materials that can be dissolved by propane. Each time propane is moved through a hose, a small amount of these soluble hose materials can be added to the propane. This requirement is intended to reduce the potential for hose products to contaminate LP-Gas.

5.9.6.2 When wire braid is used for reinforcement, it shall be of corrosion-resistant material such as stainless steel.

Carbon steel is not permitted to be used for wire braid reinforcement for hose. This prohibition is based on experience with hose that weakened as the carbon steel wire braid corroded.

5.9.6.3 Hose and quick connectors shall be approved.

5.9.6.4 Hose, hose connections, and flexible connectors used for conveying LP-Gas liquid or vapor at pressures in excess of 5 psig (34 kPag), and as provided in Section 6.19 regardless of the pressure, shall comply with 5.9.6.4(A) through 5.9.6.4(E).

(A) Hose shall be designed for a working pressure of at least 350 psig (2.4 MPag), with a safety factor of 5 to 1 and comply with ANSI/UL 569, *Standard for Pigtails and Flexible Hose Connectors*, or ANSI/UL 21, *Standard for LP-Gas Hose*.

In the 2011 edition, the requirement was revised to provide two standards for hose, which formerly appeared in the definition of *flexible connector*. They were relocated to Chapter 5 because it is not appropriate to include mandatory requirements in definitions. The provisions of 5.9.6.4(A) for hose, hose connections, and flexible connectors apply only to those involved with pressures in excess of 5 psig (34 kPag). Requiring continuous marking permits identification of short pieces of hose used as connectors. In the 2008 edition, the word *propane* was substituted for *LP-Gas* to carry out the intent for international industry identification.

(B) Hose shall be continuously marked to provide at least the following information:

(1) LP-GAS HOSE or LPG HOSE
(2) Maximum working pressure
(3) Manufacturers' name or coded designation
(4) Month or quarter and year of manufacture
(5) Product identification

(C) Hose assemblies, after the application of couplings, shall have a design capability of not less than 700 psig (4.8 MPag).

The words *design capability* have been carefully chosen to convey the committee's intent that hose assemblies be capable of withstanding the anticipated pressure and that testing is an option. If testing is done, such assemblies must be pressure-tested at 120 percent of the maximum working pressure of the hose, which is required to be at least 350 psig (2.4 MPag).

(D) If a pressure test is performed, such assemblies shall be pressure tested at 120 percent of the maximum working pressure [350 psig (2.4 MPag) minimum] of the hose.

Note that pressure testing of hose is not required. Because the maximum hose working pressure is 350 psig (2.4 MPag), this optional testing is done at 420 psig (2.9 MPag).

(E) Hose assemblies shall be leak tested at the time of installation at not less than the operating pressure of the system in which they are installed.

5.9.6.5 Hoses at a pressure of 5 psig (34 kPag) or less in agricultural buildings not normally occupied by the public shall be designed for the working pressure of the system and shall be constructed of material resistant to the action of LP-Gas.

Paragraph 5.9.6.5 is an exception to the requirements of 5.9.6.4 for hose used in agricultural applications operating at a maximum pressure of 5 psig.

5.9.6.6 Hoses or flexible connectors used to supply LP-Gas to utilization equipment or appliances shall be installed in accordance with the provisions of 6.9.6 and 6.20.3.

5.10 Reserved

5.11 Internal Valves. (Reserved)

5.12 Valves Other Than Container Valves

5.12.1 Pressure-containing metal parts of valves shall be of steel, ductile (nodular) iron, malleable iron, or brass.

(A) Ductile iron shall meet the requirements of ASTM A 395, *Standard Specification for Ferritic Ductile Iron Pressure-Retaining Castings for Use at Elevated Temperatures,* or equivalent.

(B) Malleable iron shall meet the requirements of ASTM A 47, *Standard Specification for Ferritic Malleable Iron Castings,* or equivalent.

(C) All materials used, including valve seat discs, packing, seals, and diaphragms, shall be resistant to the action of LP-Gas under service conditions.

What is meant by "resistant to the action of LP-Gas" in 5.12.1(C)?
FAQ ▶

The requirement in 5.12.1(C) uses language that is found in other areas of the code (e.g., 5.7.1.1, 5.7.1.4, and 5.9.6.1) to establish performance criteria for materials. The material must be resistant to LP-Gas such that it will not degrade, decompose, warp, or otherwise deteriorate to the point that it can no longer serve its intended function safely. Although this "criterion" is certainly subjective, the code relies upon product and material standards to establish more quantifiable performance criteria. For example, ANSI/UL 125, *Standard for Valves for Anhydrous Ammonia and LP-Gas (Other than Safety Relief)* [25], provides testing criteria to establish the resistance of materials used in valves to the action of LP-Gas. Product standards of this type include tests intended for newly produced products and not intended to verify that products in use are suitable for continued use. Good judgment should be used in the selection of tests.

5.12.2 Valves shall have a service pressure rating as specified in Table 5.9.4.1.

5.12.3 Manual shutoff valves, emergency shutoff valves, excess-flow check valves, and backflow check valves used in piping systems shall comply with the provisions for container valves.

5.12.4 Emergency shutoff valves shall be approved and shall incorporate all of the following means of closing:

(1) Automatic shutoff through thermal (fire) actuation
(2) Manual shutoff from a remote location
(3) Manual shutoff at the installed location

The emergency shutoff valve (ESV) is a key valve in the protection of liquid transfer operations at bulk plants and industrial plants. Two ESVs from different manufacturers are shown in Exhibit 5.49. The installation requirements for these emergency shutoff valves are located in Section 6.12. The actuating means for remote shutoff is not specified. Electrical, mechanical, and pneumatic systems are all used. Many systems use a pneumatic valve with a plastic gas tubing system in which the tubing itself acts as a fusible element. When the tubing melts due to high temperatures (from a fire), it releases the pressure holding the valve open, and the flow of fuel is stopped. Note, however, that the plastic tubing must fail to hold pressure at 250°F (121°C) or less, as it must release the pressure even if the fire does not impinge on it. The failure point cannot increase to a temperature above 250°F as it ages or is exposed to weather or the sun. The ESV pneumatic operator can be fitted with a fuse plug that will allow any pressure in the line to escape before the temperature reaches 250°F. Regardless of whether continuous tubing or a discrete fusible element is used, thermal activation must be located within 5 ft (1.5 m) of the point established in 6.12.6. If the ESV is closed remotely by a cable attachment, it is recommended that the remote closing feature of the ESV be operated occasionally to verify proper operation, especially in winter. Cables can become disabled if they lie in water that freezes. Also, the entire system must be tested at least annually. (See 6.12.9.)

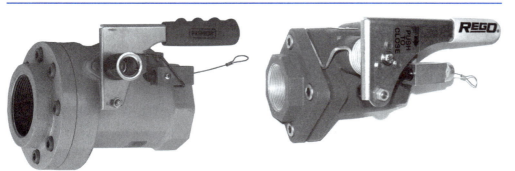

EXHIBIT 5.49 Two Emergency Cutoff Valves. [Courtesy of Emerson Process Management Regulator Technologies Inc. (left) and Engineered Controls International, Inc. (right)]

The committee issued formal interpretations on the intent of the requirements for emergency shutoff valves, after a propane company was cited for not complying with all of the requirements for the installation of an emergency shutoff valve that was not required by the code. The code was revised in the 2004 edition to address this subject with the addition of a new Section 4.4. Readers are referred to the commentary on Section 4.4 for more information.

5.12.5 Where fusible elements are used, they shall have a melting point not exceeding 250°F (121°C).

5.12.6 Valves in polyethylene piping systems shall be manufactured from thermoplastic materials listed in ASTM D 2513, *Standard Specification for Thermoplastic Gas Pressure Pipe, Tubing and Fittings,* that have been shown to be resistant to the action of LP-Gas and comply with ASTM D 2513. Valves in polyamide piping systems shall be manufactured from polyamide material as defined in ASTM D 2513. Metallic valves in polyethylene and polyamide piping systems shall be protected to minimize corrosion in accordance with Section 6.16.

5.12.7 Valves shall be recommended for LP-Gas service by the manufacturer.

5.13 Hydrostatic Relief Valves

5.13.1 Hydrostatic relief valves designed to relieve the hydrostatic pressure that can develop in sections of liquid piping between closed shutoff valves shall have pressure settings not less than 400 psig (2.8 MPag) or more than 500 psig (3.5 MPag), unless installed in systems designed to operate above 350 psig (2.4 MPag).

A hydrostatic pressure relief valve is shown in Exhibit 5.50. It is usually a small valve, because there is no capacity requirement for a hydrostatic relief valve in the code. Hydrostatic pressure relief valves usually equipped with a ¼ in. male National Pipe Thread (MNPT) inlet connection. Hydrostatic pressure relief valves are required by Section 6.13 to be installed in sections of piping that can be isolated between positive shutoff valves or other devices that stop liquid flow.

EXHIBIT 5.50 Hydrostatic Relief Valve. (Courtesy of Engineered Controls International, Inc.)

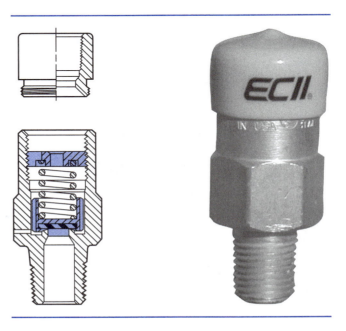

Hydrostatic pressure relief devices have a set point between 400 psig and 500 psig (2.8 MPag and 3.5 MPag) for piping systems with a design pressure of 350 psig (2.4 MPag). This pressure difference (400 psig vs. 350 psig) does not pose a problem for the piping because 350 psig represents the maximum operating pressure at the maximum operating temperature of the piping. Because the actual operating temperature of LP-Gas systems is much less than the maximum temperature, the system is capable of withstanding much higher pressures.

It is significant to note that piping systems are designed for an operating pressure of 350 psig, whereas ASME containers are usually designed for a maximum working pressure of 250 psig. This lower value is why pressure relief valves for ASME containers are rated at 250 psig.

◄ FAQ
Why are hydrostatic relief valves required to be set at a higher activation pressure than pressure relief valves?

5.13.2 Hydrostatic relief valves for use in systems designed to operate above 350 psig (2.4 MPag) shall have settings not less than 110 percent or more than 125 percent of the system design pressure.

If the design pressure of the piping system exceeds 350 psig (2.4 MPag), hydrostatic relief valves must be set to operate between 110 percent and 125 percent of the system design pressure, because it is not practical to specify the hydrostatic pressure relief valve to operate exactly at the system design pressure of the piping. The hydrostatic pressure relief valve minimum is set to operate above the piping system pressure to minimize unnecessary operation, and the maximum is well below piping system burst pressure. The design pressure of propane piping systems can be higher than 350 psig if a positive displacement pump with a discharge pressure in excess of 350 psig is used. Such pumps are not normally used in the United States and Canada, but are used in other parts of the world.

5.14 Reserved

5.15 Reserved

5.16 Reserved

5.17 Equipment

Section 5.17 provides requirements for propane equipment, such as pumps, compressors, vaporizers, regulators, and other devices used to regulate, transfer, or vaporize propane.

5.17.1 General.

5.17.1.1 This section shall apply to pressure-containing metal parts of LP-Gas equipment.

5.17.1.2 The service pressure rating of equipment shall be in accordance with Table 5.17.1.2.

5.17.1.3 Equipment shall be fabricated of materials that are compatible with LP-Gas under service conditions and shall be in accordance with Table 5.17.1.3.

(A) Pressure-containing metal parts shall be made from the following materials:

(1) Steel
(2) Ductile (nodular) iron (ASTM A 395, *Standard Specification for Ferritic Ductile Iron Pressure-Retaining Castings for Use at Elevated Temperatures,* or ASTM A 536, *Standard Specification for Ductile Iron Castings,* Grade 60-40-18 or 65-45-12)

TABLE 5.17.1.2 *Service Pressure Rating*

Fluid	Pressure	Equipment Design Pressure
LP-Gas vapor	≤20 psig (≤138 kPag)	Maximum anticipated pressure
	20 psig–125 psig (138 kPag–0.9 MPag)	125 psig (0.9 MPag)
	> 125 psig (>0.9 MPag)	250 psig (1.7 MPag) or the anticipated pressure, whichever is higher
LP-Gas liquid	≤250 psig (≤1.7 MPag)	250 psig (1.7 MPag)
	> 250 psig (>1.7 MPag)	350 psig (2.4 MPag) or the anticipated pressure, whichever is higher

TABLE 5.17.1.3 *Materials for Equipment Used in LP-Gas Service*

Equipment Material	Service Condition
Steel Ductile (nodular) iron (ASTM A 395, *Standard Specification for Ferritic Ductile Iron Pressure-Retaining Castings for Use at Elevated Temperatures,* or ASTM A 536, *Standard Specification for Ductile Iron Castings,* Grade 60–40–18 or 65–45–12) Malleable iron (ASTM A 47, *Standard Specification for Ferritic Malleable Iron Castings*) Higher strength gray iron (ASTM A 48, *Standard Specification for Gray Iron Castings,* Class 40B) Brass Materials equivalent to 5.17.1.3(A)(1) through 5.17.1.3(A)(5) in melting point, corrosion resistance, toughness, and strength	Pressure-containing metal parts
Cast iron	Not to be used as a material of construction for strainers or flow indicators
Aluminum	For approved meters, approved regulators, and indirect vaporizers
Zinc (ASTM B 86, *Standard Specification for Zinc-Alloy Die Casting*)	For approved regulators
Nonmetallic materials	Not to be used for upper or lower casings of regulators

(3) Malleable iron (ASTM A 47, *Standard Specification for Ferritic Malleable Iron Castings*)
(4) Higher strength gray iron (ASTM A 48, *Standard Specification for Gray Iron Castings,* Class 40B)
(5) Brass
(6) Materials equivalent to 5.17.1.3(A)(1) through 5.17.1.3(A)(5) in melting point, corrosion resistance, toughness, and strength

(B) Cast-iron shall not be used as a material of construction for strainers or flow indicators.

(C) Aluminum shall be used only for cylinders, gaskets, regulators, approved meters, and indirect electric vaporizers.

Note that despite the history of widespread aluminum use in products other than those listed in 5.17.1.3(C), the requirement restricts the use of aluminum because of its significantly lower melting point compared to brass and steel.

(D) Zinc shall be used for approved regulators only, complying with ASTM B 86, *Standard Specification for Zinc-Alloy Die Casting*.

(E) Nonmetallic materials shall not be used for upper or lower casings of regulators.

Materials used in equipment components must be suitable for use with LP-Gas. Equipment should not be purchased until the manufacturer has verified its suitability.

Restrictions on the use of cast iron in 5.17.1.3(B) reflect its tendency to crack under low temperature conditions and under fire control conditions when heated and suddenly cooled (for example, by water). The use of metals, such as aluminum and zinc, which melt at less than 1000°F (538.8°C), is restricted to situations in which their failure will not constitute an undue hazard. The prohibition of plastic for use in regulator casings reflects a concern for the material melting during fire conditions, allowing gas to flow freely and feed the fire.

Note that zinc can be used only in pressure regulators. Prior to the 2008 edition, the use of zinc in regulators was required to comply with ASTM B 86, *Standard Specification for Zinc-Alloy Die Casting* [26], but other uses were not specifically prohibited. The restriction was imposed because of the low melting point of zinc, which is 787°F (419°C) (by comparison, the melting point of copper is 1984°F (1084°C). The use of zinc in regulators is allowed because of a long history of safe use. Note that metals become structurally unusable at about one-half their melting point in degrees Fahrenheit. Refer to the commentary following 5.7.1.2 for information on this subject.

5.17.2 Pumps.

Pumps shall be designed for LP-Gas service.

It is important that pumps be designed and built for use with LP-Gas. There are many types of pumps, and some of these may not work satisfactorily in propane service. If necessary, the pump manufacturer can be contacted to determine if the pump is recommended for propane service and if it is capable of a discharge pressure higher than 350 psig (2.4 MPag). If the latter is the case, provisions must be made either to limit the pressure to 350 psig (2.4 MPag) or to design the system for the higher pressure.

Because pumps deliver a liquefied gas that will vaporize if the pressure drops even slightly, LP-Gas pumps are either positive displacement pumps or special types of centrifugal pumps, such as regenerative turbine pumps. (See Exhibits 5.51 through 5.54.) Standard centrifugal pumps may "vapor lock" easily and thus are ineffective. There are other types of pumps that can be used effectively for LP-Gas service, but they are not currently used in the United States. If required, such a pump can be used by referring to the Equivalency section (Section 1.5), and providing documentation to the authority having jurisdiction that the pump provides equivalent safety to those designed for LP-Gas service.

Prior to the 1998 edition, the discharge pressure of propane pumps was limited to 350 psig (2.4 MPag). This limitation was based on practice in the U.S. propane industry, in which the pumps used did not exceed this pressure. A proposal was made to delete the restriction based both on the use of pumps with higher discharge pressures in Mexico and other countries, and on the fact that this restriction was not based on safety, but reflected practice. Pumps and piping systems can be safely designed and operated at pressures above 350 psig (2.4 MPag).

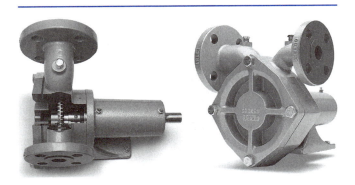

 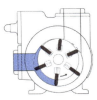 

Vanes move out, trapping liquid at the pump inlet.

Liquid is transferred toward the outlet between the vanes.

As the vanes move back into their slots, liquid is discharged through the outlet.

EXHIBIT 5.51 *(Left) A Continuous Duty, Regenerative Turbine Pump. (Right) A Positive Displacement Sliding Vane Pump Designed for Stationary and Truck Applications such as Loading and Unloading Single and Dual Bobtails. (Courtesy of Corken, Inc., a member of Liquid Controls Group)*

EXHIBIT 5.52 *Operation of Sliding Vane Pump. (Courtesy of Blackmer, a Dover Company)*

EXHIBIT 5.53 *Gear Pump. (Courtesy of Smith Precision Products Company, Inc.)*

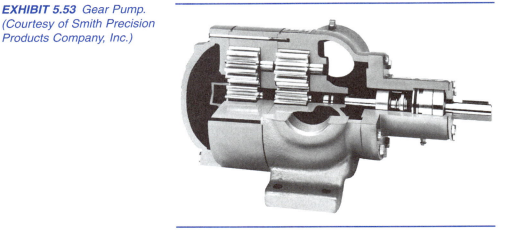

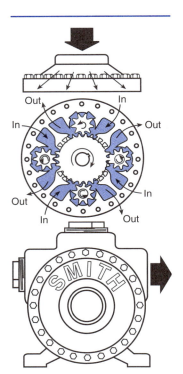

EXHIBIT 5.54 *Operation of Gear Pump. (Courtesy of Smith Precision Products Company, Inc.)*

5.17.3 Compressors.

5.17.3.1 Compressors shall be designed for LP-Gas service.

Care should be taken in selecting compressors designed for LP-Gas service. Compressors designed for noncombustible gases may not provide the required leak protection for flammable LP-Gases.

Compressors are used to transfer liquid by pumping vapor from the receiving storage containers into the supply transport truck or railcar that is supplying the LP-Gas. Increasing pressure in the vapor space of the supply container while at the same time lowering the pressure in the receiving container forces liquid from the supply tank to the receiving container. This type of loading or unloading operation is preferred when it is impractical or impossible to use liquid pumps, such as when unloading railroad tank cars. Tank cars have all fittings installed at the top in the protective tank car dome. The use of pumps is impractical because of the extended length of piping to the bottom of the tank car plus the additional hose and piping to the pump suction, which results in pump cavitation and reduced capacity. When compressors are used to unload railroad tank cars, it is common practice to reverse the vapor flow from the compressor with a three-way valve after all liquid is removed from the tank car, and recover a large amount of the remaining vapor in the tank car. Normally, this vapor recovery continues until the pressure in the tank car is about 30 psig (207 kPag). Refer to Exhibit 7.7 for an illustration of liquid transfer using a compressor.

5.17.3.2 Compressors shall be constructed or shall be equipped with auxiliary devices to limit the suction pressure to the maximum for which the compressor is designed.

Exhibit 5.55 shows a compressor complete with motor and all accessories.

5.17.3.3 Compressors shall be constructed or shall be equipped with auxiliary devices to prevent the entrance of LP-Gas liquid into the compressor suction.

Because all liquids, including liquid LP-Gas, are for all practical purposes noncompressible, liquid must not be allowed to enter an operating compressor. If it does, the compressor will probably be damaged and may fail. A number of compressors manufactured for LP-Gas service include relief devices built into the cylinder head to prevent destruction of the compressor in case small amounts of liquid are allowed to enter. Continuously operating relief devices, however, eventually will damage the compressor.

Several float-operated devices, as shown in Exhibit 5.56, are designed to prevent liquid from entering the compressor. The liquid trap shown on the left is a standard trap with a mechanical float assembly and drain valve. The trap in the center shows an automatic liquid trap with one NEMA 7 liquid-level switch for compressor shutdown and a drain valve. The trap on the right is an ASME Code-stamped automatic liquid trap with two NEMA 7 liquid-level switches for compressor shutdown and an alarm. The trap shown on the right is equipped with a relief valve, pressure gauge, demister pad, and drain valve. Some manufacturers use these types of liquid traps, others simply use a large receiver as a liquid trap on the suction side of the compressor.

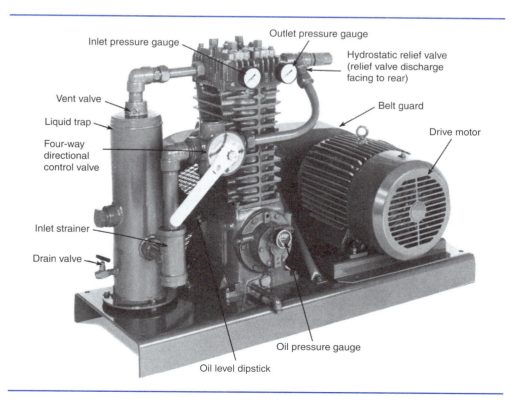

EXHIBIT 5.55 Compressor with Protection Devices. (Courtesy of Blackmer, a Dover Company)

EXHIBIT 5.56 *Compressor Liquid Traps. (Courtesy of Corken, Inc., a member of Liquid Controls Group)*

5.17.3.4 Portable compressors used with temporary connections shall not require means to prevent liquid entrance into the compressor suction.

Portable compressors are exempt from the requirement to prevent liquid LP-Gas from entering a compressor, because the temporary connections used are empty at the time they are connected and thus usually prevent liquid from entering the compressor. Also, portable units are operated under continuous surveillance by an operator.

5.17.4 Reserved.

5.17.5 Meters.

5.17.5.1 Vapor meters of the tin or brass case type of soldered construction shall not be used at pressures in excess of 1 psig (7 kPag).

Meters are designed for either vapor or liquid service. Vapor meters are commonly used where one propane container serves more than one customer in vapor service (e.g., in an apartment house or mobile home park, or where vapor service to an industrial user or farm is provided from a tank where a propane company loads bobtails). Liquid meters are commonly used on bobtails, at bulk plants, at dispensing stations, and on transports that deliver to large accounts.

There are several meter technologies in propane use, including positive displacement meters, turbine meters, mass meters, and ultrasonic meters.

• Positive displacement meters are intended for liquid service. They operate by forcing the liquid to travel through metering chambers that have a precise, known volume. The number of times the chambers are filled and emptied is counted, resulting in a direct volume measurement.

• Turbine meters can be designed for either (but not both) vapor or liquid service. The flowing product rotates blades within the known volume turbine meter body. The number of times the blades rotate is counted, resulting in a direct volume measurement.

- Mass meters can be designed for either (but not both) vapor or liquid service. As the flowing product passes through vibrating tubes, the phase of the vibration changes in direct proportion to the mass of the flowing product. This permits a direct mass measurement utilizing the coriolis effect principle.

- Ultrasonic meters can be designed for either (but not both) vapor or liquid service. Ultrasonic pulses are transmitted through the flow, and the difference in propagation between various transmission paths is used to calculate the average flow velocity across a known volume section of pipe or meter. This permits a direct volume measurement.

About three-quarters of the states require that meters and registers used to deliver product to paying customers (other than contract sales) be controlled under the states' weights and measures programs. Specifically, this requires

1. "Type approval" to National Institute of Standards and Technology (NIST) Handbook 44 [27] by the National Type Evaluation Program (NTEP), operated by the National Conference on Weights and Measures (NCWM)
2. Field calibration in the final installation by a person or agency approved by the state

Several positive displacement meters and a few mass flow meters are type-approved for LP-Gas delivery. A master meter is often used for field calibration. Some states require the use of a prover, a precisely calibrated container, to calibrate the meter. Meters tested for type approval and on the initial field testing must have errors within ±0.6 percent. Subsequent meter errors must be within ±1.0 percent. Under NTEP rules, vehicle-mounted metering systems must be equipped with a delivery ticket printer and all meters must have a provision for sealing such that an adjustment to the measuring element cannot be made without breaking the security seal.

The meter shown in Exhibit 5.57 is a positive displacement liquid meter. Note the differential back pressure valve located at the right (downstream), which is required by 6.24.3.5. The item to the left (upstream) is the vapor eliminator, which, working with the differential backpressure valve, prevents anything but liquid from being measured and delivered. The measuring chamber is between these units and has a register, or display of the quantity delivered, mounted above it.

EXHIBIT 5.57 *Positive Displacement Liquid Meter. (Courtesy of Corken, Inc., a member of Liquid Controls Group)*

5.17.5.2 Vapor meters of the die cast or iron case type shall not be used at any pressure higher than the working pressure for which they are designed and marked.

5.17.5.3 Liquid meters shall be installed so that the meter housing is not subject to excessive strains from the connecting piping. Where used to provide flexibility in the fixed piping system, flexible connectors shall not exceed 36 in. (1 m) in total length.

The design of a liquid meter installation on cargo tank motor vehicles must take into account the vibration typically experienced on cargo tank motor vehicles to avoid potential failure of the meter housing or liquid piping. Where vibration is anticipated, flexible connectors can be used. The term *flexible connector* is defined as follows:

> **3.3.23 Flexible Connector.** A short [not exceeding 60 in. (1.52 m) overall length] piping system component that is fabricated from a flexible material and equipped with connections at both ends.

Note that while a flexible connector is limited in length to 60 in. (1.52 m) in the definition, the more specific requirement in this paragraph limits flexible connectors used with meters to 36 in. (1 m).

5.17.6 Engines.

Engines used to drive portable pumps and compressors shall be equipped with exhaust system spark arresters and shielded ignition systems.

FAQ ▶
Are internal combustion engines acceptable to drive portable compressors?

Internal combustion engines have been used safely to drive portable pumps, as shown in Exhibit 5.58, as well as portable compressors. This requirement is included in the code to provide specific guidance for the selection of portable engines for these uses.

EXHIBIT 5.58 *Portable LP-Gas–Fueled Engine-Driven Pump. (Courtesy of Smith Precision Products Company, Inc.)*

The use of portable internal combustion engines has resulted in a disproportionate number of interpretation requests. These sometimes follow a local prohibition by enforcement officials on the use of internal combustion engines, because of the belief that "explosion-proof" motors or engines must be used. This confusion is understandable because Table 6.22.2.2, Electrical Area Classification, Part F, requires that the area within 15 ft (4.6 m) of an outdoor pump or vapor compressor be a Class I, Division 2 area. The following information is relevant in applying Table 6.22.2.2:

- Table 6.22.2.2 applies only to fixed electrical equipment and wiring and not to portable equipment.

• Internal combustion engines that are in good working order and are equipped with the required accessories are not a source of ignition. LP-Gas releases have occurred without causing ignition where cars have driven into, stalled, and coasted out of vapor clouds of LP-Gas that have been accidentally released [28].

The fact that these devices are portable indicates that, in many cases, they will be operated by an internal combustion engine. Subsection 5.17.6 requires the same level of protection for internal combustion engines driving portable pumps as for operating compressors.

5.17.7 Sight Flow Indicators.

Where installed, sight flow indicators shall either be the simple observation type or be combined with a backflow check valve.

Sight flow indicators are used when it is necessary to visually verify the flow of liquid LP-Gas through a piping system. (See Exhibits 5.59 and 5.60.) These indicators are found at cargo tank vehicle and railroad tank car loading and unloading facilities.

EXHIBIT 5.59 *Sight Flow Indicator with Backflow Check Valve. (Courtesy of Engineered Controls International, Inc.)*

EXHIBIT 5.60 *Flow Indicator with Backflow Check Valve. (Courtesy of Emerson Process Management Regulator Technologies Inc.)*

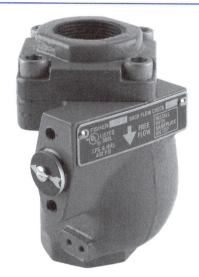

 No flow— when pointer is down, there is no flow in system

 Erratic flow— unstable position indicates vapor or cavitation

 Full flow— when pointer is in position shown, there is flow in system

5.18 Reserved

5.19 Reserved

5.20 Appliances

In the United States, Canada, and other economically developed countries, there are standards for LP-Gas and natural gas appliances. In many instances, private or governmental listing agencies have achieved an increasing level of safety for these appliances by evaluating them against these standards or through the exercise of their judgment. Because of these requirements, it has been unnecessary to provide detailed technical coverage in NFPA 58. Such coverage could create correlation problems. Therefore, NFPA 58 coverage has been limited to the following situations:

• Equipment not addressed in separate standards. The coverage may be due either to a small number or limited use of appliances or to the use of appliances in an environment under the control of specialists. Neither situation warrants the level of activity necessary to develop a separate standard.

• Coverage needed as an interim measure. It takes a considerable period of time to develop a separate standard, and frequently such a standard cannot be promulgated unless the use of the appliance is at least permitted by NFPA 58.

In such instances, although NFPA 58 serves a useful function, the technical committee must be careful to amend the code as necessary when a separate, specific code or standard is developed. Such amendment could include deletion of provisions in NFPA 58. In general, a specific appliance standard should govern in recognition of its more complete and intensive coverage, provided the code has suitable status. Many of the appliances addressed in Section 5.20 are actually installed under circumstances that place them under the scope of NFPA 54, *National Fuel Gas Code,* rather than NFPA 58, in accordance with 1.3.2(6) of NFPA 58.

5.20.1 New residential, commercial, and industrial LP-Gas consuming appliances shall be approved.

The manufacturing of most residential and commercial LP-Gas appliances is covered by specific codes and standards. The largest of these documents are the ANSI Z21/83 series of standards promulgated by the ANSI Z21/83 Committee on Performance and Installation of Gas-Burning Appliances and Related Accessories [29]. (A partial list of current ANSI Z21/83 standards is included at the end of this chapter.) Underwriters Laboratories Inc. (UL) also develops some product standards. Most authorities having jurisdiction accept appliances listed to these standards, as well as to UL requirements. UL requirements are found in published UL standards and outlines of investigations. Outlines of investigations contain requirements used by UL to investigate products prior to their publication in a UL standard.

The requirement for approval does not include listing. The decision is that of the authority having jurisdiction, and many authorities usually prefer, or even require, listed appliances and equipment whenever they are available. Refer to 3.2.1 for the definition of *approved* and to 3.2.5 for the definition of *listed*.

Some appliance manufacturers have their appliances listed by organizations acceptable to most authorities having jurisdiction. One of these organizations is CSA America Inc. In addition, many LP-Gas appliances and equipment are listed by UL and other organizations. In the industrial area, FM Global listings are frequently found for industrial heat-processing equipment.

5.20.2 Any appliance originally manufactured for operation with a gaseous fuel other than LP-Gas shall not be used with LP-Gas unless it is converted to use LP-Gas and is tested for performance with LP-Gas before being placed into use.

FAQ ▶

Can a natural gas appliance be used with LP-Gas?

Most appliances are produced to operate on one fuel gas only, but can be converted to operate on another fuel gas. The conversion of a natural gas appliance to LP-Gas, for example, is not a complex operation, but it must be done safely by a qualified, trained individual. When in doubt about such cases, check with the manufacturer or the listing laboratory. The appliance manufacturer may offer conversion parts for the appliance to use another fuel gas.

Some appliances are designed to operate on more than one fuel. These appliances are easily converted by turning a knob or lever. One example of such an appliance is a water heater designed for installation in manufactured housing. Other appliances must be converted in accordance with the appliance manufacturer's instructions to operate safely on LP-Gas.

5.20.3 Unattended heaters used inside buildings for animal or poultry production or care shall be equipped with approved automatic devices to shut off the flow of gas to the main burners and to pilots, if used, in the event of flame extinguishment or combustion failure.

5.20.4 Approved automatic devices to shut off the flow of gas to the main burners and pilots shall not be required in structures without enclosing walls with the approval of the authority having jurisdiction.

The provisions in 5.20.3 and 5.20.4 are examples of the use of NFPA 58 to fill a gap created by the absence of a specific code. (See the commentary following 5.20.1.) The use of unattended heaters inside a building used for animal or poultry production can be a hazard if the flame is extinguished and a flame safety device is not part of the appliance, because the released gas can be ignited. Because buildings used for animals in warmer climates may not have enclosing walls, NFPA 58 does not mandate the safety device with portable heaters used in these buildings, although the code requires local officials to approve such installations.

5.20.5 Appliances using vaporizing burners shall comply with 5.21.5.

5.20.6* Appliances used in mobile homes and recreational vehicles shall be approved for such service.

A.5.20.6 See NFPA 1192, *Standard on Recreational Vehicles*, for additional requirements where used on recreational vehicles.

At present, recreational vehicles are covered by NFPA 1192, *Standard on Recreational Vehicles* [11], and this requirement is consistent with the requirements of NFPA 501, *Standard on Manufactured Housing* [30]. New manufactured homes sold in the United States are covered under federal regulations issued by the Department of Housing and Urban Development (HUD). The HUD regulations apply only to the manufacture of such homes. This provision applies to appliances installed in manufactured homes after the original manufacture and sale.

5.20.7* LP-Gas appliances used on commercial vehicles shall be approved for the service.

(A) Gas-fired heating appliances and water heaters shall be equipped with automatic devices designed to shut off the flow of gas to the main burner and the pilot in the event the pilot flame is extinguished.

(B) Catalytic heating appliances shall be equipped with an approved automatic device to shut off the flow of gas in the event of combustion failure.

(C) Gas-fired heating appliances and water heaters to be used in vehicles intended for human occupancy shall be designed for complete separation of the combustion system and the living space.

(D) If the separation between the combustion system and the living space is not integral with the appliance, it shall be provided in accordance with installation requirements in 6.23.7.5.

A.5.20.7 Combustion air inlets and flue gas outlets should be included in the listing of the appliance.

The requirements of 5.20.7(A) and (B) are basic gas safety requirements.

Where gas appliances are used in vehicles intended for people, there are concerns about proper removal of the products of combustion and the possibility of carbon monoxide production. The requirements of 5.20.7(C) and (D) are intended to ensure proper appliance operation, to remove the products of combustion from vehicles, and to prevent production of carbon monoxide. Carbon monoxide alarms are not required by NFPA 58, but they are required by NFPA 1192, *Standard on Recreational Vehicles*, for recreational vehicles with gas appliances.

5.21 Vaporizers, Tank Heaters, Vaporizing Burners, and Gas–Air Mixers

FAQ ▶
What is the difference between a vaporizer and a tank heater?

This section addresses equipment that is used for providing an external heat source to assist in the vaporization of LP-Gas. LP-Gas cannot be burned by an appliance while it is a liquid. It must be converted to a vapor in order to be utilized. Any liquid will vaporize at its boiling point if heat is added to it. The amount of heat required per unit of propane is known as *the latent heat of vaporization*. From Table B.1.2(a), propane requires about 773 Btu of energy to vaporize one gallon of liquid.

In a typical propane fuel distribution system, the latent heat of vaporization is provided by the surroundings of the tank: for aboveground tanks, it is the surrounding air; for belowground tanks, the surrounding soil. As soon as vapor is removed from the tank, the pressure inside the container drops and the liquid begins to boil to try to achieve equilibrium between the vapor pressure of the liquid at its temperature and the vapor pressure in the container. In order to vaporize, however, the liquid must be provided with heat energy. In those locations where the surrounding air or soil is too cold to provide sufficient heat to the liquid through the walls of the container, an external source of heat, such as a vaporizer, tank heater, or vaporizing burner, can be used.

A vaporizer is a piece of equipment that is really a heat exchanger. It transfers heat from an external source, such as a flame or electric resistance heating element to liquid LP-Gas as it passes through the vaporizer. Liquid enters the vaporizer at one point, and vapor leaves it at another point. A tank heater, on the other hand, never contacts liquid LP-Gas. A tank heater provides a source of heat energy to the walls of an LP-Gas container, which in turn transfer the heat into the liquid within the container. The source of heat can be an electric resistance heating element or a gas-fired burner. See 3.3.70 for definitions of various types of vaporizers.

5.21.1 Reserved.

5.21.2 Indirect Vaporizers.

5.21.2.1 Indirect vaporizers shall be constructed in accordance with the applicable provision of the ASME Code for a MAWP of 250 psig (1.7 MPag) and shall be permanently and legibly marked with the following:

(1) Marking required by the ASME Code
(2) Maximum allowable working pressure and temperature for which designed
(3) Name of the manufacturer

Indirect vaporizers are heat exchangers that transfer heat from a "working" fluid heated outside the vaporizer to the liquid LP-Gas. The working fluid can be air, water or other fluid, steam, or other heated liquid. Indirect vaporizers must be built in accordance with the ASME *Boiler and Pressure Vessel Code* [1] to a MAWP of 250 psig (1.7 MPag). This pressure is the same as that required by the ASME Code for most propane containers. If the vaporizer is designed to be fed by a pump, the MAWP must be equal to or greater than the maximum pump discharge pressure.

5.21.2.2 Indirect vaporizers that have an inside diameter of 6 in. (152 mm) or less are exempt from the ASME Code and shall not be required to be marked. They shall be constructed for a MAWP of 250 psig (1.7 MPag).

Small indirect vaporizers that have an inside diameter of 6 in. (152 mm) or less must also be designed for an operating pressure of 250 psig (1.7 MPag), but need not be inspected by an ASME-approved inspector or marked with the code marking. This requirement is consistent with the ASME *Boiler and Pressure Vessel Code*, which is not applicable to pressure vessels with an inside diameter of 6 in. (152 mm).

5.21.2.3 Indirect vaporizers shall be provided with an automatic means to prevent the passage of liquid through the vaporizer to the vapor discharge piping.

Liquid cannot be allowed to leave a vaporizer through the vapor discharge piping at any time during normal operation or during a malfunction of the vaporizer. If the vaporizer is sized and functioning properly, liquid will not be present in the vapor outlet. The requirement is intended to protect against a vaporizer malfunction in which the heat source of the vaporizer fails or the unit becomes overloaded. The hazard of liquid being present in the vapor piping is that none of the vapor control equipment, such as regulators, control valves, and burners, is designed to handle liquid. Liquid passing through vapor regulators will flash to vapor and can result in significantly increased flame size that can present a fire hazard. In addition, if liquid water is present anywhere downstream of the vaporizer, it can be frozen to form ice by the vaporizing liquid, which can then plug a regulator.

5.21.2.4 Indirect vaporizers, including atmospheric-type vaporizers using heat from the surrounding air or the ground and of more than 1 qt (0.9 L) capacity, shall be equipped with a spring-loaded pressure relief valve providing a relieving capacity in accordance with 5.21.9. Fusible plug devices shall not be used.

The prohibition of fusible plugs (instead of spring-loaded pressure relief valves) is included because fusible plugs (and rupture discs) cannot re-close and will allow the entire contents of the system to be discharged into the atmosphere in case of overpressure. Spring-loaded pressure relief valves can minimize the quantity of vapor discharged because they close after the pressure returns to a normal level.

5.21.2.5 Indirect atmospheric-type vaporizers of less than 1 qt (0.9 L) capacity shall not be required to be equipped with pressure relief valves but shall be installed in accordance with 6.21.2.11.

Vaporizers with an internal capacity less than 1 qt (0.9 L) are not required to be provided with a relief valve, but must be installed in accordance with 6.21.2.11 and Table 6.21.3.6 (which is referenced in 6.21.2.11). The table provides minimum separation distances between direct-fired vaporizers and specific exposures that may present a source of ignition.

5.21.3 Direct-Fired Vaporizers.

5.21.3.1 Design and construction of direct-fired vaporizers shall be in accordance with the applicable requirements of the ASME Code for the working conditions to which the vaporizer will be subjected, and the vaporizer shall be permanently and legibly marked with the following:

(1) Markings required by the ASME Code
(2) Maximum vaporizing capacity in gallons per hour
(3) Rated heat input in British thermal units per hour
(4) Name or symbol of the manufacturer

All direct-fired vaporizers must be constructed in accordance with the ASME Code, which includes inspection and marking. (See Exhibits 5.61 and 5.62.) The term *markings required by the code* refers directly to the markings required by the ASME Code. The term *outside surface* used in the marking requirements of the ASME Code does not refer to the surface of the outside of the cabinet or enclosure. The outside surface is that surface that can be in

EXHIBIT 5.61 *Direct-Fired Vaporizer. (Courtesy of Ransome Manufacturing)*

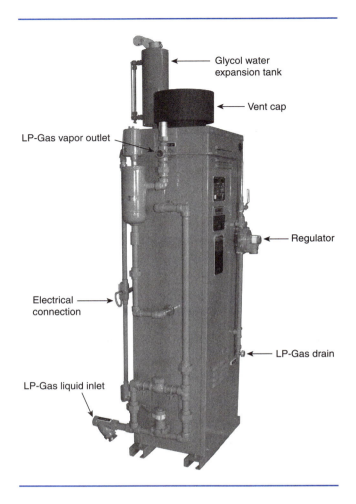

Glycol water expansion tank

Vent cap

LP-Gas vapor outlet

Regulator

Electrical connection

LP-Gas drain

LP-Gas liquid inlet

contact with LP-Gas on the inside and the atmosphere on the outside, which could add to the vaporization rate of the vaporizer if subjected to fire outside the vaporizer. The outside surface includes the heat exchange surface plus the top of the vessel.

5.21.3.2 Direct-fired vaporizers shall be equipped with a spring-loaded pressure relief valve that provides a relieving capacity in accordance with 5.21.9.

5.21.3.3 The relief valve shall be located so as not to be subject to temperatures in excess of 140°F (60°C). Fusible plug devices shall not be used.

The relief valve must be located or protected in such a manner that it will not be subjected to a temperature above 140°F (60°C). This requirement is included because a direct-fired unit contains a burner that can create high temperatures from the products of combustion, and excessive temperature near a relief valve could destroy the seats and damage the mechanism inside the relief valve.

The prohibition against fusible plugs and rupture discs addresses the same concerns as the similar provisions for indirect vaporizers. (See the commentary on 5.21.2.4.)

5.21.3.4 Direct-fired vaporizers shall be provided with automatic means to prevent the passage of liquid from the vaporizer to its vapor discharge piping.

5.21.3.5 A means for manually turning off the gas to the main burner and pilot shall be provided.

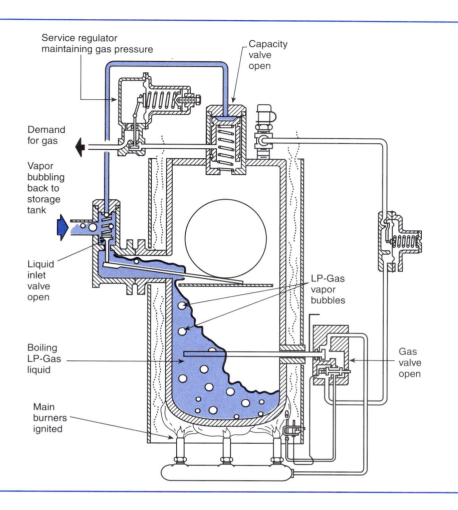

Service regulator
maintaining gas pressure

Capacity
valve
open

Demand
for gas

Vapor
bubbling
back to
storage
tank

Liquid
inlet
valve
open

LP-Gas
vapor
bubbles

Boiling
LP-Gas
liquid

Gas
valve
open

Main
burners
ignited

EXHIBIT 5.62 *Direct-Fired Vaporizer Operating on Demand. (Courtesy of National Propane Gas Association)*

5.21.3.6 Direct-fired vaporizers shall be equipped with an automatic safety device to shut off the flow of gas to the main burner if the pilot light is extinguished.

5.21.3.7 If the pilot flow exceeds 2000 Btu/hr (2 MJ/hr), the safety device shall also shut off the flow of gas to the pilot.

5.21.3.8 Direct-fired vaporizers shall be equipped with a limit control to prevent the heater from raising the product pressure above the design pressure of the vaporizer equipment, and to prevent raising the pressure within the storage container above the pressure specified in the first column of Table 5.2.4.2 that corresponds with the design pressure of the container (or its ASME Code equivalent). *(See notes to Table 5.2.4.2.)*

Paragraph 5.21.3.6 reiterates the requirement for a 100 percent shutoff for the gas burner. This requirement is not unique to a direct-fired vaporizer burner.

Although 5.21.3.8 implies that the limit control should be a pressure-operated device, temperature-sensing devices are also commonly used for this purpose. Controlling the temperature of the vapor output of the vaporizer is a practical method of preventing the burner from overheating the vapor. The vaporizer cannot produce a vapor pressure higher than that provided to the liquid inlet of the vaporizer. If the pressure in the vaporizer were to exceed the inlet pressure, the flow of liquid into the vaporizer would stop and would be reversed into the supply container.

This provision to limit the pressure within the storage container was intended to protect a type of system seldom used today, one in which liquid is fed by gravity from a storage container into a vaporizer and vapor is returned from the vaporizer back into the top of the tank. Vapor is removed from the tank through a pressure regulator into the distribution system. With this type of system, it is theoretically possible, in extremely hot weather, for a vaporizer connected in this manner to raise the pressure in the container. A severe increase in pressure, of course, would cause the container pressure relief valves to operate, discharging vapor that, because of the presence of the direct-fired vaporizer, would almost certainly become ignited. Again, temperature controls in the vaporizer prevent this type of malfunction from taking place. Accordingly, a temperature control is the only practical type of control to satisfy this requirement.

5.21.4 Tank Heaters.

Subsection 5.21.4 covering tank heaters was revised in the 2011 edition by changing the title from "Direct-Fired Tank Heaters" to "Tank Heaters," because the requirements are applicable to all types of tank heaters. In addition, 5.21.4.8 was relocated from Chapter 6 because it is a product requirement and not an installation requirement.

5.21.4.1 Direct gas-fired tank heaters shall be designed exclusively for outdoor aboveground use and so that there is no direct flame impingement upon the container.

5.21.4.2 Tank heaters shall be approved and shall be permanently and legibly marked with the following:

(1) Rated input to the burner in British thermal units per hour
(2) Maximum vaporizing capacity in gallons per hour
(3) Name or symbol of the manufacturer

5.21.4.3 The tank heater shall be designed so that it can be removed for inspection of the entire container.

5.21.4.4 The fuel gas supply connection to a direct gas-fired tank heater shall originate in the vapor space of the container being heated and shall be provided with a manually operated shutoff valve at the heater.

5.21.4.5 The heater control system of direct gas-fired tank heaters shall be equipped with an automatic safety shutoff valve of the manual reset type arranged to shut off the flow of gas to both the main and pilot burners if the pilot flame is extinguished.

5.21.4.6 Where installed on a container exceeding 1000 gal (3.8 m³) water capacity, the heater control system shall include a valve to automatically shut off the flow of gas to both the main and pilot burners if the container becomes empty of liquid.

5.21.4.7 Tank heaters shall be equipped with a limit control to prevent the heater from raising the pressure in the storage container to more than 75 percent of the pressure shown in the first column of Table 5.2.4.2 that corresponds with the MAWP of the container (or its ASME *Boiler and Pressure Vessel Code* equivalent).

Direct gas-fired tank heaters are no longer widely used, but there is no reason to prohibit them. These heaters attach to the bottom of the container to heat the container shell at the point of contact, thereby heating the liquid product inside. In order to avoid the loss of container strength, however, no flame impingement on the container itself can occur. Most of these units were constructed so that they can be easily removed to inspect for possible corrosion of the container at the point of installation. Direct gas-fired tank heaters must be engineered so that there will be automatic means to prevent overheating the product in the container, to shut off the heater in case the container empties, and to shut off the gas flow to the heater in case the pilot light goes out. The need for direct-fired tank heaters exists only in very cold climates, where temperatures can go below about −40°F (−40°C). Below this temperature, container pressure will be negative and no gas will flow from the container.

5.21.4.8 If the tank heater is of the electric immersion type, the heater shall be automatically de-energized when the liquid level falls below the top of the heater.

5.21.5 Vaporizing Burners.

Vaporizing burners are a form of direct-fired vaporizers where the vaporizing burner is actually part of the appliance. The vapor is produced by heating liquid propane in a heat exchanger in the burner. Only a small portion of the heat is used to vaporize the liquid, and the appliance delivers the remainder as useful heat energy. Vaporizing burners are used where large quantities of vapor are required — for example, for crop dryers and for smaller applications such as for roofing equipment and portable weed burners. The need for a separate vaporizer and pressure controls is eliminated by the use of a vaporizing burner, with corresponding cost savings. The minimum design pressure must be 250 psig (1.7 MPag), which is the same as that of the container. The coils and jackets must be made of ferrous metals or high-temperature alloys because of the high temperature created by the flame.

The vaporizing burner shown in Exhibit 5.63, which is incorporated into a portable weed burner, operates by delivering liquid through a tube (shown in the cutaway), which is encased in a shell with a concentric space between them. The liquid then reverses direction and proceeds back between the tube and the shell in a spiral flow pattern induced by the wire. This spiral flow pattern creates turbulence and enhances heat transfer from the flame impinging on the outside of the shell to the vaporizing liquid. The vapor created is then consumed in the burner that encloses the area outside of the concentric shell and tube.

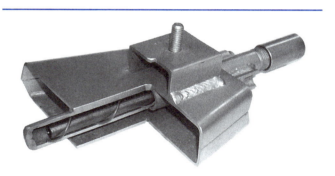

EXHIBIT 5.63 *Vaporizing Burner. (Courtesy of Flame Engineering, Inc.)*

5.21.5.1 Section 5.21 shall not apply to engine fuel vaporizers or to integral vaporizer burners, such as those used with weed burning equipment and tar kettles.

This new paragraph clearly states that the requirements for vaporizing burners are intended for large vaporizing burners and are not intended to be applied to small vaporing burners that are used on portable equipment, such as those used with small engines and weed burners. It would be impractical to incorporate the safety devices required for larger vaporizing burners into the smaller units incorporated into portable appliances.

5.21.5.2 Vaporizing burners shall be constructed with a pressure rating of 250 psig (1.7 MPag), with a safety factor of 5 to 1.

5.21.5.3 The vaporizing burner or the appliance in which it is installed shall be permanently and legibly marked with the following:

(1) Maximum burner input in British thermal units per hour
(2) Name or symbol of the manufacturer

5.21.5.4 Vaporizing coils or jackets shall be made of ferrous metals or high-temperature alloys.

5.21.5.5 The vaporizing section shall be protected by a relief valve, located where it will not be subject to temperatures in excess of 140°F (60°C), and with a pressure setting sufficient to protect the components involved but not lower than 250 psig (1.7 MPag).

5.21.5.6 The relief valve discharge shall be directed upward and away from the component parts of the vaporizing burner. Fusible plug devices shall not be used.

5.21.5.7 A valve shall be provided to turn off the gas supply to the main burner and the pilot.

5.21.5.8 Vaporizing burners shall be provided with an automatic safety device to shut off the flow of gas to the main burner and pilot in the event the pilot is extinguished.

5.21.5.9* Dehydrators and dryers utilizing vaporizing burners shall be equipped with automatic devices both upstream and downstream of the vaporizing section. These devices shall be installed and connected to shut off in the event of excessive temperature, flame failure, and, if applicable, insufficient airflow.

A.5.21.5.9 See NFPA 61, *Standard for the Prevention of Fires and Dust Explosions in Agricultural and Food Processing Facilities*, for ignition and combustion controls applicable to vaporizing burners associated with grain dryers.

The intent of 5.21.5.9 is to provide safety devices installed at the specified locations that will automatically shut down the dehydrator or dryer (used to dry grain in agricultural applications) in order to avoid unsafe situations that could lead to overheating of the equipment.

5.21.5.10 Pressure-regulating and control equipment shall be so located or so protected to prevent its exposure to temperatures above 140°F (60°C), unless designed and recommended for use at a higher temperature by the manufacturer.

5.21.5.11 Pressure-regulating and control equipment located downstream of the vaporizing section shall be designed to withstand the maximum discharge temperature of hot vapor.

Because liquid is fed to the vaporizing burner, a hydrostatic relief valve in the burner is required to protect the piping when the burner is shut off and the liquid is trapped in the burner and piping. Without a hydrostatic relief valve, an increase in the temperature of the liquid would create a pressure that could burst the heater or the attached piping. Vaporizing burners are often used for temporary heating during construction or emergencies and are left unattended. As a result, the careful use of automatic equipment is extremely important. The units are also used as agricultural product dehydrators and dryers and should be properly equipped with automatic devices on both the inlet and the outlet of the vaporizer section of the burner. Because these units are generally portable, extreme care must be taken in their placement and to ensure that fuel connections are not subjected to mechanical damage.

5.21.6 Waterbath Vaporizers.

The waterbath vaporizer differs from a direct-fired vaporizer because there is no flame impingement on the vaporizer chamber itself. The flame is directed into the water under pressure, creating a boiling, swirling effect. This turbulence results in excellent heat transfer to the water. The liquid propane is circulated in pipes in the water chamber and is heated by the turbulent hot water.

Waterbath vaporizers are used where a very high vaporization requirement exists. The use of waterbath vaporizers in LP-Gas systems under the scope of NFPA 58 is not common. Waterbath vaporizers are more commonly found in larger systems under the scope of NFPA 59, *Utility LP-Gas Plant Code* [31].

5.21.6.1 The vaporizing chamber, tubing, pipe coils, or other heat exchange surface containing the LP-Gas to be vaporized, hereinafter referred to as heat exchanger, shall be constructed in accordance with the applicable provisions of the ASME Code for a MAWP of 250 psig (1.7 MPag) and shall be permanently and legibly marked with the following:

(1) Marking required by the ASME Code
(2) MAWP and temperature for which the heat exchanger is designed
(3) Name or symbol of the manufacturer

A waterbath vaporizer is a cross between a direct-fired vaporizer and an indirect-fired vaporizer. The portion of such a unit that contains and vaporizes the LP-Gas must be built in accordance with the provisions of the ASME Code for a minimum pressure of 250 psig (1.7 MPag) and be marked as required in 5.21.6.1. Again, vaporizers less than 6 in. (152 mm) in diameter are exempt from the ASME Code but must be constructed to a minimum MAWP of 250 psig (1.7 MPag). (See also the commentary following 5.21.2.1.) The same automatic safety controls used with indirect-fired and direct-fired vaporizers to prevent liquid passing into the vapor discharge piping must be provided. The immersion heater that provides heat to the waterbath must not be in contact with the LP-Gas heat exchanger surface in order to avoid overheating it. It also must be equipped with an automatic shutoff device to prevent overheating of the liquid waterbath, should the level of the waterbath liquid fall below the top of the heat exchanger.

5.21.6.2 Heat exchangers for waterbath vaporizers that have an inside diameter of 6 in. (150 mm) or less are exempt from the ASME Code and shall not be required to be marked.

5.21.6.3 Heat exchangers for waterbath vaporizers shall be provided with automatic control to prevent the passage of liquid through the heat exchanger to the vapor discharge piping. This control shall be integral with the vaporizer.

5.21.6.4 Heat exchangers for waterbath vaporizers shall be equipped with a spring-loaded pressure relief valve that provides a relieving capacity in accordance with 5.21.9. Fusible plug devices shall not be used.

5.21.6.5 Waterbath sections of waterbath vaporizers shall be designed to prevent pressure from exceeding the design pressure.

5.21.6.6 The immersion heater that provides heat to the waterbath shall be installed so as not to contact the heat exchanger.

Note that 5.21.6.6 was revised in the 2011 edition to delete reference to fuels that can be used.

5.21.6.7 A control to limit the temperature of the waterbath shall be provided.

5.21.6.8 Gas-fired immersion heaters shall be equipped with an automatic safety device to shut off the flow of gas to the main burner and pilot in the event of flame failure.

5.21.6.9 Gas-fired immersion heaters with an input of 400,000 Btu/hr (422 MJ/hr) or more shall be equipped with an electronic flame safeguard and with programming to provide for prepurge prior to ignition, proof of pilot before the main burner valve opens, and full shutdown of the main gas valve and pilot upon flame failure.

5.21.6.10 The heat source shall be shut off if the level of the heat transfer medium falls below the top of the heat exchanger.

5.21.7 Reserved.

5.21.8 Gas–Air Mixers.

Gas–air mixers are devices used to "pre-mix" air into LP-Gas so that it can be used as a direct replacement for natural gas. Mixers are used most often in "stand-by" systems, which provide an alternate source of fuel to a facility when the primary source (natural gas) is not available. The concept of this system is to mix air with LP-Gas such that the concentration of the propane–air mix is still greater than the higher limit of flammability. The mixture is then distributed through the piping system to the fuel-burning equipment. As the mixture enters the appliance, it is mixed further with air to bring it within the flammability range.

The entire subsection on gas–air mixers (5.21.8) contains requirements that are intended to prevent both flammable gas–air mixers from entering the system and air from entering the gas distribution line.

5.21.8.1 Gas–air mixers shall be designed for the air, vapor, and mixture pressures to which they are subjected.

5.21.8.2 Gas–air mixers that are capable of producing combustible mixtures shall be equipped with safety interlocks on both the LP-Gas and air supply lines to shut down the system if combustible limits are approached.

5.21.8.3 In addition to the interlocks required in 5.21.8.2, a method shall be provided to prevent air from accidentally entering gas distribution lines without LP-Gas being present. Gas-mixing control valves installed in the air and LP-Gas supply lines that fail closed when actuated by safety trip devices shall meet this requirement.

5.21.8.4 Check valves shall be installed in the air and LP-Gas supply lines close to the mixer to minimize the possibility of backflow of gas into the air supply lines or of air into the LP-Gas system. Gas-mixing control valves installed in the air and LP-Gas supply lines that fail closed when actuated by safety trip devices shall meet this requirement.

5.21.8.5 Gas–air mixers that utilize the kinetic energy of the LP-Gas vapor to entrain air from the atmosphere, and are so designed that maximum air entrained is less than 85 percent of the mixture, shall comply with the following:

(1) They shall be exempt from the interlock provisions in 5.21.8.2 through 5.21.8.4.
(2) They shall be equipped with a check valve at the air intake to prevent the escape of gas to atmosphere when shut down.

5.21.8.6 Gas–air mixers of the type specified in 5.21.8.5 receiving air from a blower, compressor, or any source of air other than directly from the atmosphere shall prevent air without LP-Gas, or mixtures of air and LP-Gas within the flammable range, from entering the gas distribution system accidentally.

The flammable limits for propane in air are approximately 2.15 percent to 9.6 percent. A venturi-type blender or mixer uses the kinetic energy of the LP-Gas vapor to entrain air from the atmosphere. Venturi mixers should be designed so that the maximum air entrained is less than 85 percent of the mixed gas formed. The mixture of 85 percent or less air with the remainder of 15 percent or more LP-Gas is not flammable (a flammable mixture is between 90.4 percent and 97.85 percent air), and the interlock provisions of 5.21.8.2 are specifically excluded, as are 5.21.8.3 and 5.21.8.4. A check valve at each air inlet venturi prevents any LP-Gas from escaping into the atmosphere when the system is not operating.

To prevent malfunction, most venturi mixers have high and low vapor pressure interlocks, high and low mixed LP-Gas–air pressure interlocks, and a low incoming vapor temperature interlock. The latter interlock prevents any LP-Gas liquid from entering the gas–air mixer. To prevent any possible vapor condensation problems, the mixer should be located as close as possible to the vaporizer, and the mixer vapor inlet connection should be sloped back toward the vaporizer vapor outlet connection. If this is not practical, a drip leg with heater should be installed or the piping can be heated to prevent low temperatures by wrapping electric tracer heater cable around such piping. Unless ambient temperatures are very low, insulating the piping may be sufficient to prevent too low a temperature of the gas vapor.

Usually venturi mixers employing atmospheric air have an output mixture pressure of less than 3 psig (21 kPag) in order to produce a viable mixed gas. For mixer pressures greater than 3 psig, air under pressure must be supplied to the venturi mixer from an external source, such as a plant air system or an air compressor. For this external air supply system, a method must be provided on the venturi mixer to prevent 100 percent air or a flammable LP-Gas–air mixture from being supplied to the user's gas distribution piping. This prevention is usually accomplished through special controls and low air pressure interlocks that will shut down the mixer in the event of a malfunction.

Consideration also should be given to the method of installation of the downstream piping for the LP-Gas–air mixture from the mixer to the plant utilization point, relative to possible recondensation of the LP-Gas–air mixture. For most cases, when commercial propane is the LP-Gas–air feedstock and the LP-Gas–air mixture is at or below 100 psig (690 kPag), there would be no recondensation of propane in the mix until the mixed gas temperature is lowered to 20°F (−7°C) or colder. But if commercial butane is the LP-Gas–air feedstock, considerable care must be taken in the mixed gas piping design. At a mixed gas pressure of 10 psig (69 kPag), butane will start to condense at about 20°F.

Thus, for higher mixed gas send-out pressures, condensation of butane will occur at higher temperatures; for example, at 50 psig (345 kPag), the condensation temperature is about 60°F (15.6°C). Heat for the butane–air mix gas line must thus be provided in the form of heat tracing or insulation to guard against possible butane condensation.

The venturi-type gas–air mixer uses the kinetic energy of LP-Gas vapor to entrain air from the atmosphere to provide a desired LP-Gas–air mixture. Each venturi includes a solenoid valve on the gas inlet side of the venturi. A controller monitors the outlet manifold pressure of the mixer and energizes each individual solenoid valve to provide a constant flow to the process at the required pressure. The air inlet of the venturi includes a backflow check valve to prevent the escape of LP-Gas to the atmosphere. In addition, the controller is interlocked with a low-vapor inlet temperature switch and high- and low-pressure switches on the gas inlet at gas–air outlet manifolds.

Exhibit 5.64 shows a high-pressure [greater than 3 psig (21 kPag)] variable-orifice type of gas–air mixer with inlet air and gas control trains located in a room complying with Chapter 10. Both the air and gas control trains include pressure regulators, check valves, shutoff valves, safety shutoff valves, temperature and pressure indicators, and high-low pressure switches. Process air for the mixer may be furnished from an air compressor in a separate room or from the plant air system. Air and gas pressures are both regulated to equal pressures on the inlet to the mixer. The variable orifice in the mixing valve will open and

EXHIBIT 5.64 *High-Pressure Orifice Gas–Air Mixer. (Courtesy of Al-Gas SDI)*

close, depending on flow, to provide a constant Btu value. The propane–air mixture is then distributed within the plant process piping.

5.21.9 Vaporizer Pressure Relief Valve.

The minimum rate of discharge in cubic feet of air per minute for pressure relief valves for LP-Gas vaporizers, either of the indirect type or direct-fired type, shall comply with 5.21.9(A) through 5.21.9(C).

(A) Based on conservative heat transfer calculations (assuming that the vaporizing chamber is liquid full), the maximum vapor generating capacity (rate) shall be determined when maximum heat is available. That vapor rate shall be converted to an equivalent air rate.

The phrase "conservative heat transfer calculations" is explained by the statement in parentheses. This calculation is considered conservative because the maximum vapor rate occurs when propane is in contact with the entire surface of the vaporizer and maximum heat is available.

Pressure relief valves and all other safety devices are designed for the worst-case condition, which is fire exposure over the entire surface of the vessel. In the event of fire exposure to a vaporizer, the pressure relief valve must be sized to handle vapor produced as a result of the liquid heating by both the normal heat source and the fire exposure.

Subsection 5.21.9 provides three separate criteria for sizing pressure relief valves for use on vaporizers. The size of the pressure relief valve must comply with each criterion that is applicable to the specific vaporizer.

(B) If the vaporizer is direct fired or if a substantial exterior surface is in contact with the LP-Gas, the sum of the vaporizer surface and the LP-Gas wetted exterior surface shall be used in conjunction with Table 5.7.2.6 to determine the required relief valve capacity.

(C) The minimum rate of discharge in cubic feet of air per minute for pressure relief valves for LP-Gas vaporizers, of either the indirect type or direct-fired type, shall be at least 150 percent of the rated vaporizing capacity.

REFERENCES CITED IN COMMENTARY

1. ASME *Boiler and Pressure Vessel Code*, 2007 edition, American Society of Mechanical Engineers, New York, NY.
2. AAR *Manual of Standards and Recommended Practices*, Section C, Part III, "Specifications for Tank Cars," 2007, Association of America Railroads, Washington, DC.
3. ANSI/UL 132, *Standard for Safety Relief Valves for Anhydrous Ammonia and LP-Gas*, 2007 edition, Underwriters Laboratories Inc., Northbrook, IL.
4. CSA B149.2, *Propane Storage and Handling Code,* 2010 edition, Canadian Standards Association, Mississauga, Ontario, Canada.
5. Title 49, Code of Federal Regulations, Part 178.50, U.S. Government Printing Office, Washington, DC.
6. Title 49, Code of Federal Regulations, Part 178.68, U.S. Government Printing Office, Washington, DC.
7. *National Board Inspection Code*, 2007 edition, National Board of Boiler and Pressure Vessel Inspectors, Columbus, OH.
8. CGA C-6, *Standard for Visual Inspection of Steel Compressed Gas Cylinders*, 2009 edition, Compressed Gas Association, Chantilly, VA.
9. CGA C-6.3, *Guidelines for Visual Inspection and Requalification of Low Pressure Aluminum Compressed Gas Cylinders*, 2005 edition, Compressed Gas Association, Chantilly, VA.
10. Title 49, Code of Federal Regulations, Part 180.213, U.S. Government Printing Office, Washington, DC.

11. NFPA 1192, *Standard on Recreational Vehicles*, 2008 edition, National Fire Protection Association, Quincy, MA.

12. ASME E-119, *Standard Test Methods for Fire Tests of Building Construction and Materials*, 2009 edition, American Society for Testing and Materials, West Conshohocken, PA.

13. CGA S-1.1, *Pressure Relief Device Standards, Part I — Cylinders for Compressed Gases*, 2007 edition, Compressed Gas Association, Chantilly, VA.

14. CGA C-14, *Methods for Hydrostatic Testing of Compressed Gas Cylinders*, 2005 edition, Compressed Gas Association, Chantilly, VA.

15. Title 49, Code of Federal Regulations, Part 173.304(d)(3)(ii), U.S. Government Printing Office, Washington, DC.

16. ANSI/UL 2227, *Overfilling Prevention Devices*, 2008 edition, Underwriters Laboratories Inc., Northbrook, IL.

17. CGA V-1, *Standard for Compressed Gas Cylinder Valve Outlet and Inlet Connections*, 2008 edition, Compressed Gas Association, Chantilly, VA.

18. API 607, *Fire Test for Soft-Seated Quarter Turn Ball Valves*, 2008 edition, American Petroleum Institute, Washington, DC.

19. NFPA 54, *National Fuel Gas Code*, 2009 edition, National Fire Protection Association, Quincy, MA.

20. ANSI/UL 144, *Standard for LP-Gas Regulators*, 1999 edition, Underwriters Laboratories Inc., Northbrook, IL.

21. ANSI/UL 651, *Schedule 40 or 80 Rigid PVC Conduit*, 1995 edition, Underwriters Laboratories Inc., Northbrook, IL.

22. UL 1660, *Liquid-Tight Flexible Nonmetallic Conduit*, 2004 edition, Underwriters Laboratories Inc., Northbrook, IL.

23. UL 514B, *Conduit, Tubing, and Cable Fittings*, 2004 edition, Underwriters Laboratories Inc., Northbrook, IL.

24. ASTM D 2513, *Standard Specification for Thermoplastic Gas Pressure Pipe, Tubing, and Fittings*, 2007 edition, American Society for Testing and Materials, West Conshohocken, PA.

25. ANSI/UL 125, *Standard for Valves for Anhydrous Ammonia and LP-Gas (Other than Safety Relief)*, 2009 edition, Underwriters Laboratories Inc., Northbrook, IL.

26. ASTM B 86, *Standard Specification for Zinc-Alloy Die Casting*, 2009 edition, American Society for Testing and Materials, West Conshohocken, PA.

27. NIST Handbook 44, *Specifications, Tolerances, and Other Technical Requirements for Weighing and Measuring Devices*, 2006 edition, National Institute of Standards and Technology.

28. Isner, M. S. "Propane Tank Truck Incident, Eight People Killed, Memphis, TN, December 23, 1988," Fire Investigation Report, February 6, 1990, National Fire Protection Association, Quincy, MA.

29. ANSI Z21 and Z83 series standards, CSA-America, Cleveland, Ohio

    a. ANSI Z21.1, *Household Cooking Gas Appliances*, 2005 edition.
    b. ANSI Z21.5.1, *Gas Clothes Dryers, Volume I, Type 1, Clothes Dryers*, 2006 edition.
    c. ANSI Z21.5.2, *Gas Clothes Dryers, Volume II, Type 2, Clothes Dryers*, 2005 edition.
    d. ANSI Z21.10.1/CSA 4.1, *Gas Water Heaters, Volume I, Water Heaters with Input Ratings of 75,000 Btu per Hour or Less*, 2009 edition.
    e. ANSI Z21.10.3, *Gas Water Heaters, Volume III, Storage Water Heaters with Input Ratings Above 75,000 Btu per Hour, Circulating and Instantaneous Water Heaters*, 2004 edition.
    f. ANSI Z21.11.1, *Gas-Fired Room Heaters, Volume I, Vented Room Heaters*, 1991 edition.
    g. ANSI Z21.11.2b, *Gas-Fired Room Heaters, Volume II, Unvented Room Heaters*, 2004 edition.

h. ANSI Z21.11.3, *Propane-Fired Portable Heater Systems* (draft).

i. ANSI Z21.13/CSA 4.9, *Gas-Fired Low Pressure Steam and Hot Water Boilers*, 2005 edition.

j. ANSI Z21.19, *Refrigerators Using Gas Fuel*, 2002 edition.

k. ANSI Z21.40.1/CSA 2.91A-M97, and Addenda, Z21.40.1A and B, *Gas-Fired Heat-Activated Air Conditioning and Heat Pump Appliances*, 1997 edition (Revised 2002).

l. ANSI Z21.42, *Gas-Fired Illuminating Appliances*, 2004 edition.

m. ANSI Z21.47/CSA 2.3, *Gas-Fired Central Furnaces*, 2006 edition.

n. ANSI Z21.50, *Vented Decorative Gas Appliances*, 2007 edition.

o. ANSI Z21.56, *Gas-Fired Pool Heaters*, 2006 edition.

p. ANSI Z21.57, *Recreational Vehicle Cooking Gas Appliances*, 2005 edition.

q. ANSI Z21.58, *Outdoor Cooking Gas Appliances*, 2007 edition.

r. ANSI Z21.60, *Decorative Gas Appliances for Installation in Solid-Fuel Burning Fireplaces*, 2004 edition.

s. ANSI Z21.61, *Toilets, Gas-Fired*, 1983 (Reaffirmed, 2004) edition.

t. ANSI Z21.86, *Vented Gas-Fired Space Heating Appliances*, 2008 edition.

u. ANSI Z83.4, *Non-Circulating Direct Gas-Fired Industrial Air Heaters*, 2004 edition.

v. ANSI Z83.7, *Gas-Fired Construction Heaters*, 2000 (Reaffirmed 2005) edition.

w. ANSI Z83.8, *Gas Unit Heaters and Gas-Fired Duct Furnaces*, 2009 edition.

x ANSI Z83.11, *Gas Food Service Equipment*, 2006 edition.

y. ANSI Z83.19, *Gas-Fired High-Intensity Infrared Heaters*, 2001 edition.

z. ANSI Z83.20, *Gas-Fired Low-Intensity Infrared Heaters*, 2008 edition.

30. NFPA 501, *Standard on Manufactured Housing*, 2010 edition, National Fire Protection Association, Quincy, MA.

31. NFPA 59, *Utility LP-Gas Plant Code*, 2008 edition, National Fire Protection Association, Quincy, MA.

Installation of LP-Gas Systems

CHAPTER 6

Chapter 6 is organized by numbering many of the sections to align with the sections in Chapter 5, LP-Gas Equipment and Appliances. This alignment makes it easy to go from product to installation requirements, because they will carry similar numbering. For example, Section 6.9, Piping Systems, contains the requirements for the installation of piping systems, and Section 5.9, Piping (Including Hose), Fittings, and Valves, contains the requirements for all piping materials. Because of the alignment with Chapter 5, a number of sections in Chapter 6 are reserved (not used).

Chapter 6 includes all the information needed for the installation of the most commonly encountered LP-Gas systems and individual components. Systems that are installed on vehicles, that are highly specialized, or that are not as common have been separated into the following chapters:

- Chapter 9, Vehicular Transportation of LP-Gas
- Chapter 11, Engine Fuel Systems
- Chapter 12, Refrigerated Containers

Chapter 6 comprises the following sections:

- Scope — Includes both the scope of application and the scope of nonapplication of the chapter (See Section 6.1.)
- Location of Containers — A directory to specific text throughout the code that addresses the location of containers, whether installed for use or put into storage (See Section 6.2.)
- Container Separation Distances — Addresses the siting location of aboveground and underground containers, with respect to buildings, lot lines, public streets, and more (See Section 6.3.)
- Other Container Location Requirements — Addresses miscellaneous requirements with respect to the location of containers, including separation from utility installations, flammable and combustible liquids, other gas storage containers, and the construction of barriers around containers (See Section 6.4.)
- Location of Transfer Operations — Addresses the transfer of LP-Gas from one container to another by providing requirements for locating the point of liquid transfer with respect to potential sources of ignition and other hazards (See Section 6.5.)
- Installation of Containers — Provides requirements for the installation of all containers, including aboveground and underground stationary installations, exchange and stationary cylinder installations, and containers installed either horizontally or vertically (See Section 6.6.)
- Installation of Container Appurtenances — Addresses any hardware that is installed in an opening in a container, whether it is for liquid or vapor transfer, or even just to seal the container to maintain it as a pressure-containing vessel. Examples of appurtenances are service valves, relief valves, and plugs. (See Section 6.7.)
- Regulators — Provides requirements for installing vapor pressure regulation systems, including first- and second-stage regulators, line pressure regulators, and pressure relief valves (See Section 6.8.)

- Piping Systems — Provides requirements for installing piping systems, including sizing parameters, material-specific limitations on installation, and location-specific requirements (See Section 6.9.)
- Remote Shutoff Actuation — Provides the requirements for using LP-Gas as the pressure source for remote shutoff systems for internal valves and emergency shutoff valves (See Section 6.10.)
- Internal Valves — Provides the requirements for installing internal valves in containers, including ancillary safety hardware (See Section 6.11.)
- Emergency Shutoff Valves — Specifies the type and location of installations that are required to be protected by emergency shutoff valves, and also addresses the required safety activation devices (See Section 6.12)
- Hydrostatic Relief Valve Installation — States where hydrostatic relief valves are required to be installed (See Section 6.13.)
- Testing Piping Systems — Addresses the requirements for testing piping systems after assembly (See Section 6.14.)
- Installation in Areas of Heavy Snowfall — Addresses the protection of installations from the forces associated with heavy snowfall (See Section 6.15.)
- Corrosion Protection — Provides requirements where corrosion protection is required for LP-Gas systems (See Section 6.16.)
- Equipment Installation — Provides requirements for the installation of pumps, compressors, strainers, and meters (See Section 6.17.)
- Bulk Plant and Industrial LP-Gas Systems — Addresses the specific requirements for bulk plant and industrial systems, including requirements for gas distribution facilities, security and tampering protection, and electrical equipment requirements (See Section 6.18.)
- LP-Gas Systems in Buildings or on Building Roofs or Exterior Balconies — Provides detailed requirements for installing containers and systems in or on buildings. The requirements are listed according to the use, or occupancy, of the building. The section also addresses buildings under construction, those undergoing minor or major renovation, and installations used for temporary heating or cooking purposes. (See Section 6.19.)
- Installation of Appliances — Contains requirements for the installation of hose for portable appliances (See Section 6.20.)
- Vaporizer Installation — Addresses the installation of vaporizers, except for those used on vehicles (see Section 6.21 and Chapter 11, weed burners, or tar kettles. The section also covers spacing requirements for vaporizers from exposures such as "point of transfer" and property lines. (See Section 6.21.)
- Ignition Source Control — Provides requirements for the control of sources of ignition, such as electrical equipment, cigarettes, open flames, and other potential sources (See Section 6.22.)
- LP-Gas Systems on Vehicles (Other Than Engine Fuel Systems) — Addresses the requirements for LP-Gas systems on vehicles, but only those that are not part of the engine fuel system. Engine fuel systems are addressed in Chapter 11. (See Section 6.23.) This section also addresses appliances installed on vehicles. (See 6.23.7.)
- Vehicle Fuel Dispenser and Dispensing Stations — Addresses the location, installation, and operation of vehicle fuel dispensers and dispensing stations (See Section 6.24.)
- Fire Protection — Provides requirements for all fire protection for LP-Gas facilities. It addresses the planning for the response to inadvertent releases of LP-Gas, fire protection for LP-Gas containers, and "special" protection methods for containers, both active and passive. (See Section 6.25.)
- Alternate Provisions for Installation of ASME Containers — Provides requirements for using alternate methods of protecting installations, including burying and mounding containers, redundant fail-safe product control methods, and low emission transfer practices (See Section 6.26.)

6.1 Scope

Note that for most propane installations, both Chapters 5 and 6 must be used because both contain relevant requirements. The chapters are organized to enable the user to find the requirements easily. The sections in Chapters 5 and 6 have coordinated numbers; for example, the requirements for propane storage containers are located in Section 5.2, and the container installation requirements are located in Section 6.2. Note that when there are no equipment requirements in Chapter 5 for some of the installation subjects covered in Chapter 6, the equivalent section in Chapter 5 is reserved. For example, Section 6.3 covers container separation distances, but because there are no material requirements for separation distances, Section 5.3 is reserved.

6.1.1* Application.

This chapter shall apply to the following:

(1) Location and field installation of LP-Gas systems that use components, subassemblies, container assemblies, and container systems that are fabricated in accordance with Chapter 5
(2) Location of containers and liquid transfer systems
(3) Installation of container appurtenances and regulators
(4) Installation of piping (including flexible connectors and hose), hydrostatic relief valves, and piping service limitations
(5) Installation of equipment
(6) Testing of piping systems

A.6.1.1 Section 6.4 includes general provisions that are applicable to most stationary systems. Sections 6.5 through 6.13 extend and modify Section 6.4 for systems installed for specific purposes.

6.1.2 Nonapplication.

This chapter shall not apply to the following:

(1) Refrigerated containers
(2) Installation of systems used in the highway transportation of LP-Gas

Refrigerated containers are addressed in Chapter 12, and transportation of LP-Gas is addressed in Chapter 9.

6.1.3* Additional Features.

For any purpose or application addressed within the scope of this chapter, if the requirements of the chapter are met, any or all additional features or components of equipment not prohibited by the chapter shall be permitted to be used.

A.6.1.3 This installation of safety-enhancing equipment that is not otherwise required by the code is permitted by the code. This includes any device that performs a safety-related function even though the device is designed or designated to perform a required function. For example, if an emergency shutoff valve (ESV) is installed in a location where it is not required, and the installation is not intended to perform the function of an ESV but is to provide a function or feature that is available in the ESV, the valve is not required to comply with all of the closing requirements described in 5.12.4.

Subsection 6.1.3 results from a disagreement between a propane marketer and an official. The propane marketer installed an emergency shutoff valve in the liquid outlet of a container that was not required by the code to provide automatic shutoff in the event of fire at the container.

The authority having jurisdiction interpreted Section 6.10 as mandating that the remote actuation feature be installed. When this interpretation was brought to the committee's attention, they agreed that remote operation was not needed because the valve was not mandated and revised the code to so state.

6.2 Location of Containers

6.2.1 LP-Gas containers shall be located outside of buildings unless they are specifically allowed to be located inside of buildings.

6.2.2 LP-Gas containers shall be allowed in buildings only for the following applications:

(1) Cylinders as specifically provided for in Section 6.19
(2) Containers of less than 125 gal (0.5 m^3) water capacity for the purposes of being filled in buildings or structures complying with Chapter 10
(3) Containers on LP-Gas vehicles complying with, and parked or garaged in accordance with, Chapter 9
(4) Containers used with LP-Gas portable engine fuel systems shall comply with 11.15.1
(5) Containers used with LP-Gas stationary engine fuel systems shall comply with 11.15.2
(6) Containers used with LP-Gas–fueled industrial trucks complying with 11.13.4
(7) Containers on LP-Gas–fueled vehicles garaged in accordance with Section 11.16
(8) Cylinders awaiting use, resale, or exchange when stored in accordance with Chapter 8

Because propane is a flammable gas, NFPA 58 has always required that LP-Gas containers be located outdoors, with the stated exceptions in 6.2.2. A flammable gas leak outdoors dissipates much more quickly and with less chance of reaching a source of ignition than a leak occurring indoors.

FAQ ▶
Can I use or store my propane cylinder indoors?

The committee recognizes that there are a limited number of necessary uses of propane cylinders in buildings and structures, and these uses are listed in 6.2.2. These permitted uses are based on safeguards to minimize the possibility of a release of LP-Gas that can lead to ignition. The safeguards include limiting the size of the container, controlling the presence of ignition sources, and even designing the room or building to control its reaction to explosion or fire.

There are reports of fires and explosions caused by leakage from propane cylinders used indoors. In one Nevada incident, a maintenance worker at an apartment building brought a propane cylinder into the building to work away from the wind. He opened and closed the cylinder valve, and then lit a cigar with a match. The propane ignited, and the resulting fire caused $75,000 in damage [1].

Interestingly, some other countries (for example, some European nations) use LP-Gas in a totally different manner. In those countries, it is standard practice for LP-Gas containers to be located not only within buildings, but within multi-story apartment buildings, providing fuel for cooking and other applications where central heating systems are not utilized. The LP-Gas distribution system in these countries also has some differences in the manner in which LP-Gas is delivered. Most residences in those countries use LP-Gas cylinders that are exchanged rather than filled on site. Note that there may be significant differences in building construction, cylinder refilling, and cylinder filling practices between the United States (and Canada) and these other countries that allow different uses of cylinders.

In addition to the general prohibition on using cylinders indoors, it is also prohibited to store cylinders, either empty or full, inside a residential building. Requirements for storage of cylinders awaiting use or sale are located in Chapter 8, and there are exceptions for necessary uses in Chapter 8.

Storing cylinders indoors can be hazardous. In an incident in Old Fort, North Carolina, in 1996, a 100 lb (45 kg) cylinder fueled a furnace and was set indoors near the furnace. A spare cylinder was stored in the same space. The spare had been brought in from the cold, where it may have been overfilled. As it warmed, it vented and ignited, causing an explosion that blew out several windows and caused some fire damage.

6.3 Container Separation Distances

6.3.1* Containers installed outside of buildings, whether of the portable type replaced on a cylinder exchange basis or permanently installed and refilled at the installation, shall be located with respect to the adjacent containers, important building, group of buildings, or line of adjoining property that can be built upon, in accordance with Table 6.3.1, Table 6.4.2, Table 6.4.5.8, and 6.3.2 through 6.3.11.

TABLE 6.3.1 Separation Distances Between Containers, Important Buildings, and Line of Adjoining Property That Can Be Built Upon

Water Capacity per Container		Minimum Distances					
		Mounded or Underground Containers[a]		Aboveground Containers[b]		Between Containers[c]	
gal	m³	ft	m	ft	m	ft	m
<125[d]	<0.5[d]	10	3	0[e]	0[e]	0	0
125–250	0.5–1.0	10	3	10	3	0	0
251–500	>1.0–1.9	10	3	10	3	3	1
501–2,000	>1.9–7.6	10	3	25[f]	7.6	3	1
2,001–30,000	>7.6–114	50	15	50	15	5	1.5
30,001–70,000	>114–265	50	15	75	23		
70,001–90,000	>265–341	50	15	100	30	¼ of sum of	
90,001–120,000	>341–454	50	15	125	38	diameters of	
120,001–200,000	>454–757	50	15	200	61	adjacent	
200,001–1,000,000	>757–3785	50	15	300	91	containers	
>1,000,000	>3785	50	15	400	122		

[a] See 6.3.4.
[b] See 6.3.12.
[c] See 6.3.11.
[d] See 6.3.9.
[e] See 6.3.7, 6.3.8, and 6.3.9.
[f] See 6.3.3.

The requirement in 6.3.1 has been in NFPA 58 since the second edition. In the editor's opinion, it is the most important part of the code and the most widely used. The most commonly asked question NFPA staff receives on the code is, "Where do I put my tank in relation to. . . ?" This is not a simple question (note the length of commentary on this subject).

The provisions in Sections 6.3 through 6.5 and Section 6.25 provide requirements for the location of containers and the point of transfer into a container. These provisions should be studied together because there are some related requirements that address special cases to allow a reduction in the required separation distances provided in Table 6.3.1.

The siting criteria in 6.3.1 require that a container be located a specified distance from other containers, an important building or group of buildings, and a line of adjoining property that can be built upon. These separation distances are intended to reflect the relative exposure hazard of the container due to the presence of the items cited, and vice versa.

◄ **FAQ**
How close can propane containers be installed to a building or a property line?

The distances are based on a combination of the following factors:

- Potential hazard of LP-Gas
- Size and type of equipment used to contain it
- The possibility of leaks, which can ignite
- Need for fuel in buildings

The distances are not based on a "worst-case scenario" in which the LP-Gas container fails catastrophically, releasing its contents in a few seconds. Experience with LP-Gas containers at buildings over the more than 70 years that NFPA 58 has been published has not identified that such incidents occur.

Research has been conducted to evaluate the effects of radiant heat from fires on LP-Gas containers. This evaluation, the associated mathematical model, and detailed results with and without the effects of wind have been published in a peer-reviewed technical journal [2]. The results describe the maximum temperature attained by the vapor-wetted wall of a propane container exposed to heat radiation from an external, non-impinging fire, for various sized containers. The assumptions made in regard to the size and location of the external fire included the following:

- The fire used in the model was representative of a highly radiative liquid hydrocarbon pool fire. The value assumed for the heat radiation emanating from this liquid pool fire was greater than that from fires occurring due to the burning of wooden buildings, tires, forest trees, and other flammable liquids such as in oil fires, which burn with a high degree of smoke production.
- A fire diameter of 100 ft (30.5 m), which is larger than an average fire diameter, was used for a duration of 30 minutes.
- The edge of the fire was located at a distance from the container using the minimum separation distances from containers to buildings as required by Table 6.3.1 of NFPA 58 for each size of container.
- Convective cooling of the heated surface and the effects of reflective paint on the containers were included in the analysis.
- Bending of the fire plume toward the containers due to the effects of wind was also included.

The maximum temperatures calculated for the steel surface of the container in contact with vapor in different sizes of containers are presented in Commentary Table 6.1.

COMMENTARY TABLE 6.1 *Maximum Steel Container Surface Temperatures in Contact with Vapor Space Where Exposed to Fire*

Container Size (w.c.)		Maximum Temperature Attained in 30 min. Exposure	
gal	*m³*	*°F*	*°C*
1,000	3.8	660	349
2,000	7.6	648	342
4,000	15.1	507	264
12,000	45.4	507	264
18,000	68.1	437	225
30,000	114.0	384	195
60,000	227.0	340	171

The temperature at which the yield strength of steel of a propane tank begins to decrease is close to 800°F (427°C). Based on this, there is no threat of propane tank failure from radiant heat due to an external fire occurring at the minimum separation distances specified in Table 6.3.1 of NFPA 58.

Questions asked of the NFPA staff indicate continuing confusion with respect to two phrases that appear in the text of 6.3.1: "important building" and "line of adjoining property that can be built upon." The following commentary is intended to clarify these phrases.

Important Building. A building can be "important" for a number of reasons, including the following:

- Replacement value
- Human occupancy
- Value of the contents
- Vital role of its production equipment or business records to a business
- Effect of the building on product release and fire control activities by fire fighters and other emergency responders

Human occupancy in a building does not automatically make it important. Occupancy for brief periods, such as one might find in a garage while a vehicle is being loaded, should not be a factor in classifying a building as important.

Clearly, buildings that house assembly occupancies, such as theaters and churches, are "important" because the general public will be there, as well as at mercantile occupancies (stores). Homes, apartments, hotels, dormitories, and prisons should also be considered "important." Storage occupancies may not be considered "important" if workers only occasionally enter the building.

Buildings with characteristics that (1) hinder emergency responders from being able to gain access to a position where they can safely apply water to a tank or (2) act as an impediment to applying water should also be considered a part of this category. There is such a wide assortment of physical configurations of industrial and bulk plant sites that each location must be considered on its own. Items such as railroad tracks, containers for storage of other fuels, fences obstructing access from preferred directions, topography, and even rows of trees can present unique challenges for access and, with the location of buildings on congested sites, can by themselves, or in combination, make applying water on the tanks extremely difficult.

Line of Adjoining Property. Questions to NFPA staff on the application of "line of adjoining property that can be built upon" are most frequently on the application of local zoning ordinances. In many areas, local zoning laws prohibit building within a specified distance of a property line. In some areas, variances to these setbacks are easily obtained, whereas in other areas, variances are very difficult, if not impossible, to obtain. Any discrepancy in the zoning laws should be taken into account by the authority having jurisdiction when reviewing applications.

The effect of setbacks is that LP-Gas containers might be set closer to a property line than would be allowed without a setback. The intent of the code is to provide separation from buildings — those that are existing or those that could be built in the future — not an imaginary line. One useful method to provide the separation from buildings is to state a required separation from a property line. In some locations, particularly on small lots, the required separation from a building is difficult to provide. Being able to utilize part of the setback distance sometimes allows the container to be set closer to the property line, claiming some distance to the "line that can be built upon." However, it must be noted that setbacks can be problematic. In some locations, the setback may not apply to heat pumps, gas packs, air-conditioning units, and other devices that may be sources of ignition. Proper separation from those devices must be provided, as required elsewhere in this code, even though the setback might otherwise allow setting the container the required distance from the building.

In 1957, the NFPA technical committee issued Formal Interpretation LPG-5, concerning the phrase "line of adjoining property that may be built upon." This formal interpretation remains valid and is reproduced here and as a diagram in Exhibit 6.1. Paragraph B.6(b) in the

---

Formal Interpretation LPG-5

Reference: 3.2.2.2

The following interpretation of the *Standard for the Storage and Handling of Liquefied Petroleum Gases*, NFPA Standard No. 58, has been released by the Interpretation Subcommittee of the NFPA Committee on Gases following concurrence by the entire Committee on Gases.

Question: Does the quoted language in Section B.6(b) of NFPA Standard No. 58, 1957 Edition, when referring to the location of a domestic tank, mean the lot line of the property on which the tank is located or the center line of the street or alley, or is it intended that this language indicate the lot line of an adjoining property that may be built upon?

Answer: It is the Committee's opinion that the "Line of adjoining property which may be built upon" refers to the property boundaries of the plot adjacent to the one upon which the tank is located. This is illustrated in Figure 3.1 taking into consideration a condition that involves property on the other side of a street, highway, or other right of way. It is the Committee's opinion that the minimum distance limitation is from the tank to the property line where that property line is common to plots of ground of different ownership and would also apply between the tank and the property line of the far side of a street or other public right of way.

Issue Edition: 1957

1957 edition of NFPA 58 is the predecessor of the current 6.3.1 and Table 6.3.1. See also Exhibit 6.2, which has been included to provide additional illustrations to demonstrate multiple-container installations, including the provisions of 6.3.3.

In Table 6.3.1, note that the first column, Water Capacity per Container, means that the aggregate (total) capacity of multiple containers is not used when determining separation distances of containers to an important building, group of buildings, or line of adjoining property that can be built upon. The only time the aggregate capacity is used is when the water capacity of containers of less than 125 gal (0.5 m^3) exceeds 500 gal (1.9 m^3), as stated in 6.3.6. Use the capacity of the largest container in a group when using Table 6.3.1.

When separation distances are measured between aboveground containers, the measurement is made to the closest surface of the container. Separation distances between underground or mounded containers are made from the container surface (see 6.3.4.1). In addition, no part of an underground or mounded container may be less than 10 ft (3 m) from a building or line of adjoining property that can be built upon (see 6.3.4.2 and 6.26.2.3).

A.6.3.1 When applying Table 6.3.1 to cylinders, which have their capacities expressed in pounds, the first table entry, <125 gal (<0.5 m^3), includes all cylinders. Cylinders have a maximum capacity of 1000 lb or 119 gal (454 kg or 3.8 m^3) (water capacity).

6.3.2 When the provisions of 6.26.3 through 6.26.5 are met, the minimum distance from an ASME container to a building shall be reduced by one-half for ASME containers of 2001 gal through 30,000 gal (7.6 m^3 through 114 m^3) water capacity.

Subsection 6.3.2 recognizes the alternate installation requirements of 6.26.4 and 6.26.5 for low emission transfer and redundant fail-safe product control methods. In accordance with these subsections, the separation distance can be reduced. Section 6.26 is applicable to one container, 30,000 gal (114 m^3) maximum capacity, that is buried or mounded.

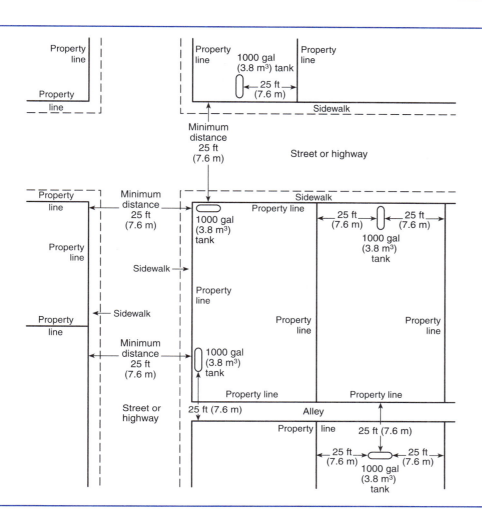

EXHIBIT 6.1 *Illustration of Separation Distances from Containers to the Line of Adjoining Property That Can Be Built Upon.*

6.3.3 The 25 ft (7.6 m) minimum distance from aboveground ASME containers of 501 gal through 2000 gal (1.9 m³ through 7.6 m³) water capacity to buildings, a group of buildings, or the line of adjoining property that can be built upon shall be reduced to 10 ft (3 m) for a single ASME container of 1200 gal (4.5 m³) or less water capacity where such container is at least 25 ft (7.6 m) from any other LP-Gas container of more than 125 gal (0.5 m³) water capacity.

Subsection 6.3.3 provides a special case that allows the installation of one LP-Gas container of 1200 gal (4.5 m³) or less 10 ft (3 m) from a building, rather than the 25 ft (7.6 m) required in Table 6.3.1. The 10 ft (3 m) spacing of one 1200 gal (4.5 m³) or less water capacity container is allowed if only one such container is installed and there are no other LP-Gas containers of more than 125 gal (0.5 m³) water capacity within 25 ft (7.6 m). The provision was created because of the limited space often found in commercial areas and has continued to be used because fire records do not indicate a problem with the reduced distance. (See Exhibit 6.2.) Note that the 25 ft separation distance to other LP-Gas containers is applicable in all cases, even if two different users would like to install containers less than 25 ft apart.

◀ **FAQ**
Can two 1000 gal (3.8 m³) LP-Gas containers 3 ft (1 m) apart serving different uses be installed 10 ft (3 m) from a building?

6.3.4 Minimum distances for underground or mounded ASME containers of 2001 gal through 30,000 gal (7.6 m³ through 114 m³) water capacity incorporating all the provisions of Section 6.26 shall be reduced to 10 ft (3 m).

The alternate requirements of Section 6.26 are enabled here as an exception to the distances established in Table 6.3.1. The reduced distances for underground or mounded containers

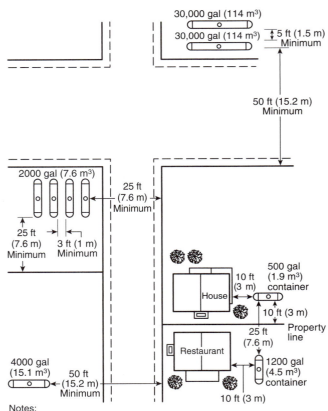

EXHIBIT 6.2 *Example of Multiple Container Installation and Various Sizes of Containers. (Illustration of the requirement of 6.3.3)*

Notes:
1. The requirements of Table 6.5.3 must also be considered.
2. Installations over 4000 gal (15.2 m³) aggregate water capacity must comply with Section 6.25.

reflect the fact that these containers are not subject to boiling liquid expanding vapor explosions (BLEVEs) from fire exposure, and the features provided in Section 6.26 reduce the potential for the uncontrolled release of product that can result in an explosion hazard.

Paragraphs 6.3.4.1 and 6.3.4.2 provide important information in measuring the distances required in 6.3.4. Although they may appear redundant to one another, 6.3.4.1 and 6.3.4.2 are not addressing the same issues. Paragraph 6.3.4.1 is addressing the clearances for fire safety purposes, and 6.3.4.2 is addressing spacing requirements to allow heavy equipment to have access to the containers, as well as to create an access easement for utilities.

6.3.4.1 Distances for all underground and mounded ASME containers shall be measured from the container surface.

Note that 6.3.4.1 requires that the measurement of separation distances from an underground or mounded ASME container be taken from the nearest surface of the container rather than the pressure relief valve and the filling connection, which is used in some cases for spacing requirements for aboveground containers.

6.3.4.2 No part of an underground or mounded ASME container shall be less than 10 ft (3 m) from a building or line of adjoining property that can be built upon.

Enforcing this provision in a crowded area can be challenging. In one case that occurred in Moorehead, North Carolina, in 2008, an underground tank was installed on a very small piece of property in the compact coastal community. Local ordinances requiring runoff provisions and other considerations for this site resulted in the tank being installed less than 10 ft (3 m) from the property line. Setback requirements did not exist in this area, and an aboveground tank was not acceptable. Because the intent of the "line of adjoining property" requirement is to keep a tank from being too close to a building, an agreement was reached to allow the underground tank to remain in place as long as a building was not constructed on the adjacent property within 10 ft of the underground tank. The tank should not have been installed initially but, in this instance, it was allowed to stay.

6.3.5 The minimum separation distances specified in Table 6.3.1 between containers and buildings of other than wood-frame construction devoted exclusively to gas manufacturing and distribution operations shall be reduced to 10 ft (3 m).

Paragraph 6.3.5 allows a reduction of the separation distances of containers to buildings used only for gas manufacturing and distribution from 50 ft (15 m) to 10 ft (3 m), because workers in a building covered by this provision are employed in the transfer of liquid LP-Gas and have had initial and refresher training in the hazards of LP-Gas. In addition, because the building is constructed of noncombustible materials, the potential exposure to the container from a building fire is greatly reduced. Buildings affected by this reduction are usually cylinder filling buildings at bulk plants. The separation distance from containers to other buildings on the site, such as office buildings, and to buildings on adjacent sites is not reduced.

6.3.6 If the aggregate water capacity of a multicontainer installation is 501 gal (1.9 m³) or more and the installation is comprised of individual containers, each with a water capacity of less than 125 gal (0.5 m³), the minimum distance shall comply with Table 6.3.1 and the following:

(1) The aggregate capacity shall be used rather than the capacity per container.
(2) If more than one such installation is made, each installation shall be separated from any other installation by at least 25 ft (7.6 m).
(3) The minimum distances between containers shall not be applied to installations covered by 6.3.6.

During its entire history, the code has permitted containers of less than 125 gal (0.5 m³) water capacity to be installed alongside a building, but some distance away from building openings, per 6.3.7 and 6.3.8. The number of such containers was not limited. The presumption was that the number would not exceed 10 or 12 containers, because normal practice would result in a large, single container being used under such service conditions. In the mid-1960s, the technical committee became aware of several installations of a large number of manifolded containers installed adjacent to buildings due to limited available space. An example of one such installation is shown in Exhibit 6.3, where fifty 100 lb (45 kg) LP-Gas capacity [about 29 gal (0.11 m³) water capacity each] U.S. Department of Transportation (DOT)–specification containers in two manifolds are installed alongside a multi-story office building. The installation is approximately equivalent to a single 1200 gal (4.5 m³) water capacity container, which requires a minimum 10 ft (3 m) separation from the building in accordance with 6.3.4.

Subsection 6.3.6 addresses loopholes in the requirements, such as the one illustrated in Exhibit 6.3, by placing an aggregate capacity limit on such multicontainer installations.

6.3.7 Cylinders shall not be located and installed underneath any building unless the space is open to the atmosphere for 50 percent of its perimeter or more.

Subsection 6.3.7 provides guidance to code users who install cylinders outdoors that are protected from the weather. It clarifies the committee's intent on what *outdoors* means by establishing that a minimum of 50 percent of the perimeter of an enclosed area be open to the atmosphere.

◀ **FAQ**
What is meant by "50 percent of its perimeter"?

EXHIBIT 6.3 *Manifolded Cylinders Adjacent to Building. (Courtesy of Wilbur Walls)*

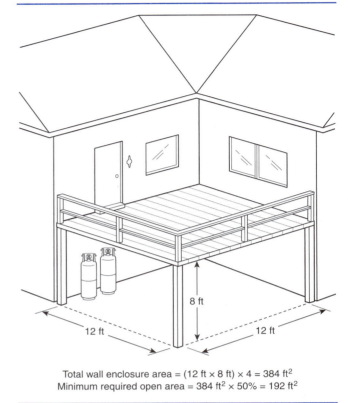

Total wall enclosure area = (12 ft × 8 ft) × 4 = 384 ft²
Minimum required open area = 384 ft² × 50% = 192 ft²

EXHIBIT 6.4 *Illustration of 50 Percent Open Perimeter of the Space Below a Deck.*

The requirement is actually based on the perimeter. See Exhibit 6.4, which shows a deck with two sides completely open. Cylinders can be installed under a deck like this one.

Although NFPA 58 is not a building code, it does provide safety requirements for the installation of propane containers that help achieve the safe occupancy and use of buildings. Note that NFPA *101®*, *Life Safety Code®* [3], prohibits LP-Gas containers from being located under egress paths from upper-level rooms. This would preclude locating containers under a stairway or ramp that is the best practical way to evacuate, for example, a second-floor apartment or elevated beach house.

6.3.8 The distance measured horizontally from the point of discharge of a container pressure relief valve to any building opening below the level of such discharge shall be in accordance with Table 6.3.8.

Note that while this paragraph, and its corresponding Table 6.3.8, were not revised in the 2011 edition, former paragraph 6.3.7 covering cylinders installed alongside buildings was deleted, as the requirements were identical to 6.3.8 and Table 6.3.8. Also, the phrase "filled on site" has been replaced by "filled on site at the point of use" to clarify the intent. Some enforcement officials interpreted "site" to include any site, including a cylinder-filling location, which was not the intent of the requirement.

Table 6.3.8 highlights the differences in location requirements between cylinders and ASME containers and between containers filled on site and those that are exchanged. An exchanged cylinder is one that is transported full to the consumer site, to be exchanged with an empty cylinder. Note that the distance is greater for containers (both cylinders and ASME tanks) filled at the point of use because the fixed liquid level gauge (referred to as "Vent Discharge" in the table) is usually open and discharges propane into the air while the cylinder is

TABLE 6.3.8 *Separation Distance Between Container Pressure Relief Valve and Building Openings*

Container Type	Exchange or Filled on Site at the Point of Use	Distance Horizontally from Relief Valve Discharge to Opening Below Discharge		Discharge from Relief Valve, Vent Discharge, and Filling Connection to Exterior Source of Ignition, Openings into Direct-Vent Appliances, and Mechanical Ventilation Air Intakes	
		ft	m	ft	m
Cylinder	Exchange	3	0.9	5	1.5
Cylinder	Filled on site at the point of use	3	0.9	10	3.0
ASME	Filled on site at the point of use	5	1.5	10	3.0

being filled. There is also a small discharge of propane when the hose assembly is disconnected from the container filler valve.

Table 6.3.8 applies to cylinders installed alongside a building. The requirements are intended to achieve the following:

- Minimize the possibility of LP-Gas escaping through the cylinder pressure relief valve and entering a building, through a window, door, or a mechanical system opening. Pressure relief valve operation is most likely to occur if the cylinder has been overfilled and the cylinder is heated due to exposure to intense sunlight or another source of heat.
- Minimize the possibility of any gas that may be released through the relief valve from providing fuel for a fire.

Note that the required distance to a pressure relief valve on a cylinder from a building opening is 3 ft (1 m), and the required distance for a pressure relief valve on an ASME container is 5 ft (1.5 m). (See Table 6.3.8.) This difference recognizes the following:

1. The start-to-discharge setting for a relief valve on a cylinder is higher than that for an ASME container [nominally 375 psig (2.6 MPag) and 250 psig (1.7 MPag), respectively], resulting in a lower probability of a discharge of LP-Gas occurring from a DOT cylinder than an ASME container.
2. The cylinder relief valve is smaller than the relief valves used on large ASME containers. The discharge flow is correspondingly less.

The building opening cited in 6.3.8 is normally a door or a window, which can be either closed or open. When open, doors and windows can have airflow through them in either direction due to natural breezes. Where the airflow is caused by a mechanical air movement system, such as a direct–vent appliance or a mechanical ventilation air intake, a 5 ft (1.5 m) distance for exchanged cylinders or a 10 ft (3 m) distance for cylinders or ASME containers filled at the point of use is specified in Table 6.3.8.

Building openings also include crawl space vents. Recent construction trends have resulted in these vents on residences being spaced 6 ft on center. As such, a container may not be placed between them and next to the building and still have the required separation from the opening. Sealing the vent could be an option if it does not violate the venting requirements of the crawl space; however, doing so may result in inadequate ventilation of the space.

◄ **FAQ**
Can crawl space vents be sealed?

Although direct-vent appliances do not represent a pathway for LP-Gas into the building interior, they do draw in outside air for combustion. If this air contains LP-Gas in ignitible proportions, the appliance ignition or burner flame can be an ignition source and, because of the small volume that the flammable mixture is contained within, an overpressure event may be possible.

Mechanical ventilation system air intakes are an obvious pathway for LP-Gas into a building interior. A mechanical ventilation system air outlet — for example, a kitchen exhaust fan — is considered to be a building opening, like a door or window, and it may actually draw air into the building when it is not operating. While the fan may incorporate a damper to minimize reverse flow, such dampers rarely seal very tightly and are known to deform and allow some reverse flow after some time in use.

See Exhibit 6.5 for an illustration of the requirements of Tables 6.3.1 and 6.3.8.

6.3.9 The distance measured in any direction from the point of discharge of a container pressure relief valve, vent of a fixed maximum liquid level gauge on a container, and the container filling connection to exterior sources of ignition, openings into direct-vent (sealed combustion system) appliances, and mechanical ventilation air intakes shall be in accordance with Table 6.3.8.

Table 6.3.8 is referenced in both 6.3.8 and 6.3.9 for distances from cylinders and container pressure relief valve outlets to building openings and outdoor sources of ignition.

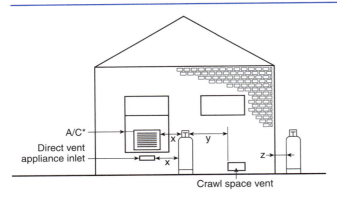

Distance to outdoor sources of ignition and building openings (source: Table 6.3.8)

Filling method	Distance X	Distance Y
Filled by exchange	5 ft	3 ft
Filled at the point of use	10 ft	5 ft

* or other exterior source of ignition

Distance to building, cylinders - Z (source: Table 6.3.1)

One container 125 gal or less	0 ft
Multiple containers, 125 gal or less with aggregate < 501 gal	0 ft
Multiple containers, 125 gal or less with aggregate > 501 gal	Per Table 6.3.1 (using aggregate water capacity)

(a) Location of Cylinders

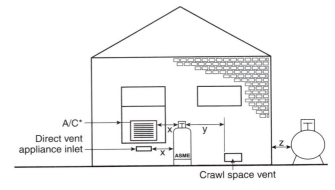

Distance to outdoor sources of ignition and building openings (source: Table 6.3.8)

Filling method	Distance X	Distance Y
Filled by exchange	5 ft	5 ft
Filled at the point of use	10 ft	5 ft

* or other exterior source of ignition

Distance to building - Z, ASME Containers up to 2000 gal (source: Table 6.3.1)

One container 125 gal or less	0 ft
126 – 500 gal	10 ft
One container, 501 – 1200 gal	10 ft (see 6.3.3)
501 – 1200 gal	25 ft

(b) Location of ASME Containers

EXHIBIT 6.5 *Location of Cylinders and ASME Containers.*

Work on dispersion of flammable gases from relief valves has been conducted by Batelle Memorial Institute and is reported in the paper, "The Effect of Velocity, Temperature, and Gas Molecular Weight on Flammability Limits in Wind-Blown Jets of Hydrocarbon Gases" [4]. This report forms a basis for API RP 521, *Guide for Pressure-Relieving and Depressuring Systems* [5]. Anyone interested in more information in this area can review these references.

The results of one such test are shown in Exhibit 6.6. While this reports one test, which was not intended to be a thorough study, it is the only data available. Discharge of liquid from a fixed liquid level gauge for as long as three minutes is an abnormal condition because, normally, the gauge discharge valve is closed by the person filling the container when liquid first appears. A lack of wind is conducive to the formation of high concentrations of LP-Gas, but calm conditions are seldom found. In spite of the severity of this test, the concentration of LP-Gas at 10 ft (3 m) did not exceed 20 percent, which is one-fifth of the lower flammable limit, or a safety factor of 5.

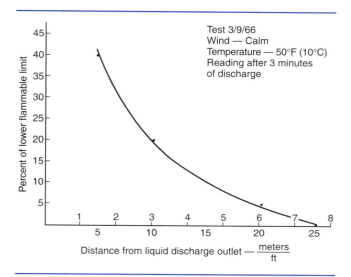

Test 3/9/66
Wind — Calm
Temperature — 50°F (10°C)
Reading after 3 minutes
of discharge

y-axis: Percent of lower flammable limit

x-axis: Distance from liquid discharge outlet — $\frac{\text{meters}}{\text{ft}}$

EXHIBIT 6.6 *Concentration of Propane–Air Mixture Resulting from Discharge of Liquid Propane from a Fixed Liquid Level Gauge on a Cylinder. (Courtesy of Wilbur Walls)*

The required separation for containers filled on site also reflects the small but distinct possibility that the fill valve may not close properly after filling the container. If the fill valve fails to close when the fill nozzle is removed, gas will be released through the valve and can result in fire and injury to transfer personnel.

6.3.10 Access at the ends or sides of individual underground containers having a water capacity of 125 gal (0.5 m³) or more shall be provided in multicontainer installations to facilitate working with cranes or hoists.

Subsection 6.3.10 requires that access to an underground container installation be provided to allow cranes and hoists to service or remove the containers. The text does not require a minimum clearance around the container installation because many cranes can "boom out" to allow access to the containers from a single point.

6.3.11 The horizontal distance between the portion of a building that overhangs out of the building wall and an ASME container of 125 gal. (0.5 m³) or more water capacity shall comply with the following:

(1) The horizontal distance shall be measured from a point determined by projecting the outside edge of the overhanging structure vertically downward to grade or other level upon which the container is installed.

(2) The horizontal distance specified in 6.3.11(1) shall be at least 50 percent of the separation distance required in Table 6.3.1.

(3) The horizontal distance requirement shall apply only when the overhang extends more than 5 ft (1.5 m) from the building.

(4) The horizontal distance requirement shall not apply when the overhanging structure is 50 ft (15 m) or more above the relief valve discharge outlet.

(5) The horizontal distance requirement shall not apply to ASME containers of 2001 gal through 30,000 gal (7.6 m^3 through 114 m^3) water capacity where the container distance from a building is in accordance with 6.26.2.

The requirements of 6.3.11 address releases of gas through the pressure relief valve. Because the ASME pressure relief valve start-to-discharge point is 250 psig (1.7 MPag), temperatures exceeding 110°F (43°C) can begin to approach this set point. Because the pressure relief valve in ASME containers is installed so that any release would be directed straight up, it is important that, if such a release occurs, there is no opportunity for it to accumulate under a building overhang, where a source of ignition may be present.

The requirement in 6.3.11(3) applies only to building extensions that project more than 5 ft (1.5 m) from a building and to building extensions less than 50 ft (15 m) above the pressure relief valve discharge outlet. See Exhibit 6.7, in which labels A through D illustrate the distances required in 6.3.11.

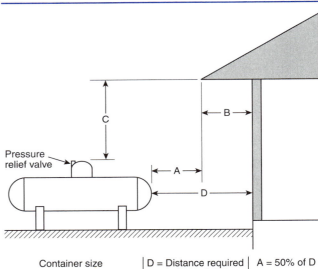

EXHIBIT 6.7 *Distance from ASME Containers to Building Projections.*

Container size	D = Distance required by Table 6.3.1	A = 50% of D
125 – 500 gal (0.5 – 1.0 m³)	10 ft (3 m)	5 ft (1.5 m)
501 – 1200 gal (1.94 – 4.5 m³)	25 ft (7.6 m)	12.5 ft (3.8 m)
501 – 2000 gal (1.94 – 7.6 m³)	10 ft (3 m)	5 ft (1.5 m)

Note: Distances apply only where B is 5 ft or more and C is less than 50 ft.

- **Label A** illustrates the separation distance from a building projection. [See 6.3.11(2).]
- **Label B** illustrates the minimum projection of a building overhang for which the requirement is applicable. [See 6.3.11(3).]
- **Label C** illustrates the maximum elevation of the projection to which the requirement applies. [See 6.3.11(4).]
- **Label D** illustrates the minimum separation from the container to the (important) building from Table 6.3.1.

The requirement is, in reality, only applicable to containers of 125 gal (0.5 m³) through 2000 gal (7.6 m³). Below 125 gal, a container can be installed next to a building, and above 2000 gal, the separation distance to a building is 50 ft (15 m). It is highly unlikely to have a building projection of 25 ft (7.5 m) or more.

6.4 Other Container Location Requirements

6.4.1 Where storage containers having an aggregate water capacity of more than 4000 gal (15.1 m³) are located in heavily populated or congested areas, the siting provisions of 6.3.1 and Table 6.3.1 shall be permitted to be modified as indicated by the fire safety analysis described in 6.25.3.

The text in 6.4.1 establishes an additional requirement for larger installations in populated and congested areas, allowing the authority having jurisdiction to require an analysis of local conditions. Refer to the commentary on Section 6.25, Fire Protection, Supplement 1, and the *Fire Safety Analysis Manual* [6] for more information on fire safety analysis.

In the United States and Canada, LP-Gas installations are usually, but not always, found in rural and suburban areas or in commercial and industrial areas where the hazards are commensurate with other operations, and thus exposure to the public has been limited accordingly. Inevitably, exceptions occur and the versatility of LP-Gas has increased the number of LP-Gas installations. Installations are common in towns and cities not supplied by a utility gas system. In other countries, propane installations can be found in similar locations or throughout the country, depending on the availability of other fuels. In Mexico, for example, natural gas is available but is not widely distributed as a heating and cooking fuel. Propane installations are common at homes, offices, hotels, and factories throughout the country. In some other countries, natural gas is not available. Although manufactured gas is still used in a limited number of locations, it is being replaced with both natural gas pipelines and propane systems.

In addition, the popularity of LP-Gas–powered vehicles has resulted in an increase in the number of refueling stations, some of which are located in populated or congested areas.

Subsection 6.4.1 recognizes that larger installations in populated or congested areas may warrant further attention to the general siting criteria in 6.3.1. Some code users misinterpret 6.4.1 to mean that where storage exceeds 4000 gal (15.1 m³), the separation distances of Table 6.3.1 should be increased, but this is not necessarily the case. In addition, attempts have been made to force propane facilities to be relocated if buildings have been allowed to be constructed closer than the spacing requirements of Table 6.3.1 after the propane facility has been installed. Increasing the distances may be impossible in a heavily populated or congested area. What 6.4.1 does state is that the distances provided in 6.3.1 and Table 6.3.1 can be modified based on the results of a fire safety analysis. The requirements for the fire safety analysis are provided in 6.25.3.

The fire safety analysis first evaluates the total product control system installed. This evaluation recognizes the important safety equipment mandated by NFPA 58 and other safety equipment that may have been installed. Other factors in the evaluation include the availability of fire-fighting resources. In populated or congested areas, emergency response resources are usually more readily available than in more remote areas. A fire safety analysis can frequently conclude that the separation distances needed are no greater than those provided for in Table 6.3.1, based on the installation of product control measures and, where necessary, appropriate planning and fire protection provisions. In a small number of cases, such a review may result in the determination that a proposed site is not appropriate.

The phrase "heavily populated or congested areas" is not defined. The phrase is always subject to the interpretation of the authority having jurisdiction, and often zoning criteria come into play. For example, a congested or heavily populated area may be considered to

◄ **FAQ**
What is meant by "heavily populated or congested areas"?

include buildings housing an institutional occupancy, such as a prison or hospital, in which the occupants are incarcerated or are nonambulatory and not able to respond to an emergency without assistance.

6.4.2 Aboveground multicontainer installations comprised of ASME containers having an individual water capacity of 12,000 gal (45 m³) or more and installed for use in a single location shall be limited to the number of containers in one group, with each group separated from the next group in accordance with the degree of fire protection provided in Table 6.4.2.

TABLE 6.4.2 *Maximum Number of Containers in a Group and Their Separation Distances*

Fire Protection Provided by	*Maximum Number of Containers in One Group*	*Minimum Separation Between Groups*	
		ft	*m*
Hose streams only *(see 6.4.2 and 6.25.3.1)*	6	50	15
Fixed monitor nozzles per 6.25.6.3	6	25	7.6
Fixed water spray per 6.25.3.1	9	25	7.6
Insulation per 6.25.5.1	9	25	7.6

Table 6.4.2, which was added to the code in 1986, applies to containers larger than 12,000 gal (45 m³) water capacity and establishes minimum distances between groups of those containers. If a container releases product and that product is ignited, any containers in the immediate vicinity are subject to the radiant heat flux and flame impingement from the fire. To mitigate this potential exposure, the number of containers in each group is limited and a minimum separation distance between groups is required. The provision for reduced spacing of container groups and number of containers in a group with fixed fire protection systems reflects the committee's belief that fixed fire protection equipment, including monitor nozzles, fixed water spray sprinklers, or tank insulation, can also be used to mitigate the threat.

6.4.3 Where the provisions of 6.26.3 and 6.26.4 are met, the minimum separation distance between groups of ASME containers protected by hose stream only shall be one-half the distances required in Table 6.4.2.

Subsection 6.4.3 permits reduced spacing for groups of aboveground containers addressed by 6.4.2 installed in accordance with the provisions of 6.26.3 and 6.26.4. This reduced spacing is allowed because the provisions of 6.26.3 and 6.26.4 enhance the product control performance of the containment system. For example, 6.26.3 requires internal valves to be installed having both remote and automatic (temperature-activated) shutoff capability, as well as positive shutoff valves. In addition, 6.26.4 requires emergency shutoff valves with remote and thermal activation as well.

6.4.4 Underground or mounded ASME containers shall be located in accordance with 6.4.4.1 through 6.4.4.5.

6.4.4.1 Underground or mounded containers shall be located outside of any buildings.

6.4.4.2 Buildings shall not be constructed over any underground or mounded containers.

6.4.4.3 The sides of adjacent containers shall be separated in accordance with Table 6.3.1 but shall not be separated by less than 3 ft (1 m).

6.4.4.4 Where containers are installed parallel with ends in line, the number of containers in one group shall not be limited.

6.4.4.5 Where more than one row of containers is installed, the adjacent ends of the containers in each row shall be separated by not less than 10 ft (3 m).

The requirement that underground and mounded containers be installed outdoors (and not beneath buildings) is consistent with the requirements for aboveground containers. A minimum separation distance for underground and mounded containers of 3 ft (1 m) is required in 6.4.4.3 to allow for movement, which cannot be observed. The separation between rows of containers allows heavy equipment to access the containers for replacement, if needed. (See Exhibit 6.8.)

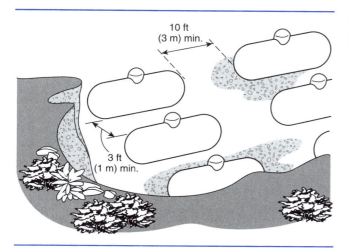

EXHIBIT 6.8 *Separation of Mounded or Underground Containers.*

6.4.5 Additional container installation requirements shall comply with 6.4.5.1 through 6.4.5.12, 6.4.6, and 6.4.7.

The requirements mentioned in 6.4.5 are additional requirements that address the location of a container with respect to various external safety concerns.

6.4.5.1 Containers shall not be stacked one above the other.

The purpose of the requirement in 6.4.5.1 is to avoid bonfire-type incidents where a gas release from one container can cause fire impingement on a container installed above it.

Although a literal reading of the words would lead one to believe that such an installation is prohibited, an understanding of the intent of the requirement usually leaves one in doubt. The intent is to prevent interaction of containers in a fire situation. It is difficult to imagine a scenario where (a) fire attacks an underground container or (b) an aboveground container on fire affects an underground container installed beneath it.

The concern of such an installation would be the location of the relief valve discharge of the underground container. However, the operation of a relief valve on an underground container is highly unlikely, unless the container is overfilled. Depending on the installation, it may be prudent to pipe the relief valve discharge of the underground container to a point where it is higher than the top of, or cannot impinge on, an aboveground container installed above it. In such cases, care must be taken to ensure that the relief valve discharge piping cannot affect the operation of the relief valve.

Because this requirement is located in Chapter 6, Installation of LP-Gas Systems, it applies to these subjects only. It does not apply to portable cylinders awaiting use or sale, which are covered in Chapter 8.

◄ **FAQ**
Can an aboveground container be installed over an underground container?

6.4.5.2 Loose or piled combustible material and weeds and long dry grass shall be separated from containers by a minimum of 10 ft (3 m).

The 10 ft (3 m) separation helps prevent a possible grass or brush fire from affecting an LP-Gas container. Note that the separation requirement does not apply to live vegetation and to wood fences, which are not piled material.

FAQ ▶
How is the requirement in 6.4.5.2 applied to vegetation that is seasonally dormant?

Note that the requirement applies only to weeds, and not bushes and trees. The 10 ft (3 m) separation applies equally to weeds whether seasonally dormant or not. It is not intended that bushes and trees that are seasonally dormant, as occurs in winter in colder climates, be considered "loose or piled combustible material."

6.4.5.3* The area under containers shall be graded or shall have dikes or curbs installed so that the flow or accumulation of flammable liquids with flash points below 200°F (93.4°C) is prevented.

A.6.4.5.3 For information on determination of flash points, see NFPA 30, *Flammable and Combustible Liquids Code.*

The requirement in 6.4.5.3 is intended to be applied when LP-Gas containers are installed in close proximity to other flammable liquid storage containers. Paragraph 6.4.5.4 indicates the required separation from containers used to store flammable or combustible liquids that have a wall or dike constructed between them and the LP-Gas container.

Flash point is the temperature at which a flammable liquid can vaporize in sufficient quantity to form a flammable mixture of vapor and air. A liquid's flash point is determined by a test in which a sample of the liquid in an open cup is heated until its vapors can be ignited. Gases, such as propane and butane, do not have a flash point, because they cannot be contained in an open cup at room temperature, although it is possible to measure a flash point by refrigerating propane or butane and using a refrigerated cup. One data source provides a flash point for butane of −76°F (−60°C), and −156° F (−104°C) for propane [Praxair Material Safety Data Sheet] [7]. Propane will remain a liquid at below −40°F (−40°C), but, even at such low temperatures, a flash point provides no useful information because the presence of flammable gas is assumed in the event of leakage. Flash point has value in dealing with flammable liquids because it advises when to be concerned about ignition of vapors (i.e., with gasoline) and when not to be concerned (i.e., with motor oil).

Liquids with flash points below 100°F (37.8°C) are classified as Class I (flammable) liquids in NFPA 30, *Flammable and Combustible Liquids Code* [8]. Examples of Class I (flammable) liquids are gasoline and many alcohols. Liquids with a flash point between 100°F and 140°F (37.8°C and 60.0°C) are classified as Class II (combustible) liquids. Examples of Class II (combustible) liquids include diesel fuel and kerosene.

Flash point should not be confused with boiling point. Although propane has a boiling point of −44°F (−42°C), for practical purposes, propane does not have a flash point. The rules in NFPA 30 for storing flammable liquids do not apply to propane or any LP-Gas.

6.4.5.4 LP-Gas containers shall be located at least 10 ft (3 m) from the centerline of the wall of diked areas containing flammable or combustible liquids.

6.4.5.5 The minimum horizontal separation between aboveground LP-Gas containers and aboveground tanks containing liquids having flash points below 200°F (93.4°C) shall be 20 ft (6 m).

Paragraphs 6.4.5.3 and 6.4.5.4 are intended to keep flammable or combustible liquids from accumulating under or around LP-Gas containers. Paragraph 6.4.5.5 addresses the mutual exposure between flammable liquids tanks and LP-Gas containers. This requirement was derived through a cooperative effort between the NFPA technical committees responsible for NFPA 30 and NFPA 58. The minimum separation distance of 20 ft (6 m) facilitates cooling and fire-extinguishing activities by fire departments. Succeeding paragraphs 6.4.5.6 and 6.4.5.7 point out exceptions to this 20 ft (6 m) separation distance where mitigation measures are utilized.

6.4.5.6 The requirements of 6.4.5.5 shall not apply where LP-Gas containers of 125 gal (0.5 m³) or less water capacity are installed adjacent to fuel oil supply tanks of 660 gal (2.5 m³) or less capacity.

The requirement in 6.4.5.6 is in recognition of the reduced hazard that smaller storage containers present and the fact that many installations are limited in space, making it impractical to comply with the 20 ft (6 m) separation distance. Industry experience has shown that these installations are not a safety problem.

6.4.5.7 No horizontal separation shall be required between aboveground LP-Gas containers and underground tanks containing flammable or combustible liquids installed in accordance with NFPA 30, *Flammable and Combustible Liquids Code*.

The provision in 6.4.5.7 is essentially an exception to 6.4.5.5 and takes advantage of the inherently safer installations of flammable and combustible liquid containers when they are installed in compliance with NFPA 30.

6.4.5.8* The minimum separation between LP-Gas containers and oxygen or gaseous hydrogen containers shall be in accordance with Table 6.4.5.8.

A.6.4.5.8 Also see NFPA 51, *Standard for the Design and Installation of Oxygen–Fuel Gas Systems for Welding, Cutting, and Allied Processes*, for oxygen systems, and NFPA 55, *Compressed Gases and Cryogenic Fluids Code*, for gaseous hydrogen systems.

The separation distances for oxygen or gaseous hydrogen containers are derived from NFPA standards covering oxygen and gaseous hydrogen container installations and are included in NFPA 58, as shown in Table 6.4.5.8. Installations having both LP-Gas and oxygen containers include factories where oxy-propane cutting torches are used. Because oxygen is an oxidizer, it creates a hazard when mixed with LP-Gas as it enhances combustion. Note that NFPA 50 and NFPA 50A have been incorporated in NFPA 55, *Standard for the Storage, Use, and Handling of Compressed Gases and Cryogenic Fluids in Portable and Stationary Containers, Cylinders, and Tanks*, as Chapters 9 and 10, respectively, and are no longer being produced as separate standards.

6.4.5.9 Where protective structures having a minimum fire resistance rating of 2 hours interrupt the line of sight between uninsulated portions of the oxygen or hydrogen containers and the LP-Gas containers, no minimum distance shall apply.

TABLE 6.4.5.8 *Separation Distances of LP-Gas Containers and Oxygen and Hydrogen Containers*

LP-Gas Containers Aggregate Water Capacity		Separation from Oxygen Containers Aggregate Capacity					Separation from Gaseous Hydrogen Containers Aggregate Capacity				
		400 ft³ (11 m³)* or Less	More than 400 ft³ to 20,000 ft³* (11 m³ to 566 m³)*, Including Unconnected Reserves		More than 20,000 ft³ (566 m³)*, Including Unconnected Reserves		Less than 400 ft³ (11 m³)*	400 ft³* to 3000 ft³ (11 m³ to 85 m³)*		More Than 3000 ft³ (85 m³)*	
gal	m³		ft	m	ft	m		ft	m	ft	m
≤1200	≤4.5	None	20	6	25	7.6	—	—	—	—	—
>1200	>4.5	None	20	6	50	15	—	—	—	—	—
≤500	≤1.9	—	—	—	—	—	None	10	3	25	7.6
>500	>1.9	—	—	—	—	—	None	25	7.6	50	15

* Measurement of ft³ (m³) at 70°F (21°C) and atmospheric pressure.

Paragraph 6.4.5.9 is an exception to 6.4.5.8 and permits an elimination of separation where the required 2-hour fire resistance–rated assembly is installed. This assembly is considered sufficient to protect the container from impingement fire.

6.4.5.10 The minimum separation between LP-Gas containers and liquefied hydrogen containers shall be in accordance with NFPA 55, *Compressed Gases and Cryogenic Fluids Code*.

The requirement in 6.4.5.10 is separate from the requirement in 6.4.5.8 because the characteristics of gaseous hydrogen storage differ greatly from those of liquid hydrogen installations. The reference to NFPA 55, *Standard for the Storage, Use, and Handling of Compressed Gases and Cryogenic Fluids in Portable and Stationary Containers, Cylinders, and Tanks* [9], recognizes that liquefied hydrogen systems, because of the very low temperature of the liquid in storage (about 4 Fahrenheit degrees above absolute zero), present very different hazards.

6.4.5.11 Where LP-Gas cylinders are to be stored or used in the same area with other compressed gases, the cylinders shall be marked to identify their content in accordance with ANSI/CGA C-7, *Guide to the Preparation of Precautionary Labeling and Marking of Compressed Gas Containers*.

6.4.5.12 An aboveground LP-Gas container and any of its parts shall not be located within 6 ft (1.8 m) of a vertical plane beneath overhead electric power lines that are over 600 volts, nominal.

The requirement in 6.4.5.12 (illustrated in Exhibit 6.9) reflects the possibility of an accident occurring should the power line break and lead to container failure through arc penetration or ignition of the pressure relief valve discharge.

EXHIBIT 6.9 Overhead Electric Power Line Spacing from LP-Gas Containers.

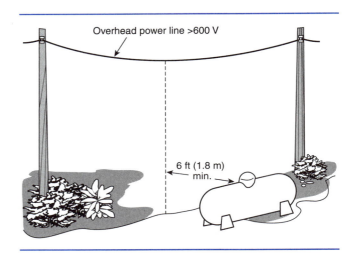

6.4.6* Refrigerated LP-Gas containers shall be located within an impoundment in accordance with Section 12.3.

A.6.4.6 Because of the anticipated flash of some nonrefrigerated LP-Gases when released to the atmosphere, dikes normally serve no useful purpose for these nonrefrigerated installations.

The need to dike refrigerated propane storage containers has long been recognized, because refrigerated liquid does not vaporize as quickly as LP-Gas released from pressurized storage. A spill from a refrigerated container puddles or runs as a liquid on the ground until the liquid can absorb sufficient heat from the ground.

This situation is very different from that of pressurized liquid propane, which vaporizes rapidly when it escapes from a container and the ambient temperature is above its normal boiling point of about $-44°F$ ($-42°C$). Much of the heat necessary for vaporization is contained in the liquid itself, and the remainder needed is readily available from the air, ground, or other material with which the liquid comes in contact. Therefore, the establishment of a pool or flowing stream of propane on the ground or water is unlikely, except in Arctic and Antarctic regions, because a dike has no function to perform around a pressurized propane storage tank.

Where butane is stored, a dike may be recommended because the normal boiling point of butane is about $15°F$ ($-9°C$), a temperature that can be reached in many parts of the world.

6.4.7* Structures such as fire walls, fences, earth or concrete barriers, and other similar structures shall not be permitted around or over installed nonrefrigerated containers unless specifically allowed as follows:

(1) Structures partially enclosing containers shall be permitted if designed in accordance with a sound fire protection analysis.
(2) Structures used to prevent flammable or combustible liquid accumulation or flow shall be permitted in accordance with 6.4.5.3.
(3) Structures between LP-Gas containers and gaseous hydrogen containers shall be permitted in accordance with 6.4.5.9.
(4) Structures such as fences shall be permitted in accordance with 6.18.4.

A.6.4.7 The presence of such structures can create significant hazards, such as the following:

(1) Pocketing of escaping gas
(2) Interference with application of cooling water by fire departments
(3) Redirection of flames against containers
(4) Impeding the egress of personnel in an emergency

Subsection 6.4.7 was inspired by a serious BLEVE of an aboveground propane container that had been enclosed by a roofed-over enclosure for aesthetic reasons. The enclosure not only contributed to ignition, but also made it difficult for the fire department to apply cooling water to the container. The technical committee also was aware of an increasing use of fences to hide LP-Gas containers. Paragraph 6.4.7(1) recognizes that the problems associated with such structures can be prevented by designs that eliminate the problems cited in A.6.4.7.

If a structure is used to hide an LP-Gas container, it is important to use materials that allow air to circulate freely. Examples of such materials are chain-link fence or materials that have significant openings on all sides. Wood can be used, but its combustibility must be considered. Wood cannot be stacked around an LP-Gas container per 6.4.5.2, but its use in a structure is not prohibited. A light fence constructed of wood, if ignited, would probably be consumed before generating enough heat to affect an LP-Gas container.

6.5 Location of Transfer Operations

Section 6.5 deals with the filling of portable containers and with the filling of stationary containers when not filled at the container (i.e., via fixed piping to a point remote from the container where the filling hose is connected). It does not apply to the filling of stationary containers where the point of transfer is located at the container. In the editor's experience, Section 6.5 is the most widely misunderstood section in NFPA 58, with many users attempting to apply it to all installed containers. Section 6.5 is not in conflict with Section 6.3, Container Separation Distances, as is sometimes thought. Section 6.3 applies to the location of containers, while Section 6.5 applies to points of transfer — that is, the point where the filling

◄ **FAQ**
What is the difference between the requirements of Section 6.5 and Section 6.3?

hose connection is made and broken. Commentary Table 6.2 shows the applicability of Sections 6.3 and 6.5.

COMMENTARY TABLE 6.2 Applicability of Sections 6.3 and 6.5

Container Type	Container Location	Point of Transfer	Applicable Sections
Stationary container	See Section 6.3	At the container	6.5.2
	See Section 6.3	Piped away from the container	6.5.3
Portable container	N/A	At the container	6.5.4

Where a container in a stationary installation complies with Section 6.3, 6.5.2 permits the container to be filled at the container itself. Where the filling point is piped to another location (not at the container), 6.5.3 becomes applicable.

The location of portable cylinders being filled is not covered in Section 6.3. Section 6.5 is the applicable section, with the pertinent requirements found in 6.5.4. Note that the storage of cylinders awaiting sale or use is covered in Chapter 8.

6.5.1* Liquid shall be transferred into containers, including containers mounted on vehicles, only outdoors or in structures specially designed for such purpose.

A.6.5.1 It is the intent to allow transfer of liquid into containers in open areas under canopies or roofs where 50 percent or more of the perimeter is not enclosed.

The location of portable containers being filled is of concern, and such filling is encouraged to be done outdoors. If filling is to be done in a building, the building must meet the requirements of Chapter 10. If filling occurs in a structure that is open to the outdoors for at least 50 percent of its perimeter, the filling is being done "outdoors."

6.5.1.1 The transfer of liquid into containers mounted on vehicles shall not take place within a building but shall be permitted to take place under a weather shelter or canopy. *(See 6.24.3.3.)*

The reference to 6.24.3.3 guides the reader to more information on the limits of a weather shelter. For example, that paragraph requires that a minimum of 50 percent of the perimeter under a weather shelter or canopy be open to the atmosphere.

6.5.1.2 Structures housing transfer operations or converted for such use after December 31, 1972, shall comply with Chapter 10.

6.5.1.3 The transfer of liquid into containers on the roofs of structures shall be permitted, provided that the installation conforms to the requirements contained in 6.6.7 and 6.19.11.

The installation of ASME containers on roofs of buildings is covered in 6.6.7, which requires fire-resistant building construction and allows the filling of ASME containers. The requirements for the installation of cylinders on roofs of buildings are covered in 6.19.11.

6.5.1.4 The transfer hose shall not be routed in or through any building except those specified in 6.5.1.2.

The prohibition of routing delivery hoses through buildings resulted from the committee's becoming aware that this was being done in at least one area where row houses are common and where there is no street access for the bobtail to the containers. The shortest route for the hose was into the building through the front door and out the back door to the cylinder. The committee believed that the possibility of hose damage with subsequent leakage was sufficiently large to prohibit the procedure.

6.5.2 Filling of containers located outdoors in stationary installations in accordance with Section 6.3 shall be permitted to be filled at that location.

This code requirement, which is often misunderstood, simply states that if the hose end valve of a delivery vehicle is connected to a fill valve that is attached directly to the container, the provisions of Section 6.5 do not apply as long as the container itself has been installed in accordance with the spacing requirements of Section 6.3.

◄ **FAQ**
If a stationary container is filled at the container itself, do the requirements of Section 6.5 and Table 6.5.3 apply?

6.5.3 If the point of transfer of containers located outdoors in stationary installations is not located at the container, it shall be located in accordance with Table 6.5.3.

Where a portable container is filled, or where the filling connection of a stationary container is located remote from the container, hazards exist that are not addressed by the spacing distances in Section 6.3. Table 6.5.3 addresses these hazards, which include hazards to the surroundings due to the filling process and hazards to the LP-Gas installation from the surroundings.

TABLE 6.5.3 *Distance Between Point of Transfer and Exposures*

Part	Exposure	Minimum Horizontal Distance	
		ft	*m*
A	Buildings,[a] mobile homes, recreational vehicles, and modular homes with at least 1-hour fire-rated walls[b]	10[c]	3.1
B	Buildings[a] with other than at least 1-hour fire-rated walls[b]	25[c]	7.6[c]
C	Building wall openings or pits at or below the level of the point of transfer	25[c]	7.6[c]
D	Line of adjoining property that can be built upon	25[c]	7.6[c]
E	Outdoor places of public assembly, including schoolyards, athletic fields, and playgrounds	50[c]	15[c]
F	Public ways, including public streets, highways, thoroughfares, and sidewalks		
	(1) From points of transfer in LP-Gas dispensing stations and at vehicle fuel dispensers	10	3.1
	(2) From other points of transfer	25[c]	7.6[c]
G	Driveways[d]	5	1.5
H	Mainline railroad track centerlines	25	7.6
I	Containers[e] other than those being filled	10	3.1
J	Flammable and Class II combustible liquid[f] dispensers and the fill connections of containers	10[c]	3.1[c]
K	Flammable and Class II combustible liquid containers, aboveground containers, and containers under ground	20	6.1

[a]For the purpose of the table, buildings also include structures such as tents and box trailers at construction sites.

[b]See NFPA 251, *Standard Methods of Tests of Fire Resistance of Building Construction and Materials.*

[c]See 6.5.4.4.

[d]Not applicable to driveways and points of transfer at vehicle fuel dispensers.

[e]Not applicable to filling connections at the storage container or to dispensing vehicle fuel dispenser units of 2000 gal (7.6 m³) water capacity or less when used for filling containers not mounted on vehicles.

[f]NFPA 30, *Flammable and Combustible Liquids Code,* defines these as follows: Flammable liquids include those having a flash point below 100°F (37.8°C) and having a vapor pressure not exceeding 40 psia (276 kPa) at 100°F (37.8°C). Class II combustible liquids include those having a flash point at or above 100°F (37.8°C) and below 140°F (60°C).

Part A of Table 6.5.3 includes mobile homes, recreational vehicles, and modular homes. This part recognizes that the added items present a fire hazard similar to buildings. Part J identifies a safe spacing from points of LP-Gas transfer to flammable liquids and Class II combustible liquids dispensers and the fill connections of aboveground and underground containers. Formal Interpretation 95-1 clarifies how to measure this distance. When installing propane-dispensing facilities at service stations that also dispense other vehicle fuels such as gasoline, diesel fuel, compressed natural gas, and hydrogen, refer to NFPA 30A, *Code for Motor Fuel Dispensing Facilities and Repair Garages* [10].

Formal Interpretation
NFPA 58
Liquefied Petroleum Gas Code
2011 Edition

Reference: Table 6.5.3

F.I.: 95-1

Question: Was it the intention of the Committee that the 20 ft (6.1 m) minimum horizontal distance refer to the fill and vent connections of underground containers rather than the shells and heads of the containers?

Answer: Yes.

Issue Edition: 1995

Reference: Table 3-2.3.3

Issue Date: April 3, 1995

Effective Date: April 23, 1995

Note that Table 6.5.3 was revised in the 2011 edition by specifying a 1-hour fire–rated building wall, rather than fire-resistive walls, and a table note was added referring to NFPA 251, *Standard Methods of Tests of Fire Resistance of Building Construction and Materials* [11], which provides the test method. This change results from different interpretations of what "fire resistive" means. Some code users assumed it was intended to allow only masonry and metal buildings, and others assumed that any degree of fire resistance would allow a building to qualify.

See Exhibit 6.10, which illustrates the distances in Table 6.5.3.

6.5.4 Containers not located in stationary installations shall be filled at a location determined by the point of transfer in accordance with Table 6.5.3.

6.5.4.1 If the point of transfer is a component of a system covered by Section 6.23 or Chapter 11, the requirements of parts A, B, and C of Table 6.5.3 shall not apply to the structure containing the point of transfer.

Paragraph 6.5.4.1 recognizes that some LP-Gas systems will be installed on vehicles, as either engine fuel systems (Chapter 11) or other systems installed on the vehicle (Section 6.23). As such, it would not be practical to apply the requirements of Parts A, B, and C of Table 6.5.3 since the transfer operation may be taking place inside of the building itself.

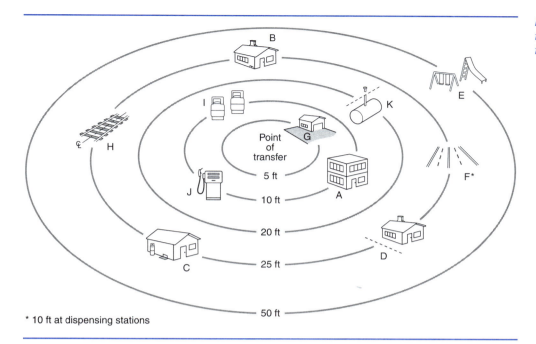

EXHIBIT 6.10 *Illustration of the Distance Requirement from Table 6.5.3.*

6.5.4.2 If LP-Gas is vented to the atmosphere under the conditions stipulated in 7.3.1(5), the distances in Table 6.5.3 shall be doubled.

The pump cited in 7.3.1(5) refers to a piston pump used to transfer liquid LP-Gas that is no longer manufactured and — to the editor's knowledge — no longer used, although a few "antiques" may still exist that are used occasionally. The pump used propane vapor as a power source to operate a piston that moved liquid propane from one container to another, and the propane vapor discharged to the atmosphere could not exceed that equivalent to a No. 31 orifice, which has a diameter of 0.120 in. (3.1 mm). Note that a No. 54 orifice, allowed in other parts of the code, is smaller, with a diameter of 0.055 in. (1.4 mm). The doubled separation distances recognize the larger discharge of gas from a larger orifice.

6.5.4.3 If the point of transfer is housed in a structure complying with Chapter 10, and the common walls comply with 10.2.1, separation distances in Table 6.5.3 shall not be required where the common walls comply with 10.3.1.3.

This requirement was revised in the 2011 edition to clarify the intent. Although compliance with 10.2.1, Construction of Structures or Buildings, is mandated by Chapter 10, the reference was added here because the technical committee believed that providing a specific reference in 6.5.4.3 would help users locate the appropriate requirement and ensure compliance.

The requirements of Chapter 10 pertain to buildings or structures housing LP-Gas facilities. Paragraph 10.3.1.3 requires a fire resistance rating of at least 1 hour for the common walls separating the portion of the structure housing the LP-Gas facility from the rest of the structure, with openings protected by a fire door with a rating of at least 1½ hours. In addition, the wall must be designed to withstand a static pressure of 100 lb/ft². Under these conditions, the distances in Table 6.5.3 can be reduced, and as no lower limit is provided, the distances can be reduced to zero. Consultation with the authority having jurisdiction may be appropriate regarding distance reductions.

6.5.4.4 The distances in Table 6.5.3, parts B, C, D, E, F(2), and J, shall be reduced by one-half where the system incorporates the provisions of low emission transfer as provided in 6.26.5.

6.6 Installation of Containers

Installation of containers is covered in Section 6.6. It is divided into the following six subsections:

- 6.6.1, General Requirements (applicable to all containers)
- 6.6.2, Installation of Cylinders
- 6.6.3, Installation of Horizontal Aboveground ASME Containers
- 6.6.4, Installation of Vertical ASME Containers
- 6.6.5, Temporary Container Installations
- 6.6.6, Installation of Underground and Mounded Containers

Prior to the 2001 edition, this information was included in one section. It was reorganized and split into six separate headings for the convenience of users.

Section 6.6 provides requirements for the installation of cylinders and augments Section 6.3, which provides location requirements.

6.6.1 General Requirements.

6.6.1.1 Containers shall be positioned so that the pressure relief valve is in direct communication with the vapor space of the container.

Positioning the container so that the pressure relief valve is in direct communication with the vapor space ensures a minimal release of LP-Gas should abnormal conditions cause the relief valve to open. Tilting or laying a cylinder on its side so that liquid LP-Gas can be withdrawn is not permitted, in part because liquid in the container comes into contact with the pressure relief device. Liquid withdrawal fittings are available that allow the proper position of the relief valve to be maintained.

When the relief valve releases vapor, the fluid inside the container auto-refrigerates, or self cools, and the pressure decreases, allowing the relief valve to reclose and stopping the release. If, instead, liquid is released, the self cooling does not occur nearly as much and the pressure is not reduced significantly. When liquid is released, much more fuel is released and it is released for a longer time. Integrity of the container is protected, but at the expense of a large amount of fuel, with the possibility of fire.

Because cylinders do not normally have liquid withdrawal valves, it is common practice when emptying a cylinder at a bulk plant to temporarily orient the container to allow the withdrawal of liquid from the service (vapor) valve. While the container is tilted or otherwise positioned to put the liquid in contact with the service valve, the liquid is also in communication with the pressure relief valve. This action is not a violation of 6.6.1.1 because the text is addressing containers that are being installed. Liquid withdrawal fittings are available for cylinders in liquid service that allow the proper position of the relief valve to be retained.

6.6.1.2 LP-Gas containers or systems of which they are a part shall be protected from damage from vehicles.

FAQ ▶
Is a specific form of protection from vehicular impact required for LP-Gas installations?

Paragraph 6.6.1.2 is intentionally written as a performance requirement, rather than providing specific guidelines addressing when protection is needed or the nature of the protection. The technical committee believes that it can neither anticipate all the ways a vehicle might potentially threaten a container nor specify the type of protection that is appropriate. The determination of threat to containers and means of mitigation of potential threats are the responsibility of the code user or the authority having jurisdiction. Many code users would prefer to have the requirement stated in a "how-to" format, providing specific requirements for protective structures for different traffic situations. This format is not possible; therefore, the user must reasonably determine the possibility and extent of physical damage to each installation.

Discussions about the intent of this paragraph and others dealing with protection are widespread. As a result, a number of different devices and concepts have been proposed. One recent proposal was that "virtual" barriers could protect containers and systems. Such barriers would include signs and painted stripes on pavement. However, the intent of this paragraph is to require physical protection.

At least one authority having jurisdiction provides a listing of devices that would be accepted as suitable protection from damage from vehicles. This listing recognizes that absolute protection is impossible; that a high level of protection may be possible from prohibitively expensive barriers; and that a reasonable amount of protection can be provided by a reasonably priced barrier. The local authority having jurisdiction should be contacted to determine the expected level of protection and acceptable types of barriers.

Other questions about this provision usually are the result of an incident that has occurred and pertain to the intent of the committee. For example, an incident occurred in which a tractor-trailer that was transporting 63 head of cattle veered off a road and traveled almost 500 ft (150 m) before striking the piping associated with two LP-Gas containers. The 18,000 gal (68 m^3) and 30,000 gal (114 m^3) containers were installed about 110 ft (34 m) from the edge of the road. Escaping LP-Gas ignited, and the torch flame impinged on the 18,000 gal (68 m^3) container, resulting in a BLEVE after about 30 minutes [12].

In this case, the installer could not reasonably have been expected to protect containers located a significant distance from a road from impact by a stray tractor-trailer. Other incidents have occurred on construction sites where LP-Gas containers have been installed close to roadways or driveways used by delivery trucks and construction vehicles. In these cases, the installer would be expected to provide protection against impact from vehicles that pass close to the container.

6.6.1.3 Field welding on containers shall be limited to nonpressure parts such as saddle plates, wear plates, or brackets installed by the container manufacturer.

Field welding on pressure vessels can be done only by persons qualified in accordance with the relevant pressure vessel code requirements. Heating a pressure vessel may affect the properties of the steel and must not be done unless the individual has the proper qualifications. Therefore, only those parts of the system that do not affect the pressure vessel itself are permitted to be welded in the field unless the person possesses the proper qualifications.

◀ **FAQ**
Is it permissible to perform welding on a container without being certified to perform welding operations on pressure vessels?

Welding on an ASME pressure vessel can only be performed by welders who have received an "R" stamp certification from the National Board of Boiler and Pressure Vessel Inspectors. This certification permits them to repair pressure vessels such as LP-Gas containers. After the weld is complete, the National Board "R" will be stamped on the vessel near the weld. Exhibit 5.8 shows an R stamp certificate.

Paragraph 6.6.1.3 does, however, permit welding to take place on parts that are not part of the pressure vessel container, such as saddle plates, wear plates, and brackets.

6.6.1.4* Aboveground containers shall be painted.

A.6.6.1.4 Generally, a light-reflecting color paint is preferred unless the system is installed in an extremely cold climate.

Steel LP-Gas cylinders and ASME containers are painted for corrosion protection. Although NFPA 58 does not stipulate paint colors, color does affect the rate of heat absorption from solar radiation and the consequent pressure in the container. This heat absorption can result in operation of a pressure relief device in very warm climates. In very cold climates, a dark color may be appropriate to enhance propane vaporization in the container. Vaporization will not occur below about −40°F (−40°C).

White paint with a titanium oxide pigment is able to reflect 90 percent to 95 percent of solar light. Yellow paint made with a medium yellow chrome pigment reflects about

80 percent of the light. Aluminum reflects about 70 percent of solar light. Other colors reflect less than 15 percent, and black reflects no solar radiation.

6.6.1.5 Containers shall be installed so that all container operating appurtenances are accessible.

Although the requirement in 6.6.1.5 would appear to be obvious, it is necessary to state this practical requirement because it helps prevent containers from being installed with valves, gauges, or controls that are inaccessible. Occasionally a storage container must be evacuated before it is moved or for other reasons. Fittings for container evacuation eliminate the need to roll a container on its side to pump it out. Many other installation situations in which the container appurtenances may not be accessible will occur unless attention is given to the container position before installation.

6.6.1.6 Where necessary to prevent flotation due to possible high flood waters around aboveground or mounded containers, or high water table for those underground and partially underground, containers shall be securely anchored.

Anchorage of ASME containers usually consists of strapping or bolting the container to concrete pads or foundations. The design of an anchorage system can be complicated and may require a civil engineer to determine an appropriate method, based on the soil conditions and anticipated flood levels. However, some jurisdictions may have published approved methods for use based on the type of flooding that may occur.

Anchorage of larger cylinders can be accomplished by strapping or chaining through the lifting lugs or foot-ring. Chaining or strapping the cylinder to a building or other support can anchor smaller cylinders. When using chains to anchor a cylinder, care should be taken not to damage cylinder paint. Anchors are available for securing manufactured housing, and these have been used for propane containers.

In practice, only ASME containers are anchored. Cylinders (which are usually smaller than ASME containers) are not anchored because of their size, unless required by local ordinance. Therefore, smaller cylinders can be torn from their connections and be carried away in a flood. Even with their valves open, these cylinders generally do not significantly contribute to overall flood damage, but they can complicate the recovery effort, especially if houses moved by flooding are on top of containers. There are also concerns related to the loss of property (the containers) and hazards to navigation.

The anchoring system should be designed in such a way as to keep the container from inverting. Cables through lifting lugs only can allow the container to float upside down, causing the connecting piping to break and release liquid propane.

6.6.2 Installation of Cylinders.

6.6.2.1 Cylinders shall be installed only aboveground and shall be set upon a firm foundation or otherwise be firmly secured. The cylinder shall not be in contact with the soil.

FAQ ▶
What is meant by "firm foundation"?

Cylinders are designed primarily for transportation purposes, but with the understanding that they are used as storage for fuel. Cylinders are allowed to be installed below grade, but not buried in the ground. In an earlier edition of NFPA 58, an explanation was given that cylinders could be installed in a niche of a slope or terrace wall as long as the container and regulator did not contact the ground and the compartment or recess was ventilated and drained.

Although traditional materials such as concrete blocks and treated wood may be used, the technical committee intentionally used the words "firm foundation" to provide a performance criterion that would avoid unnecessary restrictions on the use of innovative materials, such as plastics and composite materials. Wood can be used as a foundation for cylinders, but must be monitored. If the wood rots it no longer provides a "firm foundation" and can allow the cylinder to come in contact with the soil; corrosion of the cylinder can then occur.

6.6.2.2 Flexibility shall be provided in the connecting piping. Where flexible connectors are used, they shall comply with 6.9.6.

Flexibility in the connecting piping is generally obtained by the use of a "pigtail," which is a short length of copper tubing with POL connectors on both ends. Pigtails are available from suppliers in a variety of lengths and are shipped without bends. They are bent into a circular shape when installed. They connect the cylinder service valve to the regulator that is attached to the piping system downstream. Copper is a good material for POL connectors because it allows small amounts of vibration and movement due to settling without fracturing the connector; however, significant vibration and repeated movement can cause copper to become brittle and fail. If this occurs, a pigtail with a larger diameter may be successful, or an alternate means must be provided.

During the processing of the 2011 edition a proposal was submitted to allow nonmetallic flexible connectors, noting successful experience with such connectors for recreational vehicle service. (Paragraph 6.8.1.1 requires that regulators be connected to cylinders using flexible metallic connectors.) The proposal was rejected because the committee had concerns about issues of durability; data on the aging and pressure retention of such connectors are not available. In addition, the potential problem of rodents gnawing on connectors was noted. There may be similar recommendations for the 2014 edition of NFPA 58.

The letters "POL" stand for Prest-o-Lite®, a trademark of a pioneer LP-Gas operator (Pyrofax-Union Carbide). Because these fittings have a left-hand thread, they have also been identified as "Put-on-Left." The Compressed Gas Association (CGA) identifies these fittings as a CGA 510 connection.

6.6.3 Installation of Horizontal Aboveground ASME Containers.

6.6.3.1 Horizontal ASME containers designed for permanent installation in stationary service above ground shall be placed on masonry or other noncombustible structural supports located on concrete or masonry foundations with the container supports.

The primary considerations in the installation of horizontal ASME containers are to ensure that the integrity of the supports is retained and that damage under fire conditions is minimized. Proper installation of large containers over 2000 gal (7.6 m³) is usually accomplished through the use of masonry foundations and supports that are called "saddles." Smaller containers of 2000 gal (7.6 m³) water capacity or less usually utilize steel legs that are welded to the container. The container is set with its legs placed on a noncombustible foundation, with a minimum distance from the container bottom to the ground as specified in Table 6.6.3.3(A). These minimum heights, together with the provision that flexibility is provided in the piping, ensure that the installation will not be compromised if the container settles a reasonable amount. Exhibit 6.11 illustrates a domestic container installation, and Exhibit 6.12 illustrates the use of a noncombustible masonry block foundation.

(A) Where saddles are used to support the container, they shall allow for expansion and contraction and prevent an excessive concentration of stresses.

Saddles are concrete supports formed to the shape of the container. Saddles are a common installation method for tanks larger than 2000 gal (7.6 m³) water capacity. The saddle shown in Exhibit 6.13 supports a 30,000 gal (144 m³) water capacity ASME container 3 ft (1 m) above grade. The installation shown uses a concrete saddle with a ½ in. (13 mm) thick bitumastic felt pad installed between the steel container and concrete foundation to minimize corrosion of the container.

The correct placement of saddles along the axis of the container is critical to achieving proper balancing of the stresses. If the saddles are too close to the ends of the container, excessive tensile stresses will occur at the bottom of the container in its middle. Conversely, if

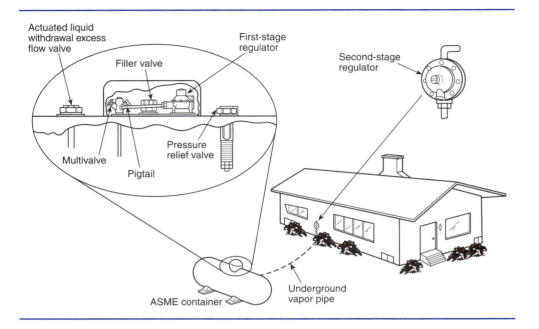

EXHIBIT 6.11 *Typical LP-Gas Domestic Container Installation. (Courtesy of Engineered Controls International, Inc.)*

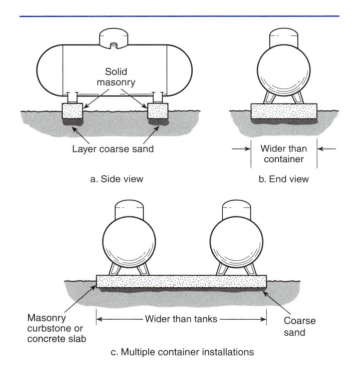

EXHIBIT 6.12 *Domestic ASME Container Installation on Noncombustible Foundation. (Courtesy of National Propane Gas Association)*

EXHIBIT 6.13 *ASME Storage Container with Concrete Saddles.*

saddles are placed too close to the middle, excessive tensile stresses will occur at the top of the container in its middle. In any event, the saddles should be placed equidistant from each end of the container. If questions arise regarding a specific installation, contact the tank fabricator if the tank is new, or a pressure vessel engineer if the tank is not new.

(B) Where structural steel supports are used, they shall comply with 6.6.3.3.

(C) Containers of more than 2000 gal (7.6 m³) water capacity shall be provided with concrete or masonry foundations formed to fit the container contour or, if furnished with saddles in compliance with Table 6.6.3.3(A), shall be placed on flat-topped foundations.

(D) Containers of 2000 gal (7.6 m³) water capacity or less shall be installed either on concrete or masonry foundations formed to fit the container contour or in accordance with 6.6.3.1(E).

(E) Containers of 2000 gal (7.6 m³) water capacity or less and equipped with attached supports complying with Table 6.6.3.3(A) shall be installed on a fire-resistive foundation if the bottoms of the horizontal members of the container saddles, runners, or skids are more than 12 in. (300 mm) above grade.

(F) Containers of 2000 gal (7.6 m³) water capacity or less shall not be mounted with the outside bottom of the container shell more than 5 ft (1.5 m) above the surface of the ground.

(G) Containers of 2000 gal (7.6 m³) water capacity or less and container-pump assemblies mounted on a common base complying with Table 6.6.3.3(A) shall be placed either on paved surfaces or on concrete pads at ground level within 4 in. (102 mm) of ground level.

6.6.3.2 ASME containers that have liquid interconnections shall be installed so that the maximum permitted filling level of each container is at the same elevation.

The arrangement described in 6.6.3.2 prevents overfilling of interconnected horizontal ASME containers. If the filling process was not carefully monitored, and the maximum filling level was not the same for all containers connected to a manifold, one or more containers could be overfilled. This type of overfilling resulted in the failure of a tank at an industrial site when individual tanks were isolated after being filled from a manifold. The containers were of different diameters and were installed with the bottoms at the same elevation.

A problem can exist if a group of manifolded containers with their maximum filling levels at different levels are filled to their maximum filling limit with their interconnecting valves open. If the valves to one or more containers are closed at a later time, an overfilling condition in one or more of the containers can occur because of the following:

- Liquid can migrate to the other container due to the natural effect of gravity.
- One container is at a higher pressure than the other.
- Solar heating of a manifolded container creates vapor, which will migrate to and condense in cooler containers.

Interconnecting piping is any piping connecting containers below the maximum filling level. Because the requirement was added in the 1998 edition and has not been made retroactive to installations existing at that time, it should be used as a reminder to use proper filling practices for installations that do not comply with this provision.

6.6.3.3 Support of Horizontal ASME Containers.

(A) Horizontal ASME containers with attached supports and designed for permanent installation in stationary service shall be installed in accordance with Table 6.6.3.3(A).

Table 6.6.3.3(A) was formerly located in the equipment chapter (now Chapter 5), but was moved to its present location because the technical committee believed it covers the installation of containers, rather than the requirements for a container. The requirements in Table 6.6.3.3(A) apply to horizontal ASME containers installed with attached steel "legs."

Note that the requirement in Table 6.6.3.3(A) for supports for containers of 2000 gal (7.6 m³) water capacity or less allow materials meeting the performance requirements of 6.6.3.3(B). These performance requirements do not prohibit nonmetallic materials as long as they provide the necessary structural support when exposed to the range of temperatures that

TABLE 6.6.3.3(A) *Installation of Permanently Installed Horizontal ASME Containers with Attached Supports*

Container Size		Attached Support	Height of Bottom of the Container
gal	*m³*		
≥2000	≥7.6	Non-fireproofed steel on flat-topped concrete foundations	6 in. (150 mm) maximum above concrete foundations
≤2000	≤7.6	Non-fireproofed steel on masonry or concrete foundations more than 12 in. (300 mm) above the ground	2 in.–12 in. (51 mm–300 mm) above concrete foundation
≤2000	≤7.6	Non-fireproofed steel on paved surfaces or concrete pads within 4 in. (100 mm) of the ground	24 in. (610 mm) maximum above paved surface or top of concrete pads
≤2000	≤7.6	Foundations or supports for horizontal LP-Gas containers per 6.6.3.3(B)	24 in. (610 mm) maximum above paved surface

can be anticipated. Any new nonmetallic material considered for this application must be capable of withstanding the environmental conditions described in the code, and verification of its performance should be documented in a research report describing the results of tests performed by an independent testing agency. Note that the new requirements also permit materials that could be combustible, as long as they are self-extinguishing materials. The definition of self-extinguishing is referenced to NFPA 99, *Standard for Health Care Facilities* [13], which states:

> **3.3.165 Self-Extinguishing.** A characteristic of a material such that, once the source of ignition is removed, the flame is quickly extinguished without the fuel or oxidizer being exhausted. [**NFPA 99**, 2005]

(B) Horizontal ASME containers of 2000 gal (7.6 m³) or less, on foundations in their installed condition, shall meet the following:

(1) Structurally support the containers when subject to deteriorating environmental effects including, but not limited to, ambient temperature of −40°F to 150°F (−40°C to 66°C) or local conditions if outside this range, ultraviolet rays, radiant heat from fires, and moisture

(2) Be of either noncombustible or self-extinguishing material (per the definition in NFPA 99, *Standard for Health Care Facilities* 3.3.165)

6.6.3.4 Where a single ASME container complying with Table 6.6.3.3(A) is installed in isolated locations with non-fireproofed steel supports resting on concrete pads or footings and the outside bottom of the container shell is not more than 5 ft (1.5 m) above the ground level, the approval of the authority having jurisdiction shall be obtained.

The provision in 6.6.3.4 is an exception to the requirements in Table 6.6.3.3(A) and is applicable only in isolated locations. Note that it allows tanks to be installed with greater distance between the container shell and the ground level than what is permitted by Table 6.6.3.3(A), but only where one tank is installed and only with the approval of the authority having jurisdiction. It does not allow an increase in the non-fireproofed steel distance from the concrete support to the bottom of the tank.

6.6.3.5 The part of an ASME container in contact with saddles or foundations or masonry shall be coated or protected to minimize corrosion.

6.6.3.6 In locations where the monthly maximum depth of snow accumulation, as determined from the National Weather Service or other published statistics, is more than the height of aboveground containers, excluding the dome cover, the following requirements shall apply:

(1) A stake or other marking shall be installed higher than the average snow cover depths, up to a height of 15 ft (4.6 m).
(2) The container shall be installed to prevent its movement resulting from snow accumulation.

The requirements in 6.6.3.6 resulted from a severe problem in the Sierra Nevada mountains of Northern California during the winter of 1992–1993. The requirements apply to areas where very heavy snowfall can be expected, even if infrequently. In the Sierra Nevada mountains, similar heavy snowfalls have been recorded at approximately 10-year intervals.
   The requirements serve the following two purposes:

1. The stake enables the gas company to locate the container for refilling and ensures that snow removal operations will not further bury the container. In the Sierra Nevada mountains, the LP-Gas companies have adopted a color code, which is painted on the top of the stakes.
2. The container must be installed to withstand the weight of the snow without being displaced from its foundation.

In addition to the problem of locating containers, several significant leaks resulted when meters and regulators were ripped from building sides when snow slid off the roof. Several methods have been developed to minimize the occurrences of damage, including recessing meters and regulators into the buildings and protecting the meters. An example of meter protection is shown in Exhibit 6.14.

EXHIBIT 6.14 *A Method of Meter Protection in Heavy Snow Areas. (Courtesy of Dead River Company)*

   Note that the height of the snow stake of 15 ft (4.6 m) is not intended to be higher than all possible snowfall accumulations, but is intended to provide a reasonable height to assist in locating tanks after heavy snowfall.
   The issue of snow depth continues to be addressed by the committee, and further revisions may be made in future editions. In the 2011 edition a proposal was submitted to revise how a determination of a "heavy snow" area is made. The current requirement, unchanged from the 2004 edition, relies on the depth of monthly average snow accumulation. While this is important, the weight of the snow is more important. (Wet snow is significantly heavier

than dry snow.) The proposal recommended using minimum roof loads of 125 lb/ft² (6 kPa) and was accepted. The change was rejected at the comment stage because the committee had concerns whether 125 lb/ft² was the correct threshold and noted that no data or other substantiation was provided for the value.

6.6.3.7 If the container is mounted on or is part of a vehicle in accordance with 5.2.7.2(A), the unit shall be located in accordance with 6.3.1.

(A) The surface on which the vehicle is parked shall be level and, if not paved, shall be able to support heavy vehicular traffic and shall be clear of dry grass and weeds and other combustible material within 10 ft (3 m) of the container.

(B) Flexibility shall be provided in the connecting piping in accordance with 6.9.6.

Paragraph 6.6.3.7 addresses the installation of portable storage containers, such as farm carts or fuel tenders, in a "stationary" installation. Such installations must be in accordance with the requirements of 6.3.1 for separation distances from buildings and property lines. In addition, the installation must be made on a level surface that is firm enough to support the weight of the cargo tank vehicle that would be sent to fill the container. Also see the commentary after 6.6.5.4.

6.6.3.8 Portable tanks of 2000 gal (7.6 m³) water capacity or less that comply with 5.2.7.3 shall be installed in accordance with 6.6.3.1(E).

Paragraph 6.6.3.8 permits DOT portable containers to be installed as permanent storage containers. The paragraph from Chapter 5 referenced in 6.6.3.8 states the following:

> **5.2.7.3** Portable tank design and construction of a full framework, skids, or lugs for the attachment of skids, and protection of fittings shall be in accordance with DOT portable tank specifications. The bottom of the skids shall be not less than 2 in. (50 mm) or more than 12 in. (300 mm) below the outside bottom of the tank shell.

6.6.4 Installation of Vertical ASME Containers.

6.6.4.1 Vertical ASME containers of over 125 gal (0.5 m³) water capacity designed for permanent installation in stationary service above ground shall be installed on reinforced concrete or steel structural supports on reinforced concrete foundations that are designed to meet the loading provisions established in 5.2.4.3.

Although vertical containers, as shown in Exhibit 6.15, are not used as extensively as horizontal containers, they are useful for certain applications, such as dispensers in service stations and in other locations where space is at a premium. The three vertical 30,000 gal (114 m³) containers shown in Exhibit 6.15 are an example of vertical tank installations. Larger vertical containers are usually selected because of either the high value of land or the inavailability of land.

6.6.4.2 The requirements in 6.6.4.3 through 6.6.4.5 shall also apply to the installation of vertical ASME containers.

6.6.4.3 Steel supports shall be protected against fire exposure with a material that has a fire resistance rating of at least 2 hours, except that continuous steel skirts that have only one opening that is 18 in. (460 mm) or less in diameter shall have fire protection applied to the outside of the skirts.

The requirements for fire protection for the structural base of vertical containers ensure that the containers will be able to withstand flame impingement without toppling over.

EXHIBIT 6.15 *Vertical 30,000 gal (114 m³) Containers. (Courtesy of Quality Gas Service)*

6.6.4.4 Vertical ASME containers used in liquid service shall not be manifolded to horizontal ASME containers.

6.6.4.5 Vertical ASME containers of different dimensions shall not be manifolded together.

The requirements in 6.6.4.4 and 6.6.4.5 are in place to ensure that the filling of manifolding containers does not lead to a situation in which the "shorter" containers become liquid-full due to the effects of gravity.

6.6.5 Temporary Container Installations.

6.6.5.1 Single containers constructed as portable storage containers for temporary stationary service in accordance with 5.2.7.2(A) shall be placed on concrete pads, paved surfaces, or firm earth for such temporary service (not more than 12 months at a given location).

6.6.5.2 The surface on which the containers are placed shall be level and, if not paved, shall be clear of dry grass and weeds and other combustible material within 10 ft (3 m) of the container.

6.6.5.3 Flexibility shall be provided in the connecting piping in accordance with 6.9.6.

6.6.5.4 Where portable storage containers are installed at isolated locations with the bottoms of the skids or runners above the ground, either fire-resistive supports shall be provided or non–fire-resistive supports shall be permitted when all the following conditions are met:

(1) The height of the outside bottom of the container does not exceed 5 ft (1.5 m) above the ground.
(2) The approval of the authority having jurisdiction is obtained.

A single portable storage container can be used in a temporary installation for applications such as fuel supplies, crop drying, road construction, building construction, and commercial cooking at fairs. Note that 4.3.2 requires that the authority having jurisdiction be notified before starting temporary installations using storage containers of over 2000 gal (7.6 m³) individual water capacity or with aggregate water capacity exceeding 4000 gal (15.1 m³) that will be used for no more than 12 months.

The requirement in 6.6.5.4, which covers only isolated locations, emphasizes the concern over the integrity of the container should its supports be subjected to fire. The height limitation ensures that, in the event non–fire-resistive supports are used, the container is not installed at an extremely high elevation, which may result in damage to the container should the supports be affected by the heat of a fire.

6.6.6 Installation of Underground and Mounded Containers.

6.6.6.1* ASME container assemblies intended for underground installation, including interchangeable aboveground–underground container assemblies, shall be installed underground in accordance with 6.6.6.1(A) through 6.6.6.1(O).

The requirements in 6.6.6.1 cover only containers listed for underground installations and interchangeable aboveground–underground container assemblies. (See Exhibits 6.16 and 6.17.) Exhibit 6.17 shows underground containers installed in an excavated area ready for backfilling. Note that sand has been placed in the bottom of the pit and that the anodes (white bags connected with wires) are in place. Prior to the backfilling, the coating should be inspected for chips and scratches that may have been created during shipping and rigging, and it should be repaired as needed with a can of spray paint.

Manufacturers of ASME containers for underground installation must mark the containers as suitable for underground use or for the interchangeable aboveground–underground type of service. While it is possible to install a container built for aboveground service under ground, modifications would probably be required to locate all the container appurtenances within a dome, and repainting would be required. Likewise, a container built for underground

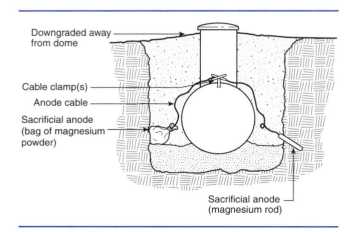

Downgraded away from dome

Cable clamp(s)

Anode cable

Sacrificial anode (bag of magnesium powder)

Sacrificial anode (magnesium rod)

EXHIBIT 6.16 *Typical Small ASME Container Underground Installation. (Courtesy of National Propane Gas Association)*

EXHIBIT 6.17 *Installation of Underground Tanks, Showing Placement of Anodes. (Courtesy of H&H Gas)*

installation could be installed above ground, but the pressure relief valve would have to be replaced with one sized for aboveground use, and a new container connection may be required. Some users prefer underground or mounded container installations for fire protection or for the aesthetics of the installation.

Because of the demand for underground containers, some tank manufacturers have significant operations to remanufacture used aboveground tanks for underground service. This work will normally require closing some existing openings and creating a new opening to mount the multi-valve normally found on underground tanks. An "R stamp" must be applied to the tank with sufficient information to trace the work done to the tank, and the original dataplate must be modified to show the new service for the tank. This conversion is not complicated, but the documentation has been found to be insufficient in some recent conversions.

Underground and mounded containers must be protected against corrosion through application of a coating, or by both coating and cathodic protection. Where coatings are used, it is especially important not to allow any scarring of the protective coating while installing the containers, because just one small, unprotected spot can concentrate corrosion and lead to quicker degradation of the container. There is an adage among metallurgists that a coating can be 99 percent perfect and 100 percent useless. This is true because any pinhole in the coating will cause severe localized corrosion. Some metallurgists are of the opinion that there can never be a perfect tank coating that will last indefinitely.

Chains or cables should never be wrapped around containers in order to move them without some cushioning material between the chain or cable and the container coating.

A concrete or metal saddle is not necessary for an underground container installation, provided the container rests on firm sand or earth. However, where the conditions of the soil are not suitable, underground containers should be placed on a foundation or slab. When the backfill is placed, it should be free of rocks and similar abrasives that can adversely affect the coating. Backfill should be tamped to prevent settling.

An underground container should not be installed in a pit until the pit is partially backfilled with sand or suitable earth, as shown in Exhibit 6.16.

If an underground container is installed in a flood plain area, it may be necessary to anchor the tank to prevent flotation. Mobile home tie-downs and straps can be used for this purpose, especially for underground tanks of 2000 gal (7.6 m³) or smaller. If the tank is larger it may be more effective to place a concrete slab in the hole and anchor the tank to the slab. Whatever anchoring method is used, the restraining system should be sized for the buoyancy of an empty tank, as the high water could come when the tank is empty or nearly so.

A.6.6.6.1 See Annex K.

Annex K, Burial and Corrosion Protection for Underground and Mounded ASME Containers, was introduced in the 2008 edition of the code. Annex K is not mandatory but does provide some direction for the owners of tanks who want to learn more about the techniques and practices used for protecting underground LP-Gas tanks from corrosion.

(A) Containers installed in areas with no vehicular traffic shall be installed at least 6 in. (150 mm) below grade.

The determination of what constitutes "vehicular traffic" is not specified. As the intent of this subparagraph is to prevent damage to the tank, precautions must be taken to keep heavy loads from being driven across the tank. A typical riding lawn mower would not be a significant load.

(B) In areas where vehicular traffic is expected, a noninterchangeable underground container shall be installed at least 18 in. (460 mm) below grade, or the container shall be protected from damage from vehicles.

A burial depth of 6 in. (15 cm) is sufficient where no vehicular traffic and only pedestrian traffic is expected above or near the container [per 6.6.6.1(A)]. When heavier loads are expected from vehicles, the burial depth is increased to 18 in. (460 mm) to distribute the loads more evenly, protecting the container. If a burial depth of 18 in. is impossible, protection must be provided by other means.

A civil engineer familiar with soils should be consulted when alternate means are used to ensure that the container is properly protected from damage by vehicles. When containers are installed in areas where gardening is expected, the deeper burial depth is a means to protect the container coating (if relied on for corrosion protection) from damage. The container user should be notified of the need to avoid digging in the area of the container.

(C) Protection against vehicular damage shall be provided for the fitting housing, housing cover, container connections, and piping.

Underground container appurtenances and their housings should be protected from vehicular traffic. The requirement in 6.6.6.1(C) protects both the container and the initial length of pipe or tubing at the container. Protection can be provided by using a visual marker or a physical barrier.

(D) Approved interchangeable aboveground–underground container assemblies installed underground shall not be placed with the container shell more than 12 in. (300 mm) below grade.

Interchangeable aboveground–underground containers are constructed in accordance with UL 644, *Container Assemblies for LP-Gas* [14]. The UL standard specifies a relatively short sleeve to which the cover is attached. The requirement results in the 12 in. (0.30 m) burial depth called for in the code. The use of this type of container is limited to warmer climates, because the relatively shallow burial depth puts the container above the frost line in colder climates, and the container can be forced above ground after a number of freeze/thaw cycles.

(E) The installation of a buried container shall include protection for the container and piping against physical damage from vehicular traffic.

This requirement was revised in the 2011 edition by splitting the paragraph into new subparagraphs (E) and (F). The new subparagraph (E) is a general requirement and does not assign responsibility. Formerly, it stated that "any party involved in construction or excavation in the vicinity of a buried container" was responsible for the location and protection of an underground container from vehicular traffic. While this was clear, the revised text simply makes it a requirement applicable to potentially anyone, without stating specifically who has to ensure compliance.

The requirement makes it clear that those digging or excavating around an underground propane container must be aware of the consequences of their actions.

(F) Prior to digging, the location of underground and mounded containers and piping in the vicinity of construction and excavation activities shall be determined and the installation shall be protected from damage.

Note that the requirement has been revised to clarify that before digging, the container must be located and digging be conducted so that the container is not damaged.

(G) Where a container is to be abandoned underground, the following procedure shall be followed:

(1) As much liquid LP-Gas as practical shall be removed through the container liquid withdrawal connection.
(2)* As much of the remaining LP-Gas vapor as practical shall be removed through a vapor connection.

A.6.6.6.1(G)(2) If vapor is vented too rapidly, the pressure drop due to the refrigeration of the liquid can lead to the erroneous conclusion that no liquid remains in the container.

The safe abandonment of underground containers is important. If a container were to be abandoned without the precautions required in 6.6.6.1(G)(1) through 6.6.6.1(G)(5) being taken, the container could corrode and result in gas leakage that could cause a fire. Also, collapse of an underground container could cause ground subsidence if not filled. Note that an abandoned tank filled with water could eventually cause ground subsidence, as it will eventually rust away.

Because of the difficulty of removing underground containers when they are no longer needed, and the damage to landscaping and vegetation by the equipment needed to dig up and remove an underground container, it is not unusual for an underground container to be abandoned, rather than moved to another location. As all propane containers do not have the capability of being completely emptied, propane vapor and some propane liquid will remain in the container.

Leaking underground gasoline and heating oil tank leaks have caused much concern because the U.S. Environmental Protection Agency (EPA) considers both of those fuels toxic. Gasoline and heating oil are groundwater contaminants that cause environmental damage. Propane is not a groundwater contaminant, however, and there is no need to remove underground propane containers for environmental reasons.

(3) The vapor shall be either recovered, burned, or vented to the atmosphere.
(4) Where only vapor LP-Gas at atmospheric pressure remains in the container, the container shall be filled with water, sand, or foamed plastic or shall be purged with an inert gas.
(5) If purged, the displaced vapor shall be either recovered, burned, or vented to the atmosphere.

(H) The discharge of the regulator vent shall be above the highest probable water level.

Discharging the regulator vent above the highest probable water level prevents the container relief valve vent from being blocked as a result of water freezing. If the container relief valve vent is blocked, overpressure of downstream piping may result, with serious consequences.

(I)* A corrosion protection system shall be installed on new installations of underground steel containers, unless technical justification is provided to and is approved by the authority having jurisdiction. The corrosion protection system shall include the following:

(1) A container coating complying with 5.2.1.11
(2) A cathodic protection system that consists of a sacrificial anode(s) or an impressed current anode
(3) A means to test the performance of the cathodic protection system

This significant new requirement in the 2011 edition mandates the use of cathodic protection systems on all new underground containers. It recognizes that cathodic protection is a practical way to protect underground containers from the normal type of corrosion that is encountered. The cathodic protection system normally used for underground propane containers consists of the tank, an anode, a sacrificial mass of metal (usually magnesium), and a wire to electrically connect the anode to the tank. When the tank coating fails, the magnesium will corrode before the steel tank does. Note that 6.6.6.1(I)(3) requires the cathodic protection system to have a means to test the performance of the system, and 6.6.6.1(K) specifies the testing schedule. Monitoring is done with a voltmeter and copper/copper sulfate reference cell. Another type of cathodic protection system exists, one in which a voltage is provided to the tank, but this type of system is normally used for pipelines and installations of a large number of underground propane tanks. For more information on the subject, refer to Supplement 5, Cathodic Protection.

The requirement for providing cathodic protection is not retroactive. Thus, there is no requirement to install cathodic protection systems on all existing underground tanks. Note that the new requirements do not require testing of all previously installed underground tanks with cathodic protection systems for the effectiveness of the cathodic protection system. This does not prohibit testing of existing cathodic protection systems, and it may be a good practice.

It makes sense that all underground tanks must be protected from corrosion, just as all aboveground tanks must be kept painted to control corrosion. Corrosion of propane containers, whatever its source, must be minimized, as failure to do so leads to leaks and tank failures. Some authorities having jurisdiction already have active inspection programs to test underground tanks for corrosion and require correction of those tanks that fail a test very similar to that described later in this section. Generally, the addition of an anode to an already-buried tank will allow the tank to pass the test.

A.6.6.6.1(I) Installing cathodic corrosion protection systems on new installations will help assure the integrity of underground storage systems. Technical reports or other data can be presented to the authority having jurisdiction in support of waiving the requirement for a cathodic protection system.

For information on the proper sizing and installation of corrosion protection systems for containers and piping systems, see the following:

(1) National Association of Corrosion Engineers Standard SP-01-69, *Control of External Corrosion on Underground or Submerged Metallic Piping Systems*
(2) National Association of Corrosion Engineers Standard RP-02-85, *Corrosion Control of Underground Storage Tank Systems by Cathodic Protection*
(3) API Publication 1632, *Cathodic Protection of Underground Petroleum Storage Tanks and Piping Systems,* 3rd ed.

For information on complete cathodic protection systems installed on containers at the factory, see the following:

(1) Underwriters Laboratories Inc., UL 1746, *External Corrosion Protection Systems for Steel Underground Storage Tanks*
(2) Underwriters Laboratories of Canada, CAN/ULC S603.1, *Standard for External Corrosion Protection Systems for Steel Underground Tanks for Flammable and Combustible Liquids*

Corrosion protection systems include not only the anode system, but also the coating on the container and a means to test the performance of the system. All elements contribute to the overall performance of the system and are needed in order to provide the most comprehensive protection to the container.

The sacrificial galvanic anode system protects the container from corrosion by generating a low voltage electrical current that protects the container while the anode deteriorates over time. While impressed current systems can also be used, those systems are typically used on containers larger than 2000 gal (WC) and are not found on typical residential or commercial ASME underground container installations.

It is important that, when a cathodic protection system is designed, there is a clear understanding of the limits of the surface area and materials being protected. Electrical isolation of the container from metallic piping may be necessary using a dielectric fitting or other component designed for that purpose. For example, the cathodic system that protects a steel tank that is not electrically isolated from the attached metallic piping system will be forced to provide protection for the connected piping system as well. Therefore, the sacrificial anode will have to be sized to protect both the container and the piping. Additionally, if the piping is of a different material (such as copper) from the container, further complications could result, and it is possible that the steel may corrode even though a sacrificial anode is connected to the container.

The importance of electrical isolation of the tank from metallic piping can not be overly stated. While the code does not specifically require electrical isolation between the tank and gas line, failure to isolate will make it difficult to achieve the voltages specified in the testing procedure and may lead to shortened anode life.

◀ **FAQ**
Is electrical separation between tank and gas piping required?

Anodes are usually sized to protect a tank with an assumed percentage of coverage by the coating material. The initial percentage will be higher than what is expected later in its underground life, with the coating deteriorating over time. With that assumption, a certain size and number of anodes will protect stated sizes of tanks for a specified amount of time. However, if the percentage of coating deterioration is higher than expected or if the anode is called on to protect more metal, then failure or depletion of the anode will occur much sooner.

Two situations illustrating this have occurred in North Carolina. In one, a 30,000 gal (114 m^3) tank was buried and several anodes were buried with it and properly connected to the tank. However, the tank was not electrically isolated from the bulkhead at the loading/unloading station. The bulkhead had an attached switch for operating the pump, with the appropriate grounding connection. It was determined after a relatively short time that the cathodic protection system was not functioning properly. Investigation showed that the anodes were protecting the underground electrical system in that part of town where the tank was installed. As the tank was not isolated from the town's underground electrical system, the anodes were consumed well before the end of their expected lifetime.

In the other situation, an underground tank installation was observed. The tank was well coated and ready for installation. The anode was placed in a hole so that it was located under the tank. Using a copper/copper sulfate half cell, the anode was tested and the expected voltage was observed, about −1.6 volts, which is an acceptable value. Then the tank was installed, buried, and wired to the anode. Another reading was taken and was in the range expected, about −1.4 volts, which is also an acceptable value. (It should be noted that, even immediately after installation, the presence of some coating imperfections was indicated by a change in the voltage.) Then the metallic piping to the house was attached. The voltage dropped to about −0.45 volts, a failing reading. The one hundred feet (30 m) or so of copper tubing to the house pulled the voltage down. It was not a fault in the house, because when the tubing was disconnected at the house, the voltage stayed the same. When a dielectric union, an electrically isolating pipe fitting, was placed between the tank and the piping to the house, the expected voltage of about −1.4 volts was re-established. A dielectric union is shown in Exhibit 6.18.

It is important that no part of the piping downstream of the dielectric union touch the tank or the tank collar after the installation is complete. If it does, then the anode may be shorted to the piping, causing a failing reading and/or shortened anode life.

(J)* Cathodic protection systems installed in accordance with 6.6.6.1(I) shall be monitored by testing and the results documented. Confirming tests shall be described by one of the following:

(1) Producing a voltage of −0.85 volts or more negative, with reference to a saturated copper-copper sulfate half cell
(2) Producing a voltage of −0.78 volts or more negative, with reference to a saturated KCl calomel half cell
(3) Producing a voltage of −0.80 volts or more negative, with reference to a silver-silver chloride half cell
(4) Any other method described in Appendix D of Title 49 of the Code of Federal Regulations, Part 192

Note that this requirement was added to the 2011 edition in conjunction with others to provide requirements for cathodic protection. The new requirement assumes that a passive cathodic protection system will be used and recognizes the three types of reference cells that are likely

EXHIBIT 6.18 *Dielectric Union Used to Isolate a Tank from Metallic Gas Piping. (Courtesy of Richard Fredenburg, North Carolina Department of Agriculture and Consumer Services)*

to be used to obtain a voltage reading. The copper/copper sulfate half cell is most widely used. Exhibit 6.19 shows the equipment used to measure the voltage. It consists of a voltmeter (any voltmeter can be used), a copper/copper sulfate half cell (in front of the voltmeter), and a cable with a clamp that is connected to the container, usually in the dome of the underground container. See Supplement 5, Cathodic Protection, for more information on the use of this measuring equipment.

FAQ ▶

Underground containers come with coatings designed for underground service. If an underground container is installed with no damage to the coating, or if any damage to the coating is repaired as instructed by the container manufacturer, is the container protected from corrosion?

The importance of maintaining a complete coating of underground tanks cannot be over-stressed. If the coating is perfect, and remains perfect over time, there will be no contact between the container and the soil, and no corrosion will occur. Unfortunately, this is not possible, as all coatings will fail at some time. If there is a pinhole in the coating, either at the time of installation or later, it will allow contact and an electrochemical action will begin. The action will result in all the corrosion occurring at the point of the pinhole.

An investigator called NFPA staff for assistance in investigating leakage from an underground propane container that had been installed for less than three years. The tank was dug up, and one small round hole was found in the shell. It was assumed to be a bullet hole, but how could only one bullet hole be present, with no bullet in the tank? Consultation with members of the NFPA LP-Gas committee resulted in the conclusion that the hole was caused by corrosion due to a point failure of the coating of the container (sometimes called a "pinhole," or "holiday"). Because there was only one point of coating failure, the electrochemical action of the entire container surface passed through that point and all the corrosion occurred at that point. If the container had not been coated, it would have lasted much longer, but its eventual failure would be certain. Installing a cathodic protection system when the container is installed can prevent this electrochemical action.

It is interesting to quantify the rate of corrosion in the example cited above. If the tank wall was 0.375 in. (9.5 mm), this is a corrosion rate of 0.375 in. divided by three years, or 0.125 in. (3.175 mm) per year, which is a significant corrosion rate. If the coating failed some

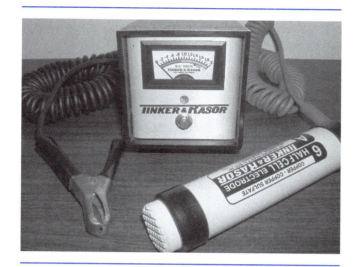

EXHIBIT 6.19 *Copper/Copper Sulfate Half Cell and Test Meter. (Courtesy of Richard Fredenburg, North Carolina Department of Agriculture and Consumer Services)*

EXHIBIT 6.20 *Corrosion Hole. (Courtesy of Richard A. Hoffmann, P.E., Hoffmann & Feige)*

time after the container was installed, and the tank failed in three years of service, then the corrosion rate was greater than 0.125 in. per year. A metallurgist advises the editor that a corrosion rate of 0.125 in. per year is significant. In reality, the rate of corrosion is not equal over time and varies with soil moisture. The soil itself is a significant variable in corrosion. Experience with soils in a local area can be very valuable in determining the need for protection from corrosion.

Exhibit 6.20 shows a corrosion hole in an LP-Gas container. It shows the localized leakage failure in a buried LP-Gas tank in a humid climate. The corrosion hole is about ½ in. (13 mm) in diameter and originated on the outside surface of the tank. This tank was coated, but the coating failed locally, and over time leakage occurred. The general corrosion shown in the photograph took place after the tank was removed from the ground.

A.6.6.6.1(J) Once the monitoring tests required by 6.6.6.1(K) have been performed, the results can be compared to the criteria listed in this paragraph. The system is functioning properly if it develops −0.85 volt or greater negative voltage when tested with a copper-copper sulfate reference electrode.

The use of a copper-copper sulfate half cell to confirm that the cathodic protection system is functioning properly is anticipated to be the most common method of testing sacrificial anode systems on propane containers. Other standard reference half cells can be substituted for the saturated cooper-copper sulfate half cell. In addition to the standard reference half cells, other means of testing cathodic systems can be employed, and they are explained in more detail in 49 CFR 192, Appendix D.

(K)* Sacrificial anodes installed in accordance with 6.6.6.1(I) shall be tested in accordance with the following schedule:

(1) Upon installation of the cathodic protection system, unless prohibited by climactic conditions, in which case testing shall be done within 180 days after the installation of the system.
(2) For continued verification of the effectiveness of the system, 12 to 18 months after the initial test.
(3) Upon successful verification testing and in consideration of previous test results, periodic follow-up testing shall be performed at intervals not to exceed 36 months.

(4) Systems failing a test shall be repaired as soon as practical unless climactic conditions prohibit this action, in which case the repair shall be made not more than 180 days thereafter. The testing schedule shall be restarted as required in 6.6.6.1(K)(1) and (2) and the results shall comply with 6.6.6.1(J).

(5) Documentation of the results of the two most recent tests shall be retained.

The annex material for this section clearly explains the requirement for periodic testing of the corrosion protection system. The testing can be accomplished by any of a number of methods. The most common methods are expected to be the following:

1. Testing by the propane company that owns the tank. The propane company will be the familiar with the location of their tanks and with the tanks' testing status. It is expected that they will implement a test program that schedules the testing timing and stores the results of the testing, as required in 6.6.6.1(K)(5). Deleting older test results so that the two most recent test results are maintained is allowed. However, retaining the results for a longer time may yield valuable data for the individual tank condition and for the protection program as a whole.

2. Testing by a contractor. A "cottage industry" of contractors who provide testing services could arise. These contractors could provide a service to multiple propane companies by testing a whole area at a time, based on the information provided by the propane companies they are serving. They could also provide this service to individuals who own their own tank.

3. Testing by the AHJ. The authority having jurisdiction in many states will likely do some testing on a random or representative sampling of tanks. Few, if any, states have enough inspection staff or the time to test all underground tanks. However, as with inspections of a sampling of containers in domestic use, testing some underground tanks will provide information to the AHJ's office about the general compliance rate for the protection of these tanks.

Who is responsible for testing and maintenance of the cathodic protection system on a customer-owned tank?
FAQ ▶

NFPA 58 does not assign responsibility for testing or other procedures. Any competent person can test the anode. What is important is that the testing be done, and that the tank not be filled unless the original and follow-up testing is done and documented.

FAQ ▶
How does a delivery person know if a tank he or she is getting ready to fill is properly protected from corrosion?

A practical problem is how to inform a tank filler that the tank has been tested and that the results of the test were acceptable. This is especially troublesome if the customer owns the tank and is not present to show the test results. A propane company in Colorado developed plastic tags that can be affixed to tanks after they are tested. (Colorado implemented a requirement for cathodic protection prior to the LP-Gas Code requirement.) These tags are shown in Exhibit 6.21. The left tag, with a white background color, is used to show that the tank was tested and was "found to be protected." It shows the month and year of the test and states that another test must be repeated within three years. The appropriate dates are punched. It also gives the location of the test report. The right tag, with a red background color, is used if the test of the anode fails, and the tank is not protected. This tag is used where the tank was determined to not have any cathodic protection or it is no longer effective. There is a warning that the tank must not be filled until the cathodic protection situation is corrected. Again, the month and year of the test are punched, and contact information for the propane company is provided.

This same type of tag can be developed by any testing entity. If the authority having jurisdiction tests underground tanks, they can have a distinctive method of providing the test information. Note that the new code requirements do not restrict how the information is provided, and it is anticipated that several equally effective systems will be developed.

A.6.6.6.1(K) The installation of a cathodic protection system on an underground container introduces a need to periodically verify that the system is functioning properly and protecting the container from corrosion. Sacrificial anode systems are anticipated to be the most frequently installed systems for propane underground storage containers. The testing program

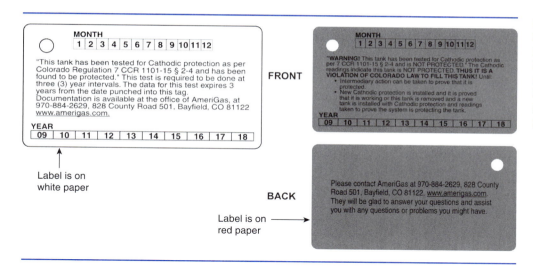

required for sacrificial anode systems is consistent with nationally recognized practices [see A.6.6.6.1(I)]. Initial testing is required as soon as practical after installing the system, and then the verification test is required approximately 12 to 18 months after the initial testing was done. The time periods for the initial and verification tests are allowed to be adjusted to accommodate installations that, due to inclement weather, unsuitable soil conditions, or other environmental conditions, cannot be tested immediately.

If the initial test and verification test are successful, a suitable period for follow-up testing of the system should be established. A review of available standards, federal and state regulations, and recommended practices indicates that a maximum time period of 3 years is an acceptable interval for periodic testing. Should a test of the installation not achieve the required results, the sacrificial anode system must be repaired and the testing program begun again.

Training material on the installation and testing of cathodic protection systems can be found in the following publications:

(1) Propane Education and Research Council (PERC) video titled "Cathodic Protection Systems"
(2) Propane Education and Research Council (PERC) publication *Cathodic Protection Manual and Quiz #20689590*

The requirement in 6.6.6.1(K)(5) is to provide protection for the container owner and to permit the AHJ to verify that the container is in compliance with the code. Retaining test results also permits easy verification of the continued effectiveness of the cathodic protection system. The retention of the two most recent tests will permit comparison with the current test results, resulting in a trend curve of performance for the system. The observed trend may be used to increase the testing frequency as needed.

(L)* Where an impressed current cathodic protection system is installed, it shall be inspected and tested in accordance with the following schedule:

(1) All sources of impressed current shall be inspected and tested at intervals not exceeding two months.
(2) All impressed current cathodic protection installations shall be inspected and tested annually.

A.6.6.6.1(L) Impressed current cathodic protection systems are typically engineered systems that must be maintained and inspected according to a more frequent schedule. The requirements contained in this section are based on information published in the NACE documents referenced in A.6.6.6.1(I). In 6.6.6.1(L)(1), evidence of proper functioning may be current output, normal power consumption, or a signal indicating normal operation. In 6.6.6.1(L)(2), a preventive maintenance program to minimize in-service failure is necessary. Inspections should include a check for electrical shorts, ground connections, meter accuracy, efficiency, and circuit resistance. The effectiveness of isolating devices and continuity bonds should be evaluated during the periodic surveys. This can be accomplished by on-site inspection or by evaluating corrosion test data.

It is not anticipated that impressed current cathodic protection systems will be installed on underground propane tanks. There are a small number of installations of a large number of underground tanks at storage facilities that may use impressed current systems.

(M) Prior to burial, the container shall be visually examined for damage to the coating. Damaged areas shall be repaired with a coating recommended for underground service and compatible with the existing coating.

Note that the container must be checked for damage to the coating, and for repairs to be made prior to backfilling. This is very important, as any gaps in the coating will result in rapid depletion of the anode.

Care must be taken to use the proper coating when repairing damage to the factory-applied coating. Often, a small amount of coating material is provided with the tank for the purpose of repairing damage sustained during shipping of the tank. Also, some coatings can fail if they are "augmented" by being covered with another coating. For example, if a mastic coating is applied over a phenolic coating, the mastic can trap water between the coatings, causing faster degradation of the phenolic coating.

(N)* Containers shall be set level and shall be surrounded by earth or sand firmly tamped in place.

A.6.6.6.1(N) Firm earth can be used.

(O) Backfill shall be free of rocks and abrasives.

Underground containers must be installed so that they will not shift, because the shifting of the container could place excessive loads on the piping system. Coarse material, such as rock and other abrasives, can damage coatings; therefore, earth or sand is used to surround the container.

> Subsections A.6.6.6.1(I) through A.6.6.6.1(L) were added by a tentative interim amendment (TIA).

6.6.6.2 Partially underground, unmounded ASME containers shall be installed as follows:

(1) The portion of the container below the surface of the ground, and for a vertical distance of at least 3 in. (75 mm) above that surface, shall comply with the corrosion protection requirements of 6.6.6.1(I) through (M). The aboveground portion of the container shall comply with 6.6.1.4.

•

With the new requirements for cathodic protection, reference is made to 6.6.6.1 (I) through (M), which cover this topic in detail.

(2) Containers shall be set level and shall be surrounded by earth or sand firmly tamped in place
(3) Backfill shall be free of rocks and abrasives.
(4) Spacing provisions shall be as specified for aboveground containers in 6.3.1 and Table 6.3.1.
(5) The container shall be located so as not to be subject to vehicular damage or shall be protected against such damage.

Partially underground, unmounded containers are essentially half-buried containers. They are rarely installed. The requirements for these containers are a combination of underground and aboveground container installation requirements. See the commentary following 6.6.1.2 for information on providing protection for an installation from vehicular damage.

6.6.6.3 Mounded containers shall be installed as follows:

Mounded containers during installation are shown in Exhibit 6.22. Note that the containers are installed above grade and shown partially covered, with sand in this case. Earth or other material can also be used so that the containers are not affected by flame impingement. Mounded containers are also placed out of sight, which has aesthetic advantages. Mounding provides insulation from low or high temperatures and is, therefore, a means of special protection. (See the definition of *special protection* in 3.3.65.) Mounded containers must be protected from corrosion in the same manner required for underground containers. Note the tunnel, which provides access to the tank's bottom connections.

Exhibit 6.22 illustrates three 80,000 gal (302 m³) storage containers mounded for special protection. These containers have an epoxy coal tar coating for corrosion protection in addition to cathodic protection. A 12 in. (300 mm) covering of sand was provided around each container and a 6 in. (150 mm) layer of gravel was installed over the three containers. The containers were provided with extended manways and relief valve nozzles to permit installation of all container trim above the top surface of the final layer of gravel.

EXHIBIT 6.22 *Storage Containers Mounded for Special Protection. (Courtesy of Superior Energy Systems, Inc.)*

(1)*Mounding material shall be earth, sand, or other noncombustible, noncorrosive materials and shall provide a minimum thickness of cover for the container of at least 1 ft (0.3 m).

A.6.6.6.3(1) Noncombustible, noncorrosive materials include vermiculite and perlite.

A mounded container can be above or partially buried below the ground surface, but it must be completely covered by at least 1 ft (0.3 m) of earth, sand, or other noncombustible, noncorrosive material. Burying a tank completely can be undesirable because of the water table, rock formations, and other reasons.

Prior to the 1992 edition, only earth or sand was permitted to be used as mounding material. The list of covering materials has since been expanded to include noncombustible, noncorrosive materials such as vermiculite and perlite. These materials have significant advantages over sand and earth in certain installations. For example, creating a mounded container by erecting walls around it and filling the space with earth or sand would require a very strong wall to contain the heavy material. By permitting a lighter material, the option of mounding in this manner is encouraged. Of course, measures have to be taken to ensure that these lighter materials remain in place. These measures include covering the lighter materials with an upper layer of sand or installing a fabric to stabilize the surface.

(2) A protective cover shall be provided on top of mounding materials subject to erosion.

(3) Container valves and appurtenances shall be accessible for operation or repair, without disturbing mounding material, as follows:

(a) Where containers are mounded and the bottom of the container is 30 in. (0.76 m) or more above the surrounding grade, access to bottom connections shall be provided by an opening or tunnel with a 4 ft (1.2 m) minimum diameter and a 3 ft (0.9 m) minimum clear area.

Refer to Exhibit 6.22, which shows a mounded container during installation. The bottom of the container is more than 30 in. (0.76 m) above grade, and access to the tank bottom connections is provided by the tunnel.

(b) Bottom connections that extend beyond the mound shall be part of the ASME container or shall be installed in compliance with the ASME Code and shall be designed for the forces that can act on the connections.

Bottom connections that extend beyond the mound provide a safe means of withdrawing liquid and a safe means of accessing mounded containers.

(4) Mounded containers shall comply with the corrosion protection requirements of 6.6.6.1(I) through (M).

The potential for corrosion of mounded containers must be addressed prior to installation, and the text was revised in the 2011 edition to reference the cathodic protection requirements of 6.6.6.1. See the references listed in A.6.6.6.1(I), the commentary following 6.6.6.1(H) and 6.6.6.1(I), and Supplement 5 for more information on cathodic protection.

> Subsection 6.6.6 was revised by a tentative interim amendment (TIA).

6.6.7 Installation of Containers on Roofs of Buildings.

The installation, filling, and use of ASME containers on roofs of buildings has been permitted since the 1998 edition. Rooftop installation is limited to ASME containers of 2000 gal (7.6 m³) water capacity or less. The maximum quantity allowed on a roof is that contained in 4000 gal (15.1 m³) of container volume, unless additional containers are located at least 50 ft (15.2 m) apart from one another. Furthermore, the building on which the containers are installed can only be of construction Type I, 443 or 332, or Type II, 222 as specified in NFPA 220, *Standard on Types of Building Construction* [15]. This requirement mandates an essentially noncombustible building providing fire resistance ratings for the main structural elements. Each installation must be acceptable to the authority having jurisdiction and requires the prior approval of the authority having jurisdiction and the fire department.

The requirements for rooftop containers were made more stringent in the 2001 edition by stating that the installation of propane containers on roofs was prohibited unless the approval of both the authority having jurisdiction and the fire chief was obtained. When approval is granted, 6.6.7.2 permits such installations in accordance with a list of requirements, which remain unchanged from the previous edition.

For many years, the code has allowed 100 lb (45 kg) LP-Gas cylinders on roofs. Other NFPA codes and standards allow fuels on roofs. For example, NFPA 37, *Standard for the Installation and Use of Stationary Combustion Engines and Gas Turbines* [16], allows fuel tanks supplying emergency generators to be located on roofs, and NFPA 407, *Standard for Aircraft Fuel Servicing* [17], permits fueling of helicopters on roofs.

The proposal to add rooftop containers to NFPA 58 was made by a committee member from Mexico, where rooftop container installations are common. In 1996, the technical committee met in Mexico City and observed ASME container installations on roofs of residences, commercial buildings, and multi-story hotels. The technical committee inspected the propane containers on the roof of the parking garage adjacent to a hotel. The containers were filled from a bobtail at ground level, four stories below, during the committee's inspection. Rooftop installations are also used in other countries that do not have piped natural gas and where space is limited.

In considering the proposal, the technical committee noted that the typical roof construction in Mexico is concrete. Therefore, the committee limited installations to buildings of fire-resistant construction as defined in NFPA 220. The other requirements were based on practices observed in use in Mexico.

6.6.7.1 Installation of containers on roofs of buildings shall be prohibited, unless approved by the authority having jurisdiction and the fire department.

An unanticipated use of 6.6.7 is shown in Exhibit 6.23. Roofers are using two 250 gal (0.95 m³) propane tanks in applying the roof of a high-rise building under construction. The tanks are refilled by lowering them to grade using the construction crane visible at the bottom

EXHIBIT 6.23 *Installation of Rooftop Propane Tanks: (top) rooftop view and (bottom) building under construction. (Courtesy of Richard Fredenburg, North Carolina Department of Agriculture and Consumer Services)*

of the photograph. Each tank weighs as much as 8½ 100 lb (45 kg) propane cylinders, and, at least on this construction site, the handling of tanks was considered safer than handling cylinders. Some building codes prohibit the use of tar kettles on roofs, so this type of installation should not be allowed in the jurisdictions with this prohibition.

6.6.7.2 Where the authority having jurisdiction and the fire department have approved an installation of a container, it shall comply with the following:

(1) The building shall be of Type I, 443 or 332, or Type II, 222, construction as specified in NFPA 220, *Standard on Types of Building Construction*.

The minimum fire resistance ratings for the types of construction specified in NFPA 220 are shown in Commentary Table 6.3.

COMMENTARY TABLE 6.3 *Fire Resistance Rating (Hours) for Type I and Type II Construction*

Wall Type	Type I		Type II
	443	332	222
Exterior Bearing Walls			
Supporting more than one floor, columns, or other bearing wall	4	3	2
Supporting one floor only	4	3	2
Supporting a roof only	4	3	1
Interior Bearing Walls			
Supporting more than one floor, columns, or other bearing wall	4	3	2
Supporting one floor only	3	2	2
Supporting a roof only	3	2	1

Source: Extracted from Table 4.1.1 of NFPA 220, *Standard on Types of Building Construction*, 2009 edition.

(2) LP-Gas containers installed on roofs shall be of 2000 gal (7.6 m³) water capacity or less.
(3) The aggregate water capacity of LP-Gas containers installed on the roof or terrace of a building shall meet the following criteria:
  (a) It shall not exceed 4000 gal (15.1 m³) in one location.
  (b) Additional installations on the same roof or terrace shall be located at least 50 ft (15 m) apart.

The largest container permitted to be installed on a rooftop is 2000 gal (7.6 m³) water capacity with a maximum aggregate capacity of 4000 gal (15.1 m³) in one location. Additional installations on the same building must be at least 50 ft (15 m) apart from other installations.

(4) An ASME container installed on the roof of a building shall always be filled by two operators, one at the controls of the vehicle supplying LP-Gas and another at the controls of the container.

The requirement for two operators is based on the practice in Mexico, where one operator remains near the liquid transfer controls on the truck while the other operator is on the roof. Communication between the two operators can be by hand signals or by radios. The use of two operators ensures that the ASME containers will not be overfilled.

(5) Containers shall be installed in external locations only.
(6) Where a fill line to the container is required, it shall be located entirely outside the building.
(7) The fill connection shall be located entirely outside the building.
(8) The fill connection shall be located at least 8 ft (2.4 m) above ground level.
(9) Containers shall be installed on a level surface.

(10) The container shall be secured to the building structure.

(11) The support of the container shall be designed to the same seismic criteria as the building.

Seismic considerations must be included when installing containers. ASCE 7 and local building officials are a good source of information on foundations and anchorage in seismic areas.

(12) The roof on which the container is located shall be able to support the weight of the container filled with water, with the safety margins required by local codes.

(13) Containers shall be located in areas where there is free air circulation, at least 10 ft (3 m) from building openings (such as windows and doors), and at least 20 ft (6.1 m) from air intakes of air-conditioning and ventilating systems.

(14) The location of containers shall allow access to all valves and controls and shall have enough surrounding area to allow the required maintenance.

(15) The location of the container shall have fixed stairs or another method to reach it.

(16) If the installation requires the use of more than one container, the distances between containers from Table 6.3.1 shall apply.

(17) If the container location is higher than 23 ft (7 m) from the ground, or if the filling hose cannot be observed by the operators in its entire length, the container shall have a filling line constructed to withstand liquid transfer, and it shall have the following appurtenances:

    (a) Filler valve with back check valve

    (b) Filler valve cap

    (c) Two control valves

    (d) Hydrostatic relief valve

    (e) Venting line

Containers on roofs must be in the open, not in penthouses or rooms. It is recommended that the containers be installed in open areas where any leakage will dissipate rapidly. If a fill line is required, it must be installed completely in the open and cannot be run inside the building. (See Exhibit 6.24.) A fill line is required by 6.6.7.2(17) if the roof on which the container is located is higher than 23 ft (7 m) or if the operators cannot see the entire length of hose.

EXHIBIT 6.24 *A Fixed Fill Line Used for Filling a Rooftop Propane Tank.*

(18) The liquid and vapor fill connections shall be conspicuously marked or labeled.

(19) A fire safety analysis shall be prepared in accordance with 6.25.3.

6.7 Installation of Container Appurtenances

Container appurtenances are defined as follows:

> **3.3.14 Container Appurtenances.** Devices installed in container openings for safety, control, or operating purposes.

The only appurtenances that the code currently addresses in terms of installation requirements are regulators and pressure relief valves. Regulators are found in Section 6.8 and pressure relief devices are found in 6.7.2.

6.7.1 Reserved.

6.7.2 Installation of Pressure Relief Devices.

6.7.2.1 Pressure relief devices shall be installed so that the relief device is in direct communication with the vapor space of the container.

It is important that the pressure relief device be installed so that it is always in the vapor space in normal operation. Paragraph 5.2.5.6 requires that ASME containers be constructed with the pressure relief valve in direct communication with the vapor space. In locating such devices, remember that what seems to be the normal filling point in a container is radically changed if the container is filled at a low temperature and then is subjected to a rising temperature that expands the liquid. If the pressure relief device is not properly located, the liquid expansion could be enough to then place the pressure relief device in the liquid space.

6.7.2.2 Pressure relief devices on cylinders shall be installed to minimize the possibility of relief device discharge impingement on the cylinder.

Burning gas discharged from a pressure relief device that impinges on the cylinder or adjacent cylinders is the most common reason for fire that spreads from cylinder to cylinder, possibly resulting in BLEVEs. Because the relief valves on most cylinders discharge horizontally when the cylinder is in its normal position, the provision in 6.7.2.2 is difficult to implement where more than one or two cylinders are present. If the cylinder has a protective collar, the collar should have an opening opposite the relief valve discharge outlet for the gas to pass through.

6.7.2.3 Pressure relief devices on the following ASME containers shall be so installed that any gas released is vented away from the container upward and unobstructed to the open air:

(1) Containers of 125 gal (0.5 m³) or more water capacity installed in stationary service
(2) Portable storage containers
(3) Portable tanks
(4) Cargo tanks

FAQ ▶
Why must relief devices on ASME containers be oriented so they vent upward?

Relief valves on ASME containers are set to operate at 250 psig (1.7 MPag), and the volume they discharge is much larger than the volume discharged by the devices used on cylinders. It is important that the discharge be unobstructed and vented upward in order to allow greater dispersion of the gas in an area that will most likely not contain a source of ignition.

6.7.2.4 Rain caps or other means shall be provided to minimize the possibility of the entrance of water or other extraneous matter into the relief device or any discharge piping. Provision shall be made for drainage where the accumulation of water is anticipated.

6.7.2.5 The rain cap or other protector shall be designed to remain in place, except during pressure relief device operation, and shall not restrict pressure relief device flow.

Rain caps, as their name implies, are used to keep rain and snow from accumulating on top of a pressure relief valve. A "weep hole" is required to allow any water to drain, but the small opening can become clogged with dirt or other material, allowing water to collect. If the water freezes, the pressure relief valve may not be able to open. In climates where freezing does not occur, the cap is needed because debris can collect in the discharge piping, insects can build nests in the pipe above the relief valve, and accumulated water can cause corrosion. All these conditions can compromise relief valve operations.

Rain caps that direct gas discharge downward or to the side should not be used. Because any rain cap that remains in place during discharge can throttle the discharge to some extent, rain caps should be used only after accounting for their effect on the relieving capacity of the relief device.

6.7.2.6 The design of the pressure relief valve drain opening shall provide the following:

(1) Protection of the container against flame impingement resulting from ignited product escaping from the drain opening
(2) Direction of the pressure relief valve drain opening so that an adjacent container, piping, or equipment is not subjected to flame impingement

6.7.2.7 Pressure relief valve discharge on each container of more than 2000 gal (7.6 m³) water capacity shall be directed vertically upward and unobstructed to the open air.

This paragraph was revised in the 2011 edition to remove the long-standing requirement for a 7 ft (2.1 m) "discharge stack," or pipe, to be attached to all pressure relief valves on aboveground containers of 2000 gal (7.6 m³) and larger. The requirement was removed because the technical committee could find no reason to justify its existence. The relief valve extension moves the discharge to a point 7 ft (2.1 m) above the pressure relief valve, and thus elevates the discharge, which serves to isolate the container from heat radiated from an ignited discharge. However, a research report, "The Effect of Velocity, Temperature, and Gas Molecular Weight on Flammability Limits in Wind-Blown Jets of Hydrocarbon Gases," issued by Battelle Memorial Institute, demonstrated that flame effect on a container from an ignited discharge jet would not affect the container [4]. It was also noted that similar flammable liquefied gas containers are not required to have such 7 ft stacks. On the positive side, it was noted that without the stack, visual inspection of the pressure relief valve is possible without having to remove and replace the stack.

6.7.2.8 Shutoff valves shall not be installed between pressure relief devices and the container unless a listed pressure relief valve manifold meeting the requirements of 6.7.2.9 is used.

Note that shutoff valves are not permitted between a propane container and its pressure relief valves, unless incorporated into a listed pressure relief valve manifold. This requirement addresses the concern that the valve could be closed by operators who do not understand the importance of pressure relief. This requirement is very strict and does not allow a pressure relief valve to be shut off for removal or inspection unless a listed pressure relief valve manifold is installed.

6.7.2.9 Listed pressure relief valve manifolds shall be exempt from the requirements of 6.7.2.8 when the following conditions are met:

(1) Two or more pressure relief devices are installed in the manifold.
(2) Only one pressure relief device in the manifold is designed to shut off at any one time.
(3) The remaining pressure relief device(s) remains open and provides the rated relieving capacity required for the container.

6.7.2.10 Shutoff valves shall not be installed at the outlet of a pressure relief device or at the outlet of the discharge piping where discharge piping is installed.

The requirements of 6.7.2.8 through 6.7.2.10 are intended to ensure that under no circumstances can containers be isolated from their pressure relief valves by an inadvertently closed valve. They were revised in the 2011 edition to recognize that the requirement for pressure relief valve stacks on aboveground containers has been removed from 6.7.2.7. Relief valve stacks are not prohibited; however, if installed a shutoff valve cannot be installed between the pressure relief valve and the stack (see Exhibit 6.25).

EXHIBIT 6.25 *Relief Valve Stacks. Note that these stacks are no longer required by NFPA 58, but do not need to be removed from current installations. (Courtesy of Richard Fredenburg, North Carolina Department of Agriculture and Consumer Services)*

Shutoff valves are not permitted between a container and its relief device because the relief device is a necessary safety feature that must always be available to operate and prevent a catastrophic failure of the container. The downside of this requirement is that if maintenance must be done on a relief device, the container must be emptied, which can discourage the testing or replacement of pressure relief valves.

The use of a relief valve manifold provides a way to replace a pressure relief valve without emptying the container and taking it out of service, which is especially important in larger containers. When a container is emptied, not all of the propane vapor can be recovered and some must be flared.

6.7.2.11 The pressure relief valve discharge piping from underground containers of 2000 gal (7.6 m^3) or less water capacity shall extend beyond the manhole or housing or shall discharge into the manhole or housing, where the manhole or housing is equipped with ventilated louvers or their equivalent, in accordance with 5.7.8.4.

The requirement in 6.7.2.11 recognizes that pressure relief valve discharge from aboveground containers and that from underground containers are different subjects. It allows discharge into a dome only if the dome has a ventilated louver or opening. Ventilation openings are required in 5.7.8.4.

Permitting the discharge of a relief valve into the housing of an underground container recognizes that the relief devices seldom operate on underground containers and that the discharge rate of underground containers of 2000 gal (7.6 m³) and less is 30 percent of aboveground containers of the same size.

Note that relief discharge devices for underground containers of 2000 gal (7.6 m³) water capacity and less do not have to be installed vertically upward and straight. If they are installed using elbows or bends, it is important to verify that the added resistance to flow will not reduce the relief valve capacity. The relief valve manufacturer may be able to provide assistance.

6.7.2.12 Pressure relief valve discharge on underground containers of more than 2000 gal (7.6 m³) water capacity shall be piped vertically and directly upward to a point at least 7 ft (2.1 m) above the ground.

The 7 ft (2.1 m) elevation of the discharge ensures that the discharge cannot impinge on nearby containers and should be above any person standing in the area.

6.7.2.13 Pressure relief devices installed in underground containers in dispensing stations shall be piped vertically upward to a point at least 10 ft (3 m) above the ground.

Underground containers serving dispensing stations, where vehicular traffic is routine and pedestrian traffic can be expected, present a hazard that is different from most other installations. The discharge piping from the pressure relief devices must extend 10 ft (3 m) above the ground. The increased height facilitates vapor dispersal. Discharge piping must be protected against physical damage.

6.7.2.14 Where installed, the discharge piping shall comply with the following:

Paragraph 6.7.2.14 was changed in the 2011 edition to cover six items related to the installation of pressure relief valve stacks on all containers by combining and revising former 6.7.2.14 and 6.7.2.15. Formerly, 6.7.2.14 contained only item (1). The additional requirements were contained in former 6.7.2.15 and are unchanged. These requirements ensure that the piping does not restrict the flow from the pressure relief valve.

(1) Piping shall be supported and protected against physical damage.
(2) Piping from aboveground containers shall be sized to provide the rate of flow specified in 5.7.2.5.
(3) Piping from underground containers shall be sized to provide the rate of flow specified in 5.7.2.7.
(4) Piping shall be metallic and have a melting point over 1500°F (816°C).
(5) Discharge piping shall be so designed that excessive force applied to the discharge piping results in breakage on the discharge side of the valve, rather than on the inlet side, without impairing the function of the valve.
(6) Return bends and restrictive pipe or tubing fittings shall not be used.

Several requirements are provided in 6.7.2.14 for discharge piping from relief devices, as follows:

• Piping must be protected against physical damage. The flow from the relief device must not be reduced by restrictions in the piping system. The piping must be designed so that if excessive force is applied to it, the piping will break on the discharge side of the relief valve and maintain the integrity of the valve itself.

• Discharge piping must be sized to provide the rate of flow specified in 5.7.2.7 for aboveground containers and 5.7.2.8 for underground or mounded containers. The piping must not restrict the flow of gas.

• Discharge piping must be constructed of metals with a melting point over 1500°F (816°C), which is the same specification for piping materials. (See Commentary Table 6.4 for melting points of some metals and alloys that can be used for relief valve discharge piping.) This requirement ensures the integrity of the discharge piping in a fire condition. Note that the PVC pipe that is allowed for regulator venting cannot be used for this application.

• Discharge piping cannot have restrictions of any type, including pipe fittings.

If it were necessary to extend the discharge pipe and fittings required by the installation, the provisions of Section 1.5 could apply if approved by the authority having jurisdiction. In such a case, the discharge piping could be designed in accordance with API RP 520, *Sizing, Selection, and Installation of Pressure-Relieving Devices in Refineries (Part I — Sizing and Selection, and Part II — Installation)* [18] to size the discharge piping system so that it would not restrict the proper operation of the relief valve.

COMMENTARY TABLE 6.4 *Melting Points of Some Metals and Alloys*

Metal or Alloy	Typical Melting Points (Solidus Temperature) °F*	
	Elemental Form	Typical Alloys
Tin	450	—
Lead/White Metal	<500	<500
Zinc	787	715–780
Magnesium	1202	850–1200
Aluminum	1220	980–1200
Copper	1981	1550–2000+
Nickel	2651	2300+
Iron/Carbon Steel	2797	2600+ (est)
Stainless Steel	—	2500+
Titanium	3035±	—

*The temperatures in this table may not agree with other reported data as the start-to-melt (solidus) temperature. Other data may report the point at which the metal is completely molten (liquidus temperature). The start-to-melt temperature is of value when strength of piping materials is of concern. The complete melting temperature is of value in fire investigations.
Note: °C = 5/9 (°F − 32).
Source: Richard Hoffmann, Hoffmann & Feige.

6.7.2.15 Where installed, the discharge piping shall be supported and protected against physical damage.

6.7.3 Reserved.

6.7.4 Reserved.

6.7.5 Reserved.

6.7.6 Reserved.

6.7.7 Reserved.

6.7.8 Reserved.

6.7.9 Reserved.

6.7.10 Reserved.

6.8 Regulators

6.8.1 Regulator Installation.

6.8.1.1 First-stage or high-pressure regulators shall be directly attached, or attached by flexible metallic connectors, to the vapor service valve used on stationary (permanent) container installations, and to interconnecting piping of manifolded stationary (permanent) container installations, or to a vaporizer outlet.

6.8.1.2 Regulators shall be directly attached, or shall be permitted to be attached by flexible hose connector or flexible metallic connector, to portable-type cylinders that are installed and replaced on a cylinder exchange basis.

6.8.1.3 First-stage regulators installed downstream of high-pressure regulators shall be exempt from the requirement of 6.8.1.1.

In a single container installation, the first-stage regulator must be connected directly to the container service valve or, in a single vaporizer installation, to the vaporizer outlet. As an alternative, a flexible metallic connector such as a pigtail, which is a short length of copper tubing, may be used between the container and the first-stage regulator or integral two-stage regulator. A proposal was received for the 2011 edition to allow a nonmetallic connector. The technical committee rejected the proposal, citing a concern over the use of nonmetallic materials in this service, due to several potential threats, including fire.

In the case of manifolded containers or vaporizers, it is impractical to install a regulator at each container service valve or vaporizer. Pressure imbalances could occur and cause regulators to counteract each other and result in an unstable pressure condition. Thus, a single regulator may be used with this type of system with interconnecting piping in the manifolded system.

The requirement in 6.8.1.1 that the regulator be connected directly to the container shutoff valve can be met in a manifolded container installation by connecting the regulator to a tee. The tee is directly connected to the container shutoff valves with connectors only, as required for spacing or flexibility. Flexibility in the piping system is necessary to allow for expansion and contraction.

A serious fire hazard could occur if LP-Gas vapor were allowed to recondense in long lengths of piping in cold weather conditions and then were fed to an appliance. Liquid LP-Gas would be present at the point of use where vapor usage was intended. To prevent this from happening, first-stage regulators must be located as close to the supply container or the outlet of the vaporizer as practical.

6.8.1.4 First-stage and high-pressure regulators shall be installed outside of buildings, except as follows:

(1) Regulators on cylinders installed indoors in accordance with Section 6.17
(2) Regulators on containers of less than 125 gal (0.5 m^3) water capacity for the purpose of being filled or in structures complying with Chapter 10

(3) Regulators on containers on LP-Gas vehicles complying with, and parked or garaged in accordance with, Chapter 11

(4) Regulators on containers used with LP-Gas stationary or portable engine fuel systems complying with Chapter 11

(5) Regulators on containers used with LP-Gas–fueled industrial trucks complying with 11.13.4

(6) Regulators on containers on LP-Gas–fueled vehicles garaged in accordance with Section 11.16

(7) Regulators on cylinders awaiting use, resale, or exchange when stored in accordance with Chapter 8

Regulators control the pressure in LP-Gas piping systems and incorporate safety features to prevent overpressure. The safety features vent propane gas from the regulator in the event of component failure to prevent pressure in the downstream piping from becoming too high and possibly leaking from appliance controls. These safety features are important because propane leakage into a building must be avoided to prevent fires and explosions.

Because propane gas can be discharged from a regulator vent in the event of component failure, the code requires that regulators be installed outside of buildings.

An automatic changeover regulator, as shown in Exhibit 6.26, is a first-stage regulator connected to two cylinders that automatically draws LP-Gas from the second when the first is empty.

EXHIBIT 6.26 *Automatic Changeover Regulator. (Courtesy of Engineered Controls International, Inc.)*

Several exceptions are provided to this broad requirement in recognition that there are some cases in which pressure regulators can be safely installed in buildings that do not serve fixed piping systems:

• Special applications where first-stage pressure regulators must be located indoors (See Section 6.19.)

- Engine fuel uses (See Chapter 11.)
- Industrial applications
- Some gas distribution facilities

All the provisions in 6.8.1.4 cover regulators used on other-than-fixed piping systems in residential and commercial buildings.

6.8.1.5 All regulators for outdoor installations shall be designed, installed, or protected so their operation will not be affected by the elements (freezing rain, sleet, snow, ice, mud, or debris).

To minimize the possibility of regulator vents being blocked by ice, the vents on all regulators used outdoors (except for portable industrial uses) must be protected against the elements. Either enclosing the regulator in a housing or mounting the regulator with the vent opening pointing vertically downward can protect the vents, as shown in Exhibit 6.27. Mounting the regulator with the vent pointing downward is designed to protect the vent opening from freezing over if the vent has a drip lip as required by UL 144, *LP-Gas Regulators* [19], with an inside diameter of not less than $1\frac{1}{16}$ in. (17 mm) and an outside diameter of at least $\frac{3}{4}$ in. (19 mm).

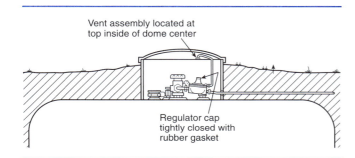

Vent assembly located at top inside of dome center

Regulator cap tightly closed with rubber gasket

EXHIBIT 6.27 *Use of Vent Extension on Underground Container to Protect Regulator Operation from Elements. The termination of the vent assembly must be above grade level. (Courtesy of Emerson Process Management Regulator Technologies Inc.)*

The specified diameter dimensions provided here evolved from a test project by Underwriters Laboratories Inc. (UL) in which different designs were subjected to freezing rain and wind conditions. Current UL-listed regulators are marked according to whether they must be installed under a protective cover or in the downward position or its equivalent. It is also important to ensure that the protective housing, if used, is installed correctly.

(A) This protection shall be permitted to be integral with the regulator.

(B) Regulators used for portable industrial applications shall be exempt from the requirements of 6.8.1.5.

6.8.1.6 The point of discharge from the required pressure relief device on regulated equipment installed outside of buildings or occupiable structures in piping systems shall be located not less than 3 ft (1 m) horizontally away from any building or occupiable structure opening below the level of discharge, and not beneath or inside any building or occupiable structure unless this space is not enclosed for more than 50 percent of its perimeter.

The use of the term *occupiable structure* clearly conveys the committee's intent that this provision apply to structures that are designed for human occupancy. An occupiable structure includes tents.

6.8.1.7 The point of discharge shall also be located not less than 5 ft (1.5 m) in any direction away from any source of ignition, openings into direct-vent (sealed combustion system) appliances, or mechanical ventilation air intakes.

The fire protection requirements of 6.8.1.6 and 6.8.1.7 are intended to reduce the potential for a flammable gas being brought into a building or forming outside the building, in the event that the pressure relief device on the regulator operates.

6.8.1.8 Where a vent line is used to comply with the point of discharge requirements, it shall comply with 6.8.1.8(A)(1) through 6.8.1.8(A)(7).

(A) The discharge from the required pressure relief device of a second-stage regulator, other than a line pressure regulator, installed inside of buildings in piping systems shall comply with the following:

(1) The discharge shall be directly vented with supported piping to the outside air.
(2) The vent line shall be at least the same nominal pipe size as the regulator vent connection pipe size.
(3) Where there is more than one regulator at a location, either each regulator shall have a separate vent to the outside or the vent lines shall be manifolded in accordance with accepted engineering practices to minimize back pressure in the event of high vent discharge.
(4) The material of the vent line shall comply with 5.8.3.
(5) The discharge outlet shall be located not less than 3 ft (1 m) horizontally away from any building opening below the level of such discharge.
(6) The discharge outlet shall also be located not less than 5 ft (1.5 m) in any direction away from any source of ignition, openings into direct-vent appliances, or mechanical ventilation air intakes.
(7) The discharge outlet shall be designed, installed, or protected from blockage so it will not be affected by the elements (freezing rain, sleet, snow, ice, mud, or debris) or insects.

(B) The requirement in 6.8.1.8(A) shall not apply to appliance regulators otherwise protected, to line pressure regulators listed as complying with ANSI Z-21.80/CSA 6.22, *Standard for Line Pressure Regulators*, or to regulators used in connection with containers in buildings as provided for in 6.2.2(1), 6.2.2(2), 6.2.2(4), 6.2.2(5), and 6.2.2(6).

The two-stage regulation system required on fixed piping systems can protect against overpressure by venting LP-Gas outside of a building in the event of component failure. The provisions in 6.8.1.8(A) address this infrequent occurrence and further minimize the possibility of entry and ignition of flammable gas in the building.

Paragraphs 6.8.1.8(A)(1) through 6.8.1.8(A)(7) are intended to convey any discharge from the second-stage regulator vent outside the building in a manner that will not reduce the vent capacity of the regulator. If a manifold is not made correctly or the vent pipe is too small, the resulting backpressure in the vent system will reduce the capacity of the pressure relief device and possibly cause the fuel gas distribution system to experience elevated pressures.

The discharge from the relief valve vent of a second-stage regulator (not an appliance regulator) installed outdoors cannot be less than 3 ft (1 m) horizontally from a building opening (below the level of this discharge) and 5 ft (1.5 m) from a source of ignition or building ventilation inlet. The same is true of the discharge from the termination end of a vent pipe to the outdoors from an indoor second-stage regulator installation. In piping the vent of the relief valve discharge from second-stage regulators to the outside, a properly sized and supported piping system must be installed. For information on sizing vent lines from relief valve discharge of second-stage regulators, see API RP 520.

The elevation of the vent discharge when piped outside the building is not specified in the code. Its elevation should be above reasonably expected snow levels to prevent blockage of the vent by drifting snow. (See Exhibit 6.28.)

(C) The requirement in 6.8.1.8(A) shall not apply to vaporizers.

6.8.1.9 Single-stage regulators shall be permitted to be used only on portable appliances and outdoor cooking appliances with input ratings of 100,000 Btu/hr (29 kW) maximum.

Single-stage regulators are not completely prohibited, but they cannot be replaced or reinstalled in most building systems. Their continued use on portable appliances and outdoor cooking gas appliances is specifically permitted.

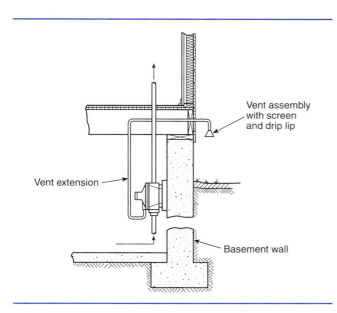

EXHIBIT 6.28 Venting Regulator Installed in a Building. (Courtesy of Emerson Process Management Regulator Technologies Inc.)

Vent assembly with screen and drip lip

Vent extension

Basement wall

6.8.1.10 Line pressure regulators shall be installed in accordance with the requirements of NFPA 54, *National Fuel Gas Code*.

As line pressure regulators are outside of the scope of NFPA 58, because they are installed downstream of the second-stage pressure regulator, reference is made to NFPA 54 for their installation.

6.8.2 Selection of Pressure Regulators.

A two-stage regulator system, an integral two-stage regulator, or a 2 psi regulator system shall be required on all piping systems that serve ½ psig (3.4 kPag) appliance systems [normally operated at 11 in. water column (2.7 kPag) pressure].

(A) The requirement for two-stage regulation shall include piping systems for appliances on recreational vehicles, mobile home installations, manufactured home installations, catering vehicles, and food service vehicle installations.

(B) Single-stage regulators shall not be installed in piping systems after June 30, 1997, except for installations covered in 6.8.2(C).

As of June 30, 1997, the installation of single-stage pressure regulators is no longer allowed. Since then, all LP-Gas systems have been required to use two-stage pressure regulation for fixed piping systems (excluding small portable appliances). Two-stage pressure regulation systems can prevent overpressure conditions that may result in leakage of LP-Gas in buildings, leading to fires. The commentary throughout Section 5.8 explains in detail the reasons for this change.

Single-stage pressure regulation is not permitted for fixed piping systems that serve ½ psig (3 kPag) appliance systems. The reason that single-stage regulation is not acceptable for large [greater than 100,000 Btu/hr (29 kW)] systems is that the outlet pressure of the regulator is difficult to maintain precisely if the inlet pressure is allowed to vary over a wide range. Therefore, the first-stage regulator will handle container pressure and deliver consistent pressure of 10 psig (69 kPag) to the second-stage regulator, which in turn can deliver much more consistent pressure to the appliances. In addition, the two-stage system provides a redundancy in case one of the stages were to completely fail. Perhaps even more important, the single-stage system has no way to control the pressure to the appliance should a catastrophic failure occur. Because the pressure to the regulator from the container could be extremely high, the capacity of a relief valve on a single-stage regulator would not be able to prevent the pressure to the appliance from reaching 5 psig (34 kPag).

(C) Single-stage regulators shall be permitted on small portable appliances and outdoor cooking appliances with input ratings of 100,000 Btu/hr (29 kW) or less.

Small portable appliances under 100,000 Btu/hr (29 kW) — for example, gas grills, portable heating appliances, portable cooking stoves, and similar appliances — do not require two-stage regulation because they are attended appliances that will be shut off in the case of malfunction.

(D) Gas distribution systems utilizing multiple second-stage regulators shall be permitted to use a high-pressure regulator installed at the container, provided that a first-stage regulator is installed downstream of the high-pressure regulator and ahead of the second-stage regulators.

A high-pressure regulator [outlet pressures greater than 10 psig (69 kPag)] can be used where the first-stage regulators are installed upstream of each second-stage regulator, ensuring that the second-stage regulator does not receive an inlet pressure in excess of 10 psig. Where this is done, three stages of pressure regulation exist.

(E) High-pressure regulators with an overpressure protection device and a rated capacity of more than 500,000 Btu/hr (147 kW) shall be permitted to be used in two-stage systems where the second-stage regulator incorporates an integral or separate overpressure protection device.

(F) The overpressure protection device described in 6.8.2(E) shall limit the outlet pressure of the second-stage regulator to 2.0 psig (14 kPag) when the regulator seat disc is removed and with an inlet pressure equivalent to the maximum outlet pressure setting of the high-pressure regulator.

Paragraphs 6.8.2(E) and 6.8.2(F) recognize that a high-pressure regulation system that limits fixed piping system pressure to 2 psig (14 kPag) or less under failure conditions can be used. It is recommended that a system that has been listed by an independent agency be used to ensure that the equipment will perform as intended.

(G) Systems consisting of listed components that provide an equivalent level of overpressure protection shall be exempt from the requirement of 6.8.2.

The use of alternative means to provide an equivalent level of safety has been accepted in NFPA 58 for a long time. Two-stage pressure regulation accomplishes equivalent safety by venting gas to the atmosphere rather than leaking it into a building if the regulator fails. Shutting off the flow of gas into the building can provide an equivalent level of safety if a regulator fails. Equipment that shuts off the flow of gas is available, but it is not offered for propane systems at present. However, 6.8.2(G) would allow such equipment and other means that provide equivalent safety, so that the deployment of new technology is not hindered.

(H)* A 2 psi regulator system shall consist of a first-stage regulator and a 2 psi service regulator in compliance with the requirements of 5.8.1.2 in conjunction with a line pressure regulator in compliance with ANSI Z-21.80/CSA 6.22, *Standard for Line Pressure Regulators.*

A.6.8.2(H) Two psi regulator systems operate with 2 psi (13.8 kPa) downstream of the 2 psi service regulators to the line pressure regulator, which reduces the pressure to an appropriate inches-of-water-column pressure.

The use of "2 psi systems" is becoming more popular, especially with the increased use of corrugated stainless steel tubing (CSST) systems. The higher pressures allow reduced pipe sizing and the use of CSST allows for fewer joints to be made, with the potential points of leakage correspondingly reduced.

6.9 Piping Systems

6.9.1 Piping System Service Limitations.

There are limits on the use of liquid LP-Gas and the pressures at which LP-Gas vapor can be used in buildings. The requirements of 6.9.1 limit the amount of flammable gas that can escape into a building in the event of leakage in a piping system. If a leak exists, the flow of gas through an opening is a function of the pressure in the piping system. The lower the pressure, the smaller the amount that leaks for a given size opening. The use of liquid LP-Gas piping is severely restricted in most buildings because liquid LP-Gas expands to a greater volume of vapor (by a factor of 270) when leaking.

6.9.1.1 The physical state (vapor or liquid) and pressure at which LP-Gas is transmitted through piping systems shall be as follows:

(1) Outdoor LP-Gas liquid or vapor metallic piping systems shall have no pressure limitations.

Although the code states that there are no limitations on the pressure in metallic piping located outdoors, the installer must recognize the pressure design limitations of the piping material and joints used.

(2) Outdoor underground LP-Gas liquid or vapor polyamide piping systems shall have pressure limitations as defined by the design pressure of the piping being installed.

Polyamide piping systems are permitted to be used outside, underground, for the purposes of distributing fuel gas to a building, in addition to the use of polyethylene systems. The restrictions on the pressure limitation for polyamide differ and are more liberal than those attached to the use of polyethylene systems [see 6.9.1.1(2)], because liquid LP-Gas does not have an adverse effect on polyamide material, as it does on polyethylene.

(3) Polyethylene piping systems shall be limited to the following:
    (a) Vapor service not exceeding 30 psig (208 kPag)
    (b) Installation outdoors and underground

The restriction on polyethylene piping reflects its unsuitability where LP-Gas liquid may be present. The presence of liquid propane can lead to the development of excessive pressure and cause polyethylene to lose strength. Polyethylene is restricted from use inside buildings and from aboveground installations for the following reasons:

- Polyethylene has no resistance to fire and could release LP-Gas and enhance a fire.
- Polyethylene's physical properties could result in its being easily cut or severed.

Note that polyethylene is often the preferred piping material in underground service due to its excellent corrosion resistance compared with metallic piping materials. It is softer than metallic piping materials and must be protected by its burial depth or other means. Both polyethylene and polyamide gas piping are completely prohibited in buildings, without exception, because they can easily melt in a fire, releasing fuel gas into the fire.

(4)* LP-Gas vapor at pressures exceeding 20 psig (138 kPag) or LP-Gas liquid shall not be piped into any building unless the installation is in accordance with one of the following:
    (a) The buildings or structures are under construction or undergoing major renovation, and the temporary piping systems are in accordance with 6.19.2 and 6.19.12.
    (b) The buildings or separate areas of the buildings are constructed in accordance with Chapter 10 and used exclusively to house the following:

    i. Equipment for vaporization, pressure reduction, gas mixing, gas manufacturing, or distribution

    ii. Internal combustion engines, industrial processes, research and experimental laboratories, or equipment or processing having a similar hazard

    iii. Engine-mounted fuel vaporizers

(c) Industrial occupancies are in accordance with 6.9.1.2.

(5) Corrugated stainless steel piping systems shall be limited to vapor service not exceeding 5 psig (34 kPag).

FAQ ▶
What is the maximum pressure at which LP-Gas can be piped into a building?

When piping vapor is at elevated pressures, condensation of LP-Gas vapor must be avoided, or liquid can be fed directly to the gas utilization equipment with potentially dangerous results. If the ambient temperature can fall below −5°F (−21°C) at any time, it may be necessary to heat-trace and insulate the outdoor portion of the piping. The condensation temperature of propane at different pressures is shown in Commentary Table 6.5. It is the same as the vapor pressure of liquid propane at the temperature shown.

COMMENTARY TABLE 6.5 *Vapor Pressure of Propane at Selected Temperatures**

Pressure		Temperature	
psig	*kPag*	*°F*	*°C*
20	138	−5	−21
40	276	20	−7
63	434	40	4

*For more information, see Tables B.1.2(a) and B1.2(b) in Annex B.

    The provisions of 6.9.1.1(4)(b) rely on construction of a building utilizing damage-resistant construction. Such buildings are constructed so that if an explosion occurred, the pressures of the explosion would vent either through panels or windows that are designed for that purpose, or through the roof. Other features of the building of this construction can be found in Chapter 10.

    The condition appearing in 6.9.1.1(4)(c) provides an exception to the maximum 20 psig (138 kPag) limitation for industrial occupancies because of the frequent need for higher pressures in those occupancies. See the commentary for 6.9.1.2.

A.6.9.1.1(4) Construction of buildings or separate areas of buildings housing certain internal combustion engines is covered in NFPA 37, *Standard for the Installation and Use of Stationary Combustion Engines and Gas Turbines*.

Corrugated stainless steel tubing (CCST), as shown in Exhibit 6.29, was added to the code in the 1998 edition. This relatively new piping material — CCST coated with a smooth plastic coating — has been recognized in NFPA 54, *National Fuel Gas Code* [20], since 1988. The tubing is supplied in coils and is connected using special fittings. The pressure limitation means that it can only be used downstream of the second-stage pressure regulator.

6.9.1.2* LP-Gas vapor fixed piping systems at pressures of 20 psig through 50 psig (138 kPag through 345 kPag) in industrial occupancies shall be approved and shall comply with the following:

(1) The industrial equipment shall require inlet pressures greater than 20 psig (138 kPag).

(2) Pressure relief valve protection shall be provided for the vapor piping system that will limit any overpressure in the piping system to not more than 10 percent of the design pressure of the system.

(3) Pressure relief valve discharge shall be vented directly to the outdoors.

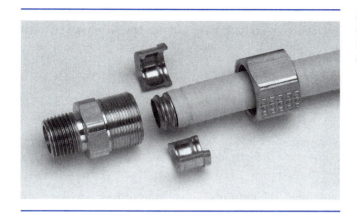

EXHIBIT 6.29 *Corrugated Stainless Steel Tubing. (Courtesy of Gastite, Division of Titeflex)*

(4) A low-temperature control system shall positively shut off the flow of LP-Gas into the vapor piping system when the temperature of the LP-Gas vapor is reduced to its condensation point at the maximum design operating pressure of the system.

A.6.9.1.2 This section addresses the numerous industrial applications that require pressures higher than 20 psig (138 kPag), which are historically above the upper limit for LP-Gas fixed piping systems in buildings. Such processes could include flame cutting, heat treating, and fuel for microturbines used to generate electricity.

Any installation with design pressures of 20 psig through 50 psig (138 kPag through 345 kPag) must first receive the approval of the authority having jurisdiction. Such approval need not be based on buildings or separate areas of buildings that are constructed in accordance with Chapter 10, because the low-temperature shutoff control system precludes the re-liquefaction of the LP-Gas vapor.

In designing the systems permitted by this section, it is necessary for one to be knowledgeable of, and experienced with, the properties and behavior of LP-Gases, especially with respect to re-liquefaction of vapor in closed fixed piping systems. For this reason, the text requires a low-temperature shutoff control system if low temperatures are anticipated. The most appropriate location for the low temperature sensor is determined by the system designer.

Paragraph 6.9.1.2 provides the specific conditions under which LP-Gas can be piped at pressures between 20 psig and 50 psig (138 kPag and 345 kPag) into a building housing an industrial occupancy. All of the conditions must be met in order to permit these higher pressures. Editorial revisions were made in the 2011 edition, but the requirements remain unchanged.

6.9.1.3 Liquid piping systems in buildings or structures feeding a vaporizer other than those covered by 6.9.1.1(4) shall comply with the material requirements of Chapter 11.

6.9.2 Sizing of LP-Gas Vapor Piping Systems.

6.9.2.1 LP-Gas vapor piping systems downstream of the first-stage pressure regulator shall be sized so that all appliances operate within their manufacturer's specifications.

6.9.2.2 LP-Gas vapor piping systems shall be sized and installed to provide a supply of gas to meet the maximum demand of all gas utilization equipment using Table 15.1(a) through Table 15.1(q) or engineering methods.

Requirements for the sizing of LP-Gas vapor piping systems were added in the 1998 edition of NFPA 58, following a change in the scope of NFPA 54. [Refer to the commentary following 1.3.2(6) for an explanation of the split between NFPA 54 and NFPA 58.] Since the 1998 edition, NFPA 58 covers piping between the first- and second-stage pressure regulators, so sizing of such piping is included here.

Tables for sizing piping systems are located in Chapter 15 for the convenience of the designer and installer. Note that the tables are not mandated and that any sizing method that provides a sufficient quantity of gas to operate the appliances properly can be used.

6.9.3 Installation of Metallic Pipe, Tubing, and Fittings.

6.9.3.1* All metallic LP-Gas piping shall be installed in accordance with ASME B 31.3, *Process Piping,* for normal fluid service, or in accordance with Section 6.9.

A.6.9.3.1 Normal fluid service is described in ASME B31.3, *Process Piping,* as any fluid service covered by ASME B31.3, other than toxic fluids, flammable fluids, and fluids under high pressure.

Rules for the installation of metallic pipe; tubing; fittings, including valves; and hose are necessary because fuel gas piping is exposed to hazards that could result in leakage, and its failure, with an accompanying risk of fire.
 The installer of piping under NFPA 58 has a choice of the following two sets of rules:

1. Section 6.9, which provides specific guidance; for example, pipe schedules are specified.
2. ASME B31.3, *Process Piping* [21]. This code is widely used in the chemical and petrochemical industries; however, it is more difficult to use than Section 6.9 because the code covers many materials that can be piped. Users with experience in using ASME B31.3 in the chemical or petrochemical industries may prefer to use B31.3, and it may allow thinner piping to be used.

The 2008 edition introduced the criterion of "normal fluid service" with the requirements of ASME B31.3, *Process Piping.* This change implemented the NFPA 58 technical committee's formal interpretation of December 1995 and provides clear directions for welded and brazed piping systems. As used in ASME B31.3, normal fluid is a fluid that is not toxic and not used at very high pressure [over 2500 psi (17 mPa)]. The category Normal Fluid clarifies which welding inspection procedures are to be used.

6.9.3.2 All welding and brazing of metallic piping shall be in accordance with ASME *Boiler and Pressure Vessel Code,* Section IX.

Section IX of the ASME *Boiler and Pressure Vessel Code* [22] requires that all welders be qualified by completing a qualification test that involves submitting welding samples and an examination of the samples in accordance with the procedures established in Section IX.

6.9.3.3 Metallic piping shall comply with the following:

(1) Piping used at pressures higher than container pressure, such as on the discharge side of liquid transfer pumps, shall be designed for a pressure rating of at least 350 psig (2.4 MPag).

The maximum allowable working pressure for containers and piping in nonengine fuel applications is normally 250 psig (1.7 MPag), and 100 psig is added to allow for pump head. Where the system pressure is known to exceed 350 psig (2.4 MPag), the higher pressure must be used.

(2) Vapor LP-Gas piping with operating pressures in excess of 125 psig (0.9 MPag) and liquid piping not covered by 6.9.3.3(1) shall be designed for a working pressure of at least 250 psig (1.7 MPag).

At a temperature of 70°F (21°C), the pressure in a container of propane, which is the most volatile LP-Gas covered by NFPA 58, is in the range of 125 psig to 130 psig (about 0.9 MPag), and that pressure increases with increased temperature. LP-Gas vapor piping that is connected to the container upstream of any reducing regulator must be suitable for a working pressure of 250 psig (1.7 MPag). The piping connected to the storage tanks of LP-Gas systems must be suitable for a working pressure of 250 psig, whether the piping is in liquid or vapor service.

(3) Vapor LP-Gas piping subject to pressures of not more than 125 psig (0.9 MPag) shall be designed for a pressure rating of at least 125 psig (0.9 MPag).

6.9.3.4 Pressure relief valve discharge piping shall be exempt from the requirement of 6.9.3.3(3).

The requirement in 6.9.3.4 applies to vapor piping connected downstream of a regulator pressure relief discharge outlet. Because the discharge piping relieves to the atmosphere, the pressure in the discharge piping will be slightly higher than atmospheric pressure.

6.9.3.5 Metallic pipe joints shall be permitted to be threaded, flanged, welded, or brazed using pipe and fittings that comply with 5.9.3 and 5.9.4 as follows:

(1) Metallic threaded, welded, and brazed pipe joints shall be in accordance with Table 6.9.3.5.
(2) Fittings and flanges shall be designed for a pressure rating equal to or greater than the required working pressure of the service for which they are used.
(3) Brazed joints shall be made with a brazing material having a melting point exceeding 1000°F (538°C).

Note that the minimum melting point of a braze of 1000°F (538°C) includes most brazes commercially available. Solder, which melts at a lower temperature, must not be used.

(4) Gaskets used to retain LP-Gas in flanged connections in piping shall be resistant to the action of LP-Gas.
(5) Gaskets shall be made of metal or material confined in metal having a melting point over 1500°F (816°C) or shall be protected against fire exposure.
(6) When a flange is opened, the gasket shall be replaced.
(7) Aluminum O-rings and spiral-wound metal gaskets shall be permitted.
(8) Nonmetallic gaskets used in insulating fittings shall be permitted.

Gaskets are an essential component of flanged piping systems because they maintain the integrity of piping systems by preventing leakage at flanges. The requirements in 6.9.3.5(4) through 6.9.3.5(8) ensure the integrity of the piping systems under both normal and fire conditions. The replacement of gaskets after opening a flanged connection is important, because used or reinstalled gaskets often leak. The minimum melting point of 1500°F (816°C) for gaskets excludes the use of elastomeric or rubber gaskets, unless they are protected from exposure to a fire.

TABLE 6.9.3.5 *Types of Metallic Pipe Joints in LP-Gas Service*

Service	Schedule 40	Schedule 80
Liquid	Welded or brazed	Threaded, welded, or brazed
Vapor, ≤125 psig (≤0.9 MPag)	Threaded, welded, or brazed	Threaded, welded, or brazed
Vapor, ≥125 psig (≥0.9 MPag)	Welded or brazed	Threaded, welded, or brazed

6.9.3.6 Metallic tubing joints shall be flared or brazed using tubing and fittings in accordance with 5.9.3 and 5.9.4.

6.9.3.7 Piping in systems shall be run as directly as is practical from one point to another, with as few fittings as practical.

The number of fittings (ells, tees, and so forth) is usually minimized in a piping system when the system is designed economically and for ease of installation. Frequently, however, piping is field run or modified, resulting in excessive fittings. The intent of 6.9.3.7 is to minimize the number of fittings, because each fitting is a potential source of leakage. Also, the more fittings there are, the more resistance there is to flow and the slower the flow will be. A large number of fittings is not detrimental if a piping system is designed for them; the use of excess fittings can be especially critical in pump suction piping and can cause pump cavitation.

Although the number of fittings is usually minimized, the need to design for the allowance of movement in the piping system cannot be ignored, because the piping will shrink when liquid vaporizes, cooling to about −40°F (−40°C), and it will expand when it warms up. Expansion loops, which require extra pipe and fittings, are one way to design for pipe expansion and contraction, and incorporating short flexible connectors is another.

6.9.3.8 Where condensation of vapor can occur, piping shall be sloped back to the container, or means shall be provided for revaporizing the condensate.

The temperature at which LP-Gas vapor condenses depends on the properties of the specific LP-Gas involved and its pressure. For example, at 10 psig (69 kPag), condensation of propane occurs at about −20°F (−29°C) and below; at 20 psig (140 kPag), it occurs at about −5°F (−21°C) and below; and at 60 psig (414 kPag), it occurs at about 30°F (−1°C) and below. (Additional data on the temperature–pressure relationship of LP-Gas are available in the commentary on Annex B.)

When piping between first- and second-stage regulators is installed, precautions must be taken to ensure that any liquid that may condense does not reach the second-stage regulator. If the condensed liquid reached the second-stage regulator, liquid could pass through the regulator and vaporize, in turn overfeeding the appliance and increasing the flame size, which can be a significant fire hazard. Sloping the piping away from the second-stage regulator, toward the first-stage regulator, usually prevents liquid from reaching it.

6.9.3.9 Piping systems, including the interconnection of permanently installed containers, shall compensate for expansion, contraction, jarring, vibration, and settling.

(A) Flexible metallic connectors shall be permitted to be used.

(B) The use of nonmetallic pipe, tubing, or hose for permanently interconnecting containers shall be prohibited.

Paragraph 6.9.3.9(B) prohibits the use of hose for permanent connections between containers because metallic pipe or tubing is less likely to degrade over time.

6.9.3.10 Aboveground piping shall be supported and protected against physical damage by vehicles.

Aboveground piping must be supported so that there are no sags in the piping. In addition, the pipe supports must be substantial enough to prevent side pressure from putting stress on the pipe. If pipe is not supported properly it can fail. Protection from vehicular damage is a necessity where vehicles may reasonably be anticipated to be present. See the commentary following 6.6.1.2.

6.9.3.11 The portion of aboveground piping in contact with a support or a corrosion-causing substance shall be protected against corrosion.

6.9.3.12 Buried metallic pipe and tubing shall be installed underground with a minimum 12 in. (300 mm) of cover. The minimum cover shall be increased to 18 in. (460 mm) if external damage to the pipe or tubing from external forces is likely to result. If a minimum 12 in. (300 mm) of cover cannot be maintained, the piping shall be installed in conduit or shall be bridged (shielded).

The 2004 edition of NFPA 58 included a change to the requirements for the minimum burial depth of metallic pipe and tubing. The minimum burial depth was changed to 12 in. (300 mm) from 18 in. (460 mm) because it was recognized that the majority of installations were permitted to be at a minimum depth of 12 in. (300 mm).

Field experience indicates that the majority of underground piping installations are not subjected to external forces such as vehicular traffic (when located under driveways), nor are they located under gardens or flowerbeds, where damage to piping may result from frequent digging or tilling the soil. For this reason, the code was changed to address the most common installations as the general rule and those that are less common as exceptions to the general rule.

There may be areas where a rock formation would be difficult to remove or where other underground obstructions exist, such as utility pipes that cannot be relocated. In these and similar cases, the piping or tubing can be protected from damage by shielding it or inserting it in a protective pipe or casing.

6.9.3.13 Where underground piping is beneath driveways, roads, or streets, possible damage by vehicles shall be taken into account.

6.9.3.14 Underground metallic piping shall be protected against corrosion as warranted by soil conditions. *(See Section 6.16.)*

Where soil conditions warrant, corrosion protection for underground piping should be provided. Section 6.16 provides guidance on the type of corrosion protection for piping systems. Not all underground piping installations require the same level of corrosion protection. Underground copper piping may not require any corrosion protection, unless it is buried in an extremely hostile soil; for example, agriculture installations and refuse landfills. All underground steel piping requires some corrosion protection. Local experience plays an important role in determining what types of protection are required. Types of protection include neutral soil backfill, pipe coating, di-electric unions, cathodic protection anodes, and routine testing. In the 2011 edition, a requirement for cathodic protection was added for all underground propane containers. Cathodic protection systems can also be installed on underground piping.

In 2006, an incident occurred in Milwaukee, Wisconsin, in a gear factory where underground piping failed due to corrosion. The piping carried liquid propane from six 30,000 gal (114 m^3) tanks to a building where it was used as a backup for natural gas. As the system was being restarted in the fall, a significant amount of liquid propane was released below ground from a corroded pipe section. The propane vaporized and was drawn into a building, where it ignited, causing fatalities and injuries to workers. When the pipe was unearthed the wires connected to the pipe were found. They were assumed to have been connected to the anodes, but no anodes were found. A total of six pipe connections, with one test station, were uncovered. It is assumed that the anodes were consumed earlier, leaving the pipe susceptible to corrosion. This unfortunate incident demonstrates that where cathodic protection systems are installed, they must be monitored periodically.

6.9.3.15 LP-Gas piping shall not be used as a grounding electrode.

The text reflects the requirements of Article 250 of *NFPA 70®, National Electrical Code®* [23]. Gas piping must not be intentionally used as a ground conductor — that is, connected to the third pin of a standard electrical plug. Gas piping should be bonded to the building ground, either directly or via other grounded steel or metallic building piping.

Note that Article 250 of the *National Electrical Code* is concerned with protection of people from electric shock, not lightning. Additional bonding may be installed to minimize the potential damage from a lightning strike without conflicting with the requirements of the *National Electrical Code.*

6.9.3.16 Underground metallic piping, tubing, or both that convey LP-Gas from a gas storage container shall be provided with dielectric fittings at the building to electrically isolate it from the aboveground portion of the fixed piping system that enters a building. Such dielectric fittings shall be installed above ground and outdoors.

6.9.4 Installation of Polyamide and Polyethylene Pipe, Tubing, and Fittings.

Only nonmetallic pipe and tubing made of polyethylene or polyamide material are allowed by the code. Polyamide 11 is the specific type of material that can be used with fuel gas piping systems. It complies with ASTM D 2513, *Standard Specification for Thermoplastic Gas Pressure Pipe, Tubing and Fittings* [24], and provides increased performance in temperature rating, pressure rating, and LP-Gas resistance over that of polyethylene, although its significantly higher cost may limit its use.

6.9.4.1 Polyethylene and polyamide pipe, tubing, and fittings shall be installed outdoors underground only.

FAQ ▶
Why does the code restrict the installation of plastic pipe and tubing to outside and underground applications only?

Note that polyethylene and polyamide piping material cannot be used indoors because it would fail quickly in a fire and the released gas would accelerate a fire. When used outdoors underground, both materials provide excellent resistance against corrosion.

6.9.4.2 Polyethylene and polyamide pipe and tubing shall be buried as follows:

(1) With a minimum of 12 in. (300 mm) of cover
(2) With a minimum of 18 in. (460 mm) of cover if external damage to the pipe or tubing is likely to result
(3) With piping installed in conduit or bridged (shielded) if a minimum of 12 in. (300 mm) of cover cannot be provided

The requirements for burial depth of polyethylene and polyamide pipe and tubing are the same as for metallic pipe and tubing. Refer to the commentary following 6.9.3.12 for more information.

6.9.4.3 Assembled anodeless risers shall be used to terminate underground polyamide and polyethylene fixed piping systems above ground.

(A) The horizontal portion of risers shall be buried at least 12 in. (300 mm) below grade, and the casing material used for the risers shall be protected against corrosion in accordance with Section 6.16.

(B) Either the aboveground portion of the riser casing shall be provided with a plastic sleeve inside the riser casing, or the pipe or tubing shall be centered in the riser casing.

Anodeless risers are used to make a transition between the underground polyethylene or polyamide pipe or tubing and aboveground metallic pipe or tubing.
    The requirements in 6.9.4.3(A) and 6.9.4.3(B) apply to either factory-assembled or field-assembled anodeless risers.

(C) Factory-assembled risers shall be sealed and leak tested by the manufacturer.

The manufacturer verifies the integrity of the riser assembly for its ability to carry gas without leaking during the pressure test and leak tests of the system. This requirement is for the manufacturer of the riser and does not require any testing by the installer.

6.9.4.4 Field-assembled risers shall be supplied only in kit form with all necessary hardware for installation.

(A) Field-assembled risers shall comply with the following:

(1) They shall be design certified.
(2) They shall be sealed and pressure tested by the installer.
(3) They shall be assembled and installed in accordance with the riser manufacturer's instructions.

Field-assembled risers must be design-certified (see 3.3.17), meaning that the design of the product has been evaluated by an independent, third-party agency (for example, UL, CSA, or other testing agency) for compliance with a specific set of performance criteria.

The requirement in 6.9.4.4(A)(2) for the installer to pressure test the riser assembly relates to the integrity of the riser to convey fuel gas without leaking. This pressure test is conducted after the riser has been installed and connected to the system.

(B) The casing of the riser shall be constructed of one of the following materials:

(1) ASTM A 53, *Standard Specification for Pipe, Steel, Black and Hot-Dipped, Zinc-Coated Welded and Seamless,* Schedule 40 steel pipe
(2) ASTM A 513, *Standard Specification for Electric-Resistance-Welded Carbon and Alloy Steel Mechanical Tubing,* mechanical steel tubing with a minimum wall thickness of 0.073 in. (1.9 mm)
(3) Flexible metal tubing with a minimum crush strength of 1000 lb (453.6 kg) and a tensile strength of 300 lb (136 kg), including the transition connection as tested by the manufacturer

The requirements of 6.9.4.4(B) apply to both factory-assembled and field-installed anodeless risers.

6.9.4.5* Polyamide and polyethylene piping shall be installed in accordance with the following:

(1) Thrust forces caused by contraction or expansion of the piping or by anticipated external or internal loading shall be minimized.
(2) Each joint shall be designed to sustain the thrust forces.

A.6.9.4.5 Polyethylene will expand or contract 1 in. for every 10°F (25 mm for every 18°C) temperature change for every 100 ft (30.5 m) of pipe.

The thermal expansion and contraction of polyethylene and polyamide plastic are greater than those of steel. Therefore, greater attention must be paid to the possibility of excessive stress on the piping due to thermal contraction. Plastic piping is usually laid in trenches in a wavy pattern, rather than in a straight line, to accommodate the effects of thermal contraction. Also, plastic pipe fittings are designed and tested for a high pullout force. This installation method and these design specifications provide a safety margin and allow for some displacement of pipe due to soil movement.

6.9.4.6 An electrically continuous corrosion-resistant tracer wire (minimum AWG 14) or tape shall be buried with the polyamide or polyethylene pipe to facilitate locating the pipe.

(A) One end of the tracer wire shall be brought above ground at a building wall or riser.

(B) The tracer wire or tape shall not be in direct contact with the polyamide or polyethylene pipe.

It is often necessary to locate underground piping, especially polyethylene and polyamide pipe and tubing, to prevent damage from the use of excavating equipment in the area, which can result in the release of flammable gas. In order to be able to locate the underground, nonmetallic gas piping, either a tracer wire or tape must be used. When a wire is used, special equipment is needed to connect to the wire and generate a magnetic field that is detected with a portable detector. When tape is used, a metal detector is used to locate the tape. The tracer wire system is used more often in natural gas systems, and the tape is used more often in propane systems.

Although it is possible that the location of electrical wiring in the same trench as gas piping could create an explosion or fire hazard, it is highly unlikely. There are no prohibitions on placing electrical wiring or conduit in a trench with gas piping because too many events would have to take place before a true hazard would be present. For example, there must be a leak in the gas piping; furthermore, there must be oxygen underground where the gas is leaking in order to combine to form a flammable mixture (between 2.15 percent and 9.6 per-

◄ **FAQ**
Will electrical wire in the same trench as gas piping create a hazardous situation?

cent fuel/air ratio); also, a source of ignition must be present, which means that the electrical wiring must be arcing at the same location and time that the flammable mixture is present. The potential for all these things to simultaneously occur underground is extremely remote. It is possible for lightning to energize a wire and for the developed electrical current to jump to an electrical ground, and to pass through a gas piping, and for the arc to create a hole in the gas piping, which the arc could ignite. Again, while the editor is aware of one such incident, it is considered highly unlikely.

6.9.4.7 Polyamide and polyethylene piping that is installed in a vault, the dome of an underground container, or any other belowground enclosure shall be completely encased in one of the following:

(1) Gastight metal pipe and fittings that are protected from corrosion
(2) An anodeless riser

Paragraph 6.9.4.7 was revised in the 2011 edition by adding "the dome of an underground container," changing the format to a list of requirements, and adding "anodeless risers."

- The "dome of an underground container" was added following interpretation requests on the use of polyethylene tubing therein. Some users interpreted the code to allow such installations, because the previous text did not specifically cover the dome of an underground container, while others interpreted the code to mean that such installations were not allowed. The additional text clarifies the intent of the committee.
- The requirement was revised to include a list for clarity.
- "Anodeless risers" were added to clarify that the protection provided by an anodeless riser to the encased polyethylene or polyamide tubing is equal to that provided by metal pipe and fittings.

The requirement for installation in a vault recognizes that a vault, although underground, is not encased in soil and the piping must be protected to prevent possible damage and the formation of a flammable mixture in the vault.

6.9.4.8 Polyamide and polyethylene piping shall be installed in accordance with the manufacturer's installation instructions.

6.9.4.9 Where polyamide or polyethylene pipe or tubing is inserted into an existing steel pipe, the following shall apply:

(1) The polyamide or polyethylene pipe or tubing shall be protected from being damaged during the insertion process.
(2) The leading end of the polyamide or polyethylene pipe or tubing being inserted shall also be closed prior to insertion.

It is important when inserting plastic pipe or tubing into a steel pipe for protection that not only is the plastic pipe not damaged, but also that debris is kept from entering the pipe or tubing. Debris can cause regulators and appliance controls to malfunction, jeopardizing the distribution system and the safe operation of appliances.

6.9.4.10 Polyamide and polyethylene pipe that is not encased shall have a minimum wall thickness of 0.090 in. (2.3 mm).

6.9.4.11 Polyamide or polyethylene pipe with an outside diameter of 0.875 in. (22.2 mm) or less shall be permitted to have a minimum wall thickness of 0.062 in. (1.6 mm).

6.9.4.12 Each imperfection or damaged piece of polyamide or polyethylene pipe shall be replaced by fusion or mechanical fittings.

6.9.4.13 Repair clamps shall not be used to cover damaged or leaking sections.

Repairing polyethylene and polyamide pipe and tubing systems must be done using the proper equipment and tools. Clamping damaged or leaking sections is not an appropriate method for repairing piping sections because of the inability of clamps to maintain a leak-free system over an extended period of time. Therefore, damaged sections must be replaced using the procedures described in 6.9.4.12.

6.9.5 Valves in Polyamide and Polyethylene Piping Systems.

6.9.5.1 Valves in polyamide and polyethylene piping shall comply with following:

(1) Valves shall protect the pipe from excessive torsional or shearing loads when the valve is operated.
(2) Valve boxes shall be installed so as to minimize transmitting external loads to the valve or pipe.

Valve boxes are available from polyethylene and polyamide valve manufacturers. The valve boxes stabilize the valve so that the force of turning the valve stem or handle will not place excessive stress on the piping.

6.9.5.2 Valves shall be recommended for LP-Gas service by the manufacturer.

6.9.5.3 Valves shall be manufactured from thermoplastic materials fabricated from materials listed in ASTM D 2513, *Standard Specification for Thermoplastic Gas Pressure Pipe, Tubing and Fittings,* that have been shown to be resistant to the action of LP-Gas, or from metals protected to minimize corrosion in accordance with Section 6.16.

6.9.6 Flexible Connectors.

6.9.6.1 Flexible connectors shall be installed in accordance with the manufacturer's instructions.

6.9.6.2 Flexible metallic connectors shall not exceed 5 ft (1.5 m) in overall length when used with liquid or vapor piping on stationary containers of 2000 gal (7.6 m^3) water capacity or less.

Flexibility is often necessary in LP-Gas piping to allow for thermal expansion and contraction of the piping and settling of containers and equipment. Flexible connections often fit well in an LP-Gas system, but should not be used unless necessary, because the service life of flexible connectors is generally not as long as that of permanent piping. Flexible connectors must be limited in length because the possibility of damage to the connector increases with its length. Flexibility can be designed into metallic piping systems, and an engineer experienced in piping design should be consulted if that approach is to be taken.

Note that in the 2011 edition, the requirement in 6.9.6.2 was not revised, but in Chapter 3 the definitions of *flexible hose connector* and *flexible metallic connector* were revised, and a new definition of *metallic-protected hose connector* was added. It is anticipated that further revisions to these definitions will be made in future editions of the code, as changes to the UL standards for flexible connectors are finalized. The maximum length of flexible metallic connectors is 60 in. (1.5 m); however, in specific applications the length is reduced. For example, 6.23.5.1(E) allows longer lengths for installations on vehicles, where approved.

6.10 Remote Shutoff Actuation

6.10.1 Where LP-Gas vapor is used as a pressure source for activating the remote shutoff mechanisms of internal valves and emergency shutoff valves, the following shall apply:

(1) Actuators and pressure supply line components shall be compatible with LP-Gas vapor.
(2) Supply line piping materials shall be limited to a maximum of ⅜ in. (9.0 mm) outside diameter.
(3)*Supply pressure shall be controlled to prevent condensation of the LP-Gas vapor.

A.6.10.1(3) If LP-Gas vapor is supplied at container pressure and there is no flow, an ambient temperature drop below the container liquid temperature will result in condensation of the LP-Gas vapor. If the system is activated, the presence of liquid could result in a delay or malfunction of the system operation.

(4) The LP-Gas supply maximum flow rate to the system shall not exceed that from a No. 54 drill orifice.

Numerous bulk plant installations in warmer climates of the United States and in other countries are successfully using LP-Gas vapor as a pressure source for activating remote shutoffs, in lieu of air compressors and compressed gas cylinders. The technical committee recognizes the viability of this type of installation as evidenced by the 2004 edition provision that allows venting of LP-Gas for this application.

Various pressure sources offer different characteristics that must be considered in the design of a remote shutdown system. The requirements in Section 6.10 provide the necessary provisions to ensure that a system is properly installed, using any of a variety of materials for the safe design of remote shutdown systems. When using LP-Gas vapor, the installer must be sure that the materials are approved to be used with the vapor.

The maximum tubing size of ⅜ in. (9 mm) OD allows flexibility in system design. The quantity of gas released in the event of tubing failure is limited by the No. 54 inlet orifice.

It must be noted that the tubing used for the pressure to hold the valves open, whether for LP-Gas vapor or for another gas, does not qualify as the thermal actuation element unless it is specifically stated that it will melt at 250°F (121°C) or less. The thermal element must function when heated, whether impinged upon by flame or not. If the design specification for the tubing does not include a melting point, then it cannot be assumed that it will melt by 250°F (121°C) or that it will continue to do so after prolonged exposure to weather and UV light.

Note, however, that the tubing used must fail to hold pressure at 250°F (121°C) or less, as it must release the pressure even if the fire does not impinge on it. The failure point cannot increase to a temperature above 250°F (121°C) as it ages or is exposed to weather or the sun.

6.10.2 Where compressed air is used as a pressure source for activating internal valves and emergency shutoff valves, the air shall be clean and kept at a moisture level that will not prevent the system from operating.

6.11 Internal Valves

6.11.1 The requirements of 6.11.2 through 6.11.5 shall be required for internal valves in liquid service that are installed in containers of over 4000 gal (15.2 m³) water capacity by July 1, 2003.

6.11.2 Internal valves shall be installed in accordance with 5.7.4.2 and Table 5.7.4.2 on containers of over 4000 gal (15.2 m³) water capacity.

6.11.3 Automatic shutdown of internal valves in liquid service shall be provided using thermal (fire) actuation. The thermal sensing element of the internal valve shall be within 5 ft (1.5 m) of the internal valve.

6.11.4 At least one remote shutdown station for internal valves in liquid service shall be installed not less than 25 ft (7.6 m) or more than 100 ft (30 m) from the liquid transfer point. This requirement shall be retroactive to all internal valves required by the code.

6.11.5 Emergency remote shutdown stations shall be identified by a sign, visible from the point of transfer, incorporating the words "Propane — Container Liquid Valve Emergency Shutoff" in block letters of not less than 2 in. (51 mm) in height on a background of contrasting color to the letters.

Section 6.11 establishes performance and identification requirements for internal valves installed in containers of over 4000 gal (15.1 m³). As part of the retrofit requirements in 5.7.4.2, these requirements were first added to the 2001 edition of NFPA 58 and were made retroactively applicable to all existing valves as of July 1, 2003. That date is carried in the code for the convenience of users in states that skipped the adoption of the 2001 through 2008 editions of NFPA 58. The following are required for internal valves:

- Automatic shutdown if fire is sensed within 5 ft (1.5 m) of the internal valve, as specified in 6.11.3
- Remote manual shutdown from a remote location from within distances specified in 6.11.4
- Identification of the remote shutdown station using 2 in. (51 mm) letters for visibility in 6.11.5

These requirements are similar to those of an emergency shutoff valve, which also requires operation at the valve. There are different retrofit requirements in 5.7.4.2 for existing containers that do not have an internal valve installed. These requirements take effect July 1, 2011, and are also given in 5.7.4.2.

The purpose of requiring an internal valve is to provide protection against external physical damage to the valve and to allow remote shutdown of flow from a propane container in the event of uncontrolled release. There have been incidents where damage to propane tank installations has caused extensive property damage and loss of life that could have been prevented if the flow of propane from damaged piping could have been stopped from a remote location or by automatic shutoff using thermal actuation.

Internal valves are required, and their installation is mandated by 5.7.4.2 in all existing LP-Gas storage containers with water capacities of more than 4000 gal (15.2 m³) in response to a number of incidents where piping system failure allowed release of significant amounts of LP-Gas with resulting fire. While excess flow valves are required in such installations, they will not operate if the pipe breakage results in less than full flow. In such incidents there is no way to shut off the flow of gas without operating the manual valve under the propane storage container, which can be dangerous or impossible under fire conditions. The internal valve includes features that close the valve in a fire and allow for remote closure.

The schematic in Exhibit 6.30 shows how the internal valve operates. In part (A), the valve is closed, permitting a tight seal by both tank pressure and the valve's closing spring. In part (B), moving the operating lever to approximately the midpoint in its 70° angle of travel allows the cam to place the rapid equalization portion of the valve stem in the pilot opening. This permits a larger amount of product to bleed downstream than if the operating lever were moved into the full open position. In part (C), after a few seconds, when the tank and the downstream pressure equalize, the excess flow spring pushes open the main poppet. The operating lever is moved to the full open position to ready the system for transfer operation. The pump or compressor should not be engaged until the valve is fully opened. In part (D), during the transfer operation, a flow, or sufficient flow surge, greater than the valve's excess flow spring rating will force the main poppet closed. A small amount of product will continue to bleed through the downstream side, but much less than in part (B).

EXHIBIT 6.30 Operational
Schematic for Internal Valves.
(Courtesy of Emerson
Process Management
Regulator Technologies Inc.)

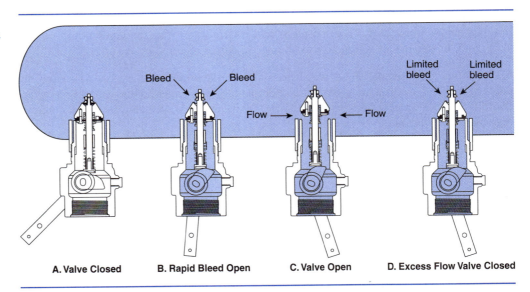

Bleed   Bleed   Flow →   ← Flow   Limited bleed   Limited bleed

A. Valve Closed   B. Rapid Bleed Open   C. Valve Open   D. Excess Flow Valve Closed

Should this occur, the operating lever should be moved to the full closed position in part (A) and the step repeated.

6.12 Emergency Shutoff Valves

Prior to 1980, accident experience at LP-Gas storage facilities was dominated by release of liquid and vapor during liquid transfer operations resulting from hose failures, hose coupling failures, and piping and component failures. In many instances, these failures resulted from a cargo tank motor vehicle being driven away before the transfer hose was disconnected. In some cases, valves were torn out of the vehicle connections, especially brass valves inserted into steel fittings. (This problem was solved by requiring steel, malleable iron, or ductile iron fittings and primary valves on cargo tank containers, as stated in 9.4.3.8.) These incidents also led to the development of the emergency shutoff valve and the addition to NFPA 58 of retroactive requirements for their installation.

Section 6.12 requires both an automatic and manual means of stopping the escape of LP-Gas, other than by an excess-flow check valve, from the storage container downstream of the emergency shutoff valve. There are installations in which the aggregate container capacity exceeds 4000 gal (15.1 m³), which would require an emergency shutoff valve, but the size of the hoses or swivel-type piping for handling liquid and vapor is smaller than 1½ in. (38 mm) and 1¼ in. (44 mm), respectively, and thus an emergency shutoff valve is not required.

Exhibit 6.31 shows how emergency shutoff valves (ESVs) are installed. Two ESVs are shown in the drawing, one for liquid and one for vapor, as is commonly used for transfers to and from bobtails, transports, and rail cars. Pull away protection is accomplished by the bulkhead, which anchors the plant side piping if the hose is pulled away by the vehicle. This installation uses a mechanically operated ESV. Note the lead cables leading away from the hoses. These are connected to the shutoff point required in 6.12.10(1) and close the ESV when pulled. The cable on the vehicle side of the ESV demonstrates a way to shut off the valve if a pull away occurs, in which case the cable will be pulled by the hose or dislocated piping, closing the valve. This method is not specifically required by NFPA 58, but it is an inexpensive way to provide a quicker closing of an ESV in a pull away incident.

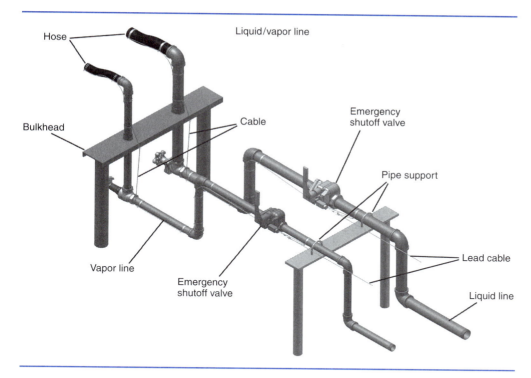

EXHIBIT 6.31 *Installation of Emergency Shutoff Valves at Unloading Station. (Courtesy of Engineered Controls International, Inc.)*

At least one state requires that a pull away initiate an automatic closure of the ESVs. A North Carolina regulation adds a requirement in its reference to the *LP-Gas Code* that "[T]he bulkhead shall incorporate a mechanical, pneumatic, or other acceptable means to automatically close emergency valves in the event of a pull away." This requirement is known to have stopped some releases almost before they started.

The plant transport unloading area must have the following safety devices:

- Anchorage, with a predictable breakaway point to retain the valves and piping intact on the plant side of the connections
- An emergency shutoff valve in the vapor line with means for manual shutoff, thermal shutoff, and remote shutoff
- Either a backflow check valve (may be part of the sight flow unit) or an emergency shutoff valve in the liquid line with means for manual shutoff, thermal shutoff, and remote shutoff control

Tank car unloading risers must have the following safety devices:

- An emergency shutoff valve with thermal shutoff on liquid hoses at the tank car end of the liquid hose
- Remote control of the emergency shutoff valve
- Backflow check valves at riser ends of liquid hose connections
- An emergency shutoff valve at the tank car end of the vapor hose with means for manual shutoff and thermal activation

Where two hoses or swivel-type piping are used on a tank car unloading riser, each leg of the piping should be protected by backflow check valve(s) or an emergency shutoff valve.

Exhibit 6.32 shows the installation of a pneumatically operated emergency shutoff valve/unloading adapter combination at a tank car unloading station.

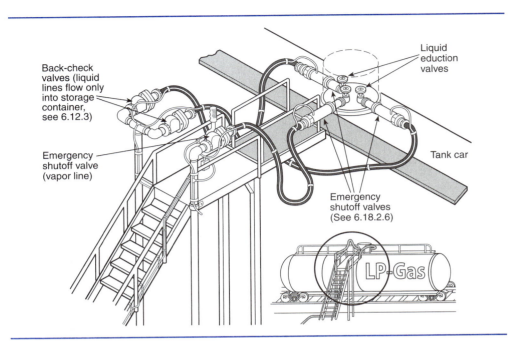

EXHIBIT 6.32 Pneumatically Operated Emergency Shutoff Valve/Unloading Adapter Combination Installation. (Courtesy of Emerson Process Management Regulator Technologies Inc.)

Back-check valves (liquid lines flow only into storage container, see 6.12.3)

Liquid eduction valves

Tank car

Emergency shutoff valve (vapor line)

Emergency shutoff valves (See 6.18.2.6)

6.12.1 On new installations and on existing installations, stationary container storage systems with an aggregate water capacity of more than 4000 gal (15.1 m³) utilizing a liquid transfer line that is 1½ in. (39 mm) or larger, and a pressure equalizing vapor line that is 1¼ in. (32 mm) or larger, shall be equipped with emergency shutoff valves.

Loading and unloading from tank cars are shown in Exhibit 6.33, but note that storage tanks are not shown. Emergency shutoff valves are installed at the tank car dome in the transfer piping during loading and unloading. A backflow check valve can be used in place of an emergency shutoff valve where flow is only into the tank car per 6.18.2.6(2). Also, where flow is only into a stationary tank, a backflow check valve can be used in place of an ESV per 6.12.3.

EXHIBIT 6.33 Transfer from a Tank Car. (Courtesy of Superior Energy Systems, Inc.)

6.12.2 An emergency shutoff valve shall be installed in the transfer lines of the fixed piping transfer system within 20 ft (6 m) of lineal pipe from the nearest end of the hose or swivel-type piping connections.

In order to comply with 6.12.8, this backflow check valve must be installed in the part of the plant piping that would not be damaged by a pull away incident.
     See Formal Interpretations 79-1 and 79-2.

Formal Interpretation
NFPA 58
Liquefied Petroleum Gas Code
2011 Edition

Reference: 6.12.2

F.I.: 79-1

Question: Is it the intent of 6.10.2 to require either an emergency shutoff valve or a backflow check valve in each leg of the piping when two or more hoses are used?

Answer: Yes.

Committee Comment: Unless these provisions are made, it would be possible for flow from one leg of the piping to escape through a leak in the other leg.

Issue Edition: 1979

Reference: 3168(a)

Date: November 1979

6.12.3 When the flow is only into the container, a backflow check valve shall be permitted to be used in lieu of an emergency shutoff valve if installed in the piping transfer system downstream of the hose or swivel-type piping connections.

6.12.4 The backflow check valve shall have a metal-to-metal seat or a primary resilient seat with metal backup, not hinged with combustible material, and shall be designed for this specific application.

6.12.5 Where there are two or more liquid or vapor lines with hoses or swivel-type piping connected of the sizes designated, an emergency shutoff valve or a backflow check valve, where allowed, shall be installed in each leg of the piping.

Where flow is in two directions, an emergency shutoff valve is required. Listing of emergency shutoff valves is not required, but most manufacturers elect to list the valves because listing facilitates approval. Where flow is only into the container, a check valve can be used, provided it is "designed for the specific application." The phrase "designed for the specific application" is not defined in NFPA 58, but is intended to mean a check valve that will be able to withstand the forces and flows of the fluid on the valve and its moving parts over an extended time where it is used.
     Exhibit 6.34 illustrates a pneumatically operated emergency shutoff valve. A mechanically operated emergency shutoff valve is illustrated in Exhibit 6.31.

Formal Interpretation
NFPA 58
Liquefied Petroleum Gas Code
2011 Edition

Reference: 6.12.2

F.I.: 79-2

Question: In an LP-Gas installation subject to the provisions of 6.10.1 of NFPA 58 by virtue of the container capacity qualifications, the vapor piping used in liquid transfer operations is 1½-inches nominal size. However, a vapor hose permanently affixed to the delivery end of this piping (by the use of a 1½-inch-to-1-inch reducing elbow) is 1-inch nominal size. No backflow check valve is installed in this piping.

Is it the intent of 6.10.2 of NFPA 58 to require that an emergency shutoff valve be installed in the fixed vapor piping?

Answer: No.

Committee Comment: The Committee notes that, in the absence of either an emergency shutoff valve or a backflow check valve, 6.16.2.6(a) or (b) would require an excess flow valve in the fixed vapor piping cited.

Issue Edition: 1979

Reference: 3168(a)

Date: December 1980

EXHIBIT 6.34 *Installation of Pneumatically Operated Emergency Shutoff Valve. (Courtesy of National Propane Gas Association)*

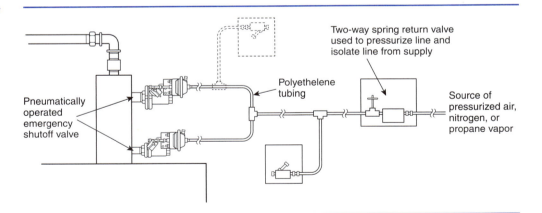

6.12.6 Emergency shutoff valves shall be installed so that the temperature-sensitive element in the valve, or a supplemental temperature-sensitive element that operates at a maximum temperature of 250°F (121°C) that is connected to actuate the valve, is not more than 5 ft (1.5 m) from the nearest end of the hose or swivel-type piping connected to the line in which the valve is installed.

Automatic actuation of an emergency shutoff valve occurs through sensing of heat from a fire with the sensing element that is part of or attached to the valve. The sensing element could also be the pressurized plastic tubing that carries the compressed air, nitrogen, or LP-Gas vapor (see Section 6.10) used to operate the emergency shutoff valve. The plastic tubing system is actually a line sensor capable of sensing fire at other locations. Refer to the commentary on 6.10.1(3) where the properties of plastic tubing are discussed.

The paragraph states that a supplemental sensing element within 5 ft (1.5 m) of the ESV can be installed in lieu of incorporating the temperature-sensitive element in the ESV. Some installations utilize additional sensors to shut the valve in the event of fire in a location remote from the ESV. A "continuous" sensor can be easily added to pneumatically actuated ESVs by installing plastic tubing along all or part of the piping and hose and pressurizing the tubing as part of the pressurized gas used to open the ESV.

6.12.7 Temperature-sensitive elements of emergency shutoff valves shall not be painted, nor shall they have any ornamental finishes applied after manufacture.

6.12.8* The emergency shutoff valves or backflow check valves shall be installed in the fixed piping so that any break resulting from a pull will occur on the hose or swivel-type piping side of the connection while retaining intact the valves and piping on the plant side of the connection.

A.6.12.8 Anchorage can be accomplished by the use of concrete bulkheads or equivalent anchorage or by the use of a weakness or shear fitting.

The feature described in 6.12.8 is known as "pull away protection." The valve, or more commonly, the piping system, is designed so that if the vehicle moves away, a break from a pull on the piping system results in failure of the "vehicle" side of the valve or anchorage, with the "plant" side of the valve or anchorage remaining intact, thereby preventing the release of product. Exhibit 6.31 shows one common way to accomplish "pull away protection." Exhibit 6.35 illustrates a pull away valve.

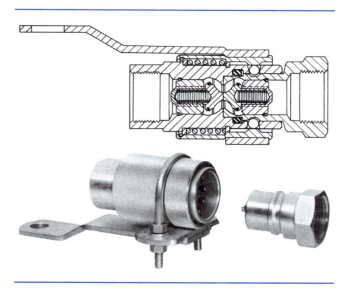

EXHIBIT 6.35 *Pull Away Valve. (Courtesy of Engineered Controls International, Inc.)*

The provision in 6.12.8 also applies to transfer from railroad tank cars directly into tank trucks with no intermediate storage. LP-Gas distributors have reportedly sent trucks to railroad tracks to unload tank cars that, before sections of rail track were abandoned, formerly could be delivered to a bulk plant. The code requires the same safety and pull away protection for trackside transfer, shown in Exhibit 6.36, as for fixed installations.

EXHIBIT 6.36 *Rail Car Unloading Using Hoses and Bobtail Filling Site with Pull Away Protection. Note that the small tank in the foreground is not part of the liquid transfer operations and note the wheel chock sign at the tank car. (Courtesy of Brian Clayton)*

6.12.9 Emergency shutoff valves required by the code shall be tested annually for the functions required by 5.12.4(2) and (3). Backflow check valves installed in lieu of emergencyshutoff valves shall be checked annually for proper operation. The results of the test shall be documented.

The requirement in 6.12.9 references 5.12.4 and includes testing for activation of the emergency shutoff valve by manual shutoff at the installed location and by manual shutoff from the remote location. The requirement to test the thermal means of closing the valve was removed in the 2011 edition, because testing the thermal means is a destructive test and would require replacement of the thermal element after the test.

An incident in Sanford, North Carolina, occurred on September 18, 1996, in which the delivery hose from a transport truck failed, releasing into the atmosphere all 9700 gal (36.7 m³) of propane on the truck and about 30,000 gal (114 m³) of propane from the two 30,000 gal (114 m³) storage tanks. Fortunately, neither fire nor personal injuries occurred in this case. Follow-up inspections at all propane bulk storage facilities in North Carolina by the state's Department of Agriculture found about 8 percent of the check valves and emergency shutoff valves to be inoperative. For this reason, all emergency shutoff valves mandated in Section 6.10 must be inspected annually for proper operation.

Exhibit 6.31 illustrates the installation of emergency shutoff valves on ASME storage containers.

The method of test for emergency shutoff valves is not specified in NFPA 58, and the valves can be tested in place by releasing propane from a storage tank into the atmosphere or into an empty bobtail or transport. The valves can also be removed and tested in a test facility.

Documentation of these tests is important so that the authority having jurisdiction can verify that the tests were done. In some areas, the authority having jurisdiction requests permission to observe the tests. In locations where the authority having jurisdiction performs an inspection that includes testing the ESVs, and a written record of the test exists, that test and record meet the requirements of 6.12.9.

6.12.10 All new and existing emergency shutoff valves shall comply with the following:

(1) Each emergency shutoff valve shall have at least one clearly identified and easily accessible manually operated remote emergency shutoff device.
(2) The shutoff device shall be located not less than 25 ft (7.6 m) or more than 100 ft (30 m) in the path of egress from the emergency shutoff valve.
(3) Where an emergency shutoff valve is used in lieu of an internal valve in compliance with 5.7.4.2(D)(2), the remote shutoff device shall be installed in accordance with 6.11.4 and 6.11.5.

Note that these requirements have been made retroactive to all installations by the phrase "new and existing."

In addition to automatic actuation, an emergency shutoff valve must be installed so that it can be operated manually both from a remote location and from its installed location. This requirement was revised in the 1998 edition to specify the meaning of the term *remote,* which describes the ability to activate the emergency shutoff valve from a location far enough from the point of transfer to be considered safe. Here, in the installation chapter, remote has been mandated to be between 25 ft and 100 ft (7.6 m and 30 m) from the valve and in the path of egress from where the emergency shutoff valve is installed. It has been recognized in some locations that strict compliance with the distance requirement can present problems. For instance, if the section of a yard from 20 ft to 110 ft (6 m to 33.5 m) from the valve is where trucks travel, putting the remote location in at exactly 100 ft (30 m) may mean it is likely to be destroyed by a passing truck. In this case, the authority having jurisdiction could approve a location at 115 ft (35 m) away as a common sense solution to the problem. The intent of having the remote location in the path of egress recognizes that the transfer employee will be more able to actuate the remote closure device if it is located along the route that he is likely to travel as he flees from the release incident. It will also keep from drawing him further into the site, possibly into a more dangerous location.

6.12.11 Emergency shutoff valves for railroad tank car transfer systems shall be in accordance with 6.18.2.6, 6.26.4, 7.2.3.7, and 7.2.3.8.

6.13 Hydrostatic Relief Valve Installation

A hydrostatic relief valve or a device providing pressure-relieving protection shall be installed in each section of piping and hose in which liquid LP-Gas can be isolated between shutoff valves so as to relieve the pressure that could develop from the trapped liquid to a safe atmosphere or product-retaining section.

If liquid LP-Gas is trapped in a length of pipe between two closed valves, there is no room for expansion of the liquid. The pressure developed can be very high (thousands of psi) and can result in pipe or valve failures. Operation of a hydrostatic relief valve prevents this pressure from developing by discharging liquid. Liquid, however, represents a greater quantity of discharged flammable gas than vapor, and its presence can present a hazard of fire and skin freezing (as the liquid vaporizes it absorbs heat) to personnel.

Over a temperature range from 30°F to 90°F (0°C to 32°C), liquid propane expands an average of about 1.6 percent for each 10 Fahrenheit degrees (5.5 Celsius degrees). Because liquid propane and most other liquids are not compressible, this thermal expansion results in a tremendous pressure rise.

Hydrostatic relief valves are usually small [about ¼ in. (6 mm) pipe size], because only a small amount of liquid has to be released to lower pressure enough to prevent an overpressure hazard.

Refer to Formal Interpretation 58-04-01.

6.14 Testing Piping Systems

6.14.1 After assembly, piping systems (including hose) shall be tested and proven free of leaks at not less than the normal operating pressure.

After assembly of piping, but before appliances are connected, standard practice is to admit full container pressure to the system and check all connections for leaks with a leak-testing solution or other means. There are specific leak-test solutions listed for this purpose because

Formal Interpretation
NFPA 58
Liquefied Petroleum Gas Code
2011 Edition

Reference: 6.13

F.I. No.: 58-04-1

Question: Is it the intent of 6.11 of NFPA 58 to allow a maintenance valve (locked in the open position) to be placed between a hydrostatic relief valve and the pipe upon which it is installed?

Answer: No.

Issue Edition: 2004

Reference: 6.11

Issue Date: September 23, 2004

Effective Date: October 12, 2004

some soap solutions can be corrosive to piping. It is important, particularly with copper and brass tubing or fittings, that the leak-test solution contain no ammonia.

A widely used and sensitive leakage test is that of using a tee block fitting with a pressure gauge between the container service shutoff valve and the first-stage regulator. This test is described in Annex D of NFPA 54, *National Fuel Gas Code* [20]. Essentially, the test consists of admitting full container pressure to the system, closing the container shutoff valve, closing off the shutoff valve at the end of the piping system being tested, and lowering the pressure reading on the gauge by 10 psig (69 kPag) by bleeding off a small amount of gas in the system. NFPA 54 suggests a test duration of three minutes. A very small leak will be accentuated in the small volume involved at the pressure gauge location. If leakage occurs and the pressure drops, the source is detected by checking all fittings and connections with a leak-testing solution. If the pressure actually rises during the test, it is an indication that the service valve is leaking past the seat.

6.14.2 Piping within the scope of NFPA 54, *National Fuel Gas Code*, shall be pressure tested in accordance with that code.

Pressure testing of piping is required by NFPA 54, *National Fuel Gas Code* [20] for piping within the scope of that code, which is typically piping downstream of the second-stage regulator. In NFPA 54, the minimum test pressure is at least 1.5 times the maximum working pressure of the system, but not less than 3 psig (21 kPag).

6.14.3 Tests shall not be made with a flame.

6.15 Installation in Areas of Heavy Snowfall

In areas where the local building codes have specified a minimum design snow load for roofs equal to, or exceeding, 125 psf (610 kg/m²), piping, regulators, meters, and other equipment installed in the piping system shall be protected from the forces anticipated as a result of accumulated snow.

The requirement was revised in the 2011 edition to make the requirement applicable in areas where the roof load exceeds 125 psf (610 kg/m²). The technical committee is aware that building codes have such requirements and that they are based on experience with snow conditions. The former requirement stated that it applied to areas where "heavy snowfall is anticipated," which left much room for interpretation. There were several comments submitted to the committee not to accept this revision, or to utilize different criteria. While the committee agrees that other criteria can be used to trigger enforcement of extra provisions in areas of heavy snow, having a specific numerical value will make the requirement much clearer and provide for uniform application.

The force of accumulated snow can damage piping, meters, and regulators outside of buildings. Specific protection requirements are not mandated, however, because it is difficult to make one rule that covers all potential snowfalls. In the area of the Sierra Nevada mountains, a model law to cover this subject has been developed, and several municipalities have enacted specific rules on the subject of heavy snowfall. Also see the container installation requirements in heavy snow areas in 6.6.3.6.

6.16* Corrosion Protection

A.6.16 For information on protection of underground components, see NACE SP-01-69, *Control of External Corrosion on Underground or Submerged Metallic Piping Systems.*

6.16.1 All metallic equipment and components that are buried or mounded shall be coated or protected and maintained to minimize corrosion.

6.16.2 Corrosion protection of all other materials shall be in accordance with accepted engineering practice.

Corrosion protection is required for buried and mounded equipment, components, and piping where soils can have a corrosive action on metal. Coatings have traditionally been relied upon for protection, although cathodic protection increasingly is being used to protect containers, and polyethylene piping is replacing some metallic piping underground. There are two types of cathodic protection: active and passive. Active systems are not normally used either for buried and mounded propane containers or for buried propane piping. Note that cathodic protection is required in the 2011 edition for all underground ASME containers. A passive cathodic protection system consists of an underground or mounded container, or other underground metal component, and a buried sacrificial anode that is connected by a wire to the container. See Exhibit 6.17 showing underground containers with anode bags prior to backfilling.

The sacrificial anode is usually made of magnesium or other electrochemically active metal in powder form in a bag, or in a rod or ribbon. The sacrificial anode will corrode before the tank corrodes, similar to galvanized pipe, where the zinc coating corrodes and in doing so protects the steel from corroding. All passive cathodic protection systems should be monitored when installed using a half-cell meter, to verify that the system is working. Using a copper/copper sulfate half cell, a voltage of −0.85 or lower (more negative) indicates that the system is working. The voltage should be recorded and additional annual readings are recommended by most corrosion engineers. The system can be checked at intervals longer than one year, but if a failure occurs, corrosion of the container will occur from the time of failure to the time it is identified and corrected.

Failure of cathodic protection systems can occur by severance of the wire connecting the sacrificial anode to the container, by depletion of the anode, by grounding of the container to a building wiring system, and by other mechanisms.

Where a coating is used, fittings such as collars must be coated after installation. Coated piping should not be installed in soil where there are rocks that can scrape the coating and expose the pipe to corrosion. If a coating is used, the coating must be completely free of openings or pinholes to prevent corrosion. Where dissimilar metals are connected together, it is also important that an insulating fitting be installed to eliminate cathodic action on the piping. If this insulating fitting is not used, the piping system can be adversely affected rather rapidly.

6.17 Equipment Installation

6.17.1 Reserved.

6.17.2 Pump Installation.

6.17.2.1 Pumps shall be installed in accordance with the pump manufacturers' installation instructions.

6.17.2.2 Installation shall be made so that the pump casing is not subjected to excessive strains transmitted to it by the suction and discharge piping. Such protection shall be accomplished by piping design, the use of flexible metallic connectors that do not exceed 36 in. (1 m) in overall length, or by other means.

Note that flexible metallic connectors used with pumps are limited to a maximum length of 36 in. (1 m) This is shorter than the 60 in. (1.5 m) flexible connector length allowed in 6.9.6.2. This requirement does not prevent other systems from being used to isolate the pump itself from vibration. Vibration can lead to stresses imposed on the casing, and it can damage the pump bearing and cause the pump to fail.

6.17.2.3 Positive displacement pumps shall incorporate a bypass valve or recirculating device to limit the normal operating discharge pressure.

(A) The bypass valve or recirculating device to limit the normal operating discharge pressure shall discharge either into a storage container or into the pump inlet.

(B) If the bypass valve or recirculating device is equipped with a shutoff valve, a secondary device shall be required and designed to do one of the following:

(1) Operate at not more than 400 psig (2.8 MPag)
(2) Operate at a pressure of 50 psig (345 kPag) above the operating pressure where the design pressure exceeds 350 psig (2.4 MPag)

(C) The secondary device shall be incorporated, if not integral with the pump, in the pump piping and shall be designed or installed so that it cannot be rendered inoperative and shall discharge either into a storage container or into the pump inlet.

(D) A pump operating control or disconnect switch shall be located near the pump. Remote control points shall be provided for other plant operations such as container filling, loading or unloading of cargo tank vehicles and railroad tank cars, or operation of the engine fuel dispenser.

Because LP-Gas liquid under pressure in a container or pipeline vaporizes when the pressure is reduced, the selection of a pump for propane service and its installation must anticipate and prevent vaporization of liquid being sent to the pump. Pumps are designed and sized to handle liquid and not vapor. The pump will not operate properly if a mixture of liquid and vapor is sent to the pump. (A mixture of liquid and vapor can be created if conditions result in vaporization of some of the liquid being fed into the pump.) When this occurs, delivery from the pump will be reduced because the vapor created takes up more space than liquid, and the pump will vibrate. This condition is called *cavitation*. The types of pumps commonly used in installations covered by NFPA 58 are installed so that the pressure in the pump inlet is not reduced to the point where vaporization can occur. This is called a *positive suction head*. In practice, pump suction inlets are installed well below the lowest liquid level in a container, and the suction piping is large enough to minimize friction loss, which can contribute to lowered pressure at the pump inlet.

The suction inlet pressure of a pump is the pressure of the LP-Gas container, which can be as high as 250 psig (1.7 MPag) for propane. The pump discharge pressures, therefore, can also be substantial. For this reason, a bypass is required for the positive displacement pumps most often used. The bypass must operate at not more than 400 psig (2.8 MPag) or 50 psig (345 kPag) above the operating pressure of the system, whichever is greater. This bypass can be provided integrally with the pump or installed in the piping system. Exhibit 6.37 shows an automatic pump bypass valve.

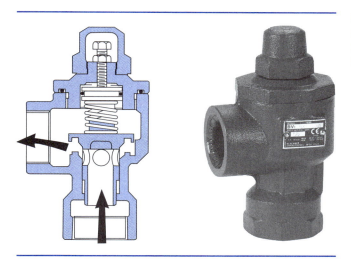

EXHIBIT 6.37 *Automatic Pump Bypass Valve. (Courtesy of Blackmer, a Dover Company)*

The off or on operation of the typical pump installation requires provisions to prevent excessive vibration and strain to inlet and discharge connections.

Many pumps are started and stopped from a location remote from the pump; for example, cylinder filling areas and dispensers. For the safety of anyone who might be working on a pump, a means is required to prevent startup of the pump using a "lock out" procedure. This requirement is also part of workplace safety requirements, including the "lock out/tag out" procedures of the U.S. Occupational Safety and Health Administration (OSHA).

Exhibit 6.38 shows a typical pump installation. Note the external bypass piping from the pump discharge to the tank with a pressure relief valve. This piping protects the pump from overpressure by allowing liquid to flow back to the tank if the outlet valve is shut off. If this bypass were not present, the pump could continue to run in a no-flow situation and the liquid would use the heat generated by the pump to vaporize. This situation could result in the pump overheating and being damaged.

6.17.3 Compressor Installation.

6.17.3.1 Compressors shall be installed in accordance with the compressor manufacturers' installation instructions.

6.17.3.2 Installation shall be made so that the compressor housing is not subjected to excessive stresses transmitted to it by the suction and discharge piping. Where used to provide flexibility in the piping system, flexible metallic connectors or metallic-protected flexible hose connectors shall not exceed 36 in. (1 m) in overall total length.

Refer to the commentary on 6.17.2.2.

6.17.3.3 Engines used to drive portable compressors shall be equipped with exhaust system spark arresters and shielded ignition systems.

6.17.3.4 Where the compressor is not equipped with an integral means to prevent the LP-Gas liquid from entering the suction, a liquid trap shall be installed in the suction piping as close to the compressor as practical.

6.17.3.5 Portable compressors used with temporary connections shall be excluded from the requirement in 6.17.3.4 unless used to unload railroad tank cars.

Portable compressors are usually small, gasoline or propane engine-driven units that are attended, and the operator provides the necessary safety measures. These features do not apply to compressors used to unload railroad tank cars, which are larger and less likely to be closely attended.

The use of a compressor piped with four-way valves for liquid transfer is shown in Exhibit 6.39. First, vapor from the receiver tank is sent into the vapor space of the supply tank, causing the pressure to rise and liquid to flow from the supply tank into the receiving tank. This process is continued until liquid flow ceases. Next, the valves are operated and vapor is taken from the supply tank, compressed, and discharged into the liquid portion of the receiver tank, where it bubbles up through the liquid, cools, and partially liquefies. This process is continued until the supply tank pressure drops to 25 percent to 30 percent of the starting pressure.

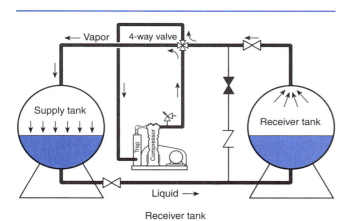

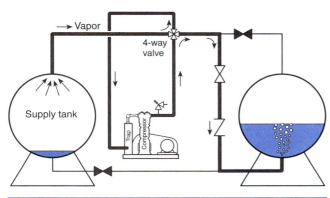

EXHIBIT 6.39 *Transferring with a Compressor Liquid Transfer (top) and Vapor Recovery (bottom). (Courtesy of Blackmer, a Dover Company)*

6.17.4 Installation of Strainers.

Strainers shall be installed so that the strainer element can be removed without removing equipment or piping.

Per 6.17.4, a strainer installed at the inlet of a pump must have clearance to allow for the removal of the strainer element. The installation of valves to isolate the assembly should also be considered, to minimize the purging of product when removal of the strainer element is required.

6.17.5 Installation of Meters.

6.17.5.1 Liquid or vapor meters shall be installed in accordance with the manufacturers' installation instructions.

6.17.5.2 Liquid meters shall be installed so that the meter housing is not subject to excessive strains from the connecting piping. If not provided in the piping design, the use of flexible connectors shall be permitted.

6.17.5.3 Vapor meters shall be installed so as to minimize the possibility of physical damage.

Meters are precisely calibrated pieces of equipment. Most states, and other countries, have regulatory agencies that require periodic calibration of customer custody transfer meters used in the LP-Gas industry. Meters are expected to remain reasonably within calibration parameters between periodic calibrations or be subject to legally mandated correction, and possibly a citation. The requirements of 6.17.5 are intended to provide protection for the meter and its housing in order to assist in maintaining the precision of the meter as long as possible.

6.18 Bulk Plant and Industrial LP-Gas Systems

Bulk plants and industrial plants are facilities where relatively large quantities of LP-Gas either are stored for further distribution or are used on site. One of the primary characteristics of bulk plants is that liquid transfer operations are frequent occurrences. Examples are shown in Exhibits 6.40 and 6.41.

The purpose of Section 6.18 is to provide a convenient reference to other sections of the code that provide specific requirements for the installation of bulk plants.

6.18.1 Operations and Maintenance.

The provisions of Chapter 14 shall apply to all new and existing LP-Gas installations at bulk plants, industrial occupancies, and industrial plants.

Chapter 14 is a compilation of all the operations and maintenance procedures found throughout the code.

6.18.2 Installation of Liquid Transfer Facilities.

The transfer of liquid LP-Gas can be accomplished by the use of pumps or compressors or by differential pressure between containers. The only prohibited method of transfer is the use of

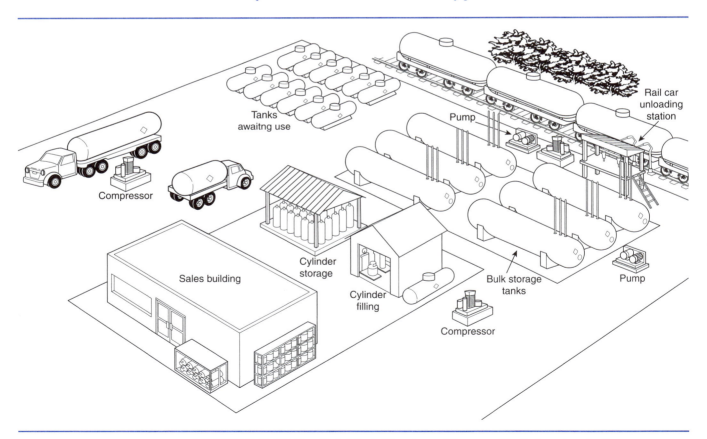

EXHIBIT 6.40 *LP-Gas Bulk Plant. (Courtesy of Cavagna North America, Inc.)*

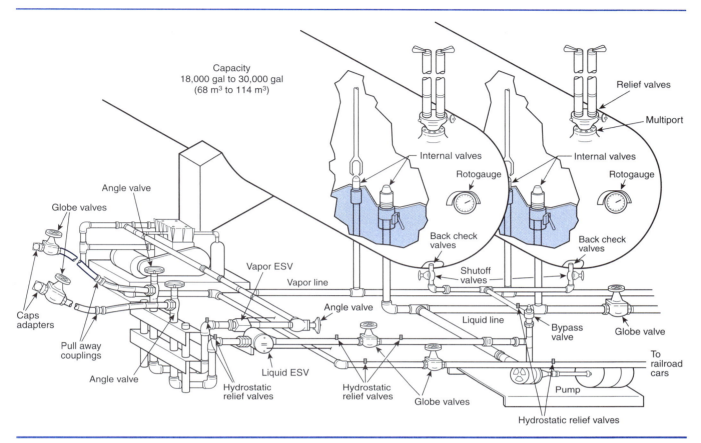

EXHIBIT 6.41 *Typical Bulk Plant Container and Piping Details. (Courtesy of Engineered Controls International, Inc.)*

compressed air or gas. Using another nonliquefied gas would result in the pressure relief valve opening at some time during the filling, or a subsequent filling, because the gas cannot be condensed and pressure would rise above the pressure relief valve setting. The use of air, oxygen, or another oxidizing gas would create a potential explosion and is therefore prohibited per 7.2.2.3.

6.18.2.1 Points of transfer or the nearest part of a structure housing transfer operations shall be located in accordance with 6.5.3 and 6.5.4.

6.18.2.2 Buildings used exclusively for housing pumps or vapor compressors shall be located in accordance with 6.5.4, considering the building as one that houses a point of transfer.

6.18.2.3 Liquid transfer facilities at rail sidings shall comply with 6.18.2.3(A) through 6.18.2.3(C).

(A) The track of the railroad siding or the roadway surface at the transfer points shall be relatively level.

(B) Clearances from buildings, structures, or stationary containers shall be provided for the siding or roadway approaches to the unloading or loading points to prevent the railroad tank car or cargo tank vehicle from contacting buildings, structures, or stationary containers.

(C) Barriers shall be provided at the ends of railroad sidings.

The primary reason for the track of railroad sidings and the roadway surfaces to be relatively level at tank truck transfer points is so that the gauging device in the unit will be as accurate as possible and be unaffected by the transport unit being on a slope. Also, this requirement ensures that the entire contents of the rail car or cargo tank truck can be unloaded, because the unloading connections are usually located in the center of the tank. A level surface also helps prevent a "runaway" situation from occurring in the event wheel chocks become dislodged or are not used.

Note the mobile railcar unloading system shown in Exhibit 6.42. This is a self-contained liquid transfer package that includes a compressor and all the necessary safety flow controls required by the code. It is used to transfer product from railcars to either permanent storage or cargo tank motor vehicles. If transfer is being made into a cargo tank vehicle, the provisions in 7.2.3.9 must be followed.

EXHIBIT 6.42 *Mobile Railcar Unloading System. (Courtesy of Superior Energy Systems)*

6.18.2.4 Pumps and compressors shall comply with 6.18.2.4(A) through 6.18.2.4(C).

(A) Compressors used for liquid transfer normally shall withdraw vapor from the vapor space of the container being filled and discharge into the vapor space of the container from which the withdrawal is being made.

Compressors transfer liquid from one container to another by removing gas from the container to be filled and transferring it to the container to be emptied. This transfer creates the pressure difference that causes liquid to flow. It is important that a compressor draw from the vapor space of a container so that liquid is not drawn into the compressor, which would probably cause damage to the compressor. Damage can occur because liquid is not compressible and the compressor will bend or break parts trying to compress the liquid. A compressor must also discharge into the vapor space of a container to obtain the maximum pressure for transfer.

(B) An operating control or disconnect switch shall be located nearby.

(C) Remote shutoff controls shall be provided as necessary in other liquid transfer systems.

Paragraphs 6.18.2.4(B) and 6.18.2.4(C) are purely safety-related issues. Section 6.12, Emergency Shutoff Valves, should be reviewed because it contains specific requirements for remote shutoff location in 6.12.10.

6.18.2.5* System piping shall be designed to prevent debris from impeding the action of valves and other components of the piping system. This requirement shall be effective for existing installations on July 1, 2011.

A.6.18.2.5 Debris and foreign material can enter a propane system from hose and connectors used to fill containers. Using strainers or screens is one method to prevent debris from interfering with the action of valves and other components.

The requirement of 6.18.2.5 first appeared in the 2001 edition and was a response to the incident in Sanford, North Carolina, described in the commentary following 6.12.9. The effective date for existing installations was added in the 2008 edition and requires that existing bulk plants be provided with screens or other means to prevent debris from entering the system and affecting the safe operation of the liquid transfer system by mid-2011. The date was chosen to coincide with the effective date for requirements of 5.7.4.2(H) for internal valves, emergency shutoff valves, positive shutoff valves, and backflow check valves in liquid inlet openings. The technical committee believes that this requirement is important to safety and must to be implemented at all sites by the effective date.

6.18.2.6 Where a hose or swivel-type piping is used for liquid transfer, it shall be protected as follows:

(1) An emergency shutoff valve shall be installed at the railroad tank car end of the hose or swivel-type piping where flow into or out of the tank car is possible.
(2) An emergency shutoff valve or a backflow check valve shall be installed on the tank car end of the hose or swivel piping where flow is only into the railroad-type tank car.

The requirement for an emergency shutoff valve provides safety requirements for liquid transfer facilities. Although redundant to 7.2.3.7, locating the requirement here helps ensure that this important safety requirement is not overlooked.

6.18.2.7 Transfer hose larger than ½ in. (12 mm) internal diameter shall not be used for making connections to individual containers being filled indoors.

6.18.2.8 If gas is to be discharged from containers inside a building, the provisions of 7.3.2.1 shall apply.

6.18.3 Installation of Electrical Equipment.

Installation of electrical equipment shall comply with 6.22.2.

6.18.4 Security and Protection Against Tampering for Section 6.18 and Section 6.24 Systems.

6.18.4.1 The following security measures shall be provided to minimize the possibility of entry by unauthorized persons:

(1) Security awareness training
(2) Limitation of unauthorized access to plant areas that include container appurtenances, pumping equipment, loading and unloading facilities, and container filling facilities

The security requirements were revised in the 2011 edition to require specific training and limitation of access to deter criminal or terrorist activities. The requirement for security awareness training is new and allows each location to have security awareness training appropriate for the location.

6.18.4.2 Areas that include features required in 6.18.4.1(2) shall be enclosed with a minimum 6 ft (1.8 m) high industrial-type fence, chain-link fence, or equivalent protection.

(A) There shall be at least two means of emergency egress from the enclosure, except as follows:

(1) The fenced or otherwise enclosed area is not over 100 ft^2 (9 m^2).
(2) The point of transfer is within 3 ft (1 m) of the gate.
(3) Containers are not filled within the enclosure.

(B) Clearance of at least 3 ft (1 m) shall be provided to allow emergency access to the required means of egress.

(C) Fencing shall not be required where devices are provided that can be locked in place and prevent unauthorized operation of valves, equipment, and appurtenances.

Of the two security methods mentioned in 6.18.4.2 and 6.18.4.2(C), fences and equipment locks, fencing is the most commonly used. Locking devices are used mostly in dispensing stations. A chain-link fence is the type most frequently used for security. A solid fence should not be used, because it is important to allow air to circulate freely. (See the commentary following 6.4.7.)

Access to and from a fenced enclosure is necessary for operating, maintenance, and emergency personnel, and two exits are required for safety in most cases. Please note that a locked gate is not an exit unless workers in an area can quickly open the gate if necessary. It is important for safety that two usable exits be available when personnel are working in the fenced area, except where the area is small and only one exit is required. A simple and effective way to accomplish this is to unlock and open all exits while workers are in a fenced area. Fencing protects against tampering with valves, appurtenances, transfer equipment, and other equipment. It is possible to provide this protection without enclosing the entire storage tank and by enclosing only the operable valves and appurtenances.

6.18.4.3 Where guard service is provided, it shall be extended to the LP-Gas installation, and the requirements of Section 4.4 shall apply to guard personnel.

6.18.5 Lighting.

If operations are normally conducted during other than daylight hours, lighting shall be provided to illuminate storage containers, containers being loaded, control valves, and other equipment.

6.18.6 Ignition Source Control.

Ignition source control shall comply with Section 6.22.

6.19 LP-Gas Systems in Buildings or on Building Roofs or Exterior Balconies

Section 6.19 identifies the situations in which LP-Gas cylinders that are connected for use can be located inside buildings or on the roofs of buildings. In addition, this section also covers the piping of liquid LP-Gas into buildings or onto the roofs of buildings from containers located outside. This important requirement of the code dates back to the first NFPA standard on LP-Gas in 1927 (which preceded NFPA 58) and has been part of the requirements since that time.

Before any installation of an LP-Gas container in a building can be considered, Section 6.19 should be read in its entirety. Transportation of containers within a building is covered by 6.19.3.6.

Note that Chapter 8 covers the storage of containers awaiting sale and use. Chapter 11 covers engine fuel systems inside a building. Chapter 9 covers the storage, service, and repair of LP-Gas transport or cargo vehicles.

The following list of subsections within Section 6.19 may help the user understand and identify the various situations that allow the use of containers inside buildings and on the roofs of buildings:

- 6.19.2, Additional Equipment Requirements for Cylinders, Equipment, Piping, and Appliances Used in Buildings, Building Roofs, and Exterior Balconies
- 6.19.3, Installation Requirements for Cylinders, Equipment, Piping, and Appliances in Buildings, Building Roofs, and Exterior Balconies
- 6.19.4, Buildings Under Construction or Undergoing Major Renovation
- 6.19.5, Buildings Undergoing Minor Renovation When Frequented by the Public
- 6.19.6, Buildings Housing Industrial Occupancies
- 6.19.7, Buildings Housing Educational and Institutional Occupancies
- 6.19.8, Temporary Heating and Food Service Appliances in Buildings in Emergencies
- 6.19.9, Use in Buildings for Demonstrations or Training, and Use of Small Cylinders for Self-Contained Torch Assemblies and Food Service Appliances
- 6.19.10, Use in Building for Flame Effects Before a Proximate Audience
- 6.19.11, Cylinders on Roofs or Exterior Balconies
- 6.19.12, Liquid LP-Gas Piped into Buildings or Structures

6.19.1 Application.

6.19.1.1 Section 6.19 shall apply to the installation of the following LP-Gas systems in buildings or structures:

(1) Cylinders inside of buildings or on the roofs or exterior balconies of buildings
(2) Systems in which the liquid is piped from outside containers into buildings or onto the roof

6.19.1.2 *Cylinders in use* shall mean connected for use.

(A) The use of cylinders indoors shall be only for the purposes specified in 6.19.4 through 6.19.9.

(B) The use of cylinders indoors shall be limited to those conditions where operational requirements make the indoor use of cylinders necessary and location outside is impractical.

The use of cylinders indoors, as well as on balconies and roofs of buildings, is permitted only for the purposes specified in this section. All other uses, including normal, routine comfort heating, are prohibited. The use of cylinder systems having capacities larger than 1 lb (0.45 kg) of LP-Gas and the associated storage of such cylinders indoors are limited to the following uses:

- Construction and renovation of buildings
- Industrial applications
- Education
- Research
- Training
- Temporary heating in cases of emergency

These limited applications acknowledge the good experience and presence of trained personnel in industrial uses and the temporary nature and lack of alternative fuel sources for certain appliances needed at certain times in buildings.

Where the indoor use of LP-Gas cylinders is permitted, the user or installer must first attempt to locate the cylinders outdoors. Only if it is impractical to locate the cylinders outdoors may the installer locate the cylinders indoors. In determining whether an outdoor location is impractical, consultation with the authority having jurisdiction may be required.

(C) The use of cylinders on roofs shall be limited to those conditions where operational requirements make the use of cylinders necessary and location other than on roofs of buildings or structures is impractical.

Provisions for the installation of cylinders on roofs were originally incorporated into the code to provide fuel for emergency generators and microwave relay stations. The provisions also have been applied when providing cylinders on roofs serving penthouses and in hospitals. Again, such systems are permitted only when the use of cylinders is necessary and other outdoor locations are impractical.

(D) Liquid LP-Gas shall be piped into buildings or structures only for the purposes specified in 6.9.1.1(4).

Although LP-Gas vapor at pressures up to and including 20 psig (138 kPag) can be piped into buildings, there are certain limitations for piping liquid LP-Gas at pressures exceeding 20 psig into buildings. These limitations are covered in 6.9.1 and 6.9.1.2.

6.19.1.3 Storage of cylinders awaiting use shall be in accordance with Chapter 8.

Stored cylinders that are not connected for use, including cylinders that are part of an appliance but are not connected to the appliance, are addressed in Chapter 8.

6.19.1.4 Transportation of cylinders within a building shall be in accordance with 6.19.3.6.

6.19.1.5 The following provisions shall be required in addition to those specified in Sections 6.2 and 6.3:

(1) Liquid transfer systems shall be in accordance with Chapter 7.
(2) Engine fuel systems used inside buildings shall be in accordance with Chapter 11.
(3) LP-Gas transport or cargo tank vehicles stored, serviced, or repaired in buildings shall be in accordance with Chapter 9.

6.19.2 Additional Equipment Requirements for Cylinders, Equipment, Piping, and Appliances Used in Buildings, Building Roofs, and Exterior Balconies.

6.19.2.1 Cylinders shall be in accordance with the following:

(1) Cylinders shall not exceed 245 lb (111 kg) water capacity [nominal 100 lb (45 kg) propane capacity] each.

(2) Cylinders shall comply with other applicable provisions of Section 5.2, and they shall be equipped as provided in Section 5.7.
(3) Cylinders shall be marked in accordance with 5.2.8.1 and 5.2.8.2.
(4) Cylinders with propane capacities greater than 2 lb (0.9 kg) shall be equipped as provided in Table 5.7.4.1, and an excess-flow valve shall be provided for vapor service when used indoors.
(5) Cylinder valves shall be protected in accordance with 5.2.6.1.
(6) Cylinders having water capacities greater than 2.7 lb (1.2 kg) and connected for use shall stand on a firm and substantially level surface.

(7) Cylinders shall be secured in an upright position if necessary.

(8) Cylinders and the valve-protecting devices used with them shall be oriented to minimize the possibility of impingement of the pressure relief device discharge on the cylinder and adjacent cylinders.

Basic considerations are given in 6.19.2.1 regarding the type of cylinder to be used. The cylinder must have a maximum LP-Gas capacity of 100 lb (45 kg). This size is the largest size that can be easily moved by personnel, from a practical standpoint. There have been some 500 gal (1.9 m³) ASME tanks used at different floor levels on large construction sites. This use was, and continues to be, prohibited by the code. The NFPA 58 approach to the use of ASME bulk tanks is to locate them at ground level on the outside or on the roof (with approval of the authority having jurisdiction) and pipe the LP-Gas into the building.

The requirements in 6.19.2.1(4) refer the code user to Table 5.7.4.1 for the proper appurtenances to be installed on the cylinder. This table has two separate columns for cylinders and the requirements differ, based on the type of service.

In addition to the requirements of Table 5.7.4.1, cylinders in vapor service used indoors must have an excess-flow valve installed per 6.19.2.1(5). This provides a higher level of safety by providing excess-flow protection in the event of a pipe or hose failure inside a building. Therefore, standard vapor service cylinders, including those used for gas grills, cannot be used in buildings unless they are fitted with an excess-flow valve. The excess-flow valve must be selected for proper closing flow. This sizing can be difficult for excess-flow valves used on portable cylinders, because the flow can vary with tank pressure (and temperature) and the length of the discharge hose or piping.

Paragraph 6.19.2.1(5) refers to 5.2.6.1, which requires that all cylinder valves be protected against physical damage by a ventilated cap or collar. Recessing the valve into the container is also permitted by DOT cylinder regulations, but this procedure is rarely used for LP-Gas cylinders. Note that when a removable cap is used, it must be in place when the container is not in use.

In 6.19.2.1(6), the use of the term *firm* (surface) is not defined in the code. It is intended to mean a level surface on which the cylinder will not sink or tip due to its weight. Concrete and masonry surfaces can be used, but are not required for cylinders in buildings.

Paragraph 6.19.2.1(7) emphasizes the importance of maintaining the cylinder in the proper orientation so that the following occurs:

- The pressure relief device is in communication with the vapor space in the cylinder, so that in the event the pressure relief device operates, it discharges vapor and not liquid. Liquid released to the atmosphere expands to 270 times its volume and represents a much greater hazard.
- Stress is not placed on piping attached to the cylinder, which could cause a break or leakage.
- The cylinder does not become subject to being impacted, if there is traffic nearby.

As required in 6.19.2.1(8), it is important that the cylinder pressure relief discharge be directed through a hole in the cap or collar. In positioning a group of cylinders, attention should be given to ensure that pressure relief valves are not directed at adjacent cylinders.

6.19.2.2 Only regulators recommended by the manufacturer for use with LP-Gas shall be used.

There are many types of regulators made for many purposes, and some that are intended for other uses may operate successfully. The use of regulators not specifically recommended for use with LP-Gas is not allowed, because they will probably not have all the specific safety features that regulators intended for LP-Gas service have. Note that the revisions made to 5.8.1.1 in the 2011 edition require that all first- and second-stage regulators meet the requirements of UL 144, *LP-Gas Regulators* [19].

6.19.2.3 Manifolds and fittings connecting cylinders to pressure regulator inlets shall be designed for at least 250 psig (1.7 MPag) service pressure.

Since the manifold will be carrying gas at the same pressure as the gas in the cylinder, it must be designed with a pressure rating of at least 250 psig (1.7 MPag).

6.19.2.4 Piping shall comply with Section 5.9 and shall have a pressure rating of 250 psig (1.7 MPag).

6.19.2.5 Liquid piping and vapor piping at pressures above 125 psig (0.9 MPag) shall be installed in accordance with 6.9.3.

The requirements in 6.9.3 include Table 6.9.3.5, which requires piping used for liquid and piping used for vapor systems greater than 125 psig (0.9 MPag) to be (1) designed in accordance with ASME B 31.3, *Process Piping*, (2) welded or brazed if it is Schedule 40 pipe, or (3) either welded, brazed, or threaded if it is Schedule 80 pipe. Most installers use the second option.

6.19.2.6 Hose, hose connections, and flexible connectors shall comply with the following:

(1) Hose used at pressures above 5 psig (34 kPag) shall be designed for a pressure of at least 350 psig (2.4 MPag).
(2) Hose used at a pressure of 5 psig (34 kPag) or less and used in agricultural buildings not normally occupied by the public shall be designed for the operating pressure of the hose.
(3) Hose shall comply with 5.9.6.
(4) Hose shall be installed in accordance with 6.20.3.
(5) Hose shall be as short as practical, without kinking or straining the hose or causing it to be close enough to a burner to be damaged by heat.
(6) Hoses greater than 10 ft (3 m) in length shall be protected from damage.

Although basic provisions for hose are given by reference to 5.9.6, two important exceptions are taken:

1. Hose used in buildings must be designed for a 350 psig (2.4 MPag) working pressure. This requirement is not so much for the pressures involved, but to ensure that a stronger type of hose is used in this service, particularly at construction sites where abrasions and damage due to rough usage may be encountered. [Note that this hose is required in 5.9.6.4 only for pressures over 5 psig (34 kPag) used in all other applications.]
2. The length of hose is not limited for connecting to appliances [see 6.20.3.2(1)], although it must be kept as short as practical. In addition, if the length of hose exceeds 10 ft (3 m), either it must be installed in a manner that protects it from damage or additional external protective devices, such as conduit, must be used.

Note that 6.19.2.6(2) provides an alternative to the hose designed for a pressure of 350 psig (2.4 MPag), which is used at low pressures of 5 psig (34 kPag) in agricultural buildings that are not normally occupied by the public. This alternative came about because LP-Gas installations are frequently located in buildings used for poultry breeding, and the 350 psig (2.4 MPag) hose was a problem due to its stiffness, which resulted in kinking where bends were needed. The life safety concerns that are paramount in Section 6.19 are relaxed for poultry breeding buildings, which are infrequently occupied by people.

6.19.2.7* Portable heaters, including salamanders, shall comply with the following:

(1) Portable heaters shall be equipped with an approved automatic device to shut off the flow of gas to the main burner and to the pilot, if used, in the event of flame extinguishment or combustion failure.
(2) Portable heaters shall be self-supporting unless designed for cylinder mounting.
(3) Portable heaters shall not be installed utilizing cylinder valves, connectors, regulators, manifolds, piping, or tubing as structural supports.

(4) Portable heaters having an input of more than 50,000 Btu/hr (53 MJ/hr) shall be equipped with either a pilot that must be lighted and proved before the main burner can be turned on or an approved electric ignition system.

A.6.19.2.7 The requirement for a pilot or an electronic ignition system became effective for heaters with inputs over 50,000 Btu/hr manufactured on or after May 17, 1967.

Although standards exist for the listing of portable heaters, not all heaters are tested and listed. Paragraph 6.19.2.7 is intended to provide basic requirements for the authorities to use in approving portable heaters.

6.19.2.8 The provisions of 6.19.2.7 shall not be applicable to the following:

(1) Tar kettle burners, hand torches, or melting pots
(2) Portable heaters with less than 7500 Btu/hr (8 MJ/hr) input if used with cylinders having a maximum water capacity of 2.7 lb (1.2 kg) and filled with not more than 16.8 oz (0.522 kg) of LP-Gas

All portable heaters used indoors must have flame failure protection, except for the following:

- Attended appliances, such as tar kettle burners, hand torches, or melting pots
- Smaller heaters of less than 7500 Btu (8 MJ/hr) capacity connected to a 1 lb (0.45 kg) LP-Gas cylinder
- Catalytic heaters, which must have combustion failure protection

Flame failure protection is provided by an approved automatic device that shuts off the flow of gas to the main burner and pilot (where a pilot is used), if the flame is not sensed. Additionally, these portable heaters designed for cylinder mounting must not use valves, piping, regulators, or other equipment as structural supports for the heater.

If the provisions of 6.19.2.7(4) are not followed, the possibility of operators being burned during the ignition of heaters may exist when using larger heaters designed to operate at higher inlet pressures. Unless a proven pilot light or electronic ignition is used, a large flame rollout may occur. Pilots on these larger heaters may encounter problems of premature thermocouple failure or outages due to wind or other factors. This problem can result in operators bypassing controls. Therefore, when igniting portable heaters not equipped with flame failure protection, care must be taken to prevent the release of large amounts of unignited gas, which can result in an explosion hazard.

6.19.3 Installation Requirements for Cylinders, Equipment, Piping, and Appliances in Buildings, Building Roofs, and Exterior Balconies.

6.19.3.1 Cylinders having water capacities greater than 2.7 lb (1.2 kg) and connected for use shall stand on a firm and substantially level surface. If necessary, they shall be secured in an upright position.

6.19.3.2 Cylinders, regulating equipment, manifolds, pipe, tubing, and hose shall be located to minimize exposure to the following:

(1) Abnormally high temperatures (such as might result from exposure to convection and radiation from heating equipment or installation in confined spaces)
(2) Physical damage
(3) Tampering by unauthorized persons

6.19.3.3 Heat-producing equipment shall be installed with clearance to combustibles in accordance with the manufacturer's installation instructions.

6.19.3.4 Heat-producing equipment shall be located and used to minimize the possibility of the ignition of combustibles.

FAQ ▶
Why is it necessary to prevent
cylinders used indoors from
reaching temperatures higher
than room temperature?

When cylinders are exposed to abnormally high temperatures, liquid LP-Gas expands. This expansion could cause the container to become liquid-full, causing high internal pressures that result in the discharge of the container pressure relief valve. For this reason, heating equipment should be positioned so that infrared heaters do not direct heat onto containers. In addition, particular attention should be given to avoid installing cylinders in poorly ventilated spaces where temperatures may rise, such as in pits or tunnels in construction areas.

Cylinders must also be provided with physical protection from reasonably anticipated damage to the cylinders themselves, to piping, or to any nearby appliances.

6.19.3.5 Where located on a floor, roof, or balcony, cylinders shall be secured to prevent falling over the edge.

Cylinders are normally secured by strapping them to walls, posts, or other anchorage. Smaller cylinders, specifically the popular 20 lb (9.1 kg) gas grill cylinders, have many other uses besides gas grills and often are used indoors. Their collar protects the valve if the cylinders do fall over. These cylinders require securing, which can be accomplished by chaining through the collar in lieu of strapping.

6.19.3.6 Transportation (movement) of cylinders having water capacities greater than 2.7 lb (1.2 kg) within a building shall be restricted to movement directly associated with the uses covered by Section 6.19.

(A) Valve outlets on cylinders having water capacities greater than 2.7 lb (1.2 kg) shall be tightly plugged, capped, or sealed with a listed quick-closing coupling or a listed quick-connect coupling.

(B) Only emergency stairways not normally used by the public shall be used, and precautions shall be taken to prevent the cylinder from falling down the stairs where freight or passenger elevators are used.

(C) Emergency stairways shall be occupied only by those engaged in moving the cylinder.

The use and transportation of cylinders within a building apply to full, partially full, and empty containers and are permitted only in conjunction with their use as described in Section 6.19.

At one time, the code required a plug or cap exclusively, when cylinder valves used the old-style POL valve exclusively. However, when the CGA 791 and 810 connections came into use in the 1990s, these connections incorporated a flow-check mechanism that prevented the flow of LP-Gas unless the mating connection was fully attached. Therefore, gas was prevented from flowing even if the valve handle was opened. Installing a plug into the CGA 791 connection can defeat this important safety feature. By doing so, the flow-check is opened and, if the plug was not fully inserted, LP-Gas can escape. Therefore, plugs or caps are neither required nor recommended for cylinder valves having either the CGA 791 or 810 connection.

6.19.4 Buildings Under Construction or Undergoing Major Renovation.

6.19.4.1 Where cylinders are used and transported in buildings or structures under construction or undergoing major renovation and such buildings are not occupied by the public, the requirements of 6.19.4.2 through 6.19.4.10 shall apply.

The requirement was revised editorially in the 2011 edition to state more clearly that the only uses of cylinders in buildings are those specifically stated in Section 6.19. All other uses of cylinders in buildings are not allowed by NFPA 58, except those allowed by the authority having jurisdiction as stated in 6.19.4.10.

6.19.4.2 The use and transportation of cylinders in the unoccupied portions of buildings or structures under construction or undergoing major renovation that are partially occupied by the public shall be approved by the authority having jurisdiction.

The requirement in 6.19.4.2 specifically extends coverage to the movement and use of cylinders in buildings that are under construction or undergoing major renovation. The term *major renovation* is not defined in NFPA 58; therefore, the authority having jurisdiction should be consulted before cylinders are used in a building being renovated. Buildings undergoing "minor" renovations are addressed in 6.19.5. Note that approval is required prior to using or transporting cylinders in unoccupied portions of buildings that are partially occupied by the public.

6.19.4.3 Cylinders, equipment, piping, and appliances shall comply with 6.19.2.

6.19.4.4 Heaters used for temporary heating shall be located at least 6 ft (1.8 m) from any cylinder. *(See 6.19.4.5 for an exception to this requirement.)*

6.19.4.5 Integral heater-cylinder units specifically designed for the attachment of the heater to the cylinder, or to a supporting standard attached to the cylinder, and designed and installed to prevent direct or radiant heat application to the cylinder shall be exempt from the spacing requirement of 6.19.4.4.

6.19.4.6 Blower-type and radiant-type units shall not be directed toward any cylinder within 20 ft (6.1 m).

The concern of 6.19.4.4 through 6.19.4.6 is the protection of cylinders used to fuel heating appliances from overheating due to proximity of the cylinders to another heating appliance. Overheating can result in the release of propane through the pressure relief device. A minimum 6 ft (1.8 m) separation between heaters used for temporary heating and other LP-Gas cylinders is required under all circumstances. In addition, blower-type and radiant-type heaters cannot be directed toward any cylinder within a 20 ft (6.1 m) distance. The infrared or larger blower-type units have a more pronounced effect on heat transmission in the direction they are aimed, and therefore, the greater separation distance to cylinders is required.

6.19.4.7 If two or more heater-cylinder units of either the integral or nonintegral type are located in an unpartitioned area on the same floor, the cylinder(s) of each such unit shall be separated from the cylinder(s) of any other such unit by at least 20 ft (6.1 m).

6.19.4.8 If heaters are connected to cylinders manifolded together for use in an unpartitioned area on the same floor, the total water capacity of cylinders manifolded together serving any one heater shall not be greater than 735 lb (333 kg) [nominal 300 lb (136 kg) propane capacity]. If there is more than one such manifold, it shall be separated from any other by at least 20 ft (6.1 m).

The LP-Gas maximum of 300 lb (136 kg) for manifolded systems has a long history in NFPA 58. The requirement in 6.19.4.8 limits the amount of propane in an area to a reasonable amount, based on experience. A distance of 20 ft (6.1 m) is set out for the separation of different manifolded systems in the same unpartitioned floor area.

6.19.4.9 Where cylinders are manifolded together for connection to a heater(s) on another floor, the following shall apply:

(1) Heaters shall not be installed on the same floors with manifolded cylinders.
(2) The total water capacity of the cylinders connected to any one manifold shall not be greater than 2450 lb (1111 kg) [nominal 1000 lb (454 kg) propane capacity].
(3) Manifolds of more than 735 lb (333 kg) water capacity [nominal 300 lb (136 kg) propane capacity], if located in the same unpartitioned area, shall be separated from each other by at least 50 ft (15 m).

Where cylinders are installed on a different floor level than the location of the heaters, the allowable quantities of propane gas are greater. Of course, this is due to the fact that the heaters, which represent a source of ignition, are not on the same floor level as the cylinders.

6.19.4.10 Where compliance with the provisions of 6.19.4.6 through 6.19.4.9 is impractical, alternate installation provisions shall be allowed with the approval of the authority having jurisdiction.

Paragraph 6.19.4.10 recognizes that at construction and renovation sites, it is sometimes not possible to meet all the requirements of this section, and although flexibility is allowed, safety cannot be compromised. This is a restatement of the equivalency requirement of Section 1.5, and by restating it here the committee is encouraging its use for construction and renovation sites.

6.19.5 Buildings Undergoing Minor Renovation When Frequented by the Public.

6.19.5.1 Cylinders used and transported for repair or minor renovation in buildings frequented by the public during the hours the public normally occupies the building shall comply with the following:

(1) The maximum water capacity of individual cylinders shall be 50 lb (23 kg) [nominal 20 lb (9.1 kg) propane capacity], and the number of cylinders in the building shall not exceed the number of workers assigned to the use of the propane.
(2) Cylinders having a water capacity greater than 2.7 lb (1.2 kg) shall not be left unattended.

6.19.5.2 During the hours the building is not open to the public, cylinders used and transported within the building for repair or minor renovation and with a water capacity greater than 2.7 lb (1.2 kg) shall not be left unattended.

Building renovation during hours when the public is present requires special considerations. For example, the number of cylinders must not exceed the number of workers assigned to them, and the cylinders are not to be left unattended at any time.

When the building is not occupied by the general public, 6.19.5.2 lifts the restrictions on cylinder size and number of cylinders in the space.

6.19.6 Buildings Housing Industrial Occupancies.

6.19.6.1 Cylinders used in buildings housing industrial occupancies for processing, research, or experimental purposes shall comply with 6.19.6.1(A) and 6.19.6.1(B).

(A) If cylinders are manifolded together, the total water capacity of the connected cylinders shall be not more than 735 lb (333 kg) [nominal 300 lb (136 kg) propane capacity]. If there is more than one such manifold in a room, it shall be separated from any other by at least 20 ft (6.1 m).

(B) The amount of LP-Gas in cylinders for research and experimental use in the building shall be limited to the smallest practical quantity.

6.19.6.2 The use of cylinders to supply fuel for temporary heating in buildings housing industrial occupancies with essentially noncombustible contents shall comply with the requirements in 6.19.4 for cylinders in buildings under construction.

6.19.6.3 The use of fuel cylinders for temporary heating shall be permitted only where portable equipment for space heating is essential and a permanent heating installation is not practical.

6.19.7 Buildings Housing Educational and Institutional Occupancies.

6.19.7.1 The use of cylinders in classrooms shall be prohibited unless they are used temporarily for classroom demonstrations in accordance with 6.19.9.1.

6.19.7.2 Where cylinders are used in buildings housing educational and institutional laboratory occupancies for research and experimental purposes, the following shall apply:

(1) The maximum water capacity of individual cylinders used shall be 50 lb (23 kg) [nominal 20 lb (9.1 kg) propane capacity] if used in educational occupancies and 12 lb (5.4 kg) [nominal 5 lb (2 kg) propane capacity] if used in institutional occupancies.

(2) If more than one such cylinder is located in the same room, the cylinders shall be separated by at least 20 ft (6.1 m).

(3) Cylinders not connected for use shall be stored in accordance with Chapter 8.

(4) Cylinders shall not be stored in a laboratory room.

The maximum size cylinder for educational buildings is 20 lb (9.1 kg) of propane and 12 lb (5.4 kg) of propane for institutional occupancies, with a separation of 20 ft (6.1 m) if more than one container is located in the same room. Containers are not allowed in classrooms, unless they are used in accordance with 6.19.9 for demonstration purposes. The storage of containers in educational and institutional occupancies must be in accordance with Chapter 8.

Note that the NFPA *101*, *Life Safety Code* [3], definition of an educational occupancy covers through grade 12 in high school. Educational facilities beyond the 12th grade are considered to be the following occupancies:

- Instructional building: business occupancy
- Classrooms under 50 persons: business occupancy
- Classrooms 50 persons and over: assembly occupancy
- Laboratories, instructional: business occupancy
- Laboratories, noninstructional: industrial occupancy

For additional information, see NFPA *101* for proper occupancy classification of educational facilities beyond the 12th grade. Note that NFPA *101* classifications are for life safety purposes. The limits of propane cylinder size in NFPA 58 still apply.

The requirements of NFPA 45, *Standard on Fire Protection for Laboratories Using Chemicals* [25], apply to laboratories used for educational purposes above grade 12 and for other laboratories.

See Formal Interpretation 89-2 regarding the use of a cylinder in a high school laboratory.

Formal Interpretation
NFPA 58
Liquefied Petroleum Gas Code
2011 Edition

Reference: 6.19.7.1

F.I.: 89-2

Question: Is it a violation of NFPA 58, 6.17.7.1 to install a 20 lb LP-Gas tank in a high school chemistry laboratory to supply Bunsen burners on the student lab tables, connected by permanently installed piping which complies with NFPA 58?

Answer: Yes.

Issue Edition: 1989

Reference: 3-4.6.1

Issue Date: May 22, 1990

Effective Date: June 10, 1990

6.19.8 Temporary Heating and Food Service Appliances in Buildings in Emergencies.

6.19.8.1 Cylinders shall not be used in buildings for temporary emergency heating purposes except when all of the following conditions are met:

(1) The permanent heating system is temporarily out of service.
(2) Heat is necessary to prevent damage to the buildings or contents.
(3) The cylinders and heaters comply with, and are used and transported in accordance with, 6.19.2 and 6.19.4.
(4) The temporary heating equipment is not left unattended.
(5) Air for combustion and ventilation is provided in accordance with NFPA 54, *National Fuel Gas Code*.

Cylinders used for temporary heating are strictly an emergency measure, to be used only if the permanent heating system is temporarily out of service. The requirement in 6.19.8.1 is not intended to apply to supplemental or zone heating. Emergency heating equipment must be attended at all times. The provision in 6.19.8.1(5) that refers to the *National Fuel Gas Code* was introduced in the 2008 edition. NFPA 54 contains extensive requirements to ensure that gas-burning appliances have sufficient air for complete combustion and ventilation to ensure that no harmful products of combustion can accumulate in buildings. These requirements are located in Section 8.3 of NFPA 54 and should be reviewed prior to installing temporary heating equipment. This is especially important if the temporary heating equipment does not use the same venting provisions as the equipment it temporarily replaces.

During the development of the 2008 and 2011 editions of NFPA 58, proposals were submitted to allow nonmetallic 20 lb (9.1 kg) cylinders in buildings in conjunction with propane fueled space heaters. These proposals were rejected in the 2008 edition and were again submitted for the 2011 edition for limited use in emergencies only. The technical committee rejected the proposals, stating that the temporary use of cylinders (that meet all requirements in the code for cylinders) in buildings in emergencies is allowed, and that no further code text is needed.

6.19.8.2 When a public emergency has been declared and gas, fuel, or electrical service has been interrupted, portable listed LP-Gas commercial food service appliances meeting the requirements of 6.19.9.4 shall be permitted to be temporarily used inside affected buildings.

6.19.8.3 The portable appliances used shall be discontinued and removed from the building at the time the permanently installed appliances are placed back in operation.

LP-Gas is an excellent fuel for the portable cooking appliances addressed in 6.19.8.2. These appliances are needed following natural disasters such as floods and hurricanes, where service from utilities supplying gas and electricity may be interrupted. It is common for these types of appliances to be used following natural disasters such as hurricanes and ice storms. Note that, per 6.19.8.3, the portable appliances, and the cylinders used to fuel them, must be removed from the building when permanent appliances are back in service.

6.19.9 Use in Buildings for Demonstrations or Training, and Use of Small Cylinders for Self-Contained Torch Assemblies and Food Service Appliances.

6.19.9.1 Cylinders used temporarily inside buildings for public exhibitions or demonstrations, including use in classroom demonstrations, shall be in accordance with the following:

(1) The maximum water capacity of a cylinder shall be 12 lb (5.4 kg) [nominal 5 lb (2 kg) propane capacity].
(2) If more than one such cylinder is located in a room, the cylinders shall be separated by at least 20 ft (6.1 m).

Cylinders up to 5 lb (2 kg) propane capacity may be used temporarily in buildings for exhibitions or demonstrations. The use of a 20 lb (9.1 kg) cylinder filled with 5 lb (2 kg) of propane is not permitted, however, because there is no easy way to verify that only 5 lb (2 kg) of propane is in the cylinder. This provision permits the demonstration of a portable cooking device with a 5 lb (2 kg) LP-Gas cylinder at an indoor trade show to demonstrate cooking equipment, but it does not permit an identical device to be used at the show to prepare food for sale. For cooking in restaurants and by caterers, 6.19.9.4 does permit the use of stoves fueled by 10 oz (0.28 kg) nonrefillable butane cylinders.

If the food preparation itself is primarily for demonstration, then the use is allowed. If the preparation is primarily for the sale of the prepared food, then 5 lb (2 kg) cylinders are prohibited. The reasoning behind this distinction is that a demonstration of cooking is not "rushed" and is being monitored closely by the cook and his audience. A commercial cooking operation, however, may be characterized by a lower level of supervision of the equipment and a much higher volume of food. Simply stated, if the food is given away, as would be done in a school or trade show, 5 lb cylinders are allowed. If the food is sold, the preparation method is considered normal use and not a demonstration, and 5 lb cylinders are not allowed.

See Formal Interpretation 89-3 for more information on this subject.

◀ **FAQ**

Can a 5 lb (2 kg) LP-Gas cylinder be used to prepare food for sale, where the preparation method is a demonstration of the chef's skill, such as in preparing a flambé dessert?

Formal Interpretation
NFPA 58
Liquefied Petroleum Gas Code
2011 Edition

Reference: 6.19.9.1

F.I.: 89-3

Question: Does the use of an approved portable cooking appliance utilizing a 2 lb LP-Gas container as its fuel supply for temporary table side cooking within a restaurant meet the intent of "public exhibition" as described in 6.17.9.1?

Answer: No.

Issue Edition: 1989

Reference: 3-4.8.1

Issue Date: March 19, 1991

Effective Date: April 8, 1991

6.19.9.2 Cylinders used temporarily in buildings for training purposes related to the installation and use of LP-Gas systems shall be in accordance with the following:

(1) The maximum water capacity of individual cylinders shall be 245 lb (111 kg) [nominal 100 lb (45 kg) propane capacity], but not more than 20 lb (9.1 kg) of propane shall be placed in a single cylinder.

(2) If more than one such cylinder is located in the same room, the cylinders shall be separated by at least 20 ft (6.1 m).

(3) The training location shall be acceptable to the authority having jurisdiction.

(4) Cylinders shall be promptly removed from the building when the training class has terminated.

Where used for LP-Gas–related training in buildings, 100 lb (45 kg) propane cylinders may be used, but they may be filled with only 20 lb (9.1 kg) of propane, and approval of the authority having jurisdiction is required. Note that the requirement in 6.19.9.2 differs from 6.19.9.1, which covers public exhibitions or demonstrations, where only small containers of 12 lb (5.4 kg) maximum are permitted.

6.19.9.3* Cylinders used in buildings as part of approved self-contained torch assemblies or similar appliances shall be in accordance with the following:

(1) Cylinders used in buildings shall comply with ANSI/UL 147A, *Standard for Nonrefillable (Disposable) Type Fuel Gas Cylinder Assemblies.*
(2) Cylinders shall have a maximum water capacity of 2.7 lb (1.2 kg).

A.6.19.9.3 The weight of the cylinders will be affected by the specific gravity of the LP-Gas. Weights varying from 16.0 oz to 16.8 oz (454 g to 476 g) are recognized as being within the range of what is nominal.

A cylinder of 2.7 lb (1.2 kg) water capacity will hold about 1.09 lb (0.49 kg) of propane [2.7 lb water capacity × 0.504 specific gravity (lb propane/lb water) × 80 percent (fill level)]. The cylinders are sometimes called "one pound cylinders" and are usually sold with a net weight as required by consumer protection laws. These small cylinders are usually filled by automatic filling machinery, and some weight variation is normal and expected. Therefore, a filling target of over 1 lb (0.45 kg) is set so that, at the lowest filling level, 1 lb (0.45 kg) will be provided. The normal weight ranges for these 1 lb (0.45 kg) cylinders are provided in A.6.19.9.3. Note that the vast majority of the 1 lb cylinders are disposable, are prohibited by DOT regulations and 7.2.2.8 from being refilled, and must be disposed of or recycled after use. Refillable 1 lb cylinders are available, and only this type can be refilled.

Paragraph 6.19.9.3 relates to, and limits the use of, LP-Gas cylinders with a propane capacity of up to 1 lb (0.45 kg). The provision permits the use of portable appliances that are fueled by butane and propane, such as curling irons and cigarette lighters, and the cylinders used to refill them. The requirement that the 1 lb (0.45 kg) cylinders comply with UL 147A, *Nonrefillable (Disposable) Type Fuel Gas Cylinder Assemblies* [26], establishes minimum safety standards for these cylinders above those required by DOT.

Note that the use of cylinders of this size with portable cooking appliances is not mentioned and is therefore prohibited in buildings, except as permitted in restaurants and attended commercial food catering in 6.19.9.4 and in emergency cooking as permitted by 6.19.8.2. This prohibition is clearly stated in 6.19.1.2, which limits the use of cylinders indoors to those applications listed in Section 6.19.

6.19.9.4 Cylinders used with commercial food service appliances shall be used inside restaurants and in attended commercial food catering operations in accordance with the following:

(1) Cylinders and appliances shall be listed.
(2) Commercial food service appliances shall not have more than two 10 oz (296 ml) nonrefillable butane gas cylinders, each having a maximum capacity of 1.08 lb (0.490 kg).
(3) Cylinders shall comply with ANSI/UL 147B, *Standard for Nonrefillable (Disposable) Type Metal Container Assemblies for Butane.*
(4) Cylinders shall be connected directly to the appliance and shall not be manifolded.
(5) Cylinders shall be an integral part of the listed, approved, commercial food service device and shall be connected without the use of a rubber hose.
(6) Storage of cylinders shall be in accordance with 8.3.1.

LP-Gas cylinders of any size that are used to fuel cooking appliances in buildings were prohibited from the first edition of NFPA 58 until 1992. (See Exhibit 6.43 for examples of butane-fueled portable cooking appliances.)

Despite their prohibition, 20 lb (9.1 kg) cylinders were being used in restaurants, and fires occurred because of their use. By permitting small butane containers used only in listed

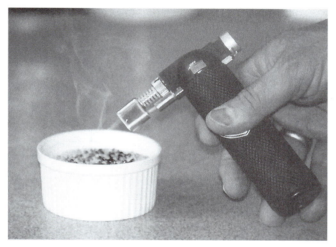

EXHIBIT 6.44 Listed Butane Cylinder for Portable Cooking Appliance. (Courtesy of ChefMaster, a Division of Mr. Bar-B-Q, Inc.)

EXHIBIT 6.43 Butane-Fueled Portable Cooking Appliances. (Top: Courtesy of ChefMaster, a Division of Mr. Bar-B-Q, Inc.)

stoves, a safe alternative was provided for restaurants that require portable cooking appliances for such applications as breakfast buffets and tableside cooking. These stoves must be listed for use with butane. The fuel containers must also be listed and be directly connected to the appliance without using hose. Direct connection enhances safety, because hoses are inherently subject to wear and abuse. The number of cylinders connected at one time is limited to two, and the containers cannot be manifolded. This arrangement permits a two-burner stove to have each burner fed from a separate cylinder and limits the amount of leakage in the event of a problem.

Note that only certain small cylinders with strict limitations are allowed. Cylinders must be nonrefillable, must be listed to UL 147B, *Nonrefillable (Disposable) Type Metal Container Assemblies for Butane* [27], and cannot contain more than 10 oz (0.28 kg) of butane.

Exhibit 6.44 shows a listed butane cylinder for use with portable cooking appliances. Note the indentations on the upper rim seal of the cylinder. These indentations are known as "rim relief," which is a designed weak point that fails upon overpressure. The failure mode ensures that "rocketing" of the cylinder is minimized. The cutaway section shows the internal vapor tube that is in the top of the cylinder when the cylinder is properly placed in the cylinder area of the stove. A notch in the flange at the top of the cylinder ensures proper orientation.

6.19.10 Use in Building for Flame Effects Before a Proximate Audience.

6.19.10.1 Where cylinders are used temporarily in buildings for flame effects before an audience, the flame effect shall be in accordance with NFPA 160, *Standard for the Use of Flame Effects Before an Audience*.

6.19.10.2 The maximum water capacity of individual cylinders shall be 48 lb (22 kg) [nominal 20 lb (9.1 kg) propane capacity].

6.19.10.3* If more than one cylinder is located in the same room, the cylinders shall be separated by at least 20 ft (6.1 m).

A.6.19.10.3 The use of LP-Gas containers inside of assembly occupancies for flame effects before a proximate audience requires compliance with this code and NFPA 160, *Standard for the Use of Flame Effects Before an Audience*. Storage of idle cylinders should be in accordance with Chapter 8. In cases where the minimum 20 ft (6.1 m) separation distance required by 6.19.10 cannot be satisfied, the authority having jurisdiction, in determining equivalency, can consider additional safety controls such as the following:

(1) Construction of a noncombustible line-of-sight barrier to protect adjacent cylinders from fire exposure
(2) Installation of piped flammable gas fixed piping systems instead of hose

6.19.10.4 Where a separation of 20 ft (6.1 m) is not practical, reduction of distances shall be permitted with the approval of the authority having jurisdiction.

6.19.10.5 Cylinders shall not be connected or disconnected during the flame effect or performance.

Subsection 6.19.10 addresses an important use of propane because of its portability and recognizes the work done by the NFPA Technical Committee on Special Effects in developing NFPA 160, *Standard for the Use of Flame Effects Before an Audience* [28], which was first published in 2001.

Cylinders now can be used in buildings where these "flame effects" displays are used. Flame effects are being used widely in the entertainment industry where the visual impact of the flame is desired, and sometimes the audience can feel the heat of the flame. Such effects are used in concerts, theatrical productions, amusement parks, and other locations.

NFPA 160 takes a different approach to safety from NFPA 58, which is reasonable considering that the flame effects are always operated and attended by trained employees.

6.19.11 Cylinders on Roofs or Exterior Balconies.

Subsection 6.19.11 addresses the installation of cylinders on the roofs and balconies of buildings. Until the 1998 edition, cylinder installations were the only rooftop installations of propane permitted in the code. Installation of ASME containers on roofs is now permitted, with significant limits. Refer to 6.6.7 for the requirements for these installations.

Permanent installations of cylinders on roofs are generally related to the use of microwave stations and emergency electricity-generating units. These systems can be installed only on roofs of buildings that are unlikely to sustain major structural failure from fire, hence the requirement that the building be constructed of fire-resistant or noncombustible construction. Specific conditions for installation are outlined in the requirement, but it is noteworthy that no cylinder refilling can take place on roofs and that the storage of cylinders on roofs is not permitted either by this section or by Chapter 8 (specifically 8.2.1.5).

6.19.11.1 Where cylinders are installed permanently on roofs of buildings, the buildings shall be of fire-resistant construction or noncombustible construction having essentially noncombustible contents, or of other construction or contents that are protected with automatic sprinklers.

(A) The total water capacity of cylinders connected to any one manifold shall be not greater than 980 lb (445 kg) [nominal 400 lb (181 kg) propane capacity]. If more than one manifold is located on the roof, it shall be separated from any other by at least 50 ft (15 m).

(B) Cylinders shall be located in areas where there is free air circulation, at least 10 ft (3 m) from building openings (such as windows and doors), and at least 20 ft (6.1 m) from air intakes of air-conditioning and ventilating systems.

The requirement for separating cylinders from air intakes into buildings relates to the release of gas that may occur and the need to prevent that gas from being brought into the building and potentially being ignited.

(C) Cylinders shall not be located on roofs that are entirely enclosed by parapets more than 18 in. (460 mm) high unless the parapets are breached with low-level ventilation openings not more than 20 ft (6.1 m) apart, or unless all openings communicating with the interior of the building are at or above the top of the parapets.

(D) Piping shall be in accordance with 6.19.2.4 through 6.19.2.6.

(E) Hose shall not be used for connection to cylinders.

(F) The fire department shall be advised of each installation.

6.19.11.2 Cylinders having water capacities greater than 2.7 lb (1 kg) [nominal 1 lb (0.5 kg) LP-Gas capacity] shall not be located on decks or balconies of dwellings of two or more living units above the first floor unless they are served by exterior stairways.

Exhibits 6.45 and 6.46 illustrate the only permitted location for a 20 lb (9.1 kg) cylinder in a multiple family dwelling of two units or more located one above the other.

EXHIBIT 6.45 Prohibited and Permitted Locations of Cylinders on Balconies of a Multiple Family Dwelling with Four Living Units, One Above the Other.

EXHIBIT 6.46 Permitted Location of Cylinders on Balconies Located One Above the Other in a Two-Unit Dwelling.

The prohibition of cylinders above the first floor in multiple family dwellings of two or more living units reflects concerns for storage and transportation within these buildings, including elevators, egress of occupants from the upper floors in the event of an emergency, and the exposure to surrounding living units in the event of a leak or fire on a balcony. (Note that a living unit may have more than one floor.)

In multiple family dwellings of two living units located one above the other, gas grill cylinders are permitted on balconies that are accessed from exterior stairways to each balcony, as shown in Exhibit 6.46.

6.19.12 Liquid LP-Gas Piped into Buildings or Structures.

6.19.12.1 Buildings or separate areas of buildings into which LP-Gas liquid at pressures exceeding 20 psig (138 kPag) is piped shall be constructed in accordance with Chapter 10 and shall be used for the purposes listed in 6.9.1.1(4)(b).

Liquid LP-Gas may be piped into buildings at pressures higher than 20 psig (138 kPag) only for the applications listed below, in accordance with 6.9.1.1(4)(b). The building must be constructed in accordance with Chapter 10 as an LP-Gas distribution facility.

LP-Gas liquid is permitted to be piped into buildings at pressures greater than 20 psig when the buildings or separate areas of the buildings are used exclusively to house the following:

1. Equipment for vaporization, pressure reduction, gas mixing, gas manufacturing, or distribution
2. Internal combustion engines, industrial processes, research and experimental laboratories, or equipment or processing having a similar hazard
3. Engine-mounted fuel vaporizers

Note that these applications are industrial-type processes that would not typically be open to the public.

6.19.12.2 Liquid LP-Gas piped into buildings under construction or major renovation in accordance with 6.9.1.1(4)(a) shall comply with 6.19.12.2(A) through 6.19.12.2(J).

(A) Liquid piping shall not exceed ¾ in. (20 mm) and shall comply with 6.9.1 and 6.9.3.

(B) Copper tubing with a maximum outside diameter of ¾ in. (20 mm) shall be used where approved by the authority having jurisdiction.

(C) Liquid piping in buildings shall be kept to a minimum length and shall be protected against construction hazards by fastening it to walls or other surfaces to provide protection against breakage and by locating it so as to avoid exposure to high ambient temperatures.

(D) A readily accessible shutoff valve shall be located at each intermediate branch line where it leaves the main line.

(E) A second shutoff valve shall be located at the appliance end of the branch and upstream of any flexible appliance connector.

(F) Excess-flow valves shall be installed downstream of each branch line shutoff valve.

(G) Excess-flow valves shall be located at any point in the piping system where branch lines are used and the pipe size of the branch line is reduced. The excess flow valve shall be sized for the reduced size of the branch line piping.

(H) Hose shall not be used to carry liquid between the container and building and shall not be used at any point in the liquid line.

(I) Hydrostatic relief valves shall be installed where required.

(J) The release of fuel when any section of piping or appliances is disconnected shall be minimized either by using an approved automatic quick-closing coupling that shuts off the gas on both sides when uncoupled or by closing the shutoff valve closest to the point to be disconnected and allowing the appliances on that line to operate until the fuel in the line is consumed.

Because the threat from a release of liquid in a building is much more hazardous than if the release were vapor (liquid propane expands to 270 times its original volume when released into the atmosphere), the following special limitations on piping size and flow controls are required:

- Maximum size of piping is limited to ¾ in. (19 mm), and the use of copper must be approved.
- Piping length must be minimized.
- Protection against breakage and against exposure to high ambient temperatures must be provided.

- Accessible shutoff valves and excess-flow valves must be provided and their locations specified.
- Hydrostatic relief valves are required between valves.
- Hose is not permitted.

Protection against the release of fuel when disconnecting piping is achieved either with an automatic quick-closing coupling (QCC) or by shutting off the system and allowing the appliance to burn off the fuel.

6.20 Installation of Appliances

Section 6.20 applies to the installation of LP-Gas appliances covered under the scope of NFPA 58, which, in 1.3.2(6), excludes the portions of the LP-Gas system covered by NFPA 54, *National Fuel Gas Code* [20], where it is adopted, used, or enforced. Because NFPA 54 covers building piping systems, Section 6.20 does not apply to appliances connected to fixed fuel gas piping systems in buildings. However, it does apply to appliances fueled directly from cylinders, such as gas grills, and appliances not installed in buildings, such as appliances used in agricultural and construction applications.

6.20.1 Application.

6.20.1.1 Section 6.20 shall apply to the installation of LP-Gas appliances.

6.20.1.2 Installation of appliances on commercial vehicles shall be in accordance with 6.23.7.

6.20.2 Installation of Patio Heaters.

6.20.2.1 Patio heaters utilizing an integral LP-Gas container greater than 1.08 lb (0.49 kg) propane capacity shall comply with 6.20.2.2 and 6.20.2.3.

6.20.2.2 Patio heaters shall be listed and used in accordance with their listing and the manufacturer's instructions.

The requirement addressing patio heaters in 6.20.2.1 was added in the 2008 edition and recognizes the growing use of these portable, outdoor appliances used to heat outdoor areas when the climate is too cool to sit or stand outdoors comfortably. They are used extensively in restaurants with outdoor seating areas to enable the areas to be used for a greater number of weeks each year. They are also used where attendants, such as those working for a valet parking service, wait outdoors. (See Exhibit 6.47.)

6.20.2.3 Patio heaters shall not be located within 5 ft (1.5 m) of exits from an assembly occupancy.

An assembly occupancy is defined in NFPA *101, Life Safety Code* [3], as follows:

> **3.3.178.2 Assembly Occupancy.** An occupancy (1) used for a gathering of 50 or more persons for deliberation, worship, entertainment, eating, drinking, amusement, awaiting transportation, or similar uses; or (2) used as a special amusement building, regardless of occupant load. [**NFPA 101**, 2009]

While restaurants are the most likely assembly occupancies to use patio heaters in outdoor areas, other assembly occupancies might use patio heaters as well.

6.20.3 Hose for Portable Appliances.

6.20.3.1 The requirements of Section 6.20 shall apply to hoses used on the low-pressure side of regulators to connect portable appliances.

EXHIBIT 6.47 *Patio Heaters.*
(Courtesy of Richard
Fredenburg, North Carolina
Department of Agriculture
and Consumer Services)

6.20.3.2 Where used inside buildings, the following shall apply:

(1) The hose shall be the minimum practical length and shall be in accordance with 6.19.2.6.
(2) The hose shall not extend from one room to another or pass through any partitions, walls, ceilings, or floors except as provided by 6.19.4.9.
(3) The hose shall not be concealed from view or used in concealed locations.

It is important for the hose to be visible so that any wear or damage it sustains can be readily detected. Hose that is longer than needed can be looped under equipment and be partially hidden. Hose hidden in walls, partitions, ceilings, and floors cannot be inspected for wear or damage.

6.20.3.3 Where installed outside of buildings, the hose length shall be permitted to exceed 10 ft (3.3 m) but shall be as short as practical.

The hose length limit was changed from 6 ft (1.8 m) to 10 ft (3.3 m) in 2008. The revision acknowledged that many portable appliances were being sold with 10 ft of hose, and the committee did not believe that this additional hose length, compared to the former 6 ft length limit, would lead to unsafe conditions. Note that hose used outdoors must be protected from damage in accordance with 6.19.2.6.

6.20.3.4 Hose shall be securely connected to the appliance.

6.20.3.5 The use of rubber slip ends shall not be permitted.

6.20.3.6 A shutoff valve shall be provided in the piping immediately upstream of the inlet connection of the hose.

A shutoff valve is required at the point where the hose connects to the piping system to permit the appliance to be isolated from the piping system should it be necessary to conduct maintenance or repairs on the hose or appliance.

6.20.3.7 Where more than one such appliance shutoff is located near another, the valves shall be marked to indicate which appliance is connected to each valve.

6.20.3.8 Hose shall be protected against physical damage.

Because hose is vulnerable to mechanical and thermal damage and has limited service life, hose should be used only where necessary and where it can be readily inspected and maintained. The requirements for hose and hose connectors are located in 5.9.6.

6.21 Vaporizer Installation

LP-Gas is stored as a liquid and most often used as a gas. LP-Gas vaporizes in a liquid storage container and reaches an equilibrium pressure determined by the temperature of the liquid and vapor in the container. As gas is withdrawn from the container, additional liquid will vaporize to maintain equilibrium, as long as heat is available and can be transferred through the walls of the container into the liquid.

This vaporization process requires heat that is drawn from the medium surrounding the tank — air or soil, depending on the installation. In installations where a larger quantity of vapor is required than can be provided by the container's surroundings, an external vaporizer is used.

A vaporizer plays an important role in installations where vapor demands, which vary seasonally, are higher than the container's vaporizing capacity. In warmer climates, vaporizers may not be common, because it is easier and may be less costly to install a larger storage container to increase the vaporization capacity of the system, since a larger container with a greater surface area provides more vaporizing capacity than a smaller container. A vaporizer is relatively expensive because it requires controls and a source of heat, such as a propane flame, electricity, steam, hot water, or some other source.

Vaporizers play an important role in installations where vapor demands are high during peak periods of use. A typical standby plant-type installation for emergency use must provide a high volume of vapor, and vaporizers are the key component of the system to meet this high demand period.

The types of vaporizers are as follows:

- Direct-fired, which are similar to a boiler
- Indirect-fired, which use electricity, hot water, steam, or other "intermediate" heating media as a source of heat
- Vaporizing burners, in which the heat of the flame vaporizes the liquid feeding the flame

Vaporizers used on engine fuel systems are not covered in Section 6.21, because they are covered in Chapter 11. Integral-vaporizing burners are also not covered in Section 6.21, because they are portable units that do not present a hazard greater than an open flame. Vaporizing burners installed in a fixed location are covered in 6.21.5, and their construction is covered in 5.21.5.

Vaporizers that are used for only a part of the year should receive special operational and maintenance attention. These vaporizers should be given a thorough check and a test run before they are needed to ensure that they will be equipped to handle the vaporizing load. Operators should also have refresher training when they have not operated the equipment for an extended period. Training is especially important when the system is operated by the user, where the user is not as familiar with the operation of the equipment as the propane distributor would be. Periodic testing during idle periods may be recommended by the manufacturer, as well as a program to alert the proper individuals to the need for this essential maintenance program. In the summer season, spiders, mud daubers, and other insects can get into the burner area, pilot area, and regulator vents and create operating problems. It is important to verify that the rain cap is always kept on the pressure relief valve outlet and that such an outlet is piped to a proper point for the safe discharge of LP-Gas.

Devices that prevent the return of liquid LP-Gas should not be installed between the storage tank and the vaporizer, unless recommended by the manufacturer of the vaporizer. Installation of these devices could trap liquid LP-Gas in the vaporizer when the vaporizer is not operating. Liquid in the vaporizer will then vaporize and possibly release LP-Gas to the atmosphere through the pressure relief valve.

6.21.1 Application.

Section 6.21 shall not apply to engine fuel vaporizers or to integral vaporizing burners such as those used for weed burners or tar kettles.

6.21.2 Installation of Indirect-Fired Vaporizers.

An indirect vaporizer is defined as follows:

> **3.3.70.3 Indirect (or Indirect-Fired) Vaporizer.** A vaporizer in which heat furnished by steam, hot water, the ground, surrounding air, or other heating medium is applied to a vaporizing chamber or to tubing, pipe coils, or other heat exchange surface containing the liquid LP-Gas to be vaporized; the heating of the medium used is at a point remote from the vaporizer.

Indirect vaporizers derive heat from a remote source. The term *remote* is not defined in NFPA 58. The strictest literal definition of remote would be any device not part of the unit itself. An example is a water or steam boiler mounted immediately adjacent to, or on the same skid or package with, the indirect vaporizer. Where this arrangement occurs, 6.21.2.4 specifies that such a combination be sited in the same manner as direct-fired vaporizers, because a source of ignition is present.

This "source of ignition" can have positive or negative effects. A source of ignition close to an indirect vaporizer installed outdoors has the effect of preventing a large buildup of gas if a leak occurs, because a leak would be ignited by the adjacent heat source before it became a more severe problem. With no source of ignition in the immediate area, on a calm day a large amount of gas could escape before finally reaching an ignition source. The escaped gas could result in an unconfined vapor cloud explosion.

If the indirect vaporizer were installed inside an enclosure, an adjacent source of ignition could cause a confined explosion, which can be considerably more devastating than an unconfined vapor cloud explosion. Accordingly, indirect vaporizers are generally used where the source of heat is a plant facility, such as steam or hot water from a plant heating or processing system.

Exhibit 6.48 illustrates an indirect-fired electric waterbath vaporizer. A pressure relief valve is installed in the vapor space of the unit, and the outlet of the relief valve is vented outside the building.

6.21.2.1 Indirect-fired vaporizers shall be installed outdoors, or in separate buildings or structures that comply with Section 10.2, or in attached structures or rooms that comply with Section 10.3.

6.21.2.2 The separate building or structure shall not have any unprotected drains to sewers or sump pits.

Because LP-Gases are heavier than air, and large quantities of propane vapor can be released if liquid escapes and vaporizes, it is important that there are no open drains, sewers, or sump pits in the building enclosure. Any drain that is piped away from a vaporizer room is suspect because it might connect with a general drainage system and carry flammable gases to a source of ignition in another building or open area. If a drain is necessary, it should be pro-

EXHIBIT 6.48 Electric
Waterbath Vaporizer.
(Courtesy of Ely Energy, Inc.)

tected with a trap that will not permit vapors to pass through, or should be discrete to the vaporizer room and terminate outside, in the open air, well away from other drains or sources of ignition.

6.21.2.3 Pressure relief valves on vaporizers within buildings in industrial or gas manufacturing plants shall be piped to a point outside the building or structure and shall discharge vertically upward.

The requirement for discharging the relief valve "vertically upward" relates to providing any gas that is discharged an opportunity to be dispersed more quickly into a concentration in air below the lower limit of flammability. Relief valve discharge piping that is required to discharge vertically upward must include a rain cap, weep hole, or other type of protection to prevent the piping from filling with water and freezing. (Refer to 5.7.2 for further information on pressure relief devices.)

6.21.2.4 If the heat source of an indirect-fired vaporizer is gas fired and is located within 15 ft (4.6 m) of the vaporizer, the vaporizer and its heat source shall be installed as a direct-fired vaporizer and shall be subject to the requirements of 6.21.3.

This restriction prevents a user from defeating the intent of the code by installing an indirect vaporizer with an adjacent heat source instead of a direct-fired vaporizer.

6.21.2.5 The installation of a heat source serving an indirect-fired vaporizer that utilizes a flammable or combustible heat transfer fluid shall comply with one of the following:

(1) It shall be located outdoors.
(2) It shall be located within a structure that complies with Section 10.2.
(3) It shall be located within a structure attached to, or in rooms within, a building or structure that complies with Section 10.3.

The restrictions in 6.21.2.5 recognize the hazard of flammable or combustible heat transfer fluid. Heat transfer fluids, such as Dowtherm™ and Therminol®, are used in many process plants and may be available when steam is not. These heat transfer fluids can transfer heat at temperatures higher than hot water or steam.

Not all heat transfer fluids are flammable. If any question exists, the fluid manufacturer should be contacted for information on the flammability of the heat transfer fluid at its operating temperature, the material safety data sheet (MSDS) should be consulted, or the fluid should be tested. Heat transfer systems have their fluid changed periodically, and when a change occurs, the flammability of the new fluid should be checked.

6.21.2.6 Gas-fired heating systems supplying heat for vaporization purposes shall be equipped with automatic safety devices to shut off gas to the main burners if ignition fails to occur.

Raw, unburned gas must not escape into the building or the atmosphere. Information on preventing explosions in boilers, as well as on gas-fired heating systems, is contained in NFPA 85, *Boiler and Combustion Systems Hazards Code* [29]. Note that NFPA 85 is not intended to cover small boilers and applies to boilers with a heat input of 12.5 MM Btu/hr (3663 kW) and above. Although this heat input is much greater than most propane vaporizers, NFPA 85 can be used as a guide.

6.21.2.7 The installation of a heat source serving an indirect-fired vaporizer that utilizes a noncombustible heat transfer fluid, such as steam, water, or a water-glycol mixture, shall be installed outdoors or in industrial occupancies.

6.21.2.8 Industrial occupancies in which a source of heat for an indirect-fired vaporizer is installed shall comply with Chapter 40 of NFPA *101*, *Life Safety Code*, and Section 6.3 of NFPA 54, *National Fuel Gas Code* (ANSI Z223.1).

6.21.2.9 The following shall apply to indirect-fired vaporizers installed in buildings:

(1) The heat transfer fluid shall be steam or hot water.
(2) The heat transfer fluid shall not be recirculated.
(3) A backflow preventer shall be installed between the vaporizer and the heat source.

The requirements in 6.21.2.7 through 6.21.2.9 are an exception to the general rule that heat sources for vaporizers be installed outdoors or in a structure complying with Chapter 10. Indirect vaporizers can be installed indoors in industrial occupancies only. Boilers can be used as a heat source for a vaporizer when condensate or circulating water is not returned to the boiler. If the condensate or water were returned to the boiler and the vaporizer developed an internal leak, propane at high pressure could be released at the boiler relief valve and cause a fire.

6.21.2.10 If the heat transfer fluid is recirculated after leaving the vaporizer, the heat source shall be installed in accordance with 6.22.2.5 and a phase separator shall be installed with the gas vented.

Existing steam and hot water boilers can be used as a heat source for indirect-fired vaporizers. The phase separator is required to ensure that any leaking propane vapors are prevented from entering the area where the boiler is installed. The phase separator allows vapor to be separated from the liquid and to be used appropriately.

6.21.2.11 Indirect-fired vaporizers employing heat from the atmosphere shall be installed outdoors and shall be located in accordance with Table 6.21.3.6.

Some vaporizers use heat from the atmosphere as the heat source for vaporizing liquid propane. These vaporizers are typically larger than direct-fired and indirect-fired vaporizers and must be installed outdoors. "Atmospheric heat" also can include "ground source" heat, which is becoming more popular as a heat source for heat pumps because of the increased efficiency that it provides. Heat for vaporization may be obtained in the following ways:

- Using tubing installed underground to maintain a relatively warm temperature and provide vaporizing heat in cold weather

- Using tubing or piping installed in basements or in crawl spaces to gain some heat for vaporization
- Designing the vaporizer with a large surface area exposed to the atmosphere

If such an atmospheric heat source vaporizer were to be used inside a building, it would be possible to accumulate gas in the building if the vaporizer were to be damaged. Because this type of vaporizer has a relatively large surface area, there is a greater chance that damage can occur.

6.21.2.12 Where atmospheric vaporizers of less than 1 qt (0.9 L) capacity are installed in industrial occupancies, they shall be installed as close as practical to the point of entry of the supply line in the building.

6.21.2.13 Atmospheric vaporizers of less than 1 qt (0.9 L) capacity shall not be installed in other than industrial occupancies.

Paragraph 6.12.2.12 was split into 6.21.2.12 and 6.21.2.13 in the 2011 edition to clarify the technical committee's intent that 1 qt (0.9 L) and smaller vaporizers be installed only in industrial occupancies.

6.21.3 Installation of Direct-Fired Vaporizers.

The definition of *direct-fired vaporizer* was revised in the 2011 edition to read:

> **3.3.70.1 Direct-Fired Vaporizer.** A vaporizer in which heat furnished by a flame is directly applied to a heat exchange surface in contact with the liquid LP-Gas to be vaporized.

The revised text is simpler, and the unnecessary reference to submerged combustion vaporizers, which are rarely used for the LP-Gas vaporization systems covered by NFPA 58, was removed. Direct-fired vaporizers derive heat for vaporizing liquid propane from a flame. While operating, a source of ignition is always present. A submerged-combustion vaporizer has coils containing liquid LP-Gas inside a water bath. The water bath is heated by directing a flame below the surface of the water. The subsurface flame causes turbulence in the water and results in excellent heat transfer to the fluid being vaporized. Direct-fired vaporizers are usually used for very high vaporization loads. See Exhibit 6.49, which shows an installation with multiple direct-fired vaporizers.

6.21.3.1 Where a direct-fired vaporizer is installed in a separate structure, the separate structure shall be constructed in accordance with Chapter 10.

EXHIBIT 6.49 *Installation of Multiple Direct-Fired Vaporizers. (Courtesy of Superior Energy Systems)*

FAQ ▶
Why are shutoff valves required
on liquid lines to a direct-fired
vaporizer?

Direct-fired vaporizers present a potential hazard not present in other LP-Gas equipment. When liquid is fed to the vaporizer, the surface is heated directly by a flame and the normal service life of the metal can be reduced. Therefore, installations must be outdoors or in a room or building without sources of ignition such as those provided in Chapter 10.

6.21.3.2 The housing for direct-fired vaporizers shall not have any drains to a sewer or a sump pit that is shared with any other structure.

Refer to the commentary following 6.21.2.2 for an explanation of the concerns over drains, sewers, and sump pits.

6.21.3.3 Pressure relief valve discharges on direct-fired vaporizers shall be piped to a point outside the structure or building.

6.21.3.4 Direct-fired vaporizers shall be connected to the liquid space or to the liquid and vapor space of the ASME container.

It is critical for the safe operation of the vaporizer that liquid (and not vapor) be provided to the heat exchanger.

6.21.3.5 A manually operated shutoff valve shall be installed in each connection of the ASME container supplying the vaporizer.

A key safety requirement for direct-fired vaporizers is that a means of stopping the flow of liquid into the vaporizer be made available. This requirement is based not only on the need to isolate the vaporizer itself from the container, but also to provide a means for stopping the flow of liquid in the event of an emergency.

6.21.3.6 Direct-fired vaporizers of any capacity shall be located in accordance with Table 6.21.3.6.

TABLE 6.21.3.6 Minimum Separation Distances Between Direct-Fired Vaporizers and Exposures

Exposure	Minimum Distance Required	
	ft	m
Container	10	3.0
Container shutoff valves	15	4.6
Point of transfer	15	4.6
Nearest important building or group of buildings or line of adjoining property that can be built upon	25	7.6
Nearest Chapter 10 building or room housing gas–air mixer	10	3.0
Cabinet housing gas–air mixer outdoors	0	0

Note: Do not apply distances to the building in which a direct-fired vaporizer is installed.

The distance requirements in Table 6.21.3.6 were established to isolate the vaporizer (a source of ignition) from stored fuel and to ensure that access to shutoff valves is not prevented by a problem at the vaporizer. They are based on the experience of members of the Technical Committee on Liquefied Petroleum Gases. Note that the requirements vary depending on the type of exposure. For example, a direct-fired vaporizer can be closer to a container than to the shutoff valves on the container because the possibility of leakage from the container shell is practically zero. Leakage potential is much greater from a connection to the container or at a valve. Where connections are made and broken at a transfer point, the hazard is greater than if the vaporizer is near the bare container without connections. The distance is greater from important buildings, from a group of buildings, and from the line of adjoining property that may be built upon in order to preclude mutual exposure during a fire.

6.21.4 Installation of Tank Heaters.

A direct gas-fired tank heater is defined as follows:

> **3.3.18 Direct Gas-Fired Tank Heater.** A gas-fired device that applies hot gas from the heater combustion chamber directly to a portion of the container surface in contact with LP-Gas liquid.

To the editor's knowledge, tank heaters are no longer manufactured. Tank heater coverage in NFPA 58 is needed because existing units can be reinstalled or new units manufactured. Tank heaters provide a simple means to vaporize propane in smaller applications in cold climates.

6.21.4.1 Tank heaters shall be installed only on aboveground ASME containers and shall be located in accordance with Table 6.21.4.1 with respect to the nearest important building, group of buildings, or line of adjoining property that can be built upon.

TABLE 6.21.4.1 Minimum Separation Between Tank Heaters and Exposures

Container Water Capacity		Minimum Distance Required	
gal	*m³*	*ft*	*m*
≤500	≤1.9	10	3.0
501–2,000	>1.9–7.6	25	7.6
2,001–30,000	>7.6–114	50	15.0
30,001–70,000	>114–265	75	23.0
70,001–90,000	>265–341	100	30.5
90,001–120,000	>341–454	125	38.1

Note that the distance requirements in Table 6.21.4.1 are the same as the requirements for aboveground containers shown in Table 6.3.1. In Table 6.21.4.1 there are no references to the size of the tank heater, only to the size of the associated container. This table provides information to ensure that spacing criteria are properly applied to direct-fired tank heaters. Of utmost importance is the point of transfer such as the filling connection, in relation to the pilot and burner on the tank heater. Most tank heaters are used on containers of 1000 gal (3.8 m³) capacity and smaller that have the point of transfer located at the top center of the container. The gas supply to the pilot and burner must be shut off while containers are being filled.

6.21.4.2 If the tank heater is similar in operation to an indirect-fired vaporizer, the heat source shall comply with 6.21.2.8 and 6.21.2.11.

Note that the safety devices required by 6.21.4.2 and 6.21.4.3 on direct-fired tank heaters reflect the special hazards of tank heaters, which are as follows:

- Container overpressurization that results in relief valve operation and release of LP-Gas in proximity to an ignition source
- Damage to the container, which occurs if the liquid level is allowed to fall below the level of the flame (This hazard is identical to that of fired boilers, where low water cutoff switches are mandated.)

6.21.4.3 If a point of transfer is located within 15 ft (4.6 m) of a direct-gas-fired tank heater, the heater burner and pilot shall be shut off during the product transfer and a caution notice that reads as follows shall be displayed immediately adjacent to the filling connections:

> **CAUTION:** A gas-fired device that contains a source of ignition is connected to this container. Burner and pilot must be shut off before filling the container.

Safety instructions should be provided to persons who refill containers that are equipped with direct gas-fired tank heaters. During the liquid transfer, using the fixed liquid level gauge may allow an accumulation of gas in the area of the container. The release of product when the transfer hose is disconnected may also allow gas accumulation. Before attempting to relight the pilot on the tank heater, all fugitive gases must be dissipated.

6.21.5 Installation of Vaporizing Burners.

Vaporizing burners, which are sometimes called vaporizer burners or self-vaporizing liquid burners, are defined as follows:

> **3.3.71 Vaporizing Burner (Self-Vaporizing Liquid Burner).** A burner that also vaporizes liquid LP-Gas prior to burning it.

Vaporizing burners are fed liquid LP-Gas that is vaporized internally prior to burning. Vaporizing burners are high-capacity burners that can offer significant economic advantage over a vapor burner by eliminating the need for a separate vaporizer and pressure regulator. Applications include large burners, such as grain dryers and cement kilns. Note that new paragraph 5.21.5.1 clarifies that these requirements are not applicable to engine fuel vaporizers and to integral vaporizing burners, such as weed burners. Vaporizing burners are also used as part of hot air balloon cylinders.

It is important that vaporizing burners not be used inside buildings because they are generally large-capacity units in which both liquid and vapor are present. The distance requirements in Table 6.21.5.2 reflect the potential for ignition of any gas leakage at the container and the hazard to the container if there is impinging flame from the vaporizing burner.

6.21.5.1 Vaporizing burners shall be installed outside of buildings.

6.21.5.2 The minimum distance between any container and a vaporizing burner shall be in accordance with Table 6.21.5.2.

TABLE 6.21.5.2 *Minimum Separation Distance Between Containers and Vaporizing Burners*

Container Water Capacity		Minimum Distance Required	
gal	m³	ft	m
≤500	≤1.9	10	3.0
501–2000	1.9–7.6	25	7.6
>2000	>7.6	50	15.0

6.21.5.3 Manually operated positive shutoff valves shall be located at the containers to shut off all flow to the vaporizing burners.

6.21.6 Installation of Waterbath Vaporizers.

6.21.6.1 If a waterbath vaporizer is electrically heated and all electrical equipment is designed for Class I, Group D locations, the unit shall be treated as an indirect-fired vaporizer and shall be installed in accordance with 6.21.2.

A gas-fueled waterbath vaporizer has a flame in it, and therefore is similar to a direct-fired vaporizer. Electrical equipment that is listed for installation in Class I, Group D locations (see *NFPA 70, National Electrical Code* [23]) does not provide a source of ignition. Therefore, electrically heated waterbath vaporizers with electrical equipment listed for Class 1, Group D are not a source of ignition should LP-Gas vapors be present, and they can be installed using the requirements for indirect-fired vaporizers in 6.21.2. A waterbath vaporizer is shown in Exhibit 6.48.

◀ **FAQ**
What does it mean for electrical equipment to be rated for installation in Class I, Group D locations?

6.21.6.2 All other waterbath vaporizers shall be treated as direct-fired vaporizers and shall be installed in accordance with 6.21.3.

6.21.7 Installation of Electric Vaporizers.

Electric vaporizers, whether direct immersion or indirect immersion, shall be treated as indirect-fired and shall be installed in accordance with 6.21.2.

6.21.8 Installation of Gas–Air Mixers.

Gas–air mixer is defined as follows:

> **3.3.26 Gas–Air Mixer.** A device or a system of piping and controls that mixes LP-Gas vapor with air to produce a mixed gas of a lower heating value than the LP-Gas.

Gas–air mixers are used to mix propane or butane with air to reduce the heating value and density of the LP-Gas in order to be compatible with, or be a substitute for, natural gas. This propane–air mixture can be substituted easily for natural gas. It is often used as a substitute for natural gas in areas where natural gas is not available, but it is expected to be available in the future. Propane–air mixtures are also commonly used in industry as a supplement or substitute when natural gas is purchased on an interruptible basis or when the price of propane or butane is less than that of natural gas. The use of propane–air mixtures assists natural gas utilities by providing a quantity of natural gas that can be made available quickly for domestic use in times of severe domestic demand, such as during very cold weather. The gas–air mixture is usually about 57 percent propane or 45 percent butane, well above the upper limit of flammability of about 10 percent for propane and 9 percent for butane.

Exhibit 6.50 shows a waterbath vaporizer with venturi gas–air mixer. This vaporizer was installed in conjunction with a venturi gas–air mixer as a standby for natural gas. The

EXHIBIT 6.50 *LP-Gas–Air Venturi Blending System. (Courtesy of Ely Energy, Inc.)*

vaporizer-burner control includes flame safeguard controls. The vaporizer also includes a shutoff to prevent liquid carryover in the event of burner failure or overcapacity. A mixture of water and antifreeze with a rust inhibitor was installed in the waterbath of the vaporizer. The vaporizing coil within the vaporizer waterbath is ASME Code stamped.

A test flare, as shown in Exhibit 6.51, is normally installed with a gas–air system, which is used as a standby for natural gas. This flare permits the system equipment to be checked during nonoperational months and may also be used to train new gas–air mixing system operators.

EXHIBIT 6.51 *Test Flare. (Courtesy of Flame Engineering)*

6.21.8.1 Piping and equipment installed with a gas–air mixer shall comply with 6.9.1, 6.9.3, and 6.14.

6.21.8.2 Where used without a vaporizer, a mixer shall be installed outdoors or in a building complying with Chapter 10.

6.21.8.3 Where used with an indirect-fired vaporizer, a mixer shall be installed as follows:

(1) In an outdoor location
(2) In the same compartment or room with the vaporizer
(3) In a building complying with Chapter 10
(4) In a location that is both remote from the vaporizer and in accordance with 6.21.2

6.21.8.4 Where used with a direct-fired vaporizer, a mixer shall be installed as follows:

(1) With a listed or approved mixer in a common cabinet with the vaporizer outdoors in accordance with 6.21.3.6

(2) Outdoors on a common skid with the vaporizer in accordance with 6.21.3

(3) Adjacent to the vaporizer to which it is connected in accordance with 6.21.3

(4) In a building complying with Chapter 10 without a direct-fired vaporizer in the same room

The ratio of gas to air in the mixture must be monitored to prevent the formation or distribution of a flammable mixture. Monitoring the relative pressures can prevent a flammable mixture from developing. In larger installations, an on-line instrument that measures the specific gravity or heat content of the mixed gas can be used. The mixing system must be shut down if the upper flammable limit is approached. The mixing system must also be shut down if the ratio of gas to air approaches the level at which the natural gas appliances that are connected to the system no longer fire as designed. This condition can cause poor combustion due to inadequate air, development of soot, and flame lifting, which can cause local overheating and the safety devices to activate and shut down the appliance. High BTU gases can also cause damage to process burner systems.

6.22 Ignition Source Control

Requirements for preventing the ignition of LP-Gas that can be released from LP-Gas containers, piping, and equipment are provided in Section 6.22. The section primarily covers electrical sources of ignition and refers to *NFPA 70, National Electrical Code* [23]. NFPA 58 establishes areas where flammable mixtures can be present, and *NFPA 70* establishes what equipment can be used in these areas. Note that Section 6.22 does not apply to residential and commercial occupancies because it is impossible to restrict other sources of ignition, such as matches, candles, and open flame appliances, from residential and commercial occupancies. (See 6.22.2.4.)

6.22.1 Scope.

6.22.1.1 This section shall apply to the minimization of ignition of flammable LP-Gas–air mixtures resulting from the normal or accidental release of nominal quantities of liquid or vapor from LP-Gas systems installed and operated in accordance with this code.

6.22.1.2* The installation of lightning protection equipment shall not be required on LP-Gas storage containers.

A.6.22.1.2 For information on lightning protection, see NFPA 780, *Standard for the Installation of Lightning Protection Systems.*

If a container or its piping is associated with a building or other structure equipped with lightning protection, the LP-Gas system may have to be integrated into the lightning protection system, or the lightning protection system might not protect the building. In such instances, refer to NFPA 780, *Standard for the Installation of Lightning Protection Systems* [30], especially the chapter on protection for ordinary structures.

Since LP-Gas storage containers are made of a metal of sufficient thickness to withstand a direct strike and the buried piping provides a conductive path through which the lightning protection currents may dissipate into the earth, the installation of lightning protection on LP-Gas storage containers is not required. However, where the liquefied petroleum gas system enters a structure equipped with lightning protection, the LP-Gas system must be integrated into the lightning protection system to ensure potential equalization of the conductors entering the structure. NFPA 780 requires the bonding of any conductive piping to the lightning protection grounding system at or near the entry point of the structure (see also the following discussion on A.6.22.1.3). In such instances, refer to NFPA 780 requirements on Common Grounding (Section 4.14, reprinted here).

4.14 Common Grounding

4.14.1 General. All grounding media and buried metallic conductors that can assist in providing a path for lightning currents in or on a structure shall be interconnected to provide a common ground potential.

4.14.1.1 This interconnection shall include lightning protection, electric service, communications, and antenna system grounds, as well as underground metallic piping systems.

4.14.1.2 Underground metallic piping systems shall include water service, well casings located within 7.6 m (25 ft) of the structure, gas piping, underground conduits, underground liquefied petroleum gas piping systems, and so on.

4.14.1.3 Connection to gas piping shall comply with the following requirements:

(1)* Interconnections to a gas line shall be made on the customer's side of the meter.

A.14.1.3(1) There could be installations where multiple sections of piping and associated junctions exist between the gas meter/regulator and the entrance of the line to the structure. Such junctions can create increased impedances at frequencies that are associated with overvoltages. Where there is internal piping that could be susceptible to overvoltages, care should be taken to ensure that the interconnection of the lightning protection grounding system is made to pipe sections that will not increase the impedance between the pipe and the grounding section. This could be accomplished by connection to the last section of pipe entering the structure. This interconnection could be made either external or internal to the structure.

(2) Bonding shall not be permitted to the utility side of the meter.

4.14.1.4 Main-size lightning conductors shall be used for interconnecting these grounding systems to the lightning protection system.

4.14.1.5* Where galvanic corrosion is a concern or where a direct bond is prohibited by local code, an isolating spark gap shall be permitted.
[**NFPA 780,** 2011]

6.22.1.3* Grounding and bonding shall not be required on LP-Gas systems.

A.6.22.1.3 Because LP-Gas is contained in a closed system of piping and equipment, the system need not be electrically conductive or electrically bonded for protection against static electricity. For information on grounding and bonding for protection against static electricity, see NFPA 77, *Recommended Practice on Static Electricity.*

For installations in areas where lightning is frequent, consideration should be given to bridging over small nonconductive joints in piping or other discontinuities to prevent flashover of lightning currents on the pipes due to direct or nearby lightning strikes. Such flashover on the pipes may damage the nonconductive sections, causing leaks and, in extreme cases, ignition. These bonds may be made using approved spark gap devices for those cases where the isolation of the conductive sections is intentional. For more information on grounding and bonding for protection against lightning, see NFPA 780, *Standard for the Installation of Lightning Protection Systems* [30].

Electrostatic sparks, even those too small to be seen or felt, have the capability to ignite LP-Gas vapors. The source of these small sparks includes ungrounded personnel or process equipment. In addition, if liquid LP-Gas is released at high velocity, creating a mixture of liquid drops, then vapor, air, and water drops (due to the condensation of water vapor in the air from the refrigerating effect of vaporizing liquid) can generate an electrostatic charge. This charge might be of sufficient energy to cause ignition of the mixture. See NFPA 77, *Recommended Practice on Static Electricity* [31], for a discussion of this phenomenon. Paragraph 6.22.1.3 does not prevent the installation of grounding and bonding if desired or required by other applicable standards such as NFPA 780. Many tanks at bulk and industrial sites have grounding straps. Also, many transfer stations at these sites have methods (equipment and procedures) to eliminate differences in electrical potential between the piping system and transport vehicles that could cause an electrical discharge when the transfer hoses are attached.

A training program, "Static Electricity in the Propane Industry," funded by the Propane Education & Research Council (PERC), includes a booklet (hazard assessment and employee quiz) and an accompanying video that provides information on static electricity in propane plant operations. The booklet is available for download at www.propanesafety.org. The entire program, including DVD, may be purchased at www.propanemarc.com.

6.22.2 Electrical Equipment.

6.22.2.1 Electrical equipment and wiring installed in unclassified areas shall be in accordance with *NFPA 70, National Electrical Code*.

6.22.2.2* The extent of electrically classified areas shall be in accordance with Table 6.22.2.2.

TABLE 6.22.2.2 Electrical Area Classification

Part	Location	Extent of Classified Area[a]	Equipment Shall Be Approved for Compliance with NFPA 70, National Electrical Code, Class I[a], Group D[b]
A	Unrefrigerated containers other than cylinders and ASME vertical containers of less than 1000 lb (454 kg) water capacity	Within 15 ft (4.6 m) in all directions from connections, except connections otherwise covered in this table	Division 2
B	Refrigerated storage containers	Within 15 ft (4.6 m) in all directions from connections otherwise covered in this table	Division 2
		Area inside dike to the level of the top of the dike	Division 2
C[c]	Tank vehicle and tank car loading and unloading	Within 5 ft (1.5 m) in all directions from connections regularly made or disconnected for product transfer	Division 1
		Beyond 5 ft (1.5 m) but within 15 ft (4.6 m) in all directions from a point where connections are regularly made or disconnected and within the cylindrical volume between the horizontal equator of the sphere and grade	Division 2
D	Gauge vent openings other than those on cylinders and ASME vertical containers of less than 1000 lb (454 kg) water capacity	Within 5 ft (1.5 m) in all directions from point of discharge	Division 1
		Beyond 5 ft (1.5 m) but within 15 ft (4.6 m) in all directions from point of discharge	Division 2
E	Relief device discharge other than those on cylinders and ASME vertical containers of less than 1000 lb (454 kg) water capacity and vaporizers	Within direct path of discharge	Fixed electrical equipment not permitted to be installed
F[c]	Pumps, vapor compressors, gas–air mixers and vaporizers (other than direct-fired or indirect-fired with an attached or adjacent gas-fired heat source)		
	Indoors without ventilation	Entire room and any adjacent room not separated by a gastight partition	Division 1

(continues)

TABLE 6.22.2.2 *Continued*

Part	Location	Extent of Classified Area[a]	Equipment Shall Be Approved for Compliance with NFPA 70, National Electrical Code, Class I[a], Group D[b]
		Within 15 ft (4.6 m) of the exterior side of any exterior wall or roof that is not vaportight or within 15 ft (4.6 m) of any exterior opening	Division 2
	Indoors with ventilation	Entire room and any adjacent room not separated by a gastight partition	Division 2
	Outdoors in open air at or above grade	Within 15 ft (4.6 m) in all directions from this equipment and within the cylindrical volume between the horizontal equator of the sphere and grade	Division 2
G	Vehicle fuel dispenser	Entire space within dispenser enclosure, and 18 in. (460 mm) horizontally from enclosure exterior up to an elevation 4 ft (1.2 m) above dispenser base; entire pit or open space beneath dispenser	Division 1
		Up to 18 in. (460 mm) above ground within 20 ft (6.1 m) horizontally from any edge of enclosure (Note: For pits within this area, see part H of this table.)	Division 2
H	Pits or trenches containing or located beneath LP-Gas valves, pumps, vapor compressors, regulators, and similar equipment		
	Without mechanical ventilation	Entire pit or trench	Division 1
		Entire room and any adjacent room not separated by a gastight partition	Division 2
		Within 15 ft (4.6 m) in all directions from pit or trench when located outdoors	Division 2
	With mechanical ventilation	Entire pit or trench	Division 2
		Entire room and any adjacent room not separated by a gastight partition	Division 2
		Within 15 ft (4.6 m) in all directions from pit or trench when located outdoors	Division 2
I	Special buildings or rooms for storage of cylinders	Entire room	Division 2
J	Pipelines and connections containing operational bleeds, drips, vents, or drains	Within 5 ft (1.5 m) in all directions from point of discharge	Division 1
		Beyond 5 ft (1.5 m) from point of discharge, same as part F of this table	
K[c]	Cylinder filling		
	Indoors with ventilation	Within 5 ft (1.5 m) in all directions from a point of transfer	Division 1
		Beyond 5 ft (1.5 m) and entire room	Division 2

TABLE 6.22.2.2 Continued

Part	Location	Extent of Classified Area[a]	Equipment Shall Be Approved for Compliance with NFPA 70, National Electrical Code, Class I[a], Group D[b]
	Outdoors in open air	Within 5 ft (1.5 m) in all directions from a point of transfer	Division 1
		Beyond 5 ft (1.5 m) but within 15 ft (4.6 m) in all directions from point of transfer and within the cylindrical volume between the horizontal equator of the sphere and grade	Division 2
L	Piers and wharves	Within 5 ft (1.5 m) in all directions from connections regularly made or disconnected for product transfer	Division 1
		Beyond 5 ft (1.5 m) but within 15 ft (4.6 m) in all directions from a point where connections are regularly made or disconnected and within the cylindrical volume between the horizontal equator of the sphere and the vessel deck	Division 2

[a]The classified area is prohibited from extending beyond an unpierced wall, roof, or solid vaportight partition.

[b] See Article 500, Hazardous (Classified) Locations, in NFPA 70, *National Electrical Code*, for definitions of classes, groups, and divisions.

[c]See A.6.22.2.2

A.6.22.2.2 When classifying the extent of hazardous areas, consideration should be given to possible variations in the spotting of railroad tank cars and cargo tank vehicles at the unloading points and the effect these variations of actual spotting point can have on the point of connection.

Where specified for the prevention of fire or explosion during normal operation, ventilation is considered adequate where provided in accordance with the provisions of this code.

Prevention of ignition is accomplished by the proper selection and installation of electrical equipment and wiring. A system of classification for areas where ordinary electrical equipment — that is, equipment not possessing a classification as specified — cannot be installed is used and is found in Table 6.22.2.2. Electrical wiring must be installed in accordance with *NFPA 70* [23]. In summary, NFPA 58 identifies the classified areas, and *NFPA 70* states the type of electrical equipment that can be installed within a classified area and how to install it.

The classified areas in Table 6.22.2.2 are based on the experience of the NFPA 58 committee with the types of LP-Gas system installations covered by NFPA 58. Reference is made to *NFPA 70* for the definitions of Division 1 and Division 2 areas. These areas are defined in Article 500 of the 2011 edition of *NFPA 70*, which is reprinted here for the convenience of the reader. Portions not relevant to flammable gases have been omitted.

(B) Class I Locations. Class I locations are those in which flammable gases or vapors are or may be present in the air in quantities sufficient to produce explosive or ignitible mixtures. Class I locations shall include those specified in 500.5(B)(1) and (B)(2).

(1) Class I, Division 1. A Class I, Division 1 location is a location

(1) In which ignitible concentrations of flammable gases or vapors can exist under normal operating conditions, or

(2) In which ignitible concentrations of such gases or vapors may exist frequently because of repair or maintenance operations or because of leakage, or

(3) In which breakdown or faulty operation of equipment or processes might release ignitible concentrations of flammable gases or vapors and might also cause simultaneous failure of electrical equipment in such a way as to directly cause the electrical equipment to become a source of ignition.

Informational Note No. 1: This classification usually includes the following locations:

(1) Where volatile flammable liquids or liquefied flammable gases are transferred from one container to another

(7) Gas generator rooms and other portions of gas manufacturing plants where flammable gas may escape

(8) Inadequately ventilated pump rooms for flammable gas or for volatile flammable liquids

(10) All other locations where ignitible concentrations of flammable vapors or gases are likely to occur in the course of normal operations

Informational Note No. 2: In some Division 1 locations, ignitible concentrations of flammable gases or vapors may be present continuously or for long periods of time. Examples include the following:

(1) The inside of inadequately vented enclosures containing instruments normally venting flammable gases or vapors to the interior of the enclosure

(5) The interior of an exhaust duct that is used to vent ignitible concentrations of gases or vapors

(2) Class I, Division 2. A Class I, Division 2 location is a location

(1) In which volatile flammable liquids or flammable gases are handled, processed, or used, but in which the liquids, vapors, or gases will normally be confined within closed containers or closed systems from which they can escape only in case of accidental rupture or breakdown of such containers or systems or in case of abnormal operation of equipment, or

(2) In which ignitable concentrations of gases or vapors are normally prevented by positive mechanical ventilation, and which might become hazardous through failure or abnormal operation of the ventilating equipment, or

(3) That is adjacent to a Class I, Division 1 location, and to which ignitable concentrations of gases or vapors might occasionally be communicated unless such communication is prevented by adequate positive-pressure ventilation from a source of clean air and effective safeguards against ventilation failure are provided.

Informational Note No. 1: This classification usually includes locations where volatile flammable liquids or flammable gases or vapors are used but that, in the judgment of the authority having jurisdiction, would become hazardous only in case of an accident or of some unusual operating condition. The quantity of flammable material that might escape in case of accident, the adequacy of ventilating equipment, the total area involved, and the record of the industry or business with respect to explosions or fires are all factors that merit consideration in determining the classification and extent of each location.

Informational Note No. 2: Piping without valves, checks, meters, and similar devices would not ordinarily introduce a hazardous condition even though used for flammable liquids or gases. Depending on factors such as the quantity and size of the containers and ventilation, locations used for the storage of flammable liquids or liquefied or compressed gases in sealed containers may be considered either hazardous (classified) or unclassified locations. See NFPA 30-2008, *Flammable and Combustible Liquids Code,* and NFPA 58-2008, *Liquefied Petroleum Gas Code.*
[*NFPA 70,* 2011]

NFPA 70 does not classify areas; this is left to NFPA 58 for areas containing LP-Gas (and to other NFPA codes for other flammable materials, i.e., NFPA 30 [8] for flammable liquids). Therefore, an area is electrically classified in accordance with Table 6.22.2.2, not *NFPA 70.* When using Table 6.22.2.2 it is important to understand that the table's Note b refers to *NFPA 70* for the definitions of Division 1 and Division 2 areas. In simple terms,

NFPA 70 defines a Division 1 area as one where combustible gases are normally present during operation, and a Division 2 area as one where combustible gases are present only under abnormal conditions. Therefore, a point of transfer where a hose is connected for filling is a Division 1 area because escape of some liquid is normal and expected, when the hose is disconnected. (Refer to the reprint of Section 500.5 from *NFPA 70* for the complete definition, if needed.)

The exception for residential and commercial installations incorporated into 6.22.2.4 recognizes that it is impossible to restrict the activities of the people in these occupancies. The activities of employees in industrial occupancies are more easily controlled. For example, in residential and commercial occupancies, NFPA 58 or the officials who enforce it cannot restrict smoking, lighting candles and matches, and open flame cooking. In industrial occupancies, work rules can restrict these activities to unclassified areas. In addition, these residential and commercial structures use ordinary wiring methods and contain only ordinary electrical equipment, such as switches and motors. Consideration of both the fire risk and the expense of the specialized electrical equipment specified for installations in classified areas justifies this exception.

Note that 6.3.7 and Table 6.3.8 provide separation distances from the discharge of a pressure relief valve on a cylinder installed outside of a building and an exterior source of ignition. These distances are smaller than those in Table 6.22.2.2. The requirements in Section 6.3 recognize that when a cylinder is exchanged or filled on site, or when an ASME container is filled on site, a release of propane occurs and the propane can be ignited, but these releases are small in comparison to the releases anticipated by Section 6.22.

Separation distances from sources of ignition to a propane storage container, pump, and transfer area are illustrated in Exhibit 6.52.

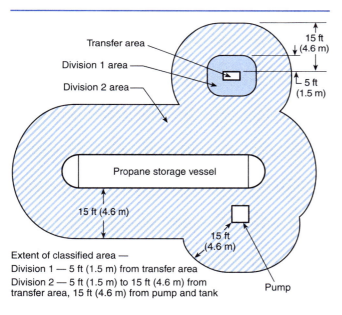

EXHIBIT 6.52 *Plan View Showing Extent of Classified Area. (Courtesy of Superior Energy Systems, Inc.)*

Some confusion remains about the requirements of Parts E and F in Table 6.22.2.2 regarding relief devices on vaporizers. Part E covers all relief valves on containers except cylinders and ASME vertical containers under 1000 lb (0.45 m³) water capacity [about 120 gal (0.45 m³)], including vaporizers. Note that Part E was revised in the 2011 edition to state that fixed electrical equipment is not permitted to be installed in areas covered by Row E. Formerly, it was a recommendation, which is not enforceable.

Part F covers area classification around vaporizers, but is not applicable to relief valves installed on vaporizers. It includes indirect or electric vaporizers. Note that direct-fired vaporizers and indirect-fired vaporizers, with an attached or adjacent gas-fired heat source, are not covered in Part F, and, therefore, no area classification is required. This information was not included because the constant presence of an ignition source (the flame) makes prohibition of other ignition sources unnecessary. If a relief valve is provided on a direct-fired or indirect-fired vaporizer with an attached or adjacent gas-fired heat source, it is covered under Part E. In such a case, no electrical area classification is required if the relief valve is directed away from sources of ignition and is locked or piped to a point at least 5 ft (1.5 m) from a source of ignition.

Part F applies only to pumps, vapor compressors, gas–air mixers, and vaporizers handling LP-Gas. A water pump or air compressor in a room or building separate from the gas equipment is not covered by this requirement. Also, gas–air mixers delivering noncombustible gas mixtures or noncombustible gas with air are not covered by this provision, nor are vaporizers handling noncombustible refrigerants and medical and industrial gases.

The other "exception" in 6.22.2.4 addresses electrical installations on vehicles, which are covered in Section 6.23. In addition to similarities with residential occupancies, noted earlier, a vehicle powered by an internal combustion engine has inherent non-electrical ignition sources, such as an exhaust system, and eliminating its electrical system as an ignition source would be of limited value.

Preventing ignition of a flammable mixture of LP-Gas is accomplished by a combination of installation and operating provisions. Installation provisions include prohibition of open flames and other sources of ignition in certain areas, such as cylinder filling rooms and the areas specified in Table 6.22.2.2. Operating provisions include prohibition of open flames and portable sources of ignition in areas specified in Table 6.22.2.2, unless all LP-Gas is removed or special precautions have been taken under carefully controlled conditions. Examples of open flames identified in the code are cutting or welding, portable electric tools, and extension lights capable of igniting LP-Gas.

6.22.2.3* The provisions of 6.22.2.2 shall apply to vehicular fuel operations.

A.6.22.2.3 See Figure A.6.22.2.3.

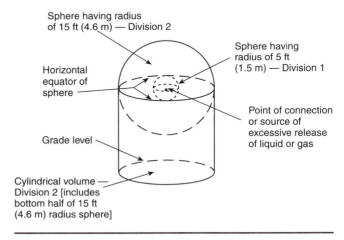

FIGURE A.6.22.2.3 *Extent of Electrically Classified Area.* (See Table 6.22.2.2.)

6.22.2.4 The provisions of 6.22.2.2 shall not apply to fixed electrical equipment at residential or commercial installations of LP-Gas systems or to systems covered by Section 6.23.

6.22.2.5 Fired vaporizers, calorimeters with open flames, and other areas where open flames are present either intermittently or constantly shall not be considered electrically classified areas.

Paragraph 6.22.2.5 covers sources of ignition other than electrical sources. These devices have LP-Gas piped to them and incorporate electrically operated components. This paragraph specifically states that they are not to be declared electrically classified areas because the operation of the devices uses an open flame, which will ignite any released LP-Gas before it can accumulate. In straightforward terms, there is no point in spending money to prevent electrical sources of ignition, when other sources of ignition are present.

6.22.2.6 Electrical equipment installed on LP-Gas cargo tank vehicles shall comply with Section 9.2.

The reference to Section 9.2 reminds the reader that the requirements of Chapter 6 apply only to the installation of fixed LP-Gas systems. Chapter 9 covers systems on LP-Gas cargo tank vehicles.

6.22.3 Other Sources of Ignition.

6.22.3.1 Open flames or other sources of ignition shall not be used or installed in pump houses, cylinder filling rooms, or other similar locations.

6.22.3.2 Direct-fired vaporizers or indirect-fired vaporizers attached or installed adjacent to gas-fired heat sources shall not be installed in pump houses or cylinder filling rooms.

6.22.3.3 Open flames, cutting or welding tools, portable electric tools, and extension lights capable of igniting LP-Gas shall not be installed or used within classified areas specified in Table 6.22.2.2.

6.22.3.4 Open flames or other sources of ignition shall not be prohibited where containers, piping, and other equipment containing LP-Gas have been purged of all liquid and vapor LP-Gas.

Note that 6.22.3.4 was revised in 2011 and now requires that all liquid *and vapor* be removed from containers, piping, and equipment prior to hot work operations. The requirement for purging prior to the use of open flames recognizes that maintenance involving cutting and welding may be needed. A procedure that permits cutting, welding, and similar operations in areas where sources of ignition are normally not permitted because of the threat of fire is provided in NFPA 51B, *Standard for Fire Prevention During Welding, Cutting, and Other Hot Work* [32]. The American Petroleum Institute, the American Gas Association, and the American Welding Society also have publications pertinent to this provision.

6.23 LP-Gas Systems on Vehicles (Other Than Engine Fuel Systems)

6.23.1* Application.

Section 6.23 shall apply to the following:

(1) Nonengine fuel systems on all vehicles
(2) Installations served by exchangeable (removable) cylinder systems and by permanently mounted containers

A.6.23.1 Typical non-engine fuel systems include those on commercial, industrial, construction, and public service vehicles such as trucks, semitrailers, trailers, portable tar kettles, road surface heating equipment, mobile laboratories, clinics, and mobile cooking units (such as catering and canteen vehicles).

A variety of LP-Gas systems are installed on vehicles where the gas is not used as a vehicle engine fuel. Examples of this include the following:

- Tar kettles used in the construction industry mounted on vehicles (usually trailers) for heating tar for roofing
- Food-warming delivery vehicles, such as pretzel/hot dog carts and larger hot dog/lunch wagons, usually mounted on pickup trucks
- Service vehicles that need a source of heated water, such as carpet cleaning services

6.23.2 Nonapplication.

Section 6.23 shall not apply to the following:

(1) Systems installed on mobile homes
(2) Systems installed on recreational vehicles
(3) Cargo tank vehicles, cargo tank vehicles (trailers and semitrailers), and similar units used to transport LP-Gas as cargo, which are covered by Chapter 9
(4) LP-Gas engine fuel systems on the vehicles, which are covered by Chapter 11

Section 6.23 is the counterpart of Chapter 11, Engine Fuel Systems. This section covers all LP-Gas systems mounted on vehicles, other than engine fuel systems, with the following exceptions:

- Manufactured housing (mobile homes). Standards for installations on mobile vehicles for cooking and heating first appeared in the 1950 edition of NFPA 58. These standards were later separated into two different chapters. One focused on systems for manufactured housing, such as mobile homes, and travel trailers, and the other focused on systems for commercial vehicle uses. These provisions formed the basis for the requirements in Chapter 4, Heating, Cooling, and Fuel Burning Systems, of NFPA 501B, *Standard for Mobile Homes* [33]. NFPA 501B was discontinued in 1979 when the U.S. Department of Housing and Urban Development (HUD) preempted NFPA 501B and issued 24 CFR 3280, "Mobile Home Construction and Safety Standard" [34]. NFPA reactivated its manufactured housing project and in 2000 issued NFPA 501, *Standard on Manufactured Housing* [35]. Refer to NFPA 501 for information on repair and maintenance of LP-Gas systems in manufactured housing.

- Recreational vehicles. The provisions of NFPA 58 are used extensively for standards on LP-Gas systems in NFPA 1192, *Standard on Recreational Vehicles* [36].

- Cargo tank vehicles. Cargo tank systems are covered in Chapter 9 of NFPA 58.

- Engine fuel systems. Engine fuel systems are covered in Chapter 11 of NFPA 58.

6.23.3 Container Installation Requirements.

6.23.3.1 Containers shall comply with 6.23.3.1(A) through 6.23.3.1(D).

(A) ASME mobile containers shall have a MAWP of 250 psig (1.7 Mpag) if constructed prior to April 1, 2001, or 312 psig (2.2 MPag) if constructed on or after April 1, 2001.

Note that two items, former (B) and (C), were deleted in the 2011 edition because they restated cylinder construction requirements in 5.2.4.4 and 5.2.4.5. As they are applicable, there is no need to restate them in the installation chapter. In Table 6.23.3.1(C), requirements limiting the capacity of LP-Gas on vehicles are provided. These were relocated from several locations in the code in the 2001 edition. These requirements have existed for many editions. The 1000 gal (3.8 m^3) water capacity limit on road surfacing vehicles [formerly 300 gal (1.14 m^3)

prior to the 1989 edition] is based on the committee's knowledge of units that have performed safely in these operations.

(B) LP-Gas fuel containers used on passenger-carrying vehicles shall not exceed 200 gal (0.8 m³) aggregate water capacity.

(C) The capacity of individual LP-Gas containers on highway vehicles shall be in accordance with Table 6.23.3.1(C).

TABLE 6.23.3.1(C) *Maximum Capacities of Individual LP-Gas Containers Installed on LP-Gas Highway Vehicles*

Vehicle	*Maximum Container Water Capacity*	
	gal	*m³*
Passenger vehicle	200	0.8
Nonpassenger vehicle	300	1.1
Road surfacing vehicle	1000	3.8
Cargo tank vehicle	Not limited by this code	

(D) Containers designed for stationary service only and not in compliance with the container appurtenance protection requirements of 5.2.6 shall not be used.

Provisions for container construction in 6.23.3.1(A) through 6.23.3.1 (D) parallel those for engine fuel containers in Chapter 11. The design pressure for new mobile containers manufactured after April 1, 2001, has been changed to 312 psig (2.2 MPag) from 250 psig (1.7 MPag) to be consistent with the requirements for engine fuel containers in Chapter 11. Paragraph 6.23.3.1(D) is particularly significant with respect to the need for protection of the container appurtenances and their connections. Refer to column 3 of Table 5.7.4.1 for mobile containers, which are defined as follows:

> **3.3.38 Mobile Container.** A container that is permanently mounted on a vehicle and connected for uses other than supplying engine fuel.

A stationary container without the protection specified in 5.2.6 must not be used, because its appurtenances would be vulnerable in the event of a vehicular accident and would not have the appurtenances required in Table 5.7.4.1.

6.23.3.2 ASME containers and cylinders utilized for the purposes covered by Section 6.23 shall not be installed, transported, or stored (even temporarily) inside any vehicle covered by Section 6.23, except for ASME containers installed in accordance with 6.23.3.4(I), Chapter 9, or DOT regulations.

6.23.3.3 The LP-Gas supply system, including the containers, shall be installed either on the outside of the vehicle or in a recess or cabinet vaportight to the inside of the vehicle but accessible from and vented to the outside, with the vents located near the top and bottom of the enclosure and 3 ft (1 m) horizontally away from any opening into the vehicle below the level of the vents.

Containers must be located on the outside of the vehicle, in a recess, or in a vented compartment that is vaportight to the inside of the vehicle, with the following exceptions:

- Those systems that are installed in the vehicle's interior and are similar to engine fuel container installations, which are covered in Section 11.8
- The transportation of cylinders as required in Chapter 9 or by DOT regulations

For example, cylinders used in connection with food warmers on delivery vehicles should be located outside or in a compartment and piped to the appliance inside. Requirements for supply systems on vehicles subject to DOT regulations are contained in 49 CFR 393, "Motor Carrier Safety Regulations" [37], and 49 CFR 177.834, Subpart B, *Hazardous Materials Regulations* [38].

6.23.3.4 Containers shall be mounted securely on the vehicle or within the enclosing recess or cabinet.

(A) Containers shall be installed with road clearance in accordance with 11.8.3.

(B) Fuel containers shall be mounted to prevent jarring loose and slipping or rotating, and the fastenings shall be designed and constructed to withstand, without permanent visible deformation, static loading in any direction equal to four times the weight of the container filled with fuel.

(C) Where containers are mounted within a vehicle housing, the securing of the housing to the vehicle shall comply with this provision. Any removable portions of the housing or cabinet shall be secured while in transit.

(D) Field welding on containers shall be limited to attachments to nonpressure parts such as saddle plates, wear plates, or brackets applied by the container manufacturer.

(E) All container valves, appurtenances, and connections shall be protected to prevent damage from accidental contact with stationary objects; from loose objects, stones, mud, or ice thrown up from the ground or floor; and from damage due to overturn or similar vehicular accident.

(F) Permanently mounted ASME containers shall be located on the vehicle to provide the protection specified in 6.23.3.4(E).

(G) Cylinders shall have permanent protection for cylinder valves and connections.

(H) Where cylinders are located on the outside of a vehicle, weather protection shall be provided.

(I) Containers mounted on the interior of passenger-carrying vehicles shall be installed in compliance with Section 11.9. Pressure relief valve installations for such containers shall comply with 11.8.5.

The container mounting arrangement must be strong enough to remain intact and to protect the container and its appurtenances and connections from damage caused by collisions, road debris, and weather. These provisions do not apply to engine fuel containers, as stated by the reference in 6.21.3.4(I) to Chapter 11.

As with vehicle propulsion engine fuel containers, exterior containers and appurtenances must be protected against material thrown up from the road, as set forth in 6.23.3.4(E). Slush and other hazards thrown up from the road must not block the regulator vent. Splashguards or the practice of locating the regulator in a compartment can protect the regulator vent. A blocked vent can lead to higher than normal pressures in the utilization system and can lead to pilot failure and improper appliance operation. Appurtenances on a container, particularly those mounted below the vehicle, should be installed so that they are accessible for maintenance and readily accessible if needed for normal operations, such as operation of the fixed maximum liquid level gauge during filling.

6.23.3.5 Cylinders installed on portable tar kettles alongside the kettle, on the vehicle frame, or on road surface heating equipment shall be protected from radiant or convected heat from open flame or other burners by the use of a heat shield or by the location of the cylinder(s) on the vehicle. In addition, the following shall apply:

(1) Cylinder valves shall be closed when burners are not in use.

(2) Cylinders shall not be refilled while burners are in use as provided in 7.2.3.2(B).

Tar kettles are used in the roofing industry and represent one of the most frequently used applications of LP-Gas systems on vehicles, and are also one of the more difficult to control, due to their portable nature. To the editor's knowledge, no standards exist for the construction and use of tar kettles. One state has issued rules to cover tar kettles, however. The State of Michigan Department of Labor & Economic Growth provides, in Part 24 of its Construction Safety Standards [39], rules for the construction and use of tar kettles.

As for the requirements in NFPA 58, cylinders should be mounted so that no wear takes place; for example, chains can cut grooves in cylinders due to vehicular motion. Most tar kettles use liquid burners, so the right type of cylinder and appurtenances must be used. The word "liquid" is stamped on the cylinder next to the liquid withdrawal connection. A metal barrier or some other physical protection is required between the tar kettle and the cylinder to protect the cylinder from becoming overheated due to its proximity to the tar kettle.

6.23.4 Installation of Container Appurtenances.

6.23.4.1 Container appurtenances shall be installed in accordance with the following:

(1) Pressure relief valve installation on ASME containers installed in the interior of vehicles complying with Section 11.9 shall comply with 11.8.5.

(2) Pressure relief valve installations on ASME containers installed on the outside of vehicles shall comply with 11.8.5 and 6.23.3.3.

(3) Main shutoff valves on containers for liquid and vapor shall be readily accessible.

(4) Cylinders shall be designed to be filled in either the vertical or horizontal position, or if they are the universal type, they are permitted to be filled in either position.

(5) All container inlets, outlets, or valves installed in container inlets or outlets, except pressure relief devices and gauging devices, shall be labeled to designate whether they communicate with the vapor or liquid space.

(6) Containers from which only vapor is to be withdrawn shall be installed and equipped with connections to minimize the possibility of the accidental withdrawal of liquid.

The three types of fuel container installations affect how the pressure relief valve is installed and located. These installations are as follows:

1. Cylinders in a cabinet or recess in accordance with 6.23.3.3, for which pipe away of the pressure relief valve is not required

2. Containers installed in the interior of passenger-carrying vehicles, which are permitted in Section 11.9, with relief valve pipe away in accordance with 11.8.5.2

3. Containers mounted on the exterior of vehicles, which is allowed per 6.23.3.3. Paragraph 11.8.5.2(F) provides specific requirements for the pressure relief valve pipe away system, if used. [See 11.8.5.2(F) for requirements for protecting the pressure relief valve outlet (valve or discharge piping) from being plugged with dirt, asphalt, or water.]

6.23.4.2 Regulators shall be installed in accordance with 6.8.2 and 6.23.4.2(A) through 6.23.4.2(E).

(A) Regulators shall be installed with the pressure relief vent opening pointing vertically downward to allow for drainage of moisture collected on the diaphragm of the regulator.

(B) Regulators not installed in compartments shall be equipped with a durable cover designed to protect the regulator vent opening from sleet, snow, freezing rain, ice, mud, and wheel spray.

(C) If vehicle-mounted regulators are installed at or below the floor level, they shall be installed in a compartment that provides protection against the weather and wheel spray.

(D) Regulator compartments shall comply with the following:

(1) The compartment shall be of sufficient size to allow tool operation for connection to and replacement of the regulators(s).
(2) The compartment shall be vaportight to the interior of the vehicle.
(3) The compartment shall have a 1 in.^{2} (650 mm^2) minimum vent opening to the exterior located within 1 in. (25 mm) of the bottom of the compartment.
(4) The compartment shall not contain flame or spark-producing equipment.

(E) A regulator vent outlet shall be at least 2 in. (51 mm) above the compartment vent opening.

Two-stage pressure regulation must be used in all systems covered in Section 6.23. Multiple regulators provide several safety features, which are described in the commentary following 6.8.2.

Regulators (and cylinders) used on vehicles are usually installed in a compartment for security and to comply with the requirement for protection of regulators from sleet, snow, freezing rain, and so forth. The enclosure cannot contain electrical devices that are a source of ignition and must be ventilated to allow any propane that might be released to disperse. Louvers in the compartment or its door are usually used to provide this required ventilation. Louvers must communicate with the outdoors and not to the interior of the vehicle.

6.23.5 Piping.

6.23.5.1 Piping shall be installed in accordance with 6.9.3 and 6.23.5.1(A) through 6.23.5.1(M).

The requirements for piping all vehicular-type installations are located in 6.23.5. The main lines and branch connections must be kept outside the vehicle so that if leakage occurs, gas will not accumulate in the vehicle. No fuel lines can be connected between two vehicular units, in order to avoid compounding problems in the event of collisions, overturns, and disconnection of vehicles. These types of risks are regarded as greater than the corresponding risks in a system located completely on one vehicle.

(A) Steel tubing shall have a minimum wall thickness of 0.049 in. (1.2 mm).

Steel tubing in vehicular installations has been specified as having a minimum 0.049 in. (1.2 mm) wall thickness to provide strength against vibration and also to provide an additional tolerance for corrosion. This provision came about as a result of experience with steel tubing during World War II, when copper tubing was not available.

(B) A flexible connector shall be installed between the regulator outlet and the fixed piping system to protect against expansion, contraction, jarring, and vibration strains.

(C) Flexibility shall be provided in the piping between a cylinder and the gas piping system or regulator.

(D) Flexible connectors shall be installed in accordance with 6.9.6.

(E) Flexible connectors longer than the length allowed in the code, or fuel lines that incorporate hose, shall be used only where approved.

The requirement in 6.23.5.1(E) was changed to reflect the new requirement that permits hoses up to 6 ft (1.8 m) in length to be used without obtaining the approval of the authority having jurisdiction. See 6.19.2.6 for hose requirements.

(F) The fixed piping system shall be designed, installed, supported, and secured to minimize the possibility of damage due to vibration, strains, or wear and to preclude any loosening while in transit.

(G) Piping shall be installed in a protected location.

(H) Where piping is installed outside the vehicle, it shall be installed as follows:

(1) Piping shall be under the vehicle and below any insulation or false bottom.
(2) Fastening or other protection shall be installed to prevent damage due to vibration or abrasion.
(3) At each point where piping passes through sheet metal or a structural member, a rubber grommet or equivalent protection shall be installed to prevent chafing.

(I) Gas piping shall be installed to enter the vehicle through the floor directly beneath or adjacent to the appliance served.

(J) If a branch line is installed, the tee connection shall be located in the main gas line under the floor and outside the vehicle.

(K) Exposed parts of the fixed piping system either shall be of corrosion-resistant material or shall be coated or protected to minimize exterior corrosion.

(L) Hydrostatic relief valves shall be installed in isolated sections of liquid piping as provided in Section 6.13.

(M) Piping systems, including hose, shall be pressure tested and proven free of leaks in accordance with Section 6.14.

Note the numerous requirements for connections to be outside of the vehicle. This helps to ensure that any leaks will occur where there will be rapid dispersion of the leaking gas.

6.23.5.2 There shall be no fuel connection between a tractor and trailer or other vehicle units.

6.23.6 Equipment Installation.

Equipment shall be installed in accordance with Section 6.17, 6.23.6.1, and 6.23.6.2.

6.23.6.1 Installation shall be made in accordance with the manufacturer's recommendations and, in the case of approved equipment, as provided in the approval.

6.23.6.2 Equipment installed on vehicles shall be protected against vehicular damage as provided for container appurtenances and connections in 6.23.3.4(C).

6.23.7 Appliance Installation on Vehicles.

6.23.7.1 Subsection 6.23.7 shall apply to the installation of all appliances on vehicles. It shall not apply to engines.

6.23.7.2 All appliances covered by 6.23.7 installed on vehicles shall be approved.

6.23.7.3 Where the device or appliance is designed to be in operation while the vehicle is in transit, such as a cargo heater or cooler, means to stop the flow of gas in the event of a line break, such as an excess-flow valve, shall be installed.

Appliances, such as cargo tank heaters, are used in vehicles, and the vibration that occurs while vehicles are in transit can result in fittings loosening or becoming disconnected. This requirement recognizes that possibility and requires a positive means of stopping the flow if fittings are disconnected. Note that excess-flow valves are given as an example of protection, but other types of protection can be used. Excess-flow valves will close only when the design flow is reached and may not operate in the event of a partial separation of a fitting. If the vehicle comes under DOT regulations, reference should be made to the DOT requirements that may apply.

6.23.7.4 Gas-fired heating appliances shall be equipped with shutoffs in accordance with 5.20.7(A), except for portable heaters used with cylinders having a maximum water capacity of 2.7 lb (1.2 kg), portable torches, melting pots, and tar kettles.

Note that the requirement was revised in the 2011 edition by removing the reference to 6.19.2.8(2) and restating the requirement here, to make it easier to use. The requirements in 5.20.7(A) refer to 100 percent pilot safety shutoffs. These safety devices are required on all heating appliances except for tar kettle burners. Hand torches, melting pots, and small heaters using a torch-type cylinder are exempted because they are attended appliances.

6.23.7.5 Gas-fired heating appliances, other than ranges and illuminating appliances installed on vehicles intended for human occupancy, shall be designed or installed to provide for a complete separation of the combustion system from the atmosphere inside the vehicle.

The concept of isolating the combustion system of appliances — except ranges in vehicle interiors where passengers might be — is consistent with all other vehicle standards on this subject, such as the standards for recreational vehicles. No portable or conventional room heaters should be used inside such vehicles. Isolation may be accomplished through the use of direct-vent-type heaters and water heaters or through separation by installing the appliance in a compartment with provisions for outside air. The range is an attended appliance and need not be isolated, but it should never be used for comfort heating.

Note that although extensive requirements for the installation of appliances fueled by LP-Gas are included in NFPA 54, that code is limited to those appliances connected to a fixed building piping system. The appliances covered under NFPA 58 are those not normally connected to a fixed building piping system.

6.23.7.6* Where unvented-type heaters that are designed to protect cargo are used on vehicles not intended for human occupancy, provisions shall be made to provide air from the outside for combustion and dispose of the products of combustion to the outside.

A.6.23.7.6 Requirements for the design of containers are located in Section 5.2. Requirements for container appurtenances are located in Section 5.3.

6.23.7.7 Appliances installed in the cargo space of a vehicle shall be readily accessible whether the vehicle is loaded or empty.

6.23.7.8 Appliances shall be constructed or otherwise protected to minimize possible damage or impaired operation due to cargo shifting or handling.

6.23.7.9 Appliances shall be located so that a fire at any appliance will not block egress of persons from the vehicle.

6.23.7.10 A permanent caution plate shall be provided, affixed to either the appliance or the vehicle outside of any enclosure and adjacent to the container(s), and shall include the following items:

CAUTION:
(1) Be sure all appliance valves are closed before opening container valve.
(2) Connections at the appliances, regulators, and containers shall be checked periodically for leaks with soapy water or its equivalent.
(3) Never use a match or flame to check for leaks.
(4) Container valves shall be closed when equipment is not in use.

6.23.8 General Precautions.

Mobile units containing hot plates and other cooking equipment, including mobile kitchens and catering vehicles, shall be provided with at least one approved portable fire extinguisher rated in accordance with NFPA 10, *Standard for Portable Fire Extinguishers*, at not less than

10-B:C. Where fire extinguishers have more than one letter classification, they can be considered as meeting the requirements of each letter class.

6.23.9 Parking, Servicing, and Repair.

6.23.9.1 Where vehicles with LP-Gas fuel systems used for purposes other than propulsion are parked, serviced, or repaired inside buildings, the requirements of 6.23.9.2 through 6.23.9.4 shall apply.

6.23.9.2 The fuel system shall be leak-free, and the container(s) shall not be filled beyond the limits specified in Chapter 7.

Specific requirements for the parking, servicing, and repair of vehicles that have non–engine fuel LP-Gas systems are provided in 6.23.9.1. Note that recreational vehicles are not addressed because they are covered by NFPA 1192, *Standard on Recreational Vehicles* [36]. Subsection 6.23.9 also does not address manufactured housing, which is covered under federal regulations, or vehicles used to transport LP-Gas as cargo, which are covered under Chapter 9 of this code.

The requirements in 6.23.9 are similar to those for vehicles using LP-Gas as an engine fuel (see Section 11.15). Vehicles having a total LP-Gas capacity of more than 300 lb (136 kg) are required to follow the more detailed requirements of Section 9.7.

6.23.9.3 The container shutoff valve shall be closed, except that the container shutoff valve shall not be required to be closed when fuel is required for test or repair.

6.23.9.4 The vehicle shall not be parked near sources of heat, open flames, or similar sources of ignition, or near unventilated pits.

6.23.9.5 Vehicles having containers with water capacities larger than 300 gal (1.1 m³) shall comply with the requirements of Section 9.7.

6.24 Vehicle Fuel Dispenser and Dispensing Stations

Section 6.24 provides requirements in one place for vehicle fuel dispensers and dispensing stations/propane vehicle fueling stations, as shown in Exhibit 6.53. The use of propane as an engine fuel is increasing to meet environmental requirements, and the number of propane fueling stations is also projected to increase significantly. Historically, propane vehicle fueling stations have been located at propane bulk plants or private fueling facilities where privately owned vehicles and fleets use propane as an engine fuel. NFPA 58 applies to such installations. It does not apply to locations where propane is dispensed with other vehicle fuels. Refer to NFPA 30A, *Code for Motor Fuel Dispensing Facilities and Repair Garages* [10], which includes a separate chapter — Chapter 12, Additional Requirements for CNG, LNG, Hydrogen, and LPG — to address the requirements for installing propane dispensers at service stations.

In the United States and in the rest of the world, propane and compressed natural gas have been identified as "alternate fuels" to gasoline for powering motor vehicles. Where this is done, engine emissions, such as carbon monoxide and unburned hydrocarbons, are significantly reduced, making these fuels more environmentally friendly.

Governments all over the world are working with industry and environmental groups to promote the use of alternate vehicle fuels, including propane, compressed natural gas, and hydrogen, in fleet operations and in privately owned personal vehicles. The selection of fuels usually is based on a combination of perceived safety, cost, and local availability. This promotion of the use of alternate fuels has led to a need to promote these fuels beyond the typical private fleet dispensing operations and to make them available at existing commercial gasoline automotive service stations.

EXHIBIT 6.53 *Dispensing Station for Propane Vehicles. (Courtesy of CleanFuel USA)*

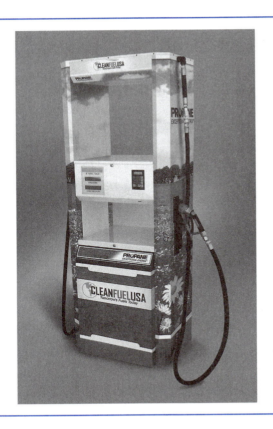

Table 6.5.3 specifies distances from points of transfer and exposures. This table applies to the location of the filling of cylinders that are not installed, which includes all cylinders brought to a dispensing station for filling. The table provides separation distances from points of transfer — for example, the hose end — to several important exposures, including public ways, buildings with and without fire-resistive walls, mainline railroad track centerlines, outdoor places of public assembly, and flammable liquids dispensers.

6.24.1 Application.

6.24.1.1 Section 6.24 includes the location, installation, and operation of vehicle fuel dispensers and dispensing stations.

6.24.1.2 The provisions of Sections 6.2 and 6.3, as modified by Section 6.24, shall apply.

6.24.2 Location.

6.24.2.1 Location of vehicle fuel dispensers and dispensing stations shall be in accordance with Table 6.5.3.

6.24.2.2 Vehicle fuel dispensers and dispensing stations shall be located away from pits in accordance with Table 6.5.3, with no drains or blow-offs from the unit directed toward or within 15 ft (4.6 m) of a sewer system's opening.

6.24.3 General Installation Provisions.

6.24.3.1 Vehicle fuel dispensers and dispensing stations shall be installed in accordance with the manufacturer's installation instructions.

Vehicle fuel dispensers and dispensing stations are typically manufactured as complete units for installation in the field. Some of these units are listed, but even if they are not, the manufacturer's installation instructions must be followed.

6.24.3.2 Vehicle fuel dispensers and dispensing stations shall not be located within a building, except as allowed in Chapter 10.

The requirement in 6.24.3.2 is another example of the restriction against piping liquid LP-Gas into a building or structure that is not specifically designed for such piping, in accordance with Chapter 10.

6.24.3.3 Where a vehicle fuel dispenser is installed under a weather shelter or canopy, the area shall be ventilated and shall not be enclosed for more than 50 percent of its perimeter.

The requirements of 6.24.3.3 are concerned with the need to disperse any vapors that may be released during the fueling process to avoid the formation of a flammable propane–air mixture. The requirement also provides guidance on how much of a weather shelter can be installed without the area being considered an indoor location. It is conceivable that the shelter could have three full-width walls and still might meet the requirement to be open for at least 50 percent of its perimeter, if an opening is provided at the base of each wall, thus providing for ventilation from all sides and decreasing the possibility that a flammable mixture could be present. The acceptability of this option should be cleared with the authority having jurisdiction prior to installing a shelter using this configuration. If an installation is considered to be an indoor installation, compliance with Chapter 10 is mandated.

6.24.3.4 Control for the pump used to transfer LP-Gas through the unit into containers shall be provided at the device in order to minimize the possibility of leakage or accidental discharge.

This requirement does not necessarily reduce the possibility of a leak occurring, but it can reduce the impact of the leak by allowing the operator to quickly stop the flow of product from the pump.

6.24.3.5 An excess-flow check valve or a differential back pressure valve shall be installed in or on the dispenser at the point at which the dispenser hose is connected to the liquid piping.

A differential back pressure valve is used with an LP-Gas meter measuring liquid. The purpose of the differential backflow pressure valve is to ensure that vapor is not introduced into the metering system. Vapor passing through a meter designed for liquid would cause an inaccurate delivery. The differential back pressure valve works in conjunction with the vapor eliminator (located upstream of the meter) to stop flow through the meter when vapor is detected in the piping upstream of the meter. See Exhibit 6.54 for a graphical explanation of the operation of a differential back pressure valve.

See the commentary following 5.17.5.1 for more information on meters.

Therefore, 6.24.3.5 requires either an excess-flow valve or a differential pressure/meter assembly to be installed at the point that the dispenser hose connects to the liquid piping in the dispenser unit.

6.24.3.6 Piping and the dispensing hose shall be provided with hydrostatic relief valves in accordance with Section 6.13.

6.24.3.7 Protection against trespassing and tampering shall be in accordance with 6.18.4.

Security is important for dispensing stations, both for filling cylinders and for buildings. Access to the dispenser and its controls must be limited to trained operators, and the equipment must be secured to prevent tampering when not attended. Options in 6.18.4 include fences and locking the equipment.

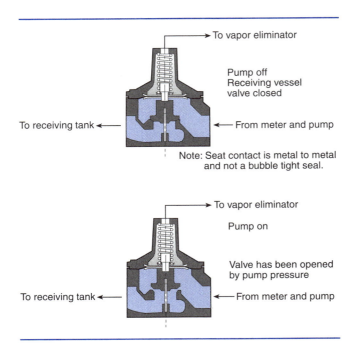

EXHIBIT 6.54 *Operation of Differential Back Pressure Valve. (Courtesy of Liquid Controls, Inc.)*

6.24.3.8 The container liquid withdrawal opening used with vehicle fuel dispensers and dispensing stations shall be equipped with one of the following:

(1) An internal valve fitted for remote closure and automatic shutoff using thermal (fire) actuation
(2) A positive shutoff valve that is located as close to the container as practical in combination with an excess-flow valve installed in the container, plus an emergency shutoff valve that is fitted for remote closure and installed downstream in the line as close as practical to the positive shutoff valve

6.24.3.9 An identified and accessible remote emergency shutoff device for either the internal valve or the emergency shutoff valve required by 6.24.3.8(1) or (2) shall be installed not less than 3 ft (1 m) or more than 100 ft (30 m) from the liquid transfer point.

6.24.3.10 Emergency shutoff valves and internal valves that are fitted for remote closure as required in this section shall be tested annually for proper operation.

Paragraphs 6.24.3.8 through 6.24.3.10 recognize that remote closures with thermal actuation are important devices for providing a safe means for shutting off product releases in the event of an emergency. Generally, dispensers are located in public areas. Equipping dispenser stations with remote shutoffs fitted with thermal actuation will provide an additional level of safety for dispensers. The requirement also requires testing to verify that the shutoff devices remain in good operating condition.

6.24.3.11 A manual shutoff valve and an excess-flow check valve shall be located in the liquid line between the pump and the dispenser inlet where the dispensing device is installed at a remote location and is not part of a complete storage and dispensing unit mounted on a common base.

6.24.3.12 All dispensers either shall be installed on a concrete foundation or shall be part of a complete storage and dispensing unit mounted on a common base and installed in accordance with 6.6.3.1(G). Protection against physical damage shall be provided for dispensers.

Anchorage of a dispenser helps to ensure that the breakaway device mandated in 6.24.4.2 operates properly. Physical protection is also required and is often needed in areas where vehicular traffic is normal.

6.24.3.13 A listed quick-acting shutoff valve shall be installed at the discharge end of the transfer hose.

A listed quick-acting shutoff valve must be installed at the end of the transfer hose, which helps the operator of the dispenser quickly shut off the flow of liquid when the vehicle fuel tank or the cylinder reaches its maximum capacity. A gate valve or globe valve does not meet this requirement, as it can take a few seconds to screw closed these valves. The container can become significantly overfilled while the valve is being closed. Also, flow can be stopped quickly should a leak suddenly become apparent.

6.24.3.14 An identified and accessible switch or circuit breaker shall be installed at a location not less than 20 ft (6.1 m) or more than 100 ft (30.5 m) from the dispensing device(s) to shut off the power in the event of a fire, an accident, or other emergency.

Specific minimum and maximum distances for a shutoff switch to the dispenser are provided. A sign or other marking (see 6.24.3.15) must identify the location of the switch so that the dispenser can be shut off either from the vicinity of the dispenser or from a remote location.

There are places where limiting the switch location to the specified distance can result in an installation that fails to meet the intent of the requirement, such as a lot where the specified distance range is nothing but an area where vehicles are moving about. In such a location, the authority having jurisdiction may allow the distance to be slightly extended in order to provide a safe and useful installation. Reducing the distance may make it inaccessible in the event of a release, especially if it results in a fire, so reducing the distance should not be considered. In all such instances, the authority having jurisdiction should be consulted prior to the installation.

6.24.3.15 The markings for the switches or breakers shall be visible at the point of liquid transfer.

It is important that the markings locating the switches or breakers be legible from the transfer point and that obstructions and signs not be placed so that the markings are hidden.

6.24.4 Installation of Vehicle Fuel Dispensers.

Additional requirements for vehicle fuel dispensers that supplement those provided in 6.24.3 are located in 6.24.4.

6.24.4.1 Hose shall comply with the following:

(1) Hose length shall not exceed 18 ft (5.5 m) unless approved by the authority having jurisdiction.
(2) All hose shall be listed.
(3) When not in use, hose shall be secured to protect them from damage.

The provision in 6.24.4.1 is modeled after 12.2.4 of NFPA 30A. The 18 ft (5.5 m) limit on hose length comes from the U.S. Bureau of Weights and Measures. The normal maximum hose length may be exceeded when needed, with the approval of the authority having jurisdiction. One consideration for the authority having jurisdiction is that the excess flow valve at the hose/piping interface will still function if the hose fails near the delivery end. A long hose can restrict flow enough so that the excess flow valve will fail to close.

6.24.4.2 A listed emergency breakaway device complying with ANSI/UL 567, *Standard Pipe Connectors for Flammable and Combustible Liquids and LP-Gas,* and designed to retain liquid on both sides of the breakaway point, or other devices affording equivalent protection approved by the authority having jurisdiction, shall be installed.

Pull away incidents have occurred with gasoline, diesel, and propane fuel dispensers. Anchorage of the breakaway device in accordance with the manufacturer's instructions is required to ensure that the dispenser operates properly. If the dispenser does not provide anchorage, a separate post or other means of anchorage may be necessary.

6.24.4.3 Dispensing devices for LP-Gas shall be located as follows:

(1) Conventional systems shall be at least 10 ft (3.0 m) from any dispensing device for Class I liquids.
(2) Low-emission transfer systems in accordance with Section 6.26 shall be at least 5 ft (1.5 m) from any dispensing device for Class I liquids.

The requirement in 6.24.4.3(2) requires a 5 ft (1.5 m) separation of a low emission propane dispenser and a dispenser for Class I flammable liquids, such as gasoline.

6.25 Fire Protection

Section 6.25 addresses fire protection provisions for LP-Gas storage containers and installations and requires coordinating control measures with local emergency response agencies through an analysis of local conditions.

The written fire safety analysis is intended to produce a report that evaluates the product control technology used and the planning activities of both plant personnel and emergency response agencies to address an incident occurring at the installation or an incident at a neighboring facility that could affect the LP-Gas storage installation. Additional information on the fire safety analysis is located in Supplement 1. A manual on preparing a fire safety analysis is available at no cost.

Note that 6.25.2.1 requires that planning be made for incidents involving security breaches of the plant.

The code does not require a fire safety analysis for installations having storage containers with an aggregate water capacity of 4000 gal (15.1 m³) or less. Storage containers and their appurtenances have specific safety features built into them. All installations must be made properly and require proper maintenance of equipment. Safe operating procedures must also be in place. All these components taken together provide effective measures to control a release or fire condition for typical installations. Although no requirements exist for installations under 4000 gal (15.1 m³) water capacity, there may be extenuating circumstances in which additional fire protection designs for smaller facilities may be considered.

Installations having storage containers with an aggregate water capacity of more than 4000 gal (15.1 m³) and installations of ASME containers on roofs must have a fire safety analysis to determine whether fire protection is necessary to protect the storage containers from exposure to a single fire. If the review determines that a "hazard to adjacent structures exists that exceeds the protection provided by the provisions of the code" (see 6.25.3.6), special protection must be provided. The following five methods of achieving special protection are specified in 6.25.5:

1. Insulation (See 6.25.5.1.)
2. Mounding (See 6.25.5.3.)
3. Burial (See 6.25.5.4.)
4. Water spray fixed systems (See 6.25.6.1.)
5. Monitor nozzles (See 6.25.6.3.)

Three important factors should be considered before and during any fire safety analysis. They are as follows:

1. Evaluate the proposed facility, product control features, and operating procedures to determine whether additional fire protection is needed.
2. If fire protection is needed, consider installation and design changes, additional product control features, and improved operating procedures to ensure that a serious hazard will not exist at the facility.
3. Ensure the safety of facility employees, members of the general public, emergency response personnel, and property surrounding the installation.

Fire department response capability and available water source(s) are also significant factors in evaluating the mitigation of hazards at a proposed installation. These factors have historically been most important in assessing the fire safety of many different buildings and occupancies. However, significant changes in NFPA 58 have shifted the focus of fire protection to the design of the facility and the mandated product control safety features. Following this path ensures that no accumulation of combustible materials will take place near tank installations. The use of product control measures eliminates exposure of storage containers to LP-Gas fires, thus greatly reducing the risks associated with the storage of LP-Gases.

A manual on conducting a fire safety analysis [6], based on the requirements of the 2001, 2004, or 2008 edition of NFPA 58, has been developed by NFPA in cooperation with the National Propane Gas Association (NPGA). The first edition of this manual based on the requirements of the 2001 edition of NFPA 58 is also available for those jurisdictions using the 2001 edition, and it is anticipated that a manual based on the requirements of the 2011 edition will be available. This manual was funded by a grant from the Propane Education and Research Council. The manual is available at no cost from www.nfpa.org. Search for "fsa" or "fire safety analysis" on nfpa.org to locate the manual. Refer to Supplement 1 of this handbook for more information on the subject.

6.25.1 Application.

Section 6.25 applies to fire protection for industrial plants, bulk plants, and dispensing stations.

Note that in 2011 the text was changed from "LP-Gas facilities" to "industrial plants, bulk plants, and dispensing stations" to be more specific and to replace the term "LP-Gas facilities," which is not defined and is not used in other parts of the code.

6.25.2* Planning.

Note that planning for inadvertent releases, fire, and security breaches must be coordinated with local police and fire agencies for all installations, not just those with storage in excess of 4000 gal (15.1 m³).

A.6.25.2 The wide range in size, arrangement, and location of LP-Gas installations covered by this code precludes the inclusion of detailed fire protection provisions completely applicable to all installations. Provisions in Section 6.25 are subject to verification or modification through analysis of local conditions.

The National Fire Protection Association, American Petroleum Institute, and National Propane Gas Association publish material, including visual aids, useful in such planning.

6.25.2.1 The planning for the response to incidents including the inadvertent release of LP-Gas, fire, or security breach shall be coordinated with local emergency response agencies.

One of the most critical aspects of effective emergency response is the ability of the emergency response agency to act on knowledge it has of the facility involved. Therefore, the code requires that facility operators coordinate the planning for the response to emergencies at their facilities with the appropriate agencies. The planning should include familiarizing emergency responders with the function and location of features and equipment that stop the release of product. Many propane plants invite local fire fighters to view the plant and be made aware of the safety features that can be used to stop escaping LP-Gas in the event of an accident.

6.25.2.2 Planning shall include consideration of the safety of emergency personnel, workers, and the public.

In establishing an incident response plan, it is important to know the variety of installations that are subject to the requirements of NFPA 58. The range of installations addressed in NFPA 58 includes the following:

- A 20 lb (9.1 kg) LP-Gas capacity cylinder that is refilled at a dispensing station or exchanged twice a year and used to fuel a gas grill at a single-family residence in a city
- One or two 100 lb (45 kg) cylinders that are filled by a bobtail or exchanged once a month and used to fuel a home in a rural area
- Several 30,000 gal (114 m³) LP-Gas containers with liquid transfer and associated transportation operations being conducted more or less continually at a bulk plant or industrial plant (and larger storage facilities at marine and pipeline terminals) in a heavily populated or congested area
- Any combination of 5000 gal to 30,000 gal (19 to 114 m³) LP-Gas containers (single or multiple) at an industrial facility that also contains a number of hazardous and/or flammable materials and may be situated in a heavily populated area, industrial park, or rural location

The need for and character of fire protection provisions in the variety of installations described here can vary widely. In fact, these requirements can be determined only by studying each installation and the hazards with which it is associated.

Fire departments and hazardous materials teams may not have as much knowledge about propane as the propane plant operator has. Therefore, planning for emergencies must include training of emergency responders to enable them to deal safely with any risks. This training should include awareness of the facility design and total product control features available to prevent a release or a fire.

Because training facilities are expensive to install and operate, there are only a few in the United States. The following are three of the largest facilities:

- Texas A&M University, Texas Engineering Extension Service, College Station, TX
- Massachusetts Firefighting Academy, Stow, MA
- Nassau County Fire Academy, Long Island, NY

The need for this hands-on training is being recognized increasingly, however, and the creation of new facilities can be anticipated.

If a facility is located within an area served by one or more emergency services such as public fire departments, police departments, and ambulance services, facility management has a right to expect assistance from these sources in the event of an emergency. Management has a duty to obtain this assistance without requiring the emergency personnel to accept undue risks. The resolution of this risk factor is a key element in the fire safety analysis process. Training and familiarization with the facility are the best ways to provide the knowledge that can minimize this risk.

In some locations, especially where many chemical and petrochemical facilities operate, agreements state that public emergency response services will not enter the facilities. Rather, the facilities maintain trained personnel at all times and provide their own mutual aid. In these cases, the facilities do not require or expect assistance from publicly funded emergency services.

Two NFPA films on propane are available: "LP-Gas: Emergency Planning and Response" [40], which is somewhat dated, but serves as a useful tactical training instrument; and "BLEVE Update" [41], which provides current information on BLEVEs. In addition, the NPGA, with assistance from the Propane Education and Research Council, has developed an educational program for emergency responders called "Propane Emergencies, Facilitator's Guide" [42]. It includes a training text, facilitator's guide with a companion video, and a presentation CD-ROM for instructors.

Supplement 1, Guidelines for Conducting a Fire Safety Analysis, contains a thorough discussion of the factors needed to plan for an LP-Gas emergency.

6.25.3* Protection of ASME Containers.

A.6.25.3 In recent years, the concept of total product control systems has been developed. Facilities that have redundant automatic product control systems provide a high level of confidence that propane will not be released during an emergency. Therefore, not only will the storage be protected from a fire that could lead to container rupture, but major fires at the facility would be prevented. The public would be protected, fire-fighting operations would be safer, and applications of large quantities of water would not be needed to prevent tank failure.

A fire safety analysis should include the following:

(1) Effectiveness of product control measures
(2) Analysis of local conditions of hazard within the container site
(3) Exposure to or from other properties, population density, and congestion within the site
(4) Probable effectiveness of plant fire brigades or local fire departments, based on adequate water supply, response time, and training
(5) Consideration for the adequate application of water by hose stream or other method for effective control of leakage, fire, or other exposures
(6) If necessary, designated time period for review of the fire safety analysis with local emergency response agencies to ensure preplanning and emergency response plans for the installation are current

The National Fire Protection Association and the National Propane Gas Association, through a grant with the Propane Education and Research Council, have developed and published the "Fire Safety Analysis Manual for LP-Gas Storage Facilities" in order to provide a format and guidance for the performance of a fire safety analysis in conjunction with the requirements of NFPA 58.

6.25.3.1 Fire protection shall be provided for installations with an aggregate water capacity of more than 4000 gal (15.1 m³) and for ASME containers on roofs.

The term *fire protection* in 6.25.3.1 is defined in 3.3.22. The primary means of fire protection provided for installations conforming to NFPA 58 is the ability to control the product (LP-Gas) within the system. Requirements in 5.7.4 and Section 6.11 for internal valves and Section 6.12 for emergency shutoff valves for larger installations provide the foundation for the most up-to-date product control systems used in the industry. Other means for providing fire protection are discussed throughout Section 6.25.

The application of 6.25.3.1 is dependent upon aggregate storage quantity. Normally the aggregate quantity is clear, but the application to a number of containers installed close to each other and serving different users has required interpretation.

◀ **FAQ**
For the purposes of 6.25.3.1, how is "aggregate storage" determined?

The technical committee recognized this and issued a formal interpretation that addresses aggregate storage not in terms of property lines, but solely on the location of multiple containers with respect to one another. In other words, the threat of fire exposure from one container to another is dependent upon the distance of that container to the second container. See Formal Interpretation 58-04-4.

Formal Interpretation
NFPA 58
Liquefied Petroleum Gas Code
2011 Edition

Reference: 6.25.3.1

F.I. No.: 58-04-4

Question: Is it the intent of the term "aggregate water capacity" as in used in Paragraph 6.23.3.1 to include only those containers separated from each other by distances less than those stated in the aboveground containers column of Table 6.3.1?

Answer: Yes.

Issue Edition: 2004

Reference: 6.23.3.1

Issue Date: November 8, 2005

Effective Date: March 22, 2006

This means that multiple storage tanks in one location, where the separation distance is less than the separation distance for aboveground containers in Table 6.3.1, are considered to be one installation for which a fire safety analysis is required. For example, if three 2000 gal (7.6 m³) propane containers are separated by less than 25 ft (7.6 m), a fire safety analysis is required by Table 6.3.1 whether the containers are manifolded together or if they serve different buildings. If the containers are located without sufficient separation, the capacities of the containers are aggregated. If this brings them to a total of more than 4000 gal (15.1 m³), then the requirements of 6.25.3.1 apply. Whether or not they are interconnected is immaterial. It also means that interconnection does not mean aggregation. For instance, if there are two groups of four 1000 gal (3.8 m³) tanks with at least 25 ft between the groups, and the tanks all deliver to a common point through one piping system, this installation does not need to meet the requirements of this paragraph.

6.25.3.2 The modes of fire protection shall be specified in a written fire safety analysis for new installations, and for existing installations that have an aggregate water capacity of more than 4000 gal (15.1 m³), and for ASME containers on roofs. Existing installation shall comply with this requirement within 2 years of the effective date of this code.

The requirement for a fire safety analysis for installations with more than 4000 gal (15.1 m³) total water capacity reflects the committee's acknowledgement of the public's concern for a greater severity of an accident where larger storage quantities are involved. The review will identify any potential threats to surrounding properties due to a release of LP-Gas from the facility. A discussion of the many aspects of the fire analysis factors given in A.6.25.3 is covered in Supplement 1, Guidelines for Conducting a Fire Safety Analysis.

Since the requirement of product control equipment was added to the 1976 edition of NFPA 58, the number of incidents involving bulk plants is believed to have decreased. Data are available beginning in 1980 and published in a report produced by the NFPA Fire Analysis Department entitled "Fires at LP-Gas Bulk Plants" [43]. The report states that caution should be used in interpreting the data due to the small number of incidents reported. The number of fires at bulk storage plants, including structure fires, vehicle fires, and outside and other fires, averaged 64 per year from 1980 through 1998, and 49 per year from 1994 through 1998. Total property damage from the types of fires contained in the data averaged $1.23 million per year from 1980 through 1998, and $754,000 per year from 1994 through 1998. Refer to the report for complete data.

See also Formal Interpretation 58-01-2.

> **Formal Interpretation**
> **NFPA 58**
> **Liquefied Petroleum Gas Code**
> **2011 Edition**
>
> *Reference:* 6.25.3.2
>
> *F.I. No.:* 58-01-2
>
> *Question:* Is it the intent of the committee that the fire safety analysis required in 6.25.3.2 be conducted only by a registered professional engineer or certified safety professional?
>
> *Answer:* No.
>
> *Issue Edition:* 2001
>
> *Reference:* 2.3.3.2 & 3.3.3.6
>
> *Issue Date:* November 7, 2001
>
> *Effective Date:* November 27, 2001
>
> Copyright © 2010 All Rights Reserved
> NATIONAL FIRE PROTECTION ASSOCIATION

6.25.3.3 The fire safety analysis shall be submitted by the owner, operator, or their designee, to the authority having jurisdiction and local emergency responders.

The need to share the fire safety analysis with both the authority having jurisdiction (usually the state fire marshal or local fire department, but sometimes another state agency, such as an LP-Gas Board or the state's Department of Agriculture) and local emergency responders (the fire department or some other trained agency) ensures that all parties potentially involved in an incident at the facility are aware of the plant layout and equipment installed. Note that NFPA 58 does not specify who should conduct the review, but specifies that it must be submitted both to the authority having jurisdiction and to local emergency responders, which could be the local fire department, a hazmat team, or a state agency.

6.25.3.4 The fire safety analysis shall be updated when the storage capacity or transfer system is modified.

The fire safety analysis must be updated if the capacity of the plant is increased or the installation is substantially reconfigured. Replacing pumps, piping, and equipment, and routine maintenance in the plant does not require an update of the fire safety analysis.

6.25.3.5 The fire safety analysis shall be an evaluation of the total product control system, such as the emergency shutoff and internal valves equipped for remote closure and automatic shutoff using thermal (fire) actuation, pullaway protection where installed, and the optional requirements of Section 6.26.

The first and best line of preventing inadvertent releases and fire in any LP-Gas installation is the equipment used to control the product, to minimize the impact of any accident. Tanks larger than 4000 gal (15.1 m³) have internal valves and emergency shutoff valves to provide remote shutoff capability, but also incorporate thermal activation to provide a high level of product control in the event of fire. Some examples of hardware used to achieve "total product control" include the following:

- Internal valves, which are required on all liquid withdrawal openings in containers larger than 4000 gal (15.1 m³)
- Excess-flow valves or check valves, which are required on vapor withdrawal openings of containers larger than 4000 gal (15.1 m³)
- Emergency shutoff valves, which are required in all piping systems used for transfer to or from trucks or railcars to containers over 4000 gal (15.1 m³).

6.25.3.6 If in the preparation for the fire safety analysis it is determined that a hazard to adjacent structures exists that exceeds the protection provided by the provisions of this code, special protection shall be provided in accordance with 6.25.5.

In most cases, the fire safety analysis will determine that no additional fire protection is needed. Paragraph 6.25.5 recognizes that the requirements in NFPA 58 for equipment in the facility first and foremost are requirements for total product control. There may be cases, however, in which the location of the plant is such that it is surrounded by "high value" occupancies such as educational, institutional (hospitals, etc.), or assembly occupancies (restaurants, nightclubs). If the proximity of these neighboring occupancies is within a distance considered to be a threat from a credible release scenario (such as a hose separation or relief valve release), "special protection," as described in 6.25.5, is an option for mitigation. The facility operator and the authority having jurisdiction may also consider other methods of reducing the risk presented by the LP-Gas installation to the adjacent "high value" occupancy.

In the event that special protection is provided for containers, the need for the fire department or plant fire brigade is not eliminated. A fire incident can involve buildings and vehicles, as well as containers. There also may be portable containers at the facility and adjacent properties that need to be protected.

The special protection provision also does not eliminate the need to consider other fire protection measures. Flammables other than LP-Gases, such as methanol and flammable paints, frequently are stored at LP-Gas facilities. Industrial sites can have large amounts of other flammable and hazardous materials on site, such as anhydrous ammonia for refrigeration or use in the process, plastic feed stocks, or agricultural chemicals.

The five modes of special protection listed in 6.25.5 and 6.25.6 — insulation, mounding, burial, water sprays, and monitor nozzles — are not the only means of special protection available for consideration. The definition of the term *special protection* in 3.3.65 also permits other means for limiting the temperature of a container. See the commentary following 6.25.5 for a further discussion of special protection.

6.25.4 Other Protection Requirements.

6.25.4.1 Roadways or other means of access for emergency equipment, such as fire department apparatus, shall be provided.

6.25.4.2 Each industrial plant, bulk plant, and distributing point shall be provided with at least one approved portable fire extinguisher having a minimum capacity of 18 lb (8.2 kg) of dry chemical with a B:C rating. Where fire extinguishers have more than one letter classification, they shall be considered to satisfy the requirements of each letter class.

See the commentary on Section 8.5, which summarizes the requirements of NFPA 10, *Standard for Portable Fire Extinguishers* [44], for the classifications of the three types of fires for which extinguishers are designed and how these extinguishers are tested.

6.25.4.3* LP-Gas fires shall not be extinguished until the source of the burning gas has been shut off.

A.6.25.4.3 LP-Gas fires should not normally be extinguished until the source of the burning gas has been shut off or can be shut off.

The danger of igniting an LP-Gas cloud that has escaped into the atmosphere can be greater than that of LP-Gas burning as it escapes. Therefore, 6.25.4.3 is an important requirement for emergency personnel involved with LP-Gas.

6.25.4.4 Emergency controls shall be conspicuously marked, and the controls shall be located so as to be readily accessible in emergencies.

6.25.5 Special Protection.

Special protection addresses flame impingement on a container that, in the worst case, can lead to a BLEVE. This hazard, although considered extremely remote, is usually of concern to the general public because of the dramatic effects associated with its occurrence. Special protection is a means to protect an LP-Gas container from elevated temperatures due to fire. This provision recognizes that other means of protecting container surfaces from fire can and probably will be used. Verification of the effectiveness of such "alternative" methods is left to independent testing laboratories. There has been some interest in designs for water application systems other than those described in 6.25.6, but the editor is unaware of any such systems listed for the purpose of protecting LP-Gas containers.

 The five modes of special protection recognized in the code are described in 6.25.5 and 6.25.6. Although not specifically cited in this provision, any combination of these five modes or other modes listed for the purpose is also acceptable. For example, a common combination consists of earth mounding for the portion of a container not fitted with appurtenances or connections, which is customarily at least 75 percent of the container surface area, and water spray or monitor protection for the remainder. Because of the rather high water demand for water spray and many monitor nozzle systems, such a combination can avoid the need for expensive water supply improvements. See Exhibits 6.55 and 6.56 for special protection examples.

EXHIBIT 6.55 Storage Containers with Special Protection. Note fixed water spray nozzles.

6.25.5.1* If insulation is used, it shall be capable of limiting the container temperature to not over 800°F (427°C) for a minimum of 50 minutes as determined by test, with insulation applied to a steel plate and subjected to a test flame applied substantially over the area of the test plate.

The temperature of 800°F (427°C) is an important threshold because that is the temperature at which the yield strength of steel begins to decrease, lowering the ability of steel to withstand deformation, which can lead to container failure.

A.6.25.5.1 For LP-Gas fixed storage facilities of 60,000 gal (227 m³) water capacity or less, a fire safety analysis could indicate that applied insulating coatings are quite often the most practical solution for special protection. It is recommended that insulation systems be evaluated on the basis of experience or listings by an approved testing laboratory.

6.25.5.2 The insulation system shall be inherently resistant to weathering and the action of hose streams.

Several types of cementitious, ablative, or intumescent coatings and steel-jacketed insulation systems have been used or been proposed for protecting LP-Gas containers. It is important, however, that they meet the LP-Gas exposure, fire, weathering, and hose stream resistance criteria specified. Hose stream resistance criteria must be known because hose streams will likely be applied in a fire emergency, even though an insulated container does not require this measure. Annex H contains a test method for evaluating insulation based on the criteria of 6.25.5.1. The NFPA Fire Test Committee has also developed NFPA 290, *Standard for Fire Testing of Passive Protection Materials for Use on LP-Gas Containers* [45], which is now available from NFPA and can be used in lieu of Annex H. It is anticipated that Annex H will be deleted in the 2014 edition of NFPA 58.

The most extensive testing and experience has been for the insulation of railroad tank cars. DOT approves a number of coatings and jacketed systems on the basis of a large-scale liquid LP-Gas torch fire exposure test. This test does not involve hose stream application because it is unlikely that hose streams will be used in an environment associated with typical multi-car derailment pileups. Hose stream resistance is not as significant with jacketed systems. Such insulated tank cars have performed well in actual fires [46].

FM Global lists coating systems for special protection on the basis of a smaller-scale modified furnace test, and their test includes hose stream application. The editor is unaware of any actual fires involving insulated stationary LP-Gas containers.

There have been cases in which containers have sustained extensive reduction in shell thickness due to corrosion caused by water trapped between the container shell and a coating applied after manufacture of the container, as shown in Exhibit 6.57. In these cases, an unlisted reinforced concrete coating was applied to a container shell to prevent moisture from penetrating the concrete. Over time, the outer coating failed and water entered the concrete and collected between the container shell and the concrete coating. This situation was discovered when discoloration and blistering of the concrete was noted and the coating was removed for inspection. Although listed coating systems are not required by the code, any system used for insulation protection against fire damage must be investigated to be sure that it will not cause damage to the container, especially concealed damage.

EXHIBIT 6.57 *Corrosion Caused by Water Trapped Under Insulation. (Courtesy of Propane Technical Services)*

6.25.5.3 If mounding is utilized, the provisions of 6.6.6.3 shall be required.

6.25.5.4 If burial is utilized, the provisions of 6.6.6.1 shall be required.

6.25.6 Water Spray Systems.

6.25.6.1 If water spray fixed systems and monitors are used, they shall comply with NFPA 15, *Standard for Water Spray Fixed Systems for Fire Protection.*

6.25.6.2 Where water spray fixed systems and monitors are used, they shall be automatically actuated by fire-responsive devices and shall also have a capability for manual actuation.

Criteria for water spray fixed systems for a number of purposes are provided in NFPA 15, *Standard for Water Spray Fixed Systems for Fire Protection* [47]. The specific purpose pertinent to special protection of LP-Gas containers is known as vessel exposure protection and is addressed in the 2007 edition of NFPA 15.

It is explained in NFPA 15 that where the temperature of a vessel or its contents should be limited, densities higher than 0.25 gpm/ft^2 [10.2 (L/min)/m^2] may be required. Several years ago, a survey of the Technical Committee on Water Spray Fixed Systems was conducted to ascertain the BLEVE experience with systems designed on the basis of 0.25 gpm/ft^2 [10.2 (L/min)/m^2]. Very little data are available, but the committee concluded that this density could not be relied on to prevent a crack from developing, but would probably prevent a crack from growing to the point of container dismemberment.

Automatic actuation is required because the nozzles and much of the piping are close to the container where they can be exposed to fire. Water must be introduced quickly to protect the system as well as the container.

Qualified personnel must maintain such systems. Maintenance of these systems can be difficult and, over time, the reliability of these systems must be verified. There are many critical parts of a water spray fixed system that, when improperly maintained, can reduce the reliability of the entire system. Performance problems include the following:

- Pump performance can be reduced if pumps are blocked or corroded.
- Pump motors can fail or have their direction of rotation changed during maintenance.
- Piping systems can become clogged with rust, dislodged system parts, and water contaminants.
- Nozzles can become partially blocked, which alters spray patterns to reduce coverage, or they may become completely blocked.

Periodic testing is a practical way to verify the effectiveness of a water spray fixed system.

6.25.6.3 Where monitor nozzles are used, they shall be located and arranged so that all container surfaces that can be exposed to fire are wetted.

NFPA standards do not provide water application design criteria for monitor nozzles in any application, including special protection of LP-Gas containers. Because of the hydraulics of fire streams, however, the pressure required to throw an effective stream from the nozzle to the container probably will result in a density on the container well in excess of 0.25 gpm/ft^2 [10.2 (L/min)/m^2]. Because of the requirement that all container surfaces likely to be exposed to fire must be wetted, considerable ingenuity may be required to avoid the need for a very large water supply.

Qualified personnel must carefully maintain these systems. Maintenance of monitor systems can be difficult and, over time, the reliability of these systems must be verified. As is the case with water spray fixed systems, the use of other modes of fire protection, principally product control systems but also such methods as mounding or insulation, can reduce the water demands greatly and, in many cases, eliminate them altogether.

6.26 Alternate Provisions for Installation of ASME Containers

Section 6.26 allows alternative installation methods that provide incentive to construct facilities that are designed to a higher level of safety. These incentives may involve the reduction of distance requirements and the easing of special protection requirements. The term used in this section, *redundant fail-safe product control measures (RFPCM)*, is self-explanatory. This section was first introduced into the code in the 1998 edition to recognize the increased safety of using redundant systems to control product flow, and it provides a tradeoff allowing reduced installation distances where additional safety devices are installed. Some of the components required to achieve RFPCM have since been added to 5.7.4 and are now routinely used. The advocate of this optional tradeoff intended to provide a safe alternative installation method for one underground or mounded container of 30,000 gal (114 m^3) or smaller to make it practical for vehicle fueling stations to economically offer propane as a vehicle fuel. This provision allows transport truck deliveries directly to vehicle fueling stations, rather than require the intermediate step of transfer to a bobtail. Of course, the option is not limited to vehicle fueling applications.

Section 6.26 allows reduced distances for one underground or mounded container of 30,000 gal (114 m^3) or smaller if all the requirements of Section 6.26 are met. These requirements include RFPCM, low emission transfer from the transport trailer to the storage tank as required in 6.26.5.2, and low emission transfer to vehicle containers where vehicle fueling is conducted.

The components of RFPCM are identified in 6.26.4. An installation built to this section of the code would provide additional features over what is currently required by the code. Employing RFPCM in a proposed installation alleviates the need for special protection and can be used to reduce separation distances for installing underground and mounded containers.

Although the provisions in 6.26.2.1 allow alternative distances for installations using underground or mounded containers, the user should understand that RFPCM could be applied to any proposed installation to alleviate the need for fire protection and/or special protection.

Subsection 6.26.5 provides alternative requirements to promote the use of propane at commercial vehicle fueling stations. Installing low emission transfer equipment allows the installation to employ reduced distances to sources of ignition.

6.26.1 Application.

Section 6.26 shall apply to alternate provisions for the location and installation of ASME containers that incorporate the use of redundant fail-safe product control measures and low-emission transfer concepts for the purpose of enhancing safety and to mitigate distance and special protection requirements.

6.26.2 Spacing Requirements for Underground and Mounded ASME Containers.

6.26.2.1 Where all the provisions of Section 6.26 are complied with, the minimum distances from important buildings and the line of adjoining property that can be built upon to underground and mounded ASME containers of 2001 gal through 30,000 gal (7.6 m³ through 114 m³) water capacity shall be reduced to 10 ft (3.0 m).

6.26.2.2 Distances for all underground and mounded ASME containers shall be measured from the container surface.

6.26.2.3 No part of an underground or mounded ASME container shall be less than 10 ft (3 m) from a building or line of adjoining property that can be built upon.

The separation distances of underground and mounded containers of 2001 gal through 30,000 gal (7.6 m³ through 114 m³) to important buildings is reduced from the normal 50 ft (15.2 m) to 10 ft (3.0 m) when all the requirements of Section 6.26 are met. (See Table 6.3.1.) This reduction can be significant in many installations and can make LP-Gas installations practical at many sites.

6.26.3 ASME Container Appurtenances.

The provisions in 6.26.3.1 through 6.26.3.5 shall be required for ASME containers of 2001 gal through 30,000 gal (7.6 m³ through 114 m³) water capacity referenced in Section 6.26.

6.26.3.1 All liquid withdrawal openings and all vapor withdrawal openings that are 1¼ in. (32 mm) or larger shall be equipped with an internal valve.

6.26.3.2 The internal valves shall remain closed except during periods of operation.

6.26.3.3 Internal valves shall be equipped for remote closure and automatic shutoff through thermal (fire) actuation.

6.26.3.4 A positive manual shutoff valve shall be installed as close as practical to each internal valve.

6.26.3.5 All liquid and vapor inlet openings shall be equipped in accordance with 6.26.3.1 through 6.26.3.4 or shall be equipped with a backflow check valve that is designed for the intended application and a positive manual shutoff valve installed as close as practical to the backflow check valve.

All withdrawal openings that are 1 ¼ in. (3.2 cm) or larger must have internal valves that are open only during transfer. The requirement in 6.26.3.5 is in addition to the other required safety features of the code. Inlet openings have the option of using the same requirements as withdrawal openings or a backflow check valve. The backflow check valve does not allow flow out of the container. These valves must be checked annually for proper operation in accordance with 6.12.9.

6.26.4 Redundant Fail-Safe Product Control.

6.26.4.1 At cargo tank vehicle and railroad tank car transfer points, protection shall be provided in accordance with Section 6.12 using approved emergency shutoff valves or backflow check valves or a combination of the two.

6.26.4.2 Automatic system shutdown of all primary valves (internal valves and emergency shutoff valves) shall be provided through thermal (fire) actuation and in the event of a hose pull-away.

6.26.4.3 Remote shutdown capability, including power supply for the transfer equipment and all primary valves (internal and emergency shutoff), shall be provided.

(A) A remote shutdown station shall be installed within 15 ft (4.6 m) of the point of transfer.

(B) At least one additional remote shutdown station shall be installed not less than 25 ft (7.6 m), or more than 100 ft (30.5 m), from the transfer point.

(C) Emergency remote shutdown stations shall be identified as such by a sign incorporating the words "Propane" and "Emergency Shutoff" in block letters not less than 2 in. (5.1 cm) in height on a background of contrasting color to the letters. The sign shall be visible from the point of transfer.

The piping system safety features listed in 6.26.4 constitute RFPCM. They include the pull away protection features of Section 6.12, which are required by reference. In addition, if fire is sensed in the area, closure of container internal valves is required. Also included is remote shutdown capability within 15 ft (4.6 m) and at least one additional remote shutdown station between 25 ft (7.6 m) and 100 ft (30.5) from the point of transfer. Shutdown capability means a station for activation of the emergency shutdown system. This station can be a push button, pull device, or anything a person can operate easily in the event of release of LP-Gas. Signs are required at each location of activation.

The commentary following 6.24.3.14 discusses a possible option where the distance requirements for remote shutoff locations for emergency shutoff valves may also be applicable to this paragraph, if approved.

6.26.5 Low Emission Transfer.

The transfer distance requirements of Table 6.5.3 and 6.24.4.3 shall be reduced by one-half where the installation is in accordance with 6.26.5. The transfer site shall be identified as "Low Emission Transfer Site" by having a sign or other marking posted in the area.

As clearly stated in 6.5.4.4, separation distances between points of transfer and various exposures are permitted to be reduced up to 50 percent if equipment complying with 6.26.5 is used. The reduction in separation distances is allowed because the amount of gas released when transfer connections are broken is so small that the fire hazard is greatly reduced. (See Exhibit 6.58.)

Table 6.5.3 covers distances between points of transfer and 11 exposures. This table should be reviewed prior to an installation of low emission transfer dispensers. The distances in 6.24.4.3 allow a low emission transfer propane dispenser to be located 5 ft (1.5 m) from a gasoline dispenser. NFPA 30A, *Code for Motor Fuel Dispensing Facilities and Repair Garages* [10], covers service stations that dispense propane and other liquid or gaseous fuels. If propane is being dispensed with other fuels, NFPA 30A should be consulted.

6.26.5.1 Transfer into permanently mounted ASME engine fuel containers on vehicles shall meet the provisions of 6.26.5.1(A) through 6.26.5.1(D).

(A) The delivery valve and nozzle combination shall mate with the filler valve in the receiving container in such a manner that, when they are uncoupled following a transfer of product, not more than 0.24 in.^{3} (4 cm^3) of product (liquid equivalent) is released to the atmosphere.

(B) Fixed maximum liquid level gauges that are installed on engine fuel and mobile containers in accordance with Table 5.7.4.1 shall not be used to determine the maximum permitted filling limit at a low emission transfer site.

(C) The maximum permitted filling limit shall be in accordance with Section 11.5 and shall be determined by an overfilling prevention device or other approved means.

(D) A label shall be placed near the fixed maximum liquid level gauge providing the following instructions: "Do not use this fixed maximum liquid level gauge at low emission transfer stations."

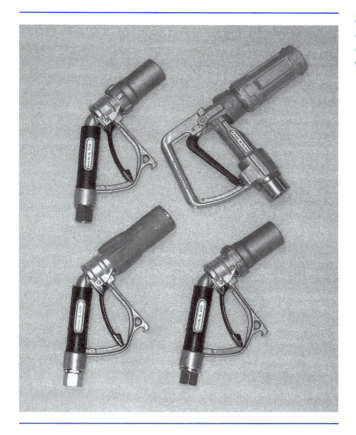

EXHIBIT 6.58 A Low Emission Nozzle for Fueling Propane Vehicles. (Courtesy of CleanFuel USA)

The following requirements are key to low emission transfer:

- By reducing the volume between the delivery nozzle and vehicle filling connection to 0.24 in.³ (4 cm³), the amount of liquid propane released following each filling is 0.24 in.³ (4 cm³). This is a much smaller amount of propane than is released with conventional filling nozzles.
- By eliminating the discharge from the fixed maximum level gauge, the amount of propane released into the atmosphere is further reduced from conventional filling systems.

Reduced propane release decreases the size and duration of any flammable propane–air mixture, with a corresponding increase in safety.

6.26.5.2 Transfer into stationary ASME containers shall meet the provisions of 6.26.5.2(A) through 6.26.5.2(F).

(A) Where transfer is made through a hose of nominal 1 in. (25 mm) size or smaller, the delivery valve and nozzle combination shall not contain an interstitial volume greater than 0.24 in.³ (4 cm³).

(B) Where transfer is made through hose larger than 1 in. (25 mm) nominal size, no more than 0.91 in.³ (15 cm³) of LP-Gas (liquid equivalent) shall be released to the atmosphere during the transfer operation, including the uncoupling of the transfer hose.

(C) Fixed maximum liquid level gauges on low emission transfer systems shall be installed and used to verify the (function) accuracy of liquid level gauges or other liquid level gauging devices.

(D) Fixed maximum liquid level gauges shall not be used in the routine filling of low emission transfer systems.

(E) The use of a float gauge or other approved nonventing device for containers of 2001 gal (7.6 m³) or larger water capacity shall be the only means for determining the maximum filling limit.

(F) The maximum filling limit for containers of less than 2001 gal (7.6 m³) water capacity in low emission transfer systems shall be controlled through the use of an overfilling prevention device or other device approved for this service.

The requirements in 6.26.5.2(A) through 6.26.5.2(F) reduce the release of LP-Gas during and following the refueling of the service station or bulk plants. The release from hose filling connections is limited to 0.24 in.³ (4 cm³) for hose 1 in. (2.5 cm) and smaller used on bobtails, and 0.91 in.³ (15 cm³) for the larger hose used on transport trucks. Note also that a nonventing liquid level device must be used on containers of 2001 gal (7.6 m³) and larger water capacity. On containers less than 2001 gal (7.6 m³) water capacity, an overfilling prevention device or other approved device must be used for determining the maximum filling limit. A fixed maximum liquid level gauge is still required on the containers, but it should be used only for periodic calibration of the nonventing device.

REFERENCES CITED IN COMMENTARY

1. NFPA's Fire Incident Data Organization, National Fire Protection Association, Quincy, MA.
2. Raj, P.K., "Exposure of a Liquefied Gas Container to an External Fire," *Journal of Hazardous Materials*, June 2005, vol. 122, Issues 1–2, pp. 37–49.
3. NFPA *101*®, *Life Safety Code*®, 2009 edition, National Fire Protection Association, Quincy, MA.
4. Hoenhe, V. O., R. G. Luce, and L. W. Miga, *The Effect of Velocity, Temperature, and Gas Molecular Weight on Flammability Limits in Wind-Blown Jets of Hydrocarbon Gases*, 1970, Batelle Memorial Institute, Columbus, OH.
5. API RP 521, *Guide for Pressure-Relieving and Depressuring Systems*, 2007 edition, American Petroleum Institute, Washington, DC.
6. *Fire Safety Analysis Manual*, National Fire Protection Association, Quincy MA, available free at www.nfpa.org.
7. Praxair Material Safety Data Sheet, www.praxair.com.
8. NFPA 30, *Flammable and Combustible Liquids Code*, 2008 edition, National Fire Protection Association, Quincy, MA.
9. NFPA 55, *Standard for the Storage, Use, and Handling of Compressed Gases and Cryogenic Fluids in Portable and Stationary Containers, Cylinders, and Tanks*, 2010 edition, National Fire Protection Association, Quincy, MA.
10. NFPA 30A, *Code for Motor Fuel Dispensing Facilities and Repair Garages*, 2008 edition, National Fire Protection Association, Quincy, MA.
11. NFPA 251, *Standard Methods of Tests of Fire Resistance of Building Construction and Materials*, 2006 edition, National Fire Protection Association, Quincy, MA.
12. Isner, M. S., "BLEVE — LP-Gas Storage Tank, Woodruff, Utah, October 16, 1986," Fire Investigation Report, National Fire Protection Association, Quincy, MA.
13. NFPA 99, *Standard for Health Care Facilities*, 2005 edition, National Fire Protection Association, Quincy, MA.
14. UL 644, *Container Assemblies for LP-Gas*, 2000 edition, Underwriters Laboratories Inc., Northbrook, IL.
15. NFPA 220, *Standard on Types of Building Construction*, 2009 edition, National Fire Protection Association, Quincy, MA.

16. NFPA 37, *Standard for the Installation and Use of Stationary Combustion Engines and Gas Turbines*, 2010 edition, National Fire Protection Association, Quincy, MA.

17. NFPA 407, *Standard for Aircraft Fuel Servicing*, 2007 edition, National Fire Protection Association, Quincy, MA.

18. API RP 520, *Sizing, Selection, and Installation of Pressure-Relieving Devices in Refineries (Part I — Sizing and Selection*, 2000, and *Part II — Installation*, 2003), American Petroleum Institute, Washington DC.

19. UL 144, *LP-Gas Regulators*, 1999 edition, Underwriters Laboratories Inc., Northbrook, IL.

20. NFPA 54, *National Fuel Gas Code*, 2009 edition, National Fire Protection Association, Quincy, MA.

21. ASME B 31.3, *Process Piping*, 2008 edition, American Society of Mechanical Engineers, New York, NY.

22. ASME *Boiler and Pressure Vessel Code*, 2007 edition, American Society of Mechanical Engineers, New York, NY.

23. *NFPA 70®, National Electrical Code®*, 2011 edition, National Fire Protection Association, Quincy, MA.

24. ASTM D 2513, *Standard Specification for Thermoplastic Gas Pressure Pipe, Tubing and Fittings*, 2009 edition, American Society for Testing and Materials, West Conshohocken, PA.

25. NFPA 45, *Standard on Fire Protection for Laboratories Using Chemicals*, 2011 edition, National Fire Protection Association, Quincy, MA.

26. UL 147A, *Nonrefillable (Disposable) Type Fuel Gas Cylinder Assemblies*, 2006 edition, Underwriters Laboratories, Inc., Northbrook, IL.

27. UL 147B, *Nonrefillable (Disposable) Type Metal Container Assemblies for Butane*, 2006 edition, Underwriters Laboratories, Inc., Northbrook, IL.

28. NFPA 160, *Standard for the Use of Flame Effects Before an Audience*, 2011 edition, National Fire Protection Association, Quincy, MA.

29. NFPA 85, *Boiler and Combustion Systems Hazards Code*, 2007 edition, National Fire Protection Association, Quincy, MA.

30. NFPA 780, *Standard for the Installation of Lightning Protection Systems*, 2011 edition, National Fire Protection Association, Quincy, MA.

31. NFPA 77, *Recommended Practice on Static Electricity*, 2007 edition, National Fire Protection Association, Quincy, MA.

32. NFPA 51B, *Standard for Fire Prevention During Welding, Cutting, and Other Hot Work*, 2009 edition, National Fire Protection Association, Quincy, MA.

33. NFPA 501B, *Standard for Mobile Homes*, 1979 edition, National Fire Protection Association, Quincy, MA.

34. Title 24, Code of Federal Regulations, Part 3280, "Mobile Home Construction and Safety Standard," U.S. Government Printing Office, Washington, DC.

35. NFPA 501, *Standard on Manufactured Housing*, 2010 edition, National Fire Protection Association, Quincy, MA.

36. NFPA 1192, *Standard on Recreational Vehicles*, 2008 edition, National Fire Protection Association, Quincy, MA.

37. Title 49, Code of Federal Regulations, Part 393, "Motor Carrier Safety Regulations," U.S. Government Printing Office, Washington, DC.

38. Title 49, Code of Federal Regulations, Part 177.834, Subpart B, "Hazardous Materials Regulations," U.S. Government Printing Office, Washington, DC.

39. Part 24, Construction Safety Standards, State of Michigan Department of Labor & Economic Growth, Lansing, MI.

40. "LP-Gas: Emergency Planning and Response," NFPA film, 1986, National Fire Protection Association, Quincy, MA.

41. "BLEVE Update," NFPA film, 1992, National Fire Protection Association, Quincy, MA.

42. "Propane Emergencies, Facilitator's Guide," third edition, 2007, Propane Education and Research Council, Washington, DC.

43. "Special Data Information Package: Fires and Explosions in Tank Farms, Cryogenic Gas Storage, and LP-Gas Bulk Plants," NFPA Fire Analysis Report, April 1998, National Fire Protection Association, Quincy, MA.

44. NFPA 10, *Standard for Portable Fire Extinguishers*, 2010 edition, National Fire Protection Association, Quincy, MA.

45. NFPA 290, *Standard for Fire Testing of Passive Protection Materials for Use on LP-Gas Containers*, 2009 edition, National Fire Protection Association, Quincy, MA.

46. "Phase 02 Report on Effectiveness of Shelf Couplers, Head Shields and Thermal Shields," Report RA-02-3.44 (AAR R-482), Railroad Tank Car Safety Research and Test Project (May 15, 1981), Association of American Railroads, Chicago, IL.

47. NFPA 15, *Standard for Water Spray Fixed Systems for Fire Protection*, 2007 edition, National Fire Protection Association, Quincy, MA.

LP-Gas Liquid Transfer

CHAPTER 7

Transfer of LP-Gas liquid to or from stationary storage containers, transportation vehicles (highway and rail), and portable containers requires connections and disconnections of couplings by transfer personnel. The likelihood of releasing LP-Gas into the atmosphere is greatest during these product transfer operations. Chapter 7 provides safety requirements when liquid LP-Gas is transferred from one container to another container and when liquid or vapor LP-Gas is vented and purged to the atmosphere.

Chapter 7 addresses the following important aspects related to liquid transfer of LP-Gas:

- Basic training and qualification requirements for persons who will be transferring product (See 7.2.1.)
- General requirements for filling and evacuating containers (See 7.2.2.)
- Operational requirements for transferring product, including the arrangement of the transfer system, controlling sources of ignition, and specific situations for transferring product (See 7.2.3.)
- Care and inspection of transfer hoses (See 7.2.4.)
- Instances in which the venting or release of LP-Gas to the atmosphere is permissible (See Section 7.3.)
- Requirements that establish the maximum allowable quantity of LP-Gas in containers (See Section 7.4.)

7.1* Scope

A.7.1 Ignition source control at transfer locations is covered in Section 6.22. Fire protection is covered in Section 6.25.

7.1.1 This chapter applies to transfers of liquid LP-Gas from one container to another wherever this transfer involves connections and disconnections in the transfer system or the venting of LP-Gas to the atmosphere.

7.1.2 This chapter also applies to operational safety and methods for determining the quantity of LP-Gas permitted in containers.

The probability of the release of LP-Gas, especially liquid LP-Gas, is greatest during liquid transfer operations. While release is an operational necessity, it can and should be minimized to the degree practical. Accurate container filling is necessary to avoid release through pressure relief devices after the container has been filled. Therefore, the code has always thoroughly addressed these operations. Exhibit 7.1 is an example of a transfer operation: filling cargo tank vehicles at a pipeline terminal.

EXHIBIT 7.1 *Transport Trailers Loading at a Pipeline Terminal.*

7.2 Operational Safety

7.2.1 Transfer Personnel.

7.2.1.1 Transfer operations shall be conducted by qualified personnel meeting the provisions of Section 4.4.

7.2.1.2 At least one qualified person shall remain in attendance at the transfer operation from the time connections are made until the transfer is completed, shutoff valves are closed, and lines are disconnected.

The liquid transfer operation is associated with the greatest risk of discharge of flammable gas into the atmosphere. The individual performing the transfer must be fully qualified in such work and be sufficiently familiar with the operation of equipment to stop the transfer operation and minimize the loss of product should an emergency arise.

The words "in attendance" in 7.2.1.2 clarify the intent of the requirement, which is that the qualified person view the transfer operation and be able to take action if needed at any time during the transfer operation. Of course, the transfer operation may not be able to be viewed from one location. For example, if an operator is filling a tank at a building, the tank may not be visible from where the bobtail is parked. In this example, the operator must choose the best location, which is usually at the tank being filled, so that the tank is not over-filled. During the time the tank cannot be seen, operators must use all their senses, for example, listening to the truck engine for speed changes that could indicate releases, listening for the escape of hissing gas, and looking for vapor clouds, to be aware of any need to take corrective action. If the operator must leave the transfer operation — for instance, to visit the location office or for personal reasons — the transfer operation must be stopped during that absence, according to U.S. Department of Transportation (DOT) regulations [1].

For some transfers, the presence of a suitable odorant is required to be verified. See the commentary following 4.2.3 for more information on this testing.

FAQ ▶
What does "in attendance" mean?

A qualified operator may be in attendance when standing at the tank vehicle, sitting in the cab of the vehicle, or sitting in a booth or guardhouse with the cargo tank vehicle in clear sight. The qualified operator must be awake and aware of the transfer during the operation. If the complete transfer system is not visible from one location and the transfer is lengthy — for example, the unloading of a transport — it is prudent for the operator to check the entire system for leakage during the transfer.

7.2.1.3 Transfer personnel shall exercise caution to ensure that the LP-Gases transferred are those for which the transfer system and the containers to be filled are designed.

Accidents can occur if propane or a mixture of propane and butane is placed in containers suitable only for butane. The lower setting for the pressure relief device can result in a release of flammable gas during its operation, possibly leading to injury and property damage. The ASME container nameplate and the cylinder collar or body are marked with the design pressure of the container.

7.2.2 Filling and Evacuating of Containers.

7.2.2.1 Transfer of LP-Gas to and from a container shall be accomplished only by qualified individuals trained in proper handling and operating procedures meeting the requirements of Section 4.4 and in emergency response procedures.

Training in emergency response procedures is required so that in the event of an incident, personnel are trained and prepared to take prompt action to minimize the extent of loss, damage, or fire. Such personnel filling the containers may be the only people regularly viewing or inspecting containers.

7.2.2.2 When noncompliance with Section 5.2 and Section 5.7 is found, the container owner and user shall be notified in writing.

When it is determined that a container does not comply with Section 5.2 or Section 5.7, the owner or operator of the container must be notified in writing. This important requirement relies on the requirement of 7.2.2.1, which mandates that personnel who transfer LP-Gas must be qualified. The requirement for qualified personnel is especially important given the trend in some areas toward greater numbers of fixed containers owned by the users, including individuals, motels, school districts, and industrial plants, who may not be aware of the requirements of Sections 5.2 and 5.7.

Note that 7.2.2.2 does not specify who must provide the notification, and there has been some confusion over who can notify the owner or operator of a container. Clearly, the qualified operator must make the determination that the container is not suitable to be filled, but the container filler is not required to notify the owner or operator. The filler can provide written notification at the container location, or it can be provided by other employees of the propane company, but there must be written notification.

The referenced Sections 5.2 and 5.7 contain requirements from pressure vessel codes (ASME and DOT) and the container appurtenance requirements. The requirement that containers not in compliance with Section 5.2 or Section 5.7 not be filled is applicable to both cylinder and ASME container filling, and its application differs depending on the filling arrangement:

Cylinder filling: The filler should check the date of the cylinder manufacture or most recent requalification. If the date is beyond 12 years from the date of manufacture or beyond 5 years from the most recent visual requalification of the cylinder, the cylinder should not be filled. If there is significant corrosion or pitting, the cylinder should not be filled. A central filling location may have procedures both to identify cylinders that should not be filled and to requalify or repair them. Dispensing stations may have a pre-printed form on which the reason for not filling is checked and returned with the cylinder. This form fulfills an important safety role. For example, operators and customers have reported incidents in which a site refuses to fill a cylinder because of some defect, so the customer takes the cylinder to have it filled at another site. However, if a written notification of the cylinder defects were given to the customer, he or she might take the danger of filling it more seriously. The form could have suggestions for taking the cylinder to a propane company that could requalify the cylinder or for exchanging it for a cylinder in good condition.

◄ **FAQ**
Who must notify the owner when a container is not suitable to be filled with LP-Gas?

ASME container filling: The largest number of fillers of ASME containers are bobtail drivers who make deliveries to ASME containers owned by the company. The driver must determine if the container should or should not be filled and should follow company policy to notify the user if the container is not filled. Reasons for not filling the ASME container include relocation of the container with respect to a building (which occurs when an addition is made to the building), significant leaks through valves or the gauge, and corrosion. Other fillers, such as transport drivers, may not know whom to contact and should follow their company policy. While location of the container with respect to a building is specified in Section 6.3 and not in Section 5.2 or Section 5.7, the code sets forth minimum spacing criteria in Chapter 6. While these spacing requirements are not specifically cited in 7.2.2.2, they are code requirements and should be communicated to the container owner and user. It is not uncommon for a container to be installed at a user location that complies with all the separation requirements of Chapter 6, but a modification to the building occurs later, as in the following examples:

- A new addition to the building places the container at a distance less than that required by 6.3.1.
- A new building air intake is found that is closer to the container filling connection than the distance required by 6.3.9.
- A new window air conditioner, an exterior source of ignition, has been installed closer than the minimum distance required by 6.3.9.

Paragraph 7.2.2.2 has a controversial history. Prior to the 1992 edition, this paragraph required that containers be filled only by the container owner or with the owner's permission. This requirement was removed in the 1992 edition after the subject was brought to the attention of the NFPA committee. In processing the 1992 edition, the committee rejected a proposal to revise the requirement to its present form, only to have the committee action reversed by the NFPA Standards Council. (The Standards Council is responsible for the entire standards-making process and all the codes and standards.) Another proposal was made to revise the 1998 edition to restore the ownership requirement. This proposal was again approved by the committee and reversed by the Standards Council. The Standards Council, in reversing the committee, stated that a code should state what should be done and not who should do it.

Since the 1992 edition, many states have enacted legislation to limit those who can fill containers, making this less of an issue for NFPA 58.

7.2.2.3 Injection of compressed air, oxygen, or any oxidizing gas into containers to transfer LP-Gas liquid shall be prohibited.

The use of compressed air, oxygen, or other oxidizing gases to transfer LP-Gas is extremely dangerous because it can create a flammable gas mixture within the container. A flammable gas mixture being fed into an appliance can result in the mixture igniting and the flame traveling back to the container. This situation can result in an explosion.

7.2.2.4 When evacuating a container owned by others, the qualified person(s) performing the transfer shall not inject any material other than LP-Gas into the container.

A number of materials could be injected into a container to force the LP-Gas out. The most common is air or water. Air, oxygen, and oxidizing gas are prohibited by 7.2.2.3. Addition of these gases can result in a flammable mixture in the container, which can flash back into it if ignited outside the container, usually resulting in a pressure rise inside the container that cannot be relieved by the pressure relief valve, and so results in an explosion. Special care should be taken where propane cylinders are sold to users that use the propane as a cutting fuel in conjunction with oxygen. NFPA 51, *Standard for the Design and Installation of Oxygen–Fuel Gas Systems for Welding, Cutting, and Allied Processes* [2], provides the necessary safety requirements to prevent oxygen and fuel gases from mixing. Injecting a foreign material into a container can degrade a container or lead to improper combustion, which can affect appliance performance. Anything other than LP-Gas is considered a foreign material.

7.2.2.5* Valve outlets on refillable cylinders of 108 lb (49 kg) water capacity [nominal 45 lb (20 kg) propane capacity] or less shall be equipped with a redundant pressure-tight seal or one of the following listed connections: CGA 790, CGA 791, or CGA 810, as described in CGA V-1, *Standard Compressed Gas Cylinder Valve Outlet and Inlet Connections.*

This paragraph was revised in the 2011 edition with the addition of the normally used specifications for containers. The CGA 790 connection is a left-handed threaded connection that was widely used for gas grill connections until the recent introduction of couplings that do not require tools. The CGA 791 is a newer threaded connection incorporating a square thread that is found on the majority of gas grills today. The CGA 810 is a newer "quick connect" fitting offered on some gas grills today.

The requirement in 7.2.2.5 was the direct result of an incident in Milford, Connecticut, in 1982, when a cylinder valve was partially (and unintentionally) opened during transportation in a passenger vehicle. Newer cylinders have one of two newer-type connections, called CGA 791 and CGA 810. Both incorporate a redundant seal, which allows flow only when the cylinder is connected for use.

It is not the intent of the provision to require a cap or plug to be installed on a cylinder using a CGA 791 connection or a CGA 810 connection, because these connections will only allow gas to be removed from the cylinder when the connection is made. This stipulation was needed because many enforcers saw the plastic plugs as proof of redundant sealing and were requiring them for the newer CGA 791 and 810 connections, for which no plug existed and for which a separate plug is not needed. In fact, putting a plug into a CGA 791 or CGA 810 connection defeats the redundant seal. A damaged O-ring on the plug would allow the cylinder to leak.

A.7.2.2.5 Examples of an effective seal are a POL plug or cap. Listed quick-closing couplings with CGA V-1 connection numbers 790 (fork lift ACME connection), 791 (portable cylinder ACME/POL connection), and 810 (socket/plug quick connection) have secondary seals. Therefore, plugs or caps for these connections are not required or recommended.

7.2.2.6 Where redundant pressure seals are used, they shall be in place whenever the cylinder is not connected for use.

This new paragraph was formerly part of 7.2.2.5. It was separated to make it more evident to readers.

7.2.2.7 Nonrefillable (disposable) and new unused cylinders shall not be required to be equipped with valve outlet seals.

While it may appear that 7.2.2.7 is in conflict with 7.2.2.5, note that 7.2.2.5 applies to cylinders of 20 lb (9.1 kg) water capacity and less, while 7.2.2.7 applies to nonrefillable (disposable) cylinders, which usually have a capacity of 1 lb (0.55 kg) or less. The largest possible disposable cylinder for flammable gases is 75 in.^{3} (1.2 L) [about 1.1 lb (0.50 kg) of propane]; therefore, a conflict does not exist where cylinders follow the DOT requirements.

Paragraph 5.7.3.4 requires these portable cylinders to be equipped with the CGA 791 or CGA 810 connection, which are described in the commentary on 5.7.3.4. These connections became a requirement in the 1998 edition of NFPA 58 wherein cylinders were required to have an overfilling prevention device valve installed. Beginning in 1997, however, these new styles of cylinder valves and grill connections were installed on new gas grills by the gas grill standard ANSI/CSA Z-21.58, *Outdoor Cooking Gas Appliances* [3].

7.2.2.8 Containers shall be filled only after determination that they comply with the design, fabrication, inspection, marking, and requalification provisions of this code.

FAQ ▶
Who is responsible for
determining that a container is
code-compliant?

NFPA 58 does not place responsibility for the determination that a container complies with the requirements of the pressure vessel code on one specific individual, for several reasons. In most cases, the individual filling a container is more qualified than a container owner to make the determination that the container complies with the code. The provision in 7.2.2.8 places a great deal of responsibility on the filler, which may not always be recognized by fillers. For example, the filler must be familiar with marking and inspection requirements, which requires considerable training. There are millions of 20 lb (9.1 kg) cylinders owned by the public, and owners of portable cylinders often are not aware of the requalification that is necessary 12 years after the date of manufacture and every 5 to 12 years thereafter. (See 5.2.2 and Annex C.)

When filling cylinders, the filler must be careful to verify that the cylinder requalification period has not been exceeded. If a cylinder is out of date, it cannot be filled, and the owner should be notified of his or her responsibility to have the cylinder requalified prior to filling. The filler should check for corrosion on easily visible surfaces and in the area within the foot ring at the bottom of portable cylinders. Many propane companies establish policies to guide cylinder fillers in this determination. Exhibit 7.2 shows a container being filled.

EXHIBIT 7.2 *Filling a Storage Container. Note the bobtail remote shutoff in the operator's left hand, which meets the DOT requirement for a remote shutdown system. The operator can stop the truck pump and close the tank valve by pressing the button on the remote. (Courtesy of Richard Fredenburg and Ferrellgas)*

Note that the newer composite cylinders must also be requalified. The methods used for metal cylinders cannot be used for composite cylinders. Refer to the information provided by the cylinder manufacturer for the frequency and method of requalification. If such information is not readily available, the U.S. Department of Transportation can provide the frequency and procedures that must be used.

The requirements of 5.7.3 for overfilling prevention device (OPD) valves on most cylinders of 4 lb to 40 lb (1.8 kg to 18 kg) propane capacity require an OPD device to be in place on every cylinder before it is filled. This was required for all new cylinders manufactured after the September 30, 1998, retrofit requirement became effective on April 1, 2002, for all cylinders. The filler must check cylinders for the OPD valve before filling. It should be noted that in the United States, some states have not adopted editions of NFPA 58 that require an OPD and some states that adopt editions of NFPA 58 that require an OPD have not adopted the OPD requirements. In such states, the OPD requirements cannot be enforced for refilling cylinders, but many propane marketers make the NFPA 58 OPD requirements their company policy. As all cylinders of 4 lb to 40 lb (1.8 kg to 18 kg) propane capacity manufactured after September 1998 have an OPD, the number of non-OPD cylinders is diminishing and will continue to diminish.

Fillers of ASME tanks must check the condition of the tank before starting to fill. The filler is not, however, expected to discover difficult-to-determine conditions such as internal corrosion, worn valve seats, or other conditions that are not reasonably apparent. The filler should be alert to visible corrosion, indications of leakage, missing piping components, and the absence of a nameplate, and should report this to the owner, as required in 7.2.2.2. Many propane suppliers' company policies do not allow subsequent refilling if the out-of-compliance condition has not been corrected. Exhibit 7.3 is an illustration of a cylinder filling facility.

◀ **FAQ**
What should the filler of an ASME container look for?

EXHIBIT 7.3 *Cylinder Filling Room with Automatic Cylinder Filling Scales. When the cylinder (not shown) is filled to its correct filling weight, the automatic shutoff valve on the hose inlet will activate and automatically stop the flow. (Courtesy of Propane Education and Research Council)*

7.2.2.9 Prior to refilling a cylinder that has a cylinder sleeve, the cylinder sleeve shall be removed to facilitate the visual inspection of the cylinder.

This requirement was added to the 2011 edition to solve a new problem created by the use of plastic sleeves by cylinder exchange companies. The sleeves contain product information and the necessary consumer warning information and are not regulated by NFPA 58. It was discovered that many of the sleeves were being left on during the refilling process, making it impossible to see if the cylinder was corroding under the sleeve, as shown in Exhibit 7.4. The sleeve can allow water to collect between the sleeve and the cylinder, causing corrosion. Requiring the sleeve to be removed prior to filling is a simple way to identify any corrosion.

7.2.2.10 "Single trip," "nonrefillable," or "disposable" cylinders shall not be refilled with LP-Gas.

Single-trip, nonrefillable, or disposable cylinders are not designed for extended service. Their small size increases the chance that they will be overfilled when commonly available filling equipment and procedures are used. The cylinders are designed for filling by weight and are equipped with filling connections that common filling equipment will not fit, in an effort to control these hazards. However, adapters for refilling are widely available because refillable cylinders come in the same sizes as nonrefillable cylinders.

Accidents have resulted from the refilling of nonrefillable cylinders, which is prohibited both by federal law in the DOT cylinder regulations and by NFPA 58.

7.2.2.11 Containers shall comply with the following with regard to service or design pressure requirements:

(1) The service pressure marked on the cylinder shall be not less than 80 percent of the vapor pressure of the LP-Gas for which the cylinder is designed at 130°F (54.4°C).

EXHIBIT 7.4 *Cylinder Showing Corrosion Under a Sleeve (Sleeve Removed). (Courtesy of Richard Fredenburg, North Carolina Department of Agriculture and Consumer Services)*

(2) The maximum allowable working pressure (MAWP) for ASME containers shall be in accordance with Table 5.2.4.2.

Table 5.2.4.2 establishes a requirement that ASME pressure vessels for propane service have a design pressure of 250 psig (1.7 MPag). If used in the interior of vehicles or as mobile containers (if built after April 1, 2001), the design pressure is increased to 312 psig (2.2 MPag).

7.2.2.12 Transfer of refrigerated product shall be made only into systems that are designed to accept refrigerated product.

See Chapter 12 for details on refrigerated storage systems.

7.2.2.13 A container shall not be filled if the container assembly does not meet the requirements for continued service.

The term *container assembly* is defined as

> **3.3.15 Container Assembly.** An assembly consisting of the container and fittings for all container openings such as shutoff valves, excess-flow valves, liquid level gauging devices, pressure relief devices, and protective housings.

7.2.2.14 Transfer hoses larger than ½ in. (12 mm) internal diameter shall not be used for making connections to individual cylinders being filled indoors.

The requirements of 7.2.2.14 limit the leakage of propane in the event of hose failure.

7.2.3 Arrangement and Operation of Transfer Systems.

LP-Gas can be transferred by pressure differential using gravity (as shown in Exhibit 7.5), pumps (as shown in Exhibit 7.6), or compressors (as shown in Exhibit 7.7), to provide the force to accomplish the transfer. Today, transfer by gravity is not common, but it is sometimes used to transfer into forklift cylinders.

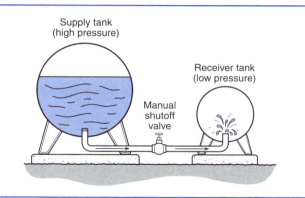

EXHIBIT 7.5 *Liquid Transfer by Pressure Differential or Gravity. (Courtesy of National Propane Gas Association)*

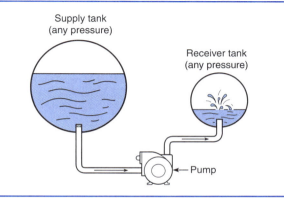

EXHIBIT 7.6 *Liquid Transfer by Pump. (Courtesy of National Propane Gas Association)*

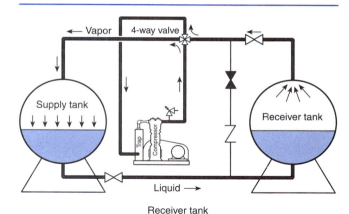

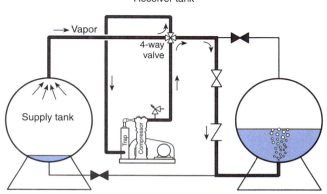

EXHIBIT 7.7 *Transferring Liquid with a Compressor. Liquid transfer is shown in the top illustration and vapor recovery is shown in the bottom illustration. (Courtesy of Blackmer, a Dover Company)*

The pressure differential method of transferring LP-Gas works when the pressure in the container to be filled is lower than that in the supply container. Liquid will flow until the pressures in the containers are equal. To fill a container, it will probably be necessary to reduce the pressure in the container being filled by opening the valve to the atmosphere prior to transferring product. The cost of this procedure, in terms of valuable product being lost and atmospheric contamination, is high.

Compressors are used to unload railroad tank cars and some transport trucks. A compressor takes vapor from the container that will be receiving the product and transfers the vapor to the container from which the liquid is being unloaded. This vapor transfer creates a higher pressure in the container being unloaded than in the receiving container, causing the liquid to flow into the receiving container. When all the liquid has been transferred, the residual vapors in the railroad tank car or transport vehicle that is being unloaded can be recovered and placed into the receiving vessel by reversing the flow through the compressor piping.

It is advantageous to have vapor enter at the bottom of the receiving container so that it will bubble up through the liquid and cool, making it easier to condense. If the vapor is put into the top of the receiving container, the heat of compression will create a higher pressure in the receiving container, slowing the transfer operation. Care also has to be taken to not open valves rapidly, which can result in the closing ("slugging") of any excess-flow check valves that have been installed.

Pumping the liquid is the usual liquid transfer method for operations such as delivery to a fixed container, transfer from bulk storage into bobtail delivery trucks, and unloading of transport vehicles. With both pump and compressor transfer methods, it is important to have proper correlation between the design size of the piping and the excess-flow check valve, so that the valve will not close prematurely. Proper excess-flow valve sizing is also important from a safety standpoint because if there is a break or rupture in the line, the size of the line must permit sufficient flow to cause the excess-flow valve to operate.

7.2.3.1 Public access to areas where LP-Gas is stored and transferred shall be prohibited, except where necessary for the conduct of normal business activities.

Areas where LP-Gas is stored or handled present hazards that are not apparent to those who are untrained in the properties of LP-Gas and the equipment used at the site. Therefore, the public normally is excluded from these areas. Many bulk plants invite their customers to bring cylinders to a drop-off point or a refilling point; these areas are normally open to the public, and this practice is permitted.

7.2.3.2 Sources of ignition shall be turned off during transfer operations, while connections or disconnections are made, or while LP-Gas is being vented to the atmosphere.

(A) Internal combustion engines within 15 ft (4.6 m) of a point of transfer shall be shut down while such transfer operations are in progress, with the exception of the following:

(1) Engines of LP-Gas cargo tank vehicles, constructed and operated in compliance with Chapter 9, while such engines are driving transfer pumps or compressors on these vehicles to load containers in accordance with 6.5.4
(2) Engines installed in buildings as provided in Section 11.13

Vehicle engines must be allowed to operate when the engine drives a pump or compressor used to transfer LP-Gas and when the truck is entering or leaving filling stations. An operating gasoline-fueled internal combustion engine normally does not create sparks or have surfaces hot enough to ignite propane and will stall in a propane-rich environment due to lack of air for proper combustion. A diesel engine, similarly, may not ignite released LP-Gas, but gas sucked into the air intake can cause the engine to accelerate uncontrollably, leading to engine damage. This is one reason for the operator to be in attendance and carefully monitoring the transfer process.

(B) Smoking, open flame, portable electrical tools, and extension lights capable of igniting LP-Gas shall not be permitted within 25 ft (7.6 m) of a point of transfer while filling operations are in progress.

The spacing of sources of ignition and LP-Gas transfer operations is consistent with DOT regulations for separation distances for smoking. Note that this requirement in 7.2.3.2(B) applies only to portable sources of ignition but does not apply to fixed electrical sources of ignition, which are covered in Section 6.20.

(C) Metal cutting, grinding, oxygen–fuel gas cutting, brazing, soldering, or welding shall not be permitted within 35 ft (10.7 m) of a point of transfer while filling operations are in progress.

The 35 ft (10.7 m) separation distance between points of transfer and sources of ignition correlates with the requirements of NFPA 51B, *Standard for Fire Prevention During Welding, Cutting, and Other Hot Work* [4]. The 35 ft distance is necessary because slag or sparks created during hot work have been shown to travel some distance horizontally, and over the years, the 35 ft distance has been shown to be safe.

(D) Materials that have been heated above the ignition temperature of LP-Gas shall be cooled before LP-Gas transfer is started.

Table B.1.2(a) in Annex B lists the ignition temperature of propane at between 920°F and 1120°F (493°C and 604°C) . Because commercial propane is a mixture of propane, butane, and other hydrocarbons, the range of ignition temperature is relatively wide in order to cover the ignition temperatures of the possible components.

(E) Sources of ignition shall be turned off during the filling of any LP-Gas container on the vehicle.

Ignition sources on vehicles waiting to be fueled and being fueled must be controlled. Special care should be taken when containers on recreational vehicles (RVs) are filled, because fires have been reported where containers were being filled without the extinguishment of pilots or other sources of ignition during refueling. Because some RVs have appliances, such as furnaces and ranges that have sources of ignition that operate automatically, it may be appropriate to turn all circuit breakers to the "off" position to prevent potential sources of ignition from operating.

7.2.3.3 Cargo tank vehicles unloading into storage containers shall be at least 10 ft (3.0 m) from the container and so positioned that the shutoff valves on both the truck and the container are readily accessible.

7.2.3.4 The cargo tank vehicle shall not transfer LP-Gas into dispensing station storage while parked on a public way.

Operations involving the unloading of cargo tank vehicles are required to have a minimum separation of 10 ft (3 m) from the cargo tank vehicle to the container receiving the product. It is important to have the cargo tank vehicle located such that the operating controls on both the truck and the tank that is being filled are accessible in an emergency.

The prohibition of street parking is intended to avoid the risks associated with accidental street vehicle collisions during a transfer operation. Traffic in the area is expected due to vehicles arriving to have their engine fuel containers filled or bringing in empty cylinders. Note that this prohibition does not apply to cargo tank vehicles transferring into containers at other locations.

The station shown in Exhibit 7.8 includes a complete bulkhead to prevent valve breakage in the event of a truck pulling away with hoses connected. In addition, the installation includes a shutoff valve, strainer, sight flow, and backflow check valve in the liquid fill line. The vapor equalizing line includes a shutoff valve, an emergency shutoff valve with remote cable release, and an excess-flow valve. Also installed are two crash posts for vehicular protection.

EXHIBIT 7.8 *Truck Unloading Station. (Courtesy of Richard Fredenburg, North Carolina Department of Agriculture and Consumer Services)*

7.2.3.5 Transfers to containers serving agricultural or industrial equipment requiring refueling in the field shall comply with 7.2.3.5(A) and 7.2.3.5(B).

(A)* Where the intake of air-moving equipment is less than 50 ft (15 m) from a point of transfer, it shall be shut down while containers are being refilled.

A.7.2.3.5(A) Air-moving equipment includes large blowers on crop dryers, space heaters, and some central heating equipment. Equipment employing open flames includes flame cultivators, weed burners, and tar kettles.

(B) Equipment employing open flames or equipment with integral containers shall be shut down while refueling.

Agricultural and industrial installations present different hazards than residential fuel applications, as they generally use more LP-Gas. The safety precautions required in 7.2.3.5 recognize common sources of ignition that can contribute to accidents during transfer. Open flames are used in weed burners, flame cultivation, vaporizing burners, some industrial heaters, and various other applications.

7.2.3.6 During the time railroad tank cars are on sidings for loading or unloading, the following shall apply:

(1) A caution sign, with wording such as "STOP. TANK CAR CONNECTED," shall be placed at the active end(s) of the siding while the car is connected, as required by DOT regulations.

Exhibit 7.9 shows a "Stop, Car Connected" warning sign on the track leading to a transfer station. Note that a derailer has been placed on the track with a sign also. The derailer will cause a car passing over it to derail, and the train's engineer will be aware of the derailing and stop the train and investigate.

EXHIBIT 7.9 *Stop and Derail Signs on a Track. (Courtesy of Eastern Propane Corp.)*

(2) Wheel chocks shall be placed to prevent movement of the car in either direction.

The provision in 7.2.3.6(2) reiterates an important DOT regulation. Accidents have occurred in cases where railroad tank cars have been moved when the unloading hose or connections were in place. In another case, a tank car was partially unloaded and the hoses disconnected, but the railroad personnel moved the tank car, thinking that it was empty. To prevent such incidents from occurring, the wheel chocks and the warning sign should always be in place until the tank car has been completely unloaded and the railroad personnel have been advised to move the tank car. (See Exhibit 7.10.)

EXHIBIT 7.10 *Wheel Chocks in Use During Unloading from a Tank Car. (Courtesy of Propane Education and Research Council)*

The value of chock blocks has been demonstrated by incidents in which trespassers have released the brake on the tank car and the tank car has moved from its unloading point. In one such instance, a string of tank cars ran down a grade and collided with a locomotive, killing two railroad workers [3].

Of course, chock blocks will fulfill their purpose only if they are physically capable. One authority having jurisdiction, visiting Star, North Carolina, in September 2004, found rail cars loaded with butane being stored in several locations around town. The cars had the brakes set and chock blocks in place. However, these "chock blocks" were pieces of scrap wood in various stages of rot. The AHJ had little faith that the chocks would perform as intended should the brakes release and required that they be replaced.

Exhibits 7.11 and 7.12 show tank car loading and unloading installations. Note the small plastic tubing strapped to the hoses in Exhibit 7.11. This tubing carries pressurized gas, which opens the emergency shutoff valves used to connect to the tank car. In case of fire, the tubing will fail, and the emergency shutoff valves will close.

7.2.3.7 Where a hose or swivel-type piping is used for loading or unloading railroad tank cars, it shall be protected as follows:

(1) An emergency shutoff valve shall be installed at the railroad tank car end of the hose or swivel-type piping where flow into or out of the railroad tank car is possible.
(2) An emergency shutoff valve or a backflow check valve shall be installed on the railroad tank car end of the hose or swivel piping where flow is only into the railroad tank car.

The requirements of 6.18.2.6 are repeated in 7.2.3.7 because they are very important and relate to railroad tank car transfer. Note that the requirements for emergency shutoff valves and check valves apply to all transfers to and from railroad tank cars, whereas in 6.12.1 they apply only to installations of 4000 gal (15.1 m³) or more.

EXHIBIT 7.11 *Tank Car Loading/Unloading Facility. Note the swing arm connected to tank car dome. (Courtesy of Eastern Propane Corp.)*

EXHIBIT 7.12 *Close-Up of Tank Car Dome. (Courtesy of Eastern Propane Corp.)*

Exhibit 7.13 shows a railroad tank car–unloading tower. Note the platform access to tank car domes. The emergency shutoff valve or check valve is located at the end of the swivel piping shown above the platform.

7.2.3.8 Where cargo tank vehicles are filled directly from railroad tank cars on a private track with nonstationary storage tanks involved, the following requirements shall be met:

(1) Transfer protection shall be provided in accordance with Section 6.12.
(2) Ignition source control shall be in accordance with Section 6.22.

EXHIBIT 7.13 Rail Car Unloading Tower. (Courtesy of Ely Energy)

(3) Control of ignition sources during transfer shall be provided in accordance with 7.2.3.2.
(4) Fire extinguishers shall be provided in accordance with 9.4.7.
(5) Transfer personnel shall meet the provisions of 7.2.1.
(6) Cargo tank vehicles shall meet the requirements of 7.2.3.
(7) The points of transfer shall be located in accordance with Table 6.5.3 with respect to exposures.
(8) Provision for anchorage and breakaway shall be provided on the cargo tank vehicle side for transfer from a railroad tank car directly into a cargo tank vehicle.

The requirements in 7.2.3.8 are needed to permit the unloading of rail cars where they cannot be unloaded directly into storage tanks. For example, this type of transfer is allowed when sections of rail mainlines are abandoned, when rail service to an area is discontinued, and when rail cars cannot reach their normal unloading location due to emergency situations. The approach taken is to require that equivalent safety features to those of fixed transfer facilities be installed to prevent the tank truck from moving and breaking a hose or piping system. The requirements in 7.2.3.8 are similar to those at storage facilities, as covered in Section 6.18.

7.2.3.9 Where cargo tank vehicles are filled from other cargo tank vehicles or cargo tanks, the following requirements shall apply:

Both cargo tank vehicles and cargo tanks are being used as an alternative to fixed storage, normally found at bulk and industrial plants. Product is transferred from one cargo tank vehicle or cargo tank to another cargo tank vehicle. Typically, transfer of product takes place from a cargo tank transport vehicle [9000 gal to 11,000 gal (34 m³ to 42 m³) water capacity] into a cargo tank vehicle known as a bobtail [typically 2500 gal to 5000 gal (9.5 m³ to 19 m³) water capacity].

The requirements in 7.2.3.9 are similar to those in 7.2.3.8 for transfer from rail cars directly to cargo tank vehicles.

(1) Transfer between cargo tanks or cargo tank vehicles where one is used as a bulk plant shall be temporary installations that comply with 4.3.2, 6.18.1, 6.18.2, 6.18.4 through 6.18.6, and 7.2.3.1.

The referenced paragraphs require the following:

- Notification of the transfer operation (4.3.2)
- Operations and maintenance for bulk plants (6.18.1)
- Clearances and other considerations to provide for safe liquid transfer (6.18.2)
- Security, lighting, and provisions for ignition source control (6.18.4, 6.18.5, and 6.18.6)
- Proper arrangement and operation of the transfer (7.2.3)

(2) Arrangements and operations of the transfer system shall be in accordance with the following:

  (a) The point of transfer shall be in accordance with Table 6.5.3.
  (b) Sources of ignition within the transfer area shall be controlled during the transfer operation as specified in 7.2.3.2.
  (c) Fire extinguishers shall be provided in accordance with 9.4.7.

(3) Cargo tanks shall comply with the requirements of 7.2.2.8.

(4) Provisions designed either to prevent a pull-away during a transfer operation or to stop the flow of products from both cargo tank vehicles or cargo tanks in the event of a pull-away shall be incorporated.

Paragraph 7.2.3.9(4) does not specify a particular device, but it does require the use of a system that will achieve the desired performance of stopping product flow in the event of a pull away event.

(5) Off-truck remote shutoff devices that meet 49 CFR 173.315(n) requirements and are installed on the cargo tank vehicle unloading the product shall satisfy the requirements of 7.2.3.9(4).

Paragraph 7.2.3.9(5) specifically permits the use of an active shutdown device, such as a "radio-controlled" device with an activator carried by the truck driver. The radio-controlled device will stop the pump, shut off the engine, and close the primary internal valve on the cargo tank vehicle that is unloading product when activated by the driver. Such devices are required by DOT for all cargo tank vehicles of 3500 gal (13 m³) or less. The device must be capable of performing at a distance of 150 ft (46 m) from the cargo tank vehicle. It must also be able to activate the shutdown system when tested at 300 ft (91 m) under optimum conditions. Cargo tank vehicles of more than 3500 gal (13 m³) in the United States are required by DOT to have a passive shutoff device that will stop the flow of propane from the cargo tank vehicle upon hose separation. Products used to comply with this requirement include a special hose incorporating a shutoff feature that activates if the hose coupling separates and a truck-mounted sensor that activates when pump discharge pressure increases. If a separation of this special hose occurs, the pump discharge pressure will increase due to the stoppage of flow.

Exhibit 7.14 shows the truck-mounted sensor on a larger cargo tank vehicle (transport). It continually monitors the offloading process for changes signifying broken or damaged hoses, fittings, or piping. A leak is detected and stopped by the closure of the tank internal valves(s). This unit also "fails safe" and closes the internal valve with a loss of power or the release of the trailer parking brake. The pressure sensor is located at the discharge of the pump. Also shown is the control box, the vapor internal valve, the manual operators that open and close the internal valves, and the air operator. Note that vapor and liquid control handles and valve caps are color coded to indicate vapor and liquid piping.

(6) Cargo tank vehicle LP-Gas transfers that are for the sole purpose of testing, maintaining, or repairing the cargo tank vehicle shall be exempt from the requirements of 7.2.3.9(1).

The provision in 7.2.3.9(6) is intended to exempt vehicles that are undergoing testing, repair, or maintenance operations that routinely occur on cargo tank motor vehicles.

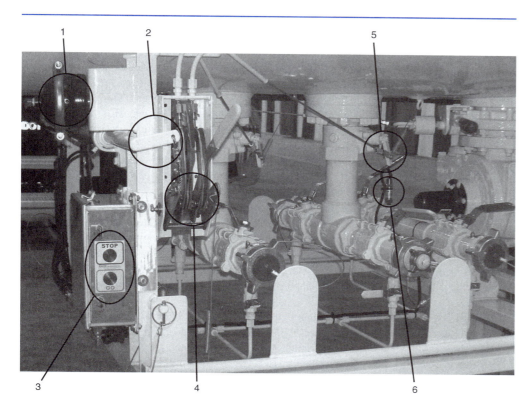

1. Air-operated shut-down actuator
2. Linkage/rod between spring chamber and valve operator
3. Passive shutdown controller
4. Manual operator to open/close vapor and liquid internal valves
5. Internal valve handle and cable linkage to valve operator with fusible link
6. Pressure sensor installed in pump discharge line, which sends signal to passive controller indicating that pump pressure is being maintained

7.2.4 Hose Inspection.

7.2.4.1 Hose assemblies shall be observed for leakage or for damage that could impair their integrity before each use.

7.2.4.2 The hose assemblies specified in 7.2.4.1 shall be inspected at least annually.

7.2.4.3 Inspection of pressurized hose assemblies shall include inspection for the following:

(1) Damage to outer cover that exposes reinforcement
(2) Kinked or flattened hose
(3) Soft spots or bulges in hose
(4) Couplings that have slipped on the hose, are damaged, have missing parts, or have loose bolts
(5) Leakage other than permeability leakage

7.2.4.4 Hose assemblies shall be replaced, repaired, or continued in service based on the results of the inspection.

7.2.4.5 Leaking or damaged hose shall be immediately repaired or removed from service.

The requirements for hose inspection provide criteria to be used to determine whether a hose assembly is suitable for continued service. These criteria emanate from the requirements for hose inspection created by DOT; this document is known as HM-225A, and became effective in 1999 [5]. HM-225A was, at least partially, a result of the hose failure incident in Sanford, North Carolina. (See the commentary following 6.12.9.) It has since been reinforced by another hose failure during a transfer in Tacoma, Washington, in October 2007.

Hose assemblies are the weak link in liquid transfer operations. Hose is inherently weaker than pipe and has a much shorter lifespan. Hose begins a gradual deterioration process from the time it is installed until the time it is removed from service. This deterioration process can be accelerated by the effects of weather and physical damage, resulting from the hose being dragged over earth, gravel, barbed wire fences, and so forth, and from other abrasive actions, such as pump-induced vibrations when in contact with gravel, concrete, or other rough surfaces. Bending hose beyond the maximum bending radius (kinking) can also cause damage. Hose ends can become loose and leak or they can separate from couplers. Hose couplers can wear and not fit tightly, and be subject to loosening from vibration.

Periodic inspection of hose assemblies is a requirement for safe transfer operations. However, disagreement remains over what should be included in hose inspection procedures. Some propane companies have established daily and periodic inspection procedures for hose assemblies.

Pressure testing of hose assemblies is a subject that has been discussed often over the years by regulatory officials, cargo tank vehicle operators, and propane companies. Recent requirements by DOT for cargo tank vehicle hose have mandated pressure testing of new and refitted hose assemblies in truck unloading service. Exhibit 7.15 shows a hose swivel end fitting, which can aid in preventing the kinking of hose.

EXHIBIT 7.15 *Hose Swivel End Fitting. (Courtesy of Full Circle)*

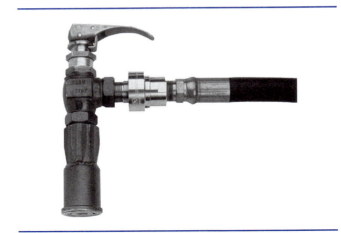

7.3 Venting LP-Gas to the Atmosphere

An increasing concern about venting LP-Gas to the atmosphere is the adverse environmental impact of the released propane. Unburned hydrocarbons in the air can combine with other chemicals to create smog or increased levels of ozone. The U.S. Environmental Protection Agency has become more interested in recent years in any releases of unburned hydrocarbons, which could result in more restrictions on venting LP-Gases.

7.3.1 General.

LP-Gas in either liquid or vapor form shall not be vented to the atmosphere unless it is vented under the following conditions:

(1) Venting of LP-Gas shall be permitted where the maximum flow from fixed liquid level, rotary, or slip tube gauges does not exceed that from a No. 54 drill orifice.

It is necessary to vent both vapor and a small amount of liquid from fixed maximum liquid level, rotary, and slip tube gauges. Venting should be done with consideration for potential ignition hazards within the surroundings. Discharged LP-Gas should not be close to a window, in order to prevent LP-Gas from entering a building. A No. 54 drill size limits the amount of LP-Gas vented to an amount that should dissipate rapidly.

(2) Venting of LP-Gas between shutoff valves before disconnecting the liquid transfer line from the container shall be permitted.
(3) Venting of LP-Gas, where necessary, shall be permitted to be performed by the use of bleeder valves.

If it is necessary to bleed off liquid from a pipe or a hose, the bleeding off must be done slowly and carefully. If bleeding off is not done correctly, a potential hazard created by the rapid discharge could result in cold liquid propane squirting into a person's eyes or coming into contact with skin. The area of the vapor ignition hazard is also increased because of the conversion of liquid to vapor. Also, if the venting it too rapid, the cooled liquid remaining in the pipe or hose can become so cold that it slows or stops vaporizing, leading to the belief that the line is empty. When the line is opened or the hose disconnected, a large release of the remaining product is likely.

(4) Venting of LP-Gas shall be permitted for the purposes described in 7.3.1(1) and (2) within structures designed for container filling in accordance with Chapter 10.

Buildings constructed to comply with Chapter 10 are built specifically to house LP-Gas transfer operations, and have no open flames or electrical sources of ignition.

(5) Venting of LP-Gas listed liquid transfer pumps using such vapor as a source of energy shall be permitted where the rate of discharge does not exceed the discharge from a No. 31 drill size orifice.

The exception in 7.3.1(5) to the general rule to minimize venting to the atmosphere has been in NFPA 58 for many years. It allows a piston pump powered by pressurized propane vapor to continue to be used; however, piston pumps have not been available for many years.

(6) Venting of LP-Gas for purging in accordance with 7.3.2 shall be permitted.
(7) Venting of LP-Gas shall be permitted for emergencies.

The need for the emergency venting is most common in cargo vehicle and railroad tank car accidents in which a tank is damaged and failure is considered possible. These situations often require the services of experts.

Teams of experts that specialize in response to rail car and truck accidents have been organized on a state or regional basis and are available to assist emergency responders in the event of a transportation emergency. One such group for chemical cargoes is the Chemical Transportation Emergency Center (CHEMTREC), which is operated by the Chemical Manufacturers Association. CHEMTREC provides a toll-free number (800-424-9300) for hazardous materials spills and incident emergencies. Frequently, local propane distributors assist in accidents involving propane cargoes through state or regional associations.

(8) Venting of LP-Gas vapor utilized as the pressure source in remote shutdown systems for internal valves and emergency shutoff valves shall be permitted.

Remote shutdown stations are often located at the gate or along the fence at a bulk plant, next to the uncontrolled area. Consideration should be given to not locating ignition sources near these remote stations, which can vent large amounts of vapor if they have many internal valves and emergency shutoff valves to close.

7.3.2 Purging.

7.3.2.1 Venting of gas from containers for purging or for other purposes shall be accomplished in accordance with 7.3.2.2 through 7.3.2.4.

7.3.2.2 Venting of cylinders indoors shall only occur in structures designed and constructed for cylinder filling in accordance with 6.5.1 and Chapter 10 and with 7.3.2.2(A) through 7.3.2.2(C).

(A) Piping shall be installed to convey the vented product outdoors at least 3 ft (1 m) above the highest point of any building within 25 ft (7.6 m).

(B) Only vapors shall be exhausted to the atmosphere.

(C) If a vent manifold is used to allow for the venting of more than one cylinder at a time, each connection to the vent manifold shall be equipped with a backflow check valve.

Purging is the process of removing the unwanted contents of a container and replacing it with something else. Purging is done for either of the following two reasons:

1. To completely empty a container of both LP-Gas liquid and vapor and replace them with air or another gas
2. To replace the air in a container with propane vapor, so that it can be filled with LP-Gas liquid and vapor

Whatever the purpose, product released from the container should be only vapor whenever feasible. Limiting the release to vapor, and not liquid, not only avoids the 270:1 liquid-to-vapor expansion ratio, but also recognizes that liquid discharge can present a greater static ignition hazard than vapor. (For additional information on static electricity, see A.6.22.1.3, which refers the reader to NFPA 77, *Recommended Practice on Static Electricity* [6].) If a container has been seriously overfilled, it is impossible to prevent liquid discharge from the container bleed valve outlet when initially correcting an overfill condition. In these circumstances, compliance with 7.3.2.2(A) is especially vital because the piping provides a safe place for vaporization.

The backflow check valve, which is required in each connection to a vent manifold by 7.3.2.2(C), minimizes the possibility of a flammable mixture being created in any one of the connections. When a container is almost completely empty of vapor and the pressure is practically at atmospheric, the possibility of a flammable mixture being created is present. Although the container could withstand the combustion explosion pressure that would develop, the piping could be subjected to detonation pressures it could not withstand.

When venting the vapor, the operator must remember that the evaporation of the liquid vapor results in refrigeration of the remaining liquid, and the temperature of the liquid may approach the normal atmospheric pressure boiling point [about –44°F (–42°C) for propane]. Because there is no pressure in the container at that liquid temperature, the operator may erroneously assume that the container is empty. When the liquid warms, vaporization will begin again and a positive pressure will be present. If the valves have been left open, a flow of vapor will occur into the atmosphere.

During the purging process when vapors are being discharged, it is important to check on conditions such as wind direction, wind speed, and the general layout of the area and structures. A given location might be perfectly satisfactory for venting the vapors under certain wind conditions, but be unsafe under other atmospheric conditions.

In some situations, it may be safer to burn off the vapors that are being vented rather than disperse them into the atmosphere. (See Exhibit 7.16.) However, when vapors are burned, a properly engineered flare stack should be used.

Purging new cylinders of air is essential; otherwise, the cylinders cannot be filled. Such purging is necessary because air will compress but not liquefy at propane tank pressures.

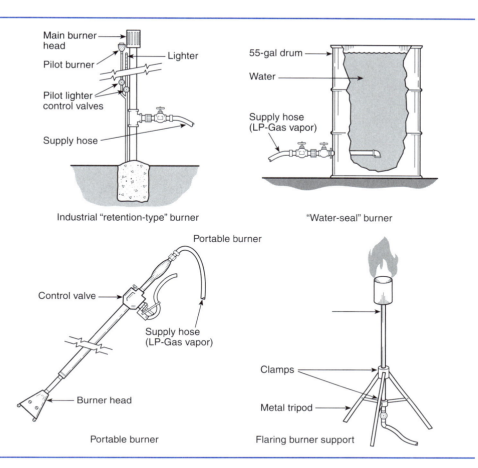

EXHIBIT 7.16 *Some Burner Arrangements for Flaring LP-Gas. (Courtesy of National Propane Gas Association)*

Industrial "retention-type" burner

"Water-seal" burner

Portable burner

Portable burner

Flaring burner support

Compressed air in a container occupies space that cannot be used for propane. Compressed air in containers creates the following two problems:

1. Containers will be underfilled because the air in the cylinder will compress but not liquefy.
2. Air–propane mixture is fed to the appliance, which will probably cause a lean fuel–air mixture and improper or no combustion.

Although it is unlikely that the mixture in the container will be flammable, the mixture will not burn properly and could result in flame lifting or a flame that is easily blown out, with a resulting danger of vapor cloud ignition.

Cylinders of 4 lb through 40 lb (1.8 kg through 18 kg) propane capacity (with some exceptions) must be equipped with an OPD. Refer to 5.7.3 for the specific requirements for OPDs. Some OPDs have been reported to incorporate a restriction orifice that limits the flow of vapor during normal withdrawal; this acts as a safety feature. The OPD also restricts the flow of vapor during the purging process. Some OPD manufacturers recommend that the fixed maximum liquid level gauge (spit gauge) be opened to expedite purging. The fixed maximum liquid level gauge can be opened outdoors but cannot be opened indoors because 7.3.2.2 requires that, in indoor purge areas, gases be piped to the outdoors. An alternate procedure is to use a vacuum pump to expedite the purging process. Some cylinder manufacturers are shipping new cylinders with a vacuum to minimize the need for purging.

7.3.2.3 Venting of containers outdoors shall be performed under conditions that result in rapid dispersion of the product being released.

7.3.2.4 If conditions are such that venting into the atmosphere cannot be accomplished safely, LP-Gas shall be burned at a distance of at least 25 ft (7.6 m) from combustibles.

7.3.2.5 Venting of containers and burning of LP-Gas from containers shall be attended.

This requirement was reinstated in 2008. Until the 2001 edition, there was a requirement that purging be done under controlled conditions, which stated:

> **4-3.2.1(c)** If conditions are such that venting into the atmosphere cannot be accomplished safely, LP-Gas shall be permitted to be burned off, providing such burning is done under controlled conditions at a distance of 25 ft (7.6 m) from combustibles or a hazardous atmosphere.

This provision was removed in the 2001 edition because it was vague and unenforceable, as "controlled conditions" were not specified. The committee added the current text in the 2008 edition in recognition that a requirement was needed, but it had to be enforceable. The phrase "shall be attended" is clearly enforceable and recognizes that all employees must be trained, and it is assumed that the training would include the necessary precautions to take while venting gas. The requirement is needed to provide some code guidance on venting of gas from containers, and the new text is enforceable and does allow procedures to be developed appropriate to each location where cylinders are purged and the gas is vented.

It was brought to the committee's attention that tanks brought back to a company for refurbishing or scrapping were being "cracked open" to allow the tanks to empty. Often, as weather conditions changed, the vented gas did not disperse well. Fire departments were receiving complaints from neighbors about the smell of gas and had to respond. At times the odor was quite strong, and fear of reaching a combustible mixture caused the fire departments to use their hoses to help disperse the gas. To comply with this requirement, a qualified employee or employees must be present during venting to respond if conditions change and hamper dispersion. They must also be in attendance during burning or flaring so they can respond to problems that might develop during that process.

7.4 Quantity of LP-Gas in Containers

7.4.1 Application.

Section 7.4 applies to the maximum permissible LP-Gas content of containers and the methods of verifying this quantity. *(See Annex F.)*

Filling containers to a proper capacity is important because LP-Gas liquids expand when heated and contract when cooled, with a corresponding change in container pressure. The degree of expansion varies with the specific gravity of LP-Gas. Table 7.4.2.2 was developed to stipulate the filling densities for different liquids, as shown by the different specific gravities in the first column. The table is used when filling a container by weight. Propane generally falls within the 0.504–0.510 range of specific gravity. (See Exhibit 7.17.)

Cylinders can be filled by weight or by volume. DOT requires that all cylinders within its jurisdiction and having water capacities less than 200 lb (91 kg) be filled by weight and that the cylinders' fill amount be verified by weight to ensure that they were not overfilled after the filling line was disconnected [7]. The jurisdiction of DOT applies to all cylinders that are transported in commerce, which means that this filling restriction does not apply to cylinders filled at the point of use and not transported on a public road. Those cylinders with water capacities greater than 200 lb (91 kg) can be filled using the volumetric method. Similarly, the quantity of product in each container must be verified after disconnecting the fill line, but use of the bleed valve for these cylinders is specified [8]. All ASME tanks are filled using the volumetric method. When filling is done by volume, Tables 7.4.2.3(a), 7.4.2.3(b), and 7.4.2.3(c) are used.

EXHIBIT 7.17 *In-Line Hygrometer for Measuring the Specific Gravity of Propane.*

In Table 7.4.2.2, the determination of the maximum quantity of propane that can be placed in a container is expressed as a percent of the water weight capacity of the container. As shown in the second column of Table 7.4.2.2, propane may be 42 percent of the water weight capacity for containers of up to 1200 gal (4.5 m³) capacity. For containers over 1200 gal (4.5 m³) capacity, the amount will be 45 percent of the water weight capacity.

Water weighs approximately 8.3 lb/gal (956 kg/m³). The application of Table 7.4.2.2 to cylinders, which are marked with the water capacity in pounds and are limited to less than 1000 lb (454 kg) total water capacity, is limited to the column of the table marked "0 to 1200 U.S. gal. . . ." For example, a 100 lb (45 kg) propane cylinder with a marked water capacity of 239 lb (108 kg) may contain 239 × 0.42, or 100.38 lb (45.4 kg), of propane.

When calculating the maximum filling limit of containers, the tables provide different filling levels for aboveground containers of 0 to 1200 gal (0 to 4.5 m³), for aboveground containers over 1200 gal (4.5 m³), and for all underground containers. Different filling levels are provided because each of the following three types of containers is assumed to have a different maximum temperature that it can reach.

◀ **FAQ**
Why does the filling limit in Table 7.4.2.2 depend on the volume of the container and whether it is installed above or below ground?

1. Cylinders and other aboveground containers with water capacities of 1200 gal (4.5 m³) or less are assumed to have a maximum temperature of 130°F (54°C). These are the smallest containers and therefore are heated most quickly by the sun. The temperature of 130°F (54°C) is the design basis of the DOT requirements in the United States because it is the highest temperature that a cylinder is expected to reach. To the editor's knowledge, it is also used in other countries.

2. Other aboveground uninsulated containers over 1200 gal (4.5 m³) are assumed to have a temperature of 115°F (46°C). These larger containers have a greater ratio of volume to surface area, so the heat from the sun is more slowly transferred to the contents, resulting in a lower temperature rise after a sunny day.

3. Underground containers are assumed to have a temperature of 105°F (41°C). These containers do not receive radiated heat directly from the sun. The sun heats the ground over the container, and the heated soil transfers some heat to the container. These containers receive the least solar heat during the day.

The basis for determining maximum filling levels is explained in Section F.2.

Proper filling is especially important for cylinders that will be used inside a building, such as industrial truck cylinders. A cylinder usually will be filled outdoors and the temperature might be extremely cold, even below zero. When the cylinder is taken inside the building, the temperature may be near 60°F (16°C). When these extreme temperature differentials are involved, the cylinder must be very carefully filled to avoid having it become liquid full within the building, which would cause the pressure relief device to open. The personnel handling such cylinders should know and understand the importance of the liquid expansion factor.

One method of filling cylinders is by weight, which is accurate when the scales are accurate. A second method of filling cylinders is by volume, using a fixed maximum liquid level gauge. If properly designed and installed, this gauge is accurate. Other volume gauges, such as a rotary gauge, should not be used for filling cylinders because they are not accurate enough. This type of gauge is normally included in an engine fuel cylinder so the operator of the vehicle can identify the quantity of fuel in the tank. The rotary gauge is used to check on gas remaining in the tank, but is not used to determine the filling level.

When the volumetric method of filling is used, it is necessary to correct the gauge reading by referencing the liquid volume temperature correction in Table F.3.3 to determine the amount of liquid at 60°F (16°C).

If the volumetric method of filling is used, using either the fixed maximum liquid level gauge or a variable liquid level gauge without liquid volume temperature correction, the liquid level indicated by such gauges must be computed on the basis of the maximum permitted filling density when the liquid is at 40°F (4°C) for aboveground containers and at 50°F (10°C) for underground containers. (See 5.7.5.8.) It is also suggested that when a variable-type gauging device such as the rotary gauge is used, its accuracy be checked regularly with the fixed liquid level gauge.

Many small cylinders incorporate only a fixed maximum liquid level gauge and are not equipped with a means of measuring the temperature of the liquid propane. The fixed maximum liquid level gauge is selected to provide a filling limit of 80 percent, as required by 7.4.3.2(A), which states that the maximum filling limit permitted must be based on a filling temperature of 40°F (4°C). Table 7.4.2.3(a) has an asterisk at the 40°F (4°C) line to note this requirement, and for the typical propane density of 0.504–0.510, the container is permitted to have an 80 percent maximum filling limit. Note that for underground containers, the filling temperature used is 50°F (10°C) when only a fixed maximum liquid level gauge is used, which corresponds to a maximum filling limit of 89 percent in Table 7.4.2.3(c).

When demand for propane is high, as will occur during very cold weather, local shortages can occur where storage is not adequate. To prevent such shortages, state authorities have permitted propane transports to be overfilled, using the provisions of Section 1.5, Equivalency. This situation requires coordination with highway officials to allow overweight vehicles on the highways and monitoring of the temperature of the loads. The practice of overfilling should be restricted to emergency periods only.

7.4.2 LP-Gas Capacity of Containers.

7.4.2.1 The capacity of an LP-Gas container shall be determined either by weight in accordance with 7.4.2.2 or by volume in accordance with 7.4.2.3.

Cylinders can be filled by either weight or volume because they are portable. Weight filling is not practical for most ASME containers because they are not portable. Exhibit 7.18 shows

EXHIBIT 7.18 Automated LP-Gas Cylinder Filling Carousel.

an automated carousel filling installation that fills cylinders for exchange cylinder cabinets. Empty cylinders are fed to the carousel on a conveyor and filled and check weighed as they travel around the circle. Filled cylinders are then removed onto a conveyor.

7.4.2.2* The maximum filling limit by weight of LP-Gas in a container shall be in accordance with Table 7.4.2.2.

TABLE 7.4.2.2 *Maximum Filling Limit by Weight of LP-Gas Containers (Percent of Marked Water Capacity in Pounds)*

	Aboveground Containers		
Specific Gravity at 60°F (15.6°C)	*0 to 1200 gal (0 to 4.5 m³) Total Water Capacity (%)*	*>1200 gal (>4.5 m³) Total Water Capacity (%)*	*Underground Containers All Water Capacities (%)*
0.496–0.503	41	44	45
0.504–0.510	42	45	46
0.511–0.519	43	46	47
0.520–0.527	44	47	48
0.528–0.536	45	48	49
0.537–0.544	46	49	50
0.545–0.552	47	50	51
0.553–0.560	48	51	52
0.561–0.568	49	52	53
0.569–0.576	50	53	54
0.577–0.584	51	54	55
0.585–0.592	52	55	56
0.593–0.600	53	56	57

Table 7.4.2.2 permits greater filling densities for containers larger than 1200 gal (4.5 m³) water capacity because of the "thermal inertia" that larger masses of material provide. In other words, it takes longer for larger tanks to heat up during the daytime, and the potential for a container to become "liquid full" due to expansion while being warmed by sunlight is less than for smaller containers. An even greater insulation against heating from sunlight is provided for containers installed under ground. Therefore, the filling densities for those containers are the highest.

A.7.4.2.2 The maximum permitted filling limit in percent by weight should be as shown in Table 7.4.2.2.

7.4.2.3* The maximum permitted volume of LP-Gas in a container shall be in accordance with Table 7.4.2.3(a), Table 7.4.2.3(b), and Table 7.4.2.3(c).

A.7.4.2.3 The maximum permitted LP-Gas volume of any container depends on the size of the container, whether it is installed above ground or under ground, the specific gravity, and the temperature of the liquid. *[See Table 7.4.2.2, Table 7.4.2.3(a), Table 7.4.2.3(b), and Table 7.4.2.3(c).]*

The difference between the requirements in 7.4.2.2 and those in 7.4.2.3 are due to the fact that Table 7.4.2.2 addresses containers that are marked with the water capacity in pounds, whereas Tables 7.4.2.3(a) through 7.4.2.3(c) are applicable to containers marked with the water capacity in gallons.

See F.5.1.2 for the method of computing the values in Table 7.4.2.3(a), Table 7.4.2.3(b), and Table 7.4.2.3(c).

TABLE 7.4.2.3(a) *Maximum Permitted LP-Gas Volume (Percent of Total Container Volume): Aboveground Containers 0 to 1200 gal (0 to 4.5 m³)*

Liquid Temperature		Specific Gravity												
°F	°C	0.496 to 0.503	0.504 to 0.510	0.511 to 0.519	0.520 to 0.527	0.528 to 0.536	0.537 to 0.544	0.545 to 0.552	0.553 to 0.560	0.561 to 0.568	0.569 to 0.576	0.577 to 0.584	0.585 to 0.592	0.593 to 0.600
−50	−45.6	70	71	72	73	74	75	75	76	77	78	79	79	80
−45	−42.8	71	72	73	73	74	75	76	77	77	78	79	80	80
−40	−40	71	72	73	74	75	75	76	77	78	79	79	80	81
−35	−37.2	71	72	73	74	75	76	77	77	78	79	80	80	81
−30	−34.4	72	73	74	75	76	76	77	78	78	79	80	81	81
−25	−31.5	72	73	74	75	76	77	77	78	79	80	80	81	82
−20	−28.9	73	74	75	76	76	77	78	79	79	80	81	81	82
−15	−26.1	73	74	75	76	77	77	78	79	80	80	81	82	83
−10	−23.3	74	75	76	76	77	78	79	79	80	81	81	82	83
−5	−20.6	74	75	76	77	78	78	79	80	80	81	82	82	83
0	−17.8	75	76	76	77	78	79	79	80	81	81	82	83	84
5	−15	75	76	77	78	78	79	80	81	81	82	83	83	84
10	−12.2	76	77	77	78	79	80	80	81	82	82	83	84	84
15	−9.4	76	77	78	79	80	80	81	81	82	83	83	84	85
20	−6.7	77	78	78	79	80	80	81	82	83	84	84	84	85
25	−3.9	77	78	79	80	80	81	82	82	83	84	84	85	85
30	−1.1	78	79	79	80	81	81	82	83	83	84	85	85	86
35	1.7	78	79	80	81	81	82	83	83	84	85	85	86	86
40*	4.4	79	80	81	81	82	82	83	84	84	85	86	86	87
45	7.8	80	80	81	82	82	83	84	84	85	85	86	87	87
50	10	80	81	82	82	83	83	84	85	85	86	86	87	88
55	12.8	81	82	82	83	84	84	85	85	86	86	87	87	88
60	15.6	82	82	83	84	84	85	85	86	86	87	87	88	88
65	18.3	82	83	84	84	85	85	86	86	87	87	88	88	89
70	21.1	83	84	84	85	85	86	86	87	87	88	88	89	89
75	23.9	84	85	85	85	86	86	87	87	88	88	89	89	90
80	26.7	85	85	86	86	87	87	87	88	88	89	89	90	90
85	29.4	85	86	87	87	88	88	88	89	89	89	90	90	91
90	32.2	86	87	87	88	88	88	89	89	90	90	90	91	91
95	35	87	88	88	88	89	89	89	90	90	91	91	91	92
100	37.8	88	89	89	89	89	90	90	90	91	91	92	92	92
105	40.4	89	89	90	90	90	90	91	91	91	92	92	92	93
110	43	90	90	91	91	91	91	92	92	92	92	93	93	93
115	46	91	91	92	92	92	92	92	92	93	93	93	94	94
120	49	92	92	93	93	93	93	93	93	93	94	94	94	94
125	51.5	93	94	94	94	94	94	94	94	94	94	94	95	95
130	54	94	95	95	95	95	95	95	95	95	95	95	95	95

*See 7.4.3.2(A).

TABLE 7.4.2.3(b) *Maximum Permitted LP-Gas Volume (Percent of Total Container Volume): Aboveground Containers Over 1200 gal (Over 4.5 m³)*

Liquid Temperature		Specific Gravity												
°F	°C	0.496 to 0.503	0.504 to 0.510	0.511 to 0.519	0.520 to 0.527	0.528 to 0.536	0.537 to 0.544	0.545 to 0.552	0.553 to 0.560	0.561 to 0.568	0.569 to 0.576	0.577 to 0.584	0.585 to 0.592	0.593 to 0.600
−50	−45.6	75	76	77	78	79	80	80	81	82	83	83	84	85
−45	−42.8	76	77	78	78	79	80	81	81	82	83	84	84	85
−40	−40	76	77	78	79	80	80	81	82	83	83	84	85	85
−35	−37.2	77	78	78	79	80	81	82	82	83	84	84	85	86
−30	−34.4	77	78	79	80	80	81	82	83	83	84	85	85	86
−25	−31.5	78	79	79	80	81	82	82	83	84	84	85	86	86
−20	−28.9	78	79	80	81	81	82	83	83	84	85	85	86	87
−15	−26.1	79	79	80	81	82	82	83	84	85	85	86	87	87
−10	−23.3	79	80	81	82	82	83	84	84	85	86	86	87	87
−5	−20.6	80	81	81	82	83	83	84	85	85	86	87	87	88
0	−17.8	80	81	82	82	83	84	84	85	86	86	87	88	88
5	−15	81	82	82	83	84	84	85	86	86	87	87	88	89
10	−12.2	81	82	83	83	84	85	85	86	87	87	88	88	89
15	−9.4	82	83	83	84	85	85	86	87	87	88	88	89	90
20	−6.7	82	83	84	85	85	86	86	87	88	88	89	89	90
25	−3.9	83	84	84	85	86	86	87	88	88	89	89	90	90
30	−1.1	83	84	85	86	86	87	87	88	89	89	90	90	91
35	1.7	84	85	86	86	87	87	88	89	89	90	90	91	91
40*	4.4	85	86	86	87	87	88	88	89	90	90	91	91	92
45	7.8	85	86	87	87	88	88	89	89	90	91	91	92	92
50	10	86	87	87	88	88	89	90	90	91	91	92	92	92
55	12.8	87	88	88	89	89	90	90	91	91	92	92	92	93
60	15.6	88	88	89	89	90	90	91	91	92	92	93	93	93
65	18.3	88	89	90	90	91	91	91	92	92	93	93	93	94
70	21.1	89	90	90	91	91	91	92	92	93	93	94	94	94
75	23.9	90	91	91	91	92	92	92	93	93	94	94	94	95
80	26.7	91	91	92	92	92	93	93	93	94	94	95	95	95
85	29.4	92	92	93	93	93	93	94	94	95	95	95	96	96
90	32.2	93	93	93	94	94	94	95	95	95	95	96	96	96
95	35	94	94	94	95	95	95	95	96	96	96	96	97	97
100	37.8	94	95	95	95	95	96	96	96	96	97	97	97	98
105	40.4	96	96	96	96	96	97	97	97	97	97	98	98	98
110	43	97	97	97	97	97	97	97	98	98	98	98	98	99
115	46	98	98	98	98	98	98	98	98	98	99	99	99	99

*See 7.4.3.2(A).

TABLE 7.4.2.3(c) *Maximum Permitted LP-Gas Volume (Percent of Total Container Volume): All Underground Containers*

Liquid Temperature		Specific Gravity												
°F	°C	0.496 to 0.503	0.504 to 0.510	0.511 to 0.519	0.520 to 0.527	0.528 to 0.536	0.537 to 0.544	0.545 to 0.552	0.553 to 0.560	0.561 to 0.568	0.569 to 0.576	0.577 to 0.584	0.585 to 0.592	0.593 to 0.600
−50	−45.6	77	78	79	80	80	81	82	83	83	84	85	85	86
−45	−42.8	77	78	79	80	81	82	82	83	84	84	85	86	87
−40	−40	78	79	80	81	81	82	83	83	84	85	86	86	87
−35	−37.2	78	79	80	81	82	82	83	84	85	85	86	87	87
−30	−34.4	79	80	81	81	82	83	84	84	85	86	86	87	88
−25	−31.5	79	80	81	82	83	83	84	85	85	86	87	87	88
−20	−28.9	80	81	82	82	83	84	84	85	86	86	87	88	88
−15	−26.1	80	81	82	83	84	84	85	86	86	87	87	88	89
−10	−23.3	81	82	83	83	84	85	85	86	87	87	88	88	89
−5	−20.6	81	82	83	84	84	85	86	86	87	88	88	89	89
0	−17.8	82	83	84	84	85	85	86	87	87	88	89	89	90
5	−15	82	83	84	85	85	86	87	87	88	88	89	90	90
10	−12.2	83	84	85	85	86	86	87	88	88	89	90	90	91
15	−9.4	84	84	85	86	86	87	88	88	89	89	90	91	91
20	−6.7	84	85	86	86	87	88	88	89	89	90	90	91	91
25	−3.9	85	86	86	87	87	88	89	89	90	90	91	91	92
30	−1.1	85	86	87	87	88	89	89	90	90	91	91	92	92
35	1.7	86	87	87	88	88	89	90	90	91	91	92	92	93
40	4.4	87	87	88	88	89	90	90	91	91	92	92	93	93
45	7.8	87	88	89	89	90	90	91	91	92	92	93	93	94
50*	10	88	89	89	90	90	91	91	92	92	93	93	94	94
55	12.8	89	89	90	91	91	91	92	92	93	93	94	94	95
60	15.6	90	90	91	91	92	92	92	93	93	94	94	95	95
65	18.3	90	91	91	92	92	93	93	94	94	94	95	95	96
70	21.1	91	91	92	93	93	93	94	94	94	95	95	96	96
75	23.9	92	93	93	93	94	94	94	95	95	95	96	96	97
80	26.7	93	93	94	94	94	95	95	95	96	96	96	97	97
85	29.4	94	94	95	95	95	95	96	96	96	97	97	97	98
90	32.2	95	95	95	95	96	96	96	97	97	97	98	98	98
95	35	96	96	96	96	97	97	97	97	98	98	98	98	99
100	37.8	97	97	97	97	97	98	98	98	98	99	99	99	99
105	40.4	98	98	98	98	98	98	98	99	99	99	99	99	99

*See 7.4.3.2(A).

7.4.3 General Provisions for the Volumetric Method of Filling Containers.

7.4.3.1 The volumetric method shall be limited to the following containers that are designed and equipped for filling by volume:

(1) Cylinders of less than 200 lb (91 kg) water capacity that are not subject to DOT jurisdiction
(2) Cylinders of 200 lb (91 kg) water capacity or more
(3) Cargo tanks or portable tanks
(4) ASME and API-ASME containers complying with 5.2.1.1 or 5.2.4.2

The volumetric filling method can be used for the services listed in 7.4.3.1. All cylinders of 200 lb (91 kg) water capacity or more can be filled by volume. Only those cylinders less than 200 lb (91 kg) water capacity that are not subject to DOT jurisdiction can be filled volumetrically. DOT jurisdiction covers cylinders transported in commerce by a common carrier or by other means. If doubt exists as to filling method, a state or federal DOT office in the United States may be contacted for a full explanation. Cylinders that are filled on the site of use do not come under DOT rules.

Proper filling of cylinders is important because overfilled cylinders are potentially hazardous. The pressure relief valve will operate and release liquid LP-Gas if the cylinder is heated sufficiently to cause the liquid to expand to the point that the cylinder becomes liquid full.

7.4.3.2 Where used, the volumetric method shall be in accordance with 7.4.3.2(A) through 7.4.3.2(C).

(A) If a fixed maximum liquid level gauge or a variable liquid level gauge without liquid volume temperature correction is used, the liquid level indicated by these gauges shall be computed based on the maximum permitted filling limit when the liquid is at 40°F (4°C) for aboveground containers or at 50°F (10°C) for underground containers.

(B) When a variable liquid level gauge is used and the liquid volume is corrected for temperature, the maximum permitted liquid level shall be in accordance with Table 7.4.2.3(a) through Table 7.4.2.3(c).

(C) ASME containers with a water capacity of 1200 gal (4.54 m^3) or less filled by the volumetric method shall be gauged in accordance with 7.4.3.2(A), utilizing the fixed maximum liquid level gauge, except that containers fabricated on or before December 31, 1965, shall be exempt from this provision.

7.4.3.3 Where containers are to be filled volumetrically by a variable liquid level gauge in accordance with 7.4.3.2(B), provisions shall be made for determining the liquid temperature.

7.4.4* Overfilling.

A.7.4.4 The overfilling prevention device is intended to be a backup safety device to prevent overfilling of cylinders. Other means as provided in the chapter must be used when filling containers, even if an overfilling prevention device is present and expected to stop flow into the container before the other means indicate the container is properly filled.

It is important to remember that even though all portable cylinders of 4 lb to 40 lb (1.8 kg to 18 kg) LP-Gas capacity are required to have an OPD, the primary means for filling the cylinder is still either a scale or the fixed maximum liquid level gauge. It is important that those who fill cylinders do not try to give the customer a "good deal" by attempting to defeat the OPD and put more product into the cylinder than the OPD allows. See the commentary following 5.7.3 for more details on this topic.

7.4.4.1 An overfilling prevention device shall not be the primary means to determine when a cylinder is filled to the maximum allowable filling limit.

7.4.4.2 Other means specified in this chapter shall be used to prevent the overfilling of cylinders.

REFERENCES CITED IN COMMENTARY

1. Title 49, Code of Federal Regulations, Parts177.834(i)(1) and (2), U.S. Government Printing Office, Washington, DC.
2. NFPA 51, *Standard for the Design and Installation of Oxygen–Fuel Gas Systems for Welding, Cutting, and Allied Processes,* 2007 edition, National Fire Protection Association, Quincy, MA.
3. ANSI/CSA Z-21.58, *Outdoor Cooking Gas Appliances,* 2007 edition, CSA America Inc., Cleveland, OH.
4. NFPA 51B, *Standard for Fire Prevention During Welding, Cutting, and Other Hot Work,* 2009 edition, National Fire Protection Association, Quincy, MA.
5. Title 49, Code of Federal Regulations, Parts 177 and 180 (HM-225A), "Hazardous Materials: Revision to Regulations Governing Transportation and Unloading of Liquefied Compressed Gases (Chlorine)," 1999, U.S. Government Printing Office, Washington, DC.
6. NFPA 77, *Recommended Practice on Static Electricity,* 2007 edition, National Fire Protection Association, Quincy, MA.
7. Title 49, Code of Federal Regulations, Part 304a (c), U.S. Government Printing Office, Washington, DC.
8. Title 49, Code of Federal Regulations, Part 304a (d)(4), U.S. Government Printing Office, Washington, DC.

Storage of Cylinders Awaiting Use, Resale, or Exchange

Chapter 8 provides storage requirements both outside and inside buildings for portable containers awaiting use, resale, or exchange. This chapter applies to cylinders — portable containers of 1000 lb (454 kg) water capacity or less — that are filled, partially filled, or empty (not purged of residual LP-Gas). These containers may be handled by dealers or resellers at dispensing locations or stored by their owners at the location of use. Chapter 8 does not apply to cylinders connected for use to LP-Gas equipment or systems. Cylinders connected for use are covered in Chapter 6. Chapter 8 also does not apply to storage of cylinders at bulk plants.

Chapter 8 includes detailed information and requirements for the following topics:

- Location and position of cylinders in storage and the protection of cylinder valves (See Section 8.2.)
- Storage within buildings, including requirements for different types of building occupancies (See Section 8.3.)
- Storage outside of buildings, including requirements for separation distances (See Section 8.4.)
- Fire extinguishers (See Section 8.5.)

8.1 Scope

Chapter 8 applies only to cylinders, which are defined as follows:

> **3.3.16 Cylinder.** A container designed, constructed, tested, and marked in accordance with U.S. Department of Transportation specifications, Title 49, *Code of Federal Regulations*, or in accordance with a valid DOT special permit.

U.S. Department of Transportation (DOT) specifications limit cylinders to 1000 lb (454 kg) water capacity, or 420 lb (191 kg) propane capacity [1]. DOT cylinders are portable storage containers that can be used in transportation, as well as installed and used in a stationary installation (see 3.3.67). The definition of *cylinder* does not include the following:

- ASME containers, which are designed to be installed at one location and are not permitted to be transported when they contain more than 5 percent propane (with one exception covered in 9.6.2.2). Chapter 8, therefore, does not apply to ASME containers not connected for use, such as at a propane distribution facility. Storage of propane tanks in these locations has not, to the editor's knowledge, been the source of fires or contributed to adding fuel to incidents. However, as might be expected, this exclusion raises questions with some fire officials. In some cases, local fire officials have contacted the state-level authority having jurisdiction to express concern with the location of some ASME tanks, especially if they are unprotected and in a location where they could be impacted by vehicles. Some AHJs share this concern. In some incidents, a tank received minor damage, and, presumably, the vehicle may have been damaged, too. However, no known significant events have occurred and therefore the exclusion remains in the 2011 edition.

- Cylinders made to specifications of other countries. Under international treaties, DOT permits these cylinders to be used, but not refilled, in the United States.

8.1.1 The provisions of this chapter apply to the storage of cylinders of 1000 lb (454 kg) water capacity or less, whether filled, partially filled, or empty, as follows:

(1) At consumer sites or dispensing stations, where not connected for use
(2) In storage for resale or exchange by dealer or reseller

8.1.2 This chapter does not apply to new or unused cylinders.

New and unused cylinders that have not been filled with propane are exempt from the requirements of Chapter 8 because they do not represent a fire hazard.

8.1.3 This chapter does not apply to cylinders stored at bulk plants.

Provisions for storing cylinders on users' premises and at locations for resale first appeared in the code in the early 1940s. By that time, many filled cylinders were being resold at locations such as hardware stores, and it was deemed necessary to regulate the manner in which these cylinders were stored. Many users, particularly industrial users, stored cylinders awaiting use on their premises, and requirements for these cylinders' storage were also needed.

The current provisions of NFPA 58 do not differentiate between storage at a resale location or a user location, but they do stipulate what is to be done if portable cylinders are stored in conventional buildings (whether frequented by the public or not), outside of buildings, and in special buildings or rooms meeting the requirements of Chapter 10. The provisions of Chapter 8 apply only to the storage of cylinders on the premises of consumers, at dispensing stations, and at locations for resale or exchange by the cylinder dealer or reseller. The requirements do not apply to storage of cylinders at propane bulk plants. Storage of cylinders at bulk plants has not, to the editor's knowledge, except in one instance, been a source of fire or contributed to adding fuel to incidents. In that incident, in Truth or Consequences, New Mexico, in January 2001, a parked pickup truck rolled into a bulk plant, breaking piping that released propane, which ignited. A major fire ensued, with filled cylinders stored at the plant exploding. See Section 6.18 and associated commentary for more information on bulk plants.

8.2 General Provisions

Section 8.2 requires the following regarding the storage of cylinders awaiting use or resale:

- Minimize exposure of the cylinders to excessive heat, physical damage, or tampering. (See 8.2.1.1.)
- Store cylinders away from exits, stairways, or areas normally used, or intended for use, as an egress inside buildings. (See 8.2.1.3.)
- Count all cylinders full, partially full, or empty (except new, unused cylinders) as full when determining the maximum quantity allowed in a building. (See 8.2.1.4.)
- Prohibit the storage of cylinders on roofs of buildings. (See 8.2.1.5.)
- Close, plug, or cap cylinder outlet valves. (See 8.2.2.3.)

8.2.1 General Location of Cylinders.

8.2.1.1 Cylinders in storage shall be located to minimize exposure to excessive temperature rises, physical damage, or tampering.

Because of the smaller size of the cylinders covered in Chapter 8, the temperature of their contents tends to fluctuate more directly with ambient air temperatures or solar radiation than the temperature of larger containers. These cylinders should not relieve LP-Gas through their pressure relief devices until the temperature of their contents exceeds 130°F (54°C), at which point the cylinder may become liquid-full. These high temperatures could be reached in some extremely hot climates or in poorly located, poorly constructed, or unventilated storage locations.

In addition to temperature control, physical damage protection may be needed in storage locations. Certain facilities have considerable vehicular traffic — for example, forklift trucks — and require these precautions. Finally, tampering is a valid consideration. Although small portable cylinders, such as those used with grills, will not flow gas even if the valve is opened by hand, it is still important to provide protection from tampering, which could affect the safety devices.

8.2.1.2 Cylinders in storage having individual water capacity greater than 2.7 lb (1.1 kg) [nominal 1 lb (0.45 kg) LP-Gas capacity] shall be positioned so that the pressure relief valve is in direct communication with the vapor space of the cylinder.

The requirement that cylinders, other than very small cylinders, be stored so that the pressure relief valve is in the vapor space of the cylinder is an important safety concept that is repeated in several locations (for example, 5.2.5.6 and 6.7.2.1) in the code. The requirement is important because the capacity of pressure relief valves is based on gas flow, not liquid flow. If the pressure in a cylinder were sufficiently high to cause the pressure relief valve to operate, and the pressure relief valve were in communication with the liquid space of the cylinder, the following would occur:

- The flow of liquid through the pressure relief valve would be lower than the flow of gas would be if gas passed through the valve. Therefore, it would take longer to reduce the pressure in the cylinder.
- The liquid being released from the cylinder would flash to vapor. Liquid release results in a significantly higher amount of propane being discharged from the cylinder (approximately 270 times by volume), because any liquid that is released to the atmosphere will vaporize almost instantly, creating a much larger amount of vapor. There can be several causes of pressure relief valve operation. These causes include overfilling, exposure to fire, and a defect in the pressure relief valve. If fire is the cause of the pressure relief valve operation, the released propane will provide more fuel to the fire.
- The cylinder would not autorefrigerate. When the vapor pressure is reduced, such as when vapor is released by the pressure relief valve, the liquid propane in the cylinder works to bring the vapor pressure back into pressure and temperature equilibrium. To do this, the liquid cools as it releases vapor. With this cooling, the pressure in the cylinder is lowered and the relief valve can close. If liquid is released, this cooling is significantly less.

Cylinders excluded from this requirement are those less than 2.7 lb (1.1 kg) water capacity [about 1 lb (0.45 kg) of propane]. Examples of such cylinders are those used for hand-held soldering torches, portable stoves, camping equipment, refillable portable appliances such as cigarette lighters, and so forth. (See Exhibit 8.1.) These small cylinders are normally stored in cardboard shipping containers, and the proper storage orientation should be indicated on the shipping container.

8.2.1.3 Cylinders stored in buildings in accordance with Section 8.3 shall not be located near exits, near stairways, or in areas normally used, or intended to be used, for the safe egress of occupants.

The provision in 8.2.1.3 is consistent with NFPA *101®*, *Life Safety Code®* [2]. In NFPA *101*, an exit is defined as that portion of a means of egress separated from all other building spaces, such as an enclosed exit stairway, and an *exit access* is that portion that leads to an exit, such as a corridor or aisle. Storage of LP-Gas cylinders is not permitted in an exit or an exit access that is used for the safe egress of the occupants.

EXHIBIT 8.1 *Cylinder Used for Portable Appliance (Camp Stove).*

8.2.1.4 If empty cylinders that have been in LP-Gas service are stored indoors, they shall be considered as full cylinders for the purposes of determining the maximum quantities of LP-Gas permitted by 8.3.1, 8.3.2.1, and 8.3.3.1.

Once filled, an LP-Gas cylinder seldom becomes completely empty. At the very least, the cylinder will usually be full of vapor and may contain some liquid or a residue that could contain the flammable odorant. If empty cylinders were not counted as full cylinders, it would be impossible for an enforcing authority to determine whether the storage limits were being exceeded without lifting or tilting all the cylinders.

8.2.1.5 Cylinders shall not be stored on roofs.

Rooftops are largely "out of sight and out of mind" and are often places where combustible materials accumulate. Although the location of cylinders connected for use is permitted on rooftops, the storage of spare cylinders is not. Even an "empty" container can complicate fire control activities in a location that is difficult for fire fighters to handle. In addition, the temperatures on roofs very often exceed the ambient temperatures by several degrees.

8.2.2 Protection of Valves on Cylinders in Storage.

8.2.2.1 Cylinder valves shall be protected as required by 5.2.6.1 and 7.2.2.5.

8.2.2.2 Screw-on-type caps or collars shall be in place on all cylinders stored, regardless of whether they are full, partially full, or empty, and cylinder outlet valves shall be closed.

Protection for all cylinder valves is required by the DOT requirements for containers of hazardous materials. Smaller portable cylinders typically use a metal protective collar around the cylinder valve, while larger cylinders typically found in stationary service may have a screw-on cap or a dome cover.

8.2.2.3 Valve outlets on cylinders less than 108 lb (49 kg) water capacity [nominal 45 lb (20 kg) propane capacity] shall be plugged, capped, or sealed in accordance with 7.2.2.5.

See the commentary following 7.2.2.5 for more details on cylinder plugs and caps, including important information about when plugs should not be used.

8.3 Storage Within Buildings

Section 8.3 applies to buildings that have public access and exposure to storage locations. The size of containers and total quantity of LP-Gas allowed are determined by code requirements for the following:

- Buildings frequented by the public (See 8.3.2.)
- Buildings not frequented by the public (See 8.3.3.)
- Special buildings or rooms (See 8.3.4.)
- Residential buildings (See 8.3.5.)

Tables that summarize the maximum allowable quantities of LP-Gas permitted in buildings, listed by building occupancy, were added in the 2004 edition. These tables use terminology that differs from the terminology used in the Chapter 8 text. The tables list the occupancy categories that are used in NFPA *101*, *Life Safety Code* [2], and *NFPA 5000®*, *Building Construction and Safety Code®* [3]. Chapter 8 uses terms historically found in NFPA 58 that are consistent with the occupancy categories of NFPA *101* and *NFPA 5000*.

Buildings frequented by the public (mercantile occupancies) include numerous types of stores selling small cylinders filled with LP-Gas. Paragraph 8.3.2.2 limits the size of those containers to 2.7 lb (1.1 kg) water capacity, which is about 1 lb (0.45 kg) of propane. The maximum quantity stored and displayed in a building without fire sprinklers cannot exceed

200 lb (91 kg). In a building with a sprinkler system meeting the requirements of 8.3.2, the amount can be increased to 1000 lb (454 kg).

A maximum of 24 nonrefillable 10 oz (283 g) butane-filled cylinders to be stored in restaurants is also allowed by 8.3.2.3. Note that 6.19.9.4 allows portable stoves that use these butane containers as fuel to be used in restaurants and attended catering operations.

Subsection 8.3.3 covers cylinders in buildings not frequented by the public (industrial occupancies), such as repair shops that use LP-Gas containers for process or equipment operations and for forklift trucks. In buildings not frequented by the public, more LP-Gas can be stored because the general public will not be exposed to the hazards or be in the area of storage. No more than 300 lb (136 kg) of propane [735 lb (334 kg) total water capacity] can be stored in one area or location. If more storage is needed, another 735 lb (334 kg) total water capacity [300 lb (136 kg) of propane] can be stored on the same floor at least 300 ft (91.4 m) from the first storage location.

If highway vehicles carrying containers as part of the service equipment on board are parked inside buildings or private garages, 8.3.3.4 permits three containers with a total capacity of 100 lb (45.4 kg) on board each vehicle. The containers in vehicles are not considered as part of the 735 lb (334 kg) total maximum water capacity allowed in the building. Paragraph 8.3.3.4 also does not limit the number of these vehicles inside a private garage.

Special buildings or rooms (meeting the requirements of Chapter 10), as discussed in 8.3.4, can store up to a maximum quantity of 10,000 lb (4540 kg) of LP-Gas. These special buildings or rooms cannot be located adjoining the line of property occupied by areas used for public gatherings, for example, schools, churches, hospitals, and athletic fields. (See 8.3.4.2.)

Storage within residential buildings (one- and two-family dwellings, lodging or rooming houses, hotels and dormitories, and apartments), as noted in 8.3.5, includes basements and any storage areas in common basement storage areas in multiple-family buildings and attached or detached garages. Storage per each living space or unit is limited to one of the following:

- Two containers, each with a maximum water capacity of 2.7 lb (1.2 kg)
- Total maximum quantity of 5.4 lb (2.4 kg) for smaller containers (no limit on the number of containers, just a total maximum quantity)

8.3.1 General.

Storage of cylinders in buildings shall be in accordance with Table 8.3.1(a) or Table 8.3.1(b) or the requirements of Section 8.3.

Tables 8.3.1(a) and 8.3.1(b) coordinate with the requirements of NFPA 58 and *NFPA 5000, Building Construction and Safety Code* [3]. Chapter 34 of *NFPA 5000* contains the "maximum allowable quantities" of many hazardous materials, including LP-Gases. The two tables referred to in 8.3.1 represent the efforts of the Technical Committee on Liquefied Petroleum Gases to consolidate the existing requirements in NFPA 58 into an easily understood format that is used in *NFPA 5000* as well.

8.3.2 Storage Within Buildings Frequented by the Public and in Residential Occupancies.

8.3.2.1 The quantity of LP-Gas in cylinders stored or displayed shall not exceed 200 lb (91 kg) in one location, with additional storage separated by 50 ft (15 m). The maximum quantity to be stored in one building shall not exceed 1000 lb (454 kg).

(A) Where the total quantity stored in a building exceeds 200 lb (91 kg), an approved sprinkler system that, at a minimum, meets the requirement of NFPA 13, *Standard for the Installation of Sprinkler Systems*, for Ordinary Hazard (Group 2) shall be installed.

TABLE 8.3.1(a) *Maximum Allowable Storage Quantities of LP-Gas in Other Than Industrial, Storage, and Mercantile Occupancies*

Occupancy	Assembly	Educational	Day Care	Health Care	Ambulatory Health Care	Detention and Correctional	One- and Two-Family Dwellings	Lodging or Rooming House	Hotel and Dormitory	Apartment	Residential Board and Care	Business
Maximum Allowable Quantity (MAQ):												
Storage (state units: lb, gal, etc.)	2 lb	2 lb	2 lb	2 lb	2 lb	2 lb	2 lb	2 lb	2 lb	2 lb	2 lb	2 lb
MAQ increases for:							Maximum 1 lb cylinders			1 lb cylinder		
Total (including cabinets)	2 lb	2 lb	2 lb	2 lb	2 lb	2 lb	2 lb	2 lb	2 lb	2 lb	2 lb	2 lb
Total for suppression	2 lb	2 lb	2 lb	2 lb	2 lb	2 lb	2 lb	2 lb	2 lb	2 lb	2 lb	2 lb
Total for both cabinets and suppression	0	2 lb	2 lb	2 lb	2 lb	2 lb	2 lb	2 lb	2 lb	2 lb	2 lb	2 lb
Attended catered food service per NFPA 58 in 10 oz maximum cylinders	15 lb	15 lb	15 lb	15 lb	15 lb	15 lb	15 lb	15 lb	15 lb	15 lb	15 lb	15 lb
			15 lb	15 lb	15 lb	15 lb	15 lb	15 lb	15 lb	15 lb	15 lb	15 lb
Additional 10 oz cylinders w/2-hr fire wall	15 lb	15 lb	15 lb	15 lb	15 lb	15 lb	15 lb	15 lb	15 lb	15 lb	15 lb	15 lb
Other												
Total (including threshold) for other	20 lb	20 lb	0	5 lb								
	Flame effects per NFPA 160. Additional 20 lb units with 20 ft (6 m) separation.	In labs, not in classrooms. Additional 20 lb units with 20 ft (6 m) separation.		In labs only. Additional 5 lb units with 20 ft separation.						Amounts per dwelling		

For SI units, 1 lb = 0.45 kg, 1 oz = 0.028 kg.

(B) The sprinkler density shall be 0.300 gpm (1.1 L/min) over the most remote 2000 ft² (18.6 m²) area, and the hose stream allowance shall be 250 gpm (946 L/min).

Paragraph 8.3.2.1 allows storage of propane cylinders for sale of more than 200 lb (91 kg) total in one store. The 200 lb limit has been in NFPA 58 since the 1965 edition, when it was

TABLE 8.3.1(b) *Maximum Allowable Storage Quantities of LP-Gas in Mercantile, Industrial, and Storage Occupancies*

Occupancy	Mercantile	Industrial	Storage
Maximum Allowable Quantity (MAQ): Storage (state units: lb, gal, etc.)	200 lb (1 lb maximum/cylinder)	300 lb	300 lb
MAQ increases for: Total (including threshold) for cabinets	200 lb	300 lb	300 lb
Total (including threshold) for suppression	200 lb	300 lb	300 lb
Total (including threshold) for both cabinets and suppression	200 lb	300 lb	300 lb
Total (including threshold) for other (describe)	1000 lb Separation of groups of 200 lb by 50 ft and a sprinkler density of 0.300 gpm (1.1 L/min) over the most remote 2000 ft² (18.6 m²) area and 250 gpm (946 L/min) hose stream allowance	Additional 300 lb 300 ft separation	10,000 lb In special rooms or buildings per Chapter 10

For SI units, 1 lb = 0.45 kg; 1 gpm = 3.8 L/min; 1 ft = 0.3 m; 1 ft² = 0.09 m².

increased from 24 cylinders of 1 lb (0.45 kg) propane or less. The increase beyond 200 lb recognizes that much larger retail stores exist today than did 40 years ago, and that they have been stocking more than 200 1 lb cylinders safely. Two options are provided to store between 200 lb and 1000 lb (454 kg) in 1 lb or smaller cylinders:

1. The specified sprinkler system must be installed to store between 200 lb and 1,000 lb in 1 lb or smaller cylinders.
2. Additional storage of 200 lb must be separated by 50 ft (15 m).

The term *most remote*, as used in 8.3.2.1(B), refers to the concept that the density of water from the sprinkler heads is not uniform across the entire sprinkler system. Those sprinklers that have longer piping runs, especially of smaller diameter pipe, are "more remote" from the water supply and provide a lower density of water. This is due to dynamic head losses as water is slowed by the friction of flow through a pipe. The system is designed so that the minimum required density is provided at the most remote specified area. Those areas closer to the water supply will then receive water density that exceeds the minimum requirements.

Note that in the 2011 edition, Table 8.3.1(b) was revised by adding storage in mercantile occupancies of up to 1000 lb (454 kg), as was allowed in this paragraph. It was inadvertently omitted from the table in the 2008 edition when 8.3.2.1(B) was added to the code.

8.3.2.2 The cylinders shall not exceed a water capacity of 2.7 lb (1.1 kg) [nominal 1 lb (0.45 kg) LP-Gas].

Early editions of the code could be interpreted to mean that 20 lb (9.1 kg) LP-Gas cylinders for steamers used in wallpaper removal could be stored at paint and wallpaper stores. A formal interpretation was issued to indicate that the intent of this provision was that the size of the cylinder be limited to 2.5 lb (1.1 kg) water capacity or approximately 1 lb (0.45 kg) LP-Gas capacity, and this limit is now explicitly stated in 8.3.2.2. The storage of cylinders larger than this is covered in 8.3.3, 8.3.4, and Section 8.4.

8.3.2.3 In restaurants and at food service locations, storage of 10 oz (283 g) butane nonrefillable containers shall be limited to not more than 24 containers and an additional 24 10 oz (283 g) butane nonrefillable containers stored in another location within the building where constructed with at least 2-hour fire wall protection.

Paragraph 8.3.2.3 permits the storage of up to forty-eight 10 oz (283 g) butane nonrefillable cylinders in restaurants and food service locations. The requirement covers fuel for the portable butane-fired cooking appliances allowed in 6.19.9.4, recognizing that spare cylinders must be on hand for these appliances and that a reasonable number of cylinders must be allowed. These cylinders are constructed to DOT specification 2P or 2Q [1] and to UL 147A, *Nonrefillable (Disposable) Type Fuel Gas Cylinder Assemblies* [4], or UL 147B, *Nonrefillable (Disposable) Type Metal Container Assemblies for Butane* [5], and are similar to aerosol containers. (See Exhibit 6.41.)

8.3.3 Storage Within Buildings Not Frequented by the Public.

8.3.3.1 The maximum quantity of LP-Gas allowed in one storage location shall not exceed 735 lb (334 kg) water capacity [nominal 300 lb (136 kg) propane capacity].

8.3.3.2 Where additional storage locations are required on the same floor within the same building, they shall be separated by a minimum of 300 ft (91.4 m).

8.3.3.3 Storage beyond the limitations described in 8.3.3.2 shall comply with 8.3.4.

FAQ ▶
Does the code permit storage of more than 300 lb of propane in one location in a building not frequented by the public?

The code originally limited storage in an industrial building to 300 lb (136 kg) water capacity of LP-Gas. This limitation proved unrealistic for large industrial complexes, where buildings may be as large as 300,000 ft² (28,000 m²). Therefore, the code was revised, in 8.3.3.2, to permit more than one storage location with a maximum of 300 lb (136 kg) of LP-Gas if such locations had a separation of 300 ft (91.4 m). If storage beyond 300 lb at a location is needed, a facility as described in 8.3.4 must be used, or the storage should be outdoors. Outdoor storage is a reasonable solution because the cylinders used in these types of facilities are commonly used to fuel industrial trucks.

8.3.3.4 Cylinders carried as part of the service equipment on highway mobile vehicles shall not be part of the total storage capacity requirements of 8.3.3.1, where such vehicles are stored in private garages and carry no more than three cylinders with a total aggregate capacity per vehicle not exceeding 100 lb (45.4 kg) of propane.

The requirement in 8.3.3.4 addresses the quantity of propane being carried by a vehicle for other than engine fuel use. It was developed originally to recognize the carrying of portable cylinders on telephone and electric utility service vehicles and the garaging of such vehicles in buildings owned and occupied by such firms. The current limit of up to three cylinders on a vehicle while maintaining the total quantity of 100 lb (45.4 kg) of LP-Gas recognizes that many utility vehicles carry multiple cylinders to meet service requirements. The fire safety experience of these vehicles, to the editor's knowledge, has been satisfactory.

8.3.3.5 Cylinder valves shall be closed when not in use.

8.3.4 Storage Within Special Buildings or Rooms.

8.3.4.1 The maximum quantity of LP-Gas stored in special buildings or rooms shall be 10,000 lb (4540 kg).

8.3.4.2 Special buildings or rooms for storing LP-Gas cylinders shall not be located where the buildings or rooms adjoin the line of property occupied by schools, churches, hospitals, athletic fields, or other points of public gathering.

8.3.4.3 The construction of all special buildings and rooms specified in 8.3.4.2 shall comply with Chapter 10 and the following:

(1) Vents to the outside only shall be provided at both the top and bottom of the building and shall be located at least 5 ft (1.5 m) from any building opening.
(2) The entire area shall be classified for purposes of ignition source control in accordance with Section 6.22.

The phrase "special buildings or rooms" refers to buildings and rooms used only to store LP-Gas. The construction of these special buildings and rooms must comply with Chapter 10 and the additional provisions of 8.3.4.

8.3.5 Storage Within Residential Buildings.

Storage of cylinders within a residential building, including the basement or any storage area in a common basement of a multiple-family building and attached or detached garages, shall be limited to cylinders each with a maximum water capacity of 2.7 lb (1.2 kg) and shall not exceed 5.4 lb (2.4 kg) aggregate water capacity per each living space unit.

The provision in 8.3.5 clearly states the code's intent on the restriction of LP-Gas cylinder storage in residential buildings, including attached and detached garages. The provision limits storage to two 1 lb (0.45 kg) (net propane content) cylinders. Previously, some code users misinterpreted the requirement to mean that a 20 lb (9.1 kg) barbecue gas grill cylinder could be stored in a building if the cylinder was not connected for use. Such misinterpretation led to incidents that resulted in injury, death, and property damage due to fire and explosion caused by leakage from 20 lb (9.1 kg) barbecue grill and recreational vehicle cylinders that were improperly stored in buildings [6]. It also increases the danger to emergency responders who do not expect these cylinders to be stored indoors. The paragraph now is clear that detached garages are also subject to these requirements.

◄ **FAQ**
Can LP-Gas cylinders be stored in residential buildings?

8.4 Storage Outside of Buildings

Section 8.4 applies to cylinders stored in outdoor areas. Paragraph 8.4.1.1 requires that containers be stored at least 5 ft (1.5 m) from any doorway or opening in a building that is frequented by the public, where there are at least two exits from the building, and at least 10 ft (3 m) from a door or opening in the building, where there is only one exit from the building. Also, cylinders must be stored at least 20 ft (6.1 m) from an automotive service station fuel dispenser and in accordance with Table 8.4.1.2, which provides spacing from cylinders to exposures.

Subsection 8.4.2 requires all outside storage containers in areas open to the public to be protected from the following:

- Trespassing or tampering by installing an enclosure (fence) or lockable ventilated metal locker or rack (See 8.4.2.1.)
- Vehicle impact where vehicle traffic normally can be expected (See 8.4.2.2.)

At locations not frequented by the public, where use of Table 8.4.1.2 is not practical, such as construction sites or buildings or structures undergoing renovation or repair, cylinder storage must be acceptable to the authority having jurisdiction. (See 8.4.3.)

8.4.1* Location of Storage Outside of Buildings.

A.8.4.1 The filling process in 8.4.1.4 refers to the time period beginning when a cylinder or cylinders are brought to a dispensing station to be filled and ending when the last cylinder is filled and all the cylinders are removed from the filling area. This is meant to define a continuous process, with the cylinders being unattended for only brief periods, such as operator breaks or lunch.

8.4.1.1 Storage outside of buildings for cylinders awaiting use or resale or that are part of a cylinder exchange point shall be located as follows:

(1) At least 5 ft (1.5 m) from any doorway or opening in a building frequented by the public where occupants have at least two means of egress as defined by NFPA *101, Life Safety Code*

(2) At least 10 ft (3 m) from any doorway or opening in a building or sections of a building that has only one means of egress

The distance between outside cylinder storage and a doorway or opening in a building that is open to the public changed in the 2001 edition. The separation distance is a function of the ability of anyone in the building to leave in the event of propane release or fire in the cylinder storage area. The distance is 5 ft (1.5 m) if there are two or more means of egress from the building and 10 ft (3 m) if there is one means of egress. The evolution to the current distance requirement involved some controversy. NFPA 58 had required a 5 ft (1.5 m) spacing through the 1995 edition. A proposal to the 1998 edition to change the distance to 20 ft (6 m) was rejected by the committee, and upon appeal the committee's rejection was overturned by the NFPA Standards Council. The Council appointed a joint task force of the LP-Gas Committee and the Life Safety Code Committee to study the issue and consider whether a Tentative Interim Agreement (TIA) was appropriate. The task force met and proposed a TIA to the 1998 edition (TIA 98-1), which was approved. The TIA revised the distance to 5 or 10 ft, depending on the number of building exits. The text of the TIA was added to the 2001 edition. The task force determined that the potential for cylinders stored in approved cabinets to contribute fuel to a fire was extremely remote because of the "shielding" effect that the cabinet provides to the cylinders from external events. The open metal mesh of the cabinets provided to prevent tampering provides some shield (shading) to the cylinders, which reduces heat flux from a fire outside the cabinet. Also, the cylinders closer to the fire shield the other cylinders. The task force also determined that more detailed information was needed to provide effective means for protecting cylinders from vehicular impact. (See 8.4.2.2.)

The term *means of egress* is defined in NFPA *101* as follows:

> **3.3.161 Means of Egress.** A continuous and unobstructed way of travel from any point in a building or structure to a public way consisting of three separate and distinct parts: (1) the exit access, (2) the exit, and (3) the exit discharge [**NFPA** *101*, 2009].

(3) At least 20 ft (6.1 m) from any automotive service station fuel dispenser

The requirement in 8.4.1.1(3) for 20 ft (6.1 m) separation between cylinder storage and gasoline or diesel fuel dispensers at a gas station addresses concerns over the possibility of vehicle impact with cylinders and failure of, or leakage from, cylinders that would affect safe means of egress from buildings. Exposure to fires occurring during vehicle fueling operations is also a concern. Cylinder exchange cabinets are frequently located near the exits of convenience stores, gas stations, and similar locations. (See Exhibit 8.2.)

8.4.1.2 Distances from cylinders in storage outside of buildings shall be in accordance with Table 8.4.1.2 with respect to the following:

(1) Nearest important building or group of buildings
(2) Line of adjoining property that can be built upon
(3) Busy thoroughfares or sidewalks on other than private property

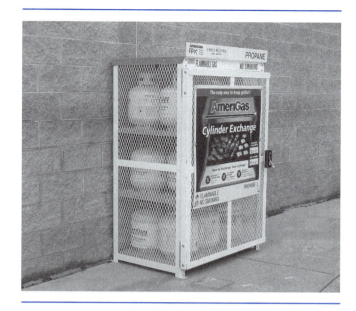

EXHIBIT 8.2 *Cylinder Exchange Cabinets at a Retail Location. (Courtesy of Amerigas)*

TABLE 8.4.1.2 *Distances from Cylinders in Storage and Exposures*

Quantity of LP-Gas Stored		Horizontal Distance to . . .					
		(1) and (2)		*(3) and (4)*		*(5)*	
lb	*kg*	*ft*	*m*	*ft*	*m*	*ft*	*m*
≤720	≤227	0	0	0	0	5	1.5
721–2,500	>227–1,134	0	0	10	3	10	3
2,501–6,000	>1,134–2,721	10	3	10	3	10	3
6,001–10,000	>2,721–4,540	20	6.1	20	6.1	20	6.1
>10,000	>4,540	25	7.6	25	7.6	25	7.6

Paragraph 8.4.1.2(3) was revised in the 2008 edition when the committee became aware that it was being used to unnecessarily restrict the location of exchange cylinder cabinets at retail locations. The former text required separation from busy thoroughfares or sidewalks, and was written to include when such storage might be on the sidewalk in front of a hardware store, with automobile traffic a few feet away at normal street speeds. With the introduction of much larger retail stores (big box stores) in malls, the threat from traffic is significantly reduced as vehicles travel more slowly in parking lots than on streets, and the requirement was revised to reflect this change by adding the words "on other than private property."

(4) Line of adjoining property occupied by schools, churches, hospitals, athletic fields, or other points of public gathering
(5) Dispensing station

8.4.1.3 The distances in Table 8.4.1.2 shall be reduced to 0 where a 2-hour fire-resistive protective structure made of noncombustible materials is provided that breaks the line of sight of the storage and the building. For buildings with exterior walls rated 2-hour fire resistance and constructed of noncombustible materials not provided with eaves over the storage, the exterior wall shall be allowed in lieu of a protective structure to reduce the distance to 0.

Prior to the 1967 edition of the code, the provisions for outside storage could be interpreted to mean that any amount of LP-Gas less than 10,000 lb (4536 kg) could be stored next to a building or be located adjoining a line of property occupied by schools, churches, hospitals, public gatherings, or thoroughfares. Also, many years ago it was customary for hardware stores in small communities to store cylinders on the sidewalk adjacent to the store. Consequently, the code was revised to state clearly how much storage could be located with respect to certain types of exposures. However, in the case of construction work, it is sometimes impractical to limit the amount of storage necessary for operations according to NFPA 58 provisions. In that case, the authority having jurisdiction must determine the conditions for storage as stated in 8.4.3.

Column (5) in Table 8.4.1.2 covers the distance from a storage location to dispensing stations, recognizing the practice of offering filled cylinders to the public on an exchange basis, rather than filling cylinders at a retail site. Column (5) requires a minimum spacing of 5 ft (1.5 m) from dispensing stations if on the same site.

Note also that 8.4.1.3 provides the option of using a noncombustible, 2-hour fire resistance–rated structure to provide a reduction in the separation distances specified in Table 8.4.1.2. The reason for this option is to bring NFPA 58 into agreement with common practices recognized for other compressed gas storage, based on alternatives that achieve the same level of fire protection.

8.4.1.4 Cylinders in the filling process shall not be considered to be in storage.

Paragraph 8.4.1.4 clarifies that cylinders in the process of being filled are not covered by the 5 ft (1.5 m) spacing requirement from dispensing stations. The vague phrase "in the filling process" recognizes efficient filling practices in that it refers not only to the cylinder being filled, but also to the group of cylinders being filled. Thus, a group of cylinders can be located within 5 ft (1.5 m) of a dispensing station, and all the cylinders in the group can be filled prior to any of them being moved to storage. No time limit is specified, but filling time is usually limited to the reasonable time it takes to perform the filling operation, allowing for other activities such as lunches and breaks. (See A.8.4.1.) Cylinders should be removed by the end of the work shift, unless the responsibility has been assigned to the workers on the next shift.

The containers shown in Exhibit 8.3 are so-called "universal" type, in which a curved tube connects the relief valve inlet to the vapor space, thus permitting the containers to be stored on their sides. All enclosure surfaces, including the roof, are open mesh, both for ventilation and so that cooling water can be applied in the event of leakage or fire.

8.4.2 Protection of Cylinders.

8.4.2.1* Cylinders at a location open to the public shall be protected by either of the following:

(1) An enclosure in accordance with 6.18.4.2
(2) A lockable ventilated enclosure of metal exterior construction

The requirements for cabinets used for exchange cylinders are listed in 8.4.2.1. (See Exhibit 8.2.) Cabinets must be ventilated and lockable. Ventilation is commonly accomplished by using expanded metal or screening for the sides of the locker. Requiring the cabinet to be locked prevents tampering with the cylinders in unattended locations. Note that the cylinder storage cabinet in Exhibit 8.3 is designed for universal (industrial truck) cylinders that are normally stored on their sides. A pin in the rack mates with a hole in the cylinder collar so that the pressure relief valve is in the vapor space of full containers, as required by 8.2.1.2. The requirement in 8.4.2.1(2) that the exterior construction of the cabinet be metal was added in 2008. The interior construction, however, can be of combustible components such as molded industrial fiberglass grates.

EXHIBIT 8.3 *Storage Rack for Engine Fuel (Industrial Truck) Containers.*

A.8.4.2.1 The shelves should be made of any material with a flame spread index, in accordance with ASTM E 84, *Standard Test Method for Surface Burning Characteristics of Building Materials*, or UL 723, *Standard for Test for Surface Burning Characteristics of Building Materials*, of less than 25 and should be of sufficient strength to support the cylinders.

8.4.2.2* Protection against vehicle impact shall be provided in accordance with good engineering practice where vehicular traffic is expected at the location.

A.8.4.2.2 There are numerous effective means to provide protection against accidental vehicle impact or damage. The method selected depends upon local conditions with regard to the kinds of traffic that can be reasonably expected and the environment surrounding the location. While additional protection over and above that used to protect the building might not be needed at some locations, others might need additional protection. Examples of such additional protection could be the following:

(1) Guard rails
(2) Steel bollards
(3) Raised sidewalks

If vehicles are operated in areas where cylinders are stored, the cylinders must be protected from possible vehicle damage. The requirement that good engineering practice be used recognizes that the protection needed varies with the size and anticipated speed of vehicles operated in the storage area and allows flexibility in design and materials. Although not specifically stated, the intent of 8.4.2.2 is that the protection be sufficient to prevent damage to the cylinders if vehicle contact should occur and to ensure that vehicles are operating at a reasonably expected speed in the storage area.

It should be noted that the cage or cabinet is not required to provide protection from vehicles. The design and construction of the cabinets vary widely, from bolted small structural steel components to welded heavy structural steel construction. The protection afforded by the cabinets is generally beyond the ability of the onsite inspector to determine. As such, most inspectors assume that the cabinet provides no protection unless there is documentation acceptable to the AHJ that shows the degree of protection provided.

8.4.3 Alternate Location and Protection of Storage.

Where the provisions of 8.4.1 and 8.4.2.1 are impractical at construction sites or at buildings or structures undergoing major renovation or repairs, alternative storage of cylinders shall be acceptable to the authority having jurisdiction.

8.5* Fire Protection

Section 8.5 addresses fire protection requirements. At least one approved portable fire extinguisher is required at most container storage locations.

A.8.5 See 6.25.4.3.

8.5.1 Storage locations, where the aggregate quantity of propane stored is in excess of 720 lb (327 kg), shall be provided with at least one approved portable fire extinguisher having a minimum capacity of 18 lb (9.2 kg) dry chemical with B:C rating.

8.5.2 The required fire extinguisher shall be located not more than 50 ft (15 m) from the storage location. Where fire extinguishers have more than one letter classification, they can be considered to satisfy the requirements of each letter class.

Section 8.5 clarifies the application of the requirements to all locations that store more than 720 lb (327 kg) of LP-Gas. However, the 50 ft (15 m) maximum distance does not apply to cylinder storage at bulk plants, because 8.1.3 exempts bulk plants from this chapter. Refer to Section 6.25 for the fire protection requirements for bulk plants.

Prior to the 1983 edition, any fire extinguisher with a B:C rating was acceptable, and the extinguisher could have had as little as 2 lb (0.9 kg) of agent and a very short discharge time. Because it is not always possible to stop the flow of escaping gas after extinguishing a fire, the committee revised the code for the safety of the operator to provide enough agent and a longer discharge time to enable the operator to extinguish a flammable gas fire. The current requirements also recognize that B ratings are not derived from tests on flammable gas fires but are based on flammable liquid pan fires, and that some extinguishers have been optimized to fight these flammable liquid pan fires rather than gas fires.

In the 2004 edition, the text was revised to allow an extinguisher with an 18 lb (9.2 kg) capacity with either a B:C rating or an A:B:C rating. This was based on committee discussion that concluded that the extinguisher was required to fight both gas fires and incendiary fires. Extinguishers with a B:C rating have a higher agent flow and are better for fighting gas fires. Extinguishers with an A:B:C rating are better for fighting other types of fires.

NFPA 10, *Standard for Portable Fire Extinguishers* [7], defines the types of fires as follows:

5.2.1 Class A Fires. Class A fires are fires in ordinary combustible materials, such as wood, cloth, paper, rubber, and many plastics.

5.2.2 Class B Fires. Class B fires are fires in flammable liquids, combustible liquids, petroleum greases, tars, oils, oil-based paints, solvents, lacquers, alcohols, and flammable gases.

5.2.3 Class C Fires. Class C fires are fires that involve energized electrical equipment. [**NFPA 10,** 2010]

NFPA 10 also requires that fire extinguishers be tested as follows:

- **Class A Rating.** Wood and excelsior
- **Class B Rating.** Two in. (5.1 cm) depth n-heptane fires in square pans
- **Class C Rating.** No fire test. Agent must be a nonconductor of electricity

8.6 Electrical Area Classification

The storage of cylinders awaiting resale shall be exempt from the electrical classification requirements of this code.

This section was added in the 2011 edition to address concerns over the location of cylinders, usually in cylinder exchange cabinets, with respect to electrical sources of ignition. Cylinder exchange locations are usually at stores that may have ice machines, electrical switches, and electrical outlets near or next to the cylinder exchange cabinets. The new text makes it clear that the area around cylinders awaiting resale is exempt from electrical area classification. The committee added this clarification for two reasons: (1) the committee is not aware of incidents involving exchange cabinets where an electrical ignition was a source of fire, and (2) DOT imposes no requirements for separation of cylinders in transportation from sources of ignition. Therefore, the committee believes that such a restriction on cylinders awaiting sale is not needed. It is understood that the subject remains of concern to many local enforcment officials, and any incidents involving propane ignition at retail cylinder storage locations, with electrical or other ignition source, should be brought to the attention of the NFPA staff to forward to the committee.

REFERENCES CITED IN COMMENTARY

1. Title 49, Code of Federal Regulations, U.S. Government Printing Office, Washington, DC.
2. NFPA *101*®, *Life Safety Code*®, 2009 edition, National Fire Protection Association, Quincy, MA.
3. *NFPA 5000*®, *Building Construction and Safety Code*®, 2009 edition, National Fire Protection Association, Quincy, MA.
4. UL 147A, *Nonrefillable (Disposable) Type Fuel Gas Cylinder Assemblies,* 2006 edition, Underwriters Laboratories Inc., Northbrook, IL.
5. UL 147B, *Nonrefillable (Disposable) Type Metal Container Assemblies for Butane,* 2006 edition, Underwriters Laboratories Inc., Northbrook, IL.
6. NFPA Fire Analysis and Research Division, "Special Data Information Package: LP-Gas Cylinders and Tanks," 1993, National Fire Protection Association, Quincy, MA.
7. NFPA 10, *Standard for Portable Fire Extinguishers,* 2010 edition, National Fire Protection Association, Quincy, MA.

Vehicular Transportation of LP-Gas

CHAPTER 9

Chapter 9 provides requirements for the highway transportation of portable containers and cargo tank vehicles containing LP-Gases. Chapter 9 applies to the delivery and return for refill of LP-Gas portable containers and to the transfer of LP-Gas liquid from a cargo tank mounted on a vehicle to stationary containers located at a residence, commercial location, or bulk storage plant. Chapter 9 does not cover all containers used to transport LP-Gas. Containers mounted on vehicles as part of LP-Gas equipment used on commercial, industrial, and construction vehicles, for example, portable tar kettles, are covered by Section 6.23, and containers used for engine fuel on vehicles are addressed in Chapter 11.

All containers used in the transportation of LP-Gas must be in compliance with Chapter 5 for construction of the container and selection of its required appurtenances. The maximum fill quantity of LP-Gas allowed in containers must be in accordance with Section 7.4, and the protection of valves on containers must be in accordance with 5.2.6 and Section 7.2.

Chapter 9 addresses the following important aspects related to the vehicular transportation of LP-Gas:

- Transportation of portable containers [U.S. Department of Transportation (DOT) cylinders and American Society of Mechanical Engineers (ASME) tanks] with an individual water capacity not exceeding 1000 lb (454 kg) and requirements for the vehicles transporting these containers (See 9.3.2.)
- Transportation of portable containers of more than 1000 lb (454 kg) water capacity that are fabricated to be transported on trucks and ships as modular units with other types of containers (See 9.3.3.)
- Transportation of LP-Gas in cargo tank motor vehicles (See Section 9.4.) These are vehicles with a container mounted or built as an integral part of the vehicle chassis or frame. Cargo tank motor vehicles usually have liquid LP-Gas piping equipment and a pump or compressor mounted on the vehicle to transfer product to a delivery point. Section 9.4 requires that these vehicles comply with all applicable DOT regulations. (See 9.4.1.3.) In addition to compliance with DOT regulations, Section 9.4 provides requirements covering the following:
  - Piping (including hose), fittings, and valves (See 9.4.3.)
  - LP-Gas equipment, such as pumps, compressors, meters, dispensers, regulators, and strainers (See 9.4.4.)
  - Fire extinguishers (See 9.4.7.)
  - Wheel stops (formerly chock blocks) (See 9.4.8.)
  - Exhaust systems (See 9.4.9.)
  - Smoking prohibition (See 9.4.10.)
- Trailers, semitrailers, and movable fuel storage tenders, including farm carts (See Section 9.5.)
- Transportation of stationary containers to and from the point of installation (See Section 9.6.)
- Parking and garaging of vehicles used to carry LP-Gas cargo (See Section 9.7.)

375

HISTORY OF LP-GAS TRANSPORTATION

Pre-1940. Little or no information on the transportation of LP-Gas existed in NFPA standards during the early years of the LP-Gas industry, because bulk transportation was generally by rail and delivery to the consumer site was usually by cylinder. Good practice requirements for the construction and operation of tank trucks for bulk transportation on highways were adopted by NFPA in 1935 and published by the National Board of Fire Underwriters as NBFU 59, *Regulations for the Design, Construction, and Operation of Automobile Tank Trucks and Tank Trailers for the Transportation of Liquefied Petroleum Gases* [1]. These provisions were incorporated into the 1940 edition of NFPA 58 as Division III.

1940 to Present. Since 1940, Division III provisions related solely to tank trucks and trailers, until the section was expanded in the 1961 edition to cover all types of truck transportation of LP-Gas, including transportation in portable containers, bulk tanks to the consumer site, movable fuel storage tenders, and farm carts. Also included in the 1961 edition were the first provisions for parking and garaging LP-Gas tank vehicles. In the 1972 edition of NFPA 58, Division III became what is now Chapter 9 as part of a general reformatting.

During this same period, the U.S. and Canadian government agencies, DOT and Transport Canada (TC), respectively, were concerned with interstate and interprovince transportation of hazardous materials, and thus expanded their regulations. Eventually, the treatment of the regulations by DOT, TC, and NFPA 58 grew very similar. For a time, this dual coverage was justified on the basis that the government regulations covered interstate and interprovince transportation — that is, state to state and province to province, respectively — and not intrastate or intraprovince transportation, which was covered in NFPA 58. This is no longer the case in the United States, as DOT now has jurisdiction over intrastate transportation as well.

Despite efforts to keep NFPA 58 consistent with DOT/TC regulations, some differences existed. The differences led to confusion, because it makes little economic sense to build a cargo tank vehicle that cannot be used in a different state or province or that cannot cross a state or province line. In the 1980s, most states and provinces adopted the federal interstate/interprovince requirements as intrastate/intraprovince transportation regulations. Today, throughout the entire United States and Canada, the federal regulations define LP-Gas cargo tank vehicle specifications and establish uniform requirements for the transportation of LP-Gases.

9.1 Scope

9.1.1 This chapter applies to containers, container appurtenances, piping, valves, equipment, and vehicles used in the transportation of LP-Gas, as follows:

(1) Transportation of cylinders
(2) Transportation in cargo tank vehicles, whether fabricated by mounting cargo tanks on conventional truck or trailer chassis or constructed as integral cargo units in which the container constitutes in whole, or in part, the stress member of the vehicle frame
(3)* Transfer equipment and piping and the protection of such equipment and the container appurtenances against overturn, collision, or other vehicular accidents

A.9.1.1(3) Most truck transportation of LP-Gas is subject to regulation by the U.S. Department of Transportation (DOT). Many of the provisions of this chapter are identical or similar to DOT regulations and are intended to extend these provisions to areas not subject to DOT regulation.

Emergency shutoff valves, flexible connectors, chock blocks, and fire extinguishers are subjects that are covered both in the DOT regulations and in Chapter 9. The requirements in Chapter 9 supplement and in some cases are more stringent than the DOT requirements. Because the DOT requirements are not updated as frequently as NFPA 58, additional safety items placed in NFPA 58 may become part of the DOT requirements in future editions.

The following are examples of some situations where DOT regulations would not apply:

- A farm-based bobtail that delivers to farm buildings and never travels on public roads
- Certain agricultural activities operating under the rules of 49 CFR Part 173.5 [2]. The requirements exempted generally apply to commercial driver's licenses and hazmat endorsements. However, the requirements addressed by DOT Special Permit 11209 still apply. (See the commentary following 9.3.4 for information on this permit.)
- Certain government-operated activities that come under the exemption specified in 49 CFR Part 390.3(f)(2) [3]

Today, cargo tank vehicles in the United States are constructed to Specification MC-331 of 49 CFR Part 178.337 [4]. All MC-331 cargo tank vehicles must also comply with 49 CFR Part 180, Subpart E, "Qualification and Maintenance of Cargo Tanks" [5]. An MC-331 vehicle is shown in Exhibit 9.1.

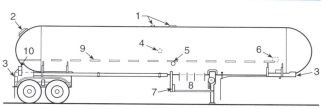

EXHIBIT 9.1 *Typical MC-331 LP-Gas Transport Trailer Features. (Courtesy of Mississippi Tank Company)*

1. Relief valve
2. Manway
3. Emergency trip release
4. Float gauge
5. Outage gauges
6. Nameplate and test inspection decal
7. Cable operator for valves
8. Typical piping location
9. Conspicuity (reflective) tape
10. Fire extinguisher

Prior to May 15, 1967, cargo tank vehicles could be constructed to MC-330 specification. Some MC-330 vehicles are still in use but have had to undergo some retrofitting. Additionally, DOT has issued a ruling to recognize those vehicles constructed to NFPA 58 provisions to allow for their continued operation, as long as certain minimum requirements are met. Title 49 CFR Part 173.315(k) [6] also mandates compliance with pertinent regulations of the DOT Office of Motor Carrier Safety.

With this dual specification often comes dual agency enforcement. Inspection to the DOT specifications is often performed by federal motor carrier enforcement officers or state highway patrol or motor carrier enforcement officers. These officers may or may not inspect the piping, pumps, valves, and other parts of the LP-Gas carrying and transfer equipment. In some states, their primary interest is in the roadworthiness of the vehicle, and officers inspect tires, brakes, running gear, placards, and a host of other items related to the safety aspects of driving. Their inspection of the LP-Gas portions varies from state to state, depending on their familiarity with the LP-Gas portions of the vehicle, their priorities on parts to inspect, and the division of responsibilities afforded by their state statutes.

Inspection of LP-Gas portions might be conducted by inspectors from a state fire marshal's office, LP-Gas Board, agricultural department, or from other state departments. In addition, meters on these vehicles are subject to inspection and calibration by state weights and measures officials, who might report to a different state agency.

9.1.2 This chapter does not apply to the following:

(1) Cylinders and related equipment incident to their use on vehicles as covered in Section 6.23 and Chapter 11

(2) Transportation of LP-Gas containers on vehicles where the containers are used to fuel the vehicle or appliances located on the vehicle as covered in Sections 6.23, 11.15, and 11.16

(3)* LP-Gas systems used for engine fuel

A.9.1.2(3) LP-Gas systems used for engine fuel are covered by Chapter 11.

FAQ ▶
Does Chapter 9 apply to the installation of vehicular fuel systems if a cargo tank provides the fuel?

Some retail bulk delivery trucks, referred to as bobtails in the propane distribution industry, use propane as an engine fuel, although today more delivery trucks use diesel fuel. (See Exhibits 9.2 and 9.3.) Although provisions for the installation of the engine fuel system are covered in Chapter 11, it is important to note that fuel for the engine can be obtained from the cargo container on delivery trucks with one chassis, but fuel cannot be obtained from cargo containers on trailers or semitrailers. An LP-Gas–fueled trailer or semitrailer requires a separate LP-Gas fuel container.

Note that former 9.1.2(4) was deleted in the 2011 edition, because it was not a requirement but an informative reference to Chapter 11 for LP-Gas used as engine fuel. As Chapter 11 is mandatory where NFPA 58 is adopted, there is no need for the reference.

EXHIBIT 9.2 *Typical Retail Delivery Cargo Tank Vehicle (Bobtail). (Courtesy of Lin's Propane Trucks)*

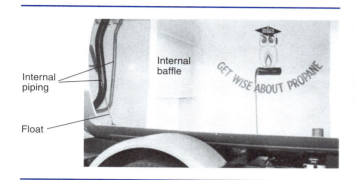

EXHIBIT 9.3 *Internal View of a Cutaway Retail Delivery Vehicle (Bobtail). Note the float gauge, internal piping connections, and internal baffle and support. (Courtesy of Lin's Propane Trucks)*

9.2 Electrical Requirements

Only electrical lighting shall be used with the vehicles covered by this chapter. Wiring shall be insulated and protected from physical damage.

In the early 1900s, some lights on vehicles were powered by burning a gas, acetylene (which was generated on the vehicle). Today, all vehicle lights are electrically powered. While it might be logical to tap the cargo vehicle's supply of propane or butane to provide lighting, it is not permitted. The requirements for lighting on trucks is found in 49 CFR Part 393.9 [7]. The requirements for lights on cargo tank vehicles are the same as for other trucks.

9.3 Transportation in Portable Containers

9.3.1 Application.

Section 9.3 shall apply to the vehicular transportation of portable containers filled with LP-Gas delivered as "packages," including containers built to DOT cylinder specifications and other portable containers.

9.3.2 Transportation of Cylinders.

9.3.2.1 Cylinders having an individual water capacity not exceeding 1000 lb (454 kg) [nominal 420 lb (191 kg) propane capacity], when filled with LP-Gas, shall be transported in accordance with the requirements of Section 9.3.

The maximum size of an individual cylinder permitted under DOT regulations is 1000 lb (454 kg) water capacity [nominal 420 lb (191 kg) of propane]. Portable ASME containers, which generally serve the same purpose as DOT cylinders, may also be encountered and are also limited to this size for transportation. Exhibit 9.4 shows portable containers transported via open delivery truck.

◄ **FAQ**
What is the maximum size of a portable cylinder or container allowed by NFPA 58?

9.3.2.2 Cylinders shall be constructed as provided in Section 5.2 and equipped in accordance with Section 5.7 for transportation as cylinders.

Section 5.2 requires construction to ASME or DOT codes and specifies minimum appurtenances and appurtenance protection. Section 5.7 provides requirements for container appurtenances such as relief valves and service valves.

9.3.2.3 The quantity of LP-Gas in cylinders shall be in accordance with Chapter 7.

All DOT cylinders are marked with the water capacity in pounds. The water capacity is required because not all LP-Gases have the same specific gravity, and therefore each gas has a

EXHIBIT 9.4 *Cylinders in an Open Portable Container Cargo Vehicle (Delivery Truck). (Courtesy of Eastern Propane Corp.)*

different filling limit. Weight is used, not volume (as is done for ASME containers), because the cylinders are portable and can be placed on a scale. For propane, with a specific gravity of between 0.504 and 0.510, the capacity of any cylinder (in pounds) is obtained by multiplying the water capacity by 0.42. See Chapter 7 for a more detailed explanation. Also, refer to the commentary following 7.4.1 for DOT requirements for verifying the amount of product in cylinders.

9.3.2.4 Cylinder valves shall comply with the following:

(1) Valves of cylinders shall be protected in accordance with 5.2.6.1.
(2) Screw-on-type protecting caps or collars shall be secured in place.
(3) The provisions of 7.2.2.5 shall apply.

The requirements for cylinder valves are located in Chapter 5. Also referenced are the requirements for cylinder valve plugs. Refer to commentary following 7.2.2.5 for more information on cylinder valve plugs. The importance of providing protection for cylinder valves from damage cannot be overstated. A damaged or separated cylinder valve could result in the uncontrolled release of LP-Gas and perhaps even the propulsion of the cylinder itself.

9.3.2.5 The cargo space of the vehicle shall be isolated from the driver's compartment, the engine, and the engine's exhaust system. Open-bodied vehicles shall be considered to be in compliance with this provision.

(A) Closed-bodied vehicles having separate cargo, driver, and engine compartments shall also be considered to be in compliance with this provision.

(B) Closed-bodied vehicles, such as passenger cars, vans, and station wagons, shall not be used for transporting more than 215 lb (98 kg) water capacity [nominal 90 lb (41 kg) propane capacity], but not more than 108 lb (49 kg) water capacity [nominal 45 lb (20 kg) propane capacity] per cylinder, unless the driver and engine compartments are separated from the cargo space by a vaportight partition that contains no means of access to the cargo space.

FAQ ▶
Is it permissible to transport a grill cylinder [20 lb (9.1 kg) propane capacity] not "in commerce" in the passenger space of an automobile? If so, how many cylinders can be transported in that manner?

The transportation of privately owned cylinders in passenger automobiles is a safety concern that is addressed based on the type of vehicle. The transportation of LP-Gas by private parties, where the transportation is not considered to be "in commerce" as defined by DOT, is not regulated by the U.S. DOT regulations, and therefore only the provisions of NFPA 58 apply. The provisions in 9.3.2.5 are easily understood as follows:

1. Will the cylinder be transported in an open-bodied vehicle (such as a pickup truck) or in a closed-bodied vehicle with a vaportight partition between the cargo space and the driver

and engine compartments? If either is the case, then up to 1000 lb (454 kg) of LP-Gas can be transported in the vehicle (total weight, including the weight of the LP-Gas and cylinders) as stated in 9.3.2.1. Beyond 1000 lb (454 kg), the requirements of 9.3.2.10 and DOT would apply to the vehicle

2. Will the cylinder be transported in a closed-body vehicle? If so, a maximum of 90 lb (41 kg) of propane can be transported in the passenger or cargo space of the vehicle. This provision allows up to four typical grill cylinders [20 lb (9.1 kg) propane capacity], up to three 30 lb (13.6 kg) cylinders, or up to two 40 lb (18 kg) cylinders to be transported.

Note that the 90 lb (41 kg) limit in closed-body vehicles rules out the transportation of 100 lb (45 kg) LP-Gas cylinder in passenger cars, vans, sport utility vehicles, and station wagons. Also, see 9.3.2.9 for requirements on cylinder orientation when being transported.

These rules apply to all transportation of cylinders, whether by propane company employees delivering cylinders to residences, exchange cabinets, or fork lift operators or by private citizens taking their grill cylinders in for filling or exchange. These rules apply in much the same way as building codes apply to a modification a citizen makes to his or her house. In the case of building codes (and this varies with location), the citizen is responsible for obtaining a building permit, for having construction done to meet the applicable code(s), and for getting an inspection by a building code official during construction and/or after the work is complete. The *LP-Gas Code* rules are less well known than building codes among citizens, which is why some jurisdictions consider it the responsibility of the propane company employees to ensure that cylinders transported by customers are properly placed and secured in their vehicles when they leave the dispensing site.

9.3.2.6 Cylinders and their appurtenances shall be determined to be leak-free before being loaded into vehicles.

9.3.2.7 Cylinders shall be loaded into vehicles with flat floors or equipped with racks for holding cylinders.

9.3.2.8 Cylinders shall be fastened in position to minimize the possibility of movement, tipping, and physical damage.

9.3.2.9 Cylinders being transported by vehicles shall be positioned in accordance with Table 9.3.2.9.

TABLE 9.3.2.9 *Orientation of Cylinders on Vehicles*

Propane Capacity of Cylinder		Open Vehicles	Enclosed Spaces of Vehicles
lb	m³		
≤45	≤0.17	Any position	
>45	>0.17	Relief valve in communication with the vapor space	
≤4.2	≤0.016		Any position
>4.2	>0.016		Relief valve in communication with the vapor space

Racks that hold cylinders in a horizontal position are commonly used for the delivery of industrial truck cylinders in open-body vehicles. The safety experience with this type of transportation has been good and is the reason that LP-Gas cylinders with a maximum propane capacity of 45 lb (20 kg) can be transported with the relief valve in contact with the liquid space of the container. This size is the maximum portable cylinder generally used in industrial trucks. Larger containers must be transported in a position such that the pressure relief valve is in communication with the vapor space of the container.

In closed-body vehicles, the requirements are much more stringent. Only cylinders less than or equal to 4.2 lb (0.016 m³) propane capacity can be transported in any position, thereby resulting in the relief valve being in communication with liquid. As a result of this provision, 20 lb (9.1 kg) cylinders (gas grill cylinders) cannot be transported on their sides inside a vehicle.

9.3.2.10 Vehicles transporting cylinders where the total weight is more than 1000 lb (454 kg), including the weight of the LP-Gas and the cylinders, shall be placarded as required by DOT regulations or state law.

FAQ ▶
What is meant when a vehicle is required to display a placard?

Placard is a term used in the DOT regulations contained in 49 CFR, Parts 172.504 and 172.532 [8]. Placards are used to warn others of hazardous materials present on the vehicle. They are signs placed on the outside of a vehicle or its cargo tank to identify the hazard class of the cargo. For LP-Gas, the identification number is "1075," the 2 in the lower part is the hazard class ("gas" in this case), and the hazard class division is "flammable," as shown by the flame. A placard must convey this information to emergency responders. A typical flammable gas placard is shown in Exhibit 9.5. DOT rules require the placard to be identical to the one shown, with a red background color.

9.3.3 Transportation of Portable Containers of More Than 1000 lb (454 kg) Water Capacity.

Note that the DOT regulations for cylinders allow the largest cylinder to be 1000 lb (454 kg) water capacity. Therefore, this subsection does not apply to cylinders. Portable containers of more than 1000 lb (454 kg) water capacity are sometimes used to transport LP-Gas in bulk to a point of use. If these portable containers were permanently installed on a vehicle and used for making deliveries, they would become cargo tanks and would be required to comply with Section 9.4. The primary difference between portable containers and storage containers is that portable containers of more than 1000 lb (454 kg) water capacity are so designed, and the fittings are of a type and so protected, that the container may be transported while filled to its maximum capacity. Storage containers do not have such features.

DOT regulations provide specifications for large portable containers designed for transporting quantities of LP-Gas greater than 1000 lb (454 kg), which are known as either Specification 51, IM101 or IM102 containers. The Specification 51 container, as shown in Exhibit 9.6, and its construction and fitting arrangement are outlined in 49 CFR Part 178.245 [9]. A counterpart that is constructed in accordance with Section 5.2 of NFPA 58 and equipped for portable use according to Section 5.7 may also be used. Vehicles transporting portable containers of this size must be placarded as required by DOT regulations, per 9.3.2.10.

EXHIBIT 9.5 *Placard for Propane Truck. (Courtesy of U.S. Department of Transportation)*

EXHIBIT 9.6 *A DOT Specification 51 Container. (Courtesy of Texas Trailer Corp.)*

DOT 51 portable containers are used primarily to transport propane to remote sites, especially islands. The containers are used in Alaska, Hawaii, the Caribbean, and other islands and remote locations. The containers can also be used temporarily at construction sites and for emergency power generation. Certain applications would dictate the use of a Specification 51 container, particularly if it were transported by a vessel that is under the jurisdiction of the U.S. Coast Guard.

9.3.3.1 Portable containers having an individual water capacity exceeding 1000 lb (454 kg) [nominal 420 lb (191 kg) propane capacity] when filled with LP-Gas shall be transported in compliance with the requirements of Section 9.3.

9.3.3.2 Portable containers shall be constructed in accordance with Section 5.2 and equipped in accordance with Section 5.7 for portable use and shall comply with DOT portable tank specifications for LP-Gas service.

9.3.3.3 The quantity of LP-Gas put into portable containers shall be in accordance with Chapter 7.

9.3.3.4 Valves and other portable container appurtenances shall be protected in accordance with 5.2.6.2.

9.3.3.5 Transportation of portable containers and their appurtenances shall be in accordance with the following:

(1) Portable containers and their appurtenances shall be leak-free before being loaded into vehicles.
(2) Portable containers shall be transported in a rack or frame or on a flat surface.
(3) Portable containers shall be fastened in a position to minimize the possibility of movement, tipping, or physical damage, relative to each other or to the supporting structure, while in transit.

9.3.3.6 Portable containers shall be transported with pressure relief devices in communication with the vapor space.

9.3.3.7 Vehicles carrying more than 1000 lb (454 kg), including the weight of the propane and the portable containers, shall be placarded as required by DOT regulations or state law.

9.3.3.8 Where portable containers complying with the requirements of Section 9.3 are installed permanently or semipermanently on vehicles to serve as cargo tanks, so that the assembled vehicular unit can be used for making liquid deliveries to other containers at points of use, the provisions of Section 9.4 shall apply.

In the event that a portable container complying with Section 9.3 is being used as a cargo tank, the assembly must comply with the requirements for cargo tank vehicles in Section 9.4.

9.3.4 Transportation of Portable Storage Containers.

ASME containers to be used as portable storage containers, including movable fuel storage tenders and farm carts for temporary stationary service (normally not more than 12 months duration at any location), when moved shall contain a liquid volume of 5 percent or less of the water capacity of the container, except for agricultural purposes where allowed in a DOT exemption.

Although DOT regulations prohibit the transportation of a movable fuel storage tender, commonly known as a farm cart, when the container has more than 5 percent liquid within it, an exemption to that requirement has been issued to the propane industry for containers used for agricultural purposes only. The exemption is numbered DOT-SP 11209, and a copy is available from the DOT web page.

◀ **FAQ**
Can movable fuel storage tenders (farm carts) be transported with more than 5 percent liquid in the container?

This exemption, a special permit, was requested by and issued to the National Propane Gas Association for the use of their member companies. Others desiring a similar exemption may apply to DOT through the web page: http://hazmat.dot.gov/sp_app/special_permits/exe_11000.htm#e11000.

9.3.5 Fire Extinguishers.

Each truck or trailer transporting portable containers in accordance with 9.3.2 or 9.3.3 shall be equipped with at least one approved portable fire extinguisher having a minimum capacity of 18 lb (8.2 kg) dry chemical with a B:C rating. Where fire extinguishers have more than one letter classification, they can be considered to satisfy the requirements of each letter class.

See the commentary following 8.5.2 for information on portable fire extinguisher requirements.

9.4 Transportation in Cargo Tank Vehicles

There are two types of cargo tank vehicles: tractor-trailer vehicles, commonly called transports, and trucks with cargo tanks mounted on them, commonly called bobtails. Exhibits 9.7 and 9.8 show typical bobtail piping systems. There is no standard piping arrangement for bobtails, and considerable variation exists. Exhibit 9.9 shows key components of a semitrailer cargo tank vehicle.

Cargo tank vehicles must comply with DOT *Federal Motor Carrier Safety Regulations*, 49 CFR Parts 100–185. The following parts of 49 CFR are relevant to cargo tank vehicles:

HAZARDOUS MATERIALS

Part 171, General information, regulations, and definitions [10]
Part 172, Hazardous materials table, special provisions, hazardous materials communication, emergency response information, and training requirements [11]
Part 173, Shippers: general requirements for shipments and packaging [2]
Part 174, Carriage by rail [12]
Part 175, Carriage by aircraft [13]
Part 176, Carriage by vessel [14]
Part 177, Carriage by highway [15]
Part 178, Shipping container specifications [16]
Part 179, Specifications for tank cars [17]
Part 180, Continuing qualification and maintenance of packaging [18]

MOTOR CARRIER SAFETY REGULATIONS

Part 383, Commercial driver's license [19]
Part 390, Motor carrier safety regulations: general requirements [3]
Part 391, Driver qualifications [20]
Part 392, Driving of motor vehicles [21]
Part 393, Parts and accessories [22]
Part 395, Hours of service [23]
Part 396, Inspection, repair of vehicles [24]
Part 397, Hazardous materials driving and parking [25]

Additional requirements for cargo tank vehicles are contained in NFPA 58, as noted in the commentary following A.9.1.1(3).

9.4.1 Application.

9.4.1.1 Section 9.4 applies to cargo tank vehicles used for the transportation of LP-Gas as liquid cargo.

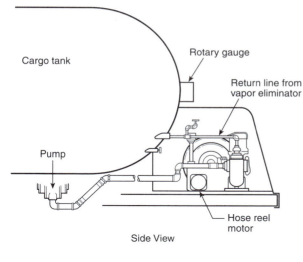

EXHIBIT 9.8 *Typical Retail Delivery Cargo Tank Vehicle (Bobtail) Transfer System. (Courtesy of Eastern Propane Corp.)*

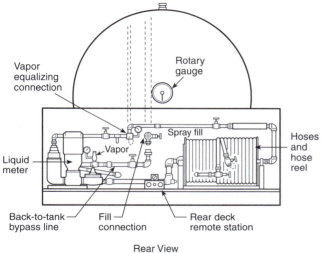

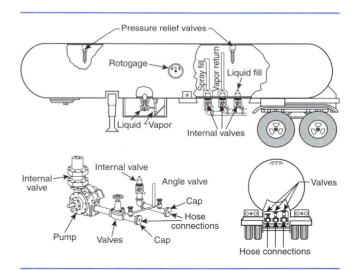

EXHIBIT 9.7 *Typical Cargo Tank Vehicle (Bobtail) Transfer System for Retail Delivery. (Courtesy of National Propane Gas Association)*

EXHIBIT 9.9 *Typical Semitrailer Cargo Tank Vehicle. (Courtesy of Engineered Controls International, Inc.)*

9.4.1.2 Transfer shall be made by a pump or compressor mounted on the vehicle or by a transfer means at the delivery point.

9.4.1.3 All LP-Gas cargo tank vehicles, whether used in interstate or intrastate service, shall comply with the applicable portion of the U.S. Department of Transportation Hazardous Materials Regulations of the DOT Federal Motor Carrier Safety Regulations (49 CFR, Parts 171–180, 393, 396, and 397) and shall also comply with any added requirements of this code.

9.4.2 Cargo Tanks Mounted on, or a Part of, Cargo Tank Vehicles.

9.4.2.1 Cargo tanks mounted on, or comprising in whole or in part, the stress member used in lieu of a frame for cargo tank vehicles shall comply with DOT cargo tank vehicle specifications for LP-Gas service.

9.4.2.2 The cargo tanks specified in 9.4.2.1 shall also comply with Section 5.2 and be equipped with appurtenances for cargo service as provided in Section 5.7.

9.4.2.3 Liquid hose of 1½ in. (nominal size) and larger and vapor hose of 1¼ in. (nominal size) and larger shall be protected with an internal valve that is fitted for remote closure and automatic shutoff using thermal (fire) actuation.

9.4.2.4 Where flow is only into the cargo tank, a backflow check valve or an internal valve shall be installed in the cargo tank.

Note that an internal valve is required by 9.4.2.3 for all liquid piping 1½ in. and larger and for vapor piping 1¼ in. and larger. The liquid outlet of a bobtail or transport truck will be 1½ in. or larger to allow a reasonable flow from the truck to storage containers installed at bulk plants (delivered by transport) or at homes and businesses (typically delivered by bobtail). The internal valve must be inside the cargo tank (internal) and must close if the flow from the container exceeds a preset maximum (excess-flow valve), which assumes that the hose has separated and the liquid is being released to the atmosphere. (See Exhibit 9.10.) Internal installation protects the valve from exposure to vehicle accidents. If flow is only in one direction, a backflow check valve may be used as an alternative to the internal self-closing stop valve.

The excess-flow valve that is incorporated in the internal valve is a safety feature that is intended to stop the flow of propane from the cargo tank vehicle in the event of the hose coupling separating from the hose. In order to stop the flow, the excess-flow valve must be sized properly. Proper sizing means that the closing flow of the excess-flow valve must be greater than the normal flow in the piping and hose, but less than the maximum flow in the hose at the maximum tank pressure. The tank's pressure is related to its temperature — the higher the temperature, the higher the tank pressure and the flow from the tank. The pump can act as a flow restrictor when not turning, preventing the excess-flow valve from closing in some cases. In one such incident, the driver shut off the truck engine when the release was observed. The pump stopped turning, causing just such a flow restriction. This was sufficient to keep the excess-flow valve from closing and allowed the entire contents of the transport to be released. (See also the commentary following 6.12.9 for an account of this incident.) Also, as the temperature is lowered, the pressure in a cargo tank vehicle is correspondingly lowered and may not be sufficient to force enough liquid from a container to operate an excess-flow valve in low temperature conditions.

As a direct result of several incidents, including the one described in the previous paragraph, in which the flow from cargo tank vehicles did not stop following a complete hose separation, DOT has required additional safety features in cargo tank motor vehicles. Bobtails must have an active shutdown system, which may or may not require operator activation. Such systems usually incorporate a radio-controlled remote shutoff. Transports must have a passive system, requiring no operator activation. This can be a specially designed hose/coupling assembly that closes upon hose separation, or sensors installed on the truck that stop the flow of gas if gas is detected. These devices were phased in over a 5-year period that ended on July 1, 2006. Although these emergency devices were recommended to the NFPA 58 committee, the committee did not mandate them for hose provided by the facility receiving the propane. In the United States, the emergency shutdown and hose management provisions are required if the hose is provided as part of the cargo tank vehicle. Paragraph 7.2.4 provides inspection criteria for all hose, including hose provided at the plant.

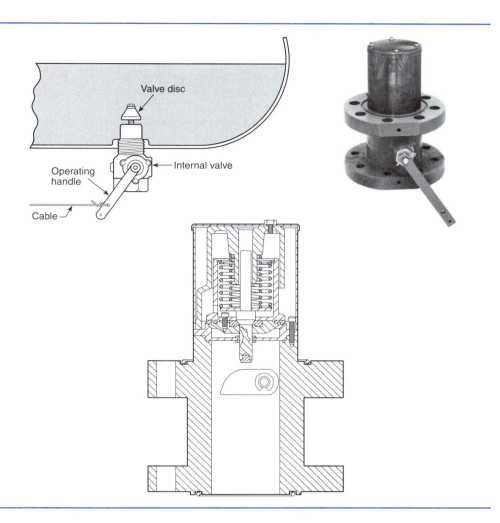

EXHIBIT 9.10 *Internal Valve in Cargo Tank Vehicle Container. [Courtesy of Emerson Process Management Regulator Technologies Inc. (top) and Engineered Controls International, Inc. (bottom)]*

9.4.3 Piping (Including Hose), Fittings, and Valves.

9.4.3.1 Pipe, tubing, pipe and tubing fittings, valves, hose, and flexible connectors shall comply with the following:

(1) Section 5.9
(2) The provisions of DOT cargo tank vehicle specifications for LP-Gas
(3) The service pressure rating specified in 5.17.1.2

9.4.3.2 The following shall also apply to pipe, tubing, pipe and tubing fittings, valves, hose, and flexible connectors:

(1) Pipe shall be wrought iron, steel, brass, or copper in accordance with 5.9.3.1.
(2) Tubing shall be steel, brass, or copper in accordance with 5.9.3.2.
(3) Pipe and tubing fittings shall be steel, brass, copper, malleable iron, or ductile (nodular) iron suitable for use with the pipe or tubing used as specified in 9.4.3.2(1) or (2).
(4) Pipe joints shall be threaded, flanged, welded, or brazed, and fittings, where used, shall comply with 9.4.3.2(3).
(5) Where joints are threaded, or threaded and back welded, pipe and nipples shall be Schedule 80 or heavier.

(6) Copper or brass pipe and nipples shall be of equivalent strength as Schedule 80 steel pipe or heavier.

(7) Where joints are welded or brazed, the pipe and nipples shall be Schedule 40 or heavier.

(8) The pressure ratings of fittings or flanges shall comply with Table 5.17.1.2

(9) Brazed joints shall be made with a brazing material having a melting point exceeding 1000°F (538°C).

(10) Tubing joints shall be brazed using a brazing material having a melting point of at least 1000°F (538°C).

The provisions for piping, fittings, and valves in NFPA 58 are more detailed than those in DOT regulations. These provisions also require compliance with 5.17.1.2, which specifies the design pressure of these materials, based on the anticipated working pressure of the system. Liquid systems must have a design pressure of at least 350 psig (2.4 MPag), but also not less than the maximum pump discharge pressure if it is higher than 350 psig (2.4 MPag).

9.4.3.3 Pipe, tubing, pipe and tubing fittings, valves, hose, and flexible connectors, and complete cargo tank vehicle piping systems including connections to equipment, after assembly, shall comply with 5.17.1.2.

The operating pressure requirements for piping and equipment in LP-Gas service are established in 5.17.1.2, and 9.4.3.3 makes them applicable to cargo tank vehicles. These requirements apply to piping on all vehicles used for transportation of LP-Gas.

9.4.3.4 Valves, including shutoff valves, excess-flow valves, backflow check valves, and remotely controlled valves, used in piping shall comply with the following:

(1) DOT cargo tank vehicle specifications for LP-Gas service

(2) Section 5.12

(3) Pressure rating requirements of 5.17.1.2

The requirements for valves are established in Section 5.12, and reference to that section makes those requirements applicable to cargo tank vehicles. Section 5.12 specifies materials and sets pressure limits similar to the requirements of 5.17.1.2 for piping.

9.4.3.5 Hose, hose connections, and flexible connectors shall comply with 5.9.6 and 9.4.3.1.

9.4.3.6 Flexible connectors used in the piping system to compensate for stresses and vibration shall be limited to 3 ft (1 m) in overall length and, when replaced, shall comply with 5.9.6.

The reference to 5.9.6 is appropriate because 5.9.6.4 specifies a minimum design pressure for hose assemblies, including flexible connectors, of 700 psig (4.8 MPag).

9.4.3.7 Flexible hose connectors shall comply with the following:

(1) Flexible hose connectors shall be permanently marked to indicate the date of installation of the flexible hose connector.

(2) The flexible hose portion of the connector shall be replaced with an unused connector within 10 years of the indicated date of installation of the connector and visually inspected before the first delivery of each day.

(3) The flexible hose portion of flexible connectors shall be replaced whenever a cargo tank unit is remounted on a different chassis, or whenever the cargo tank unit is repiped if such repiping encompasses that portion of piping in which the connector is located.

(4) Replacement of the flexible hose portion of the flexible connector shall not be required if the reinstallation or repiping is performed within 1 year of the date of assembly of the connector.

The 10-year replacement frequency coincides with each alternate 5-year inspection required by DOT. The change was made following a review of the reason for the prior required 6-year interval. The 6-year interval was determined based on experience with older hose that incorporated steel braid reinforcement. After a period of time, the hose would become slightly permeable to water from the outside, and the steel would rust and expand. The rust was causing hose failure within 6 years. Because hose is now constructed without steel braid reinforcement, this failure mode no longer occurs and the replacement frequency was lengthened. Some hose is constructed using stainless steel wire braid reinforcement. The braid wire in this hose will not rust within 10 years.

9.4.3.8 All threaded primary valves and fittings used in liquid filling or vapor equalization directly on the cargo tank of transportation equipment shall be of steel, malleable iron, or ductile iron construction.

9.4.3.9 All existing equipment shall be so equipped as described in 9.4.3.8 not later than the scheduled requalification date of the container.

Brass valves in liquid filling or vapor equalization lines are permitted on stationary containers but are prohibited from use on cargo tank vehicles. In situations where the vehicle was driven away with the hose connected, the brass threads were stripped and the valves pulled out. These accidents necessitated this provision, which prohibits brass valves from being used on cargo tank vehicles. The retrofit provision is intended to accommodate all vehicles within the 5-year hydrostatic testing requirement of DOT.

9.4.4 Equipment.

The equipment requirements in 9.4.4 are more detailed than those in the DOT regulations. Requirements for the construction and design of MC-331 LP-Gas cargo tank motor vehicles are found in 49 CFR Part 178.337 [4], and include the requirements for LP-Gas containers, including openings, outlets, inlets, and emergency discharge controls; and for LP-Gas piping system pressure relief devices, gauging devices, pumps, compressors, valve, and hose. A certificate must be issued that the cargo tank motor vehicle conforms in all respects to Specification MC-331 and the ASME *Boiler and Pressure Vessel Code* [26].

9.4.4.1 LP-Gas equipment, such as pumps, compressors, meters, dispensers, regulators, and strainers, shall comply with Section 5.17 for design and construction and shall be installed in accordance with the applicable provisions of Section 6.17.

9.4.4.2 Equipment on cargo tank vehicles shall be mounted in place and connected to the fixed piping system in accordance with the manufacturer's instructions.

9.4.4.3 Cargo tank openings whose only function is for pump bypass return shall be provided with one of the following:

(1) A positive shutoff valve capable of being secured in the open position and located as close to the tank as practical in combination with a steel backflow check valve installed in the tank
(2) An internal valve with excess flow protection
(3) A valve that is specifically recommended and listed by the manufacturer for bypass return service and that meets the requirements of 6.17.2.3

A positive shutoff of the pump bypass return line is required so that maintenance of the pumping system can be performed, even with LP-Gas in the tank.

9.4.4.4 Where an electric drive is used to power pumps or compressors mounted on vehicles and the energy is obtained from the electrical installation at the delivery point, the installation on the vehicle shall comply with 6.22.2.1.

The reference to 6.22.2.1 reminds the code user that cargo tank vehicles can have electric pumps driven by power supplied by the storage facility. At present, electric pumps are not used in the United States, but they are used in other countries such as Japan, where pumps and the electric motors that drive them are often located inside the cargo tank. The use of an electric pump has the advantage of making the cargo tank vehicle lighter by not needing a power takeoff. A power takeoff uses the vehicle engine to power the pump, resulting in increased load where vehicle weight is limited. If power is provided by the storage facility, concerns over electrical sources of ignition arise and must be addressed by installing electrical equipment appropriate for the electrically classified areas specified in 6.22.2.1.

9.4.4.5 Where wet hose is carried while connected to the truck's liquid pump discharge piping, an automatic device, such as a differential regulator, shall be installed between the pump discharge and the hose connection to prevent liquid discharge while the pump is not operating.

(A) Where a meter or dispenser is used, the automatic device specified in 9.4.4.5 shall be installed between the meter outlet and the hose connection.

(B) If an excess-flow valve is used, it shall not be the exclusive means of complying with the provision of 9.4.4.5.

Transport trucks usually carry "dry" hose, which is completely disconnected following a liquid transfer operation and carried in protective containers during travel. Smaller retail bulk delivery tank trucks carry "wet" hose, which contains liquid LP-Gas at all times. Wet hose is protected by a differential regulator on the liquid meter, which is open only when the pump is in operation. See the commentary following 6.24.3.5 for more information on differential back pressure valves.

9.4.5 Protection of Cargo Tank Appurtenances, Piping System, and Equipment.

Cargo tank appurtenances, piping, and equipment comprising the complete LP-Gas system on the cargo tank vehicle shall be mounted in position *(see 9.4.2.1 for container mounting)*, shall be protected against damage, and shall be in accordance with DOT regulations.

9.4.6 Painting and Marking Cargo Tank Vehicles.

9.4.6.1 Painting of cargo tank vehicles shall comply with 49 CFR.

U.S. Federal Regulations 49 CFR Part 178.337-1 (d) [16] states:

> (d) *Reflective design.* Every uninsulated cargo tank permanently attached to a cargo tank motor vehicle shall, unless covered with a jacket made of aluminum, stainless steel, or other bright nontarnishing metal, be painted a white, aluminum or similar reflecting color on the upper two-thirds of area of the cargo tank.

This regulation allows either a painted tank, with a light, reflective color, or a reflective metal jacket. Note that neither NFPA 58 nor the DOT regulations require a specific paint color for stationary tanks.

9.4.6.2 Placarding and marking shall comply with 49 CFR.

See the commentary following 9.3.2.10.

9.4.7* Fire Extinguishers.

Each cargo tank vehicle or tractor shall be provided with at least one approved portable fire extinguisher having a minimum capacity of 18 lb (8.2 kg) dry chemical with a B:C rating. Where fire extinguishers have more than one letter classification, they can be considered to satisfy the requirements of each letter class.

A.9.4.7 Also see NFPA 10, *Standard for Portable Fire Extinguishers*.

See the commentary following 8.5.2 for information on portable fire extinguisher requirements.

9.4.8* Wheel Stops for Cargo Tank Vehicles.

Each cargo tank vehicle or trailer shall utilize a wheel stop, in addition to the parking or hand brake, whenever the cargo tank vehicle is loading, is unloading, or is parked.

A.9.4.8 A wheel stop may consist of a chock block, curb, or parking barrier at the parking point or other means to prevent the cargo tank vehicle from unintended movement. A wheel stop is not a substitute for an operable parking brake.

These code and annex paragraphs were revised in the 2011 edition. The term *chock block* was changed to *wheel stop*. Also, the requirement to use a parking or hand brake was added. Federal Motor Carrier Safety Administration (FMCSA) regulations require that a parking brake be in good working order and used when needed. (See 49 CFR Part 392.7 [21].) By requiring in the *LP-Gas Code* that the parking brake be used, the FMCSA requirements for using the parking brake may also be invoked.

A phrase commonly used in the propane delivery community is, "When the feet hit the ground, the chock blocks go down." Despite the change in terminology, the intent remains the same. Even though the phrase is well known and often quoted, the failure to use wheel stops when leaving or parking the vehicle continues to be a fairly common violation. The authority having jurisdiction in North Carolina found this to be true while en route to visit a propane company. He saw a bobtail making a delivery to a residence that had a steep driveway, but wheel stops were not placed at the wheels. Later, at the propane company, he observed three instances of failure to use wheel stops, one of them while the truck was making a delivery to the bulk plant at the site and the hoses were connected. Net result: four violations of the wheel stop rule observed in less than two hours.

The importance of using wheel stops is borne out by an incident in Mountain City, Tennessee, on November 17, 1992. A bobtail was making a delivery near the town center. Apparently, the parking brake slipped and, not having wheel stops in place, allowed the truck to roll into a building, breaking some piping on the truck. A significant number of buildings were damaged by the ensuing explosion and fire. It was discovered the next day that some gasoline storage tanks had been damaged and were leaking and in danger of causing another fire [27].

An event relayed to the same AHJ by a former manager of a propane pipeline terminal again shows that wheel stops are important. The manager stated that a driver finished loading his transport, moved it away from the loading rack, and went into the office to complete his paperwork. The manager asked why the driver hadn't set the chock blocks. The driver responded that the parking brake would always keep his truck from rolling. The manager, with some humor, stated that the truck "was now rolling right into the gate post." The transport caused significant damage to the gate and gatepost at the pipeline terminal.

9.4.9 Exhaust Systems.

The truck engine exhaust system shall comply with Federal Motor Carrier Safety Regulations.

The FMCSA regulation that applies is 49 CFR Part 393.83 [22].

9.4.10 Smoking Prohibition.

No person shall smoke or carry lighted smoking material as follows:

(1) On or within 25 ft (7.6 m) of a vehicle that is containing LP-Gas liquid or vapor
(2) At points of liquid transfer
(3) When delivering or connecting to containers

The smoking prohibition stated here is consistent with 49 CFR Part 397.13 [28]. Note that the separation distance of 25 ft (7.6 m) for smoking is greater than the separation distance for internal combustion engines during transfer operations specified in 7.2.3.2(A), which is 15 ft (4.6 m). (See Exhibit 9.11) The technical committee determined that 25 ft (7.6 m) is the correct separation distance for separation from lit smoking materials.

It should be noted that some inspection officials consider that violation of this provision can be determined by means other than observing a person smoking. Finding cigarette butts in the cab of the vehicle or on the ground near points of transfer is sufficient evidence to generate a notice of violation in some jurisdictions.

EXHIBIT 9.11 Separation Distances for Internal Combustion Engines During Transfer Operations.

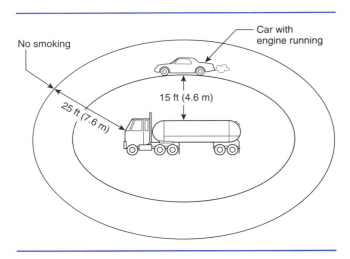

No smoking

Car with engine running

15 ft (4.6 m)

25 ft (7.6 m)

9.5 Trailers, Semitrailers, and Movable Fuel Storage Tenders, Including Farm Carts

9.5.1 Application.

Section 9.5 applies to all cargo tank vehicles, other than trucks, that are parked at locations other than bulk plants.

9.5.2 Fuel Storage Tenders Including Farm Carts.

9.5.2.1 Movable fuel storage tenders including farm carts *(see 3.3.40, Movable Fuel Storage Tender)* shall comply with Section 9.5.

Trailers or semitrailers are used where large volumes of LP-Gas are needed on a temporary basis, such as at a temporary asphalt-mixing plant for road construction or repair. These trailers are not to be used as permanent storage at a small bulk plant for filling cylinders or as retail delivery cargo vehicles.

9.5.2.2 Where used over public ways, movable fuel storage tenders shall comply with applicable state regulations.

9.5.2.3 Movable fuel storage tenders shall be constructed in accordance with Section 5.2 and equipped with appurtenances as provided in Section 5.7.

9.5.2.4 Threaded piping shall be not less than Schedule 80, and fittings shall be designed for not less than 250 psig (1.7 MPag).

9.5.2.5 Piping, hose, and equipment, including valves, fittings, pressure relief valves, and container accessories, shall be protected against collision or upset.

9.5.2.6 Movable fuel storage tenders shall comply with the following:

(1) Movable fuel storage tenders shall be so positioned that container pressure relief valves communicate with the vapor space.
(2) Movable fuel storage tenders shall not be filled on a public way.
(3) Movable fuel storage tenders shall contain no more than 5 percent of their water capacity in liquid form during transportation to or from the bulk plant.
(4) Movable fuel storage tenders shall be moved on the shortest practical route when transporting tenders between points of utilization.

Movable fuel storage tenders and farm carts, as shown in Exhibit 9.12, are limited in size to 1200 gal (4.5 m³) water capacity. These vehicles are nonhighway vehicles but occasionally are moved over roads for short distances to be used as a temporary fuel supply for farm tractors, construction equipment, and so forth. When transported over public roads, the vehicles must comply with state laws and DOT regulations where they are enforced as state law.

EXHIBIT 9.12 *Farm Cart.*

   See the commentary following 9.3.4 for information on DOT special permits that allow for transporting farm carts containing more than 5 percent liquid when used for agricultural service. The text in 9.5.2.6 does not conflict with the Special Permit 11209 because that permit permits transportation of farm carts over the road with more than 5 percent liquid level, but only between different "fields," or points of utilization.

9.6 Transportation of Stationary Containers to and from Point of Installation

9.6.1 Application.

9.6.1.1 Section 9.6 applies to the transportation of containers designed for stationary service at the point of use and secured to the vehicle only for transportation.

9.6.1.2 Containers described in 9.6.1.1 shall be transported in accordance with 9.6.2.1.

Storage containers are moved to the consumer site with a small amount of LP-Gas (5 percent maximum) for initial startup. It is impossible to measure tank contents below 5 percent with the types of gauges used in LP-Gas containers. DOT in 49 CFR Part 173.315(j) [29] also sets forth rules consistent with NFPA 58 provisions for the shipment of storage containers to consumers' premises. Occasionally, it may be necessary to move the container with more than 5 percent LP-Gas — for example, when the liquid evacuation valve does not function and the container cannot be pumped out at its installed site, or where it would be safer to transfer the contents at the propane dealer's facility rather than in a residential neighborhood. A container may be transported subject to the limitations specified by the authority having jurisdiction, which is usually DOT.

See Exhibit 9.13 for an example of a way to load ASME stationary storage containers for transport. Lifting by the lifting lugs only is limited to new tanks or to tanks that are filled to less than 5 percent of their capacity. See 9.6.2.2, including the commentary, for restrictions on the use of lifting lugs for tanks filled to more than 5 percent.

EXHIBIT 9.13 *Saddle Trailer Used to Transport Stationary Container. (Courtesy of H&H Gas)*

9.6.2 Transportation of Containers.

9.6.2.1 ASME containers of 125 gal (0.5 m³) or more water capacity shall contain no more than 5 percent of their water capacity in liquid form during transportation.

9.6.2.2 Where a container is transported with more LP-Gas than 5 percent of its water capacity in a liquid form, all of the following conditions apply:

(1) The maximum filling does not exceed the limit of Section 7.4.
(2) Transportation shall be permitted only to move containers from a stationary or temporary installation to a bulk plant.
(3) Valves and fittings shall be protected by a method approved by the authority having jurisdiction to minimize the possibility of damage.
(4) Lifting lugs shall not be used to move these containers.

The limit of 5 percent water capacity for transportation of containers of 125 gal (0.5 m³) or more is a practical one. It recognizes that the gauges on containers cannot accurately measure contents below 5 percent and that 5 percent is a small quantity of propane.

Special Permit 13341 was issued by DOT to permit the transportation of ASME containers of 500 gal (1890 L) water capacity or less containing more than 5 percent liquid, from the customer's premises to the tank owner's nearest bulk plant. The special permit also requires adherence to several operational requirements that are stated in the permit description. The special permit can be viewed at http://hazmat.dot.gov/sp_app/special_permits/exe_13000. htm#e13000. This permit may be granted to companies that wish to make use of its provisions, as party status is permitted. Information about applying for this permit is also available at this web page.

Note that the use of the lifting lugs to lift a container containing more than 5 percent liquid for and during transportation is prohibited. The lifting lugs are not fabricated to lift the weight of more than the container and 5 percent of its capacity.

The safe transportation of containers with more than 5 percent of their maximum capacity is summarized as follows:

- Transportation is permitted only to a bulk plant.
- Valve and fitting protection is required to prevent damage during transportation.
- Authorization for transportation is required.
- Lifting lugs are not to be used.

The requirements in 9.6.2.2 recognize that it is sometimes necessary to move a container in order to safely empty it and that the equipment usually available at a bulk plant can expedite the procedure, enhancing safety. In order to remove LP-Gas from a container, the actuated liquid withdrawal excess-flow valve is used. (See Exhibit 9.14.) ASME containers built prior to 1961 do not have an actuated liquid withdrawal excess-flow valve and may not have any bottom fitting. ASME containers constructed after 1961 may have an actuated liquid withdrawal excess-flow valve that is inoperable. In such a case, at the installed location, the only options are as follows:

- Roll the container on its side to withdraw liquid through the vapor withdrawal valve.
- Hold open the double-check filler valve using an unloading adapter.

When either of the above methods is used, no excess-flow protection is in place because it is not required on vapor withdrawal connections. To perform these operations as safely as possible, it is often preferable to do so away from a populated location and where the bulk

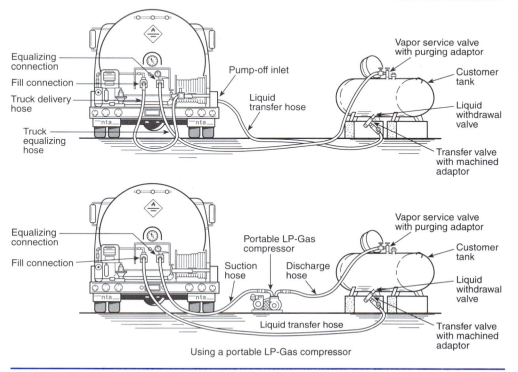

EXHIBIT 9.14 *Removing Liquid from Container to Comply with 5 Percent Provision. (Courtesy of National Propane Gas Association)*

plant has personnel better equipped to handle the procedure. In order to move the container back to the bulk plant, Special Permit 13341 was issued by DOT. See the commentary following 9.6.2.2 for more details on the special permit.

Containers smaller than 125 gal (0.5 m^3) are not required to be drained prior to shipping for the following two reasons:

1. They are not required to be equipped with a connection for liquid evacuation, so they can be difficult to drain.
2. Their weight, even when full, is not so great that they cannot be handled safely.

Exhibit 9.15 shows a container ready for transportation. The tank is supported by a cross-member and not by the tank lifting lugs. Also, the tank is securely strapped to the trailer and the chains to the lifting lugs have slack to keep from overloading the lugs.

EXHIBIT 9.15 *Boom Trailer Used to Transport a Stationary Container. (Courtesy of Richard Fredenburg, North Carolina Department of Agriculture and Consumer Services)*

9.6.2.3 Containers shall be installed to minimize movement relative to each other or to the carrying vehicle while in transit, giving consideration to vehicular operation.

9.6.2.4 Valves, regulators, and other container appurtenances shall be protected against physical damage during transportation.

9.6.2.5 Pressure relief valves shall be in direct communication with the vapor space of the container.

9.7 Parking and Garaging Vehicles Used to Carry LP-Gas Cargo

The regulations for parking cargo tank vehicles and cylinder delivery trucks cover the following:

- Outdoor parking
- Parking in public buildings
- Parking in buildings owned by the vehicle's operator
- Parking in buildings used to repair vehicles

To facilitate easier understanding of Section 9.7, see the flow charts contained in Exhibits 9.16 and 9.17.

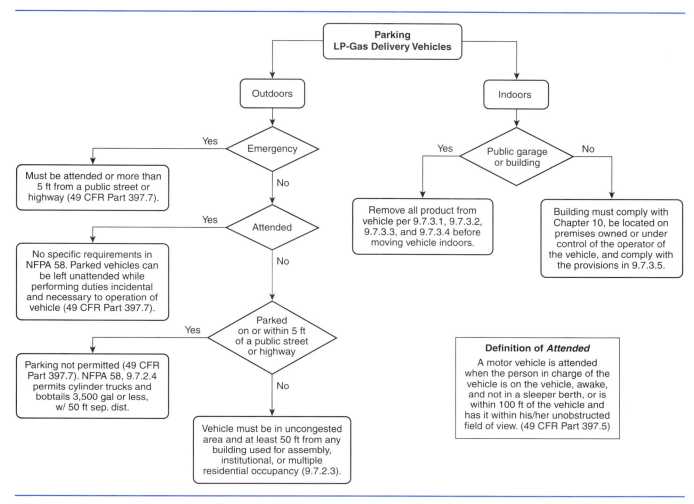

EXHIBIT 9.16 *Parking of LP-Gas Delivery Vehicles Flow Chart. (Courtesy of National Propane Gas Association)*

9.7.1 Application.

Section 9.7 applies to the parking and garaging of vehicles used for the transportation of LP-Gas.

9.7.2 Parking Outdoors.

9.7.2.1 Vehicles shall not be left unattended on any street, highway, avenue, or alley, except for necessary absences from the vehicle associated with drivers' normal duties, including stops for meals and rest stops during the day or night, except as follows:

(1) This requirement shall not apply in an emergency.
(2) This requirement shall not apply to vehicles parked in accordance with 9.7.2.3 and 9.7.2.4.

9.7.2.2 Vehicles shall not be parked in congested areas.

9.7.2.3 Where vehicles are parked off the street in uncongested areas, they shall be at least 50 ft (15 m) from any building used for assembly, institutional, or multiple residential occupancy.

EXHIBIT 9.17 *Servicing LP-Gas Cargo Vehicles Indoors Flow Chart. (Courtesy of National Propane Gas Association)*

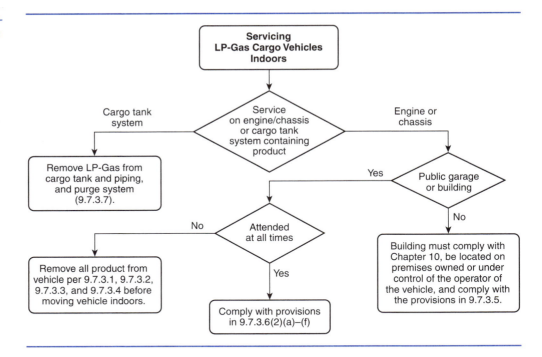

9.7.2.4 Where vehicles carrying portable containers or cargo tank vehicles of 3500 gal (13 m³) water capacity or less are parked on streets adjacent to the driver's residence in uncongested residential areas, the parking locations shall be at least 50 ft (15 m) from a building used for assembly, institutional, or multiple residential occupancy.

In remote areas, the driver's residence may be a considerable distance from bulk plant facilities, and customers may be located a considerable distance from the bulk plant but near the driver's residence. In these cases, the retail bulk delivery tank truck or cylinder delivery truck may be parked near the driver's home.

Local regulations may prohibit parking commercial vehicles in residential neighborhoods, and these regulations often supersede NFPA 58.

9.7.3 Parking Indoors.

9.7.3.1 Cargo tank vehicles parked in any public garage or building shall have LP-Gas liquid removed from the following:

(1) Cargo tank
(2) Piping
(3) Pump
(4) Meter
(5) Hose
(6) Related equipment

9.7.3.2 Vehicles used to carry portable containers shall not be moved into any public garage or building for parking until all portable containers have been removed from the vehicle.

9.7.3.3 The pressure in the delivery hose and related equipment shall be reduced to approximately atmospheric.

9.7.3.4 All valves shall be closed before the vehicle is moved indoors. Delivery hose or valve outlets shall be plugged or capped before the vehicle is moved indoors.

9.7.3.5 Vehicles carrying or containing LP-Gas shall only be parked in buildings complying with Chapter 10 and located on premises owned or under the control of the operator of such vehicles where the following provisions are met:

(1) The public shall be excluded from such buildings.
(2) Floor level ventilation shall be provided in all parts of the building where such vehicles are parked.
(3) Leaks in the vehicle LP-Gas systems shall be repaired before the vehicle is moved indoors.
(4) Primary shutoff valves on cargo tanks and other LP-Gas containers on the vehicle (except propulsion engine fuel containers) shall be closed and delivery hose outlets plugged or capped to contain system pressure before the vehicle is moved indoors.
(5) Primary shutoff valves on LP-Gas propulsion engine fuel containers shall be closed while the vehicle is parked.
(6) No LP-Gas container shall be located near a source of heat or within the direct path of hot air being blown from a blower-type heater.
(7) LP-Gas containers shall be gauged or weighed to determine that they are not filled beyond the maximum filling limit according to Section 7.4.

If it is necessary to park cargo tank vehicles in public buildings, all liquid LP-Gas must be removed from the cargo tank. Cylinder trucks parked in public buildings must have all cylinders removed. Note that the building in which the vehicle is parked must be constructed to comply with Chapter 10.

9.7.3.6 Where vehicles are serviced or repaired indoors, the following shall apply:

(1) When it is necessary to move a vehicle into any building located on premises owned or operated by the operator of such vehicle for service on engine or chassis, the provisions of 9.7.3.5 shall apply.
(2) When it is necessary to move a vehicle carrying or containing LP-Gas into any public garage or repair facility for service on the engine or chassis, the provisions of 9.7.3.1 shall apply, or the driver or a qualified representative of an LP-Gas operator shall be in attendance at all times while the vehicle is indoors, and the following shall apply:

    (a) Leaks in the vehicle LP-Gas systems shall be repaired before the vehicle is moved indoors.
    (b) Primary shutoff valves on cargo tanks, portable containers, and other LP-Gas containers installed on the vehicle (other than propulsion engine fuel containers) shall be closed.
    (c) LP-Gas liquid shall be removed from the piping, pump, meter, delivery hose, and related equipment and the pressure therein reduced to approximately atmospheric before the vehicle is moved inside.
    (d) Delivery hose or valve outlets shall be plugged or capped before the vehicle is moved indoors.
    (e) No container shall be located near a source of heat or within the direct path of hot air blown from a blower or from a blower-type heater.
    (f) LP-Gas containers shall be gauged or weighed to determine that they are not filled beyond the maximum filling capacity in accordance with Section 7.4.

If it is necessary to service cargo tank vehicles in garages, the following options are provided in 9.7.3.6:

1. If the garage is owned or operated by the vehicle operator, the requirements of 9.7.3.5 for parking of vehicles in public garages apply.
2. If the garage is a public garage, either the vehicle must be emptied of LP-Gas as required by 9.7.3.1, or the vehicle operator must be at the vehicle at all times it is in the garage, and the vehicle must meet the following very stringent criteria:

   a. The vehicle must be free of leaks.

   b. All cargo tank shutoff valves must be closed.

   c. All liquid must be removed from piping, hose, meter, and related equipment, and the pressure in these components reduced to approximately atmospheric pressure.

   d. The delivery hose and valve outlets must be plugged or capped before the vehicle is moved indoors.

   e. If the container has any residual liquid, heating of the liquid will result in increased pressure in the container, which could be released during maintenance activities.

   f. The cargo tank must be gauged or weighed to ensure that it is not overfilled.

9.7.3.7 If repair work or servicing is to be performed on a cargo tank vehicle system, all LP-Gas shall be removed from the cargo tank and piping, and the system shall be thoroughly purged before the vehicle is moved indoors.

It is extremely important to remove all LP-Gas from the cargo tank and piping, and that any residual vapor be purged. Even though the repair work may not be intended to open the piping or tank, it may occur. There have been a number of incidents where significant releases of LP-Gas have occurred in repair shops due to unintended work and worker errors [30]. One particularly tragic accident occurred as workers were converting meters on some bobtails. They had successfully completed several conversions, but one remained and it was getting dark. They pulled the truck into the company's service bay and proceeded to take the old meter off. The lines had not been purged. Propane was released and quickly found a source of ignition in the unclassified service area. A large fire ensued. Two workers died and one was terribly burned [31].

REFERENCES CITED IN COMMENTARY

1. NBFU 59 (NFPA 59), *Regulations for the Design, Construction, and Operation of Automobile Tank Trucks and Tank Trailers for the Transportation of Liquefied Petroleum Gases,* 1935, National Fire Protection Association, Boston, MA.
2. Title 49, Code of Federal Regulations, Part 173, U.S. Government Printing Office, Washington, DC.
3. Title 49, Code of Federal Regulations, Part 390, U.S. Government Printing Office, Washington, DC.
4. Title 49, Code of Federal Regulations, Part 178.337, U.S. Government Printing Office, Washington, DC.
5. Title 49, Code of Federal Regulations, Part 180, Subpart E, "Qualification and Maintenance of Cargo Tanks," U.S. Government Printing Office, Washington, DC.
6. Title 49, Code of Federal Regulations, Part 173.315(k), U.S. Government Printing Office, Washington, DC.
7. Title 49, Code of Federal Regulations, Part 393.9, U.S. Government Printing Office, Washington, DC.
8. Title 49, Code of Federal Regulations, Parts 172.504 and 172.532, U.S. Government Printing Office, Washington, DC.
9. Title 49, Code of Federal Regulations, Part 178.245, U.S. Government Printing Office, Washington, DC.
10. Title 49, Code of Federal Regulations, Part 171, U.S. Government Printing Office, Washington, DC.
11. Title 49, Code of Federal Regulations, Part 172, U.S. Government Printing Office, Washington, DC.
12. Title 49, Code of Federal Regulations, Part 174, U.S. Government Printing Office, Washington, DC.
13. Title 49, Code of Federal Regulations, Part 175, U.S. Government Printing Office, Washington, DC.

14. Title 49, Code of Federal Regulations, Part 176, U.S. Government Printing Office, Washington, DC.
15. Title 49, Code of Federal Regulations, Part 177, U.S. Government Printing Office, Washington, DC.
16. Title 49, Code of Federal Regulations, Part 178, U.S. Government Printing Office, Washington, DC.
17. Title 49, Code of Federal Regulations, Part 179, U.S. Government Printing Office, Washington, DC.
18. Title 49, Code of Federal Regulations, Part 180, U.S. Government Printing Office, Washington, DC.
19. Title 49, Code of Federal Regulations, Part 383, U.S. Government Printing Office, Washington, DC.
20. Title 49, Code of Federal Regulations, Part 391, U.S. Government Printing Office, Washington, DC.
21. Title 49, Code of Federal Regulations, Part 392, U.S. Government Printing Office, Washington, DC.
22. Title 49, Code of Federal Regulations, Part 393, U.S. Government Printing Office, Washington, DC.
23. Title 49, Code of Federal Regulations, Part 395, U.S. Government Printing Office, Washington, DC.
24. Title 49, Code of Federal Regulations, Part 396, U.S. Government Printing Office, Washington, DC.
25. Title 49, Code of Federal Regulations, Part 397, U.S. Government Printing Office, Washington, DC.
26. ASME *Boiler and Pressure Vessel Code,* 2007 edition, American Society of Mechanical Engineers, New York, NY.
27. Lee Staiger, "Explosion Rocks Mountain City," *The Tomahawk* newspaper in Mountain City, TN, November 18, 1992.
28. Title 49, Code of Federal Regulations, Part 397.13, U.S. Government Printing Office, Washington, DC.
29. Title 49, Code of Federal Regulations, Part 173.315(j), U.S. Government Printing Office, Washington, DC.
30. Kyte, Greg, "Colorado LP-Gas Explosion Kills 12, Injured 15," *Fire Journal* Nov/Dec 1986.
31. NC OSHA Inspection Number 308223502, available at http://www.osha.gov/pls/imis/establishment.inspection_detail?id=308223502

Buildings or Structures Housing LP-Gas Distribution Facilities

Chapter 10 provides requirements for buildings and structures that house specific LP-Gas systems or activities involved with the distribution of LP-Gas. These buildings, commonly called "special" buildings or structures, are used to house operations in which LP-Gas can be or is normally released. Chapter 10 includes requirements for construction, ventilation, and heating of these special-purpose buildings, structures, or rooms. The requirements of Chapter 10 apply only where specifically required elsewhere in the code.

It is important to remember that NFPA 58 is not a building code and is not trying to be one. The requirements of Chapter 10 assume compliance with building code requirements for exits, structural strength, and resistance to outside forces (e.g., wind, seismic, flood). For information on these items consult the local building code. If no building code has been adopted, reference can be made to *NFPA 5000*®, *Building Construction and Safety Code*® [1].

One impact a local building code had on a planned structure was to reduce the area for hazardous activity. The North Carolina Building Code restricts the allowable area for certain hazardous activities, but a cylinder filling operation needed more space than was allowed in a single area. The result was to divide the building in half with an acceptable fire wall to provide two areas. To allow the desired operations, openings in the wall for the conveyor belts were required. These openings had to have fusible links and other devices to move the conveyor system out of the way and close the openings if a fire was detected.

The following LP-Gas systems and operations require compliance with Chapter 10:

- Filling of containers of less than 125 gal (0.5 m³) water capacity in buildings or structures [See 6.2.2(2).]
- Transferring of liquid LP-Gas into containers inside structures (See 6.5.1.2.)
- Piping systems for LP-Gas vapor with pressure exceeding 20 psig (138 kPag) (See 6.9.1.1.)
- Indoor installation of some vaporizers in buildings or structures (See 6.21.3.1 and 6.21.8.2.)
- Venting of LP-Gas in buildings from No. 54 drill orifices [See 7.3.1(1).]
- Disconnecting liquid lines from containers during filling in buildings [See 7.3.1(4).]
- Purging of containers in buildings (See 7.3.2.)
- Storage of up to 10,000 lb (4540 kg) of LP-Gas in buildings under specific conditions (See 8.3.4.)
- Parking of vehicles carrying containers or containing LP-Gas, including bobtail and transport cargo tank vehicles, inside buildings on premises under the control of the operator of such vehicles (See 9.7.3.5.)

Note that the term *explosion venting* is used in the commentary on Chapter 10. This is a common term that is well-understood, but it is not technically correct. The correct term is *deflagration venting* and is included in the title of NFPA 68, *Standard on Explosion Protection by Deflagration Venting* [2]. NFPA 68 defines *deflagration* and *detonation* as follows:

> **3.3.4 Deflagration.** Propagation of a combustion zone at a velocity that is less than the speed of sound in the unreacted medium. [**NFPA 68**, 2007]

> **3.3.6 Detonation.** Propagation of a combustion zone at a velocity that is greater than the speed of sound in the unreacted medium. [**NFPA 68**, 2007]

Mixtures of propane and air will normally burn at a rate that causes deflagration. Confined mixtures of propane and air in buildings that are ignited can result in a pressure that is sufficient to cause the building to "explode," but detonation normally does not occur.

10.1 Scope

10.1.1 Application.

This chapter applies to the construction, ventilation, and heating of structures, parts of structures, and rooms housing LP-Gas systems where specified by other parts of the code.

Chapter 10 was introduced in the 1972 edition because certain systems or operations present combustion explosion hazards when they are located or conducted inside structures. Buildings housing LP-Gas systems in existence in 1972 were exempted, and they continue to be exempted. The accidental escape of liquid or vapor could result in the formation of a quantity of flammable vapor–air mixture that is large enough for its ignition to produce destructive pressure in the structure. In such instances, the structure's construction can limit the damage to the structure and its surroundings. For an in-depth discussion of this concept, commonly called explosion venting, see NFPA 68.

Chapter 10 is required for structures where liquid LP-Gas is used in large volumes or where high-pressure gas is present. However, the application of Chapter 10 is stipulated in specific provisions throughout the code, for example, see 6.2.2(2).

The aerosol-packaging industry, which uses LP-Gas propellants, has used Chapter 10 extensively in the design of cylinder filling rooms. (Note that NFPA 58 was not developed with such facilities in mind.) Aerosol-packaging facilities are considered chemical plants and are excluded from the requirements of this code by 1.3.2(4). Therefore, the use of Chapter 10 should be augmented with other standards, such as NFPA 68. The 2007 edition of NFPA 68 has been revised to be a standard, rather than a guide, and may be more relevant to aerosol packaging facilities than Chapter 10 of NFPA 58. NFPA 30B, *Code for the Manufacture and Storage of Aerosol Products* [3], may provide additional information.

10.1.2 Nonapplication.

This chapter does not apply to buildings constructed or converted before December 31, 1972.

Facilities constructed before 1972 when Chapter 10 was introduced are allowed to continue in use, even though they do not meet the requirements. This is typical of new requirements that are intended to increase safety, but where there is not evidence that a sufficient hazard exists to make the requirement retroactive.

10.2 Separate Structures or Buildings

Chapter 10 recognizes the following three basic locations for structures:

1. Separate — no physical connection with another structure (See Section 10.2.)
2. Attached — connected to another structure with the common walls having a perimeter length not exceeding 50 percent of the perimeter of the enclosed space (See 10.3.1.)
3. Within — wholly or partly inside another structure (See 10.3.2.)

These locations are presented in order of degree of overall safety to the facility. The first, a separate building, is the safest because loss of a separate building has the least effect on other buildings on the site. The degree of overall safety should be considered in the facility design. There should be a compelling reason to use a room within a structure if one of the other options is possible.

10.2.1 Construction of Structures or Buildings.

10.2.1.1 Separate buildings or structures shall be one story in height and shall have walls, floors, ceilings, and roofs constructed of noncombustible materials.

10.2.1.2 Either of the following shall apply to the construction of exterior walls, ceilings, and roofs:

(1) Exterior walls and ceilings shall be of lightweight material designed for explosion venting.
(2) Walls or roofs of heavy construction, such as solid brick masonry, concrete block, or reinforced concrete construction, shall be provided with explosion venting windows that have an explosion venting area of at least 1 ft² (0.1 m²) for each 50 ft³ (1.4 m³) of the enclosed volume.

From functional and economic considerations, the lightweight material designed for explosion venting construction referenced in 10.2.1.2(1) has definite advantages over the type of construction described in 10.2.1.2(2). Simple steel framing, to which roof and wall panels are affixed by fastenings just strong enough to withstand wind loadings, allows for the maximum possible explosion venting area. If these panels are made of nonbreakable, lightweight material, such as corrugated sheet steel or aluminum, they stay more or less in one piece when they blow off and do not travel very far. These panels can also be hinged or restrained with cables. Although also reasonably lightweight, cement-asbestos panels tend to fragment and present more of a flying missile hazard. (Before constructing a building with materials containing asbestos or modifying a building with asbestos-containing materials, contacting the environmental authorities or reviewing local building ordinances is recommended. Asbestos that can be released by construction activities or by damage or destruction of the building due to explosion is a known health hazard. Any activities leading to such a release may require special permits or building techniques.) When such a structure explodes, the steel framing usually survives with little damage. The roof and walls can be replaced quickly, and the structure can be returned to use promptly. Local conditions, such as a congested site, may make the construction described in 10.2.1.2(2) more attractive. NFPA 68, which is now a standard, formerly a recommended practice, should be reviewed for alternate design approaches.

Exhibit 10.1 illustrates the lightweight construction requirements of 10.2.1.2(1), and Exhibit 10.2 illustrates the heavy construction requirements of 10.2.1.2(2).

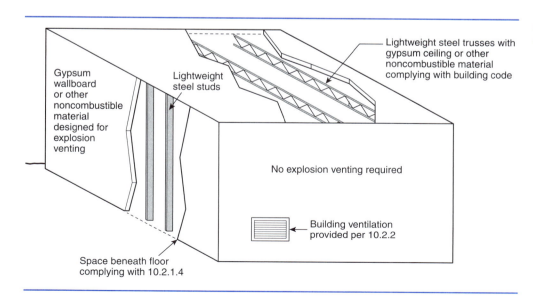

EXHIBIT 10.1 *Lightweight Construction Requirements.*

EXHIBIT 10.2 *Heavy Construction Requirements.*

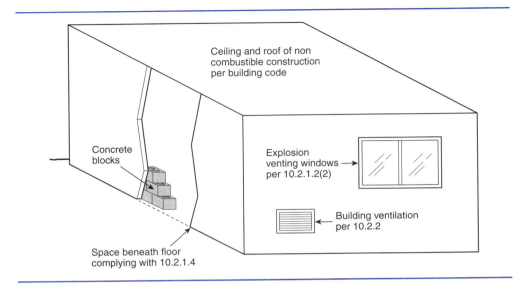

Aside from being much more costly, the heavy construction described in 10.2.1.2(2) does not have as much explosion venting area. The masonry structures also present flying missile hazards and take much longer to rebuild. Structures of heavy construction do, however, have advantages where external security is a problem and aesthetics need to be considered. Some insurance companies refer to this type of construction as damage-limiting construction and recommend its use in some applications.

10.2.1.3 The floor of separate structures shall not be below ground level.

10.2.1.4 Any space beneath the floor shall be of solid fill, or the perimeter of the space shall be left entirely unenclosed.

LP-Gas vapor is heavier than air, and the quantities of LP-Gas vapor that can be generated in some special buildings are significant. Therefore, no spaces should exist where vapor can accumulate.

10.2.2 Structure or Building Ventilation.

The structure shall be ventilated using air inlets and outlets, the bottom of which shall be not more than 6 in. (150 mm) above the floor, and ventilation shall be provided in accordance with the following:

(1) Where mechanical ventilation is used, the rate of air circulation shall be at least 1 ft³/min·ft² (0.3 m³/min·m²) of floor area.
(2) Outlets shall discharge at least 5 ft (1.5 m) from any opening into the structure or any other structure.
(3) Where natural ventilation is used, each exterior wall shall be provided with one opening for each 20 ft (6.1 m) of length.
(4) Each opening shall have a minimum size of 50 in.² (32,250 mm²), and the total of all openings shall be at least 1 in.²/ft² (6900 mm²/m²) of floor area.

Mechanical ventilation is more reliable than natural ventilation and is therefore preferred, especially in buildings used for liquid LP-Gas transfer. If the occupancy is used for storage only, natural ventilation is usually adequate.

The location for ventilation provisions in 10.2.2 reflects the fact that LP-Gas vapor is heavier than air. The criteria for mechanical ventilation are based on the practice of continuously removing a stratum of air 1 ft (0.3 m) deep along the floor. The air discharged must be made up with incoming air. The most common ventilation defect for mechanical systems is the blockage of inlets. The defect for natural arrangements is the blockage of openings in cold weather for comfort reasons. Heating the inlet is an option to solve this problem. Heating the air is considerably easier with a mechanical system because the inlets can be manifolded and a single heater can be installed in the common duct. In either ventilation system, good house-keeping practices are a must to ensure that openings are not restricted. Routine checking of the openings can be added to the plant's operating or maintenance procedure.

In large buildings, many smaller ventilation openings are preferable. Large ventilation openings in colder regions can result in high heating costs.

10.2.3 Structure or Building Heating.

Heating shall be by steam or hot water radiation or other heating transfer medium, with the heat source located outside of the building or structure *(see Section 6.22)*, or by electrical appliances listed for Class I, Group D, Division 2 locations in accordance with *NFPA 70, National Electrical Code.*

10.3 Attached Structures or Rooms Within Structures

10.3.1 Construction of Attached Structures.

The requirements for construction of attached structures in Section 10.3 maintain the explosion venting function of the attached structure while minimizing the possibility of explosion and fire damage to the structure to which it is attached. The common wall(s) is built to be strong and with a degree of fire resistance, and the presence and the character of the openings are controlled.

Although a wall designed for a static pressure of 100 lb/ft^2 (4.8 kPag) is a substantial wall [even a wall of minimal height would be at least 12 in. (0.3 m) of masonry or steel-reinforced concrete block], such a wall should be as strong as is feasible to build. Note that the wall is not required when the operation or process on the other side is of a similar hazard, unless the local building code specifies it, as was described in the opening portion of the commentary for this chapter.

10.3.1.1 Attached structures shall be spaces where 50 percent or less of the perimeter of the enclosed space is comprised of common walls.

10.3.1.2 Attached structures shall comply with 10.2.1.

10.3.1.3 Common walls of structures shall have the following features:

(1) A fire resistance rating of at least 1 hour
(2) Where openings are required in common walls for rooms used only for storage of LP-Gas, 1½-hour (B) fire doors
(3) A design that withstands a static pressure of at least 100 lb/ft^2 (4.8 kPa)

10.3.1.4 Where the building to which the structure is attached is occupied by operations or processes having a similar hazard, the provisions of 10.3.1.3 shall not apply.

10.3.1.5 Ventilation and heating shall comply with 10.2.2 and 10.2.3.

10.3.2 Construction of Rooms Within Structures.

The principle for construction of rooms within structures is similar to that for the construction of attached structures, and the requirements are similar. The following three reasons apply to the limitation to the first floor location (with no basement):

1. No lower floor can be affected in case of a gas release igniting and causing a fire or explosion.
2. Emergency responders have direct access.
3. Any cylinders being brought into or out of the room do not have to be lifted to a higher floor.

10.3.2.1 Rooms within structures shall be spaces where more than 50 percent of the perimeter of the space enclosed is comprised of common walls.

10.3.2.2 Rooms within structures shall be located in the first story and shall have at least one exterior wall with unobstructed free vents for freely relieving explosion pressures.

10.3.2.3 Walls, floors, ceilings, or roofs of the rooms shall be constructed of noncombustible materials.

10.3.2.4 Exterior walls and ceilings shall be of lightweight material designed for explosion venting.

10.3.2.5 Walls and roofs of heavy construction (such as solid brick masonry, concrete block, or reinforced concrete construction) shall be provided with explosion venting windows or panels that have an explosion venting area of at least 1 ft^2 (0.1 m^2) for each 50 ft^3 (1.4 m^3) of the enclosed volume.

10.3.2.6* Walls and ceilings common to the room and to the building within which it is located shall have the following features:

(1) Fire resistance rating of at least 1 hour
(2) Where openings are required in common walls for rooms used only for storage of LP-Gas, 1½-hour (B) fire doors
(3) Design that withstands a static pressure of at least 100 lb/ft^2 (4.8 kPa)

A.10.3.2.6 See NFPA 80, *Standard for Fire Doors and Other Opening Protectives.*

10.3.2.7 Where the building to which the structure is attached is occupied by operations or processes having a similar hazard, the provisions of 10.3.1.3 shall not apply.

10.3.2.8 Ventilation and heating shall comply with 10.2.2 and 10.2.3.

REFERENCES CITED IN COMMENTARY

1. *NFPA 5000®, Building Construction and Safety Code®,* 2009 edition, National Fire Protection Association, Quincy, MA.
2. NFPA 68, *Standard on Explosion Protection by Deflagration Venting,* 2007 edition, National Fire Protection Association, Quincy, MA.
3. NFPA 30B, *Code for the Manufacture and Storage of Aerosol Products,* 2011 edition, National Fire Protection Association, Quincy, MA.

Engine Fuel Systems

Propane has been used since the 1920s as an engine fuel for stationary engines, including agricultural water pumps and pipeline compressors. Propane has also been used since shortly thereafter for vehicle propulsion, including farm tractors and buses. Propane was the fuel used by the *Graf Zeppelin* blimp in the world voyage of 1928. Standards for LP-Gas engine fuel installations first appeared as a separate chapter in the 1937 edition of NFPA 58.

Propane has become recognized as an engine fuel that produces lower emissions than liquid fuels. Propane-powered forklifts are used widely. A number of U.S. national parks, including Acadia, Mammoth Cave, Yosemite, Zion provide in-park transportation on propane-powered buses as a way to reduce vehicle congestion and emissions. Propane-powered engines are appearing on some recently introduced lawn care products, such as consumer-oriented blowers, string trimmers, and lawn mowers. These engines are typically fueled from 1 lb propane (0.5 kg) cylinders, which are widely available and easier to manage on these small tools.

Coverage of specific applications can make the code as a whole hard to understand and can lead to inconsistencies that are difficult to explain. Engine fuel installations are a special field. It became apparent in the early 1980s that a different approach to organizing the information was needed because it was confusing to search through the entire code to find the requirements for a proper engine fuel installation. All provisions relating to LP-Gas engine installations of any sort are now located in Chapter 11, including some requirements from other parts of the code that are repeated here. This consolidation provides a complete chapter so that those who work with engine fuel systems do not have to search through the rest of the code.

Chapter 11 applies to fuel systems using LP-Gas as a fuel for internal combustion engines. The uses of LP-Gas–fueled engines include the following:

- Power units to drive automotive vehicles and trucks and to operate forklifts or other industrial equipment
- Portable engines, such as floor maintenance machines or portable electrical generators
- Stationary engines, such as gas or electric turbines

Chapter 11 addresses the requirements for these LP-Gas engines in sections based on their use as follows:

- Container Design (See 11.3.1.)
- Container Appurtenances (See Section 11.4.)
- Quantity of LP-Gas in Engine Fuel Containers (See Section 11.5.)
- Carburetion Equipment (See Section 11.6.)
- Piping, Hose, and Fittings (See Section 11.7.)
- Installation of Containers and Container Appurtenances (See Section 11.8.)
- Installation in the Interior of Vehicles (See Section 11.9.)
- Pipe and Hose Installation (See Section 11.10.)
- Equipment Installation (See Section 11.11.)
- Marking (See Section 11.12.)
- Industrial (and Forklift) Trucks Powered by LP-Gas (See Section 11.13.)

- General Provisions for Vehicles Having Engines Mounted on Them (Including Floor Maintenance Machines) (See Section 11.14.)
- Engine Installation Other Than on Vehicles (See Section 11.15.)
- Containers for Stationary Engines (See 11.15.2.)
- Garaging of Vehicles (See Section 11.16.)

11.1 Scope

Chapter 11 applies to all engine systems that use propane as a fuel for internal combustion engines, including the engine that powers the vehicle and engines that are mounted on vehicles for reasons other than propulsion. Chapter 6 covers stationary engines. A new subsection 11.15.2 covering containers for stationary engines was added in the 2011 edition. Although not included in the scope, parts of Chapter 11 may also apply to fuel cells on vehicles powered by propane.

General-purpose vehicles and industrial trucks are the two categories of vehicles that use propane engines for their propulsion. General-purpose vehicles include most non-industrial trucks using internal combustion engines. Most general-purpose vehicles are used in fleet operations serviced from central sources of supply that are not available to the public. Propane is not readily available in large enough quantities to accommodate masses of individual private vehicle owners. All over-the-road general-purpose vehicles powered by LP-Gas must be labeled by a diamond-shaped marking. (See Figure A.11.12.2.2.)

Note that NFPA 58 covers only vehicles operating on land. (See Exhibit 11.1.) NFPA 302, *Fire Protection Standard for Pleasure and Commercial Motor Craft* [1], addresses vessels that use propane. Propane has not been known to be used as an engine fuel for vessels. Propane is also not currently used as an aviation fuel, except for hot-air balloons. In the United States, the Federal Aviation Administration (FAA), an agency of the U.S. Department of Transportation (DOT), regulates the use of propane in hot-air balloons.

EXHIBIT 11.1 Typical Propane Fuel System on a Passenger Car. (Courtesy of National Propane Gas Association)

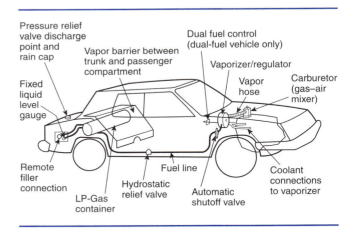

11.1.1* This chapter applies to engine fuel systems using LP-Gas in internal combustion engines, including containers, container appurtenances, carburetion equipment, piping, hose and fittings, and their installation.

A.11.1.1 Chapter 11 covers engine fuel systems for engines installed on vehicles for any purpose, as well as fuel systems for stationary and portable engines.

11.1.2* This chapter shall apply to the installation of fuel systems supplying engines used to propel all motor vehicles.

A.11.1.2 Containers for engine fuel systems can be of the permanently installed or exchange type.

11.1.3 This chapter applies to garaging of vehicles where such systems are installed.

Refer to Section 11.16 for garaging requirements.

11.2 Training

Each person engaged in installing, repairing, filling, or otherwise servicing an LP-Gas engine fuel system shall be trained.

11.3 Containers

11.3.1* General.

A significant portion of the text of 5.2.1 is repeated in 11.3.1 to provide a complete self-contained chapter that can be used without reference to other parts of NFPA 58.

A 25 percent higher design pressure [312.5 psig (2.1 MPag) compared to 250 psig (1.7 MPag) for stationary containers] is specified for engine fuel containers. This higher design pressure provides a higher pressure relief valve setting for these containers. Containers in engine fuel service may be subjected to higher temperatures due to the temperature of the road beneath them, or they can be installed on vehicles that contain large numbers of persons, especially children, as propane is used as fuel for many suburban and rural school buses. A higher setting minimizes potential discharge of propane from the pressure relief valve.

A.11.3.1 Prior to April 1, 1967, these regulations were promulgated by the Interstate Commerce Commission (ICC). In Canada, the regulations of the Canadian Transport Commission apply and are available from the Canadian Transport Commission, Union Station, Ottawa, Canada.

11.3.1.1 Containers shall be designed, fabricated, tested, and marked (or stamped) in accordance with the regulations of the U.S. Department of Transportation (DOT); the ASME *Boiler and Pressure Vessel Code*, Section VIII, "Rules for the Construction of Unfired Pressure Vessels"; or the API-ASME *Code for Unfired Pressure Vessels for Petroleum Liquids and Gases*, except for UG-125 through UG-136.

11.3.1.2 Adherence to applicable ASME Code case interpretations and addenda that have been adopted and published by ASME 180 calendar days prior to the effective date of this code shall be considered as compliant with the ASME Code.

11.3.1.3 Where containers fabricated to earlier editions of regulations, rules, or codes listed in 5.2.1.1 and of the Interstate Commerce Commission (ICC) *Rules for Construction of Unfired Pressure Vessels*, prior to April 1, 1967, are used, the requirements of Section 1.4 shall apply.

11.3.1.4 Containers that have been involved in a fire and show no distortion shall be requalified in accordance with CGA C-6, *Standard for the Visual Inspection of Steel Compressed Gas Cylinders*, or CGA C-3, *Guidelines for Visual Inspection and Requalification of Low Pressure Aluminum Compressed Gas Cylinders*, for continued service before being used or reinstalled.

(A) Cylinders shall be requalified by a manufacturer of the type of cylinder or by a repair facility approved by DOT.

(B) ASME or API-ASME containers shall be retested using the hydrostatic test procedure applicable at the time of the original fabrication.

(C) All container appurtenances shall be replaced.

(D) DOT 4E specification (aluminum) cylinders or composite cylinders involved in a fire shall be permanently removed from service.

The requirement in 11.3.1.4 that containers be requalified in accordance with CGA standards is intended to apply only to cylinders, since ASME containers are not subject to requalification requirements. Therefore, the criterion listed in 11.3.1.4(B) for ASME and API-ASME containers is the sole criterion required for those containers.

In addition, 11.3.1.4(D) now specifies both aluminum and composite cylinders are prohibited from being reintroduced into service after they have been involved in a fire.

11.3.1.5 A cylinder with an expired requalification date shall not be refilled until it is requalified by the methods prescribed in DOT regulations.

The important requirement in 11.3.1.5 serves two purposes. First, it encourages fillers to look at cylinders used for engine fuel application and to not refill them if they require recertification. Second, it extends the DOT recertification requirements to cylinders that are outside DOT's jurisdiction. Cylinders not transported over roads are not under DOT jurisdiction and would not have to be recertified if this requirement (and 11.3.1.7) were not in NFPA 58.

11.3.1.6 Cylinders shall be designed and constructed for at least a 240 psig (1.6 MPag) service pressure.

11.3.1.7 Cylinders shall be continued in service and transported in accordance with DOT regulations.

11.3.1.8 Engine fuel containers shall be of either the permanently installed or exchangeable type.

Although the requirement in 11.3.1.8 may appear to state the obvious, it is needed to inform enforcers that both permanently installed vehicle containers and exchanged cylinders can be used as a vehicle fuel source.

11.3.2 Container Maximum Allowable Working Pressure (MAWP).

11.3.2.1 ASME engine fuel and mobile containers shall be designed to provide at least the following maximum allowable working pressure (MAWP):

(1) 250 psig (1.7 MPag) or 312 psig (2.2 MPag) where required if constructed prior to April 1, 2001
(2) 312 psig (2.2 MPag) if constructed on or after April 1, 2001

11.3.2.2 ASME containers installed in enclosed spaces on vehicles and all engine fuel containers for vehicles, industrial trucks, buses, recreational vehicles, and passenger vehicles designed to carry 10 or fewer passengers shall be constructed with a MAWP of at least 312 psig (2.2 MPag).

A higher design pressure of 312 psi (2.2 MPag), is required for ASME containers installed in interior spaces of vehicles and all engine fuel containers, due to concerns over possible pressure relief valve operation. Other ASME containers have a design pressure of 250 psi (1.7 MPag). The higher design pressure requires a higher internal pressure for the pressure relief valve to operate. In addition, the higher design pressure results in a thicker shell, with greater strength and resistance to damage in the event of a vehicle accident.

11.3.3 Container Repairs and Alterations.

11.3.3.1 Containers that show excessive denting, bulging, gouging, or corrosion shall be removed from service.

The requirement in 11.3.3.1 sets a standard that allows enforcement officials to take action if dented, bulged, gouged, or corroded containers are seen. While the term *excessive* is subjective, enforcement officials should exercise good judgment when evaluating one of these conditions. If the defect is cosmetic, continued use of the container should be allowed. If the defect appears to affect the integrity of the container, especially if it significantly extends into a weld, then the container should be rejected. If there is doubt, the container manufacturer or a pressure vessel engineer should be consulted.

11.3.3.2 Repairs or alteration of a container shall comply with the regulations, rules, or code under which the container was fabricated. Repairs or alterations to ASME containers shall be in accordance with the *National Board Inspection Code*.

The National Board Inspection Code requires those who repair ASME containers to possess an "R" stamp, which certifies that they have the proper training to perform the work with the proper oversight by inspection personnel. Their work includes the application of an "R" stamp nameplate to the container in order to keep track of repairs.

11.3.3.3 Field welding shall be permitted only on saddle plates, lugs, pads, or brackets that are attached to the container by the container manufacturer.

The requirement in 11.3.3.3 permits welding only on saddle plates, lugs, pads, or brackets. However, welding on a container shell or head can be done by a welder qualified to the ASME or DOT code in accordance with the procedures of the relevant code. These codes are referenced in 11.3.1. Welding by others is not allowed.

11.3.4 ASME Container Nameplates.

The markings specified for ASME containers shall be on a stainless steel metal nameplate attached to the container, located to remain visible after the container is installed.

(A) The nameplate shall be attached in such a way as to minimize corrosion of the nameplate or its fastening means and not contribute to corrosion of the container.

(B) ASME containers shall be marked with the following information:

(1) Service for which the container is designed (e.g., underground, aboveground, or both)
(2) Name and address of container supplier or trade name of container
(3) Water capacity of container in pounds or U.S. gallons
(4) MAWP in pounds per square inch (psig)
(5) Wording that reads "This container shall not contain a product that has a vapor pressure in excess of 215 psig (1.5 MPag) at 100°F" *(see Table 5.2.4.2)*
(6) Outside surface area in square feet
(7) Year of manufacture
(8) Shell thickness and head thickness
(9) OL (overall length), OD (outside diameter), and HD (head design)
(10) Manufacturer's serial number
(11) ASME Code symbol
(12) Minimum design metal temperature: ___°F at MAWP ___ psig
(13) Type of construction: "W"
(14) Degree of radiography: "RT___"

The labeling requirements for ASME engine fuel containers are the same as other ASME containers. Obviously, the service marked will be different, and the design pressure will be different from other ASME containers. The nameplate markings must be visible after the container is installed. In some instances, a lamp and mirror may have to be used to see the nameplate.

11.3.5 Container Capacity.

11.3.5.1 The maximum capacity of individual LP-Gas containers installed on highway vehicles shall be in accordance with Table 6.23.3.1(C).

Data on the maximum capacity of LP-Gas containers installed on vehicles have been consolidated into Table 6.23.3.1(C). Reference to the table is provided in 11.3.5.1, and the table is reprinted here for the convenience of the reader. (See Commentary Table 11.1.)

COMMENTARY TABLE 11.1 *Maximum Capacities of Individual LP-Gas Containers Installed on LP-Gas Highway Vehicles*

Vehicle	Maximum Container Water Capacity	
	gal	m³
Passenger vehicle	200	0.8
Nonpassenger vehicle	300	1.1
Road surfacing vehicle	1000	3.8
Cargo tank vehicle	Not limited by this code	

Note that the maximum capacity of containers on cargo tank vehicles is not covered by NFPA 58, but is mandated in DOT regulations.

Total fuel capacity for passenger-carrying vehicles is limited to 200 gal (0.8 m³) water capacity [approximately 160 gal (0.6 m³) of LP-Gas]. If multiple tanks are used, they can be manifolded. The size limit for nonpassenger vehicles is 300 gal (1.1 m³) water capacity [approximately 240 gal (0.9 m³) of LP-Gas].

11.3.5.2 Containers larger than 30 gal (0.1 m³) water capacity shall be equipped for filling into the vapor space.

Exhibits 11.2 and 11.3 show a typical engine fuel container installed and arranged for remote filling and for external pressure relief valve discharge.

Filling in the vapor space promotes mixing of the liquid and vapor, which cools the vapor in the container. If a warm container is filled in the liquid space, with little or no surface movement, the vapor will remain warm while cooler liquid is added, and the tank pressure will be that of the vapor. This could result in operation of the pressure relief valve, which could lead to a fire.

11.3.6 Container Connections.

11.3.6.1 The connections for pressure relief valves shall communicate directly with the vapor space of the container and shall not reduce the relieving capacity of the relief device.

11.3.6.2 The connection for the pressure relief valve shall be internally piped to the uppermost point practical in the vapor space of the container if the connection is located at any position other than the uppermost point practical in the vapor space of the container.

11.3.6.3 The container openings shall be labeled on the container or valves connected to the container opening to designate whether they communicate with the vapor or with the liquid space.

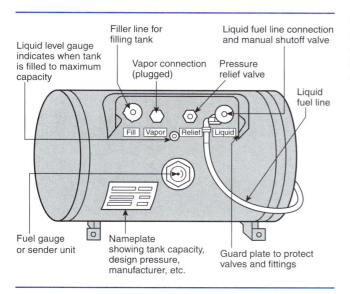

Liquid level gauge
indicates when tank
is filled to maximum
capacity

Filler line for
filling tank

Vapor connection
(plugged)

Liquid fuel line connection
and manual shutoff valve

Pressure
relief valve

Liquid
fuel line

Fill   Vapor   Relief   Liquid

Fuel gauge
or sender unit

Nameplate
showing tank capacity,
design pressure,
manufacturer, etc.

Guard plate to protect
valves and fittings

EXHIBIT 11.2 *Typical Engine Fuel Container and Appurtenances. (Courtesy of National Propane Gas Association)*

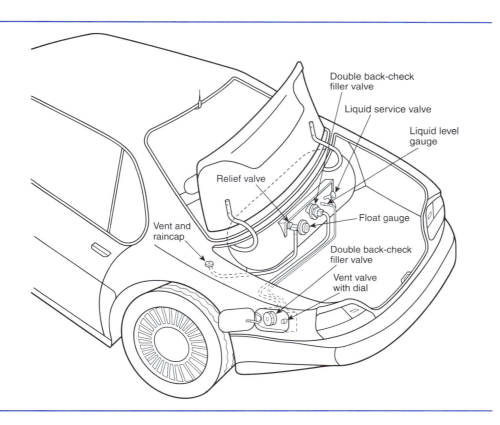

Double back-check
filler valve

Liquid service valve

Liquid level
gauge

Relief valve

Float gauge

Vent and
raincap

Double back-check
filler valve

Vent valve
with dial

EXHIBIT 11.3 *Container Shown in Exhibit 11.2 Installed and Arranged for Remote Filling and for External Pressure Relief Valve Discharge. (Courtesy of Engineered Controls International, Inc.)*

11.3.6.4 Labels shall not be required on openings for pressure relief valves and gauging devices.

Subsection 11.3.6 is concerned with avoiding or reducing the potential for releasing LP-Gas in the vicinity of a source of ignition. Paragraphs 11.3.6.1 and 11.3.6.2 address the importance of making sure the relief valve for the container is in communication with the vapor space of the container. If liquid is vented through the relief valve rather than vapor, the result will be approximately 270 times more LP-Gas released to the atmosphere. Paragraphs 11.3.6.3 and 11.3.6.4 further emphasize the importance of clearly indicating the use of each container appurtenance or opening.

11.3.7* Container Corrosion Protection.

Engine fuel containers constructed of steel shall be painted or powder coated to minimize corrosion. Stainless steel cylinders shall not be required to be painted or powder coated.

A.11.3.7 See A.6.6.1.4.

Subsection 11.3.7 recognizes the use of powder coatings, which are technically not paint, and also to clarify that the intent of the subsection is to minimize corrosion and not simply retard corrosion. While the use of stainless steel containers is not anticipated due to their higher cost, if built they do not have to be painted because they are inherently more resistant to corrosion than carbon steel containers.

This subsection is the first place in the LP-Gas code that powder coating is mentioned as a method to protect containers from corrosion. Any coating that remains in place and excludes air and moisture from reaching the steel container will minimize corrosion. Paint has traditionally been the most-used method for corrosion protection. With relatively recent environmental concerns about volatile components in paint, however, other methods of coating metal have been developed. Powder coating is one widely accepted method. A charge is applied to the metal, and it attracts a "plastic" powder that is sprayed on the metal and clings to it. The item is then run through an oven where the powder melts and flows to evenly coat the metal, providing a long-lasting coating that will exclude air and moisture. Thus, powder coating provides the same protection as paint.

The reference to A.6.6.1.4 is to a suggestion that a light-reflecting color paint is preferred in most cases. It can be inferred that a light-reflecting color powder coating is also preferred. The color is important if the containers are subjected to sunlight, in that light-reflecting colors (e.g., white, silver, and light hues of colors) will help keep containers from getting hot in the sun. Exchanged cylinders or containers mounted on the exterior of a vehicle will be subject to this solar gain. If the container is permanently installed underneath or inside a vehicle's trunk, the need for a light-reflecting color is diminished.

Note that while stainless steel has greater corrosion resistance than carbon steel, it is subject to corrosion under stress conditions with chlorides, which can come from salt. If the container is used in an area near an ocean, the danger of corrosion should be taken into consideration. Coating or an inspection program may be appropriate.

11.4 Container Appurtenances

The basic provisions for container appurtenances found in Chapter 5 are also repeated here. Requirements for container appurtenances are located in Table 5.7.4.1. Additional special considerations found in Section 11.4 recognize factors unique to the applications in Table 5.7.4.1.

11.4.1 General Requirements for Appurtenances.

11.4.1.1 Container appurtenances (such as valves and fittings) shall comply with Section 5.7 and 11.4.1.2 through 11.4.1.17.

11.4.1.2 Container appurtenances subject to pressures in excess of 125 psig (0.9 MPag) shall be rated for a pressure of at least 250 psig (1.7 MPag).

11.4.1.3 Manual shutoff valves shall be designed to provide positive closure under service conditions and shall be equipped with an internal excess-flow check valve designed to close automatically at the rated flows of vapor or liquid specified by the manufacturers.

If the manual shutoff valve is broken off at the container, the excess-flow check valve is designed to close and keep the gas from escaping. The excess-flow check valve will not close in the event of partial breakage of the manual valve or leakage in the system downstream of this valve. Note that excess-flow valves can only close when the flow exceeds the preset closing flow. Proper sizing of excess-flow valves for all expected flow conditions is extremely important or the valve may not serve its intended function.

The term *internal excess-flow valve* is defined in this code as follows:

3.3.69.4 Internal Excess-Flow Valve. An excess-flow valve constructed and installed so that damage to valve parts exterior to the container does not prevent closing of the valve.

The requirement that manual shutoff valves be designed to provide positive closure is intended to require a valve where moving the operator to the closed position stops all flow to and from the container. A check valve will not meet this requirement.

11.4.1.4 Where used, a filler valve shall comply with 5.7.4.1(F) and shall be installed in the fill opening of the container for either remote or direct filling.

11.4.1.5 Containers shall be fabricated so they can be equipped with a fixed maximum liquid level gauge as follows:

(1) The fixed maximum liquid level gauge shall be capable of indicating the maximum permitted filling level in accordance with 7.4.2.2.
(2) Fixed maximum liquid level gauges in the container shall be designed so the bleeder valve maximum opening to the atmosphere is not larger than a No. 54 drill size.
(3) The container fixed maximum liquid level gauge opening and the remote bleeder valve opening shall not be larger than a No. 54 drill size where the bleeder valve is installed at a location remote from the container.

11.4.1.6 Systems complying with the provisions of 6.26.3 shall have a water- and weather-resistant label placed near the bleeder valve with the following text: "Do not use fixed maximum liquid level gauge at low emission transfer stations."

The label requirement is consistent with the requirements for low emission transfer in 6.26.5; therefore, parts of 6.26.5 are repeated in 11.4.1.6. The water- and weather-resistant label reminds operators not to use the fixed maximum liquid level gauge required in 11.4.1.5 when filling at low emission transfer fueling stations.

11.4.1.7 ASME containers shall be equipped with full internal or flush-type full internal pressure relief valves conforming with applicable requirements of ANSI/UL 132, *Standard for Safety Relief Valves for Anhydrous Ammonia and LP-Gas,* or other equivalent pressure relief valve standards.

(A) Fusible plugs shall not be used.

(B) The start-to-leak setting of the pressure relief valves specified in 11.4.1.7, with relation to the MAWP of the container, shall be in accordance with Table 5.7.2.5(A).

Pressure relief valves on ASME containers and cylinders used in engine fuel service must be the full internal or flush-type full internal type because the working elements must remain intact within the container so they can still function in the event of an accident.

A shear section, usually a groove machined in the body of the pressure relief valve, as shown in Exhibit 5.23, is used to provide a weak spot where the piping system will break rather than allow the discharge piping to be bent, reducing the cross-sectional area of the pipe and the flow. Reduced flow can compromise the pressure relief valve.

EXHIBIT 11.4 *Lawn Care Products That Use Propane Cylinders. (Left) Blower; (Middle) String Trimmer; (Right) Lawn Mower. (Courtesy of LEHR)*

The prohibition of fusible plugs is stated in 11.4.1.7(A) to prevent misinterpretation of DOT regulations. Fusible plugs, once activated, will remain open until all of the product has been emptied from the container. Note that fusible plugs are permitted as the safety relief device for small LP-Gas containers [typically 1 lb (0.5 kg) and smaller] that would traditionally not be used for engine fuel service. Some recently introduced lawn care products (see Exhibit 11.4) use 1 lb propane cylinders as their fuel source, as these are widely available.

11.4.1.8 Permanently mounted ASME containers shall be equipped with a valve or combination of valves in the liquid outlet connection that has manual shutoff, excess-flow, and automatic closure features. The valve assembly shall prevent the flow of fuel when the engine is not in an operating mode even if the ignition switch is in the "on" position. This requirement shall not apply to industrial and forklift trucks.

The requirement for an automatic shutoff valve for ASME engine fuel containers appeared for the first time in the 2004 edition of the code. This requirement addressed a number of incidents that have been attributed to problems with shutting off flow of the liquid discharge systems on engine fuel containers. Some of these incidents were due to problems resulting from accumulations of dirt, road salt, and so on. Also, concerns have been raised when garaging vehicles and when there is a need to shut off the fuel supply after an accident. There are now commercially available solenoid-actuated valves that prevent the flow of propane when the ignition is off or the engine is not in operating mode.

11.4.1.9 Pressure relief valves shall be marked as follows:

(1) In accordance with CGA Publication S-1.3, *Pressure Relief Device Standards, Part 3 — Stationary Storage Containers for Compressed Gases*, and ASME Code, Section VIII, UG-125 through UG-136
(2) With the rated relieving capacity in cubic feet per minute of air at 60°F (15.6°C) and 14.7 psia (101 kPa)
(3) With the manufacturer's name and catalog number

Subparagraph 11.4.1.9(1) requires that the pressure relief valve be marked in accordance with the requirements of CGA S-1.3, *Pressure Relief Device Standards* Part 3 [3] and Section VIII of the ASME *Boiler and Pressure Vessel Code* [2]. The requirements from the 2008 edition of CGA S-1.3 include the following:

- Manufacturer's name or trademark and catalog number
- Year of manufacture
- Set pressure in psi (kPA)
- Full capacity in ft^3/min (m^3/hr) of free air

11.4.1.10 Cylinders, other than for industrial truck service, shall be equipped with full internal or flush-type full internal pressure relief valves.

This paragraph was added in the 2011 edition, along with 11.4.1.11, to recognize a new type of cylinder used in industrial truck service, which was inadvertently excluded from the 2008 edition. This oversight became evident with the introduction of composite cylinders for industrial truck service. One type of composite cylinder cannot accommodate more than one opening and would have been prohibited under previous editions of NFPA 58.

Pressure relief valves can now be incorporated into a cylinder valve assembly. Multiple function valves contain all the safety features that are offered on DOT industrial truck cylinders with multiple openings. The liquid opening of the multiple function valve will still have an internal excess-flow valve. Note that the substantial collar of industrial truck cylinders protects the valve assembly from mechanical damage. Also, industrial trucks travel at speeds far less than those seen with over-the-road vehicles.

11.4.1.11 Single opening cylinders in industrial truck service shall be equipped with a listed multiple function valve in accordance with 5.7.4.1(J).

11.4.1.12 A float gauge, if used, shall be designed and approved for use with LP-Gas.

11.4.1.13 A solid steel plug shall be installed in unused openings.

11.4.1.14 ASME containers fabricated after January 1, 1984, for use as engine fuel containers on vehicles shall be equipped or fitted with an overfilling prevention device.

Overfilled containers can be hazardous when liquid LP-Gas expands to the point where the container becomes liquid-full, causing the pressure relief valve to open and discharge LP-Gas. To minimize this hazard on general-purpose vehicles, containers manufactured after January 1, 1984, must be fitted or equipped with an automatic means to prevent overfilling. Valves that incorporate overfilling prevention devices (OPDs) that use a float are listed for this purpose.

The function of some OPDs can be affected by high flow rates, such as those produced from bobtail pumps. One incident of a fire on August 9, 2001, in Rolesville, North Carolina was investigated [4], and it was found that the container had been overfilled, in spite of the fact that it had an OPD installed as a fill valve. It was determined by consulting with the manufacturer that their brand of OPD fill valve would not perform its stop fill function if it was experiencing a high flow rate.

11.4.1.15 Where an overfilling prevention device is installed on the ASME container or exterior of the compartment and remote filling is used, a filler valve complying with 5.7.4.1(F) (1) or (2) shall be installed in the exterior fill opening, and a filler valve complying with 5.7.4.1(F)(3) shall be installed in the container fill valve opening.

This paragraph was revised in the 2011 edition in conjunction with revisions to the referenced paragraphs in Chapter 5 on filler valves. As the same filler valves are used on all cylinders, reference here is needed. The double backflow check valve prevents LP-Gas trapped between the OPD and the filler connection from being released to the atmosphere after the filling hose is disconnected.

11.4.1.16 Where an overfilling prevention device is installed on an ASME engine fuel container, venting of gas through a fixed maximum liquid level gauge during filling shall not be required.

FAQ ▶

Is the overfilling prevention device required by 11.4.1.14 permitted to be used as the primary means by which to fill the motor fuel container?

The requirement in 11.4.1.16 is important for two reasons. First, it acknowledges that some motor fuel dispensing facilities may be "low emission transfer" facilities built to comply with 6.26.5. As such, 6.26.5.1(B) does not permit the fixed maximum liquid level gauge to be used to determine the maximum permitted filling limit. Second, the OPD installed in the container or on the vehicle now becomes the primary means by which the maximum permitted filling limit is determined.

11.4.1.17 Where the fixed maximum liquid level gauge is not used during filling, in accordance with 11.4.1.16, the fixed maximum liquid level gauge or other approved means shall be used annually to verify the operation of the overfilling prevention device. If the container is found to be overfilled during the test, corrective action shall be taken. The result shall be documented. A label shall be affixed to the container near the fill point indicating the expiration date of the successful test.

This requirement is new in the 2011 edition. Because the OPD is a mechanical device and subject to malfunction, it was determined that the risks described in the commentary after 11.4.1.14 needed to be addressed. A test is required to be performed annually to determine that the OPD is working properly. Using the fixed maximum liquid level gauge to indicate when the container is full, either while the container is being filled or immediately thereafter, is one method. Other test methods acceptable to the authority having jurisdiction may be used. The results of the test must be documented. Note that, while not stated in the code, the results should be retained for a reasonable time period, and the test results should be available on the vehicle where the container is installed in case the filling operator wants to examine the documentation. Also required is a label affixed to the container near the fill point, which informs the filling operator whether the container has been tested in the previous year. An indication that the test has been conducted will allow filling of the container. Lack of this indication would require the customer to be refused filling or the test to be performed.

11.5 Quantity of LP-Gas in Engine Fuel Containers

The maximum permitted filling limit for engine fuel containers shall be as follows:

(1) For permanently mounted ASME engine fuel containers, the maximum permitted filling limit shall not exceed the amount shown in Table 7.4.2.3(a) when the liquid is at 40°F (4°C).

(2) For removable engine fuel containers, the maximum permitted filling limit shall be in accordance with 7.4.2 and 7.4.3.

Section 11.5 was added in the 2011 edition to clearly state the maximum permitted filling limit for containers in engine fuel service. Chapter 11 formerly had no such reference to the requirements of Chapter 7.

11.6 Carburetion Equipment

Carburetion equipment is specially designed and tested for LP-Gas service. An automatic shutoff valve is an important feature of LP-Gas carburetion systems. This valve can be either an approved electric solenoid valve controlled by vacuum or oil pressure or a vacuum lockoff that will not permit fuel flow even if the ignition is in the "on" position (the valve must not provide fuel when the engine is not running). This valve is located as close to the regulator as practicable to minimize the volume of gas involved. A primer valve is used for starting the engine.

Exhibit 11.5 shows a two-stage pressure regulator converter. Liquid propane enters through the fuel inlet port and then flows past the primary valve, which is normally open, into the primary chamber. The pressure signal travels through a port into the primary diaphragm chamber. The pressure in the primary diaphragm chamber forces the primary diaphragm to pivot against the primary valve pin and move it toward the primary valve. The movement of the primary diaphragm closes the primary valve pin against its seat, stopping fuel flow into the regulator. The liquid fuel under pressure entering the regulator is heated and expanded to a vapor by engine coolant that also prevents freezing as the liquid expands. A negative pressure signal travels from the mixer (carburetor) to the secondary chamber of the pressure regulator. Because of the negative pressure, atmospheric pressure forces down the secondary diaphragm assembly. This movement opens the secondary lever and seat assembly, allowing fuel to flow to the mixer. Part of the pressure differential is satisfied as fuel flows and the secondary diaphragm moves the secondary seat to adjust the flow.

Exhibit 11.6 shows an air–gas valve carburetor. Cranking the engine lowers pressure on the underside of the carburetor diaphragm. Lowered pressure is communicated through passages in the air–gas valve assembly to the upper side of the diaphragm. Atmospheric pressure acting on the underside of the diaphragm then lifts the diaphragm against the downward pressure of the metering spring and lifts the air–gas valve assembly.

As part of the assembly, the gas-metering valve is lifted off its seat. Lowered pressure varies with engine speed, and the air–gas valve moves in response to measure the airflow. The controlled pressure drop set up by the metering spring provides the force necessary to draw fuel into the airstream within the carburetor. There are two mixture adjustments:

1. The idle adjust bypasses a portion of incoming air around the air–gas valve. As the idle adjustment is opened, the air–gas valve partially closes, making the idle air–fuel mixtures leaner.
2. The power mixture adjustment controls mixtures when the gas-metering valve is withdrawn from its seat and is effective only when the engine approaches full-load condition.

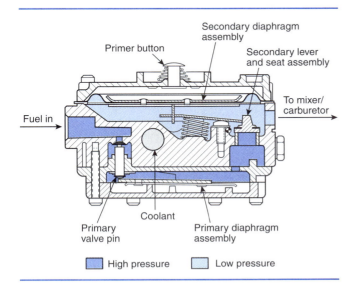

EXHIBIT 11.5 Two-Stage Pressure Regulator Converter. (Courtesy of IMPCO Technologies Inc.)

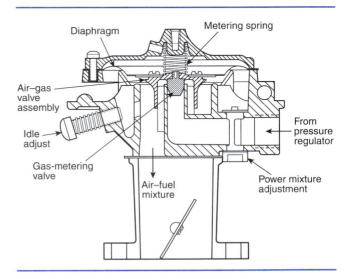

EXHIBIT 11.6 Air–Gas Valve Carburetor. (Courtesy of IMPCO Technologies Inc.)

Exhibit 11.7 shows a vacuum fuel lock. The shutoff valve required in 11.6.3 can be accomplished with a vacuum fuel lock. This shutoff can also be accomplished with oil pressure or vacuum switches. Vacuum fuel locks are normally closed. They use air valve vacuum from the air–fuel mixer to open the fuel lock. If the engine stops or is turned off, engine vacuum dissipates and the fuel lockoff closes automatically. This safety feature is desirable. When the engine is cranking or running, air valve vacuum is transmitted from the mixer to the lockoff through a vacuum hose. The vacuum acts on a diaphragm assembly, pulling it inward against the valve-operating lever. As the valve-operating lever is depressed, it moves the valve-operating pin. As the valve-operating pin moves, it lifts the valve off its seat. This movement allows propane to flow through the lockoff's 10-micron filter and on to the pressure regulator.

EXHIBIT 11.7 *Vacuum Fuel Lock. (Courtesy of IMPCO Technologies Inc.)*

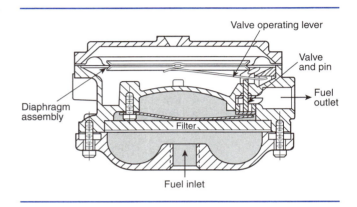

11.6.1 Pressure.

Carburetion equipment subject to a pressure of 125 psig (0.9 MPag) or greater shall be designed for a pressure rating of 250 psig (1.7 MPag) or for the MAWP of the container where the MAWP of the container is greater than 250 psig (1.7 MPag).

11.6.2 Vaporizers.

11.6.2.1 Vaporizers shall be fabricated of materials resistant to corrosion by LP-Gas under service conditions.

11.6.2.2 Vaporizers shall be designed for engine fuel service.

11.6.2.3 Vaporizers subjected to pressures up to the MAWP of the supply container shall have a pressure rating of 250 psig (1.7 MPag) or the MAWP of the container where the MAWP of the container is greater than 250 psig (1.7 MPag).

11.6.2.4 Vaporizers shall be marked with the design pressure of the fuel-containing portion in psig (MPag). The marking shall be visible when the vaporizer is installed.

11.6.2.5 The vaporizer shall not be equipped with a fusible plug.

11.6.2.6 Each vaporizer shall be capable of having the water or heating fluid drained from the engine cooling system drain or water hose or shall have a valve or plug located at or near the lowest portion of the section occupied by the water or other heating fluid to allow drainage of the water or heating fluid.

11.6.2.7 Where engine exhaust gases are used as a direct source of heat to vaporize the fuel, the materials of construction of those parts of the vaporizer in contact with the exhaust gases shall be resistant to corrosion by these gases, and the vaporizer system shall be designed to prevent a pressure in excess of 200 psig (1.4 MPag).

11.6.2.8 Devices that supply heat directly to the fuel container shall be equipped with an automatic device to cut off the supply of heat before the pressure in the container reaches 200 psig (1.4 MPag).

11.6.3 Fuel Shutoff Valve.

11.6.3.1 An automatic shutoff valve shall be provided in the fuel system as close as practical to the inlet of the gas regulator.

11.6.3.2 The valve shall prevent flow of fuel to the carburetor when the engine is not running even if the ignition switch is in the "on" position.

11.6.3.3 Atmospheric-type regulators (zero governors) shall not be considered as automatic shutoff valves for the purpose of the requirements of 11.6.3.

11.7 Piping, Hose, and Fittings

The piping and hose requirements for engine fuel systems are identical to those specified in Chapter 5 for stationary installations, with the exception of hose.

11.7.1 Pipe and Tubing.

11.7.1.1 Pipe shall be wrought iron or steel (black or galvanized), brass, or copper and shall comply with the following:

(1) Wrought-iron: ASME B36.10M, *Welded and Seamless Wrought Steel Pipe*
(2) Steel pipe: ASTM A 53, *Standard Specification for Pipe, Steel, Black and Hot-Dipped, Zinc-Coated Welded and Seamless*
(3) Steel pipe: ASTM A 106, *Standard Specification for Seamless Carbon Steel Pipe for High-Temperature Service*
(4) Brass pipe: ASTM B 43, *Standard Specification for Seamless Red Brass Pipe, Standard Sizes*
(5) Copper pipe: ASTM B 42, *Standard Specification for Seamless Copper Pipe, Standard Sizes*

11.7.1.2 Tubing shall be steel, stainless steel, brass, or copper and shall comply with the following:

(1) Brass tubing: ASTM B 135, *Standard Specification for Seamless Brass Tube*
(2) Copper tubing:
    (a) Type K or L: ASTM B 88, *Standard Specification for Seamless Copper Water Tube*
    (b) ASTM B 280, *Standard Specification for Seamless Copper Tube for Air Conditioning and Refrigeration Field Service*

Note that ASTM A 536, *Standard Specification for Electric-Resistance-Welded Coiled Steel Tubing for Gas Fuel Oil Lines*, was deleted from the list, because it has been withdrawn by ASTM with no replacement.

11.7.2 Fittings for Metallic Pipe and Tubing.

11.7.2.1 Fittings shall be steel, brass, copper, malleable iron, or ductile (nodular) iron.

11.7.2.2 Pipe fittings shall have a minimum pressure rating as specified in Table 11.7.2.2 and shall comply with the following:

(1) Cast-iron pipe fittings shall not be used.
(2) Brazing filler material shall have a melting point that exceeds 1000°F (538°C).

TABLE 11.7.2.2 Service Pressure Rating of Pipe, Tubing Fittings, and Valves

Service	*Minimum Pressure*
Higher than container pressure	350 psig (2.4 MPag) or the MAWP, whichever is higher, or 400 psig (2.8 MPag) WOG rating
LP-Gas liquid or vapor at operating pressure over 125 psig (0.9 MPag) and at or below container pressure	250 psig (1.7 MPag)
LP-Gas vapor at operating pressure or 125 psig (0.9 MPag) or less	125 psig (0.9 MPag)

See the commentary following 5.9.4.1(2) for an explanation of brazing and brazing materials.

11.7.2.3 Metal tube fittings shall have a minimum pressure rating as specified in Table 11.7.2.2.

11.7.3 Hose, Hose Connections, and Flexible Connectors.

Subsection 11.7.3 was returned to the code, after having been inadvertently deleted in the previous edition. Identical action had been taken as a Tentative Interim Amendment (TIA) to the 2008 edition.

11.7.3.1 Hose, hose connections, and flexible hose connectors *(see 3.3.26)* used for conveying LP-Gas liquid or vapor at pressures in excess of 5 psig (34.5 kPag) shall be fabricated of materials resistant to the action of LP-Gas both as liquid and vapor, and the hose and flexible hose connector and shall be reinforced with stainless steel wire braid.

11.7.3.2 Hose that can be exposed to container pressure shall be designed for a pressure rating of 350 psig (2.4 MPag) with a safety factor of 5 to 1, and the reinforcement shall be stainless steel wire braid.

11.7.3.3 Hose shall be continuously marked "LP-GAS, PROPANE, 350 PSI WORKING PRESSURE" and the manufacturer's name or trademark. Each installed piece of hose shall contain at least one such marking.

11.7.3.4 After the application of couplings, hose assemblies shall be capable of withstanding a pressure of not less than 700 psig (4.8 MPag). If a pressure test is performed, such assemblies shall be pressure tested at 120 percent of the pressure rating [350 psig (2.4 MPag) minimum] of the hose.

11.7.3.5 Hose used for vapor service at 5 psig (34.5 kPag) or less shall be constructed of material resistant to the action of LP-Gas.

11.7.3.6 Hose in excess of 5 psig (34.5 kPag) service pressure and quick connectors shall be approved.

11.7.3.7 Hose that is utilized at lower than container pressure shall be designed and marked for its maximum anticipated operating pressure.

11.8 Installation of Containers and Container Appurtenances

It is important that the container and its fittings be protected from damage resulting from collision, overturning, running over objects (such as curbs), or brushing against objects. Protection from road material thrown up from the ground and from exposure to heat from the engine or exhaust is also addressed in Section 11.8. Locations where the fuel container may be placed are limited so that the container or its fittings cannot protrude beyond the widest or highest point of the vehicle. Specifically, the container and its fittings cannot be in front of the front axle, to the rear of the rear bumper, or mounted directly on vehicle roofs.

11.8.1 Location of Containers.

11.8.1.1 Containers shall be located to minimize the possibility of damage to the container and its fittings.

11.8.1.2 Where containers are located in the rear of the vehicle, they shall be protected.

11.8.1.3 Containers located less than 18 in. (460 mm) from the exhaust system, the transmission, or a heat-producing component of the internal combustion engine shall be shielded by a vehicle frame member or by a noncombustible baffle with an air space on both sides of the frame member or baffle.

The separation of vehicle exhaust system components was increased from 8 in. (20 cm) to 18 in. (460 mm) in the 2001 edition to make it consistent with the requirements of NFPA 1192, *Standard on Recreational Vehicles* [5]. Most recreational vehicles have propane tanks used to fuel cooking and heating appliances.

11.8.1.4 After a container is permanently installed on a vehicle, container markings shall be readable either directly or with a portable lamp and mirror.

11.8.2 Protection of Containers and Appurtenances.

11.8.2.1 Container valves, appurtenances, and connections shall be protected to prevent damage due to accidental contact with stationary objects, or from stones, mud, or ice, and from damage due to an overturn or similar vehicular accident.

11.8.2.2 Protection of container valves, appurtenances, and connections shall be provided by one of the following:

(1) By locating the container so that parts of the vehicle furnish the necessary protection
(2) By the use of a fitting guard furnished by the manufacturer of the container
(3) By other means to provide equivalent protection

11.8.3 Container Clearances.

11.8.3.1 Containers shall not be mounted directly on roofs or ahead of the front axle or beyond the rear bumper of the vehicles.

11.8.3.2 No part of a container or its appurtenances shall protrude beyond the sides or top of the vehicle.

The intent of 11.8.3.2 is to locate the container where it cannot be easily damaged. A side-mounted container is permitted as long as it does not protrude beyond the widest point of the vehicle.

11.8.3.3 Containers shall be installed with as much road clearance as practical.

11.8.3.4 Clearance shall be measured to the bottom of the container or the lowest fitting, support, or attachment on the container or its housing, if any, whichever is lowest, as shown in Figure 11.8.3.4.

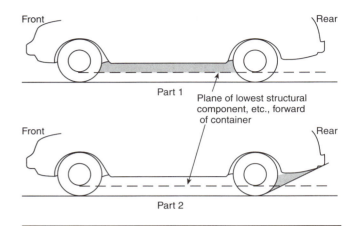

FIGURE 11.8.3.4 *Container Installation Clearances.*

11.8.3.5 Containers installed between axles shall comply with 11.8.3.6 or shall not be lower than the lowest point forward of the container on the following points:

(1) Lowest structural component of the body as illustrated in Figure 11.8.3.4
(2) Lowest structural component of the frame or subframe
(3) Lowest point on the engine
(4) Lowest point of the transmission (including the clutch housing or torque converter housing, as applicable)

11.8.3.6 Containers installed behind the rear axle and extending below the frame shall comply with 11.8.3.7 or shall not be lower than the lowest of the following points and surfaces:

(1) Containers shall not be lower than the lowest point of a structural component of the body, engine, and transmission (including clutch housing or torque converter housing, as applicable) forward of the container.
(2) Containers shall not be lower than lines extending rearward from each wheel at the point where the wheels contact the ground directly below the center of the axle to the lowest and most rearward structural interference, as illustrated in Part 2 of Figure 11.8.3.4.

11.8.3.7 Where an LP-Gas container is substituted for the fuel container installed by the original manufacturer of the vehicle, the LP-Gas container either shall fit within the space in which the original fuel container was installed or shall comply with 11.8.3.5 or 11.8.3.6.

FAQ ▶
Can a vehicle fuel container be replaced with a container of a different size?

Specific provisions are given for clearances between the road and the container and its fittings. Figure 11.8.3.4 shows shaded areas beneath the vehicle where the container can be installed. A replacement container may be installed within the space where the original fuel container was installed, but it must fit within the space provided in the vehicle for the container, or not protrude from the vehicle, as stated in the sections referenced.

11.8.4 Container Installation.

11.8.4.1 Fuel containers shall be installed to prevent their jarring loose and slipping or rotating, and the fastenings shall be designed and constructed to withstand without permanent deformation static loading in any direction equal to four times the weight of the container filled with fuel.

The strength of fasteners for mounting the container must be considered as well as the strength of that portion of the vehicle to which the container is mounted. For example, reinforcement must be used when mounting containers to thin metal decking. Installers frequently mount the container on the chassis frame, if present.

11.8.4.2 Welding for the repair or alterations of containers shall comply with 11.3.3.3.

11.8.4.3 Main shutoff valves on a container for liquid and vapor shall be readily accessible without the use of tools, or other equipment shall be provided to shut off the container valves.

The phrase "readily accessible without the use of tools" is used only in Chapter 11 — the only other use of the phrase "use of tools" is in 11.9.1.5. Its use reflects the committee's concern that vehicle manufacturers would locate the main shutoff valve behind a plate secured by screws. The committee's intent is that the valve be accessible in case of an emergency without compromising the need for the valve to be protected from accidental damage.

A recent design using the "other equipment shall be provided" option is in use. Some containers have a plate over the fuel shutoff valves. A tool is required to remove this plate. However, the valves are equipped with electrical devices that allow the valves to be closed from a control in the driver compartment.

11.8.5 Pressure Relief Valve Discharge System.

11.8.5.1 The pressure relief valve discharge from fuel containers on vehicles other than industrial (and forklift) trucks shall be in accordance with the following:

(1) It shall be directed upward or downward within 45 degrees of vertical.
(2) It shall not directly impinge on the vehicle fuel container(s), the exhaust system, or any other part of the vehicle.
(3) It shall not be directed into the interior of the vehicle.

11.8.5.2 Where the pressure relief valve discharge must be piped away, the pipeaway system shall have a breakaway adapter.

(A) The breakaway adapter shall have a melting point of not less than 1500°F (816°C).

(B) The adapter either shall be an integral part of the pressure relief valve or shall be a separate adapter attached directly to the pressure relief valve.

(C) The pipeaway system shall have a length of nonmetallic hose.

(D) The nonmetallic hose shall be as short as practical and shall be able to withstand the downstream pressure from the relief valve in the full open position, and the hose shall be fabricated of materials resistant to the action of LP-Gas.

(E) Where hose is used to pipe away the relief valve discharge on containers installed on the outside of the vehicle, the breakaway adapter and any attached fitting shall deflect the relief valve discharge upward or downward within 45 degrees of vertical and shall meet the other requirements of 11.8.5.1 without the hose attached. If an additional fitting is necessary to meet this requirement, it shall have a melting point not less than 1500°F (816°C).

(F) The pipeaway system shall have a protective cover to minimize the possibility of the entrance of water or dirt into either the relief valve or its discharge system.

(G) No portion of the system shall have an internal diameter less than the internal diameter of the recommended breakaway adapter.

(H) The breakaway adapter either shall be threaded for direct connection to the relief valve and shall not interfere with the operation of the relief valve or shall be an integral part of the pressure relief valve. It shall break away without impairing the function of the relief valve.

(I) The pipeaway system connections shall be mechanically secured and shall not depend on adhesives or sealing compounds and shall not be routed between a bumper system and the vehicle body.

(J) Where a pipeaway system is not required, the pressure relief valve shall have a protective cover in accordance with 11.8.5.2.

Pressure relief valve discharge location must be considered in the installation of engine fuel containers, because valves should not be directed in such a way as to create an unsafe condition. Vehicles must have the relief directed upward or downward within 45 degrees of vertical and located in such a way that the valve is not directed at any part of the vehicle. Prior to the 1992 edition, these requirements were more restrictive, permitting only vertical discharge. The requirements in 11.8.5 were modified based on the facts that a downward discharge could be safer than an upward discharge orientation, because the potential of water freezing in the valve is eliminated, and a downward discharge might be less likely to impinge on people or vehicles. The committee was advised that many school buses in Canada have used downward discharge for several years without problems. These restrictions do not apply to industrial trucks and forklifts, which are covered by Section 11.13.

Exhibits 11.8 and 11.9 illustrate the pressure relief valve discharge line extended above the roof of a truck cab and a line from the container to the roof of the topper or shell of a pickup truck.

11.9 Installation in the Interior of Vehicles

11.9.1 Installation of Containers and Appurtenances.

11.9.1.1 Installation of containers in the interior of vehicles shall comply with either 11.9.1.2 or 11.9.1.3.

EXHIBIT 11.8 *Pressure Relief Valve Discharge Line Extended Above the Roof of a Truck Cab. (Courtesy of Eastern Propane Corp.)*

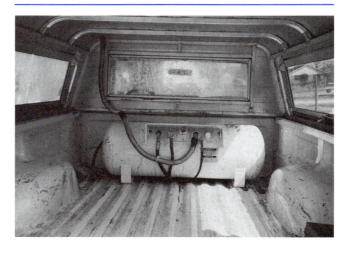

EXHIBIT 11.9 *LP-Gas Container Inside an Enclosed Pickup Truck Bed. The pressure relief valve discharge line runs from the container to the roof of the topper. (Courtesy of Eastern Propane Corp.)*

11.9.1.2* The container and its appurtenances shall be installed in an enclosure that is securely mounted to the vehicle.

(A) The enclosure shall be gastight with respect to driver or passenger compartments and to any space containing radio transmitters or other spark-producing equipment.

(B) The enclosure shall be vented to the outside of the vehicle.

A.11.9.1.2 The luggage compartment (trunk) of a vehicle can constitute such an enclosure, provided that it meets all these requirements.

11.9.1.3 The container appurtenances and their connections shall be installed in an enclosure that is securely mounted on the container.

(A) The appurtenances and their connections shall be installed in an enclosure that is gastight with respect to the driver or passenger compartments or with any space carrying radio transmitters or other spark-producing equipment.

(B) The enclosure shall be vented to the outside of the vehicle.

11.9.1.4 Fuel containers shall be installed and fitted so that no gas from fueling and gauging operations can be released inside of the passenger or luggage compartments by permanently installing a remote filling device (single or double backflow check filler valve) and a fixed maximum liquid level gauging device to the outside of the vehicle.

11.9.1.5 Enclosures, structures, seals, and conduits used to vent enclosures shall be designed and fabricated of durable materials and shall be designed to resist damage, blockage, or dislodgement through movement of articles carried in the vehicle or by the closing of luggage compartment enclosures or vehicle doors and shall require the use of tools for removal.

An alternative to mounting the fuel containers on the outside is installation in the interior of the vehicle, for example, in the trunk compartment. For fuel containers mounted inside the vehicle, certain conditions are specified to ensure that no LP-Gas is released into the passenger compartment.

The following four options are given for installation of containers mounted in the interior to seal the container appurtenances and their connections from the passenger space of the vehicle:

1. Locating the container and its appurtenances in the luggage compartment (trunk) and sealing the trunk from the passenger-carrying space (See Exhibit 11.10.)
2. Putting the entire container and its appurtenances in a sealed compartment (See Exhibit 11.11.)
3. Using a gastight enclosure totally enclosing the container appurtenances, but not the entire container (See Exhibit 11.12.)

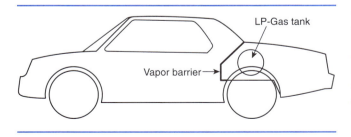

EXHIBIT 11.10 *Trunk-Mounted Fuel Container. A vapor barrier must be created between the passenger and luggage compartments. The barrier must be 100 percent gastight so no propane vapor can enter the car. (Courtesy of National Propane Gas Association)*

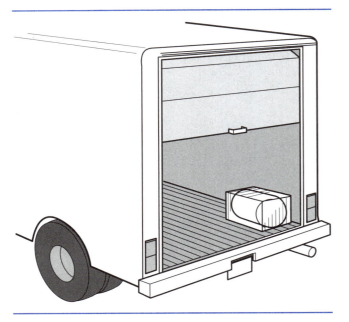

EXHIBIT 11.11 *Gastight Box Built Around the Container to Provide a Vapor Barrier in Vehicles. (Adapted from original artwork from National Propane Gas Association)*

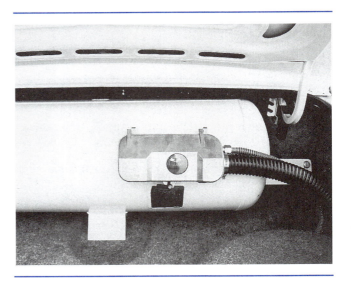

EXHIBIT 11.12 *Gastight Enclosure Installed over the Valve Fittings on the Tank Itself, Which Provides a Vapor Barrier. (Courtesy of Manchester Tank)*

4. Mounting the container so appurtenances and their connections are outside the passenger space, isolating spark-producing equipment such as radio transmitters and truck lid motors from container appurtenances and their connections

Remote filling is accomplished by permanently installing a double backflow check valve on the exterior of the vehicle in addition to one installed in the container. (See Exhibit 11.13.) Remote fixed maximum liquid level gauges are also to be permanently mounted with a maximum No. 54 drill size orifice in addition to the orificed connection on the container.

EXHIBIT 11.13 *Remote Filling Connection with Fixed Maximum Liquid Level Gauge. (Courtesy of National Propane Gas Association)*

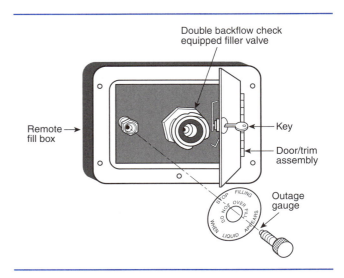

11.10 Pipe and Hose Installation

11.10.1 General Requirements.

11.10.1.1 The piping system shall be designed, installed, supported, and secured in such a manner as to minimize damage due to expansion, contraction, vibration, strains, and wear.

11.10.1.2 Piping (including hose) shall be installed in a protected location.

11.10.1.3 If piping is installed outside the vehicle, it shall be under the vehicle and below any insulation or false bottom.

11.10.1.4 Fastening or other protection shall be installed to prevent damage due to vibration or abrasion.

11.10.1.5 At each point where piping passes through sheet metal or a structural member, a rubber grommet or equivalent protection shall be installed to prevent chafing.

11.10.1.6 Fuel line piping that must pass through the floor of a vehicle shall be installed to enter the vehicle through the floor directly beneath or adjacent to the container.

11.10.1.7 If a branch fuel line is required, the tee connection shall be in the main fuel line under the floor and outside the vehicle.

11.10.1.8 Where liquid service lines of two or more individual containers are connected together, a spring-loaded backflow check valve or equivalent shall be installed in each of the liquid lines prior to the point where the liquid lines tee together to prevent the transfer of LP-Gas from one container to another.

The spring-loaded check valves are intended to prevent the transfer of LP-Gas between containers when more than one container is used. Without this protection, it would be possible for one container to transfer product into another based on each being at a different temperature and pressure, which could ultimately lead to an overfilled container.

11.10.1.9 Exposed parts of the piping system shall be of corrosion-resistant material or shall be protected to minimize exterior corrosion.

11.10.1.10 Piping systems, including hose, shall be tested and proven free of leaks at not less than normal operating pressure.

11.10.1.11 There shall be no fuel connection between a tractor and trailer or other vehicle units.

11.10.2 Hydrostatic Relief Valves.

11.10.2.1 A hydrostatic relief valve or device providing pressure-relieving protection shall be installed in each section of piping (including hose) in which liquid LP-Gas can be isolated between shutoff valves so as to relieve to the atmosphere.

11.10.2.2 Hydrostatic relief valves shall have a pressure setting of not less than 400 psig (2.8 MPag) or more than 500 psig (3.5 MPag).

11.11 Equipment Installation

11.11.1 Protection Against Damage.

11.11.1.1 Equipment installed on vehicles shall be protected against vehicular damage in accordance with 11.8.1.

11.11.1.2 The gas regulator and the automatic shutoff valve shall be installed as follows:

(1) An approved automatic shutoff valve in compliance with 11.6.3 shall be installed in the fuel system.
(2) Approved automatic pressure-reducing equipment shall be installed between the fuel supply container and the carburetor.

11.12 Marking

11.12.1 Label Requirements.

Each over-the-road general-purpose vehicle powered by LP-Gas shall be identified with a weather-resistant diamond-shaped label located on an exterior vertical or near vertical surface on the lower right rear of the vehicle (on the trunk lid of a vehicle so equipped but not on the bumper of any vehicle) inboard from any other markings.

11.12.2 Label Size.

11.12.2.1 The label shall be a minimum of 4¾ in. (120 mm) long by 3¼ in. (83 mm) high.

11.12.2.2* The marking shall consist of a border and the word PROPANE [1 in. (25 mm) minimum height centered in the diamond] in silver or white reflective luminous material on a black background.

A.11.12.2.2 See Figure A.11.12.2.2.

FIGURE A.11.12.2.2 *Example of Vehicle Identification Marking.*

11.13 Industrial (and Forklift) Trucks Powered by LP-Gas

NFPA 505, *Fire Safety Standard for Powered Industrial Trucks Including Type Designations, Areas of Use, Conversions, Maintenance, and Operations* [6], and NFPA 58 contain requirements for LP-Gas–fueled industrial trucks. While NFPA 58 sets forth installation provisions and certain conditions for their use, NFPA 505 sets forth type designations, areas containing flammables in which the truck can be used, dual-fuel trucks, truck maintenance, and fuel handling and storage.

Exhibit 11.14 shows a typical LP-Gas–powered industrial truck.

The basic provisions for engine fuel systems on general-purpose vehicles also apply to those for industrial truck engines, except for some differences that are based on the extensive use of such engines inside buildings.

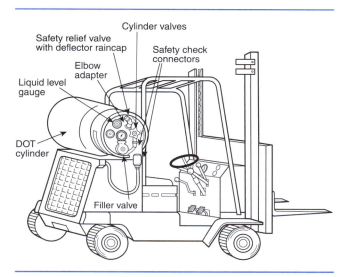

EXHIBIT 11.14 *Typical LP-Gas–Powered Industrial Truck (Forklift Truck). (Courtesy of Engineered Controls International, Inc.)*

11.13.1 Scope.

Section 11.13 applies to LP-Gas installation on industrial trucks (including forklift trucks), both to propel them and to provide the energy for their materials-handling attachments.

11.13.2 Industrial Truck Cylinders.

Cylinders for industrial trucks need not comply with 11.4.1.14; that is, they do not need to be equipped with an OPD, as is required for general-purpose vehicles. Universal cylinders are used for industrial trucks. They can be filled and used in either the horizontal or the vertical position. An OPD that will function in both positions is not available.

11.13.2.1 Cylinders shall be designed, constructed, or fitted for installation and filling in either the vertical or horizontal position or, if of the universal type, in either position.

11.13.2.2 The cylinder shall be in the design position while being filled or, if of the universal type, shall be filled in either position.

11.13.2.3 The fixed maximum liquid level gauge shall indicate the maximum permitted filling level in either position.

11.13.2.4 The pressure relief valves shall be in direct communication with the vapor space of the cylinder in either position.

11.13.2.5 The cylinder vapor or liquid withdrawal valves shall function in either position.

In addition to industrial truck cylinders designed for refilling and use specifically in either a horizontal or a vertical position, a universal cylinder is available in which the same cylinder can be filled and used in either position. With this type of cylinder, the fixed maximum liquid level gauge must indicate the maximum filling level in either the correct horizontal or the correct vertical position (for horizontal position, the relief valve must be at 12 o'clock), and, per 11.13.2.4, the pressure relief valve must communicate with the vapor space in either position.

11.13.2.6 The cylinder pressure relief valve discharge shall be directed upward within 45 degrees of vertical and otherwise shall not impinge on the cylinder, the exhaust system, or any other part of the industrial truck.

The exception in 11.13.2.6 to the general rule for orientation of the discharge of pressure relief valves recognizes that many industrial truck cylinders are used in the horizontal position, with the pressure relief valve in one of the heads (at the side of the container). The requirement for a vertical discharge would mean that the discharge would occur inside the area enclosed by the cylinder collar, and the released gas might not disperse quickly. A 45-degree angle to vertical eliminates this potential problem.

11.13.2.7 The discharge opening shall be provided with a protective cover to minimize the possibility of the entry of water or any extraneous matter.

11.13.2.8 Industrial truck cylinders shall have relief valves installed in accordance with 5.7.4.1(J).

11.13.3 Hose.

Hose 60 in. (1.5 m) in length or less shall not be required to be of stainless steel wire braid construction.

11.13.4 Operations.

The operation of industrial trucks (including forklift trucks) powered by LP-Gas engine fuel systems shall comply with 11.13.4.1 through 11.13.4.4.

11.13.4.1 Industrial trucks shall be refueled outdoors.

11.13.4.2 Where cylinders are exchanged indoors, the fuel piping system shall be equipped to minimize the release of fuel when cylinders are exchanged, in accordance with either of the following:

(1) Using an approved quick-closing coupling in the fuel line
(2) Closing the shutoff valve at the fuel cylinder and allowing the engine to run until the fuel in the line is exhausted

11.13.4.3 Where LP-Gas–fueled industrial trucks are used in buildings or structures, the following shall apply:

(1) The number of fuel cylinders on such a truck shall not exceed two.
(2) The use of industrial trucks in buildings frequented by the public, including those times when such buildings are occupied by the public, shall require the approval of the authority having jurisdiction.
(3) The total water capacity of the fuel cylinders on an individual truck shall not exceed 105 lb (48 kg) [nominal 45 lb (20 kg) propane capacity].
(4) Trucks shall not be parked and left unattended in areas occupied by or frequented by the public without the approval of the authority having jurisdiction. If left unattended with approval, the cylinder shutoff valve shall be closed.
(5) In no case shall trucks be parked and left unattended in areas of excessive heat or near sources of ignition.

11.13.4.4 All cylinders used in industrial truck service (including forklift truck cylinders) shall have the cylinder pressure relief valve replaced in accordance with 5.7.2.13.

11.14 General Provisions for Vehicles Having Engines Mounted on Them (Including Floor Maintenance Machines)

11.14.1 Scope.

Section 11.14 includes coverage of floor maintenance machines, such as the one shown in Exhibit 11.15. Use of these propane-powered floor buffers has grown since their introduction

EXHIBIT 11.15 *Floor Maintenance Machine. (Courtesy of Amano Pioneer Eclipse Corp.)*

into NFPA 58 in 1989. Their widespread use has resulted in specific coverage in NFPA 58 for the benefit of users of this equipment and enforcers of the code.

11.14.1.1 Section 11.14 applies to the installation of equipment on vehicles that supply LP-Gas as a fuel for engines installed on these vehicles.

11.14.1.2 Vehicles include floor maintenance and any other portable mobile unit, whether the engine is used to propel the vehicle or is mounted on it for other purposes.

11.14.2 General Requirements.

11.14.2.1 Industrial trucks (including forklift trucks) and other engines on vehicles operating in buildings other than those used exclusively to house engines shall have an approved automatic shutoff valve installed in the fuel system.

Although approved automatic shutoff valves are required by 11.14.2.1, it is recognized that the use of atmospheric-type regulators (zero governors) for this purpose, with portable engines of 12 horsepower or less with magneto ignition used exclusively outdoors, is acceptable. An atmospheric-type regulator, as its name implies, depends on the atmospheric pressure for its control. The regulator is not an approved vacuum lockoff, which is considered an approved automatic shutoff valve. The regulator operates on the principle that when there is no vacuum in the carburetor venturi, the regulator shuts off the flow of fuel. Atmospheric-type regulators have been used for many years on outdoor engine applications.

11.14.2.2 The source of air for combustion shall be isolated from the driver and passenger compartment, ventilating system, or air-conditioning system on the vehicle.

11.14.2.3 Non–self-propelled floor maintenance machinery (floor polishers, scrubbers, buffers) and other similar portable equipment shall be listed.

(A) A label shall be affixed to the machinery or equipment, with the label facing the operator, with the text denoting that the cylinder or portion of the machinery or equipment containing the cylinder shall be stored in accordance with Chapter 8.

(B) The use of floor maintenance machines in buildings frequented by the public, including the times when such buildings are occupied by the public, shall require the approval of the authority having jurisdiction.

Great concern exists that a propane-powered floor buffer, with its 20 lb (9 kg) LP-Gas cylinder, will be stored inside buildings in concealed areas, such as closets. The technical committee, consistent with its long prohibition (with certain exceptions) of LP-Gas cylinders larger than 1 lb (0.5 kg) in buildings, reinforced its intent that cylinders be stored properly in accordance with Chapter 8. The technical committee was especially concerned that the introduction of engine fuel cylinders would lead to improper storage and therefore require specific labeling.

Propane-powered floor buffers and forklift trucks are both categorized as industrial trucks. It is highly improbable, however, that a forklift truck will be left in a closet. If a floor buffer and its 20 lb (9 kg) LP-Gas cylinder were stored in a closet and a fire occurred, the propane in the cylinder could be a threat to fire fighters due to the storage of a fuel that can accelerate a fire. Recognition of this threat to fire fighters is especially important when one considers that the nature of the floor buffer is that it will be used in buildings such as offices, malls, schools, and other nonindustrial areas where the storage of propane cylinders is not anticipated.

Propane-powered floor buffers have been found in storage closets and backrooms of a variety of stores, such as clothing stores and big box stores. They have also been found in the areas under the seating in large arenas, such as college basketball venues. In many cases, the label required in 11.14.2.3(A) has come off, been removed, or been ignored. Also, in a few instances these machines have been found with improperly installed cylinders, so the relief valve would not be communicating with the vapor space if the cylinder were more than half full. Sometimes this is due to a broken locating pin on the machine, thus not "requiring" the cylinder to be properly installed.

Another issue is the apparent lack of concern for following the requirements of 11.14.2.3(B). Floor maintenance machines may be brought into a building by cleaning contractors and stored in the building, or may be purchased by building owners for their staff use. Both of these groups of people may be unaware of building and fire codes. Building inspectors who may inadvertently find these machines in closets or storage rooms may not be aware of these rules. The editor believes that more training and education on this issue are needed.

11.15 Engine Installation Other Than on Vehicles

This section was split into two subsections in the 2011 edition. The Committee recognized the need to specify separate requirements for portable engines and their containers and for the containers for stationary engines. Prior to the 1992 edition, containers for stationary engines were included in the chapter on LP-Gas installations, the current Chapter 6. In the 1992 edition, engine fuel systems were moved to a separate chapter, but the separation requirements that were present in former editions were not transferred. The 2011 edition provides some needed information on separation requirements.

11.15.1 Portable Engines.

11.15.1.1 The use of portable engines in buildings shall be limited to emergencies.

11.15.1.2 Air for combustion and cooling shall be supplied.

11.15.1.3 Exhaust gases shall be discharged to a point outside the building or to an area in which they will not constitute a hazard.

11.15.1.4 Where atmospheric-type regulators (zero governors) are used on engines operated only outdoors, a separate automatic shutoff valve shall not be required.

11.15.1.5 Engines used to drive portable pumps and compressors or pumps shall be equipped in accordance with 5.17.6.

11.15.2 Containers for Stationary Engines.

11.15.2.1 LP-Gas containers for stationary installations shall be located outside of buildings unless the buildings comply with the requirements of Chapter 10.

11.15.2.2 Containers for stationary engines shall be installed to meet the separation requirements of Section 6.3.

11.15.2.3 Where containers for stationary engines have a fill valve with an integral manual shutoff valve, the minimum separation distances shall be one-half of the distances specified in Section 6.3.

11.16 Garaging of Vehicles

Where vehicles with LP-Gas engine fuel systems mounted on them, and general-purpose vehicles propelled by LP-Gas engines, are stored or serviced inside garages, the following conditions shall apply:

(1) The fuel system shall be leak-free.
(2) The container shall not be filled beyond the limits specified in Chapter 7.
(3) The container shutoff valve shall be closed when the vehicle or the engine is being repaired, except when the engine is required to operate. Containers equipped with an automatic shutoff valve as specified in 11.4.1.8 satisfy this requirement.
(4) The vehicle shall not be parked near sources of heat, open flames, or similar sources of ignition or near inadequately ventilated pits.

REFERENCES CITED IN COMMENTARY

1. NFPA 302, *Fire Protection Standard for Pleasure and Commercial Motor Craft*, 2010 edition, National Fire Protection Association, Quincy, MA.
2. ASME *Boiler and Pressure Vessel Code*, 2007 edition, American Society of Mechanical Engineers, New York, NY.
3. CGA S-1.3, *Pressure Relief Device Standards* Part 3 — Stationary Storage Containers for Compressed Gases, 2008 edition.
4. Investigation Report, STEAMTECH van, October 18, 2002, conducted by Richard Fredenburg, North Carolina Department of Agriculture and Consumer Services, Standards Division, Raleigh, NC.
5. NFPA 1192, *Standard on Recreational Vehicles*, 2008 edition, National Fire Protection Association, Quincy, MA.
6. NFPA 505, *Fire Safety Standard for Powered Industrial Trucks Including Type Designations, Areas of Use, Conversions, Maintenance, and Operations*, 2011 edition, National Fire Protection Association, Quincy, MA.

Refrigerated Containers

Refrigerated LP-Gas storage systems store propane at or near its boiling point of approximately −40°F (−40°C) at atmospheric pressure. The low temperature is usually maintained by using an insulated container in which an auto-refrigeration process takes place, although some larger systems use mechanical refrigeration. Some of the liquid vaporizes due to the inevitable heat leakage into the container, which cools the liquid to maintain the low temperature. The vapor produced, or boil-off gas that is vaporized, is withdrawn from the container to control the pressure in the container. This gas is either reliquefied in an external refrigeration system or used as a fuel gas.

If a pressurized container were used for the large storage volumes normally held in refrigerated containers, the steel shell would have to be quite thick, because the thickness of a pressure vessel wall increases with the square of the diameter. So if the diameter were increased four times, the shell would have to be 16 times thicker. A steel shell this thick would be difficult, as well as very expensive, to make and weld.

◄ FAQ
Why are refrigerated containers used for larger propane storage volumes?

Refrigerated storage containers are usually quite large. The majority of the installations have tanks from 1,000,000 gal to 10,000,000 gal (3800 m³ to 38,000 m³) and larger. A few intermediate-pressure refrigerated LP-Gas systems are in operation. These intermediate-pressure systems are referred to as semi-refrigerated, and their typical operating pressures are between 15 psig and 65 psig (100 kPag and 450 kPag).

Refrigerated LP-Gas containers can be single-wall vessels with external insulation or double-wall vessels with insulation between the inner and outer tank walls.

Refrigerated storage containers are used at natural gas processing plants, petroleum refineries, petrochemical plants, import and export terminals, and at pipeline terminals, as well as by other plants requiring large storage volume. The design of these storage containers is covered in API 620, *Design and Construction of Large, Welded, Low-Pressure Storage Tanks* [1].

Prior to the 1989 edition, refrigerated storage was not specifically addressed in NFPA 58 but was covered in NFPA 59, *Utility LP-Gas Plant Code* [2]. The 1989 edition expanded the scope of NFPA 58 to include pipeline and marine terminals, which had been referenced previously to API 2510, *Design and Construction of Liquefied Petroleum Gas Installations (LPG)* [3]. At that time, some coverage specific to refrigerated storage was also added. Concurrently, the Technical Committee on Liquefied Petroleum Gases at Utility Gas Plants, which is responsible for NFPA 59, expanded the scope of NFPA 59 to include refrigerated storage containers in NFPA 59. Beginning with the 1998 edition, this chapter is extracted into NFPA 59 so that both documents have identical requirements for refrigerated containers.

Chapter 12 addresses the following topics within the scope of refrigerated storage:

- Construction and design of refrigerated containers (See Section 12.1.)
- Marking on refrigerated LP-Gas containers (See Section 12.2.)
- Container installation (See Section 12.3.)
- Refrigerated LP-Gas container instruments and controls (See Section 12.4.)
- Refrigerated LP-Gas container impoundment (See Section 12.5.)
- Inspection and testing of refrigerated LP-Gas containers and systems (See Section 12.6.)
- Container siting (See Section 12.7.)
- Relief devices (See Section 12.8.)

There have been few if any changes regarding refrigerated containers in the past few years, and consequently there are no substantive revisions to this chapter in the 2011 edition. While there are not many refrigerated containers, they are much larger than pressurized containers, and they remain an important safety concern.

12.1 Construction and Design of Refrigerated Containers

Section 12.1 contains the requirements for the construction and design of refrigerated LP-Gas containers and their foundations. A refrigerated LP-Gas container is a single-wall container with insulation on the exterior. The insulation is needed to maintain the $-40°F$ ($-40°C$) temperature in the container. Another type of refrigerated LP-Gas container uses two walls, with insulation between the two walls. A benefit of the double-wall-type container is that the outer wall can contain the LP-Gas if the inner container fails, and the outer container is made of a material that will not fail at $-40°F$ ($-40°C$). Double-wall containers are usually used for liquefied gases with lower boiling points than propane, such as liquefied natural gas, ethane, and hydrogen.

12.1.1 Container Material and Construction Requirements.

12.1.1.1 Containers designed to operate at greater than 15 psig (103 kPag) shall be designed and constructed in accordance with the ASME *Boiler and Pressure Vessel Code*, Section VIII, except that construction using joint efficiencies listed in Table UW 12, Column C, shall not be permitted.

Section VIII of the ASME *Boiler and Pressure Vessel Code* [4] is used to design and fabricate shop-built vessels or semi-refrigerated LP-Gas containers operating above 15 psig (103 kPag). While the vast majority of storage vessels are built to API 620, some plants have smaller vessels, which are built to the ASME Code. Their coverage is included to make the standard complete.

The exception of Table UW 12, Type 1, Column C, of the ASME Code strengthens inspection requirements by mandating a minimum joint efficiency of 85 percent. This efficiency requires spot or full radiography (quality control x-ray inspection) of all tank welds. In Table UW 12 of the ASME Code, Section VIII, Division 1 joint efficiencies are specified. Joint efficiency is a factor that takes into account the existence of acceptable welding defects. Column C allows Type 1 welds to be used with no weld quality inspection, which the LP-Gas Committee does not accept.

12.1.1.2 Materials used in refrigerated containers shall be selected from those included in the following:

(1) ASME *Boiler and Pressure Vessel Code*, Section VIII (materials that maintain their integrity at the boiling temperature of the liquid stored)
(2) API Standard 620, *Design and Construction of Large, Welded, Low-Pressure Storage Tanks,* Appendix R or Appendix Q

The material selection references in 12.1.1.2(2) to Appendixes R and Q of API 620, *Design and Construction of Large, Welded, Low-Pressure Storage Tanks* [1], ensure that only the materials suitable for low temperature service are used. At low temperatures, some metals become brittle and therefore are not suitable for refrigerated storage containers holding LP-Gas.

12.1.1.3 Containers designed to operate below 15 psig (103 kPag) shall be in accordance with API Standard 620, *Design and Construction of Large, Welded, Low-Pressure Storage Tanks,* including Appendix R.

API 620 is recognized worldwide as a standard for the construction of large welded storage tanks designed for pressures of 15 psig (103 kPag) or less. API 620, Appendix R, specifically addresses the design, construction, testing, and material requirements of such tanks operating at refrigerated LP-Gas temperatures.

12.1.1.4 Where austenitic stainless steels or nonferrous materials are used, API Standard 620, *Design and Construction of Large, Welded, Low-Pressure Storage Tanks,* Appendix Q, shall be used in the selection of materials.

Appendix Q of API 620 contains requirements for the use of austenitic stainless steels and nonferrous materials that are not included in Appendix R.

12.1.1.5 All new construction shall incorporate on any bottom or side penetrations that communicate with the liquid space of the container either an internal emergency shutoff valve or a back check valve. Any emergency shutoff valve shall be incorporated into a facility emergency shutdown system and be capable of being operated remotely.

This requirement in 12.1.1.5 is intended to minimize spillage in the event of piping system failure.

12.1.2 Container Design Temperature and Pressure.

12.1.2.1 The design pressure of ASME containers shall include a minimum 5 percent of the absolute vapor pressure of the LP-Gas at the design storage temperature. The margin (both positive and vacuum) for low-pressure API Standard 620 vessels shall include the following:

(1) Control range of the boil-off handling system
(2) Effects of flash or vapor collapse during filling operations
(3) Flash that can result from withdrawal pump recirculation
(4) Normal range of barometric pressure changes

The design of a typical pressurized ASME propane container usually uses a maximum allowable working pressure of 250 psig (1.7 MPag), while the design of a refrigerated storage container, where the propane is stored as a liquid at or below its normal boiling point of about −40°F (−40°C) with a pressure of roughly 0 psig, must consider both positive pressure *and* negative pressure (vacuum).

Paragraph 12.1.2.1 requires the design to include a very small (5 percent) fraction of the *absolute* vapor pressure of the product. For example, if the container is designed to contain liquid at −40°F, the absolute pressure would be about 15 psia (103 kPaa) Therefore, the design of the container must be based on a pressure of 5 percent of 15 psi (103 kPa), or 0.75 psig (5.2 kPa), at a minimum. If the container was designed for refrigerated propane that could be warmed (no refrigeration or vapor withdrawal) to 100°F (38°C), the design pressure must include 5 percent of the vapor pressure of propane at 100°F (38°C), or 5 percent of 175 psia (1.2 MPa), or 7 psi (48 kPa), and therefore the design pressure would be 182 psi (1.3 MPa).

The design of refrigerated containers using the ASME *Boiler and Pressure Vessel Code* differs from the design of typical pressure vessels for propane and requires the anticipation of a range of operating pressures. Because of the large size of LP-Gas refrigerated storage containers, even incremental changes of design pressure and vacuum can carry large costs because even a small increase in pressure or vacuum results in an increase of the thickness of the container shell. Container pressure can be significantly affected by small variations in filling rates, product composition, barometric pressure changes, and process upsets. The design pressure of refrigerated containers is usually quite low [1½ psig (10 kPag) to 5 psig (34 kPag)], and their ability to withstand vacuum is minimal [usually ¼ psig (2 kPag)]. The operator must take all these factors into account when specifying the container design pressure and ensure that the rest of the plant is designed and operated in such a way that the design pressure is not exceeded.

12.1.2.2 The design temperature for those parts of a refrigerated LP-Gas container that are in contact with the liquid or refrigerated vapor shall be equal to or lower than the boiling point of the product to be stored at atmospheric pressure. A temperature allowance shall be made for the composition of the liquid to be stored when it is flashed into the vapor space of a tank.

The requirement for a temperature allowance to account for minor variations in the composition of liquid propane provides additional safety in the selection of materials for tank construction. Propane with small amounts of other acceptable constituents, such as ethane, will produce temperatures lower than the boiling point of pure propane when flashed into the vapor space of a tank.

12.2 Marking on Refrigerated LP-Gas Containers

12.2.1 Each refrigerated LP-Gas container shall be identified by the attachment of a nameplate located either on the container or in a visible location.

12.2.2 The nameplate shall be in accordance with API Standard 620, *Design and Construction of Large, Welded, Low-Pressure Storage Tanks,* Section 6.

The marking requirements of API 620 include more information than was previously required in NFPA 58. Manufacturers must now include all information required by API 620. A change in the 2008 edition in 12.2.1 allowed the attachment of the nameplate to be in a "visible" location and not necessarily on the container itself. This change recognized that the nameplate may not be able to be readily attached to the outer covering of a container due to the presence of spray-on foam insulation or some other insulation system. In this case, the nameplate might be attached to the stairwell or some other obvious and visible location close to the container.

12.3 Container Installation

12.3.1 Wind Loading.

12.3.1.1 The design wind loading on refrigerated LP-Gas containers shall be in accordance with the projected area at various height zones above ground in accordance with ASCE 7, *Minimum Design Loads for Buildings and Other Structures.*

12.3.1.2 Design wind speeds shall be based on a mean occurrence interval of 100 years.

Wind loading can be a significant factor in the design and construction of refrigerated storage vessels because of the large size and low design pressure of the containers. Refrigerated tanks are designed to hold the weight of liquid and a very low pressure, about 2 psig (14 kPag) [versus 250 psig (1.7 MPag) for pressurized LP-Gas storage tanks]. In high winds, a refrigerated container can move if not designed and anchored properly. ASCE 7, *Minimum Design Loads for Buildings and Other Structures* [5], developed by the American Society of Civil Engineers, is the American National Standard and the authoritative resource on how to design buildings and structures to resist wind and other loads.

12.3.2 Seismic Loading.

12.3.2.1 The design seismic loading on refrigerated LP-Gas containers shall be in accordance with ASCE 7, *Minimum Design Loads for Buildings and Other Structures.*

12.3.2.2 A seismic analysis of the proposed installation shall be made that meets the approval of the authority having jurisdiction.

The large size and flammable contents of refrigerated LP-Gas storage vessels are reasons that a detailed seismic analysis may be required. A competent geotechnical or structural engineer should perform this analysis. The analysis will provide the basis for the seismic design, using ASCE 7.

12.3.3 Piping.

12.3.3.1 All piping that is part of a refrigerated LP-Gas container and refrigerated LP-Gas systems, including transfer and process piping, shall be in accordance with ASME B31.3, *Process Piping*.

The piping requirements of API 620 are supplemented with those of ASME B31.3 because the requirements of ASME B31.3, *Process Piping Code* [6], are somewhat more stringent than the piping requirements of API 620.

12.3.3.2 The container piping shall include the following:

(1) All piping internal to the container
(2) All piping within the insulation spaces
(3) All external piping attached or connected to the container up to the first circumferential external joint of the piping

12.3.3.3 Inert gas purge systems wholly within the insulation spaces shall be exempt from the provision in 12.3.3.1.

12.3.3.4 Gaskets used to retain LP-Gas in containers shall be resistant to the action of LP-Gas.

12.3.3.5 Gaskets shall be of metal or other material confined in metal, including spiral-wound metal gaskets, having a melting point over 1500°F (816°C) or shall be protected against fire exposure.

12.3.3.6 When a flange is opened, the gasket shall be replaced.

12.3.4 Foundations.

12.3.4.1 Refrigerated aboveground containers shall be installed on foundations that have been engineered for site soil conditions and loadings.

12.3.4.2* Prior to the start of design and construction of the foundation, a subsurface investigation shall be conducted by a soils engineer. Foundations shall be designed by an engineer who is experienced in foundations and soils.

A.12.3.4.2 See ASCE 56, *Sub-Surface Investigation for Design and Construction of Foundation for Buildings*, and API 620, *Design and Construction of Large, Welded, Low-Pressure Storage Tanks*, Annex C, for further information.

The importance of the tank foundation in maintaining the integrity of the tank cannot be overemphasized for refrigerated containers. If the foundation should shift, large stresses would be placed on the tank, which is not designed to hold significant pressure, potentially resulting in tank failure. This is quite different than for containers designed to hold 250 psi (1.7 MPa), which have much more strength. The publications referenced in A.12.3.4.2 can be used for guidance.

12.3.4.3 Where product storage is at less than 30°F (−1.1°C), the foundation and the tank bottom shall comply with the following:

(1) The foundation design and the container bottom insulation shall prevent damage to the tank from frost heave.

(2) If the refrigerated LP-Gas tank under bottom foundation and insulation are in contact with the soil, and the soil temperature could be less than 32°F (0°C), a heating system shall be installed to prevent the soil temperature from falling below 32°F (0°C).

(3) The under-tank heating system shall be designed to allow both functional and performance monitoring.

(4) The under-tank temperature shall be observed and logged at least weekly.

(5) Where there is a discontinuity in the foundation, such as bottom piping, the heating system in that zone shall be designed for the discontinuity.

(6) The under-tank heating system shall be installed so that any heating elements or temperature sensors used for control can be replaced while the tank is in service.

(7) Provisions shall be incorporated to minimize the effects of moisture accumulation in the conduit and other forms of deterioration within the conduit or heating element.

12.3.4.4 The refrigerated LP-Gas container foundation shall be periodically monitored for settlement during the life of the facility.

12.3.4.5 The monitoring shall include construction, hydrostatic testing, commissioning, and operation.

12.3.4.6 Any settlement in excess of that anticipated in the design shall be investigated, and corrective action shall be taken if appropriate.

FAQ ▶
Why is it important that a refrigerated LP-Gas tank's heating system be maintained?

Paragraphs 12.3.4.3 through 12.3.4.6 are concerned with maintaining the integrity of the foundation used to support the refrigerated container. When in contact with the soil, the bottom of a refrigerated propane container, with its contents at about −40°F (−40°C), transfers heat from the soil. If a heating system were not provided, the soil could freeze and expand (heave). Soil freezing must be prevented because soil heaving will cause the container foundation to move, which would probably damage the container. Heating systems are designed to prevent the soil from freezing and must be maintained. It is not uncommon to install thermocouples in or beneath the foundation to monitor the effectiveness of the undertank heating system. Undertank heating systems are usually electrically powered. However, in areas where below-freezing temperatures are not common, air circulation can be used.

12.3.4.7 For a tank having a double wall design, the bottom of the outer wall and the refrigerated LP-Gas container under-tank insulation shall be above the groundwater table or protected from contact with groundwater at all times. It shall also be protected from floodwaters.

Paragraph 12.3.4.7 recognizes the detrimental effect that water has on thermal insulation and the possibility that water can freeze and expand. When exposed to water, many thermal insulations will deteriorate or at the very least, lose much of their insulating qualities due to the presence of liquid water, which has a greater thermal conductivity than the insulation. If water under a refrigerated container should freeze, it would expand and could cause movement of part of the tank, with potentially disastrous results.

12.3.4.8 Where two or more containers are sited in a common dike, the tank foundations shall be constructed of material resistant to the effects of refrigerated LP-Gas and the temperatures to which they will be exposed.

12.3.4.9 If the foundation of a refrigerated LP-Gas container is designed to provide air circulation in lieu of a heating system, the foundation and insulating material under the bottom of the container shall be constructed of materials that are resistant to the effects of refrigerated LP-Gas and the temperatures to which they will be exposed.

12.3.4.10 The material in contact with the bottom of the container shall be selected to minimize corrosion.

12.4 Refrigerated LP-Gas Container Instruments and Controls

Requirements for controls included in Chapter 12 are not mandated for containers covered in the other parts of NFPA 58. These requirements are intended to prevent overfilling of containers and the inadvertent release of LP-Gas to the atmosphere. They are needed because of the larger size of containers covered by Chapter 12 as well as the difference in container type.

12.4.1 Gauging Devices.

12.4.1.1 Each refrigerated LP-Gas container shall be equipped with at least two independent liquid level gauging devices.

12.4.1.2 Liquid level gauging devices shall be installed so that they can be replaced without taking the container out of service.

12.4.1.3 The refrigerated LP-Gas container shall be provided with an audible and visual high–liquid level alarm.

The unusual requirement for a high–liquid level alarm with both visible and audible annunciation reflects the importance of preventing overfilling of the container. The two modes of annunciation include every reasonable step to prevent operators from ignoring the alarm.

12.4.1.4 The alarm shall be set so that the operator will have sufficient time, based on the maximum allowable filling rate, to stop the flow without exceeding the maximum permissible filling height.

12.4.1.5 The alarm shall be located so that it is visible and audible to the personnel who control the filling.

12.4.1.6 A high–liquid level flow cutoff device shall not be a substitute for the alarm.

A separate high-level sensor is required on refrigerated LP-Gas containers. This sensor cannot be a high–liquid level alarm point on a level gauge. This safety feature is required to ensure that the high–liquid level point is not changed during instrument calibration or by instrument error.

12.4.1.7 The refrigerated LP-Gas container shall be equipped with a high-high–liquid level flow cutoff device that is independent from all gauges.

A high-high–liquid level flow cutoff device is a level sensor installed above the level at which filling is not allowed. It must be independent of a level-indicating instrument (i.e., a separate device) so that it will function if the normal level indicator is not functioning correctly.

◄ **FAQ**
What is meant by "high-high–liquid level flow cutoff device"?

12.4.1.8 Where refrigerated LP-Gas containers of 70,000 gal (265 m³) or less are attended during the filling operation, they shall be equipped with either liquid trycocks or a high–liquid level alarm, and manual flow cutoff shall be permitted.

12.4.1.9 Each refrigerated LP-Gas container shall be provided with temperature-indicating devices that assist in controlling cooldown rates when placing the tank in service and monitoring product temperatures during operations.

Placing a refrigerated LP-Gas container into service is a critical process because the cooldown and contraction of the tank must be controlled to prevent cracks from developing. Temperature sensors permit the operator to monitor the process.

12.4.2 Pressure and Vacuum Control.

12.4.2.1 Provisions shall be made to maintain the container pressure within the limits set by the design specifications by releasing or admitting gas as needed. Provision for admission and release of gas shall be by any means compatible with the gas-handling facilities in the plant.

Because refrigerated propane is stored near its boiling point of about −40°F (−40°C), the pressure in the container is low and can be affected by rapid changes in atmospheric pressure due to weather systems. Pressure relief valves release pressure to reduce tank pressure if the atmospheric pressure falls. When the atmospheric pressure rises quickly, it is possible to partially implode a refrigerated container unless a means to raise the internal pressure is provided. Because the code allows gas to be released from or admitted to refrigerated containers, designers have flexibility in the means they employ to prevent over- and underpressure in these containers.

12.4.2.2 The option of gas admission (or other gas or vapor if so designed) through the vacuum relief valves provided in API Standard 620, *Design and Construction of Large, Welded, Low-Pressure Storage Tanks*, shall not be permitted.

API 620 covers tanks for all types of flammable fluids, including oils and gasoline, which normally have air in the space above the liquid. Air is not allowed in LP-Gas containers.

12.5 Refrigerated LP-Gas Container Impoundment

Diking of refrigerated LP-Gas containers is required because spillage of LP-Gas at its atmospheric boiling temperature of approximately −40°F (−40°C) will only partially vaporize, and liquid LP-Gas will be present due to the low temperature of the propane. This is quite different from pressurized propane, which will quickly vaporize completely in most spill cases.

12.5.1 Each refrigerated LP-Gas container shall be located within an impoundment that complies with Section 12.5.

12.5.2 Enclosed drainage channels for LP-Gas shall be prohibited.

12.5.3 Enclosure of container downcomers used to conduct spilled LP-Gas away from materials subject to failure upon exposure to liquid LP-Gas shall be permitted.

Enclosed drainage channels are prohibited in 12.5.2 to prevent the accumulation of vapor in enclosed spaces, which can impede the flow of liquid or promote detonation if ignition should occur. Note that 12.5.3 clarifies that downcomers, or vertical and nearly vertical passageways for conducting overflow to drainage channels, are allowed because they are needed to prevent falling liquid from contacting materials that would fail at low temperatures.

12.5.4 Impoundment for refrigerated LP-Gas containers shall have a volumetric holding capacity, with an allowance made for the displacement of snow accumulation, other containers, or equipment that is equal to the total liquid volume of the largest container served, assuming that container is full to the high–liquid level flow cutoff device.

The most commonly used means of impoundment are dikes. Dikes ensure that in the unlikely event of a refrigerated LP-Gas spill, the liquid will be contained and not allowed to spread. Diking provisions are not required for pressurized storage containers because the pressurized liquid vaporizes quickly after being released from its pressurized container. Refrigerated LP-Gas, however, will only partially vaporize, and a large part of the liquid will remain as liquid because limited heat is available from the air or the ground to vaporize the liquid.

The diking requirements are similar to those for flammable liquids diking in NFPA 30, *Flammable and Combustible Liquids Code* [7].

12.5.5 Where more than one container is installed in a single impoundment, and if an outside container wall is used as a spill containment dike, the material shall be selected to withstand exposure to the temperature of refrigerated LP-Gas liquid.

In the unlikely event of a refrigerated LP-Gas spill in a diked area containing more than one refrigerated LP-Gas container, the potential for a tank that is not leaking to be exposed to the liquid from the other leaking tank exists. This requirement for multiple refrigerated tanks in diked areas to be constructed of materials selected for exposure to the temperature of refrigerated LP-Gas recognizes several factors:

1. In the event of a spill of refrigerated LP-Gas, vaporization of the spilled liquid will take some time. Liquid can be present for a number of hours.
2. Steel, unless specially treated, can fail at a temperature of $-20°F$ ($-29°C$) or colder.
3. The temperature of liquid LP-Gas at its atmospheric boiling point is about $-40°F$ ($-40°C$).

12.5.6 Impoundment structures and any penetrations thereof shall be designed to withstand the full hydrostatic head of the impounded LP-Gas and the effects of the product composition and the resulting autorefrigeration temperatures.

12.5.7 Impoundment structures shall also be nonporous and resistant to natural forces such as wind, rain, and fire.

12.5.8 Provisions shall be made to clear rain or other water from the impounding area.

12.5.8.1 Where automatically controlled sump pumps are used, they shall be equipped with an automatic shutoff device that prevents their operation when exposed to the flash temperature of liquid LP-Gas. In addition, the sump pumps shall be de-energized if flammable vapors in excess of 25 percent of the lower flammable limit are detected within the impoundment area.

Paragraph 12.5.8.1 clarifies that electrically operated sump pumps used to keep the impounding area clear of water must be capable of being shut off when either LP-Gas vapors are detected (to prevent the possibility of igniting the vapors) or the pump is exposed to temperatures associated with liquid LP-Gas [roughly $-40°F$ ($-40°C$)], in order to prevent damage to the pump.

12.5.8.2 LP-Gas vapors shall not exceed 25 percent of the lower flammable limit or other approved methods of LP-Gas liquid or vapor detection.

12.5.8.3 Gravity drainage utilizing piping penetrations through or below impoundment dikes shall not be permitted.

12.5.9 If the container impounding area is an earthen dike system, the area topography of the impounding area floor shall be graded away from the container to prevent the accumulation of liquid under or around the container.

12.5.9.1 The grading shall move the spilled liquid to the toe of the dike system and as far away from the container as possible.

12.5.9.2 The grading shall move the spilled liquid to a subimpoundment basin that is capable of holding the quantity of liquid spilled from a line rupture, a flange leak, or a source other than container failure.

12.5.9.3 The duration of the incident shall be the amount of time that automatic systems or plant personnel could effect emergency procedures and stop the leak. The subimpoundment basin shall be located as far away from the container as possible.

The importance of clearing water and snow from diked areas frequently is not fully appreciated. Water cannot be allowed to drain from a dike because spilled propane can also drain with it. Temperature-sensitive valves can be specified, but their maintenance and operability cannot be ensured. Pumps with temperature-operated automatic shutoff are usually specified to remove rainwater and can be stopped remotely if they remove spilled propane from the dike.

Removal of snow in cold areas is not specifically addressed in the code, but should be considered by designers for plants in cold areas.

12.6 Inspection and Testing of Refrigerated LP-Gas Containers and Systems

Both the ASME and API codes contain requirements for tests and inspection, which are summarized here because of their importance.

12.6.1 During construction and prior to the initial operation or commissioning, each refrigerated LP-Gas container and system shall be inspected or tested in accordance with the provisions of this code and the codes and standards referenced herein.

12.6.2 The inspections or tests required shall be conducted by the operator or a recognized third-party engineering, scientific, insurance, or inspection organization.

The use of third-party inspectors recognizes that some plant owners may not have staff who are sufficiently knowledgeable of all the aspects of construction of refrigerated containers. If a contractor builds the container, an inspector from a different contractor will probably be very diligent.

12.6.3 Each inspector shall be qualified in accordance with the code or standard that is applicable to the test or inspection being performed.

12.6.4 After acceptance tests are completed, there shall be no field welding on the LP-Gas containers except where allowed by the code under which the container was fabricated.

12.6.5 Retesting shall be required only if the retest tests the element affected and is necessary to demonstrate the adequacy of the repair or modification.

12.7 Container Siting

The spacing requirements for refrigerated LP-Gas containers are similar to the requirements of Chapter 6 for nonrefrigerated containers. In addition, other requirements for container installation and the area around the container are provided here.

Section 12.7 contains two tables: Table 12.7.1, which applies to containers with a design pressure of more than 15 psig (103 kPag), and Table 12.7.2, which applies to containers with a design pressure of 15 psig (103 kPag) and less.

12.7.1 Spacing of refrigerated LP-Gas containers designed to operate at greater than 15 psi (103 kPa) from occupied buildings, storage containers for flammable or combustible liquids, and lines of adjoining property that can be built upon shall be in accordance with Table 12.7.1.

12.7.2 Spacing of refrigerated LP-Gas containers that operate below 15 psi (103 kPa) from occupied buildings, storage containers for flammable or combustible liquids, and lines of adjoining property that can be built upon shall be in accordance with Table 12.7.2.

TABLE 12.7.1 *Minimum Distances for LP-Gas Containers That Operate Above 15 psi (103 kPa)*

Water Capacity per Container		Aboveground Containers	
gal	*m³*	*ft*	*m*
≤70,000	≤265	75	23
70,001−90,000	>265−341	100	30
90,001−120,000	>341−454	125	38
120,001−200,000	>454−757	200	61
200,001−1,000,000	>757−3785	300	91
>1,000,000	>3785	400	122

TABLE 12.7.2 *Minimum Distances for LP-Gas Containers That Operate Below 15 psi (103 kPa)*

Water Capacity per Container		Aboveground Containers	
gal	*m³*	*ft*	*m*
≤70,000	≤265	75	25
>70,000	>265	100	30

Although the prohibition of stacking containers may seem obvious, it must be stated because smaller refrigerated containers could be installed this way.

12.7.3 The edge of a dike, impoundment, or drainage system that is intended for a refrigerated LP-Gas container shall be 100 ft (31 m) or more from a property line that can be built upon, a public way, or a navigable waterway.

12.7.4 Nonrefrigerated LP-Gas containers or flammable liquid tanks shall not be located within dikes or impoundments enclosing refrigerated LP-Gas containers.

12.7.5 Refrigerated LP-Gas containers shall not be installed one above the other.

12.7.6 The minimum distance between aboveground refrigerated LP-Gas containers shall be one-half the diameter of the larger container.

12.7.7 The ground within 25 ft (7.6 m) of any aboveground refrigerated LP-Gas container, and all ground within a dike, impoundment, or drainage area, shall be kept clear of readily ignitible materials such as weeds and long, dry grass.

The 25 ft (7.6 m) spacing to grass, weeds, and other ignitible material is similar to that for nonrefrigerated containers, except that the distance requirement is greater than the 10 ft (3 m) required for nonrefrigerated containers. This greater distance recognizes the larger size of refrigerated containers as compared to pressurized containers.

Most refrigerated container installation facilities are designed to prevent vegetation growth near containers through the use of gravel, crushed stone, or other surfacing that prevents growth of vegetation. Plant operators must take steps to ensure that any brush-clearing operations do not create hazards. At least one incident has occurred where a portable gasoline-powered weed cutter cut a pipe, resulting in liquid release and ignition.

12.8 Relief Devices

The requirements for pressure relief valve sizing are organized in the following four subsections:

12.8.1 General. Applies to all pressure and vacuum relief valves.

12.8.2 Pressure Relief Device Sizing. Establishes criteria for maximum pressure relief valve flow.

12.8.3 Vacuum Relief Device Sizing. Establishes criteria for maximum vacuum condition flow.

12.8.4 Fire Exposure Sizing. Provides equations for calculating heat transfer to a container under fire, based on the insulation used, if any.

The format of the equation for relief valve sizing is shown in 12.8.4.

12.8.1 General.

12.8.1.1 All containers shall be equipped with pressure and vacuum relief devices in accordance with Section 12.8.

Note that the sizing of pressure relief valves for API and ASME containers is not per the API and ASME codes, but is in accordance with the calculation method provided in NFPA 58. The requirements for sizing of pressure relief valves for refrigerated containers are similar to pressure relief valve sizing for pressurized containers covered in Chapter 5.

12.8.1.2 Relief devices shall communicate directly with the atmosphere. Vacuum-relieving devices shall be installed if the container can be exposed to a vacuum lower than that for which the container is designed.

Protection of a vessel from catastrophic collapse due to excessive vacuum condition is provided by a vacuum breaker, which must communicate with the atmosphere. Refer to 12.4.2.2, where the connection of a gas such as natural, propane vapor, or nitrogen is prohibited.

Many storage tanks have an additional back pressure relief valve feed with natural gas, propane vapor, or nitrogen. This valve is set to open at a pressure slightly higher than the atmospheric vacuum breaker and allows the gas to flow into the vessel to maintain proper pressure. However, if this valve fails, and the tank pressure falls too low, the vacuum breaker opens, allowing air to enter to protect the vessel from collapse.

12.8.1.3 Inlet and outlet piping connections to relief devices shall be included in the selection and sizing of relief devices.

Designers are reminded to include inlet flow losses when calculating valve size. Because of the low tank pressure, any pressure drop in piping can affect pressure relief valve sizing.

12.8.1.4 A manually operated full opening stop valve shall be installed between each pressure and vacuum safety relief valve and the LP-Gas container.

This requirement is opposite of the requirement for pressurized containers, where valves between the container and the pressure relief valve are prohibited. It is especially important to be able to isolate pressure relief valves on refrigerated storage containers for testing or replacement. The relief valves on large containers have much lower pressure settings than the relief valves used on pressurized containers and are usually pilot-operated pressure relief valves (see Exhibits 5.24 through 5.26). Direct spring-operated pressure relief valves are used on most smaller pressurized containers. Pilot-operated pressure relief valves are more complicated than direct spring-loaded pressure relief valves and have more parts that can cause the set point to change in the event of component failure. Most operators of refrigerated storage facilities test pressure relief valves regularly, and the pressure setting can be verified without removing the valve from the container.

12.8.1.5 All stop valves installed between a relief valve and a container shall be lockable or sealable in the fully open position.

12.8.1.6 A sufficient number of pressure and vacuum relief valves shall be installed on the LP-Gas container to allow each relief valve to be isolated individually while maintaining the full relieving capacities required.

12.8.1.7 Where only one relief device is required, either a full port opening three-way valve shall be installed between the container and two relief devices or separate stop valves shall be beneath each relief device.

12.8.1.8 Stop valves under individual safety relief valves shall be locked or sealed when opened and shall not be opened or closed except by an authorized person.

12.8.1.9 No more than one stop valve shall be closed at one time.

12.8.1.10 Safety relief valve discharge stacks or vents shall be designed and installed to prevent an accumulation of water, ice, snow, or other foreign matter and shall discharge vertically upward.

A pressure relief valve may not operate as designed if it becomes filled with water and debris. Also, it will not operate if ice blocks its discharge. A loose-fitting cover should be installed, or other means should be used to keep water out of the pressure relief valve.

12.8.1.11 All refrigerated storage container pressure and vacuum relief devices shall be tested or replaced at intervals not to exceed 5 years.

Pressure and vacuum relief valves on refrigerated storage containers and primary safety devices must be tested and inspected at regular intervals to ensure proper operation.

12.8.2 Pressure Relief Device Sizing.

The pressure relief devices shall be sized to relieve the flow capacity determined for the largest single contingency or any reasonable and probable combination of the following contingencies:

(1) Fire exposure
(2) Operational upset, such as failure of a control device
(3) Other circumstances resulting from equipment failures and operating errors
(4) Vapor displacement during filling
(5) Flash vaporization during filling, as a result of filling, or as a consequence of mixing of products of different compositions
(6) Loss of refrigeration
(7) Heat input from pump recirculation
(8) Drop in barometric pressure

The sizing of a pressure relief valve installed on a refrigerated LP-Gas container requires consideration of several factors, which are listed in 12.8.2. Note that reasonable engineering judgment is called for in determining which items can occur simultaneously.

12.8.3 Vacuum Relief Device Sizing.

12.8.3.1 The vacuum relief devices shall be sized to relieve the flow capacity determined for the largest single contingency or any reasonable and probable combination of the following contingencies:

(1) Withdrawal of liquid or vapor at the maximum rate
(2) Rise in barometric pressure
(3) Reduction in vapor space pressure as a result of filling with subcooled liquid

The sizing of a vacuum relief valve installed on a refrigerated LP-Gas container requires consideration of several factors, which are listed in 12.8.3.1. Note that reasonable engineering judgment is called for in determining which items can occur simultaneously. Credits (a factor less than 1.0) are not allowed for systems that can reduce vacuum because they cannot be assumed to be 100 percent reliable.

12.8.3.2 Reduction in the vacuum relief capacity to allow for the rate of vaporization resulting from minimum normal heat gain to the contents of the container shall be allowed.

12.8.3.3 No vacuum relief capacity credit shall be allowed for gas-repressuring or vapor makeup systems.

12.8.4 Fire Exposure Sizing.

12.8.4.1 The pressure-relieving capacity required for fire exposure shall be computed by the following formula:

$$W = 34{,}500\frac{F}{L}A^{0.82} + \frac{H_n}{L}$$

where:

W = relieving capacity in lb/hr or product vapor at relieving conditions

F = environmental factor from Table 12.8.4.1

L = latent heat of vaporization of the stored liquid at the relieving pressure and temperature, in Btu/lb

A = exposed wetted surface area of the container in ft^2. In the case of large containers, the exposed wetted area is the area up to a height of 30 ft (9.1 m) above grade

H_n = normal heat leak in refrigerated tanks in Btu/hr

TABLE 12.8.4.1 *Environmental Factors*

Basis	F Factor
Base container	1.0
Water application facilities	1.0
Depressuring and emptying facilities	1.0
Underground container	0
Insulation or thermal protection	$F = \dfrac{U(1660 - T_f)}{34{,}500}$
Insulation or thermal protection (metric)	$F = \dfrac{U(904 - T_f)}{71{,}000}$

Note: U is the overall heat transfer coefficient, Btu/(hr $\times$ ft^2 $\times$ °F) [W/(m^2 $\times$ °C)], of the insulation system using the mean value for the temperature range from T_f to 1660°F (T_f to 904°C). T_f is the temperature [°F(°C)] of vessel content at relieving conditions.

Fire exposure is the greatest factor affecting pressure relief valve sizing in most refrigerated propane containers in the United States. Outside the United States, double-wall containers are more common, and their insulation reduces heat input from fire to the point where it is rarely the greatest factor affecting pressure relief valve sizing.

The equations are in harmony with other NFPA standards dealing with the same subject.

The formula for sizing the pressure relief valve on refrigerated containers incorporates an insulation factor *(F)*, for which values are provided in Table 12.8.4.1. The values provided cover installation container options:

- Uninsulated (base) container
- Water application
- Depressurization and emptying facilities

(None of these permit reduction of pressure relief valve size.)

- Underground container
- Insulated container, with a formula provided based on the insulation used

(Both of these permit reduction of pressure relief valve size.)

Note that in Table 12.8.4.1, *F* does not allow credit (a factor less than 1.0) for single-wall insulated containers unless the insulation meets the requirements stated in 12.8.4.2. This requirement is intended to allow credit only for insulation that can maintain its integrity during fire-fighting efforts.

12.8.4.2 Where credit for insulation is taken in sizing of a relief valve for fire exposure, the insulation shall comply with the following:

(1) Resist dislodgment by fire-fighting equipment
(2) Be noncombustible
(3) Not decompose at temperatures up to 1000°F (538°C)

12.8.4.3 If the insulation does not meet the criteria of 12.8.4.2, no credit for the insulation shall be taken.

12.8.4.4 The equivalent airflow for relieving capacity shall be calculated by the following equation:

$$\text{SCFM (air)} = 3.09 W \left(\frac{ZT}{M}\right)^{0.5}$$

where:

SCFM (air) = equivalent airflow in standard ft^3/min

W = relieving capacity of product vapor at relieving conditions, in lb/hr

Z = compressibility factor product vapor at relieving conditions

T = absolute temperature of product vapor at relieving conditions, in °R

M = product vapor molecular weight

The flow in pounds per hour of LP-Gas calculated in 12.8.4.1 is converted in 12.8.4.4 to SCFM of air. This calculation is needed because pressure relief valves are used for many fluids and are sized and rated in terms of airflow in SCFM.

REFERENCES CITED IN COMMENTARY

1. API 620, *Design and Construction of Large, Welded, Low-Pressure Storage Tanks*, 2008 edition, American Petroleum Institute, Washington, DC.
2. NFPA 59, *Utility LP-Gas Plant Code*, 2008 edition, National Fire Protection Association, Quincy, MA.
3. API 2510, *Design and Construction of Liquefied Petroleum Gas Installations* (LPG), 2001 edition, American Petroleum Institute, Washington, DC.
4. ASME *Boiler and Pressure Vessel Code*, 2007 edition, American Society of Mechanical Engineers, New York, NY.
5. ASCE 7, *Minimum Design Loads for Buildings and Other Structures*, 2005 edition, American Society of Civil Engineers, Reston, VA.
6. ASME B31.3, *Process Piping Code*, 2008 edition, American Society of Mechanical Engineers, New York, NY.
7. NFPA 30, *Flammable and Combustible Liquids Code*, 2008 edition, National Fire Protection Association, Quincy, MA.

Marine Shipping and Receiving

CHAPTER 13

Large quantities of LP-Gas are shipped in specially equipped tankers. The requirements of Chapter 13 cover loading and unloading of tankers in ports. The chapter includes the following important requirements:

- Design and construction of piers (See Section 13.2.)
- Requirements for conducting transfer operations (See 13.2.3.)
- Location and hardware for pipelines used to connect the pier facilities to the tank (See Section 13.3.)
- Inspections conducted prior to transfer (See Section 13.4.)

The majority of the original material for Chapter 13 was drawn from NFPA 59A, *Standard for the Production, Storage, and Handling of Liquefied Natural Gas (LNG)* [1], and the existing practices at marine terminals as required by the U.S. Coast Guard and other authorities having jurisdiction. Chapter 13 is also an outgrowth of the requirements of NFPA 30, *Flammable and Combustible Liquids Code* [2], and NFPA 59, *Utility LP-Gas Plant Code* [3], which reflect the experience and practices of the marine industry.

13.1 Scope

This chapter applies to the transfer of LP-Gas between marine vessels and shore facilities.

13.2 Piers

13.2.1 Design and Construction.

Exhibit 13.1 illustrates an overhead view of an LP-Gas marine terminal. Note the two refrigerated tanks in the foreground and the pier at which a ship is unloading into the containers. This terminal is located in New Hampshire and supplies propane to the northern New England states.

13.2.1.1* Design, construction, and operation of piers, docks, and wharves shall comply with relevant regulations and the requirements of the authorities having jurisdiction.

A.13.2.1.1 Federal regulations applicable to marine terminals are contained in 33 CFR.

13.2.1.2 General cargo, flammable liquids, or compressed gases, other than ships' general stores for the LP-Gas tank vessel, shall not be handled over a pier or dock within 100 ft (30.5 m) of the point of transfer connection while LP-Gas or other flammable liquids are being transferred.

13.2.1.3 Trucks and other motorized vehicles shall be prohibited on the pier or dock within 100 ft (30.5 m) of the transfer connection while transfer operations are in progress.

EXHIBIT 13.1 An LP-Gas Marine Terminal. (Courtesy of SEA-3, Inc.)

Note that all vehicular traffic, including forklift trucks, is prohibited during transfer operations.

13.2.1.4 Authorized parking areas, if provided for in the waterfront area, shall be marked.

13.2.1.5 Warning signs or barricades shall be used to indicate when transfer operations are in progress.

13.2.1.6 Unauthorized individuals shall not be allowed access to the waterfront area while the LP-Gas vessel is alongside the pier or dock.

13.2.1.7 Security personnel shall restrict the entry of visitors, delivery trucks, and service personnel to those authorized by the facility operator.

Adequate security requires a reasonable number of security personnel to be present to control access to the berth area and to call for assistance from terminal personnel, the local police, the local fire department, the Coast Guard (or other port authorities), and local emergency responders should the need arise.

13.2.1.8 The shore mooring equipment shall be designed and maintained to safely hold the vessel to the pier or dock.

Proper design of mooring equipment is necessary to safely hold the vessel or barge to the berth during unexpected changes in wind and sea conditions.

13.2.1.9 If the terminal conducts transfers between sunset and sunrise, the pier or dock area shall have a lighting system that illuminates the following:

(1) Transfer connection area
(2) Control valves
(3) Storage containers
(4) Other equipment
(5) Walkways, fire fighting, and other emergency areas

Terminal lighting during hours of darkness must allow personnel to conduct normal and emergency operations without requiring a flashlight or other handheld lighting equipment.

13.2.1.10 All lighting shall be located or shielded so that it is not confused with any aids to navigation and does not interfere with navigation on the adjacent waterway.

13.2.1.11 Welding and cutting shall be in accordance with NFPA 51B, *Standard for Fire Prevention During Welding, Cutting, and Other Hot Work.*

13.2.1.12 Smoking shall be prohibited in all areas other than conspicuously marked, designated areas.

13.2.1.13 Medical first aid equipment and fire extinguishers shall be available at the shore facility. This equipment shall be in accordance with the following:

(1) Extinguishers shall be ready for use at all times.
(2) Emergency equipment shall be positioned and ready to operate prior to the start of the transfer operation.
(3) The locations of all fire extinguishers shall be marked and readily accessible.

Medical first aid equipment and supplies to handle minor injuries must be available for use prior to the arrival of qualified emergency medical technicians or when transporting an injured person to a medical facility. Such equipment is especially important if the shore facility is a long distance from the nearest hospital.

13.2.2 Electrical Equipment.

All electrical equipment and wiring installed on the pier or dock shall comply with 6.22.2.1.

All fixed electrical equipment operated while an LP-Gas transfer is being made must be located per the electrical requirements of Chapter 6. If a transfer is done during hours of darkness, the pier's lighting must be checked for compliance. See Exhibit 13.2, which shows a drawing of electrically classified areas at marine terminals.

Paragraph 6.22.2.2 addresses the installation of electrical equipment in classified areas in which flammable concentrations may be present.

13.2.3 Transfer Operations.

Requirements for the locations of wharves that handle flammable liquids are provided in NFPA 30. (See Exhibit 13.2.)

13.2.3.1 Prior to the start of the transfer, a warning sign that reads as shown in Figure 13.2.3.1 shall be placed in the marine transfer area and be visible from the shoreline and berth areas.

13.2.3.2 A portable LP-Gas detector calibrated to detect LP-Gas shall be readily available for use at the berth.

The portable LP-Gas detector, as shown in Exhibit 13.3, should be capable of detecting propane vapor from 0 percent to 100 percent lower flammable limit (LFL). The detector should be calibrated at least as often as recommended by the manufacturer.

13.2.3.3 Portable electrical equipment used within 100 ft (30.5 m) of the transfer connection while transfer operations are in progress either shall be listed for Class I, Division 1 or shall be intrinsically safe.

The use of intrinsically safe equipment is specifically permitted. For example, portable radios are frequently used during transfer operations.

The term *intrinsically safe* is defined in *NFPA 70®, National Electrical Code®* [4]. Section 504.2 states that intrinsically safe apparatus is apparatus in which all the circuits are intrinsically safe. An *intrinsically safe circuit* is defined in *NFPA 70,* Section 504.2, as: "A circuit in which any spark or thermal effect is incapable of causing ignition of a mixture of flammable or combustible material in air under prescribed test conditions." The definition of *intrinsically safe circuit* is followed by a Fine Print Note that states that the test conditions are described in ANSI/UL 913, *Standard for Safety, Intrinsically Safe Apparatus and*

```
WARNING

DANGEROUS CARGO

NO VISITORS

NO SMOKING

NO OPEN LIGHT
```

FIGURE 13.2.3.1 *Warning Sign to be Placed in Marine Transfer Area.*

EXHIBIT 13.2 *Marine Terminal Handling Flammable Liquids. (Source: Fig. 29.3.22, NFPA 30, 2008 edition)*

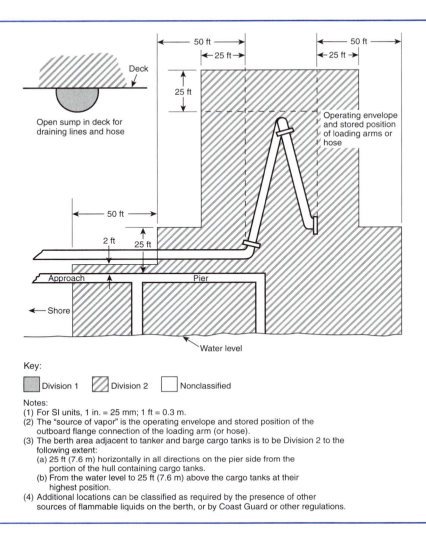

EXHIBIT 13.2 *Marine Terminal Handling Flammable Liquids. (Source: Fig. 29.3.22, NFPA 30, 2008 edition)*

Key:

▓ Division 1   ▨ Division 2   ☐ Nonclassified

Notes:
(1) For SI units, 1 in. = 25 mm; 1 ft = 0.3 m.
(2) The "source of vapor" is the operating envelope and stored position of the outboard flange connection of the loading arm (or hose).
(3) The berth area adjacent to tanker and barge cargo tanks is to be Division 2 to the following extent:
   (a) 25 ft (7.6 m) horizontally in all directions on the pier side from the portion of the hull containing cargo tanks.
   (b) From the water level to 25 ft (7.6 m) above the cargo tanks at their highest position.
(4) Additional locations can be classified as required by the presence of other sources of flammable liquids on the berth, or by Coast Guard or other regulations.

Associated Apparatus for Use in Class I, II, and III, Division 1, Hazardous (Classified) Locations [5].

NFPA 70, Section 500.5, defines a *Class I, Division 1 location* as a location (1) in which ignitible concentrations of flammable gases or vapors can exist under normal operating conditions; or (2) in which ignitible concentrations of such gases or vapors may exist frequently because of repair or maintenance operations; or (3) in which breakdown or faulty operation of equipment or processes might release ignitible concentrations of flammable gases or vapors and might also cause simultaneous failure of electrical equipment in such a way as to directly cause the equipment to become a source of ignition.

13.2.3.4 When the transfer operation is completed (secured) and the transfer piping is disconnected, the equipment used shall be in compliance with 6.22.2.1 and 6.22.2.2.

13.2.3.5 The following life safety equipment shall be positioned on the berth and be ready for immediate use while personnel are working on the berth or a vessel is alongside:

(1) Life rings with attendant rope of sufficient length
(2) Approved fire blanket

(3) Flotation vests or immersion suits suitable for the water temperature at the berth and the personnel involved in the work

In cooler climates, personnel working on the berth should wear a flotation device to protect themselves in the event they fall into the water. In areas of cold water temperatures, an immersion suit may be needed to provide additional time for rescue. The U.S. Coast Guard, or its equivalent agency in other countries, can approve life rings and other life safety equipment.

13.3 Pipelines

13.3.1* Pipelines shall be located on the dock or pier so that they are not exposed to damage from vehicular traffic or other possible cause of physical damage.

A.13.3.1 Refer to 49 CFR 195.

Safety standards for pipeline facilities used in transporting hazardous liquids are provided in 49 CFR 195 [6]. The U.S. Coast Guard recognizes the special problems presented by operations involving loading, unloading, handling, and storage of bulk cargoes of certain hazardous materials, especially if the operation occurs at a general cargo marine terminal. For this reason, the U.S. Coast Guard has defined *cargoes of particular hazard* and *facilities of particular hazard* in its regulations (33 CFR 126.10 [7] and 33 CFR 126.05 [8], respectively). Cargoes of particular hazard include flammable liquids, flammable compressed gases, and liquefied natural gas. These cargoes may be handled only at designated facilities.

13.3.1.1 Underwater pipelines shall be located or protected so that they are not exposed to damage from marine traffic.

13.3.1.2 The locations of underwater pipelines shall be posted or identified in accordance with federal regulations.

13.3.2 Isolation valving and bleed connections shall be provided at the loading or unloading manifold for both liquid and vapor return lines so that hoses and arms can be blocked off, drained or pumped out, and depressurized before disconnecting.

13.3.2.1 Liquid isolation valves and vapor valves 8 in. (20 mm) and larger in size shall be equipped with powered operators in addition to means for manual operation.

13.3.2.2 Electrical Equipment. Power-operated valves shall be capable of being closed from a remote control station located at least 50 ft (15 m) from the manifold area, as well as locally.

13.3.2.3 Unless the valve will automatically fail closed on loss of power, the valve actuator and its power supply within 50 ft (15 m) of the valve shall be protected against operational failure due to fire exposure of at least 10 minutes.

13.3.2.4 Valves shall be located at the point of hose or arm connection to the manifold.

13.3.2.5 In addition to the isolation valves at the manifold, each vapor return and liquid transfer line shall be provided with a readily accessible isolation valve located on shore near the approach to the pier or dock.

13.3.2.6 Where more than one line exists, the valves shall be grouped in one location.

13.3.2.7 Valves shall be identified as to their service.

13.3.3 Pipelines used for liquid unloading only shall be provided with a check valve located at the manifold adjacent to the manifold isolation valve.

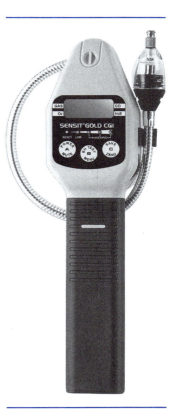

EXHIBIT 13.3 *Handheld LP-Gas Detector. (Courtesy of Sensit Technologies)*

13.3.4 All pipelines, conduits, and other conductive lines on the berth capable of carrying an electrical charge shall be equipped with insulating flanges or other means to electrically isolate them from stray currents and the rest of the terminal.

13.3.5 If a stray current (bonding) cable is not used between the facility and the vessel, insulating flanges shall be installed in the pipe risers to the off-loading connections between the vessel and the shore facility.

13.3.6 All shore facilities shall provide a low-resistance stray current (bonding) cable to be connected to the vessels.

13.3.6.1 Electrical continuity between the vessel and the berth shall be verified prior to transfer operations.

13.3.6.2 The cable shall be connected to the vessel prior to the connection of the unloading hose/arms and shall remain connected until after the hose/arms have been disconnected.

13.4 Inspections Prior to Transfer

13.4.1* Prior to starting transfer operations, the officer in charge of the vessel transfer operation and the person in charge of the shore facility shall inspect their respective facilities.

A.13.4.1 For guidance, refer to 33 CFR.

13.4.1.1 The inspection shall ensure that all cargo transfer equipment and hose have been maintained and tested and are in operating condition.

13.4.1.2 Following the inspection, the officers in charge shall meet to discuss the transfer procedures, and, when ready, each will notify the other that each facility is ready in all respects to start transfer operations.

13.4.2 The shore facility transfer system shall be equipped with a remotely operated emergency shutdown system.

13.4.3 A facilities emergency procedures manual shall be readily available and shall contain the following information:

(1) LP-Gas release response and emergency shutdown procedures
(2) Telephone number for all emergency response organizations, U.S. Coast Guard, emergency medical facilities, and hospital(s)
(3) Description and location of the facility fire systems and emergency equipment

The phrase "readily available" in 13.4.3 means that the emergency procedures manual should be located in an area that is quickly and easily accessible to terminal and emergency response personnel.

13.4.4 A facilities standard operating procedures manual shall be readily available and shall contain the following information:

(1) Procedures for start-up, operation, and shutdown of the transfer system and equipment
(2) Procedures for cooling down the transfer hose and line where refrigerated LP-Gas is transferred
(3) Telephone numbers for all emergency response organizations, U.S. Coast Guard, emergency medical facilities, and hospital(s)

(4) Description, location, and operational guidelines for the facility fire systems and emergency equipment

13.4.5 Each transfer operation shall be conducted in accordance with the operations manual.

13.4.6 At the completion of the transfer, and prior to disconnect of the transfer hose or arm, the transfer connection shall be purged of all liquid and depressurized. The liquid and vapor pressure shall be returned either to the vessel or to the shore facility. LP-Gas shall not be vented to the atmosphere.

REFERENCES CITED IN COMMENTARY

1. NFPA 59A, *Standard for the Production, Storage, and Handling of Liquefied Natural Gas (LNG)*, 2009 edition, National Fire Protection Association, Quincy, MA.
2. NFPA 30, *Flammable and Combustible Liquids Code*, 2008 edition, National Fire Protection Association, Quincy, MA.
3. NFPA 59, *Utility LP-Gas Plant Code*, 2008 edition, National Fire Protection Association, Quincy, MA.
4. *NFPA 70®, National Electrical Code®*, 2011 edition, National Fire Protection Association, Quincy, MA.
5. ANSI/UL 913, *Standard for Safety, Intrinsically Safe Apparatus and Associated Apparatus for Use in Class I, II, and III, Division 1, Hazardous (Classified) Locations*, 1997 edition, Underwriters Laboratories Inc., Northbrook, IL.
6. Title 49, *Code of Federal Regulations*, Part 195, U.S. Government Printing Office, Washington, DC.
7. Title 33, *Code of Federal Regulations*, Part 126.10, U.S. Government Printing Office, Washington, DC.
8. Title 33, *Code of Federal Regulations*, Part 126.05, U.S. Government Printing Office, Washington, DC.

Operations and Maintenance

The intent of Chapter 14 is to provide a dedicated chapter for all the operations and maintenance requirements in the code. The concept of a chapter for operations and maintenance provisions was recommended by a committee member representing the U.S. Environmental Protection Agency (EPA). The EPA enforces a Risk Management Program, which does not apply to LP-Gas retail bulk facilities or end users' facilities, but which is required for storage facilities used for wholesale or for uses of LP-Gas for other than as a fuel. Chapter 14 is intended to address all bulk plant and industrial plant facilities, in addition to refrigerated, marine, and pipeline LP-Gas systems.

To assist propane marketers in developing operations and maintenance documentation, a manual has been prepared using a grant from the Propane Education and Research Council (PERC). The *Operations & Maintenance Handbook* CD-ROM can be obtained from PERC (#005026). The *Handbook* can be downloaded at no charge from www.nfpa.org. A printed copy of the *Handbook* or a CD with the *Handbook* is available from www.propanecatalog. com for a nominal charge.

The 2004 edition expanded Chapter 14 with specific references to operations and maintenance requirements, and the committee specifically chose not to repeat or relocate information from within the code to avoid separating operation and maintenance information from the specific application to which it relates. Instead, the citations are grouped by equipment type and function to aid users in quickly finding the operations and maintenance requirements that they need.

In the 2011 edition Section 14.4, Small LP-Gas Systems, which had been added in the 2008 edition, was deleted based on a recommendation from the U.S. Department of Transportation (DOT), which has primary jurisdiction over such systems. These requirements exist in CFR 49 Part 192, which covers both natural gas and propane distribution systems of all sizes above a minimum threshold. The committee created Section 14.4 by extracting the requirements relevant to propane systems up to 100 users, but unfortunately did not include all the requirements. Further, it was recognized that the NFPA 58 committee might not be able to keep it current, and it was therefore removed.

Chapter 14 provides important requirements for the following:

- Written operating procedure manuals for all facilities (See 14.2.1.5.)
- Operating procedures that address hoses, fittings, and other equipment (See 14.2.1.1.)
- Operating procedures for personnel in the event of a release of LP-Gas in the facility (See 14.2.1.2.)
- Maintenance procedures for equipment at a facility (See Section 14.3.)
- Maintenance manuals (See 14.3.2.)
- Maintenance records for fire protection equipment (See 14.3.2.3 through 14.3.2.5.)

14.1* Scope

This chapter includes requirements related to the operations and maintenance of bulk plant, industrial plant, refrigerated, marine, and pipeline LP-Gas systems. The provisions of this chapter shall be applicable to all new and existing installations.

A.14.1 Chapter 14, Operations and Maintenance, was created to locate operating and maintenance requirements in one location for installations covered by this code. Only new operating and maintenance requirements are included in this chapter. A task force has been established to review future additions to this chapter. Users of the code are invited to submit proposals on this subject.

Chapter 14 in its entirety is retroactive to all new and existing installations. It is expected that enforcement of this new provision will allow reasonable time for those affected to comply.

14.1.1 If stated elsewhere in the code, operation and maintenance requirements are referenced to those sections.

14.1.2* Multiple containers in vapor service only, with an individual water capacity not exceeding 1200 gal (4.5 m³) water capacity, and with a maximum aggregate of 6000 gal (22.7 m³) water capacity, shall not require written operations or maintenance procedures where they are not manifolded together.

A.14.1.2 Industrial and some other installations with an capacity of 10,000 lb (454 kg) or more might be required by EPA regulations to have an operation and maintenance manual.

The committee recognizes that smaller LP-Gas storage systems do not need operations and maintenance manuals, and established a minimum size of system for which manuals are required. Operations and maintenance manuals must be prepared for the following:

- Systems with a storage container in vapor service larger than 1200 gal (4.5 m³) if the aggregate capacity is more than 6000 gal (22.7 m³)
- Systems with a total storage over 6000 gal (22.7 m³) in vapor service
- All systems in liquid service, irrespective of container size or total amount

Note that A.14.1.2 includes the capacity in pounds, which is unusual for NFPA 58 for other than cylinder capacities. The 10,000 lb (454 kg) requirement is one that was established by EPA regulations and is the amount of product "on hand." It is the propane capacity of the container unless there are administrative controls that prohibit more than a specified amount of product in the container. The other capacities are the standard capacities used in this code.

14.2 Operating Requirements

14.2.1* Operating Procedures.

A.14.2.1 The procedures should address normal start-up, operations, shutdown, emergency shutdown and operations, start-up following a major change to the system, consequences of deviations and steps required to correct or avoid deviations, and equipment inspections.

Written operating procedures are required for all bulk and industrial plants, including all LP-Gas facilities with storage of 4000 gal (15.2 m³) or more, unless the facility is exempted by 14.1.2. The written operating procedures must be updated whenever plant equipment changes are made or new equipment is added. Although a specific time frame for updating plant procedures is not provided in the code, it is reasonable to expect authorities having jurisdiction to allow a period of time after plant changes have been made for updated procedures to be developed.

Written procedures for plant operations are important because experienced operators can be temporarily or permanently removed from their jobs. For example, they might move to new jobs, become unable to work due to illness, or retire. Substitutes, including managers, for these experienced operators may not know the function and location of all controls and safety features. LP-Gas plants used for standby or supplemental fuel are not operated all year, and possibly not for a number of years, and operators in these plants may not remember all aspects of their jobs from year to year.

14.2.1.1 The procedures required in 14.2.1 shall address all aspects of LP-Gas transfer, as appropriate for the facility, including inspection of hose and fittings and connection and disconnection procedures.

Because the transfer of liquid from one container to another is considered the most potentially hazardous operation in an LP-Gas plant, the need to provide written operating procedures for training purposes and reference is important.

14.2.1.2 Operating procedures shall include operator actions to be taken if flammable concentrations of flammable liquids or gases are detected in the facility using fixed detectors, portable detectors, operating malfunctions, or the human senses.

14.2.1.3 Operating procedures for vaporizers shall include maintenance of vaporization rate, pressure control, and temperature. Procedures shall include specific actions to be taken when parameters exceed normal operating limits and criteria for emergency shutdown.

Vaporizers are more complex than other equipment used at LP-Gas installations, and the requirement draws specific attention to the critical factors related to vaporizers in LP-Gas facilities. The procedures or instructions provided by equipment vendors or manufacturers can be used. This requirement assists operators in recognizing when the operation of the equipment is outside the acceptable specifications, so that they may take appropriate action.

14.2.1.4 In facilities where propane is stored as a refrigerated liquid, operating procedures shall include monitoring of liquid temperature and pressure and procedures to be taken if the temperature or pressure exceeds operating limits. These procedures shall minimize the release of flammable gases to the atmosphere.

Refrigerated storage facilities, which are usually located at marine and pipeline terminals, are more complex and must be monitored regularly because the liquid LP-Gas is stored at about $-40°F$ ($-40°C$) and absorbs heat continuously through the tank insulation. Although this amount of heat is small, it is continuous and will result in the release of gas if equipment failures are not identified promptly.

14.2.1.5 Each facility shall prepare and maintain in a common location or locations written operating procedure manuals that contain the written operating procedures required by 14.2.1.

It is important that operating personnel know where written procedures can be found at the plant, and plant management should ensure that they are located where employees have been told they are located. If the plant has a control room, then that is the logical place for the operating procedures. If there is no control room, then the location of operating procedures must be made known to all employees who operate the plant. The plant may not be attended continuously, in which case all operators who make periodic checks must know where the written operating procedures are located.

It has been brought to the committee's attention that locating operating procedures at a remote propane bulk plant may be difficult, especially if the plant has no buildings. Water damage and mold/mildew can occur. Some sites have been successful using short lengths of PVC pipe and threaded end caps that are closed tight to prevent water entry to store written procedures. Having the procedures at an accessible location on site is a benefit to new employees and contractors working at the site, as well as to new drivers delivering product, inspectors who need to inspect the site and review the procedures, and, potentially, emergency responders.

14.2.2 Content of Operating Procedures.

14.2.2.1 Written procedures shall be the basis for conducting activities associated with the systems referenced in Section 14.1. Operating procedures shall be updated whenever a change occurs that affects the operation of a system and prior to its start-up. The written procedures shall address the requirements in 14.2.2.2 and 14.2.2.3, where applicable.

14.2.2.2 General operating procedures shall include the following:

(1) General procedures *(see 13.4.3 and 13.4.4)*

The following paragraphs, referenced in 14.2.2.2(1), are provided for the handbook user's convenience:

13.4.3 A facilities emergency procedures manual shall be readily available and shall contain the following information:
(1) LP-Gas release response and emergency shutdown procedures
(2) Telephone number for all emergency response organizations, U.S. Coast Guard, emergency medical facilities, and hospital(s)
(3) Description and location of the facility fire systems and emergency equipment

13.4.4 A facilities standard operating procedures manual shall be readily available and shall contain the following information:
(1) Procedures for start-up, operation, and shutdown of the transfer system and equipment
(2) Procedures for cooling down the transfer hose and line where refrigerated LP-Gas is transferred
(3) Telephone numbers for all emergency response organizations, U.S. Coast Guard, emergency medical facilities, and hospital(s)
(4) Description, location, and operational guidelines for the facility fire systems and emergency equipment

(2) Combustible material *(see 6.4.5.2 and 6.6.5.2)*

The following paragraphs, referenced in 14.2.2.2(2), are provided for the handbook user's convenience:

6.4.5.2 Loose or piled combustible material and weeds and long dry grass shall be separated from containers by a minimum of 10 ft (3 m).

6.6.5.2 The surface on which the containers are placed shall be level and, if not paved, shall be clear of dry grass and weeds and other combustible material within 10 ft (3 m) of the container.

(3) Sources of ignition *[see 6.22.3, 6.23.9.4, 7.2.3.2, and 9.4.10]*

The following paragraphs, referenced in 14.2.2.2(3), are provided for the handbook user's convenience:

6.22.3 Other Sources of Ignition.
6.22.3.1 Open flames or other sources of ignition shall not be used or installed in pump houses, cylinder filling rooms, or other similar locations.
6.22.3.2 Direct-fired vaporizers or indirect-fired vaporizers attached or installed adjacent to gas-fired heat sources shall not be installed in pump houses or cylinder filling rooms.
6.22.3.3 Open flames, cutting or welding tools, portable electric tools, and extension lights capable of igniting LP-Gas shall not be installed or used within classified areas specified in Table 6.22.2.2.
6.22.3.4 Open flames or other sources of ignition shall not be prohibited where containers, piping, and other equipment containing LP-Gas have been purged of all liquid and vapor LP-Gas.

6.23.9.4 The vehicle shall not be parked near sources of heat, open flames, or similar sources of ignition, or near unventilated pits.

7.2.3.2 Sources of ignition shall be turned off during transfer operations, while connections or disconnections are made, or while LP-Gas is being vented to the atmosphere.
(A) Internal combustion engines within 15 ft (4.6 m) of a point of transfer shall be shut down while such transfer operations are in progress, with the exception of the following:

(1) Engines of LP-Gas cargo tank vehicles, constructed and operated in compliance with Chapter 9, while such engines are driving transfer pumps or compressors on these vehicles to load containers in accordance with 6.5.4

(2) Engines installed in buildings as provided in Section 11.13

(B) Smoking, open flame, portable electrical tools, and extension lights capable of igniting LP-Gas shall not be permitted within 25 ft (7.6 m) of a point of transfer while filling operations are in progress.

(C) Metal cutting, grinding, oxygen–fuel gas cutting, brazing, soldering, or welding shall not be permitted within 35 ft (10.7 m) of a point of transfer while filling operations are in progress.

(D) Materials that have been heated above the ignition temperature of LP-Gas shall be cooled before LP-Gas transfer is started.

(E) Sources of ignition shall be turned off during the filling of any LP-Gas container on the vehicle.

9.4.10 Smoking Prohibition. No person shall smoke or carry lighted smoking material as follows:

(1) On or within 25 ft (7.6 m) of a vehicle that is containing LP-Gas liquid or vapor

(2) At points of liquid transfer

(3) When delivering or connecting to containers

(4) Signage and markings *[see 5.2.1.1, 5.7.3.6, 5.7.5.3, 5.7.5.8, 5.7.8.5, 6.4.5.11, 6.11.5, 6.12.6, 6.12.10(2), 6.24.3.14, 6.25.4.4, 6.26.4.3(C), 6.26.5.1(B), 7.2.3.6, 9.3.2.10, 9.3.3.7, 9.4.6, 11.3.4, Section 11.12, and 13.2.1.13]*

The following paragraphs, referenced in 14.2.2.2(4), are provided for the handbook user's convenience:

5.2.1.1* Containers shall be designed, fabricated, tested, and marked (or stamped) in accordance with the regulations of the U.S. Department of Transportation (DOT); the ASME *Boiler and Pressure Vessel Code*, Section VIII, "Rules for the Construction of Unfired Pressure Vessels"; or the API-ASME *Code for Unfired Pressure Vessels for Petroleum Liquids and Gases*, except for UG-125 through UG-136.

5.7.3.6 Exempted horizontal cylinders shall be marked with a label to indicate that they are not equipped with an overfilling prevention device.

5.7.5.3* Every container designed to be filled on a volumetric basis shall be equipped with a fixed maximum liquid level gauge(s) to indicate the maximum filling level(s) for the service(s) in which the container is to be filled or used. *(See 7.4.3.3.)*

5.7.5.8 Variable liquid level gauges shall comply with the following:

(1) Variable liquid level gauges installed on containers over 1200 gal (4.5 m³) water capacity shall be marked with the maximum liquid level, in inches, metric units, or percent of capacity of the container on which they are to be installed.

(2) If temperature correction markings are provided on variable liquid level gauges on containers greater than 1200 gal (4.5 m³) that will be used for volumetric filling as allowed by 7.4.3.2(A), 7.4.3.2(B), and 7.4.3.3, the markings shall indicate the maximum liquid level at liquid temperatures in accordance with Tables 7.4.3.3(b) or 7.4.3.3(c). Temperature markings shall be from 20°F to 115°F (−6.7°C to 46°C), with increments not to exceed 20 F° (11.1°C) for propane, for 50/50 butane-propane mixtures, and for butane.

(3) Dials of magnetic float gauges or rotary gauges shall indicate whether they are for cylindrical or spherical ASME containers and whether they are for aboveground or underground service.

(4) The dials of gauges for use only on aboveground containers of over 1200 gal (4.5 m³) water capacity shall be so marked.

5.7.8.5 Container inlet and outlet connections on ASME containers of more than 2000 gal (7.6 m³) water capacity shall be labeled either on the container service valve or on the container to designate whether they communicate with the vapor or liquid space.

6.4.5.11 Where LP-Gas cylinders are to be stored or used in the same area with other compressed gases, the cylinders shall be marked to identify their content in accordance with ANSI/CGA C-7, *Guide to the Preparation of Precautionary Labeling and Marking of Compressed Gas Containers.*

6.11.5 Emergency remote shutdown stations shall be identified by a sign, visible from the point of transfer, incorporating the words "Propane — Container Liquid Valve Emergency Shutoff" in block letters of not less than 2 in. (51 mm) in height on a background of contrasting color to the letters.

6.12.6 Emergency shutoff valves shall be installed so that the temperature-sensitive element in the valve, or a supplemental temperature-sensitive element that operates at a maximum temperature of 250°F (121°C) that is connected to actuate the valve, is not more than 5 ft (1.5 m) from the nearest end of the hose or swivel-type piping connected to the line in which the valve is installed.

6.12.10(2) The shutoff device shall be located not less than 25 ft (7.6 m) or more than 100 ft (30 m) in the path of egress from the emergency shutoff valve.

6.24.3.14 An identified and accessible switch or circuit breaker shall be installed at a location not less than 20 ft (6.1 m) or more than 100 ft (30.5 m) from the dispensing device(s) to shut off the power in the event of a fire, an accident, or other emergency.

6.25.4.4 Emergency controls shall be conspicuously marked, and the controls shall be located so as to be readily accessible in emergencies.

6.26.4.3(C) Emergency remote shutdown stations shall be identified as such by a sign incorporating the words "Propane" and "Emergency Shutoff" in block letters not less than 2 in. (5.1 cm) in height on a background of contrasting color to the letters. The sign shall be visible from the point of transfer.

6.26.5.1(B) Fixed maximum liquid level gauges that are installed on engine fuel and mobile containers in accordance with Table 5.7.4.1 shall not be used to determine the maximum permitted filling limit at a low emission transfer site.

7.2.3.6 During the time railroad tank cars are on sidings for loading or unloading, the following shall apply:
(1) A caution sign, with wording such as "STOP. TANK CAR CONNECTED," shall be placed at the active end(s) of the siding while the car is connected, as required by DOT regulations.
(2) Wheel chocks shall be placed to prevent movement of the car in either direction.

9.3.2.10 Vehicles transporting cylinders where the total weight is more than 1000 lb (454 kg), including the weight of the LP-Gas and the cylinders, shall be placarded as required by DOT regulations or state law.

9.3.3.7 Vehicles carrying more than 1000 lb (454 kg), including the weight of the propane and the portable containers, shall be placarded as required by DOT regulations or state law.

9.4.6 Painting and Marking Cargo Tank Vehicles.
9.4.6.1 Painting of cargo tank vehicles shall comply with 49 CFR.
9.4.6.2 Placarding and marking shall comply with 49 CFR.

11.3.4 ASME Container Nameplates. The markings specified for ASME containers shall be on a stainless steel metal nameplate attached to the container, located to remain visible after the container is installed.
(A) The nameplate shall be attached in such a way as to minimize corrosion of the nameplate or its fastening means and not contribute to corrosion of the container.
(B) ASME containers shall be marked with the following information:
(1) Service for which the container is designed (e.g., underground, aboveground, or both)
(2) Name and address of container supplier or trade name of container
(3) Water capacity of container in pounds or U.S. gallons
(4) MAWP in pounds per square inch (psig)
(5) Wording that reads "This container shall not contain a product that has a vapor pressure in excess of 215 psig (1.5 MPag) at 100°F" *(see Table 5.2.4.2)*

(6)   Outside surface area in square feet
(7)   Year of manufacture
(8)   Shell thickness and head thickness
(9)   OL (overall length), OD (outside diameter), and HD (head design)
(10) Manufacturer's serial number
(11) ASME Code symbol
(12) Minimum design metal temperature: ___°F at MAWP ___ psig
(13) Type of construction: "W"
(14) Degree of radiography: "RT___"

11.12 Marking

11.12.1 Label Requirements. Each over-the-road general-purpose vehicle powered by LP-Gas shall be identified with a weather-resistant diamond-shaped label located on an exterior vertical or near vertical surface on the lower right rear of the vehicle (on the trunk lid of a vehicle so equipped but not on the bumper of any vehicle) inboard from any other markings.

11.12.2 Label Size.
11.12.2.1 The label shall be a minimum of 4¾ in. (120 mm) long by 3¼ in. (83 mm) high.
11.12.2.2* The marking shall consist of a border and the word PROPANE [1 in. (25 mm) minimum height centered in the diamond] in silver or white reflective luminous material on a black background.

13.2.1.13 Medical first aid equipment and fire extinguishers shall be available at the shore facility. This equipment shall be in accordance with the following:
(1)   Extinguishers shall be ready for use at all times.
(2)   Emergency equipment shall be positioned and ready to operate prior to the start of the transfer operation.
(3)   The locations of all fire extinguishers shall be marked and readily accessible.

(5)   Containers *(see 5.7.3.3, Section 6.6, 6.26.3.1, 7.2.3.1, 7.3.2, 7.3.2.2, 7.3.2.3, 7.3.2.4, 7.4.2, 7.4.3, 8.2.1, and 9.3.2.4)*

The following paragraphs, referenced in 14.2.2.2(5), are provided for the handbook user's convenience:

5.7.3.3 No cylinder shall be filled unless it is equipped with an overfilling prevention device and a fixed maximum liquid level gauge. The length of the fixed maximum liquid level gauge dip tube shall be in accordance with 7.4.3.2(A) or Table 5.7.3.2.

6.6 Installation of Containers
6.6.1 General Requirements.
6.6.1.1 Containers shall be positioned so that the pressure relief valve is in direct communication with the vapor space of the container.
6.6.1.2 LP-Gas containers or systems of which they are a part shall be protected from damage from vehicles.
6.6.1.3 Field welding on containers shall be limited to nonpressure parts such as saddle plates, wear plates, or brackets installed by the container manufacturer.
6.6.1.4* Aboveground containers shall be painted.
6.6.1.5 Containers shall be installed so that all container operating appurtenances are accessible.
6.6.1.6 Where necessary to prevent flotation due to possible high flood waters around aboveground or mounded containers, or high water table for those underground and partially underground, containers shall be securely anchored.

6.6.2 Installation of Cylinders.
6.6.2.1 Cylinders shall be installed only aboveground and shall be set upon a firm foundation or otherwise be firmly secured. The cylinder shall not be in contact with the soil.
6.6.2.2 Flexibility shall be provided in the connecting piping. Where flexible connectors are used, they shall comply with 6.9.6.

6.6.3 Installation of Horizontal Aboveground ASME Containers.

6.6.3.1 Horizontal ASME containers designed for permanent installation in stationary service above ground shall be placed on masonry or other noncombustible structural supports located on concrete or masonry foundations with the container supports.

(A) Where saddles are used to support the container, they shall allow for expansion and contraction and prevent an excessive concentration of stresses.

(B) Where structural steel supports are used, they shall comply with 6.6.3.3.

(C) Containers of more than 2000 gal (7.6 m³) water capacity shall be provided with concrete or masonry foundations formed to fit the container contour or, if furnished with saddles in compliance with Table 6.6.3.3(A), shall be placed on flat-topped foundations.

(D) Containers of 2000 gal (7.6 m³) water capacity or less shall be installed either on concrete or masonry foundations formed to fit the container contour or in accordance with 6.6.3.1(E).

(E) Containers of 2000 gal (7.6 m³) water capacity or less and equipped with attached supports complying with Table 6.6.3.3(A) shall be installed on a fire-resistive foundation if the bottoms of the horizontal members of the container saddles, runners, or skids are more than 12 in. (300 mm) above grade.

(F) Containers of 2000 gal (7.6 m³) water capacity or less shall not be mounted with the outside bottom of the container shell more than 5 ft (1.5 m) above the surface of the ground.

(G) Containers of 2000 gal (7.6 m³) water capacity or less and container-pump assemblies mounted on a common base complying with Table 6.6.3.3(A) shall be placed either on paved surfaces or on concrete pads at ground level within 4 in. (102 mm) of ground level.

6.6.3.2 ASME containers that have liquid interconnections shall be installed so that the maximum permitted filling level of each container is at the same elevation.

6.6.3.3 Support of Horizontal ASME Containers.

(A) Horizontal ASME containers with attached supports and designed for permanent installation in stationary service shall be installed in accordance with Table 6.6.3.3(A).

(B) Horizontal ASME containers of 2000 gal (7.6 m³) or less, on foundations in their installed condition, shall meet the following:

(1) Structurally support the containers when subject to deteriorating environmental effects including, but not limited to, ambient temperature of −40°F to 150°F (−40°C to 66°C) or local conditions if outside this range, ultraviolet rays, radiant heat from fires, and moisture

(2) Be of either noncombustible or self-extinguishing material (per the definition in NFPA 99, *Standard for Health Care Facilities* 3.3.165)

6.6.3.4 Where a single ASME container complying with Table 6.6.3.3(A) is installed in isolated locations with non-fireproofed steel supports resting on concrete pads or footings and the outside bottom of the container shell is not more than 5 ft (1.5 m) above the ground level, the approval of the authority having jurisdiction shall be obtained.

6.6.3.5 The part of an ASME container in contact with saddles or foundations or masonry shall be coated or protected to minimize corrosion.

6.6.3.6 In locations where the monthly maximum depth of snow accumulation, as determined from the National Weather Service or other published statistics, is more than the height of aboveground containers, excluding the dome cover, the following requirements shall apply:

(1) A stake or other marking shall be installed higher than the average snow cover depths, up to a height of 15 ft (4.6 m).

(2) The container shall be installed to prevent its movement resulting from snow accumulation.

6.6.3.7 If the container is mounted on or is part of a vehicle in accordance with 5.2.7.2(A), the unit shall be located in accordance with 6.3.1.

(A) The surface on which the vehicle is parked shall be level and, if not paved, shall be able to support heavy vehicular traffic and shall be clear of dry grass and weeds and other combustible material within 10 ft (3 m) of the container.

(B) Flexibility shall be provided in the connecting piping in accordance with 6.9.6.

6.6.3.8 Portable tanks of 2000 gal (7.6 m³) water capacity or less that comply with 5.2.7.3 shall be installed in accordance with 6.6.3.1(E).

6.6.4 Installation of Vertical ASME Containers.

6.6.4.1 Vertical ASME containers of over 125 gal (0.5 m³) water capacity designed for permanent installation in stationary service above ground shall be installed on reinforced concrete or steel structural supports on reinforced concrete foundations that are designed to meet the loading provisions established in 5.2.4.3.

6.6.4.2 The requirements in 6.6.4.3 through 6.6.4.5 shall also apply to the installation of vertical ASME containers.

6.6.4.3 Steel supports shall be protected against fire exposure with a material that has a fire resistance rating of at least 2 hours, except that continuous steel skirts that have only one opening that is 18 in. (460 mm) or less in diameter shall have fire protection applied to the outside of the skirts.

6.6.4.4 Vertical ASME containers used in liquid service shall not be manifolded to horizontal ASME containers.

6.6.4.5 Vertical ASME containers of different dimensions shall not be manifolded together.

6.6.5 Temporary Container Installations.

6.6.5.1 Single containers constructed as portable storage containers for temporary stationary service in accordance with 5.2.7.2(A) shall be placed on concrete pads, paved surfaces, or firm earth for such temporary service (not more than 12 months at a given location).

6.6.5.2 The surface on which the containers are placed shall be level and, if not paved, shall be clear of dry grass and weeds and other combustible material within 10 ft (3 m) of the container.

6.6.5.3 Flexibility shall be provided in the connecting piping in accordance with 6.9.6.

6.6.5.4 Where portable storage containers are installed at isolated locations with the bottoms of the skids or runners above the ground, either fire-resistive supports shall be provided or non–fire-resistive supports shall be permitted when all the following conditions are met:

(1) The height of the outside bottom of the container does not exceed 5 ft (1.5 m) above the ground.

(2) The approval of the authority having jurisdiction is obtained.

6.6.6 Installation of Underground and Mounded Containers.

6.6.6.1* ASME container assemblies intended for underground installation, including interchangeable aboveground–underground container assemblies, shall be installed underground in accordance with 6.6.6.1(A) through 6.6.6.1(O).

(A) Containers installed in areas with no vehicular traffic shall be installed at least 6 in. (150 mm) below grade.

(B) In areas where vehicular traffic is expected, a noninterchangeable underground container shall be installed at least 18 in. (460 mm) below grade, or the container shall be protected from damage from vehicles.

(C) Protection against vehicular damage shall be provided for the fitting housing, housing cover, container connections, and piping.

(D) Approved interchangeable aboveground–underground container assemblies installed underground shall not be placed with the container shell more than 12 in. (300 mm) below grade.

(E) The installation of a buried container shall include protection for the container and piping against physical damage from vehicular traffic.

(F) Prior to digging, the location of underground and mounded containers and piping in the vicinity of construction and excavation activities shall be determined and the installation shall be protected from damage.

(G) Where a container is to be abandoned underground, the following procedure shall be followed:

(1) As much liquid LP-Gas as practical shall be removed through the container liquid withdrawal connection.

(2)* As much of the remaining LP-Gas vapor as practical shall be removed through a vapor connection.

(3) The vapor shall be either recovered, burned, or vented to the atmosphere.

(4) Where only vapor LP-Gas at atmospheric pressure remains in the container, the container shall be filled with water, sand, or foamed plastic or shall be purged with an inert gas.

(5) If purged, the displaced vapor shall be either recovered, burned, or vented to the atmosphere.

(H) The discharge of the regulator vent shall be above the highest probable water level.

(I)* A corrosion protection system shall be installed on new installations of underground steel containers, unless technical justification is provided to and is approved by the authority having jurisdiction. The corrosion protection system shall include the following:

(1) A container coating complying with 5.2.1.11

(2) A cathodic protection system that consists of a sacrificial anode(s) or an impressed current anode

(3) A means to test the performance of the cathodic protection system

(J)* Cathodic protection systems installed in accordance with 6.6.6.1(I) shall be monitored by testing and the results documented. Confirming tests shall be described by one of the following:

(1) Producing a voltage of -0.85 volts or more negative, with reference to a saturated copper-copper sulfate half cell

(2) Producing a voltage of -0.78 volts or more negative, with reference to a saturated KCl calomel half cell

(3) Producing a voltage of -0.80 volts or more negative, with reference to a silver-silver chloride half cell

(4) Any other method described in Appendix D of Title 49 of the Code of Federal Regulations, Part 192.

(K)* Sacrificial anodes installed in accordance with 6.6.6.1(I) above shall be tested in accordance with the following schedule:

(1) Upon installation of the cathodic protection system, unless prohibited by climactic conditions, in which case testing shall be done within 180 days after the installation of the system.

(2) For continued verification of the effectiveness of the system, 12 to 18 months after the initial test.

(3) Upon successful verification testing and in consideration of previous test results, periodic follow-up testing shall be performed at intervals not to exceed 36 months.

(4) Systems failing a test shall be repaired as soon as practical unless climactic conditions prohibit this action, in which case the repair shall be made not more than 180 days thereafter. The testing schedule shall be restarted as required in 6.6.6.1(K)(1) and (2), and the results shall comply with 6.6.6.1(J).

(5) Documentation of the results of the two most recent tests shall be retained.

(L)* Where an impressed current cathodic protection system is installed, it shall be inspected and tested in accordance with the following schedule:

(1) All sources of impressed current shall be inspected and tested at intervals not exceeding two months.

(2) All impressed current cathodic protection installations shall be inspected and tested annually.

(M) Prior to burial, the container shall be visually examined for damage to the coating. Damaged areas shall be repaired with a coating recommended for underground service and compatible with the existing coating.

(N)* Containers shall be set level and shall be surrounded by earth or sand firmly tamped in place.

(O) Backfill shall be free of rocks and abrasives.

6.6.6.2 Partially underground, unmounded ASME containers shall be installed as follows:

(1) The portion of the container below the surface of the ground, and for a vertical distance of at least 3 in. (75 mm) above that surface, shall comply with the corrosion protection requirements of 6.6.6.1(I) through (M). The aboveground portion of the container shall comply with 6.6.1.4.

(2) Containers shall be set level and shall be surrounded by earth or sand firmly tamped in place

(3) Backfill shall be free of rocks and abrasives.

(4) Spacing provisions shall be as specified for aboveground containers in 6.3.1 and Table 6.3.1.

(5) The container shall be located so as not to be subject to vehicular damage or shall be protected against such damage.

6.6.6.3 Mounded containers shall be installed as follows:

(1)* Mounding material shall be earth, sand, or other noncombustible, noncorrosive materials and shall provide a minimum thickness of cover for the container of at least 1 ft (0.3 m).

(2) A protective cover shall be provided on top of mounding materials subject to erosion.

(3) Container valves and appurtenances shall be accessible for operation or repair, without disturbing mounding material, as follows:

(a) Where containers are mounded and the bottom of the container is 30 in. (0.76 m) or more above the surrounding grade, access to bottom connections shall be provided by an opening or tunnel with a 4 ft (1.2 m) minimum diameter and a 3 ft (0.9 m) minimum clear area.

(b) Bottom connections that extend beyond the mound shall be part of the ASME container or shall be installed in compliance with the ASME Code and shall be designed for the forces that can act on the connections.

(4) Mounded containers shall comply with the corrosion protection requirements of 6.6.6.1(I) through (M).

6.26.3.1 All liquid withdrawal openings and all vapor withdrawal openings that are 1¼ in. (32 mm) or larger shall be equipped with an internal valve.

7.2.3.1 Public access to areas where LP-Gas is stored and transferred shall be prohibited, except where necessary for the conduct of normal business activities.

7.3.2 Purging.

7.3.2.1 Venting of gas from containers for purging or for other purposes shall be accomplished in accordance with 7.3.2.2 through 7.3.2.4.

7.3.2.2 Venting of cylinders indoors shall only occur in structures designed and constructed for cylinder filling in accordance with 6.5.1 and Chapter 10 and with 7.3.2.2(A) through 7.3.2.2(C).

(A) Piping shall be installed to convey the vented product outdoors at least 3 ft (1 m) above the highest point of any building within 25 ft (7.6 m).

(B) Only vapors shall be exhausted to the atmosphere.

(C) If a vent manifold is used to allow for the venting of more than one cylinder at a time, each connection to the vent manifold shall be equipped with a backflow check valve.

7.3.2.3 Venting of containers outdoors shall be performed under conditions that result in rapid dispersion of the product being released.

7.3.2.4 If conditions are such that venting into the atmosphere cannot be accomplished safely, LP-Gas shall be burned at a distance of at least 25 ft (7.6 m) from combustibles.

7.3.2.5 Venting of containers and burning of LP-Gas from containers shall be attended.

7.4.2 LP-Gas Capacity of Containers.

7.4.2.1 The capacity of an LP-Gas container shall be determined either by weight in accordance with 7.4.2.2 or by volume in accordance with 7.4.2.3.

7.4.2.2* The maximum filling limit by weight of LP-Gas in a container shall be in accordance with Table 7.4.2.2.

7.4.2.3* The maximum permitted volume of LP-Gas in a container shall be in accordance with Table 7.4.2.3(a), Table 7.4.2.3(b), and Table 7.4.2.3(c).

7.4.3 General Provisions for the Volumetric Method of Filling Containers.

7.4.3.1 The volumetric method shall be limited to the following containers that are designed and equipped for filling by volume:

(1) Cylinders of less than 200 lb (91 kg) water capacity that are not subject to DOT jurisdiction

(2) Cylinders of 200 lb (91 kg) water capacity or more

(3) Cargo tanks or portable tanks

(4) ASME and API-ASME containers complying with 5.2.1.1 or 5.2.4.2

7.4.3.2 Where used, the volumetric method shall be in accordance with 7.4.3.2(A) through 7.4.3.2(C).

(A) If a fixed maximum liquid level gauge or a variable liquid level gauge without liquid volume temperature correction is used, the liquid level indicated by these gauges shall be computed based on the maximum permitted filling limit when the liquid is at 40°F (4°C) for aboveground containers or at 50°F (10°C) for underground containers.

(B) When a variable liquid level gauge is used and the liquid volume is corrected for temperature, the maximum permitted liquid level shall be in accordance with Table 7.4.2.3(a) through Table 7.4.2.3(c).

(C) ASME containers with a water capacity of 1200 gal (4.54 m³) or less filled by the volumetric method shall be gauged in accordance with 7.4.3.2(A), utilizing the fixed maximum liquid level gauge, except that containers fabricated on or before December 31, 1965, shall be exempt from this provision.

7.4.3.3 Where containers are to be filled volumetrically by a variable liquid level gauge in accordance with 7.4.3.2(B), provisions shall be made for determining the liquid temperature.

8.2.1 General Location of Cylinders.
8.2.1.1 Cylinders in storage shall be located to minimize exposure to excessive temperature rises, physical damage, or tampering.
8.2.1.2 Cylinders in storage having individual water capacity greater than 2.7 lb (1.1 kg) [nominal 1 lb (0.45 kg) LP-Gas capacity] shall be positioned so that the pressure relief valve is in direct communication with the vapor space of the cylinder.
8.2.1.3 Cylinders stored in buildings in accordance with Section 8.3 shall not be located near exits, near stairways, or in areas normally used, or intended to be used, for the safe egress of occupants.
8.2.1.4 If empty cylinders that have been in LP-Gas service are stored indoors, they shall be considered as full cylinders for the purposes of determining the maximum quantities of LP-Gas permitted by 8.3.1, 8.3.2.1, and 8.3.3.1.
8.2.1.5 Cylinders shall not be stored on roofs.

9.3.2.4 Cylinder valves shall comply with the following:
(1) Valves of cylinders shall be protected in accordance with 5.2.6.1.
(2) Screw-on-type protecting caps or collars shall be secured in place.
(3) The provisions of 7.2.2.5 shall apply.

(6) Security and access *(see 7.2.3.1)*

The following paragraph, referenced in 14.2.2.2(6), is provided for the handbook user's convenience:

7.2.3.1 Public access to areas where LP-Gas is stored and transferred shall be prohibited, except where necessary for the conduct of normal business activities.

(7) Fire response *(see 6.25.4.3)*

The following paragraph, referenced in 14.2.2.2(7), is provided for the handbook user's convenience:

6.25.4.3* LP-Gas fires shall not be extinguished until the source of the burning gas has been shut off.

14.2.2.3 Loading and unloading procedures shall include the following:

(1) Hose *(see 6.24.4, 7.2.4, and 13.4.6)*

The following paragraphs, referenced in 14.2.2.3(1), are provided for the handbook user's convenience:

6.24.4 Installation of Vehicle Fuel Dispensers.
6.24.4.1 Hose shall comply with the following:
(1) Hose length shall not exceed 18 ft (5.5 m) unless approved by the authority having jurisdiction.
(2) All hose shall be listed.
(3) When not in use, hose shall be secured to protect them from damage.
6.24.4.2 A listed emergency breakaway device complying with ANSI/UL 567, *Standard Pipe Connectors for Flammable and Combustible Liquids and LP-Gas,* and designed to retain liquid on both sides of the breakaway point, or other devices affording equivalent protection approved by the authority having jurisdiction, shall be installed.

6.24.4.3 Dispensing devices for LP-Gas shall be located as follows:

(1) Conventional systems shall be at least 10 ft (3.0 m) from any dispensing device for Class I liquids.

(2) Low-emission transfer systems in accordance with Section 6.26 shall be at least 5 ft (1.5 m) from any dispensing device for Class I liquids.

7.2.4 Hose Inspection.

7.2.4.1 Hose assemblies shall be observed for leakage or for damage that could impair their integrity before each use.

7.2.4.2 The hose assemblies specified in 7.2.4.1 shall be inspected at least annually.

7.2.4.3 Inspection of pressurized hose assemblies shall include inspection for the following:

(1) Damage to outer cover that exposes reinforcement

(2) Kinked or flattened hose

(3) Soft spots or bulges in hose

(4) Couplings that have slipped on the hose, are damaged, have missing parts, or have loose bolts

(5) Leakage other than permeability leakage

7.2.4.4 Hose assemblies shall be replaced, repaired, or continued in service based on the results of the inspection.

7.2.4.5 Leaking or damaged hose shall be immediately repaired or removed from service.

13.4.6 At the completion of the transfer, and prior to disconnect of the transfer hose or arm, the transfer connection shall be purged of all liquid and depressurized. The liquid and vapor pressure shall be returned either to the vessel or to the shore facility. LP-Gas shall not be vented to the atmosphere.

(2) Chocks *[see 7.2.3.6(2) and 9.4.8]*

The following paragraphs, referenced in 14.2.2.3(2), are provided for the handbook user's convenience:

7.2.3.6(2) Wheel chocks shall be placed to prevent movement of the car in either direction.

9.4.8* Wheel Stops for Cargo Tank Vehicles. Each cargo tank vehicle or trailer shall utilize a wheel stop, in addition to the parking or hand brake, whenever the cargo tank vehicle is loading, is unloading, or is parked.

(3) Fire extinguishers *(see 6.25.4.2, Section 8.5, 9.4.7, and 13.2.1.13)*

The following paragraphs, referenced in 14.2.2.3(3), are provided for the handbook user's convenience:

6.25.4.2 Each industrial plant, bulk plant, and distributing point shall be provided with at least one approved portable fire extinguisher having a minimum capacity of 18 lb (8.2 kg) of dry chemical with a B:C rating. Where fire extinguishers have more than one letter classification, they shall be considered to satisfy the requirements of each letter class.

8.5* Fire Protection

8.5.1 Storage locations, where the aggregate quantity of propane stored is in excess of 720 lb (327 kg), shall be provided with at least one approved portable fire extinguisher having a minimum capacity of 18 lb (9.2 kg) dry chemical with B:C rating.

8.5.2 The required fire extinguisher shall be located not more than 50 ft (15 m) from the storage location. Where fire extinguishers have more than one letter classification, they can be considered to satisfy the requirements of each letter class.

9.4.7* Fire Extinguishers. Each cargo tank vehicle or tractor shall be provided with at least one approved portable fire extinguisher having a minimum capacity of 18 lb (8.2 kg) dry chemical with a B:C rating. Where fire extinguishers have more than one letter classification, they can be considered to satisfy the requirements of each letter class.

13.2.1.13 Medical first aid equipment and fire extinguishers shall be available at the shore facility. This equipment shall be in accordance with the following:

(1) Extinguishers shall be ready for use at all times.
(2) Emergency equipment shall be positioned and ready to operate prior to the start of the transfer operation.
(3) The locations of all fire extinguishers shall be marked and readily accessible.

(4) Sources of ignition *[see 7.2.3.2, 7.2.3.5, 7.2.3.8(2), 7.2.3.8(3), and 9.4.10]*

The following paragraphs, referenced in 14.2.2.3(4), are provided for the handbook user's convenience:

7.2.3.2 Sources of ignition shall be turned off during transfer operations, while connections or disconnections are made, or while LP-Gas is being vented to the atmosphere.
(A) Internal combustion engines within 15 ft (4.6 m) of a point of transfer shall be shut down while such transfer operations are in progress, with the exception of the following:
(1) Engines of LP-Gas cargo tank vehicles, constructed and operated in compliance with Chapter 9, while such engines are driving transfer pumps or compressors on these vehicles to load containers in accordance with 6.5.4
(2) Engines installed in buildings as provided in Section 11.13
(B) Smoking, open flame, portable electrical tools, and extension lights capable of igniting LP-Gas shall not be permitted within 25 ft (7.6 m) of a point of transfer while filling operations are in progress.
(C) Metal cutting, grinding, oxygen–fuel gas cutting, brazing, soldering, or welding shall not be permitted within 35 ft (10.7 m) of a point of transfer while filling operations are in progress.
(D) Materials that have been heated above the ignition temperature of LP-Gas shall be cooled before LP-Gas transfer is started.
(E) Sources of ignition shall be turned off during the filling of any LP-Gas container on the vehicle.

7.2.3.5 Transfers to containers serving agricultural or industrial equipment requiring refueling in the field shall comply with 7.2.3.5(A) and 7.2.3.5(B).
(A)* Where the intake of air-moving equipment is less than 50 ft (15 m) from a point of transfer, it shall be shut down while containers are being refilled.
(B) Equipment employing open flames or equipment with integral containers shall be shut down while refueling.

7.2.3.8(2) Ignition source control shall be in accordance with Section 6.22.
7.2.3.8 (3) Control of ignition sources during transfer shall be provided in accordance with 7.2.3.2.

9.4.10 Smoking Prohibition. No person shall smoke or carry lighted smoking material as follows:
(1) On or within 25 ft (7.6 m) of a vehicle that is containing LP-Gas liquid or vapor
(2) At points of liquid transfer
(3) When delivering or connecting to containers

(5) Personnel *(see 7.2.1)*

The following paragraph, referenced in 14.2.2.3(5), is provided for the handbook user's convenience:

7.2.1 Transfer Personnel.
7.2.1.1 Transfer operations shall be conducted by qualified personnel meeting the provisions of Section 4.4.
7.2.1.2 At least one qualified person shall remain in attendance at the transfer operation from the time connections are made until the transfer is completed, shutoff valves are closed, and lines are disconnected.
7.2.1.3 Transfer personnel shall exercise caution to ensure that the LP-Gases transferred are those for which the transfer system and the containers to be filled are designed.

(6) Containers *(see 5.2.2.1, 5.2.2.2, 7.2.2.1, 7.2.2.2, 7.2.2.3, 7.2.2.4, 7.2.2.5, 7.2.2.8, 7.2.2.10, 7.2.2.13, 7.2.3.3, 9.3.2.6, 9.3.2.7, and 9.3.2.8)*

The following paragraphs, referenced in 14.2.2.3(6), are provided for the handbook user's convenience:

> **5.2.2.1*** Cylinders shall be continued in service and transported in accordance with DOT regulations.
>
> **5.2.2.2** A cylinder with an expired requalification date shall not be refilled until it is requalified by the methods prescribed in DOT regulations.
>
> **7.2.2.1** Transfer of LP-Gas to and from a container shall be accomplished only by qualified individuals trained in proper handling and operating procedures meeting the requirements of Section 4.4 and in emergency response procedures.
>
> **7.2.2.2** When noncompliance with Section 5.2 and Section 5.7 is found, the container owner and user shall be notified in writing.
>
> **7.2.2.3** Injection of compressed air, oxygen, or any oxidizing gas into containers to transfer LP-Gas liquid shall be prohibited.
>
> **7.2.2.4** When evacuating a container owned by others, the qualified person(s) performing the transfer shall not inject any material other than LP-Gas into the container.
>
> **7.2.2.5*** Valve outlets on refillable cylinders of 108 lb (49 kg) water capacity [nominal 45 lb (20 kg) propane capacity] or less shall be equipped with a redundant pressure-tight seal or one of the following listed connections: CGA 790, CGA 791, or CGA 810, as described in CGA V-1, *Standard Compressed Gas Cylinder Valve Outlet and Inlet Connections.*
>
> **7.2.2.8** Containers shall be filled only after determination that they comply with the design, fabrication, inspection, marking, and requalification provisions of this code.
>
> **7.2.2.10** "Single trip," "nonrefillable," or "disposable" cylinders shall not be refilled with LP-Gas.
>
> **7.2.2.13** A container shall not be filled if the container assembly does not meet the requirements for continued service.
>
> **7.2.3.3** Cargo tank vehicles unloading into storage containers shall be at least 10 ft (3.0 m) from the container and so positioned that the shutoff valves on both the truck and the container are readily accessible.
>
> **9.3.2.6** Cylinders and their appurtenances shall be determined to be leak-free before being loaded into vehicles.
>
> **9.3.2.7** Cylinders shall be loaded into vehicles with flat floors or equipped with racks for holding cylinders.
>
> **9.3.2.8** Cylinders shall be fastened in position to minimize the possibility of movement, tipping, and physical damage.

(7) Signage *(see 7.2.3.6)*

The following paragraph, referenced in 14.2.2.3(7), is provided for the handbook user's convenience:

> **7.2.3.6** During the time railroad tank cars are on sidings for loading or unloading, the following shall apply:
> (1) A caution sign, with wording such as "STOP. TANK CAR CONNECTED," shall be placed at the active end(s) of the siding while the car is connected, as required by DOT regulations.
> (2) Wheel chocks shall be placed to prevent movement of the car in either direction.

(8) Security and access *(see 7.2.3.1)*

The following paragraph, referenced in 14.2.2.3(8), is provided for the handbook user's convenience:

> **7.2.3.1** Public access to areas where LP-Gas is stored and transferred shall be prohibited, except where necessary for the conduct of normal business activities.

(9) Fire response *(see 6.25.4.3 and 6.25.4.4)*

The following paragraphs, referenced in 14.2.2.3(9), are provided for the handbook user's convenience:

> **6.25.4.3*** LP-Gas fires shall not be extinguished until the source of the burning gas has been shut off.
>
> **6.25.4.4** Emergency controls shall be conspicuously marked, and the controls shall be located so as to be readily accessible in emergencies.

(10) Ammonia contamination *(see Section 4.5)*

The following section, referenced in 14.2.2.3(10), is provided for the handbook user's convenience:

> **4.5* Ammonia Contamination**
>
> **4.5.1** LP-Gas stored or used in systems within the scope of this code shall contain less ammonia than the quantity required to turn the color of red litmus paper to blue.
>
> **4.5.2** The initial fill of LP-Gas in a transportation or storage system that has been converted from ammonia to LP-Gas service shall be tested for ammonia contamination prior to being used or transferred from that system.

14.3* Maintenance

A.14.3 As the basis for maintenance procedures, the owner or operator can use procedures or instructions provided by equipment vendors, procedures found in industrial codes, or procedures prepared by persons or organizations knowledgeable about the process and equipment.

Written maintenance procedures are equally as important as written operating plans. For example, plants that use LP-Gas in large quantities probably have central maintenance departments, thereby making it difficult to ensure that the same mechanics work on the propane storage facility when maintenance is required. Some plants may rely on contractors for their maintenance, and maintenance contractors can change. For these situations, written procedures provide a resource for those who maintain bulk and industrial plants.

14.3.1 Maintenance Procedures.

Written maintenance procedures shall be the basis for maintaining the mechanical integrity of LP-Gas systems.

14.3.1.1 Procedures shall be updated whenever a change occurs that affects the maintenance of a system.

14.3.1.2 Persons who perform maintenance on LP-Gas systems shall be trained in the hazards of the system and in the maintenance and testing procedures applicable to the installation.

14.3.1.3 Any maintenance contractor shall ensure that each contract maintenance employee is so trained or under the immediate supervision of such a trained person to perform the maintenance procedures.

Contracted employees are held to the same standard as direct employees at LP-Gas facilities to ensure that all safety precautions are properly accounted for. Maintenance contractors must be able to provide such expertise to safely perform maintenance duties, by providing either trained personnel or supervision by such a trained person.

14.3.1.4 The written procedures shall address the following requirements, where applicable:

(1) Corrosion control *[see 5.2.1.4, 6.6.1.4, 6.6.3.5, Section 6.16, 6.6.6.1(H), 6.6.6.2(1), 6.6.6.3(1), and 6.6.6.3(4)]*

The following paragraphs, referenced in 14.3.1.4(1), are provided for the handbook user's convenience:

5.2.1.4 Containers that show excessive denting, bulging, gouging, or corrosion shall be removed from service.

6.6.1.4* Aboveground containers shall be painted.

6.6.3.5 The part of an ASME container in contact with saddles or foundations or masonry shall be coated or protected to minimize corrosion.

6.16* Corrosion Protection
6.16.1 All metallic equipment and components that are buried or mounded shall be coated or protected and maintained to minimize corrosion.
6.16.2 Corrosion protection of all other materials shall be in accordance with accepted engineering practice.

6.6.6.1(H) The discharge of the regulator vent shall be above the highest probable water level.

6.6.6.2(1) The portion of the container below the surface of the ground, and for a vertical distance of at least 3 in. (75 mm) above that surface, shall comply with the corrosion protection requirements of 6.6.6.1(I) through (M). The aboveground portion of the container shall comply with 6.6.1.4.

6.6.6.3(1)* Mounding material shall be earth, sand, or other noncombustible, noncorrosive materials and shall provide a minimum thickness of cover for the container of at least 1 ft (0.3 m).

6.6.6.3(4) Mounded containers shall comply with the corrosion protection requirements of 6.6.6.1(I) through (M).

(2) Physical protection *(see 5.7.7.2, 6.6.1.2, and 6.24.3.12)*

The following paragraphs, referenced in 14.3.1.4(2), are provided for the handbook user's convenience:

5.7.7.2 Any of the valves listed in 5.7.7.1(1), (2), or (3) that are not connected for service shall be plugged or capped.

6.6.1.2 LP-Gas containers or systems of which they are a part shall be protected from damage from vehicles.

6.24.3.12 All dispensers either shall be installed on a concrete foundation or shall be part of a complete storage and dispensing unit mounted on a common base and installed in accordance with 6.6.3.1(G). Protection against physical damage shall be provided for dispensers.

(3) Hose *(see 6.25.4.1, 7.2.4, and 9.4.3.7)*

The following paragraphs, referenced in 14.3.1.4(3), are provided for the handbook user's convenience:

6.25.4.1 Roadways or other means of access for emergency equipment, such as fire department apparatus, shall be provided.

7.2.4 Hose Inspection.
7.2.4.1 Hose assemblies shall be observed for leakage or for damage that could impair their integrity before each use.
7.2.4.2 The hose assemblies specified in 7.2.4.1 shall be inspected at least annually.
7.2.4.3 Inspection of pressurized hose assemblies shall include inspection for the following:
(1) Damage to outer cover that exposes reinforcement
(2) Kinked or flattened hose
(3) Soft spots or bulges in hose
(4) Couplings that have slipped on the hose, are damaged, have missing parts, or have loose bolts
(5) Leakage other than permeability leakage
7.2.4.4 Hose assemblies shall be replaced, repaired, or continued in service based on the results of the inspection.
7.2.4.5 Leaking or damaged hose shall be immediately repaired or removed from service.

9.4.3.7 Flexible hose connectors shall comply with the following:
(1) Flexible hose connectors shall be permanently marked to indicate the date of installation of the flexible hose connector.

(2) The flexible hose portion of the connector shall be replaced with an unused connector within 10 years of the indicated date of installation of the connector and visually inspected before the first delivery of each day.

(3) The flexible hose portion of flexible connectors shall be replaced whenever a cargo tank unit is remounted on a different chassis, or whenever the cargo tank unit is repiped if such repiping encompasses that portion of piping in which the connector is located.

(4) Replacement of the flexible hose portion of the flexible connector shall not be required if the reinstallation or repiping is performed within 1 year of the date of assembly of the connector.

(4) Piping *(see 6.9.3.10 and 6.12.7)*

The following paragraphs, referenced in 14.3.1.4(4), are provided for the handbook user's convenience:

6.9.3.10 Aboveground piping shall be supported and protected against physical damage by vehicles.

6.12.7 Temperature-sensitive elements of emergency shutoff valves shall not be painted, nor shall they have any ornamental finishes applied after manufacture.

(5) Appurtenances *(see 6.7.2.4 and 6.12.9)*

The following paragraphs, referenced in 14.3.1.4(5), are provided for the handbook user's convenience:

6.7.2.4 Rain caps or other means shall be provided to minimize the possibility of the entrance of water or other extraneous matter into the relief device or any discharge piping. Provision shall be made for drainage where the accumulation of water is anticipated.

6.12.9 Emergency shutoff valves required by the code shall be tested annually for the functions required by 5.12.4(2) and (3). Backflow check valves installed in lieu of emergency shutoff valves shall be checked annually for proper operation. The results of the test shall be documented.

(6) Containers *(see 5.2.1.2, 5.2.3.2, 5.7.1.4, 5.7.4.4, 12.3.3.4, 12.3.4.3(4), 12.3.4.4, and 12.3.4.6)*

The following paragraphs, referenced in 14.3.1.4(6), are provided for the handbook user's convenience:

5.2.1.2 Containers that have been involved in a fire and show no distortion shall be requalified for continued service before being used or reinstalled.
(A) Cylinders shall be requalified by a manufacturer of that type of cylinder or by a repair facility approved by DOT.
(B) ASME or API-ASME containers shall be retested using the hydrostatic test procedure applicable at the time of the original fabrication.
(C) All container appurtenances shall be replaced.
(D) DOT 4E specification (aluminum) cylinders and composite cylinders involved in a fire shall be permanently removed from service.

5.2.3.2 Any cylinder that fails one or more of the criteria in 5.2.3.4 shall not be refilled or continued in service until the condition is corrected.

5.7.1.4 Gaskets used to retain LP-Gas in containers shall be resistant to the action of LP-Gas.
(A) Gaskets shall be made of metal or other material confined in metal having a melting point over 1500°F (816°C) or shall be protected against fire exposure.
(B) When a flange is opened, the gasket shall be replaced.
(C) Aluminum O-rings and spiral-wound metal gaskets shall be permitted.
(D) Gaskets for use with approved or listed liquid level gauges for installation on a container of 3500 gal (13.2 m³) water capacity or less shall be exempt from the minimum melting point requirement.

5.7.4.4 ASME containers over 4000 gal (15.1 m³) water capacity shall also be equipped with the following appurtenances:
(1) An internal spring-type, flush-type full internal pressure relief valve, or external pressure relief valve *(see Annex E)*

(2) A fixed maximum liquid level gauge

(3) A float gauge, rotary gauge, slip tube gauge, or a combination of these gauges

(4) A pressure gauge

(5) A temperature gauge

12.3.3.4 Gaskets used to retain LP-Gas in containers shall be resistant to the action of LP-Gas.

12.3.4.3(4) The under-tank temperature shall be observed and logged at least weekly.

12.3.4.4 The refrigerated LP-Gas container foundation shall be periodically monitored for settlement during the life of the facility.

12.3.4.6 Any settlement in excess of that anticipated in the design shall be investigated, and corrective action shall be taken if appropriate.

(7) Cylinders *(see 5.2.3.2)*

The following paragraph, referenced in 14.3.1.4(7), is provided for the handbook user's convenience:

5.2.3.2 Any cylinder that fails one or more of the criteria in 5.2.3.4 shall not be refilled or continued in service until the condition is corrected.

(8) Underground containers *[See 6.6.6.1(J) through (O).]*

Subsection 14.3.1.4(8) was added by a tentative interim amendment (TIA).

The following paragraphs, referenced in 14.3.1.4(8), are provided for the handbook user's convenience:

(J)* Cathodic protection systems installed in accordance with (I) above shall be monitored by testing and the results documented. Confirming tests shall be described by one of the following:

(1) Producing a voltage of −0.85 volts or more negative, with reference to a saturated copper-copper sulfate half cell

(2) Producing a voltage of −0.78 volts or more negative, with reference to a saturated KCl calomel half cell

(3) Producing a voltage of −0.80 volts or more negative, with reference to a silver-silver chloride half cell

(4) Any other method described in Appendix D of Title 49 of the Code of Federal Regulations, Part 192.

(K)* Sacrificial anodes installed in accordance with 6.6.6.1(I) shall be tested in accordance with the following schedule:

(1) Upon installation of the cathodic protection system, unless prohibited by climactic conditions, in which case testing shall be done within 180 days after the installation of the system.

(2) For continued verification of the effectiveness of the system, 12 to 18 months after the initial test.

(3) Upon successful verification testing and in consideration of previous test results, periodic follow-up testing shall be performed at intervals not to exceed 36 months.

(4) Systems failing a test shall be repaired as soon as practical unless climactic conditions prohibit this action, in which case the repair shall be made not more than 180 days thereafter. The testing schedule shall be restarted as required in 6.6.6.1(K)(1) and (2) and the results shall comply with 6.6.6.1(J).

(5) Documentation of the results of the two most recent tests shall be retained.

(L)* Where an impressed current cathodic protection system is installed, it shall be inspected and tested in accordance with the following schedule:

(1) All sources of impressed current shall be inspected and tested at intervals not exceeding two months.

(2) All impressed current cathodic protection installations shall be inspected and tested annually.

(M) Prior to burial, the container shall be visually examined for damage to the coating. Damaged areas shall be repaired with a coating recommended for underground service and compatible with the existing coating.

(N)* Containers shall be set level and shall be surrounded by earth or sand firmly tamped in place.

(O) Backfill shall be free of rocks and abrasives.

14.3.2 Maintenance Manuals.

14.3.2.1 Maintenance manuals for all equipment at an attended facility shall be kept at the facility and shall be available to maintenance personnel. Manuals for unattended facilities shall be permitted to be kept at the facility or stored at a location where they will be accessible for maintenance personnel servicing the unattended location.

14.3.2.2 Maintenance manuals shall include routine inspections and preventative maintenance procedures and schedules.

14.3.2.3 Each facility shall maintain a record of all maintenance of fixed equipment used to store and transfer LP-Gas. Maintenance records for normally unattended facilities shall be maintained at the unattended facility or at another location.

14.3.2.4 Maintenance records shall be made available to the authority having jurisdiction during normal office hours.

14.3.2.5 Maintenance records shall be retained for the life of the equipment.

The section on maintenance manuals was expanded in the 2004 edition to provide more trackability and accountability of maintenance programs at LP-Gas facilities. Maintenance records are now required to include reports of when maintenance and inspections are performed to verify that the facility is properly maintained in accordance with this code. The owner or operator must be able to demonstrate through the use of a schedule that inspections and routine maintenance are being performed, in addition to nonroutine adjustments and repairs. These records must be available to the authority having jurisdiction to verify the ongoing safety of LP-Gas facilities.

See the commentary following 14.2.1.5 for problems associated with keeping operating procedures at a remote site. The same issues apply to the maintenance procedures. However, the need for onsite maintenance manuals is higher, as notes and signoffs for maintenance activities need to be made carefully at the time of such activities. Waiting to get back to the office to make the entries contributes to the possibility that something will be forgotten. In the same manner, performing the maintenance without the manual being present may contribute to forgetting to perform some required maintenance activity.

14.3.3 Maintenance of Fire Protection Equipment.

14.3.3.1 Facilities shall prepare and implement a maintenance program for all plant fire protection equipment.

14.3.3.2 Maintenance activities on fire protection equipment shall be scheduled so that a minimum of equipment is taken out of service at any time and is returned to service in a reasonable period of time.

14.3.3.3 Water-based automatic fire-extinguishing systems shall be maintained in accordance with NFPA 25, *Standard for the Inspection, Testing, and Maintenance of Water-Based Fire Protection Systems*.

14.3.3.4 Portable fire extinguishers shall be maintained in accordance with NFPA 10, *Standard for Portable Fire Extinguishers*.

NFPA 10, *Standard for Portable Fire Extinguishers* [1], covers all aspects of fire extinguishers and includes maintenance requirements. Inspection, maintenance, and recharging are covered in Chapter 7 of NFPA 10 and should be reviewed for more information on the subject.

REFERENCE CITED IN COMMENTARY

1. NFPA 10, *Standard for Portable Fire Extinguishers*, 2010 edition, National Fire Protection Association, Quincy, MA.

Pipe and Tubing Sizing Tables

CHAPTER 15

Chapter 15 contains only pipe sizing tables. These tables are needed by code users who size LP-Gas vapor piping systems that are used between first- and second-stage pressure regulators and between the second-stage pressure regulator and the appliances. New tables were added to this chapter in the 2001 edition to cover the pipe sizing situations normally encountered within the scope of NFPA 58. To assist the installer, pipe sizing tables applicable to piping downstream of the second-stage regulator have been provided, even though that piping is outside the scope of NFPA 58 and subject instead to the requirements of NFPA 54, *National Fuel Gas Code* [1]. The following text explains the use of the tables and provides an example of their use.

Sketch. The first step in using the pipe sizing tables is to make a sketch of the piping system. (See Exhibit 15.1.)

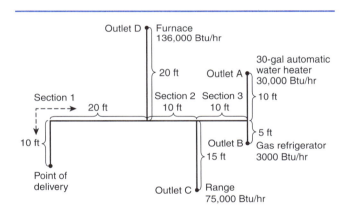

EXHIBIT 15.1 *Sketch of an LP-Gas Vapor Piping System.*

For SI units: 1 ft = 0.305 m; 1 gal = 3.785 L;
1000 Btu/hr = 0.293 kW

Demand. The quantity of gas to be provided at each outlet should be determined, whenever possible, directly from the manufacturer's Btu input rating of the equipment. If the ratings of the equipment to be installed are not known, Commentary Table 15.1 shows the approximate consumption of typical appliances in Btu/hr.

Pipe Sizing Tables. Capacities for LP-Gas pipe sizing tables are applied as shown in Commentary Table 15.2.

Use of Tables. To determine the size of each section of gas piping in a system within the range of the capacity tables, proceed as follows:

1. Determine the gas demand of each appliance to be attached to the piping system in Btu/hr.
2. Measure the length of piping from the point of delivery to the most remote outlet in the building.

COMMENTARY TABLE 15.1 *Approximate Gas Input for Typical Appliances*

Appliance	Input Btu/hr (Approx.)
Space Heating Units	
Warm air furnace	
Single family	100,000
Multifamily, per unit	60,000
Hydronic boiler	
Single family	100,000
Multifamily, per unit	60,000
Space and Water Heating Units	
Hydronic boiler	
Single family	120,000
Multifamily, per unit	75,000
Water Heating Appliances	
Water heater, automatic storage 30 gal to 40 gal tank	35,000
Water heater, automatic storage 50 gal tank	50,000
Water heater, automatic instantaneous	
Capacity at 2 gal/min	142,800
Capacity at 4 gal/min	285,000
Capacity at 6 gal/min	428,400
Water heater, domestic, circulating or side-arm	35,000
Cooking Appliances	
Range, freestanding, domestic	65,000
Built-in oven or broiler unit, domestic	25,000
Built-in top unit, domestic	40,000
Other Appliances	
Refrigerator	3,000
Clothes dryer, Type 1 (domestic)	35,000
Gas fireplace direct vent	40,000
Gas log	80,000
Barbecue	40,000
Gas light	2,500

For SI units, 1 Btu/hr = 0.293 W; 1 gal = 3.8 L

Source: NFPA 54, 2009, Table 5.4.2.1.

COMMENTARY TABLE 15.2 *Summary of Pipe Sizing Tables*

Table	Application	Material
15.1(a)	Between the first- and second-stage regulators	Schedule 40 pipe
15.1(b)	Between 2-psi service regulator and line pressure regulator	Schedule 40 pipe
15.1(c)	Between the second-stage regulator and appliance	Schedule 40 pipe
15.1(d)	Between the first- and second-stage regulators	Schedule 80 pipe
15.1(e)	Between the second-stage regulator and appliance	Schedule 80 pipe
15.1(f)	Between the first- and second-stage regulators	Type K and ACR copper tubing
15.1(g)	Between the second-stage regulator and appliance	Type K and ACR copper tubing
15.1(h)	Between the first- and second-stage regulators	Type L copper tubing
15.1(i)	Between 2-psi service regulator and line pressure regulator	Type L copper tubing
15.1(j)	Between single-stage or second-stage regulator and appliance	Type L copper tubing
15.1(k)	Between first-stage and second-stage regulators	Copper refrigeration tubing
15.1(l)	Between second-stage regulator and appliance	Copper refrigeration tubing
15.1(m)	Between 2-psi regulator and line-pressure regulator (1 psi drop)	Corrugated stainless steel tubing
15.1(n)	Between second-stage regulator and appliance (0.5 psi drop)	Corrugated stainless steel tubing
15.1(o)	Between the first- and second-stage regulators	Polyethylene pipe
15.1(p)	Between the first- and second-stage regulators	Polyethylene tubing
15.1(q)	Between the second-stage regulator and building	Polyethylene tubing

For SI units, 1 psi = 6.9 kPa.

3. Select the column in the appropriate capacity table that shows the measured length or the next longer length if the table does not give the exact length. This length is the only length used in determining the size of any section of gas piping.

Example. For the piping plan provided, calculate the demand and pipe size requirements for a propane-supplied system. It is recommended that the information in the sketch be tabulated as shown in Commentary Table 15.3. Assume that Schedule 40 pipe is available and will be used.

COMMENTARY TABLE 15.3 *Pipe Size Table*

Outlet	Demand	Pipe Size
A	Water heater	—
B	Refrigerator	—
C	Range	—
D	Furnace	—
Section 1	A through D	—
Section 2	A through C	—
Section 3	A and B	—

The longest pipe length in the system is 60 ft (18 m). This length is used in all table selections. Table 15.1(c), *Pipe Sizing Between Second-Stage Regulator and Appliance: Nominal Pipe Size, Schedule 40*, is used. (See Commentary Table 15.4.)

COMMENTARY TABLE 15.4 *Pipe Sizing Between Second-Stage Regulator and Appliance: Nominal Pipe Size, Schedule 40 [Extracted from code Table 15.1(c)]*

Pipe Length, ft	½ in. 0.622	¾ in. 0.824	1 in. 1.049
50	122	255	480
60	110	231	435
80	94	198	372

For SI units, 1 ft = 0.3 m; 1 in. = 25 mm.

Solutions to the example are shown in Calculation Worksheet 15.1.

Sizing the piping from the location of the container to the inlet of the second-stage regulator is much simpler and involves only determining the length of piping and the total input of all connected appliances that can operate simultaneously. In this example, we assume that there is 75 ft (22.86 m) of piping between the outlet of the first-stage regulator and the inlet of the second-stage regulator. If polyethylene piping IPS is used, find the total Btu load [244,000 Btu/hr (71 kW)] and the length (75 ft) in Table 15.1(o), and the proper pipe size comes out to be ½ in. (13 mm), SDR 9.33.

Alternate Methods. The method described here is one way to size propane piping downstream of the second-stage regulator. This simple method does not necessarily provide the smallest pipe size possible, but it always works. Other methods are described in Annex C of NFPA 54, *National Fuel Gas Code* [1], and the *National Fuel Gas Code Handbook* [2], as well as other publications. The user is reminded that 6.9.2.2 states the following:

> **6.9.2.2** LP-Gas vapor piping systems shall be sized and installed to provide a supply of gas to meet the maximum demand of all gas utilization equipment using Table 15.1(a) through Table 15.1(q) or engineering methods.

15.1 Tables for Sizing Pipe and Tubing

When the pipe sizing method of 6.9.2.2 is used, Table 15.1(a) through Table 15.1(q), or other approved piping tables, shall be used to size piping systems. For SI units, 1 ft³ = 0.028 m³; 1 ft = 0.305 m; 1 in. water column = 2.49 kPa; 1 psi = 6.894 kPa; and 1000 Btu/hr = 0.203 kW.

CALCULATION WORKSHEET: PIPE SIZING, LONGEST LENGTH METHOD

Step 1:
- Draw a sketch of a piping system in the space to the right. Use the back of this page or a separate sheet if more space is needed.

Step 2:
- Enter the system information. Note that demand is the amount of gas flowing through a section of pipe.
- Use total Btu/hr rating/1000 (ft³/hr) for natural gas.
- Use total Btu/hr for propane.

Step 3:
- Determine the gas used and system pressure, and enter it to the right.
- Determine the piping material and enter it to the right.
- Select the appropriate pipe sizing table from Chapter 6 and enter it to the right.

Step 4:
- On the sketch, label the section of pipe from the point of delivery (meter or regulator) to the first tee as Section 1.
- Label the section from the first tee to the second tee as Section 3. Use similar section numbers for additional sections.

Step 5:
- Determine the longest length of piping from the point of delivery to the most remote appliance. Enter this length for all pipe sections in Table 1.

Step 6:
- Enter the input rating for each appliance in Table 2. For natural gas appliances, enter the input rating in Btu/hr/1000 (ft³/hr). For propane appliances, enter the input rating in Btu/hr.

Step 7:
- From the table, determine the length of each pipe section using the appropriate table, using only the row with the longest length. Round up to the lengths in the table. Read across until a capacity equal to or greater than the required demand for the section is found. Read up to find the size. Repeat for each section of piping. Enter this size in Table 2.

Outlet D — Furnace 136,000 Btu/hr

20 ft   Outlet A — 30-gal automatic water heater 30,000 Btu/hr

Section 1   Section 2   Section 3   10 ft
---→   20 ft   10 ft   10 ft

10 ft   5 ft
Outlet B — Gas refrigerator 3000 Btu/hr
15 ft

Point of delivery

Outlet C — Range 75,000 Btu/hr

For SI units: 1 ft = 0.305 m; 1 gal = 3.785 L; 1000 Btu/hr = 0.293 kW

Pipe system sketch

Gas: _Propane_

System pressure: _11″ w.c._

Piping material: _Sch. 40 steel_

Table used: _15.1 (C)_

Pressure drop: _0.5″_

Table 1 Piping System Table

Section	Demand	Section length	Size
1	244	30 ft	1″
2	108	10 ft	½″
3	33	10 ft	½″
4			
5			

Table 2 Appliances Table

Appliance	Demand	Section length	Size
Furnace	136,000	20 ft	½″
Furnace			
Water heater	30,000	10 ft	½″
Water heater			
Range	75,000	15 ft	½″
Oven			
Dryer			
Other (Ref)	3,000	5 ft	½″
Other			
Other			
Other			
Total			

Job: _25 Elm St._   **Prepared by:** _TL_   **Date:** _9/15/10_

Calculation Worksheet 15.1 *Calculating Pipe Size Using the Longest Length Method.*

TABLE 15.1(a) *Pipe Sizing Between First-Stage and Second-Stage Regulators: Nominal Pipe Size, Schedule 40*

							Gas:	Undiluted Propane
							Inlet Pressure:	10.0 psi
							Pressure Drop:	1.0 psi
							Specific Gravity:	1.52

Pipe Length (ft)	½ in. 0.622	¾ in. 0.824	1 in. 1.049	1¼ in. 1.38	1½ in. 1.61	2 in. 2.067	3 in. 3.068	3½ in. 3.548	4 in. 4.026
30	1843	3854	7259	14904	22331	43008	121180	177425	247168
40	1577	3298	6213	12756	19113	36809	103714	151853	211544
50	1398	2923	5507	11306	16939	32623	91920	134585	187487
60	1267	2649	4989	10244	15348	29559	83286	121943	169877
70	1165	2437	4590	9424	14120	27194	76622	112186	156285
80	1084	2267	4270	8767	13136	25299	71282	104368	145393
90	1017	2127	4007	8226	12325	23737	66882	97925	136417
100	961	2009	3785	7770	11642	22422	63176	92499	128859
150	772	1613	3039	6240	9349	18005	50733	74280	103478
200	660	1381	2601	5340	8002	15410	43421	63574	88564
250	585	1224	2305	4733	7092	13658	38483	56345	78493
300	530	1109	2089	4289	6426	12375	34868	51052	71120
350	488	1020	1922	3945	5911	11385	32078	46967	65430
400	454	949	1788	3670	5499	10591	29843	43694	60870
450	426	890	1677	3444	5160	9938	28000	40997	57112
500	402	841	1584	3253	4874	9387	26449	38725	53948
600	364	762	1436	2948	4416	8505	23965	35088	48880
700	335	701	1321	2712	4063	7825	22047	32280	44969
800	312	652	1229	2523	3780	7279	20511	30031	41835
900	293	612	1153	2367	3546	6830	19245	28177	39253
1000	276	578	1089	2236	3350	6452	18178	26616	37078
1500	222	464	875	1795	2690	5181	14598	21373	29775
2000	190	397	748	1537	2302	4434	12494	18293	25483

Note: Capacities are in 1000 Btu/hr.

TABLE 15.1(b) *Pipe Sizing Between 2 psi Service Regulator and Line Pressure Regulator:
Nominal Pipe Size, Schedule 40*

								Gas:	**Undiluted Propane**
								Inlet Pressure:	**10.0 psi**
								Pressure Drop:	**1.0 psi**
								Specific Gravity:	**1.52**

Pipe Length (ft)	½ in. 0.622	¾ in. 0.824	1 in. 1.049	1¼ in. 1.380	1½ in. 1.610	2 in. 2.067	3 in. 3.068	3½ in. 3.548	4 in. 4.026
10	2687	5619	10585	21731	32560	62708	176687	258696	360385
20	1847	3862	7275	14936	22378	43099	121436	177800	247690
30	1483	3101	5842	11994	17971	34610	97517	142780	198904
40	1269	2654	5000	10265	15381	29621	83462	122201	170236
50	1125	2352	4431	9098	13632	26253	73971	108305	150877
60	1019	2131	4015	8243	12351	23787	67023	98132	136706
70	938	1961	3694	7584	11363	21884	61660	90280	125767
80	872	1824	3436	7055	10571	20359	57363	83988	117002
90	819	1712	3224	6620	9918	19102	53822	78803	109779
100	773	1617	3046	6253	9369	18043	50840	74437	103697
150	621	1298	2446	5021	7524	14490	40826	59776	83272
200	531	1111	2093	4298	6439	12401	34942	51160	71270
250	471	985	1855	3809	5707	10991	30968	45342	63166
300	427	892	1681	3451	5171	9959	28060	41083	57233
350	393	821	1546	3175	4757	9162	25814	37796	52653
400	365	764	1439	2954	4426	8523	24015	35162	48984
450	343	717	1350	2771	4152	7997	22533	32991	45960
500	324	677	1275	2618	3922	7554	21284	31164	43413
600	293	613	1155	2372	3554	6844	19285	28236	39336
700	270	564	1063	2182	3270	6297	17742	25977	36188
800	251	525	989	2030	3042	5858	16506	24167	33666
900	236	493	928	1905	2854	5496	15487	22675	31588
1000	222	465	876	1799	2696	5192	14629	21419	29838
1500	179	374	704	1445	2165	4169	11747	17200	23961
2000	153	320	602	1237	1853	3568	10054	14721	20507

Note: Capacities are in 1000 Btu/hr.

TABLE 15.1(c) *Pipe Sizing Between Second-Stage Regulator and Appliance: Nominal Pipe Size, Schedule 40*

							Gas:	Undiluted Propane
							Inlet Pressure:	10.0 psi
							Pressure Drop:	1.0 psi
							Specific Gravity:	1.52

Pipe Length (ft)	½ in. 0.622	¾ in. 0.824	1 in. 1.049	1¼ in. 1.38	1½ in. 1.61	2 in. 2.067	3 in. 3.068	3½ in. 3.548	4 in. 4.026
10	291	608	1146	2353	3525	6789	19130	28008	39018
20	200	418	788	1617	2423	4666	13148	19250	26817
30	161	336	632	1299	1946	3747	10558	15458	21535
40	137	287	541	1111	1665	3207	9036	13230	18431
50	122	255	480	985	1476	2842	8009	11726	16335
60	110	231	435	892	1337	2575	7256	10625	14801
80	94	198	372	764	1144	2204	6211	9093	12668
100	84	175	330	677	1014	1954	5504	8059	11227
125	74	155	292	600	899	1731	4878	7143	9950
150	67	141	265	544	815	1569	4420	6472	9016
200	58	120	227	465	697	1343	3783	5539	7716
250	51	107	201	412	618	1190	3353	4909	6839
300	46	97	182	374	560	1078	3038	4448	6196
350	43	89	167	344	515	992	2795	4092	5701
400	40	83	156	320	479	923	2600	3807	5303

Note: Capacities are in 1000 Btu/hr.

TABLE 15.1(d) *Pipe Sizing Between First-Stage and Second-Stage Regulators: Nominal Pipe Size, Schedule 80*

						Gas:	**Undiluted Propane**
						Inlet Pressure:	10.0 psi
						Pressure Drop:	1.0 psi
						Specific Gravity:	1.52

Pipe Length (ft)	½ in. 0.546	¾ in. 0.742	1 in. 0.957	1¼ in. 1.278	1½ in. 1.5	2 in. 1.939	3 in. 2.9	3½ in. 3.364	4 in. 3.826
30	1309	2927	5706	12185	18548	36368	104539	154295	216246
40	1121	2505	4884	10429	15875	31127	89472	132057	185079
50	993	2221	4328	9243	14069	27587	79297	117039	164032
60	900	2012	3922	8375	12748	24996	71849	106046	148625
70	828	1851	3608	7705	11728	22996	66100	97561	136733
80	770	1722	3357	7168	10911	21393	61494	90762	127204
90	723	1616	3149	6725	10237	20073	57697	85159	119351
100	683	1526	2975	6353	9670	18960	54501	80440	112738
150	548	1226	2389	5105	7765	15236	43766	64596	90533
200	469	1049	2045	4366	6646	13031	37458	55286	77484
250	416	930	1812	3870	5890	11549	33198	48999	68673
300	377	842	1642	3506	5337	10465	30080	44397	62223
350	347	775	1511	3226	4910	9627	27673	40844	57244
400	322	721	1405	3001	4568	8956	25745	37998	53255
450	303	676	1318	2816	4286	8403	24155	35652	49967
500	286	639	1245	2660	4048	7938	22817	33677	47199
600	259	579	1128	2410	3668	7192	20674	30514	42765
700	238	533	1038	2217	3375	6617	19020	28072	39344
800	222	495	966	2062	3139	6156	17694	26116	36602
900	208	465	906	1935	2946	5776	16602	24504	34342
1000	196	439	856	1828	2782	5456	15682	23146	32439
1500	158	353	687	1468	2234	4381	12593	18587	26050
2000	135	302	588	1256	1912	3750	10778	15908	22295

Notes:

(1) Capacities are in 1000 Btu/hr.

(2) To convert to capacities at a gauge pressure of 5 psi setting with 10 percent (0.5 psig) pressure drop, multiply values by 0.606. To convert to capacities at a gauge pressure of 15 psi with 10 percent (1.5 psig) pressure drop, multiply values by 1.380.

TABLE 15.1(e) *Pipe Sizing Between Second-Stage Regulator and Appliance: Nominal Pipe Size, Schedule 80*

							Gas:	**Undiluted Propane**
							Inlet Pressure:	**10.0 psi**
							Pressure Drop:	**1.0 psi**
							Specific Gravity:	**1.52**

Pipe Length (ft)	½ in. 0.546	¾ in. 0.742	1 in. 0.957	1¼ in. 1.278	1½ in. 1.5	2 in. 1.939	3 in. 2.9	3½ in. 3.364	4 in. 3.826
10	207	462	901	1924	2928	5741	16503	24357	34137
20	142	318	619	1322	2012	3946	11342	16740	23462
30	114	255	497	1062	1616	3169	9108	13443	18841
40	98	218	426	909	1383	2712	7795	11506	16125
50	87	193	377	805	1226	2404	6909	10197	14292
60	78	175	342	730	1111	2178	6260	9239	12949
80	67	150	292	625	951	1864	5358	7908	11083
100	59	133	259	553	842	1652	4748	7009	9823
125	53	118	230	491	747	1464	4208	6212	8706
150	48	107	208	444	677	1327	3813	5628	7888
200	41	91	178	380	579	1135	3264	4817	6751
250	36	81	158	337	513	1006	2892	4269	5983
300	33	73	143	305	465	912	2621	3868	5421
350	30	68	132	281	428	839	2411	3559	4987
400	28	63	122	261	398	780	2243	3311	4640

Note: Capacities are in 1000 Btu/hr.

TABLE 15.1(f) *Pipe Sizing Between First-Stage and Second-Stage Regulators: Outside Diameter Copper Tubing, Type K*

	Gas:	Undiluted Propane
	Inlet Pressure:	10.0 psi
	Pressure Drop:	1.0 psi
	Specific Gravity:	1.52

Tubing Length (ft)	⅜ in. 0.305	½ in. 0.402	⅝ in. 0.527	¾ in. 0.652	⅞ in. 0.745
30	284	587	1193	2085	2959
40	243	502	1021	1785	2532
50	216	445	905	1582	2244
60	195	403	820	1433	2033
70	180	371	754	1319	1871
80	167	345	702	1227	1740
90	157	374	659	1151	1633
100	148	306	622	1087	1542
150	119	246	500	873	1239
200	102	210	428	747	1060
250	90	186	379	662	940
300	82	169	343	600	851
350	75	155	316	552	783
400	70	144	294	514	729
450	66	136	276	482	654
500	62	128	260	455	646
600	56	116	236	412	585
700	52	107	217	379	538
800	48	99	202	353	501
900	45	93	189	331	470
1000	43	88	179	313	444
1500	34	71	144	251	356
2000	29	60	123	215	305

Notes:

(1) Capacities are in 1000 Btu/hr.

(2) To convert to capacities at a gauge pressure of 5 psi setting with 10 percent (0.5 psi) pressure drop, multiply values by 0.606. To convert to capacities at a gauge pressure of 15 psi setting with 10 percent (1.5 psi) pressure drop, multiply values by 1.380.

TABLE 15.1(g) *Copper Tube Sizing Between Second-Stage Regulator and Appliance: Outside Diameter Copper Tubing, Type K*

	Gas:	Undiluted Propane
	Inlet Pressure:	10.0 psi
	Pressure Drop:	1.0 psi
	Specific Gravity:	1.52

Tubing Length (ft)	⅜ in. 0.305	½ in. 0.402	⅝ in. 0.527	¾ in. 0.652	⅞ in. 0.745
10	45	93	188	329	467
20	31	64	129	226	321
30	25	51	104	182	258
40	21	44	89	156	221
50	19	39	79	138	196
60	17	35	71	125	177
80	15	30	61	107	152
100	13	27	54	95	134
125	11	24	48	84	119
150	10	21	44	76	108
200	9	18	37	65	92
250	8	16	33	58	82
300	7	15	30	52	74
350	7	14	28	48	68
400	6	13	26	45	63

Note: Capacities are in 1000 Btu/hr.

TABLE 15.1(h) *Copper Tube Sizing Between First-Stage and Second-Stage Regulators*

					Gas:	**Undiluted Propane**
					Inlet Pressure:	10.0 psi
					Pressure Drop:	1.0 psi
					Specific Gravity:	1.52

Tubing Length (ft)	Outside Diameter Copper Tubing, Type L					Tubing Length (ft)	Outside Diameter Copper Tubing, Type L				
	⅜ in. 0.315	½ in. 0.430	⅝ in. 0.545	¾ in. 0.666	⅞ in. 0.785		⅜ in. 0.315	½ in. 0.430	⅝ in. 0.545	¾ in. 0.666	⅞ in. 0.785
30	309	700	1303	2205	3394	350	82	185	345	584	898
40	265	599	1115	1887	2904	400	76	172	321	543	836
50	235	531	988	1672	2574	450	71	162	301	509	784
60	213	481	896	1515	2332	500	68	153	284	481	741
70	196	443	824	1394	2146	600	61	138	258	436	671
80	182	412	767	1297	1996	700	56	127	237	401	617
90	171	386	719	1217	1873	800	52	118	221	373	574
100	161	365	679	1149	1769	900	49	111	207	350	539
150	130	293	546	923	1421	1000	46	105	195	331	509
200	111	251	467	790	1216	1500	37	84	157	266	409
250	90	222	414	700	1078	2000	32	72	134	227	350
300	89	201	375	634	976						

Note: Capacities are in 1000 Btu/hr.

TABLE 15.1(i) *Copper Tube Sizing Between 2 psi Service Regulator and Line Pressure Regulator: Outside Diameter Copper Tubing, Type L*

		Gas:	**Undiluted Propane**		
		Inlet Pressure:	**10.0 psi**		
		Pressure Drop:	**1.0 psi**		
		Specific Gravity:	**1.52**		

Tubing Length (ft)	⅜ in. 0.315	½ in. 0.430	⅝ in. 0.545	¾ in. 0.666	⅞ in. 0.785
10	451	1020	1900	3215	4948
20	310	701	1306	2210	3401
30	249	563	1049	1774	2731
40	213	482	898	1519	2337
50	189	427	795	1346	2071
60	171	387	721	1219	1877
70	157	356	663	1122	1727
80	146	331	617	1044	1606
90	137	311	579	979	1507
100	130	294	547	925	1424
150	104	236	439	743	1143
200	89	202	376	636	979
250	79	179	333	563	867
300	72	162	302	511	786
350	66	149	278	470	723
400	61	139	258	437	673
450	58	130	242	410	631
500	54	123	229	387	596
600	49	111	207	351	540
700	45	102	191	323	497
800	42	95	177	300	462
900	40	89	167	282	434
1000	37	84	157	266	410
1500	30	68	126	214	329
2000	26	58	108	183	282

TABLE 15.1(j) *Copper Tube Sizing Between Single-Stage or Second-Stage Regulator and Appliance: Outside Diameter Copper Tubing, Type L*

		Gas:	**Undiluted Propane**		
		Inlet Pressure:	**10.0 psi**		
		Pressure Drop:	**1.0 psi**		
		Specific Gravity:	**1.52**		

Tubing Length (ft)	⅜ in. 0.315	½ in. 0.430	⅝ in. 0.545	¾ in. 0.666	⅞ in. 0.785
10	49	110	206	348	536
20	34	76	141	239	368
30	27	61	114	192	296
40	23	52	97	164	253
50	20	46	86	146	224
60	19	42	78	132	203
80	16	36	67	113	174
100	14	32	59	100	154
125	12	28	52	89	137
150	11	26	48	80	124
200	10	22	41	69	106
250	9	19	36	61	94
300	8	18	33	55	85
350	7	16	30	51	78
400	7	15	28	47	73

Note: Capacities are in 1000 Btu/hr.

TABLE 15.1(k) Pipe Sizing Between First-Stage and Second-Stage Regulators: Outside Diameter Refrigeration Tubing

		Gas:	Undiluted Propane
		Inlet Pressure:	10.0 psi
		Pressure Drop:	1.0 psi
		Specific Gravity:	1.52

Tubing Length (ft)	³/₈ in. 0.311	¹/₂ in. 0.436	⁵/₈ in. 0.555	³/₄ in. 0.68	⁷/₈ in. 0.785
30	299	726	1367	2329	3394
40	256	621	1170	1993	2904
50	227	551	1037	1766	2574
60	206	499	939	1600	2332
70	189	459	864	1472	2146
80	176	427	804	1370	1996
90	165	401	754	1285	1873
100	156	378	713	1214	1769
150	125	304	572	975	1421
200	107	260	490	834	1216
250	95	230	434	739	1078
300	86	209	393	670	976
350	79	192	362	616	898
400	74	179	337	573	836
450	69	168	316	538	784
500	65	158	298	508	741
600	59	144	270	460	671
700	54	132	249	424	617
800	51	123	231	394	574
900	48	115	217	370	539
1000	45	109	205	349	509
1500	36	87	165	281	409
2000	31	75	141	240	350

Notes:
(1) Capacities are in 1000 Btu/hr.
(2) To convert to capacities at a gauge pressure of 5 psi setting with 10 percent (0.5 psi) pressure drop, multiply values by 0.606. To convert to capacities at a gauge pressure of 15 psi setting with 10 percent (1.5 psi) pressure drop, multiply values by 1.380.

TABLE 15.1(l) Copper Tube Sizing Between Second-Stage Regulator and Appliance: Outside Diameter of Copper Refrigeration Tubing

		Gas:	Undiluted Propane
		Inlet Pressure:	10.0 psi
		Pressure Drop:	1.0 psi
		Specific Gravity:	1.52

Tubing Length (ft)	³/₈ in. 0.311	¹/₂ in. 0.436	⁵/₈ in. 0.555	³/₄ in. 0.68	⁷/₈ in. 0.785
10	47	115	216	368	536
20	32	79	148	253	368
30	26	63	119	203	296
40	22	54	102	174	253
50	20	48	90	154	224
60	18	43	82	139	203
80	15	37	70	119	174
100	14	33	62	106	154
125	12	29	55	94	137
150	11	26	50	85	124
200	9	23	43	73	106
250	8	20	38	64	94
300	8	18	34	58	85
350	7	17	32	54	78
400	6	16	29	50	73

Note: Capacities are in 1000 Btu/hr.

TABLE 15.1(m) *Maximum Capacity of CSST in Thousands of Btu per Hour of Undiluted Propane at a Gauge Pressure of 2 psig and a Pressure Drop of 1 psi (Based on 1.52 Specific Gravity Gas)*

	Gas:	Undiluted Propane
	Inlet Pressure:	10.0 psi
	Pressure Drop:	1.0 psi
	Specific Gravity:	1.52

EHD* Flow Designation	Tubing Length (ft)													
	10	25	30	40	50	75	80	110	150	200	250	300	400	500
13	426	262	238	203	181	147	140	124	101	86	77	69	60	53
15	558	347	316	271	243	196	189	169	137	118	105	96	82	72
18	927	591	540	469	420	344	333	298	245	213	191	173	151	135
19	1106	701	640	554	496	406	393	350	287	248	222	203	175	158
23	1735	1120	1027	896	806	663	643	578	477	415	373	343	298	268
25	2168	1384	1266	1100	986	809	768	703	575	501	448	411	355	319
30	4097	2560	2331	2012	1794	1457	1410	1256	1021	880	785	716	616	550
31	4720	2954	2692	2323	2072	1685	1629	1454	1182	1019	910	829	716	638

Notes:

(1) Table does not include effect of pressure drop across the line regulator. If regulator loss exceeds ½ psi (based on 13 in. w.c. outlet pressure), DO NOT USE THIS TABLE. Consult with regulator manufacturer for pressure drops and capacity factors. Pressure drops across a regulator can vary with flow rate.

(2) CAUTION: Capacities shown in table can exceed maximum capacity for a selected regulator. Consult with regulator or tubing manufacturer for guidance.

(3) Table includes losses for four 90-degree bends and two end fittings. Tubing runs with a larger number of bends or fittings are required to be increased by an equivalent length of tubing according to the following equation:

$$L = 1.3n$$

where:
L = additional length of tubing (ft)
n = number of additional fittings or bends

* EHD — equivalent hydraulic diameter — a measure of the relative hydraulic efficiency between different tubing sizes. The greater the value of EHD, the greater the gas capacity of the tubing.

TABLE 15.1(n) *Maximum Capacity of CSST in Thousands of Btu per Hour of Undiluted Propane at a Pressure of 11 in. Water Column and a Pressure Drop of 0.5 in. Water Column (Based on 1.52 Specific Gravity Gas)*

																		Gas:	**Undiluted Propane**

																	Inlet Pressure:	**10.0 psi**

																	Pressure Drop:	**1.0 psi**

																	Specific Gravity:	**1.52**

EHD* Flow Designation	Tubing Length (ft)																
	5	**10**	**15**	**20**	**25**	**30**	**40**	**50**	**60**	**70**	**80**	**90**	**100**	**150**	**200**	**250**	**300**
13	72	50	39	34	30	28	23	20	19	17	15	15	14	11	9	8	8
15	99	69	55	49	42	39	33	30	26	25	23	22	20	15	14	12	11
18	181	129	104	91	82	74	64	58	53	49	45	44	41	31	28	25	23
19	211	150	121	106	94	87	74	66	60	57	52	50	47	36	33	30	26
23	355	254	208	183	164	151	131	118	107	99	94	90	85	66	60	53	50
25	426	303	248	216	192	177	153	137	126	117	109	102	98	75	69	61	57
30	744	521	422	365	325	297	256	227	207	191	178	169	159	123	112	99	90
31	863	605	490	425	379	344	297	265	241	222	208	197	186	143	129	117	107

CSST: Corrugated stainless steel tubing.

Note: Table includes losses for four 90-degree bends and two end fittings. Tubing runs with a larger number of bends or fittings are required to be increased by an equivalent length of tubing according to the following equation:

$$L = 1.3n$$

where:
L = additional length of tubing (ft)
n = number of additional fittings or bends

* EHD — equivalent hydraulic diameter — a measure of the relative hydraulic efficiency between different tubing sizes. The greater the value of EHD, the greater the gas capacity of the tubing.

TABLE 15.1(o) *Polyethylene Plastic Pipe Sizing Between First-Stage and Second-Stage Regulators: Nominal Outside Diameter (IPS)*

				Gas:	**Undiluted Propane**
				Inlet Pressure:	**10.0 psi**
				Pressure Drop:	**1.0 psi**
				Specific Gravity:	**1.52**

Plastic Pipe Length (ft)	½ in. SDR 9.33 (0.660)	¾ in. SDR 11.0 (0.860)	1 in. SDR 11.00 (1.077)	1¼ in. SDR 10.00 (1.328)	1½ in. SDR 11.00 (1.554)	2 in. SDR 11.00 (1.943)
30	2143	4292	7744	13416	20260	36402
40	1835	3673	6628	11482	17340	31155
50	1626	3256	5874	10176	15368	27612
60	1473	2950	5322	9220	13924	25019
70	1355	2714	4896	8483	12810	23017
80	1261	2525	4555	7891	11918	21413
90	1183	2369	4274	7404	11182	20091
100	1117	2238	4037	6994	10562	18978
125	990	1983	3578	6199	9361	16820
150	897	1797	3242	5616	8482	15240
175	826	1653	2983	5167	7803	14020
200	778	1539	2775	4807	7259	13043
225	721	1443	2603	4510	6811	12238
250	681	1363	2459	4260	6434	11560
275	646	1294	2336	4046	6111	10979
300	617	1235	2228	3860	5830	10474
350	567	1136	2050	3551	5363	9636
400	528	1057	1907	3304	4989	8965
450	495	992	1789	3100	4681	8411
500	468	937	1690	2928	4422	7945
600	424	849	1531	2653	4007	7199
700	390	781	1409	2441	3686	6623
800	363	726	1311	2271	3429	6161
900	340	682	1230	2131	3217	5781
1000	322	644	1162	2012	3039	5461
1500	258	517	933	1616	2441	4385
2000	221	443	798	1383	2089	3753

IPS: Iron pipe size.

SDR: Standard dimension ratio.

Notes:

(1) Capacities are in 1000 Btu/hr.

(2) Dimensions in parentheses are inside diameter.

TABLE 15.1(p) *Polyethylene Plastic Tube Sizing Between First-Stage and Second-Stage Regulators: Nominal Outside Diameter (CTS)*

	Gas:	Undiluted Propane
	Inlet Pressure:	10.0 psi
	Pressure Drop:	1.0 psi
	Specific Gravity:	1.52

Plastic Tubing Length (ft)	½ in. SDR 7.00 (0.445)	1 in. SDR 11.00 (0.927)
30	762	5225
40	653	4472
50	578	3964
60	524	3591
70	482	3304
80	448	3074
90	421	2884
100	397	2724
125	352	2414
150	319	2188
175	294	2013
200	273	1872
225	256	1757
250	242	1659
275	230	1576
300	219	1503
350	202	1383
400	188	1287
450	176	1207
500	166	1140
600	151	1033
700	139	951
800	129	884
900	121	830
1000	114	784
1500	92	629
2000	79	539

CTS: Copper tube size.

SDR: Standard dimension rating.

Notes:

(1) Capacities are in 1000 Btu/hr.

(2) Dimensions in parentheses are inside diameter.

TABLE 15.1(q) *Polyethylene Plastic Tube Sizing Between Second-Stage Regulator and Building: Nominal Outside Diameter (CTS)*

	Gas:	Undiluted Propane
	Inlet Pressure:	10.0 psi
	Pressure Drop:	1.0 psi
	Specific Gravity:	1.52

Plastic Tubing Length (ft)	½ in. SDR 7.00 (0.445)	1 in. SDR 11.00 (0.927)
10	121	829
20	83	569
30	67	457
40	57	391
50	51	347
60	46	314
70	42	289
80	39	269
90	37	252
100	35	238
125	31	211
150	28	191
175	26	176
200	24	164
225	22	154
250	21	145
275	20	138
300	19	132
350	18	121
400	16	113

CTS: Copper tube size.

SDR: Standard dimension rating.

Notes:

(1) Capacities are in 1000 Btu/hr.

(2) Dimensions in parentheses are inside diameter.

REFERENCES CITED IN COMMENTARY

1. NFPA 54, *National Fuel Gas Code*, 2009 edition, National Fire Protection Association, Quincy, MA.
2. *National Fuel Gas Code Handbook*, 2009 edition, National Fire Protection Association, Quincy, MA.

Explanatory Material

Annex A is not a part of the requirements of this NFPA document but is included for informational purposes only. This annex contains explanatory material, numbered to correspond with the applicable text paragraphs.

The material contained in Annex A of the 2011 edition of NFPA 58 is interspersed among the text of Chapters 1 through 15 of this handbook and, therefore, is not repeated here.

Properties of LP-Gases

This annex is not a part of the requirements of this NFPA document but is included for informational purposes only.

Annex B provides information on the physical properties of LP-Gas. This material is included for the benefit of users of the code who may require information on the physical properties of butane and propane. Additional information not in the code is provided in graphical form.

Exhibit B.1, the pressure-temperature chart for propane-air mixtures, is used to determine the dew point of mixtures. This exhibit is needed to determine the minimum temperature

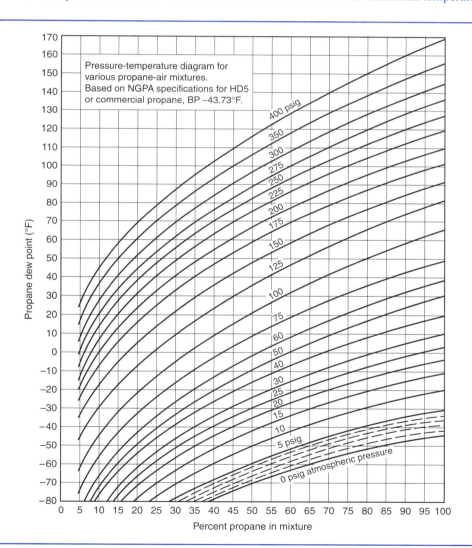

Pressure-temperature diagram for various propane-air mixtures. Based on NGPA specifications for HD5 or commercial propane, BP −43.73°F.

EXHIBIT B.1 *Pressure-Temperature Chart for Propane-Air Mixtures. (Courtesy of BP News)*

to which piping containing propane-air mixtures can be exposed without condensing liquid propane.

Exhibit B.2, the dew points of LP-Gas-air mixtures, provides three graphs. The first graph duplicates the information presented in Exhibit B.1, while the others provide corresponding information for N-butane and isobutane.

Exhibit B.3, the pressure-density chart for propane, provides the properties of propane under all pressure and temperature conditions.

Exhibit B.4, the temperature-density chart for propane, is similar to Exhibit B.3 but presents the same information plotted with different variables on each axis.

B.1 Approximate Properties of LP-Gases

B.1.1 Source of Property Values.

B.1.1.1 The property values for the LP-Gases are based on average industry values and include values for LP-Gases coming from natural gas liquid plants as well as petroleum refineries. Thus, any particular commercial propane or butane might have properties varying slightly from the values shown. Similarly, any propane–butane mixture might have properties varying from those obtained by computation from these average values *(see B.1.2 for computation method used)*. Because these are average values, the interrelationships between them (e.g., pounds per gallon, specific gravity) will not cross-check perfectly in all cases.

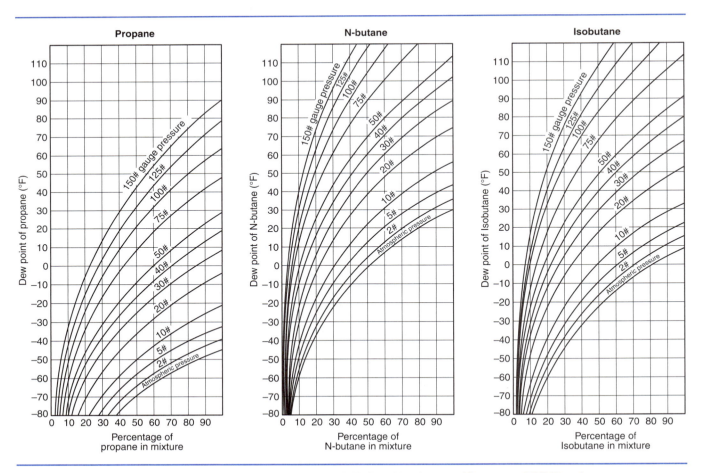

EXHIBIT B.2 *Dew Points of LP-Gas-Air Mixtures. (Courtesy of BP News)*

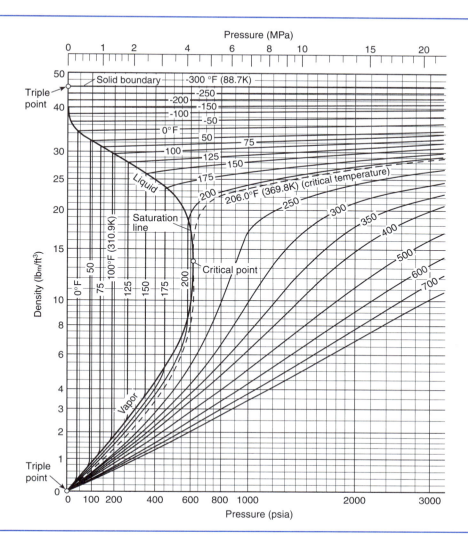

EXHIBIT B.3 *Pressure-Density Chart for Propane. (Courtesy of BP News)*

B.1.1.2 The variations specified in B.1.1.1 are not sufficient to prevent the use of average values for most engineering and design purposes. They stem from minor variations in composition. The commercial grades are not chemically pure (CP) propane or butane, or mixtures of the two, but they might also contain small and varying percentages of ethane, ethylene, propylene, isobutane, or butylene, which can cause slight variations in property values. There are limits to the accuracy of even the most advanced testing methods used to determine the percentages of these minor components in any LP-Gas.

B.1.2 Approximate Properties of Commercial LP-Gases.

The principal properties of commercial propane and commercial butane are shown in Table B.1.2(a) and Table B.1.2(b). Reasonably accurate property values for propane–butane mixtures can be obtained by computation, applying the percentages by weight of each in the mixture to the values for the property desired to be obtained. Slightly more accurate results for vapor pressure are obtained by using the percentages by volume. Very accurate results can be obtained using data and methods explained in petroleum and chemical engineering data books.

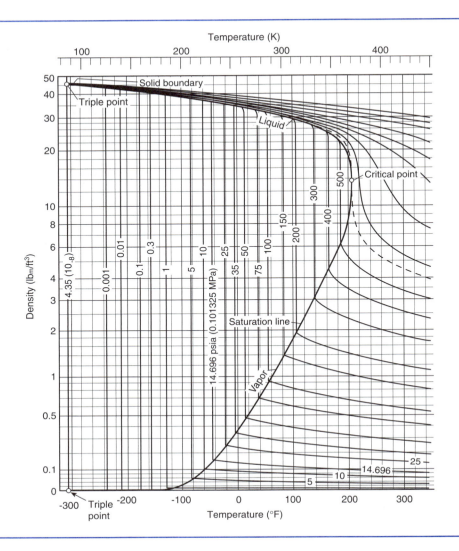

TABLE B.1.2(a) *Approximate Properties of LP-Gases (English)*

Property	Commercial Propane	Commercial Butane
Vapor pressure in psi (absolute pressure) at:		
70°F	145	32
100°F	218	52
105°F	233	56
130°F	315	84
Specific gravity of liquid at 60°F	0.504	0.582
Initial boiling point at 14.7 psia, °F	−44	15
Weight per gallon of liquid at 60°F, lb	4.20	4.81
Specific heat of liquid, Btu/lb at 60°F	0.630	0.549
Cubic feet of vapor per gallon at 60°F	36.38	31.26
Cubic feet of vapor per pound at 60°F	8.66	6.51
Specific gravity of vapor (air = 1) at 60°F	1.50	2.01

TABLE B.1.2(a) *Continued*

Property	Commercial Propane	Commercial Butane
Ignition temperature in air, °F	920−1,120	900−1,000
Maximum flame temperature in air, °F	3,595	3,615
Limits of flammability in air, percent of vapor in air–gas mixture:		
Lower	2.15	1.55
Upper	9.60	8.60
Latent heat of vaporization at boiling point:		
Btu per pound	184	167
Btu per gallon	773	808
Total heating values after vaporization:		
Btu per cubic foot	2,488	3,280
Btu per pound	21,548	21,221
Btu per gallon	91,502	102,032

TABLE B.1.2(b) *Approximate Properties of LP-Gases (Metric)*

Property	Commercial Propane	Commercial Butane
Vapor pressure in kPa (absolute pressure) at:		
20°C	1,000	220
40°C	1,570	360
45°C	1,760	385
55°C	2,170	580
Specific gravity of liquid at 15.56°C	0.504	0.582
Initial boiling point at 1.00 atm pressure, °C	−42	−9
Weight per cubic meter of liquid at 15.56°C, kg	504	582
Specific heat of liquid at 15.56°C, kJ/kg	1.464	1.276
Cubic meter of vapor per liter of liquid at 15.56°C	0.271	0.235
Cubic meter of vapor per kilogram of liquid at 15.56°C	0.539	0.410
Specific gravity of vapor (air = 1) at 15.56°C	1.50	2.01
Ignition temperature in air, °C	493−549	482−538
Maximum flame temperature in air, °C	1,980	2,008
Limits of flammability in air, percent of vapor in air–gas mixture:		
Lower	2.15	1.55
Upper	9.60	8.60
Latent heat of vaporization at boiling point:		
Kilojoules per kilogram	428	388
Kilojoules per liter	216	226
Total heating value after vaporization:		
Kilojoules per cubic meter	92,430	121,280
Kilojoules per kilogram	49,920	49,140
Kilojoules per liter	25,140	28,100

B.1.3 Specifications of LP-Gases.

Specifications of LP-Gases covered by this code are listed in GPA Standard 2140, *Liquefied Petroleum Gas Specifications for Test Methods*, or ASTM D 1835, *Standard Specification for Liquefied Petroleum (LP) Gases*.

This annex is not a part of the requirements of this NFPA document but is included for informational purposes only.

C.1 Scope

C.1.1 Application.

C.1.1.1 This annex provides general information on cylinders referred to in this code. For complete information, consult the applicable specification *(see C.2.1)*. The water capacity of such cylinders is not permitted to be more than 1000 lb (454 kg).

C.1.1.2 This annex is not applicable to Department of Transportation (DOT) specifications for tank cars, portable tank containers, or cargo tanks. Portable and cargo tanks are basically ASME containers and are covered in Annex D.

C.1.1.3 Prior to April 1, 1967, these specifications were promulgated by the Interstate Commerce Commission (ICC). On this date, certain functions of the ICC, including the promulgation of specifications and regulations dealing with LP-Gas cylinders, were transferred to DOT. Throughout this annex, both ICC and DOT are used, ICC applying to dates prior to April 1, 1967, and DOT to subsequent dates.

C.2 LP-Gas Cylinder Specifications

C.2.1 Publishing of DOT Cylinder Specifications.

DOT cylinder specifications are published in 49 CFR 178, "Specifications for Packaging," available from the U.S. Government Printing Office, Washington, DC. The information in this publication is also issued as Tarrif No. BOE-6000 by the Bureau of Explosives, American Railroads Building, 1920 L Street, N.W., Washington, DC 20036.

C.2.2 DOT Specification Nomenclature.

C.2.2.1 The specification designation consists of a one-digit number, sometimes followed by one or more capital letters, then by a dash and a three-digit number. The one-digit number alone, or in combination with one or more capital letters, designates the specification number. The three-digit number following the dash shows the service pressure for which the cylinder is designed. Thus, "4B–240" indicates a cylinder built to Specification 4B for a 240 psig (1650 kPag) service pressure. *(See C.2.2.3.)*

C.2.2.2 The specification gives the details of cylinder construction, such as material used, method of fabrication, tests required, and inspection method, and prescribes the service pressure or range of service pressures for which that specification can be used.

C.2.2.3 The term *service pressure* is analogous to, and serves the same purpose as, the ASME design pressure. However, it is not identical, representing instead the highest pressure to which the cylinder will normally be subjected in transit or in use, but not necessarily the maximum pressure to which it might be subjected under emergency conditions in transportation. The service pressure stipulated for the LP-Gases is based on the vapor pressures exerted by the product in the cylinder at two different temperatures, the higher pressure of the two becoming the service pressure, as follows:

(1) The pressure in the cylinder at 70°F (21°C) must be less than the service pressure for which the cylinder is marked.

(2) The pressure in the container at 130°F (54.4°C) must not exceed ¾ times the pressure for which the cylinder is marked.

Example: Commercial propane has a vapor pressure at 70°F (21°C) of 132 psig (910 kPag). However, its vapor pressure at 130°F (54.4°C) is 300 psig (2070 kPag), so service pressure [¾ times, which must not exceed 300 psig (2070 kPag)] is 300 divided by ¾, or 240 psig (1650 kPag). Thus, commercial propane requires at least a 240 psig (1650 kPag) service pressure cylinder.

C.2.3 DOT Cylinder Specifications Used for LP-Gas.

C.2.3.1 A number of different specifications were approved by DOT (and its predecessor, ICC) for use with LP-Gases. Some of these are no longer published or used for new construction. It should be noted that recently DOT has elected to remove certain old cylinder specifications from the list of specification cylinders that can be requalified. *(See 49 CFR 180.209.)*

C.2.3.2 DOT specifications cover primarily safety in transportation. However, for the product to be used, it is necessary for it to come to rest at the point of use and serve as LP-Gas storage during the period of use. Cylinders adequate for transportation are also deemed to be adequate for use as provided in this code. Because small-size ASME containers were not available at the time cargo tank vehicle delivery was started, ICC (now DOT) cylinders have been equipped for cargo tank vehicle deliveries and permanently installed.

C.2.3.3 The DOT cylinder specifications most widely used for the LP-Gases are shown in Table C.2.3.3. The differing materials of construction, the method of fabrication, and the date of the specification reflect the progress made in knowledge of the products to be contained and the improvement in metallurgy and methods of fabrication.

TABLE C.2.3.3 DOT Cylinder Specifications

Specification No. and Marking	*Material of Construction*	*Method of Fabrication*
3B−300	Steel	Seamless
4B−300	Steel	2-piece welded and brazed
4B−240	Steel	2-piece welded and brazed
4BA−240	Alloy steel	2-piece welded and brazed
4E−240	Aluminum	Welded and brazed
4BW−240	Steel	3-piece welded

Note: The term *service pressure* had a different connotation at the time the specification was adopted.

C.3 Requalification, Retesting, and Repair of DOT Cylinders

C.3.1 Application.

This section outlines the requalification, retesting, and repair requirements for cylinders but should be used only as a guide. For official information, the applicable DOT regulations should be consulted.

C.3.2 Requalification (Including Retesting) of DOT Cylinders.

C.3.2.1 DOT rules prohibit cylinders from being refilled, continued in service, or transported unless they are properly qualified or requalified for LP-Gas service in accordance with DOT regulations.

C.3.2.2 DOT rules require a careful examination of every cylinder each time it is to be filled, and a cylinder must be rejected if there is evidence of exposure to fire or if there are bad gouges or dents, seriously corroded areas, leaks, or other conditions indicating possible weaknesses that might render it unfit for service. The following disposition is to be made of rejected cylinders:

(1) Cylinders subjected to fire are required to be requalified, reconditioned, or repaired in accordance with C.3.3 or permanently removed from service, except that DOT 4E (aluminum) cylinders and composite material cylinders used under a special permit issued by DOT must be permanently removed from service.
(2) Cylinders showing serious physical damage or leaks or showing a reduction in the marked tare weight of 5 percent or more are required to be retested in accordance with C.3.2.4(1) or (2) and, if necessary, repaired in accordance with C.3.3.

C.3.2.3 All cylinders, including those apparently undamaged, are required to be periodically requalified for continued service. The first requalification for a new cylinder is required within 12 years after the date of manufacture. Subsequent requalifications are required within the periods specified under the requalification method used. Composite material cylinders used under a special permit issued by DOT must be requalified in accordance with the terms of the permit.

C.3.2.4 DOT regulations permit three alternative methods of requalification for most commonly used LP-Gas cylinders *(see DOT regulations for permissible requalification methods for specific cylinder specifications)*. Two methods use hydrostatic testing, and the third uses a carefully made and duly recorded visual examination by a competent person. DOT regulations cite in detail the data to be recorded for the hydrostatic test methods, the observations to be made during the visual examination for the hydrostatic and visual inspection methods, and the marking of cylinders to indicate the requalification date and the method used. The three methods — the volumetric expansion method, the proof pressure method, and the external visual inspection method — are outlined in C.3.2.4.1 through C.3.2.4.3.

C.3.2.4.1 Volumetric Expansion Method. The volumetric expansion method test, with determination of expansion readings, can be used to requalify cylinders for 12 years before the next requalification is due. A pressure of twice the marked service pressure is applied, using a water jacket (or the equivalent) so that the total expansion of the cylinder during the application of the test pressure can be observed and recorded for comparison with the permanent expansion of the cylinder after depressurization. The following disposition is made of cylinders tested in this manner:

(1) Cylinders that pass the retest and the visual examination required with it *(see C.3.2.4)* are marked with the retester identification number (RIN) and retest date. The RIN (e.g., A123) is set in a square pattern between the month and the year of the test date (e.g., 5/96). The first character of the RIN is positioned at the upper left corner of the square pattern the second character in the upper right, the third character in the lower right, and the fourth character in the lower left. Minimum character size is ⅛ in. (3 mm) [¼ in. (6 mm) minimum height is recommended for the month and year]. Following marking, cylinders can be placed back into service.
(2) Cylinders that leak, or for which the permanent expansion exceeds 10 percent of the total expansion (12 percent for Specification 4E aluminum cylinders), must be rejected. If rejected for leakage, cylinders can be repaired in accordance with C.3.3.

C.3.2.4.2 Proof Pressure Method. Cylinders are requalified for 7 years before the next requalification is due, using the proof pressure method. A pressure of twice the marked service pressure is applied, but no provision is made for measuring total and permanent expansion during the test outlined in C.3.2.4.1. The cylinder is carefully observed while under the test pressure for leaks, undue swelling, or bulging indicating weaknesses. The following disposition is made of cylinders tested in this matter:

(1) Cylinders that pass the test and the visual examination required with it *(see C.3.2.4)* are marked with the retester identification number (RIN) and retest date. The RIN (e.g., A123) is set in a square pattern between the month and the year of the test date (e.g., 5/96), followed by an S. The first character of the RIN is positioned at the upper left corner of the square pattern, the second character in the upper right, the third character in the lower right, and the fourth character in the lower left. Minimum character size is ⅛ in. (3 mm) [¼ in. (6 mm) minimum height is recommended for the month and year]. Following marking, cylinders can be placed back into service.

(2) Cylinders that are developing leaks or showing undue swelling or bulging must be rejected. If rejected for leaks, cylinders are permitted to be repaired in accordance with C.3.3.

C.3.2.4.3 External Visual Inspection Method. The recorded external visual inspection method can be used to requalify cylinders for 5 years before the next qualification is due, provided that the cylinder has been used exclusively for LP-Gas commercially free of corroding components. Inspection is to be made by a competent person, using CGA C-6, *Standard for Visual Inspection of Steel Compressed Gas Cylinders*, for steel cylinders and CGA C-6.3, *Guidelines for Visual Inspection and Requalification of Low Pressure Aluminum Compressed Gas Cylinders*, for aluminum cylinders and recording the inspection results as required by DOT regulations. The following disposition is to be made of cylinders inspected in this manner:

(1) Cylinders that pass the visual examination are marked with the retester identification number (RIN) and retest date and year of the examination, followed by an E (e.g., 6-07 A123 E, indicating requalification by the specific cylinder retester using the visual examination method in June 2007), and can be placed back into service. In certain situations, DOT has issued visual requalifier identification numbers. Those issued this identification must place the VRIN in a straight line (e.g., V108231), followed by the month and year and the letter E.

(2) Cylinders that leak or show serious denting or gouging or excessive corrosion must be either scrapped or repaired in accordance with C.3.3.

The Compressed Gas Association's *Standard for Visual Inspection of Steel Compressed Gas Cylinders*, Pamphlet C-6, is a guide that can be used to requalify cylinders as required by the U.S. Department of Transportation (DOT) regulations [1]. The standard contains examples of various types of pitting, corrosion, and failed cylinders and is very useful for persons not completely familiar with the subject. A portion of the document also provides the complete set of DOT requirements along with illustrations demonstrating the use of the gauges needed to complete the inspection and a visual inspection form.

DOT requires that anyone who requalifies cylinders must apply to DOT for registration as a requalifier. This registration will result in a Requalifier Identification Number (RIN) being assigned to that individual or company.

C.3.3 Repair of DOT Cylinders.

Repair of DOT cylinders is required to be performed by a manufacturer of the type of cylinder to be repaired or by a repair facility authorized by DOT.

Repairs normally made are for fire damage, leaks, denting, and gouges and for broken or detached valve-protecting collars or foot rings.

REFERENCE CITED IN COMMENTARY

1. CGA C-6, *Standard for Visual Inspection of Steel Compressed Gas Cylinders,* 2009, Compressed Gas Association, Chantilly, VA.

Design of ASME and API-ASME Containers

This annex is not a part of the requirements of this NFPA document but is included for informational purposes only.

D.1 General

D.1.1 Application.

D.1.1.1 This annex provides general information on containers designed and constructed in accordance with ASME or API-ASME codes, usually referred to as ASME containers. For complete information on either ASME or API-ASME containers, the applicable code should be consulted. Construction of containers to the API-ASME *Code for Unfired Pressure Vessels for Petroleum Liquids and Gases* has not been authorized since July 1, 1961.

D.1.1.2 Department of Transportation (DOT) and Interstate Commerce Commission (ICC) specifications for portable tanks and cargo tanks are for either ASME or API-ASME containers. In writing these specifications, which should be consulted for complete information, additions were made to ASME and API-ASME pressure vessel codes to cover the following:

(1) Protection of tank valves and appurtenances against physical damage in transportation
(2) Hold-down devices for securing cargo tanks to conventional vehicles
(3) Attachments to relatively large [6000 gal (22.7 m^3) or more water capacity] cargo tanks in which the tank serves as a stress member in lieu of a frame

D.1.2 Development of ASME and API-ASME Codes.

D.1.2.1 ASME-type containers of approximately 12,000 gal (45.4 m^3) or more water capacity were initially used for bulk storage in processing, distribution, and industrial plants. As the industry expanded and residential and commercial usage increased, the need grew for small ASME containers with capacities greater than the upper limit for cylinders. This ultimately resulted in the development of cargo containers for cargo tank vehicles and the wide use of ASME containers ranging in size from less than 25 gal to 120,000 gal (0.1 m^3 to 454 m^3) water capacity.

D.1.2.2 In 1911, the American Society of Mechanical Engineers (ASME) set up the Boiler and Pressure Vessel Committee to formulate "standard rules for the construction of steam boilers and other pressure vessels." The ASME *Boiler and Pressure Vessel Code*, first published in 1925, has been revised regularly since that time. During this period, changes have been made to the code as materials of construction improved and more was known about them and as fabrication methods changed and inspection procedures were refined.

D.1.2.3 One major change involved the so-called "factor of safety" (the ratio of the ultimate strength of the metal to the design stress used). Prior to 1946, a 5:1 safety factor was used. Fabrication changed from the riveting widely used when the code was first written (some forge welding was used) to fusion welding. This latter method was incorporated into the code as welding techniques were perfected, and it now predominates.

D.1.2.4 The safety factor change in the ASME Code was based on the technical progress made since 1925 and on experience with the use of the API-ASME Code. This offshoot of the ASME Code, initiated in 1931, was formulated and published by the American Petroleum Institute (API) in cooperation with ASME. It justified the 4:1 safety factor on the basis of certain quality and inspection controls not incorporated at that time in the ASME Code editions. In 1998, ASME reduced the safety factor or design margin from 4:1 to 3.5:1, noting improvements in metal manufacturing, welding techniques, X-ray quality, and pressure vessel manufacturer's quality systems.

D.1.2.5 ASME Code case interpretations and addenda are published between code editions and normally become part of the code in the new edition. Adherence to these interpretations and addenda is considered compliance with the code. *[See 5.2.1.1(B).]*

D.2 Design of Containers for LP-Gas

D.2.1 ASME Container Design.

D.2.1.1 When ASME containers were first used to store LP-Gas, the properties of the chemically pure (CP) grades of the principal constituents were available, but the average properties for the commercial grades of propane and butane were not. Also, there was no experience that demonstrated the expected temperatures and pressures for product stored in areas with high atmospheric temperatures. A 200 psig (1378 kPag) design pressure was for propane [the CP grade of which has a gauge vapor pressure of 176 psig (1210 kPag) at 100°F (37.8°C)] and 80 psig (550 kPag) for butane [CP grade has a vapor pressure of 37 psig (255 kPag) at 100°F (37.8°C)] were deemed appropriate. These containers were built with a 5:1 safety factor. *(See D.1.2.3.)*

D.2.1.2 Pressure vessel codes, following boiler pressure relief valve practice, require that the pressure relief valve start-to-leak setting be the maximum allowable working pressure (MAWP) of the container. In specifying pressure relief valve capacity, however, they stipulate that this relieving capacity be adequate to prevent the internal pressure from rising above 120 percent of the design pressure under fire exposure conditions.

D.2.1.3 Containers built in accordance with D.2.1.1 were entirely adequate for the commercial grades of the LP-Gases [the vapor pressure of propane at 100°F (37.8°C) is 220 psig (1515 kPag); the gauge vapor pressure of commercial butane at 100°F (37.8°C) is 37 psig (255 kPag)]. However, because they were equipped with pressure relief valves set to start-to-leak at the MAWP of the container, these relief valves occasionally opened on an unusually warm day. Because any unnecessary release of a flammable gas is potentially dangerous, and considering the recommendations of fire prevention and insurance groups as well as the favorable experience with API-ASME containers *(see D.2.2.1)*, relief valve settings above the design pressure [up to 250 psig (1720 kPag) for propane and 100 psig (690 kPag) for butane] were widely used.

D.2.1.4 In determining safe filling limits for compressed liquefied gases, DOT (ICC) uses the criterion that the container not become liquid full at the highest temperature the liquid is expected to reach due to the normal atmospheric conditions to which the container can be exposed. For containers of more than 1200 gal (4.5 m^3) water capacity, the liquid temperature selected is 115°F (46°C). The vapor pressure of the gas to be contained at 115°F (46°C) is specified by DOT as the minimum design pressure for the container. The gauge vapor pressure of CP propane and commercial propane at 115°F (46.1°C) is 211 psig (1450 kPag) and

255 psig (1756 kPag), respectively. The gauge vapor pressure of both normal butane and commercial butane at 115°F (46.1°C) is 51 psig (350 kPag).

D.2.1.5 The ASME *Boiler and Pressure Vessel Code* editions generally applicable to LP-Gas containers, and the design pressures, safety factors, and exceptions to these editions for LP-Gas use, are shown in Table D.2.1.5. They reflect the use of the information in D.2.1.1 through D.2.1.4.

TABLE D.2.1.5 *Container Pressure and Safety Factors/Design Margin for Various Editions of the ASME Code*

| Year ASME Code Edition Published | Maximum Allowable Working Pressure (MAWP) | | | | Safety Factor/Design Margin |
| | Butane | | Propane | | |
	psig	MPag	psig	MPag	
1931 through 1946[a]	100[a]	0.7	200	1.4	5:1
1949, paragraphs U-68 and U-69[b]	100	0.7	200	1.4	5:1
1949, paragraphs U-200 and U-201[c]	125	0.9	250	1.7	4:1
1952 through 1998	125	0.9	250	1.7	4:1
1998 to current					3.5:1

[a] Until December 31, 1947, containers designed for 80 psig (0.6 MPag) under prior (5:1 safety factor) codes were authorized for butane. Since that time, either 100 psig (0.7 MPag) (under prior codes) or 125 psig (0.9 MPag) (under present codes) is required.

[b] Containers constructed in accordance with the 1949 edition and prior editions of the ASME Code were not required to be in compliance with paragraphs U-2 to U-10, inclusive, or with paragraph U-19. Construction in accordance with paragraph U-70 of these editions was not authorized.

[c] Higher MAWP [312.5 psig (2.2 MPag)] is required for small ASME containers used for vehicular installations, because they can be exposed to higher temperatures and, consequently, develop higher internal pressure.

D.2.2 API-ASME Container Design.

D.2.2.1 The API-ASME Code was first published in 1931. Based on petroleum industry experience using certain material quality and inspection controls not incorporated at that time in the ASME Code, the 4:1 safety factor was first used. Many LP-Gas containers were built under this code with design pressures of 125 psig (860 kPag) [100 psig (690 kPag) until December 31, 1947] for butane and 250 psig (1725 kPag) for propane. Containers constructed in accordance with the API-ASME Code were not required to comply with Section 1 or with the annex to Section 1. Paragraphs W-601 through W-606 of the 1943 and earlier editions were not applicable to LP-Gas containers.

D.2.2.2 By changing the safety factor from 5:1 to 4:1 through consideration of the factors described in D.2.1.1 through D.2.1.4, the ASME Code became, in effect, nearly identical to the API-ASME Code by the 1950s. Thus, the API-ASME Code was phased out, and construction was not authorized after July 1, 1961.

D.2.3 Design Criteria for LP-Gas Containers.

To prevent confusion in earlier editions of this code, the container type nomenclature was used to designate the pressure rating of the container to be used for various types of LP-Gases. With the adoption of the 4:1 safety factor in the ASME Code and the phasing out of the API-ASME Code, the need for container type ceased to exist.

D.2.4 DOT (ICC) Specifications Utilizing ASME or API-ASME Containers.

D.2.4.1 DOT (ICC) specifications for portable tanks and cargo tanks require ASME or API-ASME construction for the tank proper *(see D.1.1.2)*. Several such specifications were written by the ICC prior to 1967, and DOT has continued this practice.

D.2.4.2 ICC specifications written prior to 1946, and to some extent through 1952, used ASME containers with a 200 psig (1380 kPag) design pressure for propane and 80 psig (550 kPag) for butane [100 psi (690 kPa) after 1947] with a 5:1 safety factor. During this period and until 1961, ICC specifications also permitted API-ASME containers with a 250 psig (1720 kPag) design pressure for propane and 100 psig (690 kPag) for butane [125 psig (862 kPag) after 1947].

D.2.4.3 To prevent any unnecessary release of flammable vapor during transportation *(see D.2.1.3)*, the use of safety relief valve settings 25 percent above the MAWP was common for ASME 5:1 safety factor containers. To eliminate confusion, and in line with the good experience with API-ASME containers, the ICC permitted the rerating of these particular ASME containers used under its specifications to 125 percent of the originally marked MAWP.

D.2.4.4 DOT (ICC) pressure specifications applicable to portable tanks and cargo tanks currently in use are listed in Table D.2.4.4. New construction is not permitted under the older specifications. However, use of these older containers is permitted to continue, provided that they have been maintained in accordance with DOT (ICC) regulations.

TABLE D.2.4.4 DOT Pressure Specification for Cargo Tanks

Specification Number	ASME Construction			API-ASME Construction		
	MAWP (psig)		Safety Factor/Design Margin	Design Pressure (psig)		Safety Factor
	Propane	Butane		Propane	Butane	
ICC-50[a]	200[b]	100[b]	5:1	250	125	4:1
ICC-51[a]	250	125	4:1	250	125	4:1
MC-320[c,d]	200[b]	100[b]	5:1	250	125	4:1
MC-330[c]	250	125	4:1	250	125	4:1
MC-331[c]	250	125	4:1	250	125	4:1

For SI units, 100 psig = 0.69 MPag; 125 psig = 0.86 MPag; 200 psig = 1.40 MPag; 250 psig = 1.72 MPag.

[a]Portable tank container.

[b]Permitted to be re-rated to 125 percent of original ASME MAWP.

[c]Cargo tank.

[d]Requires DOT exemption.

D.3 Underground ASME or API-ASME Containers

D.3.1 Use of Containers Underground.

D.3.1.1 ASME or API-ASME containers are used for underground or partially underground installation in accordance with 6.6.6.1 or 6.6.6.2. The temperature of the soil is normally low so that the average liquid temperature and vapor pressure of product stored in underground containers will be lower than in aboveground containers.

D.3.1.2 Containers listed to be used interchangeably for installation either above ground or under ground must comply as to pressure relief valve rated relieving capacity and filling limit with aboveground provisions when installed above ground *(see 5.7.2.6)*. When installed under ground, the pressure relief valve rated relieving capacity and filling limit can be in accordance with underground provisions *(see 5.7.2.8)*, provided that all other underground installation provisions are met. Containers installed partially under ground are considered as aboveground containers insofar as filling limit and pressure relief valve rated relieving capacity are concerned.

Pressure Relief Devices

This annex is not a part of the requirements of this NFPA document but is included for informational purposes only.

E.1 Pressure Relief Devices for Department of Transportation (DOT) Cylinders

E.1.1 Source of Provisions for Relief Devices.

The requirements for relief devices on Department of Transportation (DOT) cylinders are established by the DOT. Complete technical information regarding these requirements are found in CGA S-1.1, *Pressure-Relief Device Standards*, Part 1 — "Cylinders for Compressed Gases."

E.2 Pressure Relief Devices for ASME Containers

E.2.1 Source of Provisions for Pressure Relief Devices.

Capacity requirements for pressure relief devices are in accordance with the applicable provisions of CGA S-1.2, *Pressure-Relief Device Standards*, Part 2 — "Cargo and Portable Tanks for Compressed Gases"; or with CGA S-1.3, *Pressure Relief Device Standards*, Part 3 — "Compressed Gas Storage Containers."

E.2.2 Spring-Loaded Pressure Relief Valves for Aboveground and Cargo Containers.

The minimum rate of discharge for spring-loaded pressure relief valves is based on the outside surface of the containers on which the valves are installed. Paragraph 5.2.8.3(C)(6) provides that new containers be marked with the surface area in square feet. The surface area of containers not so marked (or not legibly marked) can be computed by use of the applicable formula.

(1) The following formula is used for cylindrical containers with hemispherical heads:

$$\text{Surface area} = \text{overall length} \times \text{outside diameter} \times 3.1416$$

(2) The following formula is used for cylindrical containers with other than hemispherical heads:

$$\text{Surface area} = (\text{overall length} + 0.3 \text{ outside diameter}) \times \text{outside diameter} \times 3.1416$$

NOTE: This formula is not precise but will give results within the limits of practical accuracy in sizing relief valves.

(3) The following formula is used for spherical containers:

$$\text{Surface area} = \text{outside diameter squared} \times 3.1416$$

(4) The following formula is used for flow rate for all containers:

$$\text{Flow rate CFM Air} = 53.632 \times A^{0.32}$$

where:

A = total outside surface area of container in square feet obtained from E.2.2(1), (2), or (3)

E.2.3 Pressure Relief Valve Testing.

E.2.3.1 Frequent testing of pressure relief valves on LP-Gas containers is not considered necessary for the following reasons:

(1) The LP-Gases are so-called "sweet gases" having no corrosive or other deleterious effect on the metal of the containers or relief valves.
(2) The relief valves are constructed of corrosion-resistant materials and are installed so as to be protected against the weather.
(3) The variations of temperature and pressure due to atmospheric conditions are not sufficient to cause any permanent set in the valve springs.
(4) The required odorization of the LP-Gases makes escape almost instantly evident.
(5) Experience over the years with the storage of LP-Gases has shown a good safety record on the functioning of pressure relief valves.

E.2.3.2 Because no mechanical device can be expected to remain in operative condition indefinitely, it is suggested that the pressure relief valves on containers of more than 2000 gal (7.6 m^3) water capacity be tested at approximately 10-year intervals.

Liquid Volume Tables, Computations, and Graphs

This annex is not a part of the requirements of this NFPA document but is included for informational purposes only.

F.1 Scope

F.1.1 Application.

This annex explains the basis for Table 7.4.2.2; includes the LP-Gas liquid volume temperature correction table, Table F.3.3; and describes its use. It also explains the methods of making liquid volume computations to determine the maximum permissible LP-Gas content of containers in accordance with Table 7.4.2.3(a), Table 7.4.2.3(b), and Table 7.4.2.3(c).

F.2 Basis for Determination of LP-Gas Container Capacity

The basis for determination of the maximum permitted filling limits shown in Table 7.4.2.2 is the maximum safe quantity that will ensure that the container will not become liquid full when the liquid is at the highest anticipated temperature.

F.2.1 For portable containers built to Department of Transportation (DOT) specifications and other aboveground containers with water capacities of 1200 gal (4.5 m³) or less, the highest anticipated temperature is assumed to be 130°F (54°C).

F.2.2 For other aboveground uninsulated containers with water capacities in excess of 1200 gal (4.5 m³), including those built to DOT portable or cargo tank specifications, the highest anticipated temperature is assumed to be 115°F (46°C).

F.2.3 For all containers installed under ground, the highest anticipated temperature is assumed to be 105°F (41°C).

F.3 Liquid Volume Correction Table

Table F.3.3 shows the correction of observed volume to standard temperature condition [60°F (16°C) and equilibrium pressure].

F.3.1 The volume of a given quantity of LP-Gas liquid in a container is directly related to its temperature, expanding as temperature increases and contracting as temperature decreases. Standard conditions, often used for weights and measures purposes and, in some cases, to comply with safety regulations, specify correction of the observed volume to what it would be at 60°F (16°C).

F.3.2 To correct the observed volume to 60°F (16°C), the specific gravity of LP-Gas at 60°F (16°C) in relation to water at 60°F (16°C) (usually referred to as "60°/60°F") and its average temperature must be known. The specific gravity normally appears on the shipping papers. The average liquid temperature can be obtained as follows:

(1) Insert a thermometer in a thermometer well in the container into which the liquid has been transferred, and read the temperature after the completion of the transfer. *[See F.3.2(3) for proper use of a thermometer.]*

(2) If the container is not equipped with a well but is essentially empty of liquid prior to loading, the temperature of the liquid in the container from which liquid is being withdrawn can be used. Otherwise, a thermometer can be inserted in a thermometer well or other temperature-sensing device installed in the loading line at a point close to the container being loaded. Read temperatures at intervals during transfer and averaging. *[See F.3.2(3).]*

(3) A suitable liquid should be used in thermometer wells to obtain an efficient heat transfer from the LP-Gas liquid in the container to the thermometer bulb. The liquid used should be noncorrosive and should not freeze at the temperatures to which it will be subjected. Water should not be used.

F.3.3 The volume observed or measured is corrected to 60°F (16°C) by use of Table F.3.3. The column headings, across the top of the tabulation, list the range of specific gravities for

TABLE F.3.3 *Liquid Volume Correction Factors*

	Specific Gravity at 60°F/60°F												
Observed Temperature (°F)	*0.500*	*Propane 0.5079*	*0.510*	*0.520*	*0.530*	*0.540*	*0.550*	*0.560*	*iso-Butane 0.5631*	*0.570*	*0.580*	*n-Butane 0.5844*	*0.590*
	Volume Correction Factor												
−50	1.160	1.155	1.153	1.146	1.140	1.133	1.127	1.122	1.120	1.116	1.111	1.108	1.106
−45	1.153	1.148	1.146	1.140	1.134	1.128	1.122	1.117	1.115	1.111	1.106	1.103	1.101
−40	1.147	1.142	1.140	1.134	1.128	1.122	1.117	1.111	1.110	1.106	1.101	1.099	1.097
−35	1.140	1.135	1.134	1.128	1.122	1.116	1.112	1.106	1.105	1.101	1.096	1.094	1.092
−30	1.134	1.129	1.128	1.122	1.116	1.111	1.106	1.101	1.100	1.096	1.092	1.090	1.088
−25	1.127	1.122	1.121	1.115	1.110	1.105	1.100	1.095	1.094	1.091	1.087	1.085	1.083
−20	1.120	1.115	1.114	1.109	1.104	1.099	1.095	1.090	1.089	1.086	1.082	1.080	1.079
−15	1.112	1.109	1.107	1.102	1.097	1.093	1.089	1.084	1.083	1.080	1.077	1.075	1.074
−10	1.105	1.102	1.100	1.095	1.091	1.087	1.083	1.079	1.078	1.075	1.072	1.071	1.069
−5	1.098	1.094	1.094	1.089	1.085	1.081	1.077	1.074	1.073	1.070	1.067	1.066	1.065
0	1.092	1.088	1.088	1.084	1.080	1.076	1.073	1.069	1.068	1.066	1.063	1.062	1.061
2	1.089	1.086	1.085	1.081	1.077	1.074	1.070	1.067	1.066	1.064	1.061	1.060	1.059
4	1.086	1.083	1.082	1.079	1.075	1.071	1.068	1.065	1.064	1.062	1.059	1.058	1.057
6	1.084	1.080	1.080	1.076	1.072	1.069	1.065	1.062	1.061	1.059	1.057	1.055	1.054
8	1.081	1.078	1.077	1.074	1.070	1.066	1.063	1.060	1.059	1.057	1.055	1.053	1.052
10	1.078	1.075	1.074	1.071	1.067	1.064	1.061	1.058	1.057	1.055	1.053	1.051	1.050
12	1.075	1.072	1.071	1.068	1.064	1.061	1.059	1.056	1.055	1.053	1.051	1.049	1.048
14	1.072	1.070	1.069	1.066	1.062	1.059	1.056	1.053	1.053	1.051	1.049	1.047	1.046
16	1.070	1.067	1.066	1.063	1.060	1.056	1.054	1.051	1.050	1.048	1.046	1.045	1.044
18	1.067	1.065	1.064	1.061	1.057	1.054	1.051	1.049	1.048	1.046	1.044	1.043	1.042
20	1.064	1.062	1.061	1.058	1.054	1.051	1.049	1.046	1.046	1.044	1.042	1.041	1.040
22	1.061	1.059	1.058	1.055	1.052	1.049	1.046	1.044	1.044	1.042	1.040	1.039	1.038
24	1.058	1.056	1.055	1.052	1.049	1.046	1.044	1.042	1.042	1.040	1.038	1.037	1.036
26	1.055	1.053	1.052	1.049	1.047	1.044	1.042	1.039	1.039	1.037	1.036	1.036	1.034
28	1.052	1.050	1.049	1.047	1.044	1.041	1.039	1.037	1.037	1.035	1.034	1.034	1.032

TABLE F.3.3 *Continued*

Observed Temperature (°F)	0.500	Propane 0.5079	0.510	0.520	0.530	0.540	0.550	0.560	iso-Butane 0.5631	0.570	0.580	n-Butane 0.5844	0.590
	\multicolumn{13}{c}{Volume Correction Factor}												
30	1.049	1.047	1.046	1.044	1.041	1.039	1.037	1.035	1.035	1.033	1.032	1.032	1.030
32	1.046	1.044	1.043	1.041	1.038	1.036	1.035	1.033	1.033	1.031	1.030	1.030	1.028
34	1.043	1.041	1.040	1.038	1.036	1.034	1.032	1.031	1.030	1.029	1.028	1.028	1.026
36	1.039	1.038	1.037	1.035	1.033	1.031	1.030	1.028	1.028	1.027	1.025	1.025	1.024
38	1.036	1.035	1.034	1.032	1.031	1.029	1.027	1.026	1.025	1.025	1.023	1.023	1.022
40	1.033	1.032	1.031	1.029	1.028	1.026	1.025	1.024	1.023	1.023	1.021	1.021	1.020
42	1.030	1.029	1.028	1.027	1.025	1.024	1.023	1.022	1.021	1.021	1.019	1.019	1.018
44	1.027	1.026	1.025	1.023	1.022	1.021	1.020	1.019	1.019	1.018	1.017	1.017	1.016
46	1.023	1.022	1.022	1.021	1.020	1.018	1.018	1.017	1.016	1.016	1.015	1.015	1.014
48	1.020	1.019	1.019	1.018	1.017	1.016	1.015	1.014	1.014	1.013	1.013	1.013	1.012
50	1.017	1.016	1.016	1.015	1.014	1.013	1.013	1.012	1.012	1.011	1.011	1.011	1.010
52	1.014	1.013	1.012	1.012	1.011	1.010	1.010	1.009	1.009	1.009	1.009	1.009	1.008
54	1.010	1.010	1.009	1.009	1.008	1.008	1.007	1.007	1.007	1.007	1.006	1.006	1.006
56	1.007	1.007	1.006	1.006	1.005	1.005	1.005	1.005	1.005	1.005	1.004	1.004	1.004
58	1.003	1.003	1.003	1.003	1.003	1.003	1.002	1.002	1.002	1.002	1.002	1.002	1.002
60	1.000	1.000	1.000	1.000	1.000	1.000	1.000	1.000	1.000	1.000	1.000	1.000	1.000
62	0.997	0.997	0.997	0.997	0.997	0.997	0.997	0.998	0.998	0.998	0.998	0.998	0.998
64	0.993	0.993	0.994	0.994	0.994	0.994	0.995	0.995	0.995	0.995	0.996	0.996	0.996
66	0.990	0.990	0.990	0.990	0.991	0.992	0.992	0.993	0.993	0.993	0.993	0.993	0.993
68	0.986	0.986	0.987	0.987	0.988	0.989	0.990	0.990	0.990	0.990	0.991	0.991	0.991
70	0.983	0.983	0.984	0.984	0.985	0.986	0.987	0.988	0.988	0.988	0.989	0.989	0.989
72	0.979	0.980	0.981	0.981	0.982	0.983	0.984	0.985	0.986	0.986	0.987	0.987	0.987
74	0.976	0.976	0.977	0.978	0.980	0.980	0.982	0.983	0.983	0.984	0.985	0.985	0.985
76	0.972	0.973	0.974	0.975	0.977	0.978	0.979	0.980	0.981	0.981	0.982	0.982	0.983
78	0.969	0.970	0.970	0.972	0.974	0.975	0.977	0.978	0.978	0.979	0.980	0.980	0.981
80	0.965	0.967	0.967	0.969	0.971	0.972	0.974	0.975	0.976	0.977	0.978	0.978	0.979
82	0.961	0.963	0.963	0.966	0.968	0.969	0.971	0.972	0.973	0.974	0.976	0.976	0.977
84	0.957	0.959	0.960	0.962	0.965	0.966	0.968	0.970	0.971	0.972	0.974	0.974	0.975
86	0.954	0.956	0.956	0.959	0.961	0.964	0.966	0.967	0.968	0.969	0.971	0.971	0.972
88	0.950	0.952	0.953	0.955	0.958	0.961	0.963	0.965	0.966	0.967	0.969	0.969	0.970
90	0.946	0.949	0.949	0.952	0.955	0.958	0.960	0.962	0.963	0.964	0.967	0.967	0.968
92	0.942	0.945	0.946	0.949	0.952	0.955	0.957	0.959	0.960	0.962	0.964	0.965	0.966
94	0.938	0.941	0.942	0.946	0.949	0.952	0.954	0.957	0.958	0.959	0.962	0.962	0.964
96	0.935	0.938	0.939	0.942	0.946	0.949	0.952	0.954	0.955	0.957	0.959	0.960	0.961
98	0.931	0.934	0.935	0.939	0.943	0.946	0.949	0.952	0.953	0.954	0.957	0.957	0.959
100	0.927	0.930	0.932	0.936	0.940	0.943	0.946	0.949	0.950	0.952	0.954	0.955	0.957
105	0.917	0.920	0.923	0.927	0.931	0.935	0.939	0.943	0.943	0.946	0.949	0.949	0.951
110	0.907	0.911	0.913	0.918	0.923	0.927	0.932	0.936	0.937	0.939	0.943	0.944	0.946
115	0.897	0.902	0.904	0.909	0.915	0.920	0.925	0.930	0.930	0.933	0.937	0.938	0.940
120	0.887	0.892	0.894	0.900	0.907	0.912	0.918	0.923	0.924	0.927	0.931	0.932	0.934
125	0.876	0.881	0.884	0.890	0.898	0.903	0.909	0.916	0.916	0.920	0.925	0.927	0.928
130	0.865	0.871	0.873	0.880	0.888	0.895	0.901	0.908	0.909	0.913	0.918	0.921	0.923
135	0.854	0.861	0.863	0.871	0.879	0.887	0.894	0.901	0.902	0.907	0.912	0.914	0.916
140	0.842	0.850	0.852	0.861	0.870	0.879	0.886	0.893	0.895	0.900	0.905	0.907	0.910

For SI units, °C = (5/9) (°F — 32).

the LP-Gases. Specific gravities are shown from 0.500 to 0.590 by 0.010 increments, except that special columns are inserted for chemically pure propane, isobutane, and normal butane. To obtain a correction factor, read down the column for the specific gravity of the particular LP-Gas to the factor corresponding with the liquid temperature. Interpolation between the specific gravities and temperatures shown can be used if necessary.

F.4 Use of Liquid Volume Correction Factors in Table F.3.3

F.4.1 To correct the observed volume in gallons for any LP-Gas (the specific gravity and temperature of which is known) to gallons at 60°F (16°C), Table F.3.3 is used as follows:

(1) Obtain the correction factor for the specific gravity and temperature as described in F.3.3.
(2) Multiply the gallons observed by the correction factor to obtain the gallons at 60°F (16°C).

Example: A container has in it 4055 gal (15.3 m³) of LP-Gas with a specific gravity of 0.560 at a liquid temperature of 75°F (23.9°C). The correction factors in the 0.560 column are 0.983 at 74°F (23.3°C) and 0.980 at 76°F (24.4°C), or, interpolating, 0.9815 for 75°F. The volume of liquid at 60°F is 4055 × 0.9815, or 3980 gal (15.1 m³).

F.4.2 To determine the volume in gallons of a particular LP-Gas at temperature, t, to correspond with a given number of gallons at 60°F (16°C), Table F.3.3 is used as follows:

(1) Obtain the correction factor for the LP-Gas, using the column for its specific gravity and reading the factor for temperature t.
(2) Divide the number of gallons at 60°F (16°C) by the correction factor to obtain the volume at temperature, t.

Example: It is desired to pump 800 gal (3.03 m³) at 60°F (15.5°C) into a container. The LP-Gas has a specific gravity of 0.510, and the liquid temperature is 44°F (6.7°C). The correction factor in the 0.510 column for 44°F (6.7°C) is 1.025. The volume to be pumped at 44°F (6.7°C) is 800/1.025 = 780 gal (2.95 m³).

F.5 Maximum Liquid Volume Computations

F.5.1 Maximum Liquid LP-Gas Content of a Container at Any Given Temperature.

F.5.1.1 The maximum liquid LP-Gas content of any container depends on the size of the container, whether it is installed above ground or under ground, the maximum permitted filling limit, and the temperature of the liquid. *[See Table 7.4.2.3(a), Table 7.4.2.3(b), and Table 7.4.2.3(c).]*

F.5.1.2 The maximum volume fraction, V_t (in percent of container capacity), of an LP-Gas at temperature, t, having a specific gravity, G, and a filling limit and weight percent filling limit, L, is computed by use of the following formula:

$$V_t = \frac{L}{G} \div F$$

or

$$V_t = \frac{L}{G \times F}$$

where:

V_t = percent of container capacity that can be filled with liquid

  t = liquid temperature [assumed to be 40°F (4.4°C) for aboveground containers or 50°F (10°C) for underground containers]

L = maximum permitted filling limit by weight *(see Table 7.4.2.2)*

G = specific gravity of particular LP-Gas

F = correction factor to correct volume at temperature, t, to 60°F (16°C)

  Example: The maximum liquid content, in percent of container capacity, for an aboveground 30,000 gal (114 m³) water capacity container of LP-Gas having a specific gravity of 0.508 and at a liquid temperature of 80°F (27°C) is computed as follows:
  From Table 7.4.2.2, $L = 0.45$ and, from Table F.3.3, $F = 0.967$. Thus,

$$V_{80} = \frac{0.45}{0.508 \times 0.967}$$
$$= 0.915 \ (91\%) \text{ or } 27{,}300 \text{ gal } (103 \text{ m}^3)$$

F.5.2 Alternate Method of Filling Containers.

F.5.2.1 Containers equipped with fixed maximum level gauges or with variable liquid level gauges when temperature determinations are not practical can be filled with either gauge, provided that the fixed maximum liquid level is installed or the variable gauge is set to indicate the volume equal to the maximum permitted filling limit as provided in 7.4.3.2(A). The level is computed on the basis of the liquid temperature being 40°F (4.4°C) for aboveground containers or 50°F (10°C) for underground containers.

F.5.2.2 The percentage of container capacity that can be filled with liquid is computed by use of the formula shown in F.5.1.2, substituting the appropriate values as follows:

$$V_t = \frac{L}{G \times F}$$

where:

V_t = percent of container capacity that can be filled with liquid

  t = liquid temperature [assumed to be 40°F (4.4°C) for aboveground containers or 50°F (10°C) for underground containers]

L = loading limit obtained from Table 7.4.2.2 for the following:

(1) Specific gravity of the LP-Gas to be contained
(2) Method of installation, aboveground or underground, and, if aboveground, then:

   (a) For containers of 1200 gal (4.5 m³) water capacity or less
   (b) For containers of more than 1200 gal (4.5 m³) water capacity

G = specific gravity of the LP-Gas to be contained

F = correction factor [obtained from Table F.3.3, using G and 40°F (4°C) for aboveground containers or 50°F (10°C) for underground containers]

  Example: The maximum volume of LP-Gas with a specific gravity of 0.508 that can be in a 1000 gal (3.8 m³) water capacity aboveground container that is filled by use of a fixed maximum liquid level gauge is computed as follows:
  $t = 40°F$ (4.4°C) for an aboveground container
  $L = 0.508$ specific gravity and an aboveground container of less than 1200 gal (4.5 m³) water capacity, from Table 7.4.2.2, = 42 percent
  $G = 0.508$
  $F = 0.508$ specific gravity at 40°F (4.4°C) from Table F.3.3 = 1.033

Thus,

$$V_{80} = \frac{0.42}{0.508 \times 1.033}$$
$$= 0.800 \, (80\%) \text{ or } 800 \text{ gal } (3 \text{ m}^3)$$

F.5.2.3 Percentage values, such as those in the example in F.5.2.2, are rounded off to the next lower full percentage point, or to 80 percent in this example.

F.5.3 Location of Fixed Maximum Liquid Level Gauges in Containers.

F.5.3.1 Due to the diversity of fixed maximum liquid level gauges, and the many sizes [from cylinders to 120,000 gal (454 m³) ASME vessels] and types (vertical, horizontal, cylindrical, and spherical) of containers in which gauges are installed, it is not possible to tabulate the liquid levels such gauges should indicate for the maximum permitted filling limits. *[See Table 7.4.2.2 and Table 7.4.2.3(a).]*

F.5.3.2 The percentage of container capacity that fixed maximum liquid level gauges should indicate is computed by use of the formula in F.5.1.2. The liquid level the gauge should indicate is obtained by applying the percentage to the water capacity of the container in gallons [water at 60°F (16°C)] and then using the strapping table for the container (obtained from its manufacturer) to determine the liquid level for this gallonage. If such a table is not available, the liquid level is computed from the internal dimensions of the container, using data from engineering handbooks.

F.5.3.3 Table 5.7.3.2 can be used to determine minimum dip tube length when installing an overfilling prevention device on cylinders for vapor service.

Wall Thickness of Copper Tubing ANNEX G

This annex is not a part of the requirements of this NFPA document but is included for informational purposes only.

G.1

Table G.1(a) and Table G.1(b) contain the nominal wall thicknesses of Type K, Type L, and Type ACR copper tubing.

TABLE G.1(a) *Wall Thickness of Copper Tubing (Standard Specification for Seamless Copper Water Tube, ASTM B 88)*

Standard Size (in.)	Nominal Outside Diameter (in.)	Nominal Wall Thickness (in.)	
		Type K	Type L
¼	0.375	0.035	0.030
⅜	0.500	0.049	0.035
½	0.625	0.049	0.040
⅝	0.750	0.049	0.042
¾	0.875	0.065	0.045

For SI units, 1 in. = 25 mm.

TABLE G.1(b) *Wall Thickness of Copper Tubing (Standard Specification for Seamless Copper Tube for Air Conditioning and Refrigeration Field Service, ASTM B 280)*

Standard Size (in.)	Outside Diameter (in.)	Wall Thickness (in.)
¼	0.250	0.030
⁵⁄₁₆	0.312	0.032
⅜	0.375	0.032
½	0.500	0.032
⅝	0.625	0.035
¾	0.750	0.042
⅞	0.875	0.045

For SI units, 1 in. = 25 mm.

Procedure for Torch Fire and Hose Stream Testing of Thermal Insulating Systems for LP-Gas Containers

This annex is not a part of the requirements of this NFPA document but is included for informational purposes only.

It is anticipated that Annex H is appearing for the last time in this edition of NFPA 58. The NFPA Technical Committee on Fire Tests has issued NFPA 290, *Standard for Fire Testing of Passive Protection Materials for Use on LP-Gas Containers* [1]. With the issuance of this standard, the material is no longer needed in NFPA 58. The annex was developed by the NFPA Technical Committee on Fire Tests at the request of the NFPA 58 committee, and it first appeared in the 1989 edition of NFPA 58.

Paragraph 6.25.5.1 provides a performance requirement for container insulation, and A.6.25.5.1 gives additional information. The LP-Gas committee recognized that no test methods existed for insulation where the critical condition was flame impingement with hose streams, which would be expected to prevent a boiling liquid expanding vapor explosion (BLEVE). The technical committee has placed this insulation test procedure in Annex H so that experience can be gained with it prior to making it a mandatory test procedure.

It is recommended that anyone using this annex also review NFPA 290.

H.1 Performance Standard

Thermal protection insulating systems, proposed for use on LP-Gas containers as a means of "Special Protection" under 6.25.3.1, are required to undergo thermal performance testing as a precondition for acceptance. The intent of this testing procedure is to identify insulation systems that retard or prevent the release of a container's contents in a fire environment of 50 minutes duration and that resist a concurrent hose stream of 10 minutes duration.

H.2 Reference Test Standards

The testing procedure described herein was taken with some modification from segments of the following two test standards:

(1) 49 CFR, Transportation, Part 179.105-4, "Thermal Protection"
(2) NFPA 252, *Standard Methods of Fire Tests of Door Assemblies*, Chapter 6, Section 6.2, Hose Stream Test

H.3 Thermal Insulation Test

H.3.1 A torch fire environment shall be created in the following manner:

(1) The source of the simulated torch shall be a hydrocarbon fuel. The flame temperature from the simulated torch shall be 2200°F ± 100°F (1200°C ± 56°C) throughout the test

duration. Torch velocities shall be 40 mph ± 10 mph (64 km/hr ± 16 km/hr) throughout the duration of the test.

(2) An uninsulated square steel plate with thermal properties equivalent to ASME pressure vessel steel shall be used. The plate dimensions shall be not less than 4 ft × 4 ft (1.2 m × 1.2 m) by nominal ⅝ in. (16 mm) thick. The plate shall be instrumented with not less than nine thermocouples to record the thermal response of the plate. The thermocouples shall be attached to the surface not exposed to the simulated torch and shall be divided into nine equal squares, with a thermocouple placed in the center of each square.

(3) The steel plate holder shall be constructed in such a manner that the only heat transfer to the back side of the plate is by heat conduction through the plate and not by other heat paths. The apex of the flame shall be directed at the center of the plate.

(4) Before exposure to the torch fire, none of the temperature recording devices shall indicate a plate temperature in excess of 100°F (38°C) or less than 32°F (0°C).

(5) A minimum of two thermocouples shall indicate 800°F (427°C) in a time of 4.0 ± 0.5 minutes of torch fire exposure.

H.3.2 A thermal insulation system shall be tested in the torch fire environment described in H.3.1 in the following manner:

(1) The thermal insulation system shall cover one side of a steel plate identical to that used under H.3.1(2).

(2) The back of the steel plate shall be instrumented with not less than nine thermocouples placed as described in H.3.1(2) to record the thermal response of the steel.

(3) Before exposure to the torch fire, none of the thermocouples on the thermal insulation system steel plate configuration shall indicate a plate temperature in excess of 100°F (37.8°C) or less than 32°F (0°C).

(4) The entire outside surface of the thermal insulation system shall be exposed to the torch fire environment.

(5) A torch fire test shall be run for a minimum of 50 minutes. The thermal insulation system shall retard the heat flow to the steel plates so that none of the thermocouples on the un-insulated side of the steel plate indicate a plate temperature in excess of 800°F (427°C).

H.4 Hose Stream Resistance Test

After 20 minutes exposure to the torch test, the test sample shall be hit with a hose stream concurrently with the torch for a period of 10 minutes. The hose stream test shall be conducted in the following manner:

(1) The stream shall be directed first at the middle and then at all parts of the exposed surface, making changes in direction slowly.

(2) The hose stream shall be delivered through a 2½ in. (64 mm) hose discharging through a National Standard playpipe of corresponding size equipped with a 1⅛ in. (29 mm) discharge tip of the standard-taper smooth-bore pattern without shoulder at the orifice. The water pressure at the base of the nozzle and for the duration of the test shall be 30 psig (207 kPag). [Estimated delivery rate is 205 gpm (776 L/min).]

(3) The tip of the nozzle shall be located 20 ft (6 m) from, and on a line normal to, the center of the test specimen. If impossible to be so located, the nozzle can be on a line with a deviation not to exceed 30 degrees from the line normal to the center of the test specimen. When so located, the distance from the center shall be less than 20 ft (6 m) by an amount equal to 1 ft (0.3 m) for each 10 degrees of deviation from the normal.

(4) Subsequent to the application of the hose stream, the torching shall continue until any thermocouple on the uninsulated side of the steel plate indicates a plate temperature in excess of 800°F (427°C).

(5) The thermal insulation system shall be judged to be resistant to the action of the hose stream if the time from initiation of torching for any thermocouple on the uninsulated side of the steel plate to reach in excess of 800°F (427°C) is 50 minutes or greater.
(6) One successful combination torch fire and hose stream test shall be required for certification.

REFERENCE CITED IN COMMENTARY

1. NFPA 290, *Standard for Fire Testing of Passive Protection Materials for Use on LP-Gas Containers*, 2009 edition, National Fire Protection Association, Quincy, MA.

This annex is not a part of the requirements of this NFPA document but is included for informational purposes only.

Annex I contains Figures I.1(a) through (c), which illustrate the separation distance required for the installation of LP-Gas containers up to 2000 gal (7.6 m³). The figures incorporate the distances required in Section 6.3 and Table 6.3.1. Because Table 6.3.1 is the most used item in the code, the need for clarity and unambiguous implementation of the table is of great importance. Figures I.1(a) through (c) make it much easier for all users to properly apply Section 6.3 and Table 6.3.1.

I.1 Spacing of Containers

Figure I.1(a), Figure I.1(b), and Figure I.1(c) illustrate container spacing required in 6.3.1.

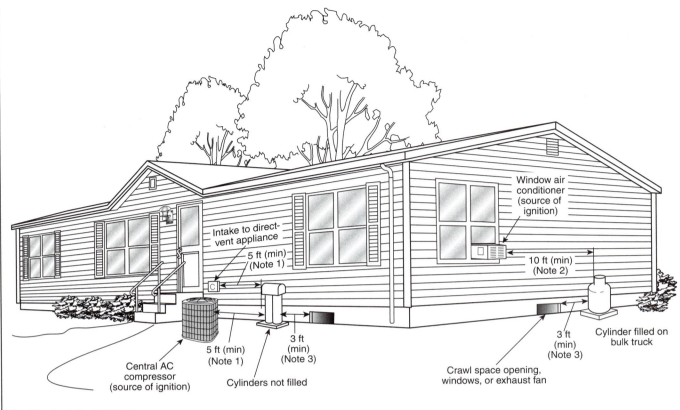

For SI units, 1 ft = 0.3048 m

Note 1: 5 ft minimum from relief valve in any direction away from any exterior source of ignition, openings into direct-vent appliances, or mechanical ventilation air intakes.

Note 2: If the cylinder is filled on site from a bulk truck, the filling connection and vent valve must be at least 10 ft from any exterior source of ignition, openings into direct-vent appliances, or mechanical ventilation air intakes. Refer to 6.3.9.

Note 3: Refer to 6.3.8.

FIGURE I.1(a) Cylinders. (Figure for illustrative purposes only; code compliance required.)

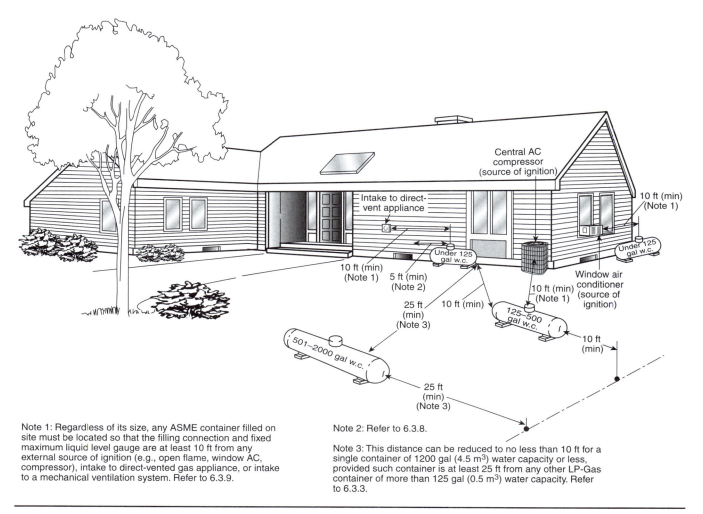

Note 1: Regardless of its size, any ASME container filled on site must be located so that the filling connection and fixed maximum liquid level gauge are at least 10 ft from any external source of ignition (e.g., open flame, window AC, compressor), intake to direct-vented gas appliance, or intake to a mechanical ventilation system. Refer to 6.3.9.

Note 2: Refer to 6.3.8.

Note 3: This distance can be reduced to no less than 10 ft for a single container of 1200 gal (4.5 m³) water capacity or less, provided such container is at least 25 ft from any other LP-Gas container of more than 125 gal (0.5 m³) water capacity. Refer to 6.3.3.

FIGURE I.1(b) *Aboveground ASME Containers. (Figure for illustrative purposes only; code shall govern.)*

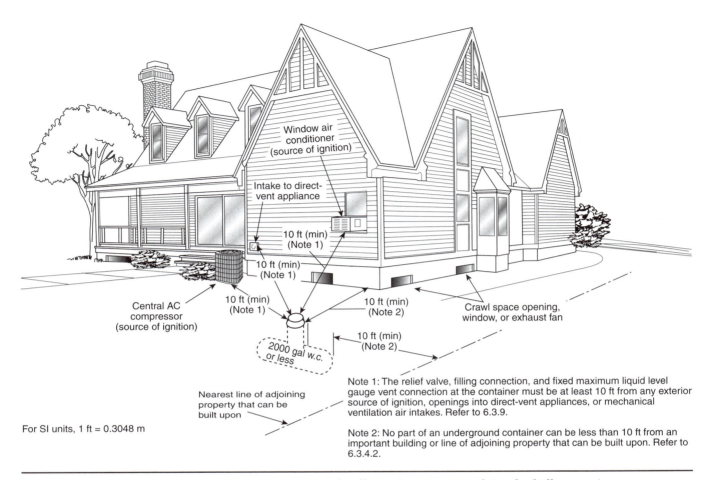

For SI units, 1 ft = 0.3048 m

Window air conditioner (source of ignition)

Intake to direct-vent appliance

10 ft (min) (Note 1)

10 ft (min) (Note 1)

Central AC compressor (source of ignition)

10 ft (min) (Note 1)

10 ft (min) (Note 2)

2000 gal w.c. or less

10 ft (min) (Note 2)

Crawl space opening, window, or exhaust fan

Nearest line of adjoining property that can be built upon

Note 1: The relief valve, filling connection, and fixed maximum liquid level gauge vent connection at the container must be at least 10 ft from any exterior source of ignition, openings into direct-vent appliances, or mechanical ventilation air intakes. Refer to 6.3.9.

Note 2: No part of an underground container can be less than 10 ft from an important building or line of adjoining property that can be built upon. Refer to 6.3.4.2.

FIGURE I.1(c) *Underground ASME Containers. (Figure for illustrative purposes only; code shall govern.)*

Sample Ordinance Adopting NFPA 58

This annex is not a part of the requirements of this NFPA document but is included for informational purposes only.

NFPA 58 is a code. The NFPA Regulations Governing Committee Projects define *code* and *standard* as follows:

Code: A standard that is an extensive compilation of provisions covering broad subject matter or that is suitable for adoption into law independently of other codes and standards.

Note: The decision to designate a standard as a "code" is based on such factors as the size and scope of the document, its intended use and form of adoption, and whether it contains substantial enforcement and administrative provisions.

Standard: A document, the main text of which contains only mandatory provisions using the word "shall" to indicate requirements and which is in a form generally suitable for mandatory reference by another standard or code or for adoption into law. Nonmandatory provisions shall be located in an appendix or annex, footnote, or fine-print note and are not to be considered a part of the requirements of a standard.

As a code, NFPA 58 is adopted into law in many jurisdictions. Therefore, the sample ordinance to adopt the code has been added for the convenience of adopters. Although many government bodies that adopt NFPA 58 and other codes write their own laws, Annex J can be and is used.

Note that Section 1.7, Enforcement, provides adopting agencies with a means to allow enforcement of NFPA 58.

J.1

The following sample ordinance is provided to assist a jurisdiction in the adoption of this code and is not part of this code.

ORDINANCE NO. _____

An ordinance of the *[jurisdiction]* adopting the 2011 edition of NFPA 58, *Liquefied Petroleum Gas Code*, documents listed in Chapter 2 of that code; prescribing regulations governing conditions hazardous to life and property from fire or explosion; providing for the issuance of permits and collection of fees; repealing Ordinance No. _____ of the *[jurisdiction]* and all other ordinances and parts of ordinances in conflict therewith; providing a penalty; providing a severability clause; and providing for publication; and providing an effective date.

BE IT ORDAINED BY THE *[governing body]* OF THE *[jurisdiction]*:

SECTION 1 That the *Liquefied Petroleum Gas Code* and documents adopted by Chapter 2, three (3) copies of which are on file and are open to inspection by the public in the office of the *[jurisdiction's keeper of records]* of the *[jurisdiction]*, are hereby adopted and incorporated into this ordinance as fully as if set out at length herein, and from the date on which this ordinance shall take effect, the provisions thereof shall be controlling within the limits of the *[jurisdiction]*. The same are hereby adopted as the code of the *[jurisdiction]* for the purpose of prescribing regulations governing conditions hazardous to life and property from fire or explosion and providing for issuance of permits and collection of fees.

SECTION 2 Any person who shall violate any provision of this code or standard hereby adopted or fail to comply therewith; or who shall violate or fail to comply with any order made thereunder; or who shall build in violation of any detailed statement of specifications or plans submitted and approved thereunder; or failed to operate in accordance with any certificate or permit issued thereunder; and from which no appeal has been taken; or who shall fail to comply with such an order as affirmed or modified by or by a court of competent jurisdiction, within the time fixed herein, shall severally for each and every such violation and noncompliance, respectively, be guilty of a misdemeanor, punishable by a fine of not less than $ _____ nor more than $_____ or by imprisonment for not less than _____ days nor more than _____ days or by both such fine and imprisonment. The imposition of one penalty for any violation shall not excuse the violation or permit it to continue; and all such persons shall be required to correct or remedy such violations or defects within a reasonable time; and when not otherwise specified the application of the above penalty shall not be held to prevent the enforced removal of prohibited conditions. Each day that prohibited conditions are maintained shall constitute a separate offense.

SECTION 3 Additions, insertions, and changes — that the 2011 edition of NFPA 58, *Liquefied Petroleum Gas Code,* is amended and changed in the following respects:

List Amendments

SECTION 4 That ordinance No. _____ of *[jurisdiction]* entitled *[fill in the title of the ordinance or ordinances in effect at the present time]* and all other ordinances or parts of ordinances in conflict herewith are hereby repealed.

SECTION 5 That if any section, subsection, sentence, clause, or phrase of this ordinance is, for any reason, held to be invalid or unconstitutional, such decision shall not affect the validity or constitutionality of the remaining portions of this ordinance. The *[governing body]* hereby declares that it would have passed this ordinance, and each section, subsection, clause, or phrase hereof, irrespective of the fact that any one or more sections, subsections, sentences, clauses, and phrases be declared unconstitutional.

SECTION 6 That the *[jurisdiction's keeper of records]* is hereby ordered and directed to cause this ordinance to be published.

[NOTE: An additional provision may be required to direct the number of times the ordinance is to be published and to specify that it is to be in a newspaper in general circulation. Posting may also be required.]

SECTION 7 That this ordinance and the rules, regulations, provisions, requirements, orders, and matters established and adopted hereby shall take effect and be in full force and effect *[time period]* from and after the date of its final passage and adoption.

Burial and Corrosion Protection for Underground and Mounded ASME Containers

This annex is not a part of the requirements of this NFPA document but is included for informational purposes only.

K.1 Scope

K.1.1 This annex provides general information for the burial of underground and mounded ASME containers of 125 gal through 2000 gal (0.5 m^3 through 7.6 m^3) water capacity.

K.1.2 The location for underground and mounded ASME containers must comply with applicable sections of Chapter 6 of this code and federal and state codes.

K.2 Container Preparation and Burial

K.2.1 Prior to burial, the container should be inspected for any coating damage that may have been caused during the installation process.

K.2.2 Cathodic protection should be considered as an additional method to minimize corrosion. Anodes are used in this process and should be attached to the container according to the anode manufacturer's instructions. The number and size of anodes installed varies, depending on the container size.

K.2.3 Dielectric couplings should be used to isolate the container from the piping when using metallic piping (e.g., copper, steel) to minimize current flow.

K.2.4 The backfill material used to cover the container should be compacted soil or coarse sand. Backfill material containing crushed rock or other material that could damage the container coating should be avoided.

K.3 Inspection and Testing of Corrosion Protection

K.3.1 A periodic test program should be established to monitor the effectiveness of the corrosion protection for the container. Inspection records should be made available to the container owner.

Informational References

Note that the mandatory referenced publications appear in Chapter 2. Many of the documents listed in Annex L also appear in Chapter 2, and although shown here for advisory purposes, they remain mandatory in the body of the code (Chapters 1 through 15).

L.1 Referenced Publications

The documents or portions thereof listed in this annex are referenced within the informational sections of this code and are not part of the requirements of this document unless also listed in Chapter 2 for other reasons.

L.1.1 NFPA Publications.

National Fire Protection Association, 1 Batterymarch Park, Quincy, MA 02169-7471.

NFPA 10, *Standard for Portable Fire Extinguishers*, 2010 edition.

NFPA 30, *Flammable and Combustible Liquids Code*, 2008 edition.

NFPA 37, *Standard for the Installation and Use of Stationary Combustion Engines and Gas Turbines*, 2010 edition.

NFPA 51, *Standard for the Design and Installation of Oxygen–Fuel Gas Systems for Welding, Cutting, and Allied Processes*, 2007 edition.

NFPA 54, *National Fuel Gas Code*, 2009 edition.

NFPA 55, *Compressed Gases and Cryogenic Fluids Code*, 2010 edition.

NFPA 61, *Standard for the Prevention of Fires and Dust Explosions in Agricultural and Food Processing Facilities*, 2008 edition.

NFPA 77, *Recommended Practice on Static Electricity*, 2007 edition.

NFPA 80, *Standard for Fire Doors and Other Opening Protectives*, 2010 edition.

NFPA 160, *Standard for the Use of Flame Effects Before an Audience*, 2011 edition.

NFPA 252, *Standard Methods of Fire Tests of Door Assemblies*, 2008 edition.

NFPA 302, *Fire Protection Standard for Pleasure and Commercial Motor Craft*, 2010 edition.

NFPA 780, *Standard for the Installation of Lightning Protection Systems*, 2011 edition.

NFPA 1192, *Standard on Recreational Vehicles*, 2008 edition.

"Fire Safety Analysis Manual for LP-Gas Storage Facilities," 2006.

L.1.2 Other Publications.

L.1.2.1 API Publications. American Petroleum Institute, 1220 L Street, N.W., Washington, DC 20005-4070.

API 620, *Design and Construction of Large, Welded, Low-Pressure Storage Tanks*, 2008.

API 1632, *Cathodic Protection of Underground Petroleum Storage Tanks and Piping Systems*, 3rd ed., 1996 (revised 2002).

API 2510, *Design and Construction of LP-Gas Installations*, 2001.

API-ASME *Code for Unfired Pressure Vessels for Petroleum Liquids and Gases*, Pre-July 1, 1961.

L.1.2.2 ASCE Publications. American Society of Civil Engineers, 1801 Alexander Bell Drive, Reston, VA 20191-4400.

ASCE 56, *Sub-Surface Investigation for Design and Construction of Foundation for Buildings*, 2006.

L.1.2.3 ASME Publications. American Society of Mechanical Engineers, Three Park Avenue, New York, NY 10016-5990.

ASME *Boiler and Pressure Vessel Code*, 2007.
ASME B31.3, *Process Piping*, 2008.

L.1.2.4 ASTM Publications. ASTM International, 100 Barr Harbor Drive, P.O. Box C700, Conshohocken, PA 19428-2959.

ASTM A 47, *Standard Specification for Ferritic Malleable Iron Castings*, 2009.
ASTM A 395, *Standard Specification for Ferritic Ductile Iron Pressure-Retaining Castings for Use at Elevated Temperatures*, 2009.
ASTM B 88, *Standard Specification for Seamless Copper Water Tube*, 2003.
ASTM B 280, *Standard Specification for Seamless Copper Tube for Air Conditioning and Refrigeration Field Service*, 2008.
ASTM D 638, *Standard Test Method for Tensile Properties of Plastics*, 2008.
ASTM D 1835, *Standard Specification for Liquefied Petroleum (LP) Gases*, 2005.
ASTM E 84, *Standard Test Method for Surface Burning Characteristics of Building Materials*, 2009.

L.1.2.5 AWS Publications. American Welding Society, 550 N.W. LeJeune Road, Miami, FL 33126, www.aws.org.

AWS Z49.1, *Safety in Welding Cutting, and Allied Processes*, 2005.

L.1.2.6 CAN/CSGB Publications. Canadian General Standards Board, Place du Portage III, 6B1, 11 Laurier Street, Gatineau, QC, K1A 1G6, Canada.

CAN/CGSB-3.0 No. 18.5, *Test for Ethyl Mercaptan Odorant in Propane, Field Method*, March 2006.

L.1.2.7 CGA Publications. Compressed Gas Association, 4221 Walney Road, 5th Floor, Chantilly, VA 20151-2923.

CGA C-6, *Standard for Visual Inspection of Steel Compressed Gas Cylinders*, 2009.
CGA C-6.3, *Guidelines for Visual Inspection and Requalification of Low Pressure Aluminum Compressed Gas Cylinders*, 2005.
CGA S-1.1, *Pressure-Relief Device Standards*, Part 1 — "Cylinders for Compressed Gases" (Errata, 1982), 2007.
CGA S-1.2, *Pressure-Relief Device Standards*, Part 2 — "Cargo and Portable Tanks for Compressed Gases," 2009.
CGA S-1.3, *Pressure Relief Device Standards,* Part 3 — "Compressed Gas Storage Containers," 2008.

L.1.2.8 GPA Publications. Gas Processors Association, 6526 East 60th Street, Tulsa, OK 74145.

Standard 2140, *Liquefied Petroleum Gas Specifications for Test Methods*, 1997.
Standard 2188, *Tentative Method for the Determination of Ethyl Mercaptan in LP-Gas Using Length of Stain Tubes*, 1989.

L.1.2.9 NACE Publications. NACE International, 1440 South Creek Drive, Houston, TX 77084-4906.

SP-01-69, *Control of External Corrosion on Underground or Submerged Metallic Piping Systems*, 2007.

RP-02-85, *Corrosion Control of Underground Storage Tank Systems by Cathodic Protection*, 2002.

L.1.2.10 PERC Publications. Propane Education and Research Council, Suite 1075, 1140 Connecticut Avenue, NW, Washington, DC 20036.

Cathodic Protection Manual and Quiz #20689590.
Cathodic Protection Systems Video.

L.1.2.11 UL Publications. Underwriters Laboratories Inc., 333 Pfingsten Rd., Northbrook, IL 60062-2096.

UL 651, *Schedule 40 or 80 Rigid PVC Conduit*, 1995.
UL 723, *Standard for Test for Surface Burning Characteristics of Building Materials*, 2008.
UL 1746, *External Corrosion Protection Systems for Steel Underground Storage Tanks*, 1993.

L.1.2.12 ULC Publications. Underwriters' Laboratories of Canada, 7 Underwriters Road, Toronto, ON M1R 3B4, Canada.

CAN/ULC S603.1, *Standard for External Corrosion Protection Systems for Steel Underground Tanks for Flammable and Combustible Liquids*, 2000.

L.1.2.13 U.S. Government Publications. U.S. Government Printing Office, Washington, DC 20402.

A New Look at Odorization Levels for Propane Gas, BERC/RI-77/1, United States Energy Research and Development Administration, Technical Information Center, September 1977.
15 U.S.C. 1261, Federal Hazardous Substances Act.
Title 16, Code of Federal Regulations, "Commercial Practices," Chapter 11, "Consumer Product Safety Commission."
Title 33, Code of Federal Regulations.
Title 49, Code of Federal Regulations, Part 178, "Specifications for Packaging."
Title 49, Code of Federal Regulations, Part 179.105-4, "Thermal Protection."
Title 49, Code of Federal Regulations, Part 180.209.
Title 49, Code of Federal Regulations, Parts 191.3, 191.9, 192.281(e), 192.283(b).
Title 49, Code of Federal Regulations, Parts 191, 192, and 195, "Transportation of Hazardous Liquids by Pipeline."

L.2 Informational References. (Reserved)

L.3 References for Extracts in Informational Sections. (Reserved)

PART TWO

Supplements

The seven supplements included in Part Two of the *LP-Gas Code Handbook* provide additional information as well as supporting reference material to assist users and enforcers of NFPA 58, *Liquefied Petroleum Gas Code*. The supplements are not part of NFPA 58 or the commentary presented in the previous part of this book. Additionally, former Supplement 3, Sizing of Independent Pressure Regulators for Large Propane Systems, from the 2008 edition of the handbook can be accessed at www.nfpa.org/58HB.

1. Guidelines for Conducting a Fire Safety Analysis
2. LP-Gas Systems Subject to DOT Pipeline Regulations
3. Fire Testing of Composite Propane Cylinders
4. Preparing Propane Companies for Natural Disasters
5. Cathodic Protection
6. Home Fires Involving Grills
7. Technical/Substantive Changes from the 2008 Edition to the 2011 Edition of NFPA 58

Guidelines for Conducting a Fire Safety Analysis

Editor's Note: *Supplement 1 is intended to assist enforcement officials and installers of LP-Gas storage facilities in conducting the fire safety analysis required in Section 6.25, Fire Protection, of NFPA 58.*

The section on fire protection was first introduced in the 1976 edition of NFPA 58. At the time, enforcement officials and installers of LP-Gas storage facilities lacked clear guidance on how to conduct a fire safety analysis. The National Propane Gas Association's (NPGA's) Safety Committee developed a safety bulletin to provide guidance in conducting the analysis, which was reprinted as this supplement up to the 1998 edition. At that time, the NPGA Safety Bulletin was withdrawn, and this supplement was revised to provide in a clear, usable form much of the information needed to conduct the fire safety analysis.

A significant change in the 2001 edition of the code required all installations having aggregate storage exceeding 4000 gal (15.1 m³) water capacity to have a fire safety analysis prepared and used as a tool for coordinating with the local emergency response agency.

In 2003, NFPA and NPGA received funding from the Propane Education and Research Council (PERC) to develop a manual for conducting the fire safety analysis required by the 2001 edition of NFPA 58, in order to assist in complying with the requirement for a written fire safety analysis. The document, "Fire Safety Analysis Manual for LP-Gas Storage Facilities" [1], is available at all three organizations' websites: www.propanecouncil.org (PERC), www.nfpa.org, and www.npga.org. The manual provides a series of drawings of containers and their appurtenances and forms to verify compliance with the product control requirements of NFPA 58. Manuals are available for both the 2001 and 2004 editions of NFPA 58. References to the appropriate code sections are included in addition to an analysis of hazards such as exposure to and from adjacent properties. It is hoped that the manual, by providing a step-by-step method to complete the analysis, will make it practical for propane system operators to comply with the requirement for the fire safety analysis.

It is anticipated that the Fire Safety Analysis Manual for LP-Gas Storage Facilities will be updated to reflect the changes that occurred in the 2011 edition of NFPA 58.

INTRODUCTION

NFPA 58 requires that fire protection be provided for all LP-Gas facilities incorporating storage of more than 4000 gal (15.1 m³) water capacity. (See Section 6.25, Fire Pro-tection, for the specific requirements.) A competent fire safety analysis (hereinafter abbreviated as FSA) is required to determine whether a serious hazard exists and to determine the type and degree of fire protection needed for the facility.

A change in the 2001 edition of the code required that all facilities storing over 4000 gal (15.1 m^3) of LP-Gas have an FSA within 3 years of the effective date of the 2001 edition of the code. Now that that date has passed, an FSA is required for all LP-Gas storage facilities with aggregate storage greater than 4000 gal (15.1 m^3) water capacity.

The FSA requirement for fire protection was introduced to the code in 1976. Several items were relocated to the appendix in the 1998 edition because they were not mandatory requirements but rather a list of items to be included in the study. The 1976 edition also instructed that the first consideration in the analysis be an evaluation of the use of water applied with hose streams by the facility's fire brigade or local fire department "for the effective control of hazardous leakage or fire exposing storage tanks, cargo vehicles, or railroad tank cars which may be present."

The 1995 edition changed the first consideration of the FSA to an evaluation of the total product control system. This total product control system includes emergency shutoff valves and internal valves having remote and thermal shutoff capability and pull-away protection, as well as the optional requirements of Section 6.26, Alternate Provisions for Installation of ASME Containers. The FSA is concerned, in part, with the factors that can lead to a boiling liquid expanding vapor explosion (BLEVE) of a storage tank at a facility. These events occur very infrequently.

A BLEVE is a failure mode of tanks containing liquids at a temperature above their normal atmospheric boiling point. Because the boiling point of propane is about –40°F (–40°C), propane is above its boiling point on all but the coldest of days in the coldest climates. A BLEVE occurs when the tank cannot continue to contain the liquid in it, and the contents begin to leak out. Because the tank is under pressure, this release of contents is rapid, and the expansion of the released liquid to vapor creates a greatly increased volume (about 260:1, vapor to liquid) that provides the energy to propel parts of the container. The following factors can contribute to the tank becoming weakened to the point that it can no longer contain the pressure it was designed to hold:

- Reduction in wall thickness due to corrosion
- Damage to wall by mechanical means (e.g., gouging)
- Softening of part of the tank wall due to heating by flame [Steel, the material used for larger LP-Gas tanks, becomes unusable for pressure containment above approximately 1000°F (538°C) to 1100°F (593°C), depending on the alloy. This temperature range is easily reached in a fire.]

An analysis of the effects of heat absorption by steel propane containers was conducted as part of the development of the *Fire Safety Analysis Manual*. The results, included in the *Manual*, show that propane containers installed at the distances specified in NFPA 58 will not be affected by fires beyond those distances. This demonstration is important because it corroborates the separation distances that have been used in NFPA 58 for several decades.

The following three important factors should be considered before and during any FSA:

1. The product control features and operating procedures must be evaluated to determine whether any fire protection is needed.
2. If fire protection is needed, installation and design changes, product control features, and improved operating procedures must be considered to ensure that a serious hazard will not occur at the facility.
3. The safety of facility employees, the public, emergency response personnel, and the property surrounding the installation must be ensured.

PURPOSE OF AN FSA

The FSA is required by 6.25.3.2. Its purpose is to determine the safety of the facility, including any fire protection features provided beyond the specific requirements of NFPA 58. If the FSA indicates that a serious hazard does not exist, then fire protection is not required. If the FSA indicates that a serious hazard does exist, then special protection in accordance with 6.25.5 is needed. The facility owner and the authority having jurisdiction determine the type of special protection.

The purpose of the FSA is not to determine whether a facility should or should not be installed. That determination is beyond the scope of NFPA 58. Local or state laws, including zoning laws, may cover the installation of an LP-Gas facility. The FSA may recommend or require fire protection features in addition to the types of special protection in 6.25.5.

CONDUCTING AN FSA

Despite efforts to eliminate hazards within an LP-Gas facility in its design and operation, prudent management must consider that accidents can occur and must therefore provide features to deal with potential accidents as well as provide training to operating staff to deal with emergencies. The FSA is primarily concerned with the evaluation of potential hazards in order to identify whether special protection is needed and the type of special protection that can be used. Recommendations for post-construction operational features can be included in the analysis.

ELEMENTS OF AN FSA

The basic components of an FSA are stated in A.6.25.3 and are as follows:

1. The effectiveness of product control measures
2. An analysis of local conditions of hazard within the container site
3. Exposure to or from other properties, population density, and congestion within the site
4. The probable effectiveness of plant fire brigades or local fire departments based on adequate water supply, response time, and training
5. Consideration for the adequate application of water by hose stream or other method for effective control of leakage, fire, or other exposures
6. If necessary, a designated time period for review of the fire safety analysis with local emergency response agencies to ensure preplanning and emergency response plans for the installation are current

It is recommended that the *Fire Safety Analysis Manual* be used to conduct the analysis. However, it must be noted that NFPA 58 does not mandate use of the *Manual*.

REFERENCE CITED

1. Raj, P. K., and T. C. Lemoff. *Fire Safety Analysis Manual for LP-Gas Storage Facilities* (2008). Available from www.nfpa.org.

LP-Gas Systems Subject to DOT Pipeline Regulations

Editor's Note: This supplement provides designers, installers, operators, and regulatory officials of systems supplying LP-Gas vapor to multiple consumers with information on how both NFPA 58 and U.S. Department of Transportation (DOT) Pipeline Safety Regulations, Title 49, Code of Federal Regulations, Part 192, are administered by the Office of Pipeline Safety of DOT. The latter is referred to in this supplement as the DOT Pipeline Regulations. To be consistent with the term used by pipeline safety regulators, the multiple consumer systems that fall under both sets of regulations will be referred to as "jurisdictional systems."

The editor thanks Kenneth Wood, Partner of Education Training & Safety Associates, and Richard Marini, retired New Hampshire director of gas safety, who authored this supplement.

JURISDICTIONAL SYSTEM

For the purposes of this supplement, a jurisdictional system is a system that is under the jurisdiction of 49 CFR 192 [1] and NFPA 58. In June of 1996 changes to federal law, as stated in 49 CFR 192, simplified compliance for operators of these jurisdictional systems by clarifying the reference to NFPA 58 in these regulations.

Prior to 1996, NFPA 58 was referenced in the DOT Pipeline Regulations, but it was not clear where NFPA 58 applied. In 1996, the DOT Pipeline Regulations were revised to state that for LP-Gas systems, NFPA 58 supersedes the DOT Pipeline Regulations where they both cover the same subject. Where NFPA 58 is silent, the DOT Pipeline Regulations apply. This change was made in order to recognize that the DOT Pipeline Regulations were primarily intended to cover fuel distribution pipelines.

Many operators of multi-consumer LP-Gas systems have usually kept their systems small enough to avoid being under the jurisdiction of the DOT Pipeline Regulations. However, the 1996 changes to the DOT Pipeline Regulations make compliance easier. The additional requirements can also enhance safety.

An LP-Gas system is jurisdictional where one of the following conditions exists:

- Ten or more customers are supplied from a single tank or multiple tanks that are manifolded together. The location in this scenario does not matter.
- More than one customer is supplied from a single tank or multiple tanks that are manifolded together where a portion of the system is located in a public place.

The interpretation of public place by the Office of Pipeline Safety of DOT 49 CFR 192.1 is as follows:

The term public place in Section 192.1 means a place that is generally open to all persons in a community as opposed to being restricted to specific persons. DOT considers churches, schools, and commercial buildings, as well as any publicly owned right-of-way or property frequented by persons, to be public places.

An LP-Gas system is not jurisdictional where a single customer and the system are located entirely on the customer's premises, even if part of the system is located in a public place.

The following comments and exhibits clarify jurisdiction:

- A system that consists of a single LP-Gas tank supplying one residence is not jurisdictional, provided that no portion of the system is located in a public place other than on the customer's premises. NFPA 58 covers this typical residential installation.
- A system that consists of five mobile homes supplied by one LP-Gas tank in a mobile home park is not jurisdictional. NFPA 58 covers systems of fewer than 10 customers.
- A system that consists of 10 or more homes supplied by a single LP-Gas tank is jurisdictional. (See Exhibit S2.1.)

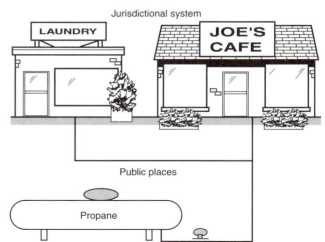

EXHIBIT S2.2 *System Consisting of a Single LP-Gas Tank Supplying More Than One Customer Where the System Is Located in a Public Place.*

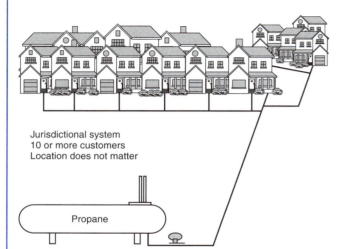

EXHIBIT S2.1 *System Consisting of 10 or More Homes Supplied by a Single LP-Gas Tank.*

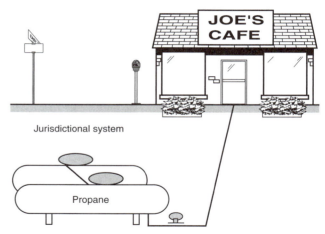

EXHIBIT S2.3 *System Consisting of Two Manifolded LP-Gas Tanks Supplying a Restaurant Where a Portion of the System Is Located in a Public Place.*

- A system that consists of a single LP-Gas tank supplying more than one customer where the system is located in a public place (e.g., a parking lot) is jurisdictional. (See Exhibit S2.2.)
- A system that consists of two manifolded LP-Gas tanks supplying a restaurant where a portion of the system is located in a public place that is not part of the customer premises is jurisdictional. (See Exhibit S2.3.)

All jurisdictional systems must follow NFPA 58. In addition, the following plans are required by the DOT Pipeline Regulations.

PLANS REQUIRED BY THE DOT PIPELINE REGULATIONS

The DOT Pipeline Regulations and NFPA 58 require the operators of all jurisdictional systems to have plans for operations and maintenance and emergency response activities. Most operators of LP-Gas systems comply with this requirement by developing and maintaining one plan that covers both the operations and the maintenance of a facility. The plan must be prepared before operations on an LP-Gas system begin and must be updated once a year. The plan must be available at locations where operations and maintenance activities are conducted. The complete requirements for these plans can be found in the DOT Pipeline Regulations, 49 CFR 192.605 and 192.615 [1,2].

Note that inspectors from the Pipeline and Hazardous Materials Safety Administration (PHMSA) of DOT or state agencies enforcing the DOT Pipeline Regulations can, after due process, require an LP-Gas operator to amend his or her plans to provide a reasonable level of safety.

Plans for Operations and Maintenance

The operations and maintenance plans required of all jurisdictional systems must be written, and they must be followed. All operations and maintenance plans must contain the following components:

1. *Investigation of Failures.* Procedures for analyzing accidents and failures in order to determine the cause and to minimize the probability of recurrence must be included.

2. *Operating Pressure.* The maximum operating pressure for an LP-Gas system must be identified. For small LP-Gas systems, this pressure is 20 psig (138 kPag) in most cases. Although higher pressures can be used, NFPA 58 requires that regulators use a 10 psig (69 kPag) interstage pressure. Higher pressures can be used for economy of pipe (i.e., the higher the pressure, the smaller the pipe). However, the minimum ambient temperature must be taken into account to prevent liquefaction of propane.

3. *Pressure Testing.* It is important to verify that systems are pressure tested to ensure that they do not leak and can safely operate within the intended pressure limits. This requirement is covered in Section 6.14 of NFPA 58. Procedures for pressure testing must be included in the plan.

4. *Tapping or Purging of Pipelines.* If tapping or purging is performed, those procedures must be included in the plan. Tapping is the addition of points of use, or taps, to an existing pipeline.

5. *Odorization.* A provision for the measurement of the odor of LP-Gas must be included. A "Bill of Lading" normally shows odorization of each transport or railroad car shipment. All transport or railroad car shipments delivered directly to a bulk plant must be checked for the presence of odorant by a sniff test or other means. For smaller systems that receive bobtail shipments of propane, a similar procedure to verify the presence of odorant must be included. This test can be as simple as smelling the gas periodically. Large jurisdictional systems, such as those serving a town distribution system, may require testing of certain areas of the distribution system to ensure that odorant can be readily detected at one-fifth of the lower flammable limit of LP-Gas.

6. *Patrolling.* Operators must include provisions for patrolling mains located in places, or on structures, where anticipated physical movement or external loading (e.g., weight, traffic) could cause failure or leakage. Patrolling is normally not necessary for small jurisdictional LP-Gas systems. However, exceptions are possible, such as a system that has already experienced some of the noted problems.

7. *Leak Surveys.* Procedures for conducting an annual leak survey must be included. (See Compliance Actions later in this supplement.)

8. *Line Markers.* If the system crosses under a public road or railroad, markers can be required at each crossing point and where necessary to locate the line to reduce the possibility of damage or interference. Line markers are usually not required for most LP-Gas jurisdictional systems.

9. *Testing for Reinstating a Service Line.* A provision for testing each service line that has been disconnected from the main in the same manner as new service, before placing it back into service, must be included.

10. *Abandonment or Deactivation of Facilities.* Provisions for shutdown, abandonment, or inactivation of facilities must be included. When gas piping is abandoned, it must be physically disconnected at both ends, and the open ends must be sealed. In addition, the operator must determine if it is necessary to purge the line.

11. *Key Valve Maintenance.* Key valves, or critical valves, are the valves needed to shut down the system, or parts of the system, in case of emergency. In a small propane system, the tank valve is the key valve. In a larger system, the key valves are the container valve and valves that can shut off branches of the system. Annual maintenance of these valves must be included. (See Compliance Actions later in this supplement.)

12. *Accidental Ignition of Gas.* Provisions to prevent the accidental ignition of gas must be included. Propane is flammable when mixed with 2.15 percent to 9.6 percent air and will ignite where an ignition source is present. Every precaution must be taken to prevent unintentional ignition of propane. When venting propane, a fire extinguisher must be available and located for immediate use.

13. *Corrosion Protection.* Provisions for corrosion protection of underground metallic piping systems and underground tanks should be included. If only polyethylene pipe is used, no protection is needed. If underground tanks are used with a sacrificial cathodic protection system, measurements of the voltage should be conducted annually or at more frequent intervals. This action can be delegated to a consultant who has the appropriate qualifications and equipment. (See Compliance Actions later in this supplement.)

14. *Construction Records, Maps, and Operating History.* The operator must have construction records, maps, and operating history of the system and must follow procedures to make them available to operating personnel.

15. *Gathering of Data Needed for Reporting Incidents.* Procedures to compile information on pipeline incidents and safety-related conditions must be included. These procedures must ensure accurate and timely reporting. This information must be readily available.

16. *Startup and Shutdown of Any Part of the System.* Step-by-step procedures for the startup and shutdown of the system must be included, as well as procedures to be followed by operating personnel during an abnormal operating condition.

Emergency Plans

Each operator is required to keep a written plan of procedures used to respond to emergencies. The emergency plan should contain at minimum the following information. (See Exhibit S2.4.)

1. *Emergency Notification List.* The names and telephone numbers of the following personnel should be included:

- System operator
- Fire department
- Gas company
- Other entity whose service may be necessary in the event of an emergency

A copy of this list should be posted in a public area.

2. *Map of Key Valve Locations.* A map of the system showing the location of key valves must be included. A small system that supplies one facility from a single tank, where a portion of the system is located in a public place, must have a map showing the tank, pipeline, and customer location, with the tank valve identified as the key valve. A small system that supplies one facility from a single tank, where no portion of the system is located in a public place, must have a map showing the tank and the tank valve, and other key valves where present.

3. *Description and Location of Emergency Equipment.* The operator must determine what emergency equipment is needed and ensure that it is available. A description of the emergency equipment and its location must be included. Most operators of small LP-Gas systems serving a limited number of users may not have emergency equipment on site, but rely on their installer or propane supplier to provide emergency equipment when needed. In a small system, closing the tank valve will stop the escape of fuel and end an incident. Of course, quick action is needed to restore service to unaffected users, especially in winter. Where emergency equipment is not on site, its location and how to obtain it should be available on site.

4. *Response to Gas Leak Reports and Interruption of Gas Service.* The operator must have written procedures to

Checklist for a Major Emergency

- ☐ Fire department called
- ☐ Persons evacuated and affected area blockaded
- ☐ Local or regional police department notified
- ☐ Repair personnel notified
- ☐ Company call list executed
- ☐ Communication established
- ☐ Outside help requested
- ☐ Ambulances called if needed
- ☐ Leak shut off or brought under control
- ☐ Civil defense authorities notified
- ☐ Emergency valves or valves to shut down or reroute gas identified and located
- ☐ Individual service of each customer shut off (if an area has been cut off from a supply of gas)
- ☐ Situation under control and the possibility of recurrence eliminated
- ☐ Surrounding area, including buildings adjacent to and across streets, checked for the possibility of additional gas leakage, if appropriate
- ☐ Proper tag placed on affected meters
- ☐ Telephone report made to the state officials
- ☐ Telephone report made to the Office of Pipeline Safety
- ☐ Local radio station notified, if necessary

EXHIBIT S2.4 *Sample Checklist for a Major Emergency.*

be followed in response to gas leaks reported by customers. The operator's responsibility is to ensure that all employees are familiar with procedures for responding to gas leak calls and reports.

5. *Reporting Requirements (Telephone Reports).* In case of an incident, a telephone report must be made immediately to the National Response Center (800-424-8802). An incident is any event involving release of gas from a pipeline and the occurrence of any of the following:

- Death or injury requiring inpatient hospitalization
- Estimated property damage of $50,000 or more
- Unusual occurrence that the operator deems necessary to report

The telephone report must be followed with a written report using DOT Form RSPA F 7100.1 and addressed to the Information Resources Manager, Office of Pipeline Safety, Research and Special Programs Administration Pipeline and Hazardous Materials Safety Administration, U.S. Department of Transportation, Room 7128, 400 Seventh Street, SW, Washington, DC 20590. The written report should be submitted as soon as practicable but no more than 30 days after the incident. Form RSPA F 7100.1 is reproduced here as Exhibit S2.5 and can be copied to file incident reports.

NOTICE: This report is required by 49 CFR Part 191. Failure to report can result in a civil penalty not to exceed $100,000 for each violation for each day the violation continues up to a maximum of $1,000,000 for any related series of violations as provided in 49 USC 60122.

Form Approved
OMB No. 2137-0522

INCIDENT REPORT - GAS DISTRIBUTION SYSTEM

U.S. Department of Transportation
Pipeline and Hazardous Materials Safety
Administration

Report Date _____
No. _____
(DOT Use Only)

INSTRUCTIONS

Important: Please read the separate instructions for completing this form before you begin. They clarify the information requested and provide specific examples. If you do not have a copy of the instructions, you can obtain one from the Office Of Pipeline Safety Web Page at http://ops.dot.gov.

PART A – GENERAL REPORT INFORMATION   Check: ☐ **Original Report**   ☐ **Supplemental Report**   ☐ **Final Report**

1. Operator Name and Address

a. Operator's 5-digit Identification Number / / / / / /

b. If Operator does not own the pipeline, enter Owner's 5-digit Identification Number / / / / / /

c. Name of Operator _____

d. Operator street address _____

e. Operator address _____
City, County or Parish, State and Zip Code

2. Time and date of the incident

/ / / /   / / /   / / /   / / /
hr.   month   day   year

3. Incident Location

a. _____
Street or nearest street or road

b. _____
City and County or Parish

c. _____
State and Zip Code

d. Latitude: / / / / / / Longitude: / / / / / /
(if not available, see instructions for how to provide specific location)

e. Class location description
○ Class 1 ○ Class 2 ○ Class 3 ○ Class 4

f. Incident on Federal Land ○ Yes ○ No

4. Type of leak or rupture

○ Leak: ○ Pinhole ○ Connection Failure *(complete sec. F5)*

○ Puncture, diameter or cross section *(inches)*____

○ Rupture (if applicable):
○ Circumferential – Separation

○ Longitudinal

–Tear/Crack, length *(inches)* _____

– Propagation Length, total, both sides *(feet)* _____

○ N/A

○ Other: _____

5. Consequences *(check and complete all that apply)*

a. ☐ Fatality   Total number of people: / / / /

Employees: / / / /   General Public: / / / /

Non-employee Contractors: / / / /

b. ☐ Injury requiring inpatient hospitalization

Total number of people: / / / /

Employees: / / / /   General Public: / / / /

Non-employee Contractors: / / / /

c. ☐ Property damage/loss *(estimated)*   Total $_____

Gas loss $_____   Operator damage $_____

Public/private property damage $_____

d. ☐ Gas ignited   Explosion ○ No Explosion

e. ☐ Gas did not ignite ○ Explosion ○ No Explosion

f. ☐ Evacuation *(general public only)* / / / / / people

Evacuation Reason:
○ Unknown
○ Emergency worker or public official ordered, precautionary
○ Threat to the public
○ Company policy

6. Elapsed time until area was made safe:

/ / / hr.   / / / min.

7. Telephone Report

/ / / / / /   / / / / / / / / /
NRC Report Number   month   day   year

8. a. Estimated pressure at point and time of incident:
_____ PSIG

b. Max. allowable operating pressure *(MAOP)*: _____ PSIG

c. MAOP established by:
○ Test Pressure _____ psig
○ 49 CFR § 192. 619 (a)(3)

PART B – PREPARER AND AUTHORIZED SIGNATURE

(type or print) Preparer's Name and Title _____   Area Code and Telephone Number _____

Preparer's E-mail Address _____   Area Code and Facsimile Number _____

Authorized Signature _____   (type or print) Name and Title _____   Date ____   Area Code and Telephone Number _____

Form PHMSA F 7100.1 (03-04)   *Reproduction of this form is permitted*   Page 1 of 3

EXHIBIT S2.5 *RSPA Form F 7100.1.*

PART C - ORIGIN OF THE INCIDENT

1. Incident occurred on
   - ○ Main   ○ Meter Set
   - ○ Service Line   ○ Other: _____
   - ○ Pressure Limiting and Regulating Facility

2. Failure occurred on
   - ○ Body of pipe   ○ Pipe Seam
   - ○ Joint   ○ Component
   - ○ Other: _____

3. Material involved *(pipe, fitting, or other component)*
   - ○ Steel
   - ○ Cast/Wrought Iron
   - ○ Polyethelene Plastic (complete all items that apply in a-c)
   - ○ Other Plastic (complete all items that apply in a-c)
     - Plastic failure was: ☐ a. ductile ☐ b. brittle ☐ c. joint failure
   - ○ Other material: _____

4. Year the pipe or component which failed was installed: / / / / /

PART D – MATERIAL SPECIFICATION (if applicable)

1. Nominal pipe size *(NPS)*   / / / / / in.
2. Wall thickness   / / / / / in.
3. Specification _____ SMYS / / / / / / /
4. Seam type _____
5. Valve type _____
6. Pipe or valve manufactured by _____ in year / / / / /

PART E – ENVIRONMENT

1. Area of incident
   - ○ Under pavement   ○ In open ditch
   - ○ Under ground   ○ Above ground
   - ○ Inside/under building   ○ Under water
                          ○ Other: _____

2. Depth of cover: _____ inches

PART F – APPARENT CAUSE

Important: There are 25 numbered causes in this section. Check the box to the left of the primary cause of the incident. Check one circle in each of the supplemental items to the right of or below the cause you indicate. See the instructions for this form for guidance.

F1 – CORROSION

If either F1 (1) External Corrosion, or F1 (2) Internal Corrosion is checked, complete all subparts a – e.

1. ☐ External Corrosion

2. ☐ Internal Corrosion

a. Pipe Coating
   - ○ Bare
   - ○ Coated
   - ○ Unknown

b. Visual Examination
   - ○ Localized Pitting
   - ○ General Corrosion
   - ○ Other: _____

c. Cause of Corrosion
   - ○ Galvanic   ○ Stray Current
   - ○ Improper Cathodic Protection
   - ○ Microbiological
   - ○ Other: _____

d. Was corroded part of pipeline considered to be under cathodic protection prior to discovering incident?
   - ○ No   ○ Yes   ○ Unknown   Year Protection Started: / / / / /

e. Was pipe previously damaged in the area of corrosion?
   - ○ No   ○ Yes   ○ Unknown   How long prior to incident: / / / / years / / / months

F2 – NATURAL FORCES

3. ☐ Earth Movement   ⇒ ○ Earthquake   ○ Subsidence   ○ Landslide   ○ Other: _____

4. ☐ Lightning

5. ☐ Heavy Rains/Floods ⇒ ○ Washouts   ○ Flotation   ○ Mudslide   ○ Scouring   ○ Other: _____

6. ☐ Temperature   ⇒ ○ Thermal stress   ○ Frost heave   ○ Frozen components   ○ Other: _____

7. ☐ High Winds

F3 - EXCAVATION

8. ☐ Operator Excavation Damage *(including their contractors)* / Not Third Party

9. ☐ Third Party Excavation Damage *(complete a-d)*
   - a. Excavator group
     - ○ General Public   ○ Government   ○ Excavator other than Operator/subcontractor
   - b. Type: ○ Road Work ○ Pipeline ○ Water ○ Electric ○ Sewer ○ Phone/Cable/Fiber ○ Landowner ○ Railroad
     - ○ Building Construction   ○ Other: _____
   - c. Did operator get prior notification of excavation activity?
     - ○ No ○ Yes: Date received: / / / mo. / / / day / / / yr.
     - Notification received from: ○ One Call System ○ Excavator ○ General Contractor ○ Landowner
   - d. Was pipeline marked?
     - ○ No ○ Yes *(If Yes, check applicable items i – iv)*
       - i. Temporary markings: ○ Flags   ○ Stakes   ○ Paint
       - ii. Permanent markings: ○ Yes   ○ No
       - iii. Marks were *(check one)*   ○ Accurate   ○ Not Accurate
       - iv. Were marks made within required time? ○ Yes ○ No

F4 – OTHER OUTSIDE FORCE DAMAGE

10. ☐ Fire/Explosion as primary cause of failure   ⇒ Fire/Explosion cause: ○ Man made   ○ Natural   *Describe in Part G*

11. ☐ Car, truck or other vehicle not relating to excavation activity damaging pipe

12. ☐ Rupture of Previously Damaged Pipe

13. ☐ Vandalism

Form PHMSA F 7100.1 (03-04)   *Page 2 of 3*

F5 – MATERIAL OR WELDS

Material

14. ☐ Body of Pipe ⇒ ○ Dent   ○ Gouge   ○ Wrinkle Bend   ○ Arc Burn   ○ Other: _____

15. ☐ Component ⇒ ○ Valve   ○ Fitting   ○ Vessel   ○ Extruded Outlet   ○ Other: _____

16. ☐ Joint ⇒ ○ Gasket   ○ O-Ring   ○ Threads   ○ Fusion   ○ Other: _____

Weld

17. ☐ Butt ⇒ ○ Pipe   ○ Fabrication   ○ Other: _____

18. ☐ Fillet ⇒ ○ Branch   ○ Hot Tap   ○ Fitting   ○ Repair Sleeve   ○ Other: _____

19. ☐ Pipe Seam ⇒ ○ LF ERW   ○ DSAW   ○ Seamless   ○ Flash Weld

    ○ HF ERW   ○ SAW   ○ Spiral   ○ Other: _____

*Complete a-f if you indicate **any** cause in part F5.*

    a. Type of failure:

      ☐ Construction Defect ⇒ ○ Poor Workmanship   ○ Procedure not followed   ○ Poor Construction Procedures

      ☐ Material Defect

    b. Was failure due to pipe damage sustained in transportation to the construction or fabrication site?   ○ Yes   ○ No

    c. Was part which leaked pressure tested before incident occurred?   ○ Yes, *complete d-f, **if known***   ○ No

    d. Date of test: /   /   / mo.   /   /   / day   /   /   / yr.

    e. Time held at test pressure: /   /   / hr.

    f. Estimated test pressure at point of incident: _____ PSIG

F6 – EQUIPMENT OR OPERATIONS

20. ☐ Malfunction of Control/Relief Equipment ⇒ ○ Valve   ○ Instrumentation   ○ Pressure Regulator   ○ Other: _____

21. ☐ Threads Stripped, Broken Pipe Coupling ⇒ ○ Nipples   ○ Valve Threads   ○ Mechanical Couplings   ○ Other: _____

22. ☐ Leaking Seals

23. ☐ Incorrect Operation

    a. Type: ○ Inadequate Procedures   ○ Inadequate Safety Practices   ○ Failure to Follow Procedures   ○ Other: _____

    b. Number of employees involved in incident who failed post-incident drug test: /   /   /   / Alcohol test: /   /   /   /

    c. Was person involved in incident qualified per OQ rule?   ○ Yes   ○ No   d. Hours on duty for person involved: /   /   /

F7 – OTHER

24. ☐ Miscellaneous, *describe:* _____

25. ☐ Unknown

    ○ Investigation Complete   ○ Still Under Investigation *(submit a supplemental report when investigation is complete)*

PART G – NARRATIVE DESCRIPTION OF FACTORS CONTRIBUTING TO THE EVENT	*(Attach additional sheets as necessary)*

***EXHIBIT S2.5** Continued.*

Note that LP-Gas operators should check with their state pipeline agency for state reporting requirements.

6. *Restoration of Gas Service After an Outage.* Qualified persons must follow proper procedures to safely restore gas service after an outage. These procedures should include details of appliance relighting procedures.

7. *Investigation Procedures.* Each operator must establish procedures for investigating incidents and failures, including the following:

- Evaluating the situation
- Protecting life and property
- Securing the area
- Conducting a leak survey
- Conducting meter and regulator checks
- Questioning persons on the scene
- Examining burn and debris patterns
- Testing odorization level
- Recording meter readings
- Recording weather conditions
- Selecting samples of the failed facility or equipment

Small LP-Gas systems not operated by an individual in the propane business will normally not have the ability to investigate accidents and will rely on their propane supplier or an outside contractor.

8. *Education and Training.* Operating personnel must be qualified to ensure understanding and competency in performance of emergency procedures.

ONE-CALL AND DAMAGE PREVENTION PROGRAM

LP-Gas operators that have jurisdictional systems must have a damage prevention plan and be members of, and participate in, a qualified one-call system to protect such systems from dig-ins. It is recommended that LP operators check with their state one-call systems to determine the laws and regulations that apply to them.

One-Call Systems

A one-call system provides a telephone communication link between excavators and operators of underground pipeline and facilities. The heart of the system is an operational center whose main function is to transfer information from excavators about their intended excavation activities to the operators of underground pipelines and facilities participating in the system. Excavators have to make only a single call to an operational center to start the process, thus the name "one-call." Upon receipt of the information, operators of pipelines and facilities that could be affected by the ex-

cavation activity arrange for the timely identification and marking of underground facilities that are in the vicinity of the intended activity. When necessary, the underground operators inspect the site being excavated and advise the excavator of the need for special measures to protect buried or exposed facilities. One-call notification systems may perform various other functions relevant to protecting underground pipelines and facilities from damage, such as record keeping and public awareness programs.

Excavation

Excavation activities must not be conducted without first ascertaining the location of all underground facilities that could be affected by the excavation. Excavation activities include excavation, blasting, boring, tunneling, backfilling, and other earth-moving operations, as well as the removal of aboveground structures by either explosive or mechanical means.

Prior to any excavation, each excavator must serve notice of intent to excavate to the One-Call Center serving the area in which the proposed excavation will occur. Notice must be given to the local One-Call Center in accordance with state regulations in advance of excavation. This requirement may vary from 24 to 72 hours, excluding weekends and holidays.

EMERGENCY EXCAVATION

An emergency excavation is an excavation performed to eliminate an imminent danger to life, health, or property. Telephone notification of the emergency excavation must be given as soon as possible to the One-Call Center. If necessary, emergency assistance should be requested from each operator to locate and protect its underground facilities.

OPERATOR QUALIFICATION

All operators of jurisdictional LP-Gas systems were required to have a written operator qualification program in place by April 27, 2001. By October 28, 2002, all employees performing covered tasks were required to be qualified to meet the requirements of 49 CFR 192 N of the federal pipeline safety regulations.

General Requirements

The operator must

- Identify covered tasks
- Determine who must be qualified
- Determine the method of qualification
- Determine requalification procedures
- Keep records

Covered Tasks

A covered task is an activity identified by the operator that fulfills all of the following four characteristics:

1. It is performed on a pipeline facility.
2. It is an operations or maintenance task. (Note: This task includes an emergency response.)
3. It is performed as a requirement of 49 CFR 192 of the federal pipeline safety regulations.
4. It affects the operation or integrity of the pipeline.

Covered tasks in a typical small LP-Gas system include the following:

*   Installing regulators and meter sets
*   Testing service lines
*   Protecting against corrosion (underground and atmospheric)
*   Joining plastic pipe or tubing with mechanical fittings
*   Purging pipelines
*   Making permanent repairs
*   Locating and marking facilities
*   Performing leak surveys
*   Tapping pipelines under pressure
*   Purging pipelines
*   Abandoning pipelines
*   Operating and maintaining vaporizers

These tasks can be carried out by the operator, contractor, or gas supplier.

Operator Qualification Program

The written qualification program must include provisions that accomplish the following:

*   Identify covered tasks
*   Ensure that individuals are qualified
*   Allow unqualified individuals to perform a covered task while under the observation of a qualified individual
*   Evaluate the individual's qualifications in the event of an incident
*   Evaluate the individual if there is reason to believe that the individual is no longer qualified
*   Inform the qualified individual of any changes affecting the covered task
*   Establish a plan that provides adequate training for performing covered tasks safely and, if any significant changes are made to the plan, inform the state agency
*   Determine intervals for requalification

Record Keeping

Qualification records must be maintained as long as the individual is performing the covered task. Records of indi-

viduals no longer performing a covered task must be kept for five years.

Records must include the following information:

*   Identification of qualified individuals
*   Covered tasks the individual is qualified to perform
*   Date of current qualification
*   Qualification method

COMPLIANCE ACTIONS

The following are some of the commonly used methods of compliance with DOT regulations. State pipeline regulations and 49 CFR 192 should always be referenced, to ensure compliance. Local pipeline regulatory officials can assist in understanding these regulations.

Leak Surveys

Leak surveys are part of periodic maintenance. Leak surveys using leak detection equipment must be conducted in business districts such as shopping malls. The surveys should include tests of the atmosphere in gas, electric, telephone, sewer, and water system manholes; at cracks in pavement and sidewalks; and at other locations providing an opportunity for finding gas leaks. These tests should be performed annually, but at intervals not exceeding 15 months. Leak surveys with leak detector equipment must be conducted outside business districts as frequently as necessary, but at intervals not exceeding 5 years.

Some operators are currently being allowed to use the pressure drop test method for compliance of their systems. It is important to remember that if any drop occurs, gas detection equipment is almost always needed to pinpoint the leak. Other factors to consider when doing a pressure drop test are the volume of the piping system being tested, the time duration necessary for performing an adequate test after considering the volume, and the accuracy of the instrument or gauge used during the test.

LP-Gas system surveys using gas detection equipment must include a subsurface survey where underground piping is a part of the system. This survey is usually done with a special tool, a bar hammer, that is used to make a hole for sampling. Both flame ionization detectors and combustible gas indicators can be used to determine whether gas is present. If any leak is found, equipment that gives a numerical reading must be used to determine the seriousness and location of the leak from multiple test holes.

Cathodic Protection of Underground Piping

Each system that is cathodically protected must be tested annually, but at intervals not exceeding 15 months, to determine whether the cathodic protection is adequate. Criteria to ensure that cathodic protection is adequate can be found in Appendix D of 49 CFR 192. A commonly used method for LP-Gas systems is determining whether a negative (cathodic) voltage of at least 0.85 volt, with reference to a saturated copper-copper sulfate half cell, exists between the pipe or underground tank and remote earth. A special voltage meter, called a half-cell potential meter, is required to conduct this test.

Protection Against Atmospheric Corrosion of Aboveground Piping

Steel pipelines exposed to the atmosphere must be cleaned and either coated or jacketed for the prevention of atmospheric corrosion. A durable paint is the usual protective system used for LP-Gas piping. Aboveground piping should be inspected during other routine maintenance to reevaluate each pipeline that is exposed to the atmosphere. Remedial action must be taken when it is necessary to maintain protection against atmospheric corrosion.

Key Valves and Their Maintenance

Each valve, the use of which can be necessary for the safe operation of a distribution system, must be checked and serviced at intervals annually, but at intervals not exceeding 15 months. Maintenance usually includes operating the valve to verify that it is operable and does stop the flow of gas and checking the valve for leakage. Appropriate replacements, repairs, or adjustments should be made as needed. In small LP-Gas systems, the key valves are generally tank valves. Larger LP-Gas systems may have other key valves to isolate a section of the main system in the event of an emergency.

First-Stage Regulator Maintenance

The first-stage regulator must be inspected and tested annually, but at intervals not exceeding 15 months, to determine the following:

- It is in good mechanical condition.
- It is adequate for the capacity of the system.
- It is set to function at the correct pressure.
- It is properly installed and protected from dirt, liquids, or conditions that could prevent proper operation.

A lockup test is one method used for compliance with these requirements.

NFPA 58 requires that two-stage pressure regulation be installed to provide system overpressure protection. The use of two-stage pressure regulation and the requirement of the first-stage regulator to have overpressure protection as required by UL 144, *Standard for LP-Gas Regulators*, provide a safe and simple alternative to the requirements of

the DOT Pipeline Regulations for overpressure protection [3]. NFPA 58 requires an interstage pressure of 10 psi (69 kPa). If a higher pressure is desired, it can be achieved without compromising safety by using a three-stage system, with the first stage at a pressure higher than 10 psi, the second stage at 10 psi, and the final stage at 11 in. w.c.

Record Keeping

Operators may use any record-keeping method that produces authentic records. The data constituting these records should be retained in a medium that has a life expectancy at least equal to the specified retention period. The retention period varies by state.

Operators must keep records necessary to administer the procedures established in their operations and maintenance manual. Some of the record-keeping requirements are listed as follows:

- *Pressure Test Records.* Initial pressure test records should be kept for the useful life of the system. The operator's name, the name of the employee or contractor responsible for conducting the test, the test medium used, the test pressure, and the test duration should all be recorded.
- *Cathodic Protection Records.* Records of the cathodic protection method used to protect underground tanks and piping must be maintained for the life of the system. Each test, survey, or inspection required by the DOT Pipeline Regulations should be recorded in sufficient detail to demonstrate the adequacy of corrosion control measures or that a corrosion condition does not exist. (If there are no underground tanks and the piping is polyethylene, no cathodic protection systems are required, and this requirement is not applicable.)
- *Emergency Plan Training Records.* The system operator must train appropriate operating personnel to ensure that they are knowledgeable in the emergency procedures and to verify that the training is effective.

The records can be as simple as a bound notebook in which all maintenance, abnormal operations, and system changes are recorded.

Annual Unaccounted for Gas Report (100 or More Customers)

LP-Gas systems serving 100 or more customers from a single source are required to file an annual report. Part of this report must be the system's percentage of unaccounted for gas. Unaccounted for gas is the difference between the amount of propane delivered into the system and the amount that is recorded through the customer's meters.

Unaccounted for gas can be caused by measurement and control errors, system leakage, and theft.

Temperature and pressure affect gas density. For this reason, temperature-compensating meters are widely used. For customers with high gas usage, the meter can be located upstream of the second-stage pressure regulator so that a smaller (less costly) meter can be used. Where the meter is located upstream of the second-stage pressure regulator, a constant pressure must be maintained. Otherwise, meter readings will not be accurate, which can lead to unaccounted for gas. Pressure-compensating meters are available. The better the control on gas measurement, the easier it is to spot problems in other areas that affect unaccounted for gas.

STATE PIPELINE SAFETY PROGRAM MANAGERS

A list of state pipeline safety program managers with their contact information can be downloaded from the following link: http://www.phmsa.dot.gov/staticfiles/PHMSA/DownloadableFiles/appendxa-slpgassystems.htm.

Note that operators of LP-Gas jurisdictional systems are required to belong to a qualified one-call notification system for protecting their systems from construction damage. In addition, the operators must also have a written damage prevention program to protect the systems against damage from "excavation activities." The state pipeline safety program managers can provide specific information on one-call notification systems in their respective states.

REFERENCES CITED

1. Title 49, Code of Federal Regulations, Part 192.605, U.S. Government Printing Office, Washington, DC.
2. Title 49, Code of Federal Regulations, Part 192.615, U.S. Government Printing Office, Washington, DC.
3. UL 144, *Standard for LP-Gas Regulators*, 1999 edition, Underwriters Laboratories Inc., Northbrook, IL.

SUPPLEMENT 3

Fire Testing of Composite Propane Cylinders

Editor's Note: This supplement provides information on the testing of composite cylinders. These tests were funded by the Propane Education and Research Council to support the proposal to allow portable heaters fueled by a composite cylinder (cabinet heaters) in buildings. The proposal has not been accepted, but may be considered for a future edition of NFPA 58. Currently, cabinet heaters can be used if a public emergency is declared, such as a hurricane or ice storm. The results of the testing showed that composite cylinders act very differently from steel cylinders in simulated room fires, and the supplement is intended to communicate the test results to anyone interested in this subject.

The editor thanks Rodney L. Osborne, Ph.D., P.E, of Battelle Memorial Institute, and Pravinray D. Gandhi, Ph.D., P.E., and Ronald R. Czischke, P.E., of Underwriters Laboratories Inc., who authored this supplement.

INTRODUCTION

Composite propane cylinders have been used in Europe for about 15 years and have recently entered the United States market for the storage, handling, and use of propane gas. In 2007, two manufacturers were marketing cylinders with nominal capacities of 10 lb, 20 lb, and 33 lb. These cylinders were imported into or manufactured in the United States under special permits from the U.S. Department of Transportation (DOT). The DOT-specified tests in these permits subject the cylinders to high temperature creep, gas permeability, vertical drop, pressure cycling, hydraulic burst, gunfire, and bonfire.

Composite cylinder manufacturers had performed various tests on their cylinders to meet European and U.S. standards. However, it was recognized that more comprehensive fire testing was needed to independently generate the data needed on the cylinders' fire performance. The test protocol and results obtained are described in this supplement.

COMPOSITE CYLINDER BACKGROUND

Users may choose composite cylinders for outdoor consumer applications such as grills, patio heaters, patio light-

ing, and similar appliances, or in industrial or commercial applications where steel and aluminum cylinders are being used. The composite cylinders offer several advantages over steel cylinders in that they weigh less and are corrosion resistant. In addition, composite cylinders have translucent walls that make the liquid level visible. No external devices or stickers are required to determine the amount of propane remaining in the cylinder.

FIRE TEST PROGRAMS

Two test programs were developed to determine the fire performance characteristics of outdoor composite propane cylinder use and the potential consequences of bringing these cylinders indoors. NFPA 58 currently prohibits bringing these cylinders indoors except in very limited cases. Composite cylinders from two manufacturers were used in each of the test programs. One design was a single piece construction, and the other was a two-piece construction.

Outdoor Fire Testing Program

In the first program, Battelle Memorial Institute (Columbus, Ohio) and ThermDyne Technologies Limited (Kingston,

Ontario, Canada) developed a protocol to test the cylinders' performance with respect to the fire exposure intensity, liquid fill levels, and cylinder orientations. Twenty-nine composite cylinders from two manufacturers and six standard steel cylinders were exposed to propane torch fires (Exhibit S3.1). The total heat release rate of the torches was approximately 540 kW (1,800,000 Btu/hr). The cylinders were placed at a fixed distance from the face of the torches. All cylinders were nominal 20 lb capacity (0.32 ft^3 or 45 to 47 lb water capacity). In this first round of testing, the cylinders were oriented either vertically (Exhibit S3.2) or horizontally (Exhibit S3.3). In the horizontal position, the flame was directed at the side (as shown in Exhibit S3.3), at the valve, or at the base for the different tests. The propane torches were shut down after all the propane

EXHIBIT S3.3 *Horizontal Cylinder Prior to Flame Impingement.*

from a test cylinder was vented or when a test cylinder ruptured.

No steel cylinders ruptured during the testing. The relief valves opened at pressures between 375 to 400 psig. Some relief valves reclosed above 300 psig, and some did not reclose until 100 psig. In all tests, the steel cylinders emptied before the cylinder walls softened and thinned enough to rupture. One steel cylinder bulged during the test.

When tested vertically and with a nominal fill level of 75 percent, the two composite cylinder designs did not fail. During these tests, propane began to leak around the valve-cylinder connection and diffused through the cylinder walls after reaching peak pressures between 98 and 118 psig. Exhibit S3.4 shows that the propane continues to

EXHIBIT S3.1 *Propane Torches for Fire Exposure.*

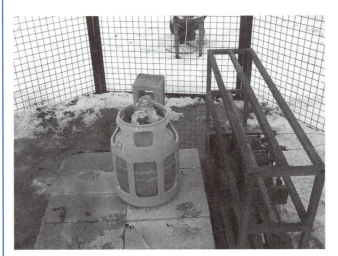

EXHIBIT S3.2 *Vertical Cylinder Prior to Flame Impingement.*

EXHIBIT S3.4 *Vertical Cylinder During Fire Test.*

permeate through the wall even though the cylinder pressure is essentially zero. The outer protective jacket was consumed on all composite cylinder tests.

When one of the composite cylinder designs (two-piece construction) was tested in the horizontal position, the cylinder ruptured. This failure was repeatable. The same result occurred with this cylinder design in the vertical position and a low fill level. Under similar conditions, the other cylinder design did not rupture.

Twenty of the 29 composite cylinders had pressure relief valves, integral to the cylinder valve. Only one of the relief valves opened, on a test where the cylinder was horizontal and the flame was aimed directly at the valve. The peak pressure for this test was 112 psig. It is suspected that the elastomers in the relief valve degraded and the valve opened. There was no appreciable difference in performance between the cylinders that had relief valves and those that did not.

Indoor Fire Testing Program

In the second test program, a performance test plan was developed to consider the potential consequences of bringing composite cylinders indoors and was based on input from the propane industry and fire protection community. Battelle and Underwriters Laboratories Inc. (UL) developed this fire test plan and performed the testing in UL's large-scale fire test facility in Northbrook, Illinois (see http://www.ul.com/fire/research.html).

The test plan was designed to address various fire safety concerns, such as the following:

- Fire hazard from an empty stored cylinder
- Contribution of potential leaking gas from a composite cylinder to fire hazards in a room fire
- Possibility of a composite cylinder rupture when exposed to an ignition source
- Contribution to room fires from a spare composite cylinder stored indoors
- Effects of fire hose spray on a burning composite cylinder

Composite cylinders from the same two manufacturers (single piece and two piece constructions) were used in this second phase of fire testing. No steel cylinders were tested in this phase.

The first set of tests (referred to as Type 1 tests) considered the smoke and heat released from ignited empty composite cylinders. These cylinders were ignited by placing an igniter (a cotton bundle soaked in gasoline) at the base of the cylinder. The heat and smoke release rates of the empty, burning composite cylinders were measured. As the jackets and the resins used in the composite cylinders

are combustible, these data can be used by fire protection engineers in considering storage requirements of empty cylinders. Maximum heat release rates ranged from 98 to 119 kW for the two manufacturers' cylinders. The maximum smoke release rates were 0.65 m^3/sec for cylinders from one manufacturer and 2.65 m^3/sec for the other manufacturer's cylinders.

In the next set of tests (referred to as Type 2 tests), a composite cylinder was tested with a space heater as a potential future application using an NFPA 286[1] configuration test room with the cylinder exposed to a standard igniter (see Exhibit S3.5 for a schematic of the test room). (As noted, NFPA 58 currently prohibits this application.) In this test, the test room was lined with gypsum wallboard. The heater with cylinder was located in the corner facing the open doorway. In one test, an additional spare cylinder, positioned next to the heater, was exposed to the igniter. The increase in temperatures and heat flux in the test room, as well as pressure in the gas cylinder were measured. The cylinders were ignited in the same manner as the Type 1 tests.

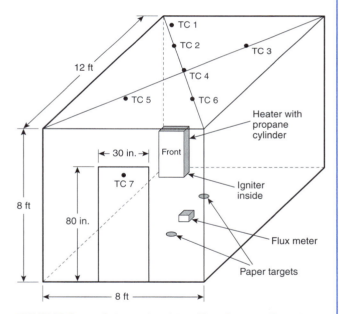

EXHIBIT S3.5   *Schematic of Fire Test Room – Type 2 Tests.*

The heater that was used in these tests was essentially a sheet metal enclosure, with air vents at the top and bottom that included a heating element, controls, and space for the propane composite cylinder.

For these tests, except for the test involving a spare cylinder, the cylinder pressure increased during the tests until propane gas began to release after 4 to 12 minutes, at a pressure level from 163 to 242 psig. The release of gas did not result in high velocity flame jets such as through a relief valve orifice. The released gas was consumed in the fire.

When gas was released, the heat flux (measured on the center of the floor) and the room temperature (measured below the ceiling) increased very quickly. The average ceiling temperatures reached 614°C to 831°C. The maximum heat flux obtained was 20 to 36 kW/m^2.

For all tests involving ignition of a full cylinder in the heater, the room reached (or was close to) flashover conditions between 5 to 12 minutes after ignition. As a general guideline, flashover with flames coming out through the doorway occur in a NFPA 286 room in the same time period as the crumpled paper targets ignite, the ceiling temperature reaches approximately 600°C, and the heat flux level on the floor reaches approximately 20 kW/m^2.

Once the cylinder began venting, it continued to release gas. In the test scenarios, the released gas was consumed in the fire. The cylinder was emptied approximately 10 to 15 minutes after the maximum pressure was reached. All cylinders showed areas were the resin was consumed at such an extent that gas could easily pass through. The photos in Exhibit S3.6 are representative of composite cylinders after the propane in the cylinder was consumed and the fire was extinguished. The photos show that the cylinder jackets were consumed, as was much of the resin in the cylinder walls.

In one of the Type 2 tests, a rupture occurred 17 minutes into the test, at a pressure of 46 psig. The rupture occurred when the pressure level was decaying, 8 minutes after the pressure had reached its maximum level of 243 psig. The burst resulted in severe heater and room damage. The failed cylinder was the same design (two piece construction) that ruptured during the first fire test program.

In the test with the spare cylinder, the burning rate of the cylinder surface was lower and the increase in cylinder pressure was slower, than for a cylinder located in a heater. The spare cylinder did not release gas throughout the test, reaching 303 psig at the test termination time of 20 minutes. The fire size of the burning spare cylinder did not result in any significant pressure increase or visible damage of the cylinder in the heater.

In the third set of tests (referred to as Type 3 tests), the fire performance of a heater with composite propane cylinder was assessed in a room fire scenario that grows to flashover conditions. In this test, the test room was lined with medium density fiberboard (see Exhibit S3.7 for a schematic of the test room). A heater with a composite propane cylinder was positioned against the wall facing the open doorway. A 300 kW or a 40 to 160 kW propane burner located in the corner of the room was used to ignite

EXHIBIT S3.6 *Composite Cylinder After Fire Test, Shown Inside Heater (top) and Composite Cylinder After Fire Test (bottom).*

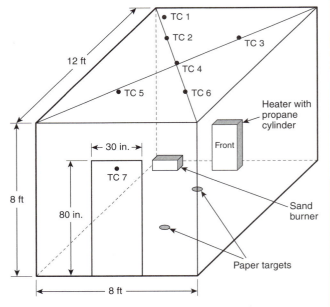

EXHIBIT S3.7 *Schematic of the Fire Test Room – Type 3 Tests.*

the medium density fiberboard, resulting in flashover conditions in the test room. In one test, an additional spare cylinder was positioned next to the heater. The increases in temperatures, ensuing from the fire growth, were measured and the performance of the heater with a composite cylinder was assessed.

The room reached flashover conditions after 1 to 2 minutes for the 300 kW initial burner size and after 4 to 7 minutes for the 40 kW/160 kW burner size, but the cylinder in the heater was not immediately affected. It was observed that the gas pressure peak and subsequent release of propane gas occurred 3 to 6 minutes after the room reached flashover conditions. The cylinders did not rupture or release gas in any high velocity jet–like fashion outside of the heater. The released gas was consumed in the fire. The release of propane gas occurred after 6 to 12 minutes, at a pressure level of 170 to 270 psig. At the conclusion of the test, the cylinders in general showed the same type of damage as in the Type 2 tests.

In the Type 3 test with a spare cylinder and a cylinder in the heater, both cylinders sustained the radiant heat from a 300 kW fire for 20 minutes without igniting or leaking propane. The spare cylinder pressure increased to 231 psig, and the pressure of the cylinder in the heater increased to 123 psig, during the 30 minute test. Exhibit S3.8 shows the exterior of the spare cylinder after this test, with the jacket partially melted, but with no significant damage to the pressure vessel walls.

EXHIBIT S3.8 *Spare Cylinder After Fire Test.*

The final test at UL was to assess the performance of a burning pressurized cylinder when impacted by a water hose stream. Two igniters were attached to a composite cylinder, filled to half of its capacity with water, which was pressurized by nitrogen following a predetermined cylinder pressure-time curve obtained in Type 2 tests. The cylinder was impacted by a water hose stream when a cylinder pressure of 220 psig was reached, 6 minutes into the test. The water hose stream was generated from an Elkhart SLO/0 adjustable nozzle on a 1½ in. rubber hose. The adjustable nozzle was set at maximum flow and a straight stream. The available water pressure to the hose was a nominal 100 psig. The stream was aimed directly at the cylinder from a distance of approximately 18 ft. The cylinder breached before the hose stream impact. However, the hose stream impact did not cause additional damage to the cylinder.

Testing Summary

The key findings of the second test program were the following:

1. Fire hazard from empty or filled stored cylinder

    a. The maximum heat release rates from the ignition and burning of the empty cylinders were approximately 100 to120 kW.

    b. A full stored cylinder sustained the radiant heat from a 300 kW fire for 20 minutes without being ignited or leaking propane (Type 3).

    c. A burning, nitrogen-pressurized stored cylinder did not violently breach or rupture when impacted with a water hose stream.

2. Contribution of leaking gas from an ignited cylinder to fire hazards in a room fire

    a. In each of the fire tests (Type 2), the ignited composite cylinder in the heater assembly released gas resulting in flashover conditions in the room.

    b. In a growing room fire that goes to flashover (Type 3), the composite cylinder breached and ignited after the flashover had occurred. Typically, there was a 3 to 5 minute lag between room flashover and breach of the cylinder. The leaking gas cylinder did not rupture.

    c. Once the cylinder started to leak, the release of gas continued during the test. A full cylinder was emptied approximately 10 to 15 minutes after the maximum pressure was reached.

3. Rupture hazard from propane filled cylinder:

    a. Cylinder design played a role in its fire performance. The design from one manufacturer with the two piece construction ruptured when partially filled and oriented horizontally during a Type 2 test.

4. High velocity jetting of propane gas flames upon leakage from the cylinder

   a. In all the Type 2 and Type 3 tests, there was no evidence of high velocity jetting of propane gas after the composite cylinder had breached and ignited. The cylinder pressure when the breach was observed (128 to 270 psig) was lower than the relief valve setting (375 psig).

The full test reports are available from the Propane Education & Research Council (Washington, DC) at www. propanecouncil.org (reference Research Docket No. 11643).

REFERENCE CITED

1. NFPA 286, *Standard Methods of Fire Tests for Evaluating Contribution of Wall and Ceiling Interior Finish to Room Fire Growth*, 2006 edition, National Fire Protection Association, Quincy, MA.

SUPPLEMENT 4

Preparing Propane Companies for Natural Disasters

Editor's Note: Supplement 5 provides information on preparing propane companies for natural disasters. It is based on a presentation, "Natural Disasters and the Propane Industry, 2006," presented by Stuart Weidie, Blossman Gas, and Eric Kuster, Tri-Gas & Oil Co., at an industry conference. The editor thanks Mr. Weidie and Mr. Kuster for sharing the information they learned after Hurricane Katrina, as well as Mr. Bruce Swiecicki, who prepared the supplement. While the information in the supplement is based on a major hurricane, it is applicable to planning for all types of natural disasters.

INTRODUCTION

Between 1996 and 2006, the United States Federal Emergency Management Agency (FEMA) declared, on average, over 56 emergencies per year due to natural events. The emergencies ranged from snow and ice storms during winter and thunderstorms during summer in the northern states; hurricanes, floods, and wild fires in the southern states; hurricanes floods and tornadoes in the eastern states; earthquakes, mudslides, and wildfires in the western states; and floods, thunderstorms, and tornadoes in the middle states.

The effect of natural disasters on the propane industry can include supply disruptions to retail marketers and propane users, damaged and missing tanks and other equipment, and an increase in the release of LP-Gas from tanks and the possible ignition of the released propane. See Exhibits S4.1 and S4.2, which show a propane container formerly located at a bulk plant and propane tank foundations after Hurricane Katrina.

It is impossible to be totally prepared for a natural disaster, given the uncertainty of when, where, and to what degree a natural disaster may occur. The allocation of personnel and financial resources to developing and maintaining a contingency plan is dependent on the ability of a propane retail marketer or user to make available the labor and assets that may be required. However, resources are available that would help a propane marketer become familiar with the basic preparations necessary to minimize

EXHIBIT S4.1 *Propane Container Moved by Hurricane Katrina.*

the impact of a natural disaster on the business. Information on areas subject to high winds, floods, and heavy snowfall is available from several sources. Exhibit S4.3 is a map from the American Society of Civil Engineers (ASCE) showing maximum wind speeds for the Gulf Coast of the United States. Wind speed maps of other areas are available in *NFPA 5000®, Building Construction and Safety Code®* [1]; ASCE 7, *Minimum Design Loads for Buildings and Other Structures* [2]; and other sources.

EXHIBIT S4.2 *Two Propane Container Foundations After the Containers Were Washed Away in Floodwaters Resulting from Hurricane Katrina.*

Flood maps are available from the Federal Emergency Management Agency (FEMA) and local sources. FEMA (www.fema.gov) is a government agency whose primary mission is to reduce the loss of life and property and protect the nation from all hazards, including natural disasters, acts of terrorism, and other man-made disasters, by leading and supporting the nation in a risk-based, comprehensive

emergency management system of preparedness, protection, response, recovery, and mitigation.

The following general topics can also be researched at www.fema.gov:

- Protecting a business
- Recovering from an emergency situation
- Flood maps and insurance
- Contractors and vendors

PRE-EMERGENCY PLANNING

While planning for a natural disaster, it is reasonable to assume the following:

- Electricity may not be available for several days
- Phone service (including cellular) may not be available for several days
- Propane storages facilities may be damaged
- Access to certain parts of a service area may not be possible for several days
- Supply of LP-Gas may be curtailed for several days

During the planning phase for emergencies, meet with emergency service providers, including the fire and police departments and other organizations such as the Red Cross, to make sure their capabilities are well understood, and also to allow those services to become familiar with the resources that the retail marketer can provide or the propane user must provide. For example, a hospital may have

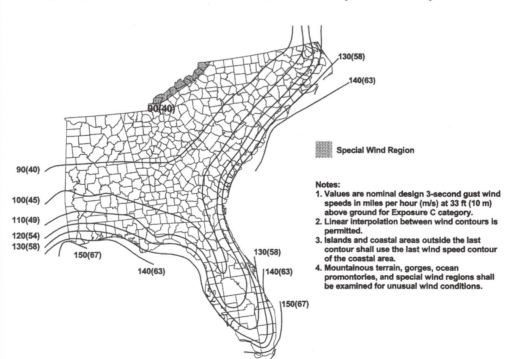

EXHIBIT S4.3 *Basic Wind Speed – Western Gulf of Mexico Hurricane and Coastline. (Courtesy of ASCE)*

emergency power systems fueled by propane when electricity is not available.

Emergency response agencies, such as the fire and police departments, will be counting on a retail marketer to supply fuel for emergency heating, cooking, and hot water. Ensure that it is clear to everyone which resources would be available in an emergency and the quantities that can be expected. Present each agency with a list that documents these resources. During the planning phase, it is useful to have a current list of parts, tanks, appliances, and vehicles that other propane marketers and key users in the area can draw from. Make contact with local financial institutions that can make cash or credit available to the propane retail marketer in the event of an emergency.

Meet with other propane retailers in the area to assign specific crews to cover specific areas, regardless of whose customers may be affected. Develop a list of employees and other persons in the area that can be called upon for additional labor during an emergency. Teaming non-experienced personnel with experienced drivers or service technicians is one means of spreading manpower over a larger area. Making sure the physical assets of a business, (equipment and personnel) are spread over a large area reduces the chances that an event will devastate the operations of a business.

Specific steps to be performed while planning for an emergency include the following:

- Create and maintain a list of contact information for all employees.
- Implement a communication system between the business and its employees, assuming no power or cellular service is available.
- At critical locations for the business, install and maintain portable or fixed generators with sufficient fuel and capacity for running pumps and basic office and plant operations
- Designate a point of communication for emergency services to contact the business. Also plan an alternate location in case the primary location is not available.
- Design an incident command team that can make critical decisions for the company regarding service operations, delivery operations, supply, finance, communications, and public relations.
- Create a new file in the system to allow for disaster-related activities and work orders performed for customers during an emergency.
- Draw on the resources of state and national associations, such as the National Propane Gas Association, the National Fire Protection Association, and the Propane Education and Research Council to assist with planning.

- Maintain check-off lists for all aspects of the plan so that it can be more easily implemented during times of extreme duress.
- Have a safe or some other secure location where the emergency plan can be accessed when needed.

If enough advanced notice is available before a disaster event occurs, the following points should be considered:

- Use radio and television to communicate safety precautions with a clear and consistent message.
- Secure additional supplies of consumables such as water, fuel, and batteries. Other materials such as rope, snow shovels, and duct tape may be useful.
- Put the emergency plan into effect and contact supply points and other retail marketers for last minute planning.
- Review the emergency plan with employees and discuss contingency plans.

When developed, pre-emergency plans should kept in one or more safe places. Review the plan at the beginning of each storm season.

EMERGENCY RESPONSE

During a disaster, the following actions should be taken:

- Do not send employees into harm's way by responding too soon.
- Prioritize all responses. Large leaks, elderly customers or customers with health issues, and critical infrastructure such as hospitals, emergency services, and shelters must be given top priority.
- Be considerate of employees' needs to ensure the safety of their own families.
- Because emergencies can last for days or weeks, take care not to overwhelm employees and ensure that they get adequate rest.
- Keep some resources in reserve and do not deploy all crews immediately. Emergency services will call for assistance, and supplies and crews will need to be immediately available at that time.

After the disaster, the following actions should be taken:

- Communicate with customers as soon as possible using radio or other available means. Arrange for a special contact number for customers to call and get information.
- Keep the focus on safety by using established safety procedures for putting services back into operation.

- Inspect all equipment and replace pressure regulators and controls that have been underwater.
- Inspect piping systems to ensure they are leak-free.
- Utilize FEMA and other assistance agencies. Have contact numbers available for customers.
- Establish contact with a financial institution for additional support if necessary.
- Determine the extent of the needs for the business and contact suppliers of products and equipment to inform them of those needs. Establish additional credit if necessary.
- Maintain a reliable accounting of extra expenses incurred, including direct property losses, damaged tanks and equipment, overtime for employees, lost production time, and extra clerical expenses.
- Document damages. Take many photographs of damages at plants and customer locations. Establish a separate file for disaster-related activities and work orders performed for customers.

Finally, for longer term issues related to disaster events, consider the following:

- Establish relationships with FEMA and other federal and state aid agency representatives sent into the area to assist with customer and business related issues.
- Utilize the assistance offered by others in the industry.
- Utilize the assistance of state and national trade associations for communications, logistics, and public relations activities.

- Establish a central collection site for orphan tanks and equipment. Communicate the location to emergency management agencies and other retail marketers in the area.
- Contact elected officials at all levels to inform them and let them know how they can help. If the area is declared a disaster area, take advantage of programs and assistance that are available. Communicate the availability of those resources to all affected customers.

SUMMARY

A natural disaster can take many forms, including a hurricane, snowstorm, flood, ice storm, or major fire. One or more of these can occur anywhere. The information provided in this supplement is applicable to any of these natural disasters and should be considered by all those in the supply chain of key fuels, including propane.

REFERENCES CITED

1. *NFPA 5000®, Building Construction and Safety Code®*, 2009 edition, National Fire Protection Association, Quincy, MA.
2. ASCE 7, *Minimum Design Loads for Buildings and Other Structures*, 2010 edition, American Society of Civil Engineers, Reston, VA.

SUPPLEMENT 5

Cathodic Protection

Editor's Note: *With the addition of requirements for the installation and maintenance of cathodic protection systems for underground propane tanks, the need for more information on cathodic protection has become important for several reasons. First, some propane tank installers have not installed cathodic protection systems. Most of those who have installed cathodic protection systems may not have had comprehensive training; rather, they rely on information supplied by the cathodic system manufacturer or local distributor. Maintenance of cathodic protection systems is done by measuring the voltage between the tank and the anode or anodes, and is now required to be done upon installation, after a year, and every 3 years thereafter, unless a deficiency is identified.*

This new supplement provides a thorough overview of the basics of corrosion of buried tanks, how cathodic protection works, the components that make up a cathodic protection system, the installation or use of the components, and how to test cathodic protection systems.

The supplement also provides an overview of impressed current systems, which are not practical for systems involving a small number of underground propane tanks. Impressed current systems are used for underground pipeline and at installations with a large number of underground tanks.

The supplement has been adapted with permission from the manual, "Cathodic Protection," published by the Propane Education and Research Council. Their generosity is appreciated.

ABOUT THE PROGRAM

Cathodic Protection is a program of training material intended for propane technicians who install residential and small commercial underground ASME tanks and piping. The program provides basic knowledge and requirements for the technician to properly and efficiently provide cathodic protection for underground steel ASME tanks and piping from corrosion.

The program is conveniently divided into five sections.

1. An Introduction covering the basics of corrosion, the principles of cathodic protection, and the methods to achieve protection.
2. Galvanic Protection including anodes, pre-installation procedures, installation procedures, electrical isolation, testing equipment, tank-to-soil potential tests, troubleshooting and retrofitting.
3. Impressed Current Overview which briefly covers installation and maintenance.
4. A 48 question fill-in-the-blank quiz with answer key. [not included in this Supplement]
5. A Skills Evaluation form. [not included in this Supplement]

The following training tools are available:

1. An instructional manual (either on CD or in paper format).
2. A companion DVD to be used as a visual aid.

ACKNOWLEDGEMENTS

The Propane Education and Research Council (PERC) gratefully acknowledges the members of the Safety & Training Advisory Committee (STAC) who served as Subject Matter Experts (SME) and reviewers. Without their help, the program could not have been produced.

Lyndon Rickards, Task Force Chairman, *Eastern Propane Gas, Inc.*

Eric Leskinen, *Griffith Energy, Inc.*

Jerry Lucas, *Heritage Propane Partners*

Sam McTier, *Propane Technologies, LLC*

Ken Mueller, *Nationwide Agribusiness*

Thomas Petru, *Railroad Commission of Texas*

Carlton Revere, *Revere Gas and Appliance*

Jeff Shaffer, *Shaffer's Bottled Gas Corp.*

Mike Walters, *Amerigas*

Ross Warnell, *Ferrellgas*

In addition, PERC acknowledges the following individuals and organizations for providing staff, equipment, technical assistance and management support during production of this program.

Hans Schmoldt, *Anode Systems, Inc.*, Grand Junction, CO.

Jim Reuscher, *Country Gas Co./Inergy LP*, Crystal Lake and Wasco, IL.

Tom Aikens, *Trinity Industries, Inc.*, Dallas, TX.

Stuart Flatow, *VP, Safety & Training, PERC*, Washington, DC.

1.0 CATHODIC PROTECTION INTRODUCTION

1.1 Basics of Corrosion

Corrosion is an aggressive form of rusting...and rust to a steel propane tank and metallic piping can be fatal. Heavy steel propane tanks and metallic piping may seem indestructible. But as steel ages, it begins to show its age as rust (see Exhibit S5.1). Some rust is superficial and does not cause serious concern. However, if the steel is in a bad environment such as wet ground that contains natural or man-made chemicals, the rusting process accelerates. This is what we call corrosion.

Over time, the corrosion causes structural problems, creating pits or holes in the steel. Left alone and ignored, these holes may leak, releasing propane into the ground. The concern is that the leaking propane can migrate into a crawl space or basement of a building. Corrosion can vir-

EXHIBIT S5.1 *Extensive Corrosion on a Tank.*

EXHIBIT S5.2 *Steel Tank with Coating.*

tually destroy a propane tank or piping, and leaking propane is potentially dangerous.

1.2 The Principles of Cathodic Protection

To live a long and productive existence, propane tanks and metallic piping also need protection . . . Cathodic Protection. In general terms, Cathodic Protection can be used to protect ASME (American Society of Mechanical Engineers) underground steel propane tanks and piping from corrosion. This is done by making the tank a cathode. Cathodes will be discussed further in the manual.

Corrosion can be defined as a disease of steel. Coating the steel tank like many of the manufacturers do in the factory is the first line of defense against corrosion (see Exhibit S5.2). Cathodic protection is the second line of defense. It will make a steel propane tank and its piping immune to the disease of corrosion.

1.3 Methods to Achieve Cathodic Protection

Underground propane tanks and metal piping can be cathodically protected in two ways. The most common way is with magnesium anodes (see Exhibit S5.3). Another is with impressed current using power from the local electric utility company. Although the two methods differ greatly, what's important to remember, is that cathodic protection can extend the life of an underground tank by helping to prevent corrosion and rust. Impressed current systems will be covered later in the manual.

2.0 GALVANIC PROTECTION

2.1. Galvanic Protection and Anodes

Galvanic Protection uses anodes. Although there are dozens of different types of anodes, the three most commonly

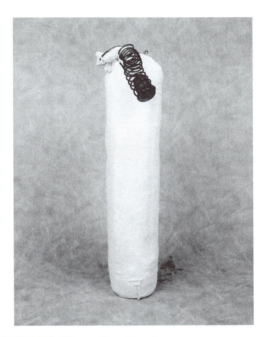

EXHIBIT S5.3 *Magnesium Anode.*

used in the propane industry include high potential magnesium (AZ-63 or H-1), magnesium alloy and zinc. Typical installations use one or more anodes based on container manufacturer's instructions, geographic location, advice from cathodic protection experts, and company procedures and policies.

High potential anodes may be used in dry or sandy areas where it's important for greater voltage, and therefore more current. These anodes produce a minimum of minus 1.75 volts, versus 1.5 volts for standard anodes. Zinc anodes can be used to protect underground propane tanks and piping in coastal areas where groundwater may be brackish or salty. However, standard minus 1.5 volt magnesium anodes are more generally used in the propane industry because they work best in the majority of underground conditions found in the United States.

The purpose of the magnesium anode is to protect the tank and connected steel piping by providing current and electrons to the entire surface area of both. In doing this, the anode acts like a light bulb, lighting up the surface of the steel tank. This happens because electrons flow from the external magnesium anode along a wire to the steel tank...the cathode (see Exhibit S5.4). At the same time, a small electric current measured in milliamps flows through the earth from the magnesium anode to the steel cathode. By using natural laws and processes where electric current flows from a high voltage source to a lower voltage receiver, man-made anodes of higher voltage metal such as magnesium will artificially prevent lower voltage metal like steel from decomposing. The electrons actually prevent the iron atoms in the steel from oxidizing into rust. And if enough electrons flow from an anode to the tank, it will not corrode, because the voltage of the tank will change.

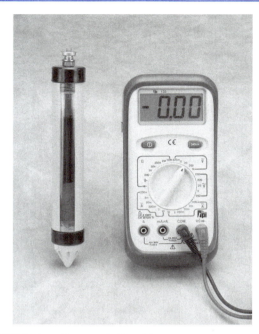

EXHIBIT S5.5 *Copper Sulfate Electrode and Voltmeter.*

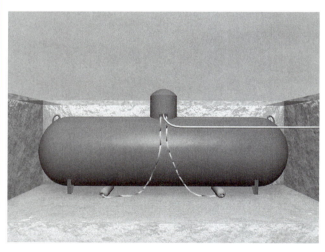

EXHIBIT S5.4 *Illustration of Wire Connecting Anodes to a Steel Tank.*

This voltage can be measured with a voltmeter and a copper sulfate electrode (see Exhibit S5.5). Although different metals have different voltage readings, the voltage reading of steel is naturally around minus 0.50 volts. A voltage of minus 0.50 volts on a propane tank would indicate that the tank is unprotected and is susceptible to corrosion. To avoid corrosion, the electrons must shift the voltage of the steel to a minimum of minus 0.85 volts or more. The rule is the higher the voltage, the better. How-

ever, the electrons should not shift the voltage above a minus 2.00 volts.

When a tank is totally protected from corrosion, it means that the entire tank has become a cathode. The length of the protection measured in years is dependent on the severity of the environment in which the tank is installed. If the tank is installed in non-corrosive dry sandy soil, it may be relatively free of corrosion and the anode will last a lifetime. However, if the tank is installed in wet, fertilized and sticky clay like under a lawn or flower bed, the anode could possibly be consumed in less time.

2.2 Pre-Installation Preparation

But remember, before you do any digging, first refer to your company's policy, or call the national Dig Safe hotline (811) or your local one-call system to prevent damage to underground structures.

Although there are several locations where an anode can be placed, one way is to dig a hole so that the anode can be placed below the bedding of the tank. If two anodes are being used, you'll dig two holes. Another way is to place the anode beside the tank. Again, if two anodes are being used, one can be placed on each side or each end of the tank. When installing two anodes, they can also be placed diagonally from each other at the ends of the tank. See Exhibit S5.6 for a depiction of possible locations for the anodes.

2.3 Installation Procedures

The first thing is to remove the outer box or plastic bag from the anode. The anode should be wetted. One good way to wet the anode is to place it in a bucket brought to the jobsite and then fill the bucket with water (see Exhibit S5.7). The idea is to let the anode soak up the water. It will do this because the anode is packaged in a bag of gypsum, sodium sulfate and bentonite clay. After a couple of minutes, turn the anode upside down in the bucket so it soaks up the remaining water. Another way to wet the anode is to pour water over it from the container. Just make sure you get it good and wet and that the water soaks in. This procedure ensures moisture retention and good soil contact. That way the anode will work more evenly.

EXHIBIT S5.7 *Wetting the Anode Prior to Installation.*

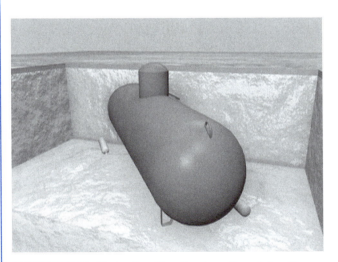

EXHIBIT S5.6 *Illustration Showing Location of Anodes Below Tank (top), Beside Tank (middle), and Diagonally at Ends of Tank (bottom).*

Once the anode is placed in the hole, unwind the wire and temporarily anchor it to the top of the hole with a dirt clog or rock. Then cover the anode with dirt from the hole. Run the anode wire to the connecting lug or tank lead wire and make the connection with a silicon filled underground wire connector (see Exhibit S5.8). This is where the manufacturers have made the job easier. There are no more Thermite welds that formerly needed to be performed.

The integrity of the tank coating is one factor in the success of the Cathodic Protection system. Once the tank has been set, make sure you've touched up any damaged areas on the tank that happened while loading, in transit, or unloading at the job site. Tank fabricators and coating manufacturers supply touch-up kits that are easy to use. Use a piece of coarse sandpaper to rough up the area around the ding. Wipe the area clean with a dry cloth and then apply the coating per manufacturer's instructions. Doing this puts less of a drain on the anode.

In desert or semi-dry parts of the country, and after the tank has been set, anodes should stay wet so that you get

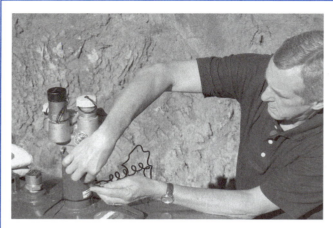

EXHIBIT S5.8 *Running the Anode Wire to the Connecting Lug.*

acceptable results on the tank-to-soil test. One way to do this is to place a two inch diameter, five foot long plastic pipe, or any kind of flexible tubing into the hole next to the anode (see Exhibit S5.9). Keep it upright while the hole is being partially backfilled. After the tank has been buried, the top of the pipe should extend a few inches above the ground. In order to keep what ground moisture there is from evaporating through the pipe, place a cap on the pipe.

EXHIBIT S5.9 *Plastic Pipes to Wet the Anodes.*

Once the installation is complete, you'll want to document it for future reference. Follow your company's policy and local codes, but remember, in snowy climates, NFPA 58 requires the tank location to be marked.

2.4 Electrical Isolation

When metal pipe like steel or copper is used, electrical isolation becomes critical. All metals have a unique voltage stored within them.

Bare copper lines must be isolated from the tank at the outlet of the regulator on the tank to prevent anodes from having to supply more electrical current than necessary to protect the tank. Care must be taken to isolate bare copper lines from metallic tank domes or the steel of the tank.

Black iron or steel lines may be protected using the same anode that protects the tank, but must be isolated from the building being served to prevent the anode from supplying electrical current to protect everything that's underground at the building that is not a propane pipe.

A dielectric union may provide the necessary isolation (see Exhibit S5.10). Without a dielectric union to isolate the tank from bare pipe, or insulation to prevent a bare copper tubing from touching the tank through a metal dome, the current can collect on interconnected underground copper and steel pipe that connects a customer's well casing or the city water system and the electrical grid. This unwanted loss of current is like having the cathodic protection "light" illuminate all the unwanted previously mentioned structures.

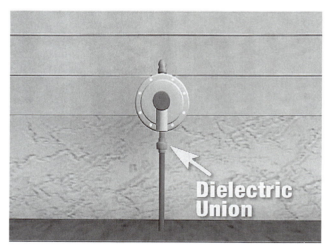

EXHIBIT S5.10 *Location of a Dielectric Union.*

2.5 Testing Equipment

Checking your cathodic protection system is vitally important. It's easy and takes just a few moments. All you need is a voltmeter and a copper sulfate electrode to measure the voltage or stored energy surrounding the tank and its piping.

2.6 Tank-to-Soil Potential Tests

First, if the ground is dry where you're going to take the readings, moisten it with water. Also, make sure the electrode has been properly maintained per the manufacturer's instructions. Next, set the voltmeter on the 2 volt DC or the 20 volt DC scale. Then connect the voltmeter to the tank, with the positive lead connected to the multivalve©, and the negative lead to the copper electrode (see Exhibit S5.11). Do this at the multivalve© rather than the dome. While many newer domes are made from a poly/plastic type of material, even if the dome is metal, it might be loose and you probably won't get a good reading. The multivalve©is well connected to the tank, and regardless of whether there is brass, steel or any other metal on the valve, the important thing is that it is a metal to metal connection between the voltmeter and the tank.

EXHIBIT S5.12 *Sticking the Tip of the Electrode into the Ground.*

EXHIBIT S5.11 *Connecting the Voltmeter to the Tank.*

Then take a couple of steps to the side of the tank opposite the dome. You'll want to be just above where the side of the tank is underground. Stick the tip of the electrode into the ground where you have moistened it, and take your reading (see Exhibit S5.12). Record your data according to company policy. Repeat the process on the opposite side of the dome, and then at both ends of the tank. It is important to take four tank-to-soil potential readings around a tank to get a complete picture of the cathodic protection level. It is possible to record a good reading above −0.85 volts on one end or one side of a tank and have a bad reading below −0.85 volts on the opposite end or opposite side of a tank. When this happens, the areas of the tank that have readings above −0.85 volts are protected while an area with a reading below −0.85 volts is not protected and could still suffer corrosion damage. A single reading would not detect an area of low protection. And remember, you'll want to record all four readings. This information can be valuable for future reference.

The voltage reading on a healthy tank should be equal to or greater than minus .85 volts. The voltage of an anode should be at least minus 1.5 volts. The voltage of an unprotected tank is usually around minus .50 volts. When the

anode is connected to the tank, the two voltages average somewhere in between. If the average voltage is high or close to the voltage of magnesium, −1.50 volts or higher, this indicates the tank's coating is good. If the voltage is low or close to the voltage of steel, there may be any variety of problems with the tank or installation. Perhaps the *anode was not connected to the tank properly*. If the copper anode wire does not make good strong metal-to-metal contact with the tank, the reading could be low. Another possibility for a low reading is that the *electrode was not making good contact with the earth*. Additional reasons might be the *rubber boot was not removed from the electrode*. The *battery in the voltmeter was dead. The electrode and the connection to the tank were not good.* Or, the *anode has been consumed and needs to be replaced.*

2.7 Troubleshooting and Retrofitting

When a reading at an existing installation is zero, you'll have to do some troubleshooting (see Exhibit S5.13 for an illustration of good and bad readings). The following is a laundry list of things to check when troubleshooting:

1. Start with the voltmeter. Is it on?
2. Is the battery good?
3. Have you taken off the rubber boot on the copper sulfate electrode?
4. Have you set the voltmeter switch to the d.c. volt scale?
5. Have you connected one lead wire to the copper sulfate electrode?
6. Have you connected the other lead wire to the multivalve© securely?
7. Does your copper sulfate electrode have a blue liquid in it?

Bad Readings		Good Readings
		−1.80
		−1.70
−0.80		−1.60
−0.70		−1.50
−0.60		−1.40
−0.50		−1.30
−0.40		−1.20
−0.30		−1.10
−0.20		−1.00
−0.10		−0.90
−0.0		−0.85

EXHIBIT S5.13 *Good and Bad Readings.*

8. Have you set the electrode firmly on the ground?
9. Have you poured a glass of water on the ground if the ground is dry?
10. Are your lead wires and their connections good?

If everything you've checked is okay, and the meter reading is below −0.85 volts, the following is a second checklist. But remember, not all of these items are going to be off mark at the same time.

1. In the dome, is there copper tubing leading from the regulator?

2. Is there a dielectric or insulating union between the copper tubing and the tank?

3. Is the coating on the tank peeling off or non-existent in the dome?

4. Is there a steel service pipe and no dielectric union in the piping at the building?

5. Is there electrical continuity between the multivalve and the pipe into the building? Check this using the ohms resistance setting and a jumper wire between the multivalve and the pipe at the building. A reading less than 20 ohms indicates there is continuity between the tank and the building.

1. The anode wire may not be securely connected to the tank.
2. The anode may have been buried still inside its plastic bag.
3. The anode may be dry.
4. The anode may be old and have been consumed.
5. The anode may have been too small (1 lb, 3 lb, 5 lb. anodes are too small).

6. The anode may be lying up against the opposite side of the tank.
7. Is there a plastic liner under decorative rock or bark between the electrode and the tank? If so, punch a small hole with a pencil and pour water at the hole before taking the reading again.
8. Are you connected to a metal dome and not the multivalve?

If everything checks out that you can see, the ground is moist and your readings are still below −0.85 volts, try this.

Take an anode out of its protective plastic bag or box, lay it on the ground next to the tank, pour water on the anode and let the water flow onto the ground.

Using a 12″ jumper wire with alligator clips on each end, connect one end to the multivalve© and the other end to an anode wire. The voltage readings on the tank should start to increase in the direction of −0.85 volts. If the voltage readings do not change, you could disconnect a copper service line at the first stage regulator inside the dome. If the tank-to-soil voltage readings immediately jump above −0.85 volts, you need to install a dielectric union inside the dome. If the voltage slowly increases, you can now think about retrofitting the tank by adding a new anode.

If you need to retrofit an existing tank, before you do any digging, refer to your company's policy, or call the national hotline (811) or your local one-call system to prevent damage to underground structures.

First, verify there are no sprinkler lines, low voltage electric wires, the propane service line or other owner installed pipes or wires where you plan to dig.

Cut out a plug of grass five feet to the side of the dome with the shovel and set it aside.

Dig a vertical hole at least 3 ft. deep. If this isn't possible, you may have to lay the anode down horizontally. In dry environments, the anode may work better if it is laid horizontally in a ditch 18 in. deep where sprinkler or rain water will wet the anode. As stated earlier, if the tank is in a desert environment, set a PVC pipe in the hole with the anode so that water can be poured into the pipe to wet the anode.

Place the anode in the hole and pour water on it.

Touch the anode wire to the multivalve© while taking a tank potential reading. The reading should be above −0.85 volts. If so, continue with the installation. If the reading is still not good, refer to the troubleshooting list in Section 2.7.

With the shovel, wedge the grass apart from the anode to the dome, and push the wire down below the grass into the dirt.

With a portable electric drill, drill a hole through the

dome...and insert a rubber grommet in the hole. Then, push the wire through the hole into the dome.

Connect the wire to the tank at the stud under the multivalve©, or to the riser pipe using a band clamp. Any water proofed secure connection between the anode wire and the riser pipe or multivalve© will cause the tank potential readings to shift to the protected level of −0.85 volts or greater.

Fill the anode hole with the dirt removed during digging and use the shovel handle to tamp the dirt around and on top of the anode. This fills in the voids between the anode and the hole you dug. If you don't do this, there will be a gap between the anode and the hole that the current cannot flow across. This will reduce the amount of current your anode creates, and cause the readings to be lower than what is possible. Replace the plug of grass on top of the anode hole and push the separated grass back together where the anode wire was run.

Once you've completed these steps, one last major thing to do is to take a tank to soil potential test. This was covered in Section 2.6 of the manual. Remember though to take four readings, one on each side of the tank and one on each end, with a healthy reading being any voltage equal to or greater than minus .85 volts. But in the unlikely event that one anode does not increase the readings to a protected level of −0.85 volts or greater all around the tank, install a second anode on the opposite side of the tank. And...just like the original installation, once done, you'll want to document your work for future reference. Follow your company's policy and local codes.

If after following all these procedures and your reading still does not increase to −0.85 volts or greater, it is possible the container is too corroded and may need to be removed from service. Check with your supervisor for company policy regarding these guidelines.

2.8 Gas Piping Protection

The following are general recommendations for protecting lines connecting underground tanks to buildings or gas utilization equipment such as generators. These recommendations are based on commonly accepted installation codes and good operating practice. Any deviations should be with the recommendation of a corrosion specialist and approval of the authority having jurisdiction.

Coated Steel or Black Iron Pipe — The anodes installed to protect the tank will also protect coated steel or black iron gas lines where a dielectric union is installed at the building or gas utilization equipment.

Coated Copper Tubing — The anodes installed to protect the tank will also protect coated copper gas lines where a

dielectric union is installed at the building or gas utilization equipment.

Uncoated Steel or Black Iron Pipe — Uncoated steel or black iron piping is not recommended. NFPA 58 and good installation practices requires black iron or steel pipe to be coated.

Uncoated Copper Tubing — Because uncoated copper tubing does not present corrosion problems in most soils that can result in reduced anode performance and life, this material must be isolated from the underground tank being cathodically protected. Use of uncoated copper tubing is dependent on local soil conditions and approval of the authority having jurisdiction.

Coated Steel or Black Iron Pipe With Uncoated Fittings — Uncoated fittings should never be used with coated black iron or steel piping. All pipe fittings must be coated and wrapped before burial.

Since coatings, pipe sizes, composition and lengths vary from one job to another, the -0.85 volt criterion will determine whether one anode or multiple anodes are needed to achieve protection. Multiple readings over and along a pipe may be needed to confirm that a single anode is protecting the gas line from the tank to the building.

3.0 IMPRESSED CURRENT OVERVIEW

3.1 Impressed Current . . . An Overview

Earlier in the manual, we said there were two ways to protect underground steel tanks and metal piping from corrosion, with the most common being galvanic protection using magnesium anodes. The second way is with impressed current. But there's a major difference in how the two work and where you use one versus the other. Whereas galvanic protection works well with small tanks usually meant for residential and small commercial applications, impressed current is meant for large bulk storage tanks. And know that a company specializing in cathodic protection should design systems for installations larger than 4,000 gallons.

Earlier, we discussed the current from an anode as light from a light bulb. Current from an impressed current anode is similar to light from a bank of stadium lights. Therefore, one or two impressed current anodes is enough to bathe in light . . . or protect the entire surface of any size commercial tank . . . its liquid lines, vapor lines and anything else nearby. How does this work? The impressed current anode gets its power from a rectifier which is like a transformer and is as small as a shoebox. This rectifier turns a.c. voltage into d.c. voltage like a battery charger.

Whereas a magnesium anode has the power of a 1 volt battery, a rectifier and its anode or anodes have the voltage of a car battery and more! With more voltage, you get more current, or as in our example here . . . more light. If there is resistance in the ground, that resistance will block the current from an anode like smoke blocks light. But the impressed current rectifier has the power to force the current through the resistant earth like a searchlight through smoke.

Although we simplified it, what we've just discussed are a few of the major differences between galvanic protection and impressed current protection. Of course there are a lot of other differences.

Impressed current anodes are made of a special alloy of cast iron, silicon and chromium. Unlike magnesium anodes which are covered with dirt from the hole that was dug, impressed current anodes are first encased in coke breeze backfill, a good electrical conductor, and then covered with dirt from the excavation. Also, if the coating on the tank disintegrates as it gets old, the additional current from the impressed current anode can compensate for the lack of coating. Finally, as alluded to earlier, if there are electrically grounded structures to the tank, or a long run of underground steel liquid or vapor lines, the rectifier system can also protect them for many years.

3.2 Installation

When it comes to installation, know that high voltage is very dangerous! Impressed current can also, on occasion, harm unrelated buried structures around a commercial tank system. Impressed current systems need to be designed and installed by people trained in the science of cathodic protection . . . people who are qualified and know exactly what they are doing. Talk with your supervisor before attempting to work with impressed current.

3.3 Maintenance

An impressed current system requires maintenance to be certain it is on, and that required current is always flowing to the anodes. Rectifiers have amp meters that show how much current is flowing to the anodes. As long as there is an amp meter in the rectifier that shows some amperage flowing into the anodes, the system is on. A person should write the amperage output down, date it and initial the reading for future reference.

If there is ever any doubt that the rectifier is on, you should check the output voltage with a voltmeter across the + and − terminals of the rectifier, just as you would across the "+" and "−" terminals of a car battery.

Because this manual has been designed around cathodic protection for residential systems, we just wanted to give you a brief overview of impressed current. For further information and training, talk with your supervisor and see what your company offers. Just remember, impressed current systems must be inspected and maintained by persons or companies specializing in cathodic protection systems.

SUPPLEMENT 6

Home Fires Involving Grills

Editor's Note: Supplement 6 was extracted from NFPA's 2009 report, Home Fires Involving Cooking Equipment, by Marty Ahrens. This new supplement provides detailed data on reported grill fires, including trends, causes, and circumstances of these fires as well as patterns of grill usage. Gas grill usage increased dramatically over the past few decades. Reported gas grill fires hit their peak in 1997. Due to changes in the data collection system, annual estimates are highly uncertain for 1999–2001. The 2003 estimate of gas grill fires was the lowest seen since 1987. After 2003, the numbers increased each year through 2006. Roughly two-thirds of the grills involved in reported home structure and outside fires in 2003–2006 were fueled by LP-Gas. The data show that the leading cause gas grill fires was a leak or break. For more information, refer to the full report, Home Fires Involving Cooking Equipment, by Marty Ahrens. The report is periodically updated after new data become available and are analyzed. Revised reports will be available from www.nfpa.org. Reports are available at no charge to NFPA members and to others at a nominal cost.

U.S. Fire Departments Responded to an Average of 7,900 Home Structure and Outdoor Fires Involving Grills per Year During 2003–2006

During the four-year period of 2003–2006, grills, hibachis or barbecues were involved in the ignition of an estimated 7,900 reported home[1] structure and outdoor fires per year. These fires caused an average of 10 civilian deaths, 120 civilian injuries, and $80 million in direct property damage annually. When a grill was involved in ignition, it provided the heat source that started the fire.

The 7,900 home grill fires reported annually included 2,900 (37%) fires per year in or on structures. All of the grill fire deaths, 90 (73%) of the associated fire injuries, and $79 million in direct property damage (99%) per year resulted from fires involving structures. The 2,900 home structure fires involving grills accounted for 2% of the reported home cooking equipment fires, 3% of associated civilian deaths, and 2% of associated civilian injuries, but 10% of the associated property damage.

On average, 5,000 (63%) outside and unclassified grill fires were reported annually during this period. These fires caused an annual average of 30 civilian injuries (27%) and less than $1 million in direct property damage.

Grill Fires Peak in the Summer

Exhibit S6.1 shows that June and July were the peak months for grill fires, with 16% of the incidents each. May and August followed with 13% each. Although the smallest share of fires occurred in the winter months, these incidents occurred throughout the year.

More People Are Grilling Year Round

The market research company NPD Group, Inc. reported that in 2007, more than one-third (38%) of American households had at least one meal cooked on an outdoor grill in an average two-week period during the year.[2] In the summer months of June, July and August, half (49%) had

---

1. Homes include one- and two-family dwellings, apartments (regardless of ownership), and manufactured housing. Fires are rounded to the nearest hundred, casualties to the nearest ten, and direct property damage to the nearest million.

2. The NPD Group, Inc. "NPD Reports Year Round Grilling at All Time High," Port Washington, New York, May 2008 15, 2008, accessed at http://www.npd.com/press/releases/press_080515a.html on April 17, 2009.

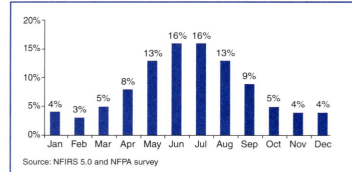

Source: NFIRS 5.0 and NFPA survey

EXHIBIT S6.1 *Home Grill Fires by Month: 2003–2006.*

a grilled meal. But even in the winter months of December, January, and February, one-quarter (27%) had eaten at least one grilled item in a 14-day period. Year-round grilling more than doubled from 17% in 1985 to 38% in 2007.

More than one-third of people who cooked from scratch prepared at least one meal per week on an outdoor grill, according to A.E. Sloan's article that referenced 2005 findings from Multi-Sponsor Surveys, Inc.[3] Twenty percent used an indoor grill at least once a week. One-quarter (27%) of convenience cooks used an outdoor grill for at least one meal a week and 19% used indoor grills every week.

Seventy Percent of Grills Involved in Home Outdoor and Structure Fires in 2003–2006 Used LP-Gas

Exhibit S6.2 shows the power source for all grills involved in reported home fires. Gas grills were involved in 81% of

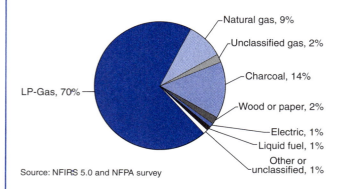

Source: NFIRS 5.0 and NFPA survey

EXHIBIT S6.2 *Home Grill Fires by Power Source: 2003–2006.*

reported home grill fires. More than two-thirds (70%) of the home grill fires involved grills fueled by liquid propane gas (LP-gas) or similar gas that is heavier than air. Nine percent were fueled by natural gas or other lighter than air gas, and 2% were fueled by an unclassified gas.

Sixteen percent of the grills involved in fires were solid-fueled, including 14% that used charcoal or coal and 2% that used wood or paper. One percent of the grills were powered by electricity, 1% by a liquid fuel, and 1% by another known or unclassified power source.

The NPD Group also noted that 76% of American households own an outdoor grill and 75% of the owners have a gas grill.[4] That means that more than half (57%) of American households have a gas grill. In a 2007 press release, NPD reported that in 2005, 30% of households had a charcoal grill and 56% a gas grill.

In 2008, the Weber GrillWatch™ Survey, conducted by Greenfield Online, reported that 53% of all grill owners have a charcoal grill, and 63% have a gas grill.[5] Fifty-six percent use gas grills more often, while 38% use charcoal grills more. Almost one-quarter (23%) use both equally. Although gas grills are used roughly 1.5 times as often as charcoal grills, they were involved in five times as many fires.

Shipments of Gas Grills Overtook Charcoal in 1995

According to the Hearth, Patio and Barbecue Association, more than twice as many charcoal grills were shipped in North America during 1985 as gas grills. Exhibit S6.3 shows that as of 1995, more gas grills were shipped for sale than charcoal grills.

Gas Grill Fires Climbed Since The Early 80s While Solid-Fueled Grill Fires Decreased

In 2005, gas grill user households outnumbered charcoal grill user households by roughly 2-to-1 (56% of U.S. households vs. 30% of U.S. households).[6] Exhibit S6.4 shows that the 9,200 grill fires in 2006 was almost twice the 5,300 reported in 1980 but still below the peak years of 1995–1998, when fires ranged between 10,500 and 12,500. These statistics include both structure and outdoor fires. Because of issues related to the gradual introduction of

---

3. A.E. Sloan. "What, When and Where America Eats," *Food Technology,* January 2006, p. 26, accessed http://members.ift.org/NR/rdonlyres/65A7B82E-0AFF-4639-95B2-733B8225D93A/0/0106americaeats.pdf on April 20, 2009.

4. The NPD Group, Inc., 2008.

5. Weber. "Outdoor Grillers Are Turning to Healthier Choices, Grilling More Often According to the 19th Annual Grillwatch™ Survey." March 24, 2008. Accessed at http://weber.mediaroom.com/index.php?s=41&cat=1.

6. The NPD Group, Inc., "NPD reveals outdoor grill usage at a 20-year high," news release, May 22, 2006, accessed at www.npd.com.

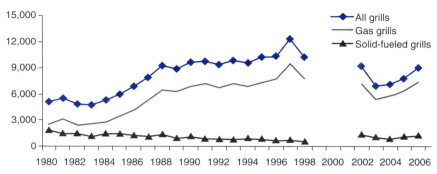

EXHIBIT S6.3 *Number of Barbecue Grills Shipped in North America, by Power Source: 1985–2007.*

Source: Data from NFIRS and NFPA survey. Estimates for the transition to Version 5.0 of NFIRS in 1999-2001 are unstable and not shown.

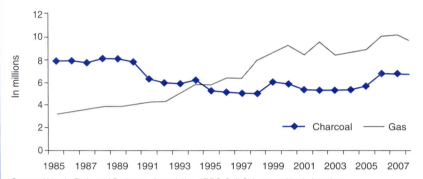

EXHIBIT S6.4 *Home Fires Involving Grills, by Year Fires Reported to U.S. Fire Departments: 1980–2006.*

Source: Hearth, Patio and Barbecue Association, "BBQ Grill Shipments-North America: 1985-2008," accessed at http://www.hpba.org/index.php?id=255 on April 17, 2009.

NFIRS 5.0, data from 1990–2001 are not depicted graphically but are included in the tables available in the full report, *Home Fires Involving Cooking Equipment.*

Gas grill fires were nearly three times as frequent in 2006 (7,500 fires) as in 1980 (2,600). In contrast, 1,400 charcoal or solid-fueled grill fires were reported in 2006, a drop of 30% from the 2,000 reported in 1980.

Exhibit S6.5 shows that gas grills accounted for roughly two-thirds to three-quarters of the outdoor and unclassified grill fires from 1980 through 1998. Since 2002, 84–89% of the outdoor grill fires involved gas-fueled equipment. Gas-fueled equipment accounted for roughly one-quarter to one-third of the structure fires involving grills in the early 1980s. In the most recent three years of data, gas-fired equipment was involved in 80–89% of the grill structure fires.

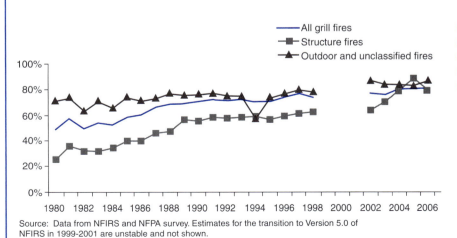

EXHIBIT S6.5 *Percent of Home Grill Fires Involving Gas-Fueled Grills, by Year Fires Reported to U.S. Fire Departments: 1980–2006.*

Source: Data from NFIRS and NFPA survey. Estimates for the transition to Version 5.0 of NFIRS in 1999-2001 are unstable and not shown.

One-Third of Home Grill Structure Fires Started on an Exterior Balcony or Open Porch

Exhibit S6.6 shows that in 2003–2006, 33% of the non-confined home grill structure fires started on an exterior balcony or unenclosed porch; 18% began on a courtyard, terrace, or patio; and 11% started along an exterior wall surface. Unlike typical cooking equipment, most grills are intended for outdoor use. Consequently, few grill fires start in kitchens (5% of non-confined home structure grill fires). The rank order of where fires start is the same for both gas grills and solid-fueled grills. It appears that grills are too often used too close to the structure.

For outdoor and unclassified grill fires (excluding outdoor rubbish fires), the leading areas of origin were courtyards, terraces, or patios (39%); unclassified outside areas (21%); exterior balconies or unenclosed porch (14%), and lawns, fields, or open areas (7%). Although the order varied slightly, these were the leading areas of origin for outdoor fires involving both gas and solid-fueled grills.

About Confined, Non-Confined, and Outside Rubbish Fires

Certain types of fires collectively referred to as "confined fires," including confined cooking fires, chimney fires, trash fires, and fuel burner or boiler fires (incident types 113-118) can be documented more easily in NFIRS 5.0. Causal data, including equipment involved in ignition, is generally not required for these incidents although it is provided in some cases. Equipment involved in ignition was reported in 22% of the non-confined fires and 4% of the confined fires. Confined

and non-confined structure fires were analyzed separately and then summed to obtain estimates of grill structure fires with different power sources.

Causal data is not required for outside rubbish fires (incident type 150-159) either. Outside rubbish fires were analyzed separately from the remaining non-structure, non-vehicle fires. These two groups (1- outside rubbish, and 2- outside non rubbish and unclassified) were also analyzed separately and summed for estimates of grill trends, power sources and months. Confined structure fires and outside rubbish fires are excluded from analysis of area of origin, factors contributing to ignition, and item first ignited.

The Grill Was Too Close to Something Combustible in One-Third of Non-Confined Home Grill Structure Fires

In 2003–2006, a heat source (the grill) was too close to something that could catch fire in 32% of all non-confined structure fires in which grills were involved in ignition. The leading factors contributing to ignition varied by power source. Heat source too close was a factor in almost half (46%) of solid-fueled grill structure fires and almost one-quarter (23%) of gas grill structure fires. Unattended equipment was a factor in 15% of all grill structure fires, 16% of gas grill structure fires, 12% of solid-fueled grill structure fires, 15% of outdoor solid-fueled grill structure fires, but only 2% of outdoor gas grill fires.

Although leaks or breaks were the leading contributing factors in all outdoor grill fires (34%) and the third leading factor in grill structure fires (13%), this is due largely to gas grill fires. Leaks or breaks were the leading

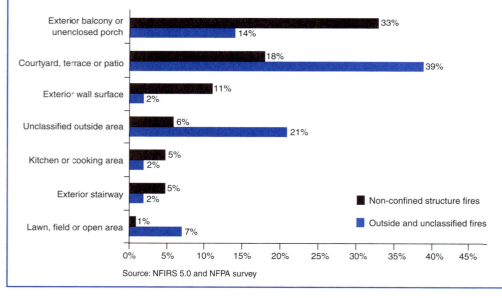

EXHIBIT S6.6 Home Grill Fires by Leading Areas of Origin 2003–2006.

contributing factors in gas grill structure fires (24%), and outdoor gas grill fires (39%). A failure to clean was a factor in 14% of all outdoor grill fires and 16% of outdoor gas grill fires.

Flammable or Combustible Gas or Liquid Was The Item First Ignited in Half of Home Outdoor Grill Fires

In 51% of the home outdoor fires in which grills were involved, 56% of the outside gas grills, and 29% of the non-confined gas grill structure fires, the fire started when a flammable or combustible gas or liquid caught fire. Exterior wall coverings and structural members or framing were in the top three items first ignited for all non-confined grill structure fires, as well as those involving solid-fueled and gas grills.

So far, the analysis has focused on fires that were reported to fire departments. These injuries are a tiny fraction of the grill-related injuries seen in the country's emergency rooms.

In 2007, 18,600 Patients Went to Emergency Rooms Because of Injuries Involving Grills

The U.S. Consumer Product Safety Commission (CPSC) maintains the National Electronic Injury Surveillance System (NEISS). A weighted sample of hospital emergency rooms provides information about the patients and injuries seen and allows projections to be made about injuries involving specific products. Gas grills accounted for an estimated 2,900 injuries and charcoal or wood-burning grills for 2,100 injuries. Unspecified other grills accounted for 13,300 injuries. The number of electric-powered grill injuries was too small to produce reliable estimates.[7]

- The 9,600 thermal burns accounted for roughly two-thirds (2,000) of the injuries involving gas grills and charcoal or wood-burning grills (1,400) and almost half (6,100) of the injuries involving unspecified grills. Children under five accounted for 2,200, or roughly one-quarter, of total thermal grill burns. Most of these were contact burns rather than flame burns.
- Roughly one-third of the gas grill injuries were thermal burns incurred while lighting the grill.
- Gasoline or lighter fluid was a factor in roughly one-quarter of the charcoal or wood burning grill burns.
- Although the number of cases was too small for reliable estimates, more people were seen for carbon monoxide exposure after using a charcoal grill inside the home compared to gas grills.

CPSC Estimates That Grills Were Involved in an Average of 7 Fatal CO Poisonings a Year in 2003–2005

In a study of non-fire deaths resulting from carbon monoxide (CO) poisoning, Matthew Hnatov of the CPSC reported that charcoal or charcoal grills were involved in an average of six such deaths a year in 2003–2005.[8] Gas-fueled grills or camp stoves were involved in an average of one CO death per year in the same period.

Additional Information

The full report, *Home Fires Involving Cooking Equipment*, or the section devoted to grills that includes supporting tables on the material here, is available to NFPA members without charge at www.nfpa.org. Non-members can order the report for a small fee by contacting osds@nfpa.org or (617) 984-7443.

---

7. Queries on charcoal or wood burning grills (code 3218), gas or LP-Grills or Stoves (for outdoor use) (code 3248), and grills, not specified (3249) were done at http://www.cpsc.gov/library/neiss.html in April 2009.

8. Matthew Hnatov Non-Fire Carbon Monoxide Deaths Associated with the Use of Consumer Products," U.S. Consumer Product Safety Commission, 2008, Table 1, p. 6 accessed at http://www.cpsc.gov/LIBRARY/co08.pdf on April 20, 2009.

Technical/Substantive Changes from the 2008 Edition to the 2011 Edition of NFPA 58

Editor's Note: *Supplement 7 contains a useful table of major code changes from the 2008 to the 2011 edition of NFPA 58, Liquefied Petroleum Gas Code. Purely editorial or formatting changes that have occurred from the 2008 edition to the 2011 edition of NFPA 58 have not been included in this supplement.*

2008 Edition	2011 Edition	Comments
Chapter 1 Administration		
1.3.2 (11) Propane dispensers located at multiple fuel refueling stations shall comply with NFPA 30A, *Code for Motor Fuel Dispensing Facilities and Repair Garages.*	**1.3.2 (11)** Propane vehicle fuel dispensers located at multiple fuel refueling stations shall comply with NFPA 30A, *Code for Motor Fuel Dispensing Facilities and Repair Garages*	Revised to clarify that NFPA 58 does not apply to propane dispensers at multiple fuel refueling stations. This falls under the scope of NFPA 30A.
Chapter 2 Referenced Publications		
Any change to a referenced publication is reflected in the section of NFPA 58 in which it appears.		
Chapter 3 Definitions		
3.3.2 Anodeless Riser. A transition assembly where polyethylene or polyamide pipe or tubing is permitted to be installed underground and is terminated above ground outside of a building.	**3.3.2 Anodeless Riser.** A transition assembly used between underground polyethylene or polyamide pipe and aboveground metal piping or equipment, and terminating aboveground outside of a building.	Revised to remove a requirement. Definitions must not include requirements.
3.3.16 Cylinder. A container designed, constructed, tested, and marked in accordance with U.S. Department of Transportation specifications, Title 49, Code of Federal Regulations, or in accordance with a valid DOT exemption.	**3.3.16 Cylinder.** A container designed, constructed, tested, and marked in accordance with U.S. Department of Transportation specifications, Title 49, *Code of Federal Regulations,* or in accordance with a valid DOT special permit.	The definition of cylinder has been updated to be consistent with changes in DOT regulations.
3.3.18 Diameter. The length of a straight line passing through the center of a cycle, terminating at the periphery.	Not in 2011 edition	Removed as it is an unnecessary definition.
3.3.24 Fixed Piping System. Piping, valves, and fittings permanently installed in a location to connect the source of the LP-Gas to the utilization equipment.	Not in 2011 edition	This is now covered by the revised definition of *piping system.*

2008 Edition	*2011 Edition*	*Comments*
3.3.25.1 Flexible Hose Connector. A component fabricated from LP-Gas hose that meets the requirements of UL 569, *Standard for Pigtails and Flexible Hose Connectors for LP-Gas,* or the following requirements of UL 21, *Standard for LP-Gas Hose*: (1) The tube or lining of a hose shall be made from a material compatible with LP-Gas. (2) The hose reinforcement shall be of cotton, synthetic fibers, or corrosion-resistant material such as stainless steel, or any combination thereof, evenly applied over the tube.	**3.3.23.1 Flexible Hose Connector.** A component fabricated from LP-Gas hose that is made from a material that is compatible with LP-gas.	Revised to remove a requirement. Definitions must not include requirements. The requirement is described in 11.7.3.1.
3.3.25.2 Flexible Metallic Connector A component fabricated from flexible metal such as stainless steel wire braid or soft copper tubing.	**3.3.23.2 Flexible Metallic Connector.** A component fabricated from metallic material that provides liquid and vapor LP-Gas confinement and is provided with connections on both ends.	
Not in 2008 edition	**3.3.23.3 Metallic-Protected Flexible Hose Connector.** A flexible hose connector that is provided with a metallic material over wrap that provides mechanical protection of the inner hose but does not provide fluid confinement.	
3.3.27 Gas. Liquefied petroleum gas in either the liquid or vapor state. The more specific terms liquid LP-Gas or vapor LP-Gas are used for clarity.	**3.3.25* Gas.** Liquefied petroleum gas in either the liquid or vapor state.	Revised to delete unnecessary text.
3.3.29.5 Rotary Gauge. A variable liquid level gauge consisting of a small positive shutoff vent valve located at the outside end of a tube that has a bent end inside the container and can be manually rotated to determine the liquid level in the container. It is equipped with a pointer and an outside dial to indicate the liquid level.	**3.3.27.5 Rotary Gauge.** A type of variable liquid level gauge that indicates the liquid level on a dial gauge installed on an ASME container by manually rotating an open ended tube inside the container, which is connected to a positive shutoff vent valve.	Distinguishes the slip tube from a fixed maximum liquid level gauge.
3.3.40 Minimum Design Metal Temperature (MDMT). As described by the ASME *Boiler and Pressure Vessel Code.*	Not in 2011 edition	This definition has been deleted because it is used only in 5.2.8.3(12) and 11.3.4(12). It has been moved to these paragraphs.
3.3.46 Multipurpose Passenger Vehicle. A motor vehicle with motive power, with the exception of a trailer, designed to carry 10 or fewer persons that is constructed on a truck chassis or with special features for occasional off-road operations.	Not in 2011 edition	This term is only used in 11.3.2.2. The revised 11.3.2.2 makes the definition unnecessary.
3.3.53 Piping System. Pipe, tubing, hose, and flexible rubber or metallic hose connectors with valves and fittings made into complete systems for conveying	**3.3.49 Piping Systems.** Pipe, tubing, hose, and flexible rubber or metallic hose connectors with valves and fittings made into complete systems for conveying	Revised to be more general, allowing the definition of *fixed piping system* to be removed.

2008 Edition	2011 Edition	Comments
LP-Gas from one point to another in either the liquid or the vapor state at various pressures.	LP-Gas from one point to another in either the liquid or the vapor state at various pressures.	
3.3.58 Pressure Relief Device. A device designed to open to prevent a rise of internal pressure in excess of a specified value due to emergency or abnormal conditions.	**3.3.54 Pressure Relief Device.** A device designed to open to prevent a rise of internal pressure in excess of a specified value.	Revised to remove unneeded text.
3.3.63 Refrigerated LP-Gas. LP-Gas that is maintained as a liquid at temperatures below ambient temperature to reduce the storage pressure including fully refrigerated LP-Gas at pressures near atmospheric pressure but not exceeding 15 psig (103 kPag) and semi-refrigerated LP-Gas at pressures above 15 psig (103 kPag).	**3.3.59* Refrigerated LP-Gas.** LP-Gas that is cooled to temperatures below ambient to maintain the product as a liquid with a vapor pressure of 15 psig or less.	Revised to improve the accuracy of the definition.
Not in 2008 edition	**3.3.69.3 Filler Valve.** A valve that is designed to allow liquid flow into a container.	New definition added to define a term used in the code.
3.3.74.4* Internal Valve. A container primary shutoff valve having the following features: (1) The seat and seat disc remain inside the container so that damage to parts exterior to the container or mating flange does not prevent effective sealing of the valve; (2) The valve is designed for the addition of a means for remote closure and is also designed for automatic shutoff when the flow through the valve exceeds its maximum rated flow capacity or when pump actuation differential pressure drops to a predetermined point.	**3.3.69.5* Internal Valve.** A container primary shutoff valve that can be closed remotely, which incorporates an internal excess flow valve with the seat and seat disc located within the container so that they remain in place should external damage occur to the valve.	Revised to describe the valve, not its use.
3.3.74.5.3* Full Internal Pressure Relief Valve. A pressure relief valve, for engine fuel and mobile container use, in which all working parts are recessed within the container connection, and the spring and guiding mechanism are not exposed to the atmosphere.	**3.3.69.6.3* Full Internal Pressure Relief Valve.** A pressure relief valve in which all working parts are recessed within a threaded connection of the valve, and the spring and guiding mechanism are not exposed to the atmosphere.	Revised to describe the valve, not its use.
3.3.74.5.4* Internal Spring-Type Pressure Relief Valve. A pressure relief valve, for use on ASME stationary containers that has a low profile and is similar to a full internal relief valve except the wrenching pads and seating section are above the container connection. The adjusting spring and the stem are below the seat and are not exposed to the atmosphere.	**3.3.69.6.4* Internal Spring-Type Pressure Relief Valve.** A pressure relief valve that is similar to a full internal relief valve except the wrenching pads and seating section are above the container connection in which the adjusting spring and the stem are below the seat and are not exposed to the atmosphere.	Revised to describe the valve, not its use.

2008 Edition	2011 Edition	Comments
3.3.75.1 Direct-Fired Vaporizer. A vaporizer in which heat furnished by a flame is directly applied to some form of a heat exchange surface in contact with the liquid LP-Gas to be vaporized. This classification includes submerged combustion vaporizers.	**3.3.70.1 Direct-Fired Vaporizer.** A vaporizer in which heat furnished by a flame is directly applied to a heat exchange surface in contact with the liquid LP-Gas to be vaporized.	Revised to delete reference to submerged combustion vaporizers, which are not covered by NFPA 58.
3.3.75.5.1 External Pressure Relief Valve. A pressure relief valve that is used on older domestic containers, on pressure relief valve manifolds, and for piping protection where all the working parts are located entirely outside the container or piping.	**3.3.69.6.1* External Pressure Relief Valve.** A pressure relief valve where all the working parts are located entirely outside the container or piping.	Revised to describe the valve, not its use.
Chapter 4 General Requirements		
4.1.1 Systems or components assembled to make up systems shall be approved as specified in Table 4.1.1.	**4.1.1** Systems or components assembled to make up systems shall be approved as specified in Table 4.1.1. Where necessary to alter or repair such systems or assemblies in the field, approved components shall be used.	The conditions of the systems that can be assembled are explained.
4.1.2 Where necessary to alter or repair containers or container assemblies in the field, such changes shall be made using approved components.	**4.1.2** Where it is necessary to alter or repair such systems or assemblies, approved components shall be used.	4.1.2 clarifies the change in 4.1.1.
4.3.2 Temporary Installations. The authority having jurisdiction shall be notified of temporary (not to exceed 12 months) installations of the container sizes covered in 4.3.1 before the installation is started.	**4.3.2 Temporary Installations.** **4.3.2.1** The authority having jurisdiction shall be notified of temporary installations of the container sizes covered in 4.3.1 before the installation is started. **4.3.2.2** Where temporary installations exceed 12 months, approval shall be obtained.	Temporary installations are now consistent at 12 months, and therefore the requirement has been added to Chapter 4 and the parenthetical statement removed.
Chapter 5 LP-Gas Equipment and Appliances		
Not in 2008 edition	**5.2.1.1 (A)** Used containers constructed to specifications of the Association of American Railroads shall not be installed.	The railroad standard to which these containers were built is not equivalent to the *ASME Boiler and Pressure Vessel Code.*
Not in 2008 edition	**5.2.1.5** Except for containers used in cargo tank vehicle service, ASME containers of 3000 gal (11.4 m³) water capacity or less used to store anhydrous ammonia shall not be converted to LP-Gas fuel service.	The conversion of these containers can pose many major risks. Cargo tanks are the exception because they are periodically inspected.
Not in 2008 edition	**5.2.1.11** ASME containers installed underground, partially underground, or as mounded installations shall incorporate provisions for cathodic protection and shall be coated with a material recommended for the service that is applied in accordance with the coating manufacturer's instructions.	This provides new corrosion protection requirements by the use of cathodic protection for underground, mounded and partially underground, unmounded containers.

2008 Edition	2011 Edition	Comments
5.2.3 Cylinders Filled on Site. DOT cylinders in stationary service that are filled on site and therefore are not under the jurisdiction of DOT either shall be requalified in accordance with DOT requirements or shall be visually inspected within 12 years of the date of manufacture and within every 5 years thereafter, in accordance with 5.2.3.1 through 5.2.3.3.	**5.2.3 Cylinders Filled on Site at the Point of Use.** **5.2.3.1** DOT cylinders in stationary service that are filled on site at the point of use and, therefore, are not under the jurisdiction of DOT shall comply with one of the following criteria: (1) They shall be requalified in accordance with DOT requirements. (2) They shall be visually inspected within 12 years of the date of manufacture and within every 5 years thereafter, in accordance with 5.2.3.2 through 5.2.3.4.	The phrase "filled on site at the point of use" is employed as it is more widely understood. The description is divided into subparts (1) and (2) to make it clearer.
5.2.5.6 (B) If the pressure relief valve is located in a protecting enclosure, the enclosure shall be designed to minimize corrosion and to allow inspection. Not in 2008 edition	**5.2.5.6 (B)** An enclosure that protects a pressure relief valve shall be painted, coated, or made from corrosion-resistant materials. **(C)** The design of an enclosure that protects a pressure relief valve shall permit inspection of the pressure relief valve.	This clarifies that corrosion protection applies to the enclosure itself.
5.2.8.3* The markings specified for ASME containers shall be on a stainless steel metal nameplate attached to the container, located to remain visible after the container is installed. **(A)** The nameplate shall be attached in such a way as to minimize corrosion of the nameplate or its fastening means and not contribute to corrosion of the container. **(B)** Where the container is buried, mounded, insulated, or otherwise covered so the nameplate is obscured, the information contained on the nameplate shall be duplicated and installed on adjacent piping or on a structure in a clearly visible location. **(C)** ASME containers shall be marked with the following information: [. . .] Not in 2008 edition	**5.2.8.3*** The markings specified for ASME containers shall be on a stainless steel metal nameplate attached to the container, located to remain visible after the container is installed. **(A)** Unchanged **(B)** Unchanged **(C)** Stationary ASME containers shall be marked with the following information: [. . .] **(D)** In addition to the markings required by this code, nameplates on cargo tanks shall include the markings required by the ASME *Boiler and Pressure Vessel Code* and the DOT.	New requirement to distinguish between marking requirements for containers in stationary service and containers used in commercial transport.
Not in 2008 edition	**5.7.2.3** Composite cylinders shall not be equipped with fusible plugs.	Fusible plugs are not needed for composite cylinders.
5.7.2.7 The flow capacity of pressure relief valves installed on underground or mounded containers shall be permitted to be reduced to 30 percent of the flow specified in Table 5.7.2.5.	**5.7.2.8** The flow capacity of pressure relief valves installed on underground or mounded containers shall be a minimum of 30 percent of the flow specified in Table 5.7.2.6.	Editorial revision to clarify the size of the pressure relief valve.

2008 Edition	2011 Edition	Comments
5.7.4.1 (A) The requirement for internal spring-type pressure relief valves that are shown in Table 5.7.4.1 for stationary ASME containers up to and including 4000 gal (15.2 m³) water capacity shall not apply to underground containers where external pressure relief valves are permitted or to containers that were originally equipped with external pressure relief valves.	**5.7.4.1 (A)** ASME containers having a propane capacity not greater than 100 gal (0.45 m³) shall be permitted to have an external pressure relief valve. The relief valve shall be permitted to be part of a multiple-function valve. Underground containers and containers originally equipped with an external pressure relief valve shall be permitted to have an external relief valve.	Revised to specifically allow external relief valves on ASME containers that are the same size as cylinders.
Not in 2008 edition	**5.7.4.1 (F)** A filler valve shall incorporate one of the following: (1) Double backflow check valves of the spring-loaded type (2) Manual shutoff valve with an internal backflow check valve of the spring-loaded type (3) Combination single backflow check valve of the spring-loaded type and an overfilling prevention device designed for containers	Added to provide guidance on the selection of filler valves. A definition has also been added to Chapter 3.
5.7.4.1 (F) Excess-flow protection shall not be required for manual shutoff valves for vapor service where an approved regulator is directly attached or attached with a flexible connector to the outlet of the manual shutoff valve for vapor service and the controlling orifice between the container contents and the shutoff valve outlet does not exceed 5/16 in. (8 mm) in diameter.	**5.7.4.1 (G)** Manual shutoff valves in vapor service shall be equipped with one of the following: (1) Orifice between the container contents and the shutoff valve outlet, not exceeding 5/16 in. (8 mm) in diameter, and an approved regulator directly attached, or attached with a flexible connector, to the manual shutoff valve outlet (2) Excess-flow valve	Editorial revision to clarify the requirement.
Not in 2008 edition	**5.7.4.1 (J)** Pressure relief valves installed in multiple function valves in single opening cylinders used in industrial truck service shall have the springs and guiding mechanism on the container pressure side of the seats, such that the springs and guiding mechanism shall not be exposed to the atmosphere. Such multiple function valves shall meet the following requirements: (1) In accordance with 5.7.2.13, the pressure relief valve shall either be replaced with a multiple function valve that incorporates the pressure relief valve described in 5.7.4.1(J) or it shall have the means to be replaced without removing the multiple function valve body from the cylinder. (2) The multiple function valve shall incorporate an internal excess flow valve for the liquid or vapor withdrawal service valve outlet.	It is important that the relief valve have its adjusting spring and stem below the seat and not exposed to the atmosphere. This reduces the likelihood of debris and other contaminants affecting the valve setting and flow capacity. New requirements are needed to allow multivalves for composite cylinders to meet the requirements for fork truck cylinders.

2008 Edition	*2011 Edition*	*Comments*
	(3) The multiple function valve shall incorporate a weak section on the service valve outlet connection to mitigate product loss. (4) The internal excess flow valve incorporated into a multiple function valve shall not restrict the flow to the pressure relief valve. (5) Multiple function valves shall be listed.	
5.7.5.8 (1) Variable liquid level gauges installed on containers over 2000 gal (7.6 m³) water capacity shall be marked with the maximum liquid level, in inches, metric units, or percent of capacity of the container where they are to be installed. (2) Markings shall indicate the maximum liquid level at liquid temperatures from 20°F to 130°F (−6.7°C to 54.4°C) and in increments not greater than 20°F (11°C) for propane, for 50/50 butane–propane mixtures, and for butane.	**5.7.5.8.** (1) Variable liquid level gauges installed on containers over 1200 gal (4.5 m³) water capacity shall be marked with the maximum liquid level, in inches, metric units, or percent of capacity of the container on which they are to be installed. (2) If temperature correction markings are provided on variable liquid level gauges on containers greater than 1200 gal (4.5 m³) that will be used for volumetric filling as allowed by 7.4.3.2(A), 7.4.3.2(B), and 7.4.3.3, the markings shall indicate the maximum liquid level at liquid temperatures in accordance with Tables 7.4.3.3(b) or 7.4.3.3(c). Temperature markings shall be from 20°F to 115°F (−6.7°C to 46°C), with increments not to exceed 20°F (11.1°C) for propane, for 50/50 butane-propane mixtures, and for butane.	(1) Size reduced from 2000 to 1200. (2) Editorial revision to clarify the use of variable liquid level gauges.
(3) Markings indicating the various liquid levels from empty to full shall be shown on the system nameplate, on the gauging device, or on both.	Not in 2011 edition	(3) Is unnecessary as the markings are covered by parts (1) and (2)
5.7.8.5 Container inlet and outlet connections on ASME containers of more than 2000 gal (7.6 m³) water capacity shall be labeled to designate whether they communicate with the vapor or liquid space.	**5.7.8.5** Container inlet and outlet connections on ASME containers of more than 2000 gal (7.6 m³) water capacity shall be labeled either on the container service valve or on the container to designate whether they communicate with the vapor or liquid space.	Labels can now be on valves as well as on containers.
(A) Labels shall be permitted to be on valves.	**(A)** Not in 2011 edition	
5.7.8.5 **(B)** Connections for pressure relief devices, liquid level gauging devices, and pressure gauges shall not be required to be labeled.	**5.7.8.6** Connections for pressure relief devices, liquid level gauging devices, and pressure gauges shall not be required to be labeled.	Editorial revision to separate into a paragraph.
5.7.8.6 Every ASME storage container of more than 2000 gal (7.6 m³) water capacity shall be provided with a pressure gauge.	Not in 2011 edition	This paragraph has been combined into 5.7.8.5.

2008 Edition	*2011 Edition*	*Comments*
Not in 2008 edition	**5.7.9* Container Refurbishment.** To prevent the intrusion of foreign matter and physical damage during the container refurbishment process, either of the following shall be required: (1) The container appurtenances shall be removed and the container openings shall be protected (2) The container appurtenances shall be protected.	This new subsection addresses the problem of minimizing intrusion of foreign matter in containers during refurbishment that could affect valve operation in emergencies.
5.8.1 Regulators. **5.8.1.1** Single-stage regulators shall have a maximum outlet pressure setting of 1.0 psig (7 kPag) and shall be equipped with one of the following *(see 6.8.1.5 for required protection from the elements)*: (1) An integral pressure relief valve on the outlet pressure side having a start to-discharge pressure setting within the limits specified in UL 144, *Standard for LP-Gas Regulators.* (2) An integral overpressure shutoff device that shuts off the flow of LP-Gas vapor when the outlet pressure of the regulator reaches the overpressure limits specified in UL144, *Standard for LP-Gas Regulators.* Such a device shall not open to permit flow of gas until it has been manually reset.	**5.8.1 Regulators.** **5.8.1.1** Pressure regulators with a maximum rated capacity of 500,000 Btu/hr (147 kW/hr), except for line pressure and appliance regulators, shall comply with ANSI/UL 144, *Standard for LP-Gas Regulators.* Line pressure regulators shall comply with ANSI Z21.80/CSA 6.22, *Standard for Line Pressure Regulators.* Appliance pressure regulators shall comply with ANSI Z21.18/CSA 6.3, *Gas Appliance Regulators.*	Section 5.8.1 has been extensively revised to recognize revisions to UL 144, the referenced standard for regulator construction. UL 144 now includes many requirements that have been deleted from this section as they are more appropriate to the construction of pressure regulators. These changes will not require changes in the way regulators are constructed.
5.8.1.2 Second-stage regulators and integral two-stage regulators shall have a maximum outlet pressure setting of 14 in. w.c. (4.0 kPag) and shall be equipped with one of the following *(see 6.8.1.5 for required protection from the elements)*: (1) An integral pressure relief valve on the outlet pressure side having a start to discharge pressure setting within the limits specified in UL144, *Standard for LP-Gas Regulators.* This relief device shall limit the outlet pressure of the second-stage regulator to 2.0 psig (14 kPag) when the regulator seat disc is removed and the inlet pressure to the regulator is 10.0 psig (69 kPag) or less, as specified in UL 144. (2) An integral overpressure shutoff device that shuts off the flow of LP-Gas vapor when the outlet pressure of the regulator reaches the overpressure limits specified in UL144, *Standard for LP-Gas Regulators.* Such a device shall not open to permit flow of gas until it has been manually reset.	**5.8.1.2** Single-stage regulators shall have a maximum outlet pressure setting of 1.0 psig. (7 kPag) and shall be equipped with one of the following *(see 6.8.1.5 for required protection from the elements)*: (1) Integral pressure relief valve on the outlet pressure side having a start-to-discharge pressure setting within the limits specified in ANSI/UL 144, *Standard for LP-Gas Regulators* (2) Integral overpressure shutoff device that shuts off the flow of LP-Gas vapor when the outlet pressure of the regulator reaches the overpressure limits specified in ANSI/UL 144, *Standard for LP-Gas Regulators*, and does not open to allow flow of gas until it has been manually reset	

2008 Edition	*2011 Edition*	*Comments*
(3) Regulators with a rated capacity of more than 500,000 Btu/hr (147 kW/hr) shall be permitted to have a separate overpressure protection device complying with 5.9.2 of NFPA 54, *National Fuel Gas Code* (ANSI Z223.1). The overpressure protection device shall limit the outlet pressure of the regulator to 2.0 psig (14 kPag) when the regulator seat disc is removed and the inlet pressure to the regulator is 10 psig (69 kPag) or less.		
5.8.1.3 Integral two-stage regulators shall be provided with a means to determine the outlet pressure of the high-pressure regulator portion of the integral two-stage regulator.	**5.8.1.3** Second-stage regulators and integral two-stage regulators shall have a maximum outlet pressure setting of 16 in. w.c. (4.0 kPa) and shall be equipped with one of the following *(see 6.8.1.5 for required protection from the elements)*: (1) An integral pressure relief valve on the outlet pressure side having a start-to-discharge pressure setting within the limits specified in ANSI/UL 144, *Standard for LP-Gas Regulators*, that limits the outlet pressure of the second-stage regulator to 2.0 psig (14 kPag) or less when the regulator seat disc is removed and the inlet pressure to the regulator is 15.0 psig (103.5 kPag), as specified in ANSI/UL 144 (2) An integral overpressure shutoff device that shuts off the flow of LP-Gas vapor when the outlet pressure of the regulator reaches the overpressure limits specified in ANSI/UL 144, *Standard for LP-Gas Regulators*, and does not open to allow flow of gas until it has been manually reset	
5.8.1.4 Automatic changeover regulators shall be exempt from the requirement in 5.8.1.3.	**5.8.1.4** Second-stage regulators with a rated capacity of more than 500,000 Btu/hr (147 kW/hr) shall either comply with ANSI/UL 144, *Standard for LP-Gas Regulators,* with respect to an integral pressure relief device or an overpressure shutoff device, or shall have a separate overpressure protection device complying with 5.9.2 of NFPA 54, *National Fuel Gas Code* (ANSI Z223.1). The overpressure protection devices shall limit the outlet pressure of the regulator to 2.0 psig (14 kPag) or less when the regulator seat disc is removed and the inlet pressure to the regulator is 15.0 psig (103.5 kPag).	

2008 Edition	2011 Edition	Comments
5.8.1.5 Integral two-stage regulators shall not incorporate an integral pressure relief valve in the high-pressure regulator portion of the unit.	**5.8.1.5** Integral two-stage regulators shall be provided with a means to determine the outlet pressure of the high-pressure regulator portion of the integral two-stage regulator.	
5.8.1.6 First-stage regulators shall incorporate an integral pressure relief valve having a start-to-discharge setting within the limits specified in UL 144, *Standard for LP-Gas Regulators*.	**5.8.1.6** Automatic changeover regulators shall be exempt from the requirement in 5.8.1.5.	
5.8.1.7 First-stage regulators with a rated capacity of more than 500,000 Btu/hr (147 kW/hr) shall be permitted to have a separate pressure relief valve.	**5.8.1.7** Integral two-stage regulators shall not incorporate an integral pressure relief valve in the high-pressure regulator portion of the unit.	
5.8.1.8 High-pressure regulators with a rated capacity of more than 500,000 Btu/hr (147 kW/hr) where permitted to be used in two-stage systems shall incorporate an integral pressure relief valve or shall have a separate relief valve.	**5.8.1.8** First-stage regulators shall incorporate an integral pressure relief valve having a start-to-discharge setting within the limits specified in ANSI/UL 144, *Standard for LP-Gas Regulators*.	
5.8.1.9 First-stage regulators shall have an outlet pressure setting up to 10.0 psig (69 kPag) in accordance with UL 144, *Standard for LP-Gas Regulators*.	**5.8.1.9** High-pressure regulators with a rated capacity of more than 500,000 Btu/hr (147 kW/hr) where permitted to be used in two-stage systems shall incorporate an integral pressure relief valve or shall have a separate relief valve.	
5.8.1.10 Regulators shall be designed so as to drain all condensate from the regulator spring case when the vent is directed down vertically.	**5.8.1.10** First-stage regulators shall have an outlet pressure setting up to 10.0 psig (69 kPag) in accordance with ANSI/UL 144, *Standard for LP-Gas Regulators*.	
5.8.1.11 Two-psi service regulators shall be equipped with one of the following: (1) An integral pressure relief valve on the outlet pressure side having a start to-discharge pressure setting within the limits specified in UL 144, *Standard for LP-Gas Regulators*. This relief device shall limit the outlet pressure of the 2 psi (14 kPa) service regulator to 5.0 psi (34.5 kPa) when the regulator seat disc is removed and inlet pressure to the regulator is 10.0 psi (69 kPa) or as specified in UL144. (2) An integral overpressure shutoff device that shuts off the flow of LP-Gas vapor when the outlet pressure of the regulator reaches the overpressure limits specified in UL144, *Standard for LP-Gas Regulators*. Such a device shall not open to permit flow of gas until it has been manually reset.	**5.8.1.11** First-stage regulators with a rated capacity of more than 500,000 Btu/hr (147 kW/hr) shall be permitted to have a separate pressure relief valve.	

2008 Edition	*2011 Edition*	*Comments*
	5.8.1.12 Regulators shall be designed to drain condensate from the regulator spring case when the vent is directed vertically down.	
	5.8.1.13 Two-psig service regulators and integral 2-psi regulators shall have a maximum outlet pressure setting of 2.5 psi (17 kPag) and shall be equipped with one of the following: (1) An integral pressure relief valve on the outlet pressure side having a start-to-discharge pressure setting within the limits specified in ANSI/UL 144, *Standard for LP-Gas Regulators*. This relief device shall limit the outlet pressure of the 2 psig service regulator to 5.0 psig when the seat disc is removed and the inlet pressure of the regulator is 15.0 psig (103.5 kPag) as specified in ANSI/UL 144. (2) An integral overpressure shutoff device that shuts off the flow of LP-Gas vapor when the outlet pressure of the regulator reaches the overpressure limits specified in ANSI/UL 144. Such a device shall not open to permit the flow of LP-Gas vapor until it has been manually reset.	
Not in 2008 edition	**5.8.3.1** (3) Flexible conduit meeting the requirements of UL 1660, *Liquid-Tight Flexible Nonmetallic Conduit*, with nonmetallic fittings meeting the requirements of UL 514B, *Conduit, Tubing, and Cable Fittings*.	Revised to recognize an alternate nonmetallic conduit that can be safely used to vent gas from regulators.
5.9.3.2 (1) Steel tubing: ASTM A 539, *Standard Specification for Electric-Resistance-Welded Coiled Steel Tubing for Gas Fuel Oil Lines.*	Not in 2011 edition	Reference to ASTM 539 has been removed as it has been withdrawn from ASTM with no replacement.
5.9.6.4 Hose, hose connections, and flexible connectors used for conveying LP-Gas liquid or vapor at pressures in excess of 5 psig (34 kPag), and as provided in Section 6.19 regardless of the pressure, shall comply with 5.9.6.4(A) through 5.9.6.4(D).	**5.9.6.4** Hose, hose connections, and flexible connectors used for conveying LP-Gas liquid or vapor at pressures in excess of 5 psig (34 kPag), and as provided in Section 6.19 regardless of the pressure, shall comply with 5.9.6.4(A) through 5.9.6.4(E).	This revision removes inconsistencies between UL 21 marking standards for LP-Gas hose and NFPA 58. Requirements that hose comply with ANSI/UL 21 or UL 569 have been removed from the definition (3.3.25.1) and placed under this section.
(A) Hose shall be designed for a working pressure of 350 psig (2.4 MPag) with a safety factor of 5 to 1 and shall be continuously marked with LP-GAS, PROPANE, 350 PSI WORKING PRESSURE, and with the manufacturer's name or trademark.	**(A)** Hose shall be designed for a working pressure of at least 350 psig (2.4 MPag), with a safety factor of 5 to 1 and comply with ANSI/UL 569, *Standard for Pigtails and Flexible Hose Connectors*, or ANSI/UL 21, *Standard for LP-Gas Hose*.	

2008 Edition	*2011 Edition*	*Comments*
Not in 2008 edition	**(B)** Hose shall be continuously marked to provide at least the following information: (1) LP-GAS HOSE or LPG HOSE (2) Maximum working pressure (3) Manufacturers' name or coded designation (4) Month or quarter and year of manufacture (5) Product identification	
5.21.4 Direct Gas-Fired Tank Heaters.	**5.21.4 Tank Heaters.**	Title changed to cover all tank heaters.
5.21.4.4 The fuel gas supply connection to the tank heater shall originate in the vapor space of the container being heated and shall be provided with a manually operated shutoff valve at the heater.	**5.21.4.4** The fuel gas supply connection to a direct gas-fired tank heater shall originate in the vapor space of the container being heated and shall be provided with a manually operated shutoff valve at the heater.	Code now addresses "tank heaters" within the equipment section, rather than only "direct gas-fired tank heaters." The requirements are made applicable to the appropriate type of tank heater. Similar revisions have been made to Section 6.21.
5.21.4.5 The heater control system shall be equipped with an automatic safety shutoff valve of the manual-reset type arranged to shut off the flow of gas to both the main and pilot burners if the pilot flame is extinguished.	**5.21.4.5** The heater control system of direct gas-fired tank heaters shall be equipped with an automatic safety shutoff valve of the manual reset type arranged to shut off the flow of gas to both the main and pilot burners if the pilot flame is extinguished.	
5.21.4.7 Direct gas-fired tank heaters shall be equipped with a limit control to prevent the heater from raising the pressure in the storage container to more than 75 percent of the pressure shown in the first column of Table 5.2.4.2 that corresponds with the MAWP of the container (or its ASME *Boiler and Pressure Vessel Code* equivalent).	**5.21.4.7** Tank heaters shall be equipped with a limit control to prevent the heater from raising the pressure in the storage container to more than 75 percent of the pressure shown in the first column of Table 5.2.4.2 that corresponds with the MAWP of the container (or its ASME *Boiler and Pressure Vessel Code* equivalent). **5.21.4.8** If the tank heater is of the electric immersion type, the heater shall be automatically de-energized when the liquid level falls below the top of the heater.	
Not in 2008 edition	**5.21.5.1** Section 5.21 shall not apply to engine fuel vaporizers or to integral vaporizer burners, such as those used with weed burning equipment and tar kettles.	This paragraph re-establishes an exception that was removed from previous editions. The deletion inadvertently required small systems to meet requirements that were not intended for and were difficult to apply to small, portable, vaporizers used in agricultural settings.
5.21.6.6 The immersion heater that provides heat to the water bath shall be installed so as not to contact the heat exchanger and shall be permitted to be electric or gas-fired. **Chapter 6 Installation of LP-Gas Systems**	**5.21.6.6** The immersion heater that provides heat to the waterbath shall be installed so as not to contact the heat exchanger.	Revised to allow any heat source to provide heat to the waterbath rather than just electric or gas-fired sources.

2008 Edition	*2011 Edition*	*Comments*
6.2.2 (4) Containers used with LP-Gas stationary or portable engine fuel systems complying with Chapter 11 (5) Containers used with LP-Gas fueled industrial trucks complying with 11.12.4	**6.2.2** (4) Containers used with LP-Gas portable engine fuel systems shall comply with 11.15.1 (5) Containers used with LP-Gas stationary engine fuel systems shall comply with 11.15.2	Revised to clarify the installation of containers serving engines in building.
6.3 Container Separation Distances.	**6.3 Container Separation Distances.**	Change in referenced sections and tables.
6.3.1 Containers installed outside of buildings, whether of the portable type replaced on a cylinder exchange basis or permanently installed and refilled at the installation, shall be located with respect to the adjacent containers, important building, group of buildings, or line of adjoining property that can be built upon, in accordance with Table 6.3.1, Table 6.4.2, Table 6.4.5.8, and 6.3.2 through 6.3.12.	**6.3.1*** Containers installed outside of buildings, whether of the portable type replaced on a cylinder exchange basis or permanently installed and refilled at the installation, shall be located with respect to the adjacent containers, important building, group of buildings, or line of adjoining property that can be built upon, in accordance with Table 6.3.1, Table 6.4.2, Table 6.4.5.8, and 6.3.2 through 6.3.11.	
6.3.7 Cylinders installed alongside of buildings shall be positioned so that the discharge from the cylinder pressure relief device is located as follows: (1) At least 3 ft (1 m) horizontally away from any building opening that is below the level of such discharge. (2) At least 5 ft (1.5 m) in any direction away from any exterior source of ignition, openings into direct-vent (sealed combustion system) appliances, or mechanical ventilation air intakes.	Not in 2011 edition	This subject is addressed in both 6.3.9 and Table 6.3.9. Including it twice is unnecessary.
Table 6.3.8 Filled at the point of use	**Table 6.3.8** Filled on site at the point of use	
Table 6.3.9 Separation Distance Between Container Pressure Relief Valve and Building Openings	**Table 6.3.8 Separation Distance Between Container Pressure Relief Valve and Building Openings**	The phrase "filled on site at the point of use" clarifies that is does not apply to central filling locations.
Table 6.5.3 Distance Between Point of Transfer and Exposures.	**Table 6.5.3 Distance Between Point of Transfer and Exposures.**	The phrase "fire resistive walls" has been replaced with "at least 1-hour fire-rated walls." This change clarifies that a specific requirement for fire protection is required.
6.5.4.3 If the point of transfer is housed in a structure complying with Chapter 10, the distances in Table 6.5.3 shall be permitted to be reduced, provided the common walls comply with 10.3.1.3.	**6.5.4.3** If the point of transfer is housed in a structure complying with Chapter 10, and the common walls comply with 10.2.1, separation distances in Table 6.5.3 shall not be required where the common walls comply with 10.3.1.3.	Revised to clearly establish the requirement.
6.6.6.1* ASME container assemblies listed for underground installation, including interchangeable aboveground–underground container assemblies, shall be installed underground in accordance with 6.6.6.1(A) through 6.6.6.1(K).	**6.6.6.1*** ASME container assemblies intended for underground installation, including interchangeable aboveground–underground container assemblies, shall be installed underground in accordance with 6.6.6.1(A) through 6.6.6.1(O).	Revised to apply to both listed and unlisted ASME container assembly.

2008 Edition	*2011 Edition*	*Comments*
6.6.6.1* **(E)** Any party involved in construction or excavation in the vicinity of a buried container shall be responsible for determining the location of, and providing protection for, the container and piping against their physical damage from vehicular traffic.	**(E)** The installation of a buried container shall include protection for the container and piping against physical damage from vehicular traffic. **(F)** Prior to digging, the location of underground and mounded containers and piping in the vicinity of construction and excavation activities shall be determined and the installation shall be protected from damage.	The two subjects that were in 6.6.6.1 (E) are now addressed in two separate paragraphs.
6.6.6.1* (H) Containers shall be coated or protected to minimize corrosion.	**(I)*** A corrosion protection system shall be installed on new installations of underground steel containers, unless technical justification is provided to and is approved by the authority having jurisdiction. The corrosion protection system shall include the following: (1) A container coating complying with 5.2.1.11 (2) A cathodic protection system that consists of a sacrificial anode(s) or an impressed current anode (3) A means to test the performance of the cathodic protection system	This revision adds requirements for cathodic protection for underground containers, including periodic inspections and clarifies how damage to tank coatings should be repaired prior to burial.
(I) Any damage to the coating shall be repaired before backfilling	**(J)*** Cathodic protection systems installed in accordance with 6.6.6.1(I) shall be monitored by testing and the results documented. Confirming tests shall be described by one of the following: (1) Producing a voltage of -0.85 volts or more negative, with reference to a saturated copper-copper sulfate half cell (2) Producing a voltage of -0.78 volts or more negative, with reference to a saturated KCl calomel half cell (3) Producing a voltage of -0.80 volts or more negative, with reference to a silver-silver chloride half cell (4) Any other method described in Appendix D of Title 49 of the Code of Federal Regulations, Part 192 **(K)*** Sacrificial anodes installed in accordance with 6.6.6.1(I) above shall be tested in accordance with the following schedule: (1) Upon installation of the cathodic protection system, unless prohibited by climactic conditions, in which case testing shall be done within 180 days after the installation of the system. (2) For continued verification of the effectiveness of the system, 12 to 18 months after the initial test.	

2008 Edition	2011 Edition	Comments
	(3) Upon successful verification testing and in consideration of previous test results, periodic follow-up testing shall be performed at intervals not to exceed 36 months. (4) Systems failing a test shall be repaired as soon as practical unless climactic conditions prohibit this action, in which case the repair shall be made not more than 180 days thereafter. The testing schedule shall be restarted as required in 6.6.6.1(K)(1) and (2), and the results shall comply with 6.6.6.1(J). (5) Documentation of the results of the two most recent tests shall be retained. **(L)*** Where an impressed current cathodic protection system is installed, it shall be inspected and tested in accordance with the following schedule: (1) All sources of impressed current shall be inspected and tested at intervals not exceeding two months. (2) All impressed current cathodic protection installations shall be inspected and tested annually. **(M)** Prior to burial, the container shall be visually examined for damage to the coating. Damaged areas shall be repaired with a coating recommended for underground service and compatible with the existing coating.	
6.6.6.2 Partially underground, unmounded ASME containers shall be installed as follows: (1) The portion of the container below the surface and for a vertical distance of at least 3 in. (75 mm) above the surface shall be coated or protected to minimize corrosion.	**6.6.6.2** Partially underground, unmounded ASME containers shall be installed as follows: (1) The portion of the container below the surface of the ground, and for a vertical distance of at least 3 in. (75 mm) above that surface, shall comply with the corrosion protection requirements of 6.6.6.1(I) through (M). The aboveground portion of the container shall comply with 6.6.1.4.	This revision provides additional corrosion protection requirements by the use of cathodic protection for underground, mounded, and partially underground, unmounded containers. 6.6.6.2 (2) was removed so that a requirement was not duplicated.
(2) Any damage to the coating shall be repaired before backfilling.	Not in 2011 edition	The new requirements for cathodic protection for underground containers are also now required for mounded containers.
6.6.6.3 (4) Mounded containers shall be coated or protected to minimize corrosion.	**6.6.6.3 (4)** Mounded containers shall comply with the corrosion protection requirements of 6.6.6.1(I) through (M).	Provides additional corrosion protection requirements by the use of cathodic protection for underground, mounded, and partially underground, unmounded containers. A reference to 6.6.6.1 is provided for clarification of the requirement.

2008 Edition	*2011 Edition*	*Comments*
6.7.2.7 Pressure relief valve discharge on each aboveground container of more than 2,000 gal (7.6 m³) water capacity shall be piped vertically upward to a point at least 7 ft (2.1 m) above the top of the container, and the discharge opening shall be unobstructed to the open air.	**6.7.2.7** Pressure relief valve discharge on each container of more than 2000 gal (7.6 m³) water capacity shall be directed vertically upward and unobstructed to the open air.	A vertical pipe-away stack of any length for pressure relief valves on aboveground containers is not necessary. The requirement to discharge upward to the open air is retained. The requirement for a 7 ft stack on pressure relief valves is deleted. No reason for requiring it could be found.
6.7.2.10 Shutoff valves shall not be installed between a pressure relief device and the pressure relief device discharge piping.	**6.7.2.10** Shutoff valves shall not be installed at the outlet of a pressure relief device or at the outlet of the discharge piping where discharge piping is installed.	The change leaves the option of using the discharge piping but does not require it for aboveground containers.
6.7.2.15 The discharge piping shall comply with the following: (1) Piping from aboveground containers shall be sized to provide the rate of flow specified in 5.7.2.5. Piping from underground containers shall be sized to provide the rate of flow in specified in 5.7.2.5. (2) Piping shall be metallic and have a melting point over 1500° F (816°C). (3) Discharge piping shall be so designed that excessive force applied to the discharge piping will result in breakage on the discharge side of the valve rather than on the inlet side without impairing the function of the valve. (4) Return bends and restrictive pipe or tubing fittings shall not be used. (5) Not in 2008 edition (6) Not in 208 edition	**6.7.2.14** Where installed, the discharge piping shall comply with the following: (1) Piping shall be supported and protected against physical damage. (2) Piping from aboveground containers shall be sized to provide the rate of flow specified in 5.7.2.5. (3) Piping from underground containers shall be sized to provide the rate of flow specified in 5.7.2.7. (4) Piping shall be metallic and have a melting point over 1500°F (816°C). (5) Discharge piping shall be so designed that excessive force applied to the discharge piping results in breakage on the discharge side of the valve, rather than on the inlet side, without impairing the function of the valve. (6) Return bends and restrictive pipe or tubing fittings shall not be used.	Paragraphs 6.7.2.14 and 6.7.2.15 have been merged to provide the requirements of discharge piping in one paragraph.
6.7.2.14 Discharge piping shall be supported and protected against physical damage.	**6.7.2.15** Where installed, the discharge piping shall be supported and protected against physical damage.	
Not in 2008 edition	**6.9.3.16** Underground metallic piping, tubing, or both that convey LP-Gas from a gas storage container shall be provided with dielectric fittings at the building to electrically isolate it from the aboveground portion of the fixed piping system that enters a building. Such dielectric fittings shall be installed above ground and outdoors.	The energizing of the underground piping makes this piping act as if it were a grounding electrode per the *National Electrical Code* (*NFPA 70*). With the addition of requirements for cathodic protection systems for underground containers, a new requirement is needed to electrically isolate the building piping from the underground container so as to not interfere with the cathodic protection system.

2008 Edition	2011 Edition	Comments
6.9.4.7 Polyamide and polyethylene piping that is installed in a vault or any other belowground enclosure shall be completely encased in gastight metal pipe and fittings that are protected from corrosion.	**6.9.4.7** Polyamide and polyethylene piping that is installed in a vault, the dome of an underground container, or any other belowground enclosure shall be completely encased in one of the following: (1) Gastight metal pipe and fittings that are protected from corrosion (2) An anodeless riser	Revised to clearly state that the polyethylene pipe or tubing in container domes must be protected from damage and fire. This includes PE in the dome of an underground tank.
Not in 2008 edition	**6.10.2** Where compressed air is used as a pressure source for activating internal valves and emergency shutoff valves, the air shall be clean and kept at a moisture level that will not prevent the system from operating.	A new minimum requirement for moisture in compressed air is needed to prevent ice formation, which can defeat safety systems. The term *properly* has been removed due to its vagueness.
6.12.6 Emergency shutoff valves shall be installed so that the temperature sensitive element in the valve, or a supplemental temperature-sensitive element [250°F (121°C) maximum] connected to actuate the valve, is not more than 5 ft (1.5 m) from the nearest end of the hose or swivel-type piping connected to the line in which the valve is installed.	**6.12.6** Emergency shutoff valves shall be installed so that the temperature-sensitive element in the valve, or a supplemental temperature-sensitive element that operates at a maximum temperature of 250°F (121°C) that is connected to actuate the valve, is not more than 5 ft (1.5 m) from the nearest end of the hose or swivel-type piping connected to the line in which the valve is installed.	The operating temperature requirement of the fusible link has been moved from parentheses into the text of the paragraph to make it clear that it is a requirement.
6.12.9 Emergency shutoff valves and backflow check valves required by the code shall be tested annually for the functions required by 5.12.4. The results of the test shall be documented.	**6.12.9** Emergency shutoff valves required by the code shall be tested annually for the functions required by 5.12.4(2) and (3). Backflow check valves installed in lieu of emergency shutoff valves shall be checked annually for proper operation. The results of the test shall be documented.	Clarifies that backflow check valves are to be tested only for closure. This clarifies that fusible links are not required to be tested.
6.15 Installation in Areas of Heavy Snowfall. In areas where heavy snowfall is anticipated piping, regulators, meters, and other equipment installed in the piping system shall be protected from the forces anticipated as a result of accumulated snow.	**6.15 Installation in Areas of Heavy Snowfall.** In areas where the local building codes have specified a minimum design snow load for roofs equal to, or exceeding, 125 psf (610 kg/m²), piping, regulators, meters, and other equipment installed in the piping system shall be protected from the forces anticipated as a result of accumulated snow.	A more available criterion for what constitutes heavy snowfall is provided. Roof loads are available throughout the country. The previous criterion was vague, and resulted in the requirements for heavy snow being applied in areas not intended by the committee.
6.18.4.1 The facility operator shall provide security measures to minimize entry by unauthorized persons, including the following: [. . .] [list unchanged]	**6.18.4.1** The following security measures shall be provided to minimize the possibility of entry by unauthorized persons: [. . .] [list unchanged]	The revision mandates compliance with the requirement, but does not specify who should provide it.
6.19.2.1 (1) Cylinders shall comply with DOT cylinder specifications.	Not in 2011 edition	This subparagraph is not needed because it repeats the requirement for compliance with DOT cylinder specifications in 5.2.1.1.

2008 Edition	*2011 Edition*	*Comments*
6.19.4.1 Cylinders shall be permitted to be used and transported in buildings or structures under construction or undergoing major renovation, where such buildings are not occupied by the public.	**6.19.4.1** Where cylinders are used and transported in buildings or structures under construction or undergoing major renovation and such buildings are not occupied by the public, the requirements of 6.19.4.2 through 6.19.4.10 shall apply.	Revised to be an introductory paragraph for the requirements in the section.
6.19.5.1 (1) The maximum water capacity of individual cylinders shall be 50 lb (23 kg) [nominal 20 lb (9.1 kg) propane capacity], and the number of cylinders in the building shall not exceed the number of workers assigned to the use of the LP-Gas.	**6.19.5.1** (1) The maximum water capacity of individual cylinders shall be 50 lb (23 kg) [nominal 20 lb (9.1 kg) propane capacity], and the number of cylinders in the building shall not exceed the number of workers assigned to the use of the propane.	The LP-Gas type is specified as propane.
6.21.2.12 Where atmospheric vaporizers of less than 1 qt (0.9 L) capacity are installed inside an industrial building, they shall be installed as close as practical to the point of entry of the supply line in the building.	**6.21.2.12** Where atmospheric vaporizers of less than 1 qt (0.9 L) capacity are installed in industrial occupancies, they shall be installed as close as practical to the point of entry of the supply line in the building.	Revised to clarify the committee's intent of where small propane vaporizers can be installed.
Not in 2008 edition	**6.21.2.13** Atmospheric vaporizers of less than 1 qt (0.9 L) capacity shall not be installed in other than industrial occupancies.	
6.21.4 Installation of Tank Heaters.	**6.21.4 Installation of Tank Heaters.**	The subsection has been revised to not contain equipment elements.
6.21.4.2 If the tank heater is gas fired, an automatic shutoff shall be provided on the fuel supply (including the pilot) that will operate at if the ASME container pressure exceeds 75 percent of the maximum allowable working pressure specified in Table 5.2.4.2 or if the liquid level in the ASME container falls below the top of the tank heater.	Not in 2011 edition	The second part of paragraph 6.21.4.2 has been deleted from Chapter 6, as it is an equipment requirement. Revised paragraph 5.21.4.7 contains the requirement.
6.21.4.3 If the tank heater is of the electric immersion type, the heater shall be automatically de-energized when the pressure or level conditions specified in 6.21.4.4 are reached.		The first part of paragraph 6.21.4.2 is relocated to (new) 6.21.4.2.
6.21.4.4 If the tank heater is similar in operation to an indirect-fired vaporizer, the flow of the heat transfer fluid shall be automatically interrupted under the pressure or temperature conditions specified in 6.21.4.2 and the heat source shall comply with 6.21.2.8 and 6.21.2.11.	**6.21.4.2** If the tank heater is similar in operation to an indirect-fired vaporizer, the heat source shall comply with 6.21.2.8 and 6.21.2.11.	Paragraph 6.21.4.3 has been revised by deleting an equipment requirement covered in 5.21.4.7.
6.22.2.1 Electrical equipment and wiring installed in unclassified areas shall be in accordance with NFPA 70, *National Electrical Code*, for nonclassified locations.	**6.22.2.1** Electrical equipment and wiring installed in unclassified areas shall be in accordance with *NFPA 70, National Electrical Code*.	Revised to clarify that the *National Electrical Code* is referenced for all electrical installation, and that Table 6.22.2.2 covers the extent of the classified area.

2008 Edition	2011 Edition	Comments
6.22.2.2* Fixed electrical equipment and wiring installed within a classified area specified in Table 6.22.2.2 shall be installed in accordance with NFPA 70, *National Electrical Code.*	**6.22.2.2*** The extent of electrically classified areas shall be in accordance with Table 6.22.2.2.	
Table 6.22.2.2 (E) Column 3 Note: Fixed electrical equipment should preferably not be installed.	**Table 6.22.2.2 (E) Column 3** Fixed electrical equipment not permitted to be installed.	Clarifies an unenforceable requirement. Revised to not use a nonmandatory term.
6.22.3.4 Open flames or other sources of ignition shall not be prohibited where LP-Gas facilities have been purged of all liquid and vapor.	**6.22.3.4** Open flames or other sources of ignition shall not be prohibited where containers, piping, and other equipment containing LP-Gas have been purged of all liquid and vapor LP-Gas.	Revised to delete the term *LP-Gas facilities*, which is not defined within this code.
6.23.3.1 (B) Cylinders installed on recreational vehicles or on other vehicles shall be constructed for at least a 240 psig (1.6 MPag) service pressure. **(C)** ASME mobile containers installed on recreational vehicles or on other vehicles shall be constructed for at least a 312 psig (2.2 MPag) MAWP.	Not in 2011 edition	Deleted because 6.23.3.1(B) duplicates 5.2.4.5, and (C) duplicates 5.2.4.4.
6.23.7.4 All gas-fired heating appliances shall be equipped with safety shutoffs in accordance with 5.20.7(A) except those covered in 6.19.2.8(2).	**6.23.7.4** Gas-fired heating appliances shall be equipped with shutoffs in accordance with 5.20.7(A), except for portable heaters used with cylinders having a maximum water capacity of 2.7 lb (1.2 kg), portable torches, melting pots, and tar kettles.	This revision returns an exception to its original intent and provides the examples in the text for ease of use.
6.25.1 Application. Section 6.25 applies to fire protection for LP-Gas facilities.	**6.25.1 Application.** Section 6.25 applies to fire protection for industrial plants, bulk plants, and dispensing stations.	Clarified to state what is covered.
6.26.1 Scope. Section 6.26 applies to alternate provisions for the location and installation of ASME containers that incorporate the use of redundant fail safe product control measures and low-emission transfer concepts for the purpose of enhancing safety and to mitigate distance and special protection requirements.	**6.26.1 Application.** Section 6.26 shall apply to alternate provisions for the location and installation of ASME containers that incorporate the use of redundant fail-safe product control measures and low-emission transfer concepts for the purpose of enhancing safety and to mitigate distance and special protection requirements.	Editorial revision. Scope statements are limited to Chapter 1 and the beginning of other chapters.
6.26.5 Low Emission Transfer. The transfer distance requirements of Table 6.5.3 and 6.24.4.3 shall be reduced by one-half where the installation is in accordance with 6.26.5.	**6.26.5 Low Emission Transfer.** The transfer distance requirements of Table 6.5.3 and 6.24.4.3 shall be reduced by one-half where the installation is in accordance with 6.26.5. The transfer site shall be identified as "Low Emission Transfer Site" by having a sign or other marking posted in the area.	Revised to clarify the requirements of the section. A requirement for a sign is also added.
6.26.5.1 Transfer into ASME containers on vehicles shall meet the provisions of 6.26.5.1(A) through 6.26.5.1(D).	**6.26.5.1** Transfer into permanently mounted ASME engine fuel containers on vehicles shall meet the provisions of 6.26.5.1(A) through 6.26.5.1(D).	

2008 Edition	*2011 Edition*	*Comments*
(A) The delivery valve and nozzle combination shall mate with the filler valve in the receiving container in such a manner that, when they are uncoupled following a transfer of product, not more than 4 cm³ (0.24 in.³) of product (liquid equivalent) is released to the atmosphere.	**(A)** Unchanged	
(B) Fixed maximum liquid level gauges shall not be used to determine the maximum permitted filling limit at a low emission transfer site.	**(B)** Fixed maximum liquid level gauges that are installed on engine fuel and mobile containers in accordance with Table 5.7.4.1 shall not be used to determine the maximum permitted filling limit at a low emission transfer site.	(B) Revision clarifies that it is applicable only to fixed maximum level gauges installed on engine fuel and mobile containers.
(C) The maximum permitted filling limit shall be determined by an overfilling prevention device or other approved means.	**(C)** The maximum permitted filling limit shall be in accordance with Section 11.5 and shall be determined by an overfilling prevention device or other approved means.	(C) Reference to the new Section 11.5 has been added.
(D) Where fixed maximum liquid level gauges are installed, a label shall be placed near the gauge providing the following instructions: "Do not use this fixed maximum liquid level gauge at low emission transfer stations."	**(D)** A label shall be placed near the fixed maximum liquid level gauge providing the following instructions: "Do not use this fixed maximum liquid level gauge at low emission transfer stations."	(D) Revised for clarity.
Chapter 7 LP-Gas Liquid Transfer 7.2.2.5* Valve outlets on cylinders of 108 lb (49 kg) water capacity [nominal 45 lb (20 kg) propane capacity] or less shall be equipped with redundant pressure-tight seal or a listed quick-connect coupling. Where seals are used, they shall be in place whenever the cylinder is not connected for use.	**7.2.2.5*** Valve outlets on refillable cylinders of 108 lb (49 kg) water capacity [nominal 45 lb (20 kg) propane capacity] or less shall be equipped with a redundant pressure-tight seal or one of the following listed connections: CGA 790, CGA 791, or CGA 810, as described in CGA V-1, *Standard Compressed Gas Cylinder Valve Outlet and Inlet Connections*. **7.2.2.6** Where redundant pressure seals are used, they shall be in place whenever the cylinder is not connected for use.	Revised to require a seal on all of the recognized connections that are suitable for refillable containers. The section has been split into two subsections.
7.2.3.8 (4) Fire extinguishers shall be provided in accordance with 6.25.4.2.	**7.2.3.8** (4) Fire extinguishers shall be provided in accordance with 9.4.7.	Revised to reference the same requirement, which has been relocated.
Chapter 8 Storage of Cylinders Awaiting Use, Resale, or Exchange **Table 8.3.1 (b) Maximum Allowable Storage Quantities of LP-Gas in Mercantile, Industrial, and Storage Occupancies.** Not in 2008 edition	**Table 8.3.1 (b) Maximum Allowable Storage Quantities of LP-Gas in Mercantile, Industrial, and Storage Occupancies.** **8.6 Electrical Area Classification.** The storage of cylinders awaiting resale shall be exempt from the electrical classification requirements of this code.	The table has been revised to include text added to 8.3.5.1 in the 2008 edition of NFPA 58. Added to clarify the intent of the code. Cylinder exchange cabinets can be located adjacent to electrical outlets, ice machines, and other sources of ignition.

2008 Edition	*2011 Edition*	*Comments*
Chapter 9 Vehicular Transportation of LP-Gas **9.1.2** (2) Vehicles and procedures under the jurisdiction of DOT	Not in 2011 edition	9.1.2 (2) has been removed as these vehicles and procedures are now a part of the scope of this code as shown in 9.1.1(4).
9.4.8* Chock Blocks for Cargo Tank Vehicles. Each cargo tank vehicle and trailer shall carry chock blocks, which shall be used to prevent rolling of the vehicle whenever it is being loaded, unloaded, or is parked.	**9.4.8* Wheel Stops for Cargo Tank Vehicles.** Each cargo tank vehicle or trailer shall utilize a wheel stop, in addition to the parking or hand brake, whenever the cargo tank vehicle is loading, is unloading, or is parked.	A new term, *wheel stop*, is introduced, replacing *chock block*. The paragraph now clearly states that the purpose of the wheel stop is to be a secondary method to prevent the cargo tank vehicle from unintended movement.
9.6.2.2 Where containers shall be permitted to be transported with more LP-Gas than 5 percent of their water capacity in a liquid form but shall not exceed the maximum permitted by Section 7.4, all the following conditions apply:	**9.6.2.2** Where a container is transported with more LP-Gas than 5 percent of its water capacity in a liquid form, all of the following conditions apply:	Revised for clarity. A requirement has been moved to the list from the main paragraph.
(1) Not in 2008 edition	(1) The maximum filling does not exceed the limit of Section 7.4.	
(2) Transportation shall be permitted only to move containers from a stationary or temporary installation to a bulk plant.	(2) Unchanged	
(3) Valves and fittings shall be protected by a method approved by the authority having jurisdiction to minimize the possibility of damage.	(3) Unchanged	
(4) Lifting lugs shall not be used to move these containers.	(4) Unchanged	

Chapter 10 Buildings or Structures Housing LP-Gas Distribution Facilities

No changes have occurred in this chapter since the 2008 edition of NFPA 58.

2008 Edition	*2011 Edition*	*Comments*
Chapter 11 Engine Fuel Systems **11.3.2.2** ASME containers installed in enclosed spaces on vehicles and all engine fuel containers for vehicles, industrial trucks, buses (including school buses), recreational vehicles, and multipurpose passenger vehicles shall be constructed with a MAWP of at least 312 psig (2.2 MPag).	**11.3.2.2** ASME containers installed in enclosed spaces on vehicles and all engine fuel containers for vehicles, industrial trucks, buses, recreational vehicles, and passenger vehicles designed to carry 10 or fewer passengers shall be constructed with a MAWP of at least 312 psig (2.2 MPag).	Revised to incorporate the former definition of *multipurpose passenger vehicle* to where it is used in the code. The definition has also been deleted from Chapter 3.
Not in 2008 edition	**11.4.1.4** Where used, a filler valve shall comply with 5.7.4.1(F) and shall be installed in the fill opening of the container for either remote or direct filling.	5.7.4.1 (F) details the use of excess-flow valves. This reference avoids repeating the same information.
11.4.1.10 Cylinders shall be equipped with full internal or flush-type full internal pressure relief valves in accordance with DOT regulations.	**11.4.1.10** Cylinders, other than for industrial truck service, shall be equipped with full internal or flush-type full internal pressure relief valves.	This revision allows industrial truck cylinders to be part of a multivalve assembly. The committee became aware that DOT regulations do not have requirements for specific types of pressure relief valves.

2008 Edition	*2011 Edition*	*Comments*
Not in 2008 edition	**11.4.1.11** Single opening cylinders in industrial truck service shall be equipped with a listed multiple function valve in accordance with 5.7.4.1(J).	This requirement recognizes single opening composite cylinders and allows their use in individual truck service.
11.4.1.14 Where an overfilling prevention device is installed on the ASME container or exterior of the compartment and remote filling is used, a double backflow check valve shall be installed in the container fill valve opening.	**11.4.1.15** Where an overfilling prevention device is installed on the ASME container or exterior of the compartment and remote filling is used, a filler valve complying with 5.7.4.1(F)(1) or (2) shall be installed in the exterior fill opening, and a filler valve complying with 5.7.4.1(F)(3) shall be installed in the container fill valve opening.	Revised to show that a filler valve can now be used rather than a double backflow check valve. The term *filler valve* is now defined, and requirements have been added to Chapter 5. This change is consistent with these other revisions.
11.4.1.15 Where an overfilling prevention device is installed on an engine fuel container, venting of gas through a fixed maximum liquid level gauge during normal filling shall not be required.	**11.4.1.16** Where an overfilling prevention device is installed on an ASME engine fuel container, venting of gas through a fixed maximum liquid level gauge during filling shall not be required.	"ASME" is added to clarify that the requirement is not applicable to cylinders.
Not in 2008 edition	**11.4.1.17** Where the fixed maximum liquid level gauge is not used during filling, in accordance with 11.4.1.16, the fixed maximum liquid level gauge or other approved means shall be used annually to verify the operation of the overfilling prevention device. If the container is found to be overfilled during the test, corrective action shall be taken. The result shall be documented. A label shall be affixed to the container near the fill point indicating the expiration date of the successful test.	Allows use of a stop-fill device, with checks every 3 months.
Not in 2008 edition	**11.5 Quantity of LP-Gas in Engine Fuel Containers.** The maximum permitted filling limit for engine fuel containers shall be as follows: (1) For permanently mounted ASME engine fuel containers, the maximum permitted filling limit shall not exceed the amount shown in Table 7.4.2.3(a) when the liquid is at 40°F (4°C). (2) For removable engine fuel containers, the maximum permitted filling limit shall be in accordance with 7.4.2 and 7.4.3	This section has been added to clearly state what the maximum permitted filling limit is for containers in engine fuel service.
11.6.1.2 (1) Steel tubing: ASTM A 539, Standard Specification for Electric-Resistance-Welded Coiled Steel Tubing for Gas Fuel Oil Lines	Not in 2011 edition	ASTM 539 has been withdrawn and not replaced.
11.6.1.2 Tubing shall be steel, stainless steel, brass, or copper *(see 6.9.4)* and shall comply with the following: (1) Steel tubing: ASTM A 539, *Standard Specification for Electric-Resistance*	**11.7.1.2** Tubing shall be steel, stainless steel, brass, or copper and shall comply with the following: Not in 2011 edition	11.6.1.2 (2) has been removed since the requirement is explained in 6.9.3.

2008 Edition	*2011 Edition*	*Comments*

Welded Coiled Steel Tubing for Gas Fuel Oil Lines
(2) Brass tubing: ASTM B 135, *Standard Specification for Seamless Brass Tube*
(3) Copper tubing:
 	
  (a) Type K or L: ASTM B 88, *Specification for Seamless Copper Water Tube*
  (b) ASTM B 280, *Specification for Seamless Copper Tube for Air Conditioning and Refrigeration Field Service*
	(1) Brass tubing: ASTM B 135, *Standard Specification for Seamless Brass Tube*
	(2) Copper tubing:
	
	  (a) Type K or L: ASTM B 88, *Standard Specification for Seamless Copper Water Tube*
	  (b) ASTM B 280, *Standard Specification for Seamless Copper Tube for Air Conditioning and Refrigeration Field Service*	

11.6.3 Hose that is utilized at lower than container pressure shall be designed and marked for its maximum anticipated operating pressure.	**11.7.3 Hose, Hose Connections, and Flexible Connectors.** **11.7.3.1** Hose, hose connections, and flexible hose connectors *(see 3.3.26)* used for conveying LP-Gas liquid or vapor at pressures in excess of 5 psig (34.5 kPag) shall be fabricated of materials resistant to the action of LP-Gas both as liquid and vapor, and the hose and flexible hose connector and shall be reinforced with stainless steel wire braid. **11.7.3.2** Hose that can be exposed to container pressure shall be designed for a pressure rating of 350 psig (2.4 MPag) with a safety factor of 5 to 1, and the reinforcement shall be stainless steel wire braid. **11.7.3.3** Hose shall be continuously marked "LP-GAS, PROPANE, 350 PSI WORKING PRESSURE" and the manufacturer's name or trademark. Each installed piece of hose shall contain at least one such marking. **11.7.3.4** After the application of couplings, hose assemblies shall be capable of withstanding a pressure of not less than 700 psig (4.8 MPag). If a pressure test is performed, such assemblies shall be pressure tested at 120 percent of the pressure rating [350 psig (2.4 MPag) minimum] of the hose. **11.7.3.5** Hose used for vapor service at 5 psig (34.5 kPag) or less shall be constructed of material resistant to the action of LP-Gas. **11.7.3.6** Hose in excess of 5 psig (34.5 kPag) service pressure and quick connectors shall be approved. **11.7.3.7** Hose that is utilized at lower than container pressure shall be designed and marked for its maximum anticipated operating pressure.	This text was inadvertently deleted from the 2004 edition of NFPA 58 and has now been returned.

2008 Edition	*2011 Edition*	*Comments*
Not in 2008 edition	**11.13.2.8** Industrial truck cylinders shall have relief valves installed in accordance with 5.7.4.1 (J).	Added to provide additional information on industrial truck cylinders. This new requirement recognizes changes in Chapter 5 for relief valves used on certain composite cylinders.
11.12.4.4 All cylinders used in industrial truck service (including forklift truck cylinders) shall have the cylinder pressure relief valve replaced by a new or unused valve within 12 years of the date of manufacture of the cylinder and every 10 years thereafter.	**11.13.4.4** All cylinders used in industrial truck service (including forklift truck cylinders) shall have the cylinder pressure relief valve replaced in accordance with 5.7.2.13.	The text has been revised to reference 5.7.2.13, rather than restate a requirement.
11.14.1 General. Not in 2008 edition	**11.15.1 Portable Engines.**	This section addresses portable engines separately from stationary ones.
Not in 2008 edition	**11.15.2 Containers for Stationary Engines.** **11.15.2.1** LP-Gas containers for stationary installations shall be located outside of buildings unless the buildings comply with the requirements of Chapter 10. **11.15.2.2** Containers for stationary engines shall be installed to meet the separation requirements of Section 6.3.	New text clarifies location requirement for containers for stationary engines. Reduced spacing is allowed where a manual shutoff is installed. This is important at cell phone towers.
Chapter 12 Refrigerated Containers **12.4.1.8** Refrigerated LP-Gas containers of 70,000 gal (265 m³) or less, if attended during the filling operation, shall be permitted to be equipped with liquid trycocks in lieu of the high–liquid level alarm, and manual flow cutoff shall be permitted.	**12.4.1.8** Where refrigerated LP-Gas containers of 70,000 gal (265 m³) or less are attended during the filling operation, they shall be equipped with either liquid trycocks or a high–liquid level alarm, and manual flow cutoff shall be permitted.	Revised to clarify the requirement.
Chapter 14 Operation and Maintenance **14.3.2.1** Maintenance manuals for all equipment at the facility shall be kept at the facility and shall be available to maintenance personnel. Manuals for normally unattended facilities shall be permitted to be stored at a location where they will be accessible for maintenance personnel servicing the unattended location.	**14.3.2.1** Maintenance manuals for all equipment at an attended facility shall be kept at the facility and shall be available to maintenance personnel. Manuals for unattended facilities shall be permitted to be kept at the facility or stored at a location where they will be accessible for maintenance personnel servicing the unattended location.	Editorial revision to clarify the definition of "at a location."
14.4* Small LP-Gas Systems (SLGSs)	Not in 2011 edition	Removed as it was conflicting with some sections of federal pipeline regulations.
Chapter 15 Pipe and Tubing Sizing Tables Not in 2008 edition	**15.1 Tables for Sizing Pipe and Tubing.** When the pipe sizing method of 6.9.2.2 is used, Table 15.1(a) through Table 15.1(q), or other approved piping tables, shall be used to size piping systems. For SI units, 1 ft³ = 0.028 m³; 1 ft = 0.305 m; 1 in. water column = 2.49 kPa; 1 psi = 6.894 kPa; and 1000 Btu/hr = 0.203 kW.	The revised format of the piping tables in NFPA 54 has been added to NFPA 58 in Chapter 15.

Index

6.26.3.3, 11.6.3, 11.11.1.2, 11.14.2.1, 11.16, A.5.20.7
Buildings, piping systems in, 6.19.12.2
Cargo tank vehicles, 9.4.3.4, 9.7.3.5, 9.7.3.6
Dispensers, 6.24.3.8 to 6.24.3.11, 6.24.3.13
Emergency *see* subhead: Emergency shutoff
Hydrostatic relief valve installation between, 6.13
Manual, 5.7.4.1(F), 5.7.4.1(G), 5.7.4.5, 5.12.3, 5.12.4, 5.21.3.5, 5.21.4.5, 6.21.3.5, 6.21.5.3, 6.24.3.11, 6.26.3.4, 6.26.3.5, 11.4.1.3, 11.4.1.8
Non-engine fuel systems, 6.23.4.1
Overpressure *see* Overpressure shutoff devices/valves
Positive, 5.7.4.1(C), 5.7.4.2, 5.7.4.5, 5.7.7.1, 5.7.7.2, 5.7.8.1, 6.21.5.3, 6.24.3.8, 6.26.3.4, 6.26.3.5, 9.4.4.3
Quick-acting, 6.24.3.13
Regulator hose use with, 6.20.3.6, 6.20.3.7
Remote control of *see* Remote shutoff controls
Venting of gas between, 7.3.1(2)
Vapor, Table 5.7.4.1, 6.8.1.1, 13.3.2.1
Vaporizers, 5.21, Table 6.22.2.2, 6.22.2.5, A.5.21.5.9
Burner *see* Vaporizing burners
Definition, 3.3.70
Direct-fired, 5.21.3, 5.21.9, 6.21.6.2
  Definition, 3.3.70.1
  Gas-air mixers used with, 6.21.8.4
  Installation, 6.21.3, 6.22.3.2
Electric
  Definition, 3.3.70.2
  Direct immersion, 6.21.7
    Definition, 3.3.70.2.1
  Indirect, 6.21.7
    Definition, 3.3.70.2.2
  Installation, 6.21.7
Indirect (indirect-fired), 5.21.2, 5.21.9, 6.21.6.1, 6.21.7
  Definition, 3.3.70.2.3
  Gas-air mixers used with, 6.21.8.3
  Installation, 6.21.2, 6.22.3.2
Installation, 6.21, 6.22.3.2
Operating procedures, 14.2.1.3
Piping systems feeding, 6.9.1.1(4), 6.9.1.3
Regulator installation, 6.8.1.1
Vehicle engines, 11.6.2
Waterbath (immersion-type), 5.21.6

Definition, 3.3.70.2.4
Installation, 6.21.6
Vaporizing burners (self-vaporizing liquid burners), 5.20.5, 5.21.5, A.5.21.5.9
Definition, 3.3.71
Installation, 6.21.5
Vapor meters, 6.17.5.1, 6.17.5.3
Vapor piping systems *see* Piping and piping systems
Vapor service valves, 6.8.1.1
Vehicle dispensing stations *see* Dispensing stations
Vehicle fuel dispensers, Table 6.22.2.2, 6.24
Definition, 3.3.72
Vehicles
Appliance installation, 6.23.7, A.6.23.7.6
Containers on/in *see* Vehicles, containers on/in
Engine fuel systems *see* Engine fuel systems
Equipment installation, 6.23.6
Garaging of *see* Parking and garaging of vehicles
Industrial trucks *see* Industrial trucks
Interiors, 11.9, A.11.9.1.2
Marking/placarding, 9.3.2.10, 9.3.3.7, 9.4.6.2, 11.12, A.11.12.2.2
Movable fuel storage tenders or farm carts *see* Movable fuel storage tenders
Non-engine fuel system installation, 6.23, A.6.23.1, A.6.23.7.6
Parking, 6.23.9, 9.7
Passenger-carrying *see* Passenger-carrying vehicles
Piers or docks, vehicles on, 13.2.1.3
Precautions, general, 6.23.8
Safety provisions, 9.4.10
Servicing and repair, 6.23.9, 9.7.3.6, 9.7.3.7
Trailers and semitrailers, 9.5
Transportation of LP-Gas, Chap. 9
Vehicles, containers on/in, 11.9, A.11.9.1.2
Cargo tank vehicles, 9.3.3.8, 9.4.2
Fuel dispensers *see* Vehicle fuel dispensers
Leakage, 9.7.3.5, 9.7.3.6
Location, 6.2.2
Non-engine fuel systems, 6.23.3
Parking of, 11.13.4.3
Transfer of liquid into, 6.5.1, A.6.5.1
Ventilation, building, 9.7.3.5, 10.2.2,

10.3.1.5, 10.3.2.8
Venting, regulator, pipe for, 5.8.3, A.5.8.3
Venting gas to atmosphere, 6.5.4.2, 6.6.6.1(H), 6.7.2.3, 6.7.2.7, 6.23.3.3, 7.3, 8.3.4.3
Vents, fixed maximum liquid level gauge, 6.3.9
Vertical filling, 5.7.5.6(B)
Volume, liquid, Annex F
Volumetric method filling (loading), 5.2.5.7, 5.7.5.3, 7.4.2.1, 7.4.2.3, Table 7.4.2.3(a) to Table 7.4.2.3(c), 7.4.3, A.5.2.5.7, A.5.7.5.3, A.7.4.2.3
Definition, 3.3.21.1

W

Walls, fire, 6.4.7, A.6.4.7
Warning signs/labels
Appliances, 6.23.7.10
ASME containers, 5.2.8.5
Cylinders, 5.2.8.4
Emergency remote shutdown stations, 6.11.5
Marine shipping and receiving, prior to transfer at, 13.2.1.5, 13.2.3.1
Tank cars, filling of, 7.2.3.6(1)
Water capacity, of containers, 5.2.1.8, 5.2.1.9, Table 7.4.2.2
Definition, 3.3.74
Portable containers of more than 1000 lb (454 kg) water capacity, 9.3.3
Stationary installations, 4.3.1
Storage of containers, 8.3.2.2, 8.3.3.1
Vehicles, containers installed on, 11.3.5
Water heaters, 5.20.7, A.5.20.7
Water spray fixed systems, 6.25.6
Weight method filling, 7.4.2.1, 7.4.2.2, Table 7.4.2.2, A.7.4.2.2
Definition, 3.3.21.2
Welding, 5.2.1.7, 5.7.3.5, 6.6.1.3, 6.9.3.2, 6.22.3.3, 7.2.3.2(C), 11.3.3.3, 11.8.4.2, 13.2.1.11
Wharves *see* Marine shipping and receiving
Wheel chocks, 7.2.3.6(2)
Wheel stops, 9.4.8, A.9.4.8
Wind loading
ASME containers, 5.2.4.3(C)
Refrigerated containers, 12.3.1
Wiring, electrical, 6.22.2, 9.2, 13.2.2, A.6.22.2.2, A.6.22.2.3
Working pressure; *see also* Maximum allowable working pressure (MAWP)
Hose, 5.9.6.5, 11.7.3.1 to 11.7.3.7

IMPORTANT NOTICES AND DISCLAIMERS CONCERNING NFPA® DOCUMENTS

NOTICE AND DISCLAIMER OF LIABILITY CONCERNING THE USE OF NFPA DOCUMENTS

NFPA® codes, standards, recommended practices, and guides ("NFPA Documents"), of which the NFPA Document contained herein is one, are developed through a consensus standards development process approved by the American National Standards Institute. This process brings together volunteers representing varied viewpoints and interests to achieve consensus on fire and other safety issues. While the NFPA administers the process and establishes rules to promote fairness in the development of consensus, it does not independently test, evaluate, or verify the accuracy of any information or the soundness of any judgments contained in NFPA Documents.

The NFPA disclaims liability for any personal injury, property or other damages of any nature whatsoever, whether special, indirect, consequential or compensatory, directly or indirectly resulting from the publication, use of, or reliance on NFPA Documents. The NFPA also makes no guaranty or warranty as to the accuracy or completeness of any information published herein.

In issuing and making NFPA Documents available, the NFPA is not undertaking to render professional or other services for or on behalf of any person or entity. Nor is the NFPA undertaking to perform any duty owed by any person or entity to someone else. Anyone using this document should rely on his or her own independent judgment or, as appropriate, seek the advice of a competent professional in determining the exercise of reasonable care in any given circumstances.

The NFPA has no power, nor does it undertake, to police or enforce compliance with the contents of NFPA Documents. Nor does the NFPA list, certify, test, or inspect products, designs, or installations for compliance with this document. Any certification or other statement of compliance with the requirements of this document shall not be attributable to the NFPA and is solely the responsibility of the certifier or maker of the statement.

ADDITIONAL NOTICES AND DISCLAIMERS

Updating of NFPA Documents

Users of NFPA codes, standards, recommended practices, and guides ("NFPA Documents") should be aware that these documents may be superseded at any time by the issuance of new editions or may be amended from time to time through the issuance of Tentative Interim Amendments. An official NFPA Document at any point in time consists of the current edition of the document together with any Tentative Interim Amendments and any Errata then in effect. In order to determine whether a given document is the current edition and whether it has been amended through the issuance of Tentative Interim Amendments or corrected through the issuance of Errata, consult appropriate NFPA publications such as the National Fire Codes® Subscription Service, visit the NFPA website at www.nfpa.org, or contact the NFPA at the address listed below.

Interpretations of NFPA Documents

A statement, written or oral, that is not processed in accordance with Section 6 of the Regulations Governing Committee Projects shall not be considered the official position of NFPA or any of its Committees and shall not be considered to be, nor be relied upon as, a Formal Interpretation.

Patents

The NFPA does not take any position with respect to the validity of any patent rights referenced in, related to, or asserted in connection with an NFPA Document. The users of NFPA Documents bear the sole responsibility for determining the validity of any such patent rights, as well as the risk of infringement of such rights, and the NFPA disclaims liability for the infringement of any patent resulting from the use of or reliance on NFPA Documents.

NFPA adheres to the policy of the American National Standards Institute (ANSI) regarding the inclusion of patents in American National Standards ("the ANSI Patent Policy"), and hereby gives the following notice pursuant to that policy:

NOTICE: The user's attention is called to the possibility that compliance with an NFPA Document may require use of an invention covered by patent rights. NFPA takes no position as to the validity of any such patent rights or as to whether such patent rights constitute or include essential patent claims under the ANSI Patent Policy. If, in connection with the ANSI Patent Policy, a patent holder has filed a statement of willingness to grant licenses under these rights on reasonable and nondiscriminatory terms and conditions to applicants desiring to obtain such a license, copies of such filed statements can be obtained, on request, from NFPA. For further information, contact the NFPA at the address listed below.

Law and Regulations

Users of NFPA Documents should consult applicable federal, state, and local laws and regulations. NFPA does not, by the publication of its codes, standards, recommended practices, and guides, intend to urge action that is not in compliance with applicable laws, and these documents may not be construed as doing so.

Copyrights

NFPA Documents are copyrighted by the NFPA. They are made available for a wide variety of both public and private uses. These include both use, by reference, in laws and regulations, and use in private self-regulation, standardization, and the promotion of safe practices and methods. By making these documents available for use and adoption by public authorities and private users, the NFPA does not waive any rights in copyright to these documents.

Use of NFPA Documents for regulatory purposes should be accomplished through adoption by reference. The term "adoption by reference" means the citing of title, edition, and publishing information only. Any deletions, additions, and changes desired by the adopting authority should be noted separately in the adopting instrument. In order to assist NFPA in following the uses made of its documents, adopting authorities are requested to notify the NFPA (Attention: Secretary, Standards Council) in writing of such use. For technical assistance and questions concerning adoption of NFPA Documents, contact NFPA at the address below.

For Further Information

All questions or other communications relating to NFPA Documents and all requests for information on NFPA procedures governing its codes and standards development process, including information on the procedures for requesting Formal Interpretations, for proposing Tentative Interim Amendments, and for proposing revisions to NFPA documents during regular revision cycles, should be sent to NFPA headquarters, addressed to the attention of the Secretary, Standards Council, NFPA, 1 Batterymarch Park, P.O. Box 9101, Quincy, MA 02269-9101; email: stds_admin@nfpa.org

For more information about NFPA, visit the NFPA website at www.nfpa.org.